Family and Succession Law in Pakistan

Family and Succession Law in Pakistan

Second Edition

Muhammad Shahid Malik

This book was originally published as a monograph in the International Encyclopaedia of Laws/Family and Succession Law.

Founding Editor: Roger Blanpain
General Editor: Frank Hendrickx
Volume Editor: Walter Pintens

Wolters Kluwer

Published by:
Kluwer Law International B.V.
PO Box 316
2400 AH Alphen aan den Rijn
The Netherlands
E-mail: lrs-sales@wolterskluwer.com
Website: www.wolterskluwer.com/en/solutions/kluwerlawinternational

Sold and distributed by:
Wolters Kluwer Legal & Regulatory U.S.
920 Links Avenue
Landisville, PA 17538
United States of America
E-mail: customer.service@wolterskluwer.com

ISBN 978-94-035-4859-3

e-Book: ISBN 978-94-035-4869-2
web-PDF: ISBN 978-94-035-4879-1

The Author

Born in 1968 in Pakistan, Mr Muhammad Shahid Malik is a registered Legal Practitioner and Petroleum Sector Lawyer working as Head of Legal and Commercial in a foreign Exploration and Production Company. He has done his Bachelor's (LLB) from the University of Punjab, Pakistan, a Master's in Law (LLM) from the University of Karachi, Pakistan and a Master's in Political Science from the University of Punjab and attended several local and international training courses in Petroleum Sector.

He has about twenty-five years' experience in Upstream Oil and Gas sector dealing with Petroleum Sector laws and provides legal advice on a whole range of commercial and governance issues with sensitivity to regulatory compliance. He is also responsible for establishing and implementing legal controls and compliance systems. He has expertise in drafting and finalizing specialized Oil & Gas Contracts which include PCAs, PSAs, Joint Operating Agreements, GSAs, COSAs, LPG SPAs, MOUs, Assignment Agreements, Novation Agreements, Pricing Agreements, Farmin/Farmout Agreements, Settlement Agreements and related Supplemental Agreements. In addition, he has also expertise in drafting Seismic Contracts, Drilling Contracts, Construction Facilities Contracts, Service Contracts, Purchase Agreements, Assets Sale & Purchase Agreements, Financial Transaction Agreements, Sale Deeds and Land Lease Agreements. He helps in developing and understanding, risk mitigation strategies for contractual risks which may arise during the project implementation phase. He also advises different departments of the Company on legal and commercial issues.

He has been involved for over twenty-five years in handling, implementation and compliance of employment laws, labour laws and industrial relations laws in the organizations. He handled several disciplinary and grievance cases, collective bargaining agents issues participated in policy development and trade union negotiations and conducted industrial relations audit of the organization.

The Author

Co-author

Ms. Shaiyza Malik, born in 1999 in Rawalpindi, Pakistan, is a dedicated legal professional with a strong academic background and practical experience in the field of law. She holds an LLB degree from Bahria University, Islamabad, and is currently pursuing her LLM from the same institution. With two years of legal practice, she has developed expertise in various areas of law, including corporate, family, and civil law.

Currently serving as a Trainee Legal Officer at Fauji Cement Limited, Ms Malik is committed to expanding her legal acumen. To enhance her knowledge, she has undertaken specialized courses in corporate, family, labour and civil law. She also obtained training in the Islamabad Court-Annexed Mediation Centre, where she gained valuable insights into Alternative Dispute Resolution (ADR). Her diverse experience and academic achievements reflect her dedication to the legal profession and her pursuit of excellence in legal practice.

Co-author

Table of Contents

The Author 3

Co-author 5

List of Abbreviations 15

Preface 17

General Introduction 19

Chapter 1. General Background of the Country 19

§1. BACKGROUND 19

§2. POPULATION 21

§3. PEOPLE OF PAKISTAN 24

§4. LAND, HERITAGE AND CULTURE 26

§5. THE ECONOMY 28

§6. CONSTITUTIONAL HISTORY 30

§7. POLITICAL, JUDICIAL AND ADMINISTRATIVE SYSTEM 33

Chapter 2. Historical Background of Family and Succession Law 43

§1. INTRODUCTION 43

Chapter 3. Sources of Family and Succession Law 45

§1. ISLAMIC LAW 45
I. *Holy Quran* 45
II. *Sunnah/Hadees* 45

III. *Ijma* or Consensus of Opinion 46
IV. The *Qiyas* or Analogical Deductions 46

§2. Constitution 46

§3. Legislation 47

§4. Court Decisions 50

§5. Customs 50

Chapter 4. The Courts Administering Family Law and Succession Law 51

§1. Arbitration Council 51

§2. Family Courts 53

§3. High Courts 56

§4. Federal Shariat Court 56

Part I. Persons 57

Chapter 1. The Status of a Person 57

§1. Definition of a Person 57

§2. Capacity 57
I. Minors 57
II. Child 57
III. Lunacy and Idiocy 57

Chapter 2. Registration of Civil Status 61

§1. Muslim Law 61

§2. Minorities Laws 62
I. Christian Law 62
II. Hindu Law 63
III. Parsi Law 63

§3. Special Marriage Act, 1872 64

Chapter 3. Personality Rights 65

§1. Minority Rights 65

§2. Minors' Responsibility for Crimes 66

§3. Juvenile Rights 67

Chapter 4. Names 73

§1. Forename 73

§2. Surname 74
I. Acquisition of the Surname 74
II. Change of the Surname 75

Chapter 5. Nationality 76

§1. Citizenship 76

§2. Acquisition of Citizenship 77

Chapter 6. Domicile and Residence 79

§1. Domicile 79

§2. Domicile of Origin 79

Chapter 7. Mentally Handicapped Persons 83

§1. Criminal Law 83

§2. Suits By or Against Lunatics 83

§3. Marriage 89

Part II. Family Law 91

Chapter 1. Marriage 91

§1. The Nature of Marriage 91

§2. Marriage Functions 92

§3. The Capacity to Marry 93

I. Different Sex 94
II. Consanguinity 94
III. Marriageable Age 95
IV. Prior Marriage 97
V. Option of Puberty 97
VI. Failure to Consent 99
A. Duress 101
B. Insanity 102
VII. Failure to Comply with Necessary Formalities 103
VIII. Formalities of Marriage 104
IX. Christian Marriage 107
X. Hindu Marriages 122
XI. Parsi Marriages 126

§4. Dower (Haq Mehr) 130

§5. Dowry and Bridal Gifts 136

§6. Effects of Marriage 141
I. General 141
II. Rights and Duties of Husband 142
III. Rights and Duties of Wife 143
IV. Maintenance of Wife 145
V. Maintenance of Children 150
VI. Sexual Intercourse 153

§7. Polygamy (Second Marriage) 155

§8. Re-marriage 158

§9. Void and Voidable Marriages 159
I. Impotency 159
II. Cruelty 161
III. Idiocy or Lunacy 163
IV. Consent Obtained by Force or Fraud 164
V. Prohibited Marriages 165

Chapter 2. Divorce 167

§1. Grounds of Muslim Divorce 167
I. Divorce by Mutual Consent 168
II. Divorce by Husband 169
III. Divorce by Wife 170
IV. Divorce Through Judicial Process (‘*Khula*’) 172

§2. Procedure of Divorce 180

§3. Different Modes of Divorce 182
A. *Talak Ahsan* (Most Approved Way for Divorce) 183
B. *Talaq Hasan* (Approved Way for Divorce) 184
C. Talaq-ul-Bidaat or Talaq-i-Badai 184
D. Divorce under Compulsion 186
E. Divorce by Ila (Vow of Continence) 187
F. Zihar (Injurious Assimilation) 187
G. '*Khula*' (Redemption) and *Mubarat* (Mutual Freeing) 188

§4. Effects of Divorce 189

§5. Iddat (Time Limitation for Woman to Remarry) 191

§6. Christian Marriage Dissolution 193

§7. Parsi Marriage Dissolution 201

Chapter 3. Cohabitation Outside Marriage 204

Chapter 4. Filiation 207

§1. Children Born in Wedlock 207

§2. Legitimacy of Child 207

§3. Ex-nupital Children 209
I. Name 210
II. Maintenance 210
III. Guardianship, Custody and Access 211
IV. Nationality and Citizenship 212
V. Inheritance 213

Chapter 5. Adoption and Foster Care 214

§1. Adoption 214

§2. Adoptees 216

§3. Foreign Adoption 217

Chapter 6. Guardianship and Custody 218

§1. Introduction 218

§2. Custody of Children 221

§3. Adopted Children 221

§4. Interim Orders 222

§5. Guardians Court 225

§6. Restriction on Removal of Children from Pakistan 226

§7. Principles on Guardianship Custody and Access Awards 227

§8. Wishes of the Child 237
I. Performance in Court 239
II. Preference for Natural Parents 240
III. Economic Factors 243

§9. Cessation of Guardianship 244

Part III. Matrimonial Property Law 245

Chapter 1. Matrimonial Property 245

§1. Introduction 245

§2. Property Regime During Marriage and Cohabitation 245

§3. Adjudication of Property Disputes 246

Part IV. Succession Law 247

Chapter 1. Intestate Succession 247

§1. The Open of the Succession 247

§2. Death 247

§3. The Heir and Other Beneficiaries 248

§4. Islamic Law of Inheritance and Succession 253
I. Sunni Laws 254
A. Shia Laws 267
III. Case Laws Inheritance and Succession 278

§5. Parsi Intestates 310

Chapter 2. Testamentary Succession 313

§1. Introduction 313

§2. Capacity to Make a Will 313

§3. Different Types of Will 314

§4. Revocation of Will 316

§5. Void Will 317

§6. Provisions and Interpretation of Will 318

§7. Consanguinity 324

§8. The Joint Will 329

§9. Bequests 330

§10. Void Bequests 337

§11. Legacies 346

§12. Grants 357

§13. Protection of Property of Deceased 361

§14. Gifts in Contemplation of Death 369

§15. Administrators or Executors 369

§16. Succession Certificates 381

§17. Case Laws 384

Index 387

Table of Contents

List of Abbreviations

ADR	Alternative Dispute Resolution
AJK	Azad Jammu & Kashmir
CEDAW	Convention on the Elimination of All Forms of Discrimination Against Women
CLC	Civil Law Cases
CNIC	Computerized National Identity Card
CPC	Code of Civil Procedure
CRC	Convention on the Rights of the Child
CrPC	Criminal Procedure Code
FATA	Federally Administered Tribal Areas
FBR	Federal Board of Revenue
FIR	First Information Report
FSC	Federal Shariat Court
GDP	Gross Domestic Product
IMF	International Monetary Fund
JJSA	Juvenile Justice System Act
LHC	Lahore High Court, Lahore
MFLO	Muslim Family Laws Ordinance, 1961
MLD	Monthly Law Digest
NADRA	National Database and Registration Authority
NICOP	National Identity Card for Overseas Pakistanis
NWFP	North-West Frontier Province
PBUH	Peace Be Upon Him
PHC	Peshawar High Court, Khyber Pakhtunkhwa
PKR	Pakistan Rupees
PLC	Pakistan Labour Cases
PLD	Pakistan Legal Decisions
POC	Pakistan Origin Card
PPC	Pakistan Penal Code
REER	Real Effective Exchange Rate

List of Abbreviations

SCMR	Supreme Court Monthly Review
SCP	Supreme Court of Pakistan
SDPO	Sub-Division Police Officer
SHC	Sindh High Court, Karachi
SMA	Succession Miscellaneous Petition
SBP	State Bank of Pakistan

Preface

This monograph of Family and Succession Laws in Pakistan includes a summary of all major laws relating to contracting and dissolution of marriages, family laws relating to Muslims, Christians, Parsis and Hindu religions, maintenance of wife and child, restitution of conjugal rights, Guardianship, Laws of Inheritance, child marriage restraints, Family Courts, Dowry and Bridal Gifts, Guardians and Succession Laws. Muhammadan Laws (Islamic Laws) have also been quoted at appropriate places. The important Court decisions have been quoted with reference to relevant Family and Succession Laws to clarify the interpretation done and the position taken by the courts in certain cases.

General Introduction

Chapter 1. General Background of the Country

§1. Background

1. Pakistan, a South Asian nation, is bordered by India to the east, Iran to the west, Afghanistan to the northwest, and China to the northeast. Spanning 796,095 square kilometres, it exceeds the combined area of France and the UK. The Indus River, originating in China, runs almost the entire length of the country, nourishing its land and people. While the Chenab, Jhelum, and Ravi rivers contribute to the Indus, the Beas and Sutlej are mostly diverted for irrigation in India. Along the Indus lie Pakistan's fertile agricultural lands, major cities, and vast hydroelectric projects, all interconnected by the world's largest canal system before reaching the Arabian Sea.

2. The geography of Pakistan is strikingly diverse, with towering mountains in the north and west, including K2 in the Pakistani-administered region of Kashmir, the world's second-highest peak. Northern Pakistan enjoys greater rainfall than the arid south and is home to remnants of moist temperate forests. To the southeast, the landscape transitions into the flat, expansive Cholistan and Thal Deserts, marking the border with India. West-central Balochistan features a high-altitude desert plateau encircled by low mountain ranges. In contrast, Punjab and parts of Sindh boast vast, fertile plains that sustain the country's thriving agricultural sector.

3. Pakistan emerged as an independent state through the enactment of the Indian Independence Act of 1947, which was passed on 18 July 1947. This legislation outlined the partition of British India and the establishment of two sovereign dominions India and Pakistan by replacing certain provisions of the Government of India Act of 1935 and addressing legal and administrative matters necessary for their transition to independence. As per the Act, both dominions were set to officially come into existence on 15 August 1947. A key provision of the Act, outlined in section 6(3), granted the Governor General of each dominion full authority to approve, amend, or enact laws. Exercising these powers, the Governor General of Pakistan issued *The Pakistan (Adaptation of Existing Pakistan Laws) Order, 1947* under Order GGP 20 on 14 August 1947. This order ensured the seamless transition of legal frameworks by adapting and continuing the laws in force prior to independence. As a result, Pakistan formally declared its sovereignty a day earlier than the appointed date, attaining independence on 14 August 1947. From its inception, Pakistan was officially recognized as the Islamic Republic of Pakistan, laying the foundation for its governance, legal system, and national identity.

4. Following independence, Quaid-e-Azam Muhammad Ali Jinnah assumed office as the first Governor General of Pakistan and appointed Liaquat Ali Khan as the country's first Prime Minister. The newly formed nation faced immense challenges, including communal riots, a large influx of refugees, the establishment of an administrative system, foreign policy formulation, and the drafting of a constitution. Recognizing the strategic and economic significance of Karachi, Quaid-e-Azam declared it as Pakistan's first Federal Capital. In the initial years, he devoted himself to stabilizing the country's fragile economy and addressing pressing national concerns. Despite his tireless efforts, he did not remain with Pakistan for long, passing away on 11 September 1948. He was laid to rest in Karachi, leaving behind an enduring legacy of leadership and resilience. After Jinnah's demise, Liaquat Ali Khan played a crucial role in shaping the country's governance. One of his significant contributions was the passage of the Objectives Resolution, which laid the foundation for Pakistan's future constitution, emphasizing its Islamic character. Unfortunately, his tenure was cut short when he was assassinated on 16 October 1951. In recognition of his service and sacrifice, the government honoured him with the title Shaheed-i-Millat (Martyr of the Nation). Pakistan was established on the foundation of Islamic ideology, fulfilling the aspirations of the Muslims of the subcontinent who sought a separate homeland where they could live in accordance with their religious and cultural values. This vision continues to shape the nation's identity and governance to this day.

5. Nestled at the foothills of the Margalla Hills in the northern part of the Pothohar Plateau, Islamabad stands as Pakistan's picturesque and modern capital. Designed with meticulous urban planning, the city boasts a serene environment, a pollution-free atmosphere, abundant water resources, and lush greenery, making it one of the most livable cities in the region. Islamabad is characterized by its broad, tree-lined avenues, spacious residences, and elegant public buildings that reflect both modernity and sophistication. The city's well-organized bazaars, markets, and shopping centres cater to diverse needs while maintaining an uncluttered aesthetic. Pedestrian walkways, shaded by rows of flame trees, jacarandas, and hibiscus, provide a safe and pleasant experience, separated from traffic for added convenience. Islamabad's parks and gardens burst with vibrant blooms of roses, jasmine, and bougainvillaea, enhancing the city's natural beauty. Scenic viewpoints, spread across the Margalla Hills, offer breathtaking panoramas, allowing visitors to admire the city's harmonious blend of nature and modern architecture. With its tranquil ambience, well-planned infrastructure, and stunning landscapes, Islamabad stands as a testament to Pakistan's vision for a progressive and eco-friendly capital.

6. Brief Facts about Pakistan are as under:

Official Name:	Islamic Republic of Pakistan
Capital:	Islamabad
Area:	881,913 sq. km
	Punjab 205,344 sq.km ; Sindh 140,914 sq.km;
	Khyber Pakhtunkhwa 101,741 sq. km
	Balochistan 347,190 sq. km
	Federally Administered Tribal Areas 27,220 sq.km; and Islamabad (Capital) 906 sq. km
Population:	240 million (estimated)
Ethnic Composition:	96.5% Muslims, 3.5% others
Per Capita Income:	USD 1650+
Currency:	Pakistani Rupee (PKR)
Languages:	Punjabi (38.78%), Pashto (18.24%), Sindhi (14.57%), Saraiki (12.1%), Urdu (7.08%), Balochi (3.02%), Bengali (0.02%), Others (including Hindko, Brahui, Kashmiri, etc.) 6.12%
Archaeological Sites:	Mohenjodaro, Harappa, Taxila, Kot Diji, Mehar Garh, Takht Bahi, Ranikot Fort, Rohtas Fort, Baltit and Altit Forts
Major Cities:	Islamabad, Karachi, Lahore, Peshawar, Quetta, Rawalpindi, Hyderabad, Faisalabad, Bahawalpur, Sialkot, Gujranwala and Multan.

§2. Population

7. As of 2010, Pakistan's population exceeded 170 million, ranking it as the world's sixth most populous country, positioned between Brazil and Russia. This marked a significant increase from the 34 million recorded in 1951. By 2020, the population had surged to approximately 235 million. In the southern regions, the majority of inhabitants reside along the Indus River, with Karachi being the nation's largest city by population. In the northern areas, a substantial portion of the populace is concentrated in an arc encompassing cities such as Lahore, Faisalabad, Rawalpindi, Islamabad, Gujranwala, Sialkot, Gujrat, Jhelum, Sargodha, and Sheikhupura.

8. The estimated existing population of major cities of Pakistan is given below:

TABLE 1 : AREA, POPULATION BY SEX, SEX RATIO, POPULATION DENSITY, URBAN POPULATION, HOUSEHOLD SIZE AND ANNUAL GROWTH RATE, CENSUS-2023

NAME OF ADMINISTRATIVE UNIT	AREA IN SQ.KM	POPULATION-2023								POPULATION 2017	2017-2023 AVG. ANNUAL G.RATE
		ALL SEXES	MALE	FEMALE	TRANS GENDER	SEX RATIO	DENSITY PER SQ.KM	URBAN PROPORTION	AVG. H.HOLD SIZE		
PAKISTAN	**796,096**	**241,499,431**	**124,324,406**	**117,154,694**	**20,331**	**106.12**	**303.35**	**38.88**	**6.3**	**207,684,626**	**2.55**
RURAL		147,614,729	75,592,790	72,017,097	4,842	104.97			6.3	132,013,789	1.88
URBAN		93884702	48,731,616	45,137,597	15,489	107.96			6.2	75,670,837	3.67
KHYBER PAKHTUNKHWA	**101,741**	**40,856,097**	**20,845,747**	**20,009,233**	**1,117**	**104.18**	**401.57**	**15.01**	**6.9**	**35,501,964**	**2.38**
RURAL		34,724,801	17,685,692	17,038,648	461	103.80			6.9	29,626,670	2.69
URBAN		6131296	3,160,055	2,970,585	656	106.38			6.7	5,875,294	0.72
PUNJAB	**205,345**	**127,688,922**	**65,448,376**	**62,226,589**	**13,957**	**105.18**	**621.83**	**40.71**	**6.4**	**109,989,655**	**2.53**
RURAL		75,712,955	38,625,841	37,083,868	3,246	104.16			6.4	69,442,450	1.46
URBAN		51975967	26,822,535	25,142,721	10,711	106.68			6.3	40,547,205	4.24
SINDH	**140,914**	**55,696,147**	**29,014,424**	**26,677,501**	**4,222**	**108.76**	**395.25**	**53.97**	**5.6**	**47,854,510**	**2.57**
RURAL		25,639,408	13,245,373	12,393,405	630	106.87			5.4	23,021,876	1.82
URBAN		30056739	15,769,051	14,284,096	3,592	110.40			5.8	24,832,634	3.24
BALOCHISTAN	**347,190**	**14,894,402**	**7,768,166**	**7,125,471**	**765**	**109.02**	**42.90**	**30.96**	**6.4**	**12,335,129**	**3.20**
RURAL		10,282,574	5,379,780	4,902,339	455	109.74			6.1	8,928,428	2.39
URBAN		4611828	2,388,386	2,223,132	310	107.43			7.0	3,406,701	5.19
ISLAMABAD	**906**	**2,363,863**	**1,247,693**	**1,115,900**	**270**	**111.81**	**2,609.12**	**46.91**	**5.7**	**2,003,368**	**2.80**
RURAL		1,254,991	656,104	598,837	50	109.56			5.5	994,365	3.97
URBAN		1108872	591,589	517,063	220	114.41			5.9	1,009,003	1.59

TABLE 3 : NUMBER OF RURAL LOCALITIES BY POPULATION SIZE AND THEIR POPULATION BY SEX, CENSUS-2023

RURAL LOCALITIES BY POPULATION SIZE	NUMBER OF RURAL LOCALITIES	POPULATION - 2023			
		ALL SEXES	MALE	FEMALE	T.GENDER
1	2	3	4	5	6
PAKISTAN	**46,697**	**147,614,729**	**75,592,790**	**72,017,097**	**4,842**
5,000 AND ABOVE	8,340	86,567,399	44,378,573	42,185,614	3,212
2,000 -- 4,999	12,417	40,261,195	20,575,171	19,684,900	1,124
1,000 -- 1,999	9,334	13,613,632	6,952,771	6,660,573	288
500 -- 999	6,950	5,148,345	2,638,118	2,510,091	136
200 -- 499	4,808	1,666,139	859,704	806,363	72
LESS THAN 200	3,821	358,019	188,453	169,556	10
UN-INHABITED	1,027	-	-	-	-
KHYBER PAKHTUNKHWA	**9,821**	**34,724,801**	**17,685,692**	**17,038,648**	**461**
5,000 AND ABOVE	1,818	23,795,646	12,155,621	11,639,701	324
2,000 -- 4,999	1,952	6,207,646	3,147,365	3,060,209	72
1,000 -- 1,999	1,988	2,853,797	1,438,813	1,414,940	44
500 -- 999	1,792	1,308,049	659,917	648,115	17
200 -- 499	1,366	477,614	242,046	235,564	4
LESS THAN 200	758	82,049	41,930	40,119	-
UN-INHABITED	147	-	-	-	-
PUNJAB	**24,700**	**75,712,955**	**38,625,841**	**37,083,868**	**3,246**
5,000 AND ABOVE	4,348	40,637,166	20,760,889	19,874,021	2,256
2,000 -- 4,999	7,386	23,964,437	12,203,845	11,759,831	761
1,000 -- 1,999	5,319	7,810,520	3,969,750	3,840,614	156
500 -- 999	3,348	2,503,449	1,277,351	1,226,054	44
200 -- 499	1,883	662,747	341,788	320,933	26
LESS THAN 200	1,657	134,636	72,218	62,415	3
UN-INHABITED		-	-	-	-
SINDH	**5,690**	**25,639,408**	**13,245,373**	**12,393,405**	**630**
5,000 AND ABOVE	1,756	16,274,570	8,407,404	7,866,736	430
2,000 -- 4,999	2,292	7,634,122	3,937,923	3,696,035	164
1,000 -- 1,999	902	1,367,151	710,128	656,996	27
500 -- 999	369	287,763	149,889	137,868	6
200 -- 499	175	63,271	33,275	29,994	2
LESS THAN 200	127	12,531	6,754	5,776	1
UN-INHABITED	69	-	-	-	-
BALOCHISTAN	**6,357**	**10,282,574**	**5,379,780**	**4,902,339**	**455**
5,000 AND ABOVE	375	4,724,898	2,460,982	2,263,755	161
2,000 -- 4,999	764	2,378,348	1,246,384	1,131,845	119
1,000 -- 1,999	1,111	1,560,815	822,698	738,056	61
500 -- 999	1,416	1,031,303	541,738	489,497	68
200 -- 499	1,376	459,917	241,225	218,652	40
LESS THAN 200	1,265	127,293	66,753	60,534	6
UN-INHABITED	50	-	-	-	-
ISLAMABAD CAPITAL TERRITORY	**129**	**1,254,991**	**656,104**	**598,837**	**50**
5,000 AND ABOVE	43	1,135,119	593,677	541,401	41
2,000 -- 4,999	23	76,642	39,654	36,980	8
1,000 -- 1,999	14	21,349	11,382	9,967	-
500 -- 999	25	17,781	9,223	8,557	1
200 -- 499	8	2,590	1,370	1,220	-
LESS THAN 200	14	1,510	798	712	-
UN-INHABITED	2	-	-	-	-

9. The population growth rates of Pakistan are as under:

Years	*Growth Rate (%)*
1951–1961	2.45
1961–1972	3.66
1972–1981	3.05
1981–1998	2.69

Years	*Growth Rate (%)*
2010	2.05
2010–2015	1.71
2015–2025	1.61

10. Official population projections of Pakistan are as under:

Year	*Both Male/Female (in Million)*
2030	276.88
2029	272.34
2028	267.88
2027	263.52
2026	259.30
2025	249.95
2024	245.21
2023	240.49
2022	235.82
2021	231.40
2020	227.20
2019	223.29
2018	219.73
2017	216.38
2016	213.52
2015	210.97
2014	208.25
2013	205.34
2012	202.21
2011	198.60

Source: Ministry of Population & Welfare, Government of Pakistan.

§3. People of Pakistan

11. Pakistan is a diverse yet culturally cohesive nation, with the vast majority of its people adhering to Islam. The country is also home to minority religious communities, including Christians, Hindus, Buddhists, and Parsees, who contribute to its rich cultural fabric. Despite ethnic and regional variations, Pakistanis share a common historical and racial heritage, with most tracing their ancestry to Aryan lineage, alongside influences from other civilizations that have shaped the region over centuries. Linguistically, Urdu serves as the national language, fostering unity among the people. However, English is widely used in government, commerce, and urban centres, playing a crucial role in administration and international communication. Each province has its own distinct regional language, reflecting the country's cultural diversity: Punjabi in Punjab, Sindhi in Sindh, Balochi in Balochistan, and Pashto in Khyber Pakhtunkhwa. These languages, along with several other dialects, enrich Pakistan's literary and cultural traditions, preserving the heritage of its people.

12. English serves as Pakistan's official language and is widely used in government, education, business, and legal affairs. It is spoken and understood by many Pakistanis, particularly among the educated elite and urban populations. Due to its prominence in higher education and professional settings, English plays a crucial role in national and international communication. Urdu, the national language, functions as a lingua franca, uniting people across diverse ethnic and linguistic backgrounds. While spoken and understood throughout the country, it coexists with a rich tapestry of regional languages that reflect Pakistan's cultural and ethnic diversity. These include Punjabi, Sindhi, Pashto, Balochi, Saraiki, Hindko, Shina, Burushaski, Khowar, Wakhi, and several other dialects spoken in various regions. This linguistic diversity is a testament to Pakistan's rich heritage and cultural pluralism.

13. Pakistan is home to a civilization that dates back over *5,000 years*, making it one of the world's oldest cultural hubs. Over the centuries, the region has witnessed successive waves of migrations and conquests, shaping its rich and diverse heritage. Aryans, Persians, Greeks, Arabs, and Mughals all left their mark, blending their traditions with local cultures and influencing the social, artistic, and architectural landscape of the land. Despite these varied influences, it was Islam and its traditions that ultimately took deep root, becoming the foundation of Pakistan's cultural identity. Islamic values, art, and philosophy became the guiding forces behind the region's social and intellectual development, shaping the customs, traditions, and way of life that define Pakistan today.

14. Since the advent of Islam in the region, Muslim rulers and artisans have left behind a remarkable architectural heritage, constructing cities, forts, palaces, mosques, religious schools (madrassas), tombs, and mausoleums. These structures, marked by elegance and simplicity, emphasize open spaces and natural light, reflecting the Islamic principle of a direct and unmediated connection with the Divine. The blend of intricate design, geometric artistry, and serene courtyards continues to define Pakistan's architectural landscape. Pakistan boasts an extensive cultural legacy, preserved and promoted through various dedicated institutions. Government bodies such as the Pakistan National Council of Arts, Lok Virsa (Folk Heritage),

National Film Development Corporation, Authority for the Preservation of Mohenjodaro, and the National Archives of Pakistan play a vital role in documenting, conserving, and celebrating the country's diverse artistic and historical heritage. Their efforts ensure that Pakistan's rich traditions remain a source of national pride and inspiration for future generations.

15. Pakistan is officially an Islamic Republic, with Islam as the State religion. The Preamble of the Constitution affirms that the sovereign authority of Pakistan belongs to Allah Almighty, and the power vested in the people is to be exercised as a sacred trust within the framework prescribed by divine guidance. The Constitution ensures that governance is conducted through elected representatives, upholding the principles of democracy, freedom, equality, tolerance, and social justice. While the State's foundation is rooted in Islamic values, the Constitution does not establish a theocracy, nor does it grant authority to a religious clergy to govern. Instead, Pakistan's legal and political system operates within a democratic structure, ensuring that faith and governance coexist in a balanced and inclusive manner.

16. Pakistan is a predominantly Muslim-majority nation, with over 97% of its population adhering to Islam. Among them, approximately 80% are Sunni, while 20% belong to the Shia sect. Religious minorities make up a small yet significant part of the population. Christians constitute around 1%, with a slightly higher proportion of Protestants compared to Catholics. Hindus, primarily residing in the southern regions, particularly in Sindh, form a minority of less than 1%. Additionally, small Buddhist communities are present in urban centres like Karachi, Lahore, Rawalpindi, and Quetta. In the remote Chitral region, near the Afghan border, a tiny indigenous group known as the Kalash people follow their ancient animist traditions, preserving a unique and distinct cultural identity.

§4. Land, Heritage and Culture

17. Pakistan is situated between 24° and 37° North latitude and 62° and 75° East longitude sharing borders with Iran to the west, India to the east, Afghanistan to the northwest, and China to the north, while the Arabian Sea lies to its south. The country's northern region is dominated by the towering mountain ranges of the Himalayas, Karakoram, and Hindukush, which include some of the world's highest peaks, such as K2. These highlands, covering Khyber Pakhtunkhwa and the Northern Areas, feature deep valleys, glaciers, and fast-flowing rivers that contribute to the Indus River system. Punjab, a fertile alluvial plain, is shaped by five major rivers – the Jhelum, Chenab, Ravi, Sutlej, and Beas that merge into the Indus, making the region the agricultural heartland of Pakistan. Further south, Sindh is bordered by the arid Thar Desert and Rann of Kutch to the east and the rugged Kirthar Range to the west, with the Indus River flowing through its centre before reaching the Arabian Sea. This province is known for its coastal belt and major ports, including Karachi, which serves as Pakistan's primary trade hub. In the west, Balochistan consists of a vast, arid plateau encircled by dry, Rocky Mountains. Though sparsely populated, this region is rich in mineral resources and features a harsh climate with limited water sources. Pakistan's diverse landscape, from its snow-capped peaks to its coastal plains, plays a crucial role in shaping its economy, climate, and way of life.

18. The land that now forms the Islamic Republic of Pakistan has been the cradle of some of the world's most advanced civilizations since ancient times. Ample evidence from both prehistoric and historic periods supports this claim, such as the discovery of fossilized ape jaws in the Pothohar region, dating back approximately 14 million years. These fossils belong to a species called *Sivapithecus Pakininsis*, believed to be an early ancestor of humans. Additionally, a two-million-year-old stone hand axe, one of the earliest known tools, is exhibited at the Islamabad Museum, showcasing the region's deep-rooted prehistoric heritage.

19. Pakistan takes great pride in its rich artistic and craft traditions, which span thousands of years. Since gaining independence, successive governments have actively supported and promoted the country's arts and crafts through various state-led initiatives. The National Crafts Council, along with organizations like the Export Promotion Bureau and Small Industries Corporations, has played a vital role in recognizing and uplifting the craftsmanship of artisans. Pakistani craftsmen are renowned for their exceptional skills in creating high-quality products from clay, stone, textiles, carpets, wood, metal, jewellery, and leather, preserving a heritage that continues to thrive both locally and internationally.

20. Pakistan experiences four distinct seasons: a chilly, dry winter from December to February; a warm, arid spring from March to May; a monsoon season with heavy summer rains from June to September; and a post-monsoon transition period in October and November. However, the timing and intensity of these seasons vary across different regions.

21. Islamabad experiences a diverse climate, with temperatures ranging from an average low of 2°C in January to a peak of 40°C in June. The city receives the majority of its annual rainfall during July and August, with an average of approximately 255 millimetres in each of these months. For the rest of the year, precipitation is considerably lower, averaging around 50 millimetres per month.

22. Karachi, Pakistan's largest city and its main industrial hub has a more humid climate than Islamabad but receives significantly less rainfall. Only in July and August does the city experience more than 25 millimetres of rain, while the rest of the year remains predominantly dry. Unlike Islamabad, Karachi's temperatures are relatively consistent, with winter nights averaging a low of 13°C and summer days reaching up to 34°C. Though the summer heat is not as intense as in Punjab, the high humidity levels make the weather considerably uncomfortable.

§5. THE ECONOMY

23. Since 2020, Pakistan's economy has navigated a tumultuous path, marked by the aftermath of the COVID-19 pandemic, global economic disruptions, and numerous domestic challenges. The pandemic severely impacted the economy in 2020, leading to a contraction of 1.0% due to lockdowns, disruptions in trade, and a slowdown in key sectors. However, the country experienced a robust recovery in FY2021, with a growth rate of 5.6%, fuelled by a surge in industrial output and an uplift in services as pandemic restrictions eased. This recovery was a testament to Pakistan's resilience, but the economy continued to face mounting challenges in subsequent years, including inflationary pressures and supply chain disruptions. In 2023, Pakistan's growth stagnated, with gross domestic product (GDP) growth standing at 0.0%, largely due to continued global economic slowdowns and rising domestic issues such as energy shortages, political instability, and high inflation. The inflation rate reached a peak of 28.3% in early 2024, driven by rising food and fuel costs, and the depreciation of the national currency. However, by January 2025, inflation had eased significantly to 2.4%, thanks to a combination of factors including base effects, the stabilization of the currency, and falling global food and energy prices. The country's central bank took a proactive step by slashing interest rates to 12% to further support economic recovery and stimulate investment. The efforts to stabilize Pakistan's economy have been bolstered by international support, particularly from the International Monetary Fund (IMF), which extended a USD 7 billion facility to help Pakistan navigate its fiscal challenges and stabilize its macroeconomic framework. The government has also implemented structural reforms aimed at boosting exports, improving tax collection, and addressing the growing fiscal deficit. These reforms, along with the stabilization of key economic indicators such as inflation and interest rates, have provided a foundation for gradual recovery, even though challenges remain. Despite facing one crisis after another, from the 2005 earthquake to the pandemic and natural disasters, Pakistan's economy has demonstrated significant resilience, showing the country's ability to adapt and survive in an increasingly volatile global environment.

24. The economic impact of external shocks, such as the devastating floods of 2022 and global supply chain disruptions, severely affected Pakistan's key sectors. Agriculture, particularly crops like rice and cotton, faced significant losses, contributing to a contraction of 4% in this sector. Manufacturing also saw limited growth, with output in textiles and petroleum products significantly reduced due to damage to refineries during the floods and the ongoing circular debt crisis. As a result, the services sector, which had originally been projected to grow by 5.4%, grew only by 4.1%, reflecting the broader slowdown in economic activities. The government's efforts to implement economic reforms were complicated by the persistent exogenous shocks. The ongoing challenges of flood rehabilitation, rising oil prices, and the need for fiscal adjustments forced difficult trade-offs. While the government pursued deregulation in the pricing of essential commodities, it had to intervene in energy and food markets to prevent prices from spiralling out of control. Although subsidies were significantly reduced compared to previous years, they still placed considerable strain on the fiscal system, impeding progress in fiscal consolidation.

By the second half of 2024, a combination of austerity measures, resource mobilization strategies, and decisive actions on pricing helped stabilize the macroeconomic framework. These efforts enabled the government to avoid further deterioration in the fiscal position, ensuring that the damage from external shocks did not worsen the overall economic outlook. A significant milestone in Pakistan's recent economic performance has been the remarkable recovery of the external sector. As of 2024, the country's exports have experienced a substantial growth increasing by 18% in the first half of the year compared to the same period in 2023. This growth has pushed exports beyond the USD 25 billion mark for the first time in Pakistan's history, signalling an optimistic outlook for the economy. Remittances, another crucial external income source, have also performed exceptionally well, surpassing USD 13 billion, reflecting a rise of 10% year-on-year. These robust remittance flows, combined with a controlled import bill, have contributed to a current account surplus, which stands at approximately USD 1.3 billion by the end of 2024. This surplus marks a positive shift, as the country previously struggled with a deficit in its external balance. The combined effect of these positive developments has also been reflected in the country's foreign reserves, which reached an all-time high of USD 20.5 billion by the end of 2024. This growth in reserves, bolstered by export performance and remittances, provides Pakistan with a buffer against external shocks and enhances investor confidence. Moreover, the country has maintained a period of relative exchange rate stability since 2022, with the Real Effective Exchange Rate (REER) appreciating by 7% in the past year, suggesting a strengthened currency in real terms. The State Bank of Pakistan (SBP) has allowed the exchange rate to be largely market-determined, reducing its interventions in the foreign exchange markets. On the inflation front, the situation has been more challenging. After a brief period of easing inflation in 2023, global commodity price hikes and rising oil costs have led to a resurgence in inflationary pressures. In 2024, inflation surged to 28.3% in the first quarter but gradually stabilized to around 15% by mid-year. Pakistan, like many other countries worldwide, has been significantly impacted by these global inflationary trends, driven by supply chain disruptions and soaring energy prices. However, in the second half of 2024, inflation started to abate as the government implemented fiscal consolidation measures, and international commodity prices began to stabilize. While inflation remains a concern, the outlook for the rest of 2025 appears more favourable, with expectations for inflation to gradually decline as supply-side pressures ease and fiscal measures take effect.

25. Inflationary pressures led to a rise in interest rates, exerting further strain on the economy. While the government sector continued to absorb much of the available credit, private sector credit growth remained weak, despite showing some improvement from previous years. The government faced significant challenges in managing its fiscal policy, as the increasing cost of flood rehabilitation efforts, rising energy and petroleum subsidies, and other unanticipated expenditures stretched public finances. As a result, the government had to significantly reduce public investment, marking one of the lowest levels of development spending in recent years. This adjustment was necessary to address immediate fiscal needs while maintaining some level of financial stability in the face of mounting external and internal pressures.

26. . In the fiscal year 2023–2024, Pakistan's economy exhibited signs of stabilization, achieving a GDP growth rate of 2.4%, a notable recovery from the previous year's contraction of 0.29%. This positive trajectory was underpinned by a substantial 41% increase in revenue collection, totalling PKR 9.8 trillion in the first nine months of the fiscal year. However, total expenditures also rose by 37% to PKR 13.7 trillion, primarily driven by a significant surge in mark-up payments due to elevated interest rates. Despite these fiscal challenges, the government successfully contained the fiscal deficit at 3.7% of GDP. Inflation, which had peaked at 38.0% in May 2023, declined to 11.8% by May 2024, attributed to factors such as exchange rate stability, monetary tightening, and improved global commodity prices. Per capita income increased to USD 1,680, reflecting both economic recovery and currency appreciation. The agriculture sector emerged as a pivotal contributor to this growth, compensating for underperformance in other areas. Nevertheless, the Federal Board of Revenue (FBR) granted record tax exemptions amounting to PKR 3.879 trillion, highlighting ongoing structural challenges within the fiscal framework. The SBP identified persistent structural impediments, including declining investment, an unfavourable business environment, lack of research and development, low productivity, and climate change risks, all of which continue to constrain the country's economic growth potential. Despite these obstacles, the government's commitment to fiscal discipline and comprehensive economic reforms aims to strengthen macroeconomic stability and foster sustainable growth in the coming years.[1]

§6. Constitutional History

27. The process of drafting Pakistan's Constitution traces back to the Lahore Resolution of 1940, where the concept of a separate homeland for the Muslims of India was first articulated. This landmark event, later known as the Pakistan Resolution, laid the foundation for the country's constitutional development.

28. On 3 June 1947, the British Government formally approved the partition of India, leading to the creation of two independent dominions: Pakistan and India. The Indian Independence Act was passed by the British Parliament on 18 July 1947, paving the way for Pakistan's emergence as a sovereign state on 14 August 1947. The newly established nation comprised East Bengal, part of Assam (Sylhet), West Punjab, Sindh, Khyber Pakhtunkhwa, and Balochistan, which were formerly provinces of British India. The partition was accompanied by one of the largest mass migrations in history, as millions of people moved across borders amid communal violence and unrest. As per section 8 of the Indian Independence Act 1947, Pakistan initially adopted a modified version of the Government of India Act 1935 as its interim constitutional framework. This temporary arrangement remained in place until Pakistan formulated and adopted its own constitution, reflecting the aspirations and governance needs of the newly independent state.

1. Government of Pakistan, Ministry of Finance, *Pakistan Economic Survey 2023–24: Overview* (Finance Division, 2024).

29. On 12 March 1949, the Constituent Assembly passed a resolution presented by Pakistan's then Prime Minister, Liaquat Ali Khan. Known as the Objectives Resolution, it set the foundational principles for the country's future Constitution. It declared that Pakistan's governance framework would not follow the European model but would be based on Islamic ideology and democratic principles. The resolution affirmed that ultimate sovereignty belongs to Allah, who has entrusted the authority to the State of Pakistan, to be exercised by its people within divine limits as a sacred responsibility. It emphasized that power and governance would rest with the elected representatives of the people. The resolution also underscored the importance of democracy, freedom, equality, tolerance, and social justice in accordance with Islamic teachings. Furthermore, it ensured that Muslims would have the freedom to lead their personal and collective lives in line with the principles of Islam as outlined in the Holy Quran and Sunnah. At the same time, provisions were made to protect the rights of minorities, allowing them to freely practice their religions and preserve their cultural identities. The resolution also established Pakistan as a federation, guaranteed fundamental rights for all citizens, and emphasized the independence of the judiciary.

30. Pakistan's Constitution (1973) is a written document that includes a framework for interpreting its provisions. The responsibility for interpreting the Constitution lies with the judiciary, particularly the High Courts and the Supreme Court of Pakistan (SCP), which have the authority to provide legal interpretations of its articles.

31. Pakistan's first Constitution came into effect on 23 March 1956, after more than eight years of challenges and delays. This Constitution was grounded in Islamic principles and established a federal system of government. It aimed to reflect the goals outlined in the Pakistan Resolution, creating a political system that ensured freedom, equality, tolerance, and social justice as envisioned by Islam. However, the 1956 Constitution proved short-lived, as it was abrogated on 7 October 1958 when Muhammad Ayub Khan declared Martial Law. In 1962, Ayub Khan introduced a new Constitution, which marked a drastic shift from its predecessor. It established a presidential system, granting the president extensive powers. This Constitution lasted until 25 March 1969 when it was annulled following Ayub Khan's resignation and replaced by Yahya Khan's military rule.

32. The first general elections in Pakistan, conducted through universal adult suffrage, took place in 1970. Despite the elections' democratic foundation, the outcome failed to result in the formation of a stable government. The tragic events that followed, particularly the revolt and the subsequent separation of East Pakistan, which became Bangladesh, left the remaining part of the country in a state of deep disillusionment. In response to the crisis, an interim Constitution was enacted in 1972. This provisional document was adopted by the National Assembly as a temporary measure until a permanent, formal Constitution could be developed for Pakistan.

33. In the final months of 1972, the government successfully presented a draft of the new Constitution to the National Assembly. The proposed Constitution underwent careful deliberation, incorporating the diverse political perspectives of various stakeholders within the system. After extensive discussions and amendments, the Constitution of the Islamic Republic of Pakistan was officially passed by the National Assembly on 10 April 1973. The Constitution came into effect on 14 August 1973, marking the twenty-sixth anniversary of Pakistan's independence, and became the foundation of the country's legal and political structure.

34. Since its adoption in 1973, the Constitution of Pakistan has undergone nineteen amendments. Following the imposition of Martial Law by General Zia-ul-Haq on 5 July 1977, several changes were introduced to the Constitution. Successive democratic governments worked to restore the Constitution to its original form. However, after General Pervez Musharraf assumed power in 1999, further alterations were made. In April 2010, the democratically elected parliament passed the 18th Amendment, which effectively reversed many of the changes imposed by previous military regimes, thereby restoring much of the original framework of the 1973 Constitution. More recently, the 19th Amendment was enacted in January 2011, primarily focusing on the procedural changes regarding the appointment of judges.

35. The Constitution of Pakistan guarantees fundamental rights to all citizens, in line with the principles of the Universal Declaration of Human Rights. The government is prohibited from enacting laws that contradict or undermine these rights, with any such laws subject to judicial review and potential nullification by the Superior Courts. These rights encompass personal security, protections against unlawful arrest, detention, and torture, as well as safeguards against practices such as slavery, forced labour, and retrospective punishment. The Constitution further protects individuals from double jeopardy, and self-incrimination, and ensures the inviolability of personal dignity. It also safeguards property rights and promotes equality before the law, regardless of race, religion, or gender. In addition, it recognizes the cultural diversity of Pakistan by ensuring the preservation of languages, scripts, and cultural identities of various communities. Citizens are granted the freedom of speech, association, and assembly, which are fundamental to the democratic framework of the nation. Moreover, the Constitution provides special protection to marginalized groups, including women, children, and minorities, ensuring their right to participate fully in the social, economic, and political life of the country.

36. The Constitution of Pakistan guarantees a wide range of fundamental freedoms to its citizens which include the right to move freely within the country, the right to assemble peacefully, and the right to form associations or organizations. It also ensures the freedom to engage in trade, commerce, and any lawful profession. Additionally, the Constitution protects the right to express opinions and ideas freely, without fear of censorship or retribution. It further upholds the right of individuals to practice their religion and to establish and manage religious institutions in accordance with their beliefs. These freedoms are essential to maintaining the democratic and pluralistic fabric of Pakistani society.

§7. Political, Judicial and Administrative System

37. The Constitution of the Islamic Republic of Pakistan establishes a federal parliamentary system, where the President serves as the ceremonial Head of State, and the Prime Minister, elected by the people, assumes the role of Head of Government. The national legislative body is the Parliament, which is bicameral, consisting of the National Assembly and the Senate. The federal structure comprises various entities including the President, the Prime Minister, the National Security Council, and both the National Assembly and Senate. Additionally, the federal government encompasses ministers, government ministries, departments, and the Attorney General. At the provincial level, each province has its own government, led by a Governor and a Chief Minister, with accompanying ministries and administrative departments overseeing local governance and regional affairs.

38. The National Assembly of Pakistan stands as the supreme legislative authority in the country, reflecting the democratic will of the people in the framework of a multi-party federal parliamentary system. It is empowered to legislate on matters specified in the Federal Legislative List, ensuring the country's legal structure aligns with constitutional mandates. Through its various functions, including rigorous debates, adjournment motions, the question hour, and active Standing Committees, the National Assembly holds the Executive accountable, ensuring that the government operates within the limits prescribed by the Constitution and upholds the Fundamental Rights of citizens. One of the core functions of the National Assembly is its oversight of public finances; through the Public Accounts Committee, it thoroughly reviews and audits government spending, maintaining checks on the expenditure of public funds. In addition to these roles, the National Assembly plays a key part in shaping national policies, approving budgets, and addressing the needs and concerns of the people through legislation. By engaging in these democratic processes, the National Assembly ensures transparency, accountability, and responsiveness in governance.

39. The Islamic Republic of Pakistan is a federated nation composed of four distinct provinces: Balochistan, Khyber Pakhtunkhwa, Punjab, and Sindh, along with the Federal Capital Territory of Islamabad. Additionally, the country formerly included the Federally Administered Tribal Areas (FATA), which were merged with Khyber Pakhtunkhwa in 2018. These provincial entities represent a rich mosaic of cultural, linguistic, and ethnic diversity, each with its own unique characteristics. The provinces vary widely in terms of socio-economic development, population distribution, and geographical features. Punjab, the most populous province, is the agricultural heartland, while Balochistan is known for its vast natural resources and arid landscape. Sindh is an economic hub, particularly in terms of its industrial output and port access, and Khyber Pakhtunkhwa holds significant historical and cultural importance. The differences in climate range from the temperate regions of the north to the arid deserts in the south, further adding to the complexity and dynamism of the federation. Together, these regions contribute to the national fabric of Pakistan, balancing both unity and regional identity.

40. Article 50 of the Constitution of Pakistan outlines the structure of the country's Parliament, which consists of the President and two chambers: the National Assembly and the Senate. The National Assembly holds a distinctive advantage over the Senate, particularly in matters related to financial legislation, as it holds exclusive authority over money bills. While the Senate plays a crucial role in representing the provinces and contributing to the legislative process, it is the National Assembly that has the final say on matters involving national finances. Beyond financial matters, both chambers collaborate in the legislative process, working together to draft, amend, and pass laws that govern the country. The National Assembly, as the lower house, is directly elected by the people, while the Senate serves as the upper house, providing a broader representation of the provinces and territories. This bicameral structure ensures a balance of power and a fair representation of both the population and the regions in the decision-making process of the country.

41. The Constitution of Pakistan establishes a parliamentary system of governance with a bicameral legislature, consisting of the National Assembly and the Senate. The Senate, initially comprising 45 members, saw its membership increase to 63 in 1977 and then to 87 in 1985. In 2002, the Senate's total membership was further expanded to 100. This expansion ensured a more inclusive representation of Pakistan's diverse provinces and territories. Today, the Senate includes 22 members from each of the four provinces: Punjab, Sindh, Khyber Pakhtunkhwa, and Balochistan. These members are elected through a combination of general seats, seats for technocrats or ulema (religious scholars), and seats reserved for women. The Federal Capital, Islamabad, is represented by four senators, two general members, one technocrat/ulema, and one woman. Additionally, the FATA, which until recently enjoyed special status, elects eight members to the Senate. While seventeen seats are specifically reserved for women in the Senate, there are no restrictions preventing women from contesting election for any of the other available seats, ensuring that they can represent their constituencies in all areas of governance. This structure aims to balance representation across Pakistan's varied regions and social groups, giving a voice to marginalized communities and ensuring gender diversity in the upper house of Parliament.

42. The Senate of Pakistan serves as a continuous legislative body that ensures stability and continuity in the governance of the nation. Its members serve for a term of six years, with half of the Senate members retiring every three years. This staggered election process allows for a consistent flow of experienced lawmakers while also providing new perspectives within the upper house. In the event of a vacancy due to reasons such as resignation, death, disqualification, or incapacity, the vacant seat is filled through a by-election. The election process is carried out by the relevant electoral college, which typically consists of members of the provincial assemblies. The newly elected senator assumes office for the remainder of the term of the member whose position has been vacated. This mechanism ensures that the Senate remains fully functional and that legislative activities continue without interruption. The Senate, with its rotating membership and careful selection process, plays a crucial role in providing long-term stability and continuity in Pakistan's legislative framework, balancing regional representation and contributing to the broader democratic process.

43. To be eligible for election to the Senate of Pakistan, a candidate must meet several key requirements. First, the individual must be at least 30 years old. In addition, the candidate must be a registered voter in the area or province from which they seek election. Beyond these basic criteria, the candidate must also fulfil the qualifications outlined in Articles 62 and 63 of the Constitution. These articles stipulate that a candidate must possess qualities such as good character, sound moral standing, and must not have been disqualified under any relevant legal or constitutional provisions. Furthermore, the individual must be capable of representing the interests and concerns of their constituency effectively, ensuring that they contribute positively to the legislative process. By setting these standards, the Constitution seeks to ensure that only qualified and credible individuals are entrusted with the responsibility of participating in the Senate's important legislative and oversight functions.

44. Pakistan's Federation comprises four provinces: Balochistan, Khyber Pakhtunkhwa, Punjab, and Sindh. Each province has its own Provincial Assembly, which serves as the legislative body empowered to make laws on matters specifically allocated to them by the Constitution. Provincial Assemblies possess legislative authority over all subjects not explicitly included in the Federal Legislative List or relating to areas under federal jurisdiction. This framework ensures that provincial governments have considerable autonomy, allowing them to address local issues and concerns effectively. The Constitution of Pakistan provides a high degree of provincial autonomy, which distinguishes the country's federal system from those of many other nations, granting significant power to the provinces while maintaining the unity of the Federation.

45. The President of Pakistan serves as the ceremonial Head of State, symbolizing the unity of the nation. To be eligible for the office of President, a candidate must be a Muslim, at least 45 years old, and qualified to be a member of the National Assembly. The President is elected by an electoral college, which consists of the members of the National Assembly, Senate, and the Provincial Assemblies, for a term of five years. Upon election, the President takes an oath of office before the Chief Justice of Pakistan. During their tenure, the President is prohibited from holding any office of profit in the public service or engaging in any remunerative positions. The President's term is fixed for five years or until the new President assumes office, but they may resign at any time by submitting a written resignation to the Speaker of the National Assembly. In addition to his symbolic role, the President possesses certain constitutional powers, including the authority to grant pardons, reprieves, and commutations of sentences, as well as the ability to remit or suspend sentences passed by courts or tribunals, offering a critical check within the justice system.

46. In Pakistan's parliamentary system, the Cabinet of Ministers is headed by the Prime Minister, who plays a crucial role in advising and assisting the President in carrying out the functions of the state. Following the general elections, and once the newly elected members of the National Assembly take their oath of office, the President invites the member who holds the confidence of the majority of the Assembly to assume the office of Prime Minister. This is confirmed through a vote of confidence in a specially convened session of the National Assembly. Once appointed, the Prime Minister takes the oath of office and is tasked with recommending the appointment of Federal Ministers and Ministers of State. These ministers, who must be members of the National Assembly or the Senate, are appointed by the President to form the Cabinet. The Prime Minister and his Cabinet work collectively to shape national policy, implement laws and advise the President on the functioning of the federal government.

47. The Cabinet led by the Prime Minister holds collective responsibility to the National Assembly for the execution of its duties and decisions. In addition to the ministers, the Prime Minister has the authority to appoint up to five advisers, whose roles are defined by the Prime Minister's discretion. These advisers assist the Prime Minister on various matters, and their appointments are made upon the advice of the Prime Minister to the President. While advisers do not hold formal cabinet positions, they provide expert counsel and strategic guidance to the Prime Minister, helping to shape government policies and initiatives. The Cabinet's responsibility to the National Assembly ensures transparency and accountability in governance, with all its actions subject to scrutiny and approval by the legislative body.

48. The Governor serves as the ceremonial head of the Provincial Government, although the executive authority within the province is exercised on the advice of the Provincial Cabinet or the Chief Minister. Appointed by the President after consulting the Prime Minister, the Governor represents the central government in the province. To qualify for the position, the individual must meet the eligibility criteria for election to the National Assembly and be at least 35 years of age. The Governor is vested with several constitutional powers, including the authority to summon the Provincial Assembly at his discretion and to prorogue it when necessary. While the Governor's role is largely formal, he plays an essential part in maintaining the balance of power between the federal and provincial governments, ensuring that provincial legislation aligns with national policies. The Governor also performs various ceremonial duties, acts as a key liaison between the provincial and federal governments, and may be called upon to intervene in exceptional circumstances, such as the dissolution of the Provincial Assembly or in cases of governmental instability.

49. The Governor has the authority to issue Ordinances when the Provincial Assembly is not in session, provided there is an urgent need for immediate legislative action. Such Ordinances are temporary laws that remain in effect for up to three months unless they are either withdrawn or disapproved before the expiration of that period. Additionally, the Governor plays a key role in the legislative process by granting assent to all Bills passed by the Provincial Assembly, which, upon approval, become Acts of the Assembly. However, the Governor may return a Bill with a request for reconsideration or revision, offering a message to the Assembly to address specific concerns. The Chief Minister is the principal executive officer of the Provincial Government and leads the Provincial Cabinet, which is composed of members of the Provincial Assembly appointed on the Chief Minister's recommendation. As the leader of the majority party in the Provincial Assembly or someone who commands the support of the majority of members, the Chief Minister holds significant authority over the administration of the province. Responsible for managing the executive affairs of the province, the Chief Minister exercises his powers either directly or through the Provincial Cabinet. He allocates responsibilities among Cabinet Ministers according to the Rules of Business, which are formulated by the Governor on the Chief Minister's advice.

50. The Judiciary plays a crucial role as a cornerstone of the government, responsible for upholding justice in any democratic society. In Pakistan, the judicial system comprises several layers, with the SCP at the apex, followed by the High Courts of each Province and Federal Territories, as well as other courts established in accordance with the law. The judicial framework in Pakistan is divided into two primary categories: Constitutional Courts and Statutory Courts. Constitutional Courts include the Supreme Court, the High Courts, and the Federal Shariat Court (FSC). These institutions are specifically empowered by the Constitution to interpret and enforce the legal framework of the country, ensuring the protection of fundamental rights and the proper functioning of the government. On the other hand, Statutory Courts are those created by laws enacted by the legislature and serve specialized functions within the legal system, handling cases related to various legal matters outside of constitutional jurisdiction. Together, these judicial bodies form an intricate system designed to ensure the fair administration of justice and the rule of law throughout Pakistan.

51. The SCP stands as the highest judicial authority in the country entrusted with the responsibility of safeguarding the Constitution and ensuring the rule of law. As the ultimate court of appeal, it serves as the final adjudicator on matters of law, interpretation of the Constitution and disputes that affect the state. The Supreme Court holds a wide range of jurisdictions including original, appellate, and advisory powers which enable it to handle cases directly or hear appeals from lower courts, as well as provide guidance on legal matters when requested by the government. Its rulings are authoritative and binding on all courts, institutions, and authorities across Pakistan, meaning that all executive bodies and other judicial organs must comply with and enforce its decisions. By exercising this role, the Supreme Court plays an essential part in upholding justice, protecting citizens' rights, and maintaining the constitutional framework of the state.

52. The Constitution of Pakistan (1973) lays down comprehensive provisions regarding the structure, jurisdiction, powers, and responsibilities of the judiciary. It specifies the qualifications required for judges, the process of their appointment, the criteria for their removal from office, as well as the age of retirement and the terms of their service. The Constitution enshrines the principle of judicial independence, ensuring that the judiciary remains separate from the executive branch of government. This separation guarantees that the judiciary can operate free from external influence, safeguarding its impartiality and integrity. Both the Supreme Court and the High Courts are granted a certain level of financial autonomy, with the Chief Justice of each court authorized to approve expenditures and reallocate funds within the court's allocated budget without requiring prior approval from the Ministry of Finance. Moreover, these courts have the authority to establish their own procedural rules and determine the terms and conditions of service for their employees. This framework reinforces the judicial independence necessary for the effective functioning of the justice system and the protection of fundamental rights within the country.

53. The Constitution of Pakistan establishes a system of checks and balances with the Supreme Court playing a critical role in ensuring the separation of powers among the three branches of government: the Legislature, the Executive, and the Judiciary. This system is designed to maintain a delicate equilibrium, ensuring that each branch operates within its defined authority and does not exceed its constitutional limits. As the guardian of the Constitution, the Supreme Court holds the responsibility to 'preserve, protect, and defend' the Constitution against any encroachments or violations. In fulfilling this duty, the Court not only safeguards the legal framework of the country but also plays an integral role in promoting national unity. By interpreting and upholding the Constitution, the Court contributes to the cohesion of the nation, helping to harmonize diverse communities, regions, and institutions. In this way, the Supreme Court holds a central position in the governance of the country, ensuring that the constitutional order remains intact and that the rights of citizens are protected.

54. The SCP plays a vital role as the protector and defender of citizens' fundamental rights, freedoms, and liberties. Entrusted with the responsibility of safeguarding these essential rights, the Court is empowered to intervene whenever it deems necessary to address matters of public significance related to the enforcement of constitutional guarantees. Specifically, under Article 184(3) of the Constitution, the Supreme Court has the authority to take suo motu action if a question arises regarding the violation or protection of any fundamental right. This provision allows the Court to proactively address issues that affect the public interest, ensuring that individuals' rights are not infringed upon and that justice is upheld in accordance with the Constitution. By taking such actions, the Court serves as a critical mechanism for ensuring that the principles of equality, liberty, and justice are preserved in the legal and social fabric of the nation.

55. The SCP holds a wide range of responsibilities, exercising original, appellate, and advisory jurisdiction, each with distinct functions. In its original jurisdiction, the Court has exclusive authority to resolve disputes between federal and provincial governments, delivering declaratory judgments to clarify legal matters. The Court can also use its original jurisdiction to address cases involving the enforcement of fundamental rights when the matter at hand carries significant public importance. As for its advisory jurisdiction, the Supreme Court is empowered to provide the President with legal opinions on questions of public significance, offering guidance on complex constitutional or legal issues referred to it. In its appellate capacity, the Supreme Court reviews decisions made by the High Courts, special tribunals, and other lower courts, ensuring that justice is served at the highest level. This appellate role reinforces the Court's central position in maintaining the consistency and integrity of legal interpretations across the country. Additionally, the Constitution grants the Supreme Court the authority to establish its own procedural rules, giving it the flexibility to adapt to evolving legal needs. The Chief Justice, as the head of the institution, plays a crucial role in the administration of the Court overseeing the assignment of cases to Judges and carrying out other essential administrative duties. Through these mechanisms, the Supreme Court ensures that justice is not only delivered effectively but also in a manner consistent with the Constitution's framework.

56. Pakistan's judicial system includes five High Courts, each serving as the principal appellate and constitutional authority within their respective jurisdictions. These courts are the Islamabad High Court, Lahore High Court (LHC), High Court of Sindh, High Court of Balochistan, and Peshawar High Court (PHC). In Pakistan, the appointment of High Court judges, including the Chief Justice, is governed by Article 175A of the Constitution, as amended by the 18th and 19th Constitutional Amendments. The process begins with the Judicial Commission of Pakistan, which is chaired by the Chief Justice of Pakistan and includes senior judges of the Supreme Court, a retired judge, the Federal Law Minister, the Attorney General, a senior advocate nominated by the Pakistan Bar Council, and representatives from the relevant provincial judiciary and bar councils. This Commission recommends suitable candidates for appointment. The nominations are then forwarded to a Parliamentary Committee, composed equally of members from the National Assembly and Senate, representing both the treasury and opposition benches. The Committee reviews the recommendations and may approve or reject them, with reasons provided in writing. Only after this approval does the President of Pakistan formally appoint the judges. The Chief Justice of a High Court is typically the senior-most judge and, like other High Court judges, retires at the age of 62. The Chief Justice takes an oath of office before the Governor, and subsequently, the Chief Justice administers the oath to the other judges. High Courts in Pakistan have a broad jurisdiction, encompassing original, appellate, and administrative functions as outlined in various laws. They are primarily responsible for overseeing and supervising all lower courts within their jurisdiction, ensuring consistency and accountability in the judicial process. High Courts also have the authority to establish rules governing the practice and procedure of the court, as well as those for subordinate courts. The decisions made by a High Court are legally binding on all courts under its jurisdiction, particularly when such decisions establish or clarify a legal principle. Moreover, the High Court possesses exclusive jurisdiction in hearing appeals related to criminal matters, especially those involving the Hudood Laws, which cover offences such as theft, intoxication, unlawful sexual relations (Zina), and the false accusation of such offences (Qazf). This role highlights the critical position of the High Courts in shaping the legal landscape and ensuring the fair application of justice in Pakistan.

57. The FSC holds a distinctive position in Pakistan's judicial system with its primary responsibility being the examination and review of laws to determine their compliance with Islamic principles. In addition to its core function of ensuring that laws are in line with the teachings of Islam, the court also has jurisdiction over matters related to personal laws, such as those concerning family issues, inheritance, and marriage, particularly when they pertain to the Islamic practices prescribed in the Quran and Sunnah. The Court has the authority to declare any law or part of a law as repugnant to Islam, and such a declaration can lead to recommendations for amendments or repeal of the law in question. The court's decisions on these matters can profoundly impact the legislative process, especially when it comes to aligning secular laws with religious mandates. One important aspect of the FSC's jurisdiction is its appellate authority over certain criminal cases. For example, the FSC has jurisdiction over appeals concerning offences related to Hudood laws, which govern crimes such as theft, adultery, and false accusations of adultery (Qazf). In such cases, the FSC ensures that the punishment for these offences is consistent with Islamic jurisprudence. In terms of its structure, while the Chief Justice of the FSC is appointed by the President of Pakistan, the court's decisions are subject to appeal before the SCP. This provides an additional level of oversight, ensuring that the interpretation of Islamic principles in legal matters is subject to the highest judicial scrutiny in the country. In essence, the FSC plays a critical role in preserving Pakistan's Islamic identity offering legal guidance that aligns the country's legal system with its constitutional commitment to Islam while ensuring justice is administered in accordance with Islamic values.

58. Courts established under or by laws are of many kinds and in the relevant laws, their composition, powers, jurisdiction and other administrative and procedural matters are prescribed. Following are important courts established under different laws:

- Income Tax Appellate Tribunals;
- Environmental Protection Tribunals;
- Insurance Appellate Tribunals;
- Customs, Excise and Sales Tax Appellate Tribunals;
- Service Tribunals;
- Special Courts (Courts of Narcotics Substances);
- Banking Courts (Recovery of Loans);
- Special Courts (Offences in Banks);
- Special Courts (Customs, Taxation and Anti-Smuggling);
- Special Judges (Central);
- Drug Courts;
- Anti-Terrorism Courts;
- Accountability Courts;
- Labour Courts; and
- Other Courts.

59. In each district of a province, the principal court of original jurisdiction for civil matters is the Court of District Judge. This court holds broad authority to hear and adjudicate civil cases with general jurisdiction over a wide range of civil disputes. Below the District Judge, there are various other courts such as the courts of Civil Judges which handle less complex civil matters. These courts operate under the oversight and supervision of the District Judge who ensures that the proceedings are conducted in accordance with the law. Civil cases are generally initiated in the courts of Civil Judges, with the District Judge having the discretion to transfer any case to themselves if deemed necessary. This allows the District Judge to exercise direct control over particularly important or complex cases that may require their expertise. In addition, if a case falls within the jurisdiction of a Civil Judge but exceeds a specific monetary threshold, it may be appealed to the District Judge for review. The District Judge also holds appellate jurisdiction over certain civil matters. Appeals from the decisions of Civil Judges are generally directed to the District Judge, especially when the value of the claim does not exceed a prescribed monetary limit. This hierarchical structure ensures that civil cases are handled efficiently at the district level and the District Judge serving as the final arbiter in cases where the matter falls within their purview. Moreover, the District Judge's office plays an integral role in maintaining the consistency and integrity of judicial decisions within the district. By overseeing the operations of Civil Judges, the District Judge helps ensure that civil justice is administered fairly and in accordance with the laws of Pakistan. This division of judicial responsibility at the district level allows for a streamlined and organized approach to civil dispute resolution.

60. In each district, there is a Court of Sessions Judge alongside various Courts of Magistrates that handle criminal matters. The Sessions Judge holds authority over more serious criminal cases particularly those involving capital punishment or offences related to the enforcement of Hudood laws. These cases which carry severe penalties are adjudicated by the Sessions Court which has the power to impose any sentence prescribed by law including the death penalty. For less severe criminal offences, Courts of Magistrates are responsible for hearing and determining cases. Magistrates are categorized into three classes based on the gravity of the offences they are authorized to handle: First Class, Second Class, and Third Class. These Magistrates have jurisdiction over criminal matters that do not carry the death penalty and can impose sentences that align with the laws applicable to the offences in question. Appeals from the decisions of Sessions Judges are directed to the High Court, particularly when the conviction involves a sentence that includes the death penalty or other significant penalties. In contrast, appeals against sentences imposed by Magistrates are generally heard by the Sessions Court, provided the sentence does not exceed a four-year term. If the sentence exceeds this limit, the appeal is then brought before the High Court for further review. This judicial framework allows for a tiered approach to criminal justice ensuring that more serious criminal cases are handled by higher courts with appropriate jurisdiction, while less severe cases are processed by Magistrates. It also provides for a clear avenue of appeal ensuring that defendants have the opportunity to seek a review of their cases by a higher court when necessary.

61. To address specific legal matters, various specialized courts and tribunals have been established. These include courts for banking offences, the recovery of bank loans, cases under the Customs Act, traffic-related offences, anti-corruption matters, commercial disputes, drug-related cases, labour issues, insurance appeals, income tax appeals, and service-related matters. Generally, appeals from these specialized courts are directed to the High Courts with the exception of Labour Courts and Special Traffic Courts which have their own designated appellate forums. Cases from tribunals are appealed to the SCP. In order to tackle the persistent challenges of delayed justice and high litigation costs, comprehensive reforms have been implemented. These reforms seek to address the historical issues of long waiting times and financial burdens on litigants. One such measure includes the expansion of the judiciary by increasing the number of judges at the High Court, Sessions Court, Civil Court, and Magistrates' level. In addition, amendments to the Code of Criminal Procedure, 1898, now mandate automatic bail for under-trial prisoners who have been detained for extended periods over one year for non-capital offences and two years for capital offences. The period of detention is also considered when determining the sentence in criminal cases. To enhance accessibility to the judicial system significant reductions in court fees have been introduced. There are no fees for criminal cases or petitions before the FSC. In civil cases, the fee requirement has been removed for cases with a value of up to PKR 25,000. These changes are intended to create a more efficient, affordable, and fair judicial process for all.

Chapter 2. Historical Background of Family and Succession Law

§1. INTRODUCTION

62. The history of family and succession laws in the subcontinent especially in relation to the Muslim community, traces its roots to the Islamic legal tradition. Before the colonial era, personal laws pertaining to marriage, divorce, inheritance, and family matters were largely governed by religious customs and interpretations of Islamic law. These practices though grounded in religious principles were not always standardized or codified leading to regional variations and, at times, inconsistent applications. During the British colonial period, the British administration refrained from codifying Muslim family law thus leaving a significant gap in the legal framework concerning marriage and divorce within the Muslim community. This approach inadvertently created a legal void where practices around family law were largely determined by individual interpretations of Islamic law, often in informal or local courts. As a result, legal disputes related to marriage, divorce, and inheritance were subjected to a disorganized and often arbitrary system with limited legal recourse or protection for women. Evidence of marriage was often based on unreliable and ambiguous sources and divorce was largely controlled by male authorities further marginalizing women's rights in a male-dominated society. The absence of a clear, codified system of family law left women vulnerable and unable to fully exercise their rights. This became particularly evident as divorce and inheritance laws were frequently contested, with women left to navigate a legal system that was not necessarily aligned with their interests or needs. The need for reform was eventually recognized, and in 1955, the Commission on Marriage and Family Laws was formed to address the growing concerns. The Commission, after extensive research and consultation, presented a report in 1956 which called for legislative action to codify Muslim family law and safeguard the rights of women, particularly in the context of marriage, divorce, and inheritance. This resulted in the promulgation of the *Muslim Family Laws Ordinance of 1961* (MFLO), a landmark piece of legislation that aimed to regulate marriage and divorce in a structured and systematic manner. The Ordinance introduced several reforms such as the requirement for marriage registration, the establishment of a family court system, and the provision for women to have greater protection in the event of divorce. It also addressed the issue of polygamy placing restrictions on the practice and ensuring that a woman had the right to petition for divorce under certain conditions. This was a significant shift from the pre-independence practices where family law was unregulated and often detrimental to women's rights.

63. The Commission recognized the need to modernize family laws in accordance with contemporary requirements, yet its recommendations leaned toward a more conservative interpretation of Islamic principles. For example, while it did not ban the practice of divorce pronounced by the husband without adhering to the Quranic guidelines, it did emphasize that marriage (nikah) must be legally registered for it to be recognized. The Commission put forward several other key proposals, which aimed at creating a more structured approach to family law while still retaining certain traditional elements. However, these reforms were met with strong opposition from religious scholars and conservative factions in 1956, who argued that the recommendations were incompatible with Islamic teachings. Following this backlash, successive civilian governments refrained from enacting the proposed reforms. It wasn't until the regime of General Ayub Khan, in 1961, that some of the Report's selective recommendations were adopted and enacted into law through the *Muslim Family Laws Ordinance*, marking a significant shift in the regulation of family matters in Pakistan.

Chapter 3. Sources of Family and Succession Law

§1. Islamic Law

I. *Holy Quran*

64. The foundation of Islamic law is rooted in the belief that the word of God is the ultimate authority and His commands must be followed. Muslims regard the *Holy Quran* as the primary and most sacred source of divine law, offering a complete guide to life. They believe that the *Quran* was revealed by *Allah* to *Prophet Muhammad* through the angel *Jibril (Gabriel)* over a span of approximately twenty-three years. It serves as a source of moral and spiritual guidance for humanity, with the original Arabic text considered the final and unalterable word of God. While the *Quran* contains around 6,000 verses, only about 200 specifically address legal matters. Among these, roughly 80 verses focus on personal status laws, including inheritance, marriage, divorce, and family affairs. These legal provisions form the foundation of *Shariah* law, influencing Muslim societies and guiding judicial and ethical conduct. However, Islamic jurisprudence is not solely based on the *Quran*; other significant sources include the *Hadith* (sayings and actions of *Prophet Muhammad*), *Ijma* (consensus of scholars), and *Qiyas* (analogical reasoning). Together, these sources ensure that Islamic law remains dynamic and applicable to changing circumstances while preserving its divine essence.

II. *Sunnah/Hadees*

65. The principles outlined in the *Holy Quran* were put into practice by *Prophet Muhammad (PBUH)*, serving as a living example of divine guidance. This practical implementation gave rise to the *Hadith*, which consists of the sayings, actions, and approvals of the Prophet. Together, the *Quran* and *Sunnah* form the primary foundation of *Islamic Law*, providing comprehensive guidelines for both spiritual and social life. As a source of law, the *Sunnah* is considered just as authoritative as the *Quran* in shaping legal and ethical conduct. In Islamic tradition, the term *Sunnah* refers to the lifestyle and practices of *Prophet Muhammad (PBUH)*, encompassing his words, actions, habits, and even his silent endorsements. It holds immense significance in Islam, offering practical guidance on various aspects of life, including personal relationships, family matters, social justice, and governance. Beyond its legal importance, the *Sunnah* plays a crucial role in the moral and spiritual development of Muslims, teaching them compassion, humility, patience, and justice. It complements the *Quran* by demonstrating how its teachings can be applied in daily life, ensuring that Islamic values remain relevant across generations and cultures.

III. *Ijma* or Consensus of Opinion

66. .In *Islamic law*,[2] it is equally obligatory for people to follow a legal principle that has been established through the consensus of highly qualified scholars, provided that it does not contradict the *Holy Quran* or *Sunnah*. This concept, known as *Ijma*, is a significant source of *Shariah* and represents the collective agreement of Islamic jurists on legal matters. The *Hanafi* school of thought supports the idea that legal rulings should evolve in response to changing circumstances ensuring that Islamic law remains adaptable over time. Similarly, the *Maliki* school holds that new situations necessitate new rulings highlighting the dynamic nature of Islamic jurisprudence. *Ijma* serves as a mechanism to address contemporary issues while maintaining the integrity of Islamic teachings. It has played a crucial role in the development of *Fiqh* (Islamic jurisprudence) allowing scholars to interpret and apply Islamic principles to emerging challenges in society.

IV. The *Qiyas* or Analogical Deductions

67. .The fourth and final source of *Islamic law* is *Qiyas*[3] or analogical reasoning. Compared to the other three primary sources the *Quran*, *Sunnah*, and *Ijma*. *Qiyas* holds lesser significance but remains an essential tool in Islamic jurisprudence. It involves deriving legal rulings for new situations by drawing analogies to established principles, provided that the underlying reasoning remains consistent with Islamic teachings. In *Qiyas*, scholars analyse the rationale behind an existing ruling and apply it to a similar case where direct textual evidence is absent. This method ensures that *Shariah* remains relevant and adaptable to evolving societal conditions. While *Qiyas* is a recognized means of legal interpretation, its validity depends on the soundness of reasoning and its alignment with the core principles of *Islamic law*. It plays a crucial role in addressing contemporary issues that were not explicitly mentioned in the foundational texts helping scholars provide guidance on modern challenges while staying true to Islamic values.

§2. Constitution

68. The Constitution of the Islamic Republic of Pakistan upholds the protection of the family as a fundamental principle. Article 35 of the Constitution of Pakistan (1973) mandates the State to safeguard marriage, family, mothers, and children, ensuring their well-being and rights. This provision reflects the importance of family as the cornerstone of society in both Islamic and legal traditions. Furthermore,

2. Mulla Principles of Mohamedan Law by M. Hidayatullah.
3. Mulla Principles of Mohamedan Law by M. Hidayatullah.

under the Constitution of Pakistan, the Federal Government has the authority to legislate on matters concerning marriage, divorce, child welfare, guardianship, adoption, wills, inheritance, and succession. Various family laws in Pakistan such as the MFLO 1961 provide guidelines on personal status matters to ensure fairness and equity in familial relationships.

§3. Legislation

69. The Government of Pakistan enacted several Acts, Rules and Regulations regarding handling of family matters, succession and inheritance matters in Pakistan. Some important and major laws enacted or opted at different times are given below:

Contracting and Dissolution of Muslim Marriages (Statutory Law):

- Azad Jammu and Kashmir Family Courts Act, 1993
- Child Marriage Restraint Act, 1929
- Dissolution of Muslim Marriages Act, 1939
- Dowry and Bridal Gifts (Restriction) Act, 1976
- Dowry and Bridal Gifts (Restriction) Rules, 1976
- Family Court Act, 1964
- Family Courts (Amendment) Act, 1997
- Family Courts (Amendment) Ordinance, 1997
- Family Courts (Amendment) Ordinance, 2002
- Family Courts (Khyber Pakhtunkhwa) (Amendment) Act, 1996
- Family Courts (Sindh Amendment) Act, 1997
- Family Courts (Sindh Amendment) Ordinance, 1997
- Family Courts Ordinance, 1964
- Kazis Act, 1880
- Muslim Family Laws Ordinance, 1961
- Muslim Family Laws Rules, 1961
- Punjab/Sindh/Khyber Pakhtunkhwa/Balochistan Family Courts Act, 1964
- Sindh Muslim Marriages and Divorces Registration Act, 1955
- West Pakistan Family Courts Rules, 1965.

Contracting and Dissolution of Christian, Parsi and Hindu Marriages:

- Births, Deaths and Marriages Registration Act, 1886
- Christian Marriage Act, 1872
- Divorce Act, 1869
- Hindu Marriage Disabilities Removal Act, 1946
- Hindu Married Woman's Right to Separate Residence and Maintenance Act, 1946
- Hindu Widow's Marriages Act, 1856
- Indian (Non-Domiciled Parties) Divorce Rules, 1927
- Parsi Marriage and Divorce Act, 1936.

Anand and Arya Marriages:

- Anand Marriages Act, 1909
- The Arya Marriage Validation Act, 1937.

Marriage Validation and other Acts:

- Majority Act, 1875
- Special Marriage Act, 1872
- The Marriages Validation Act, 1892.

Foreign Marriages:

- The Foreign Marriages Act, 1903.

Offences Relating to Marriages:

- Pakistan Penal Code (PPC) (XLV of 1860) (sections 493–498).

Maintenance of Wife and Child:

- The Claims for Maintenance (Recovery Abroad) Ordinance, 1959
- The Maintenance Orders Enforcement Act, 1921.

Guardian:

- Code of Civil Procedure, 1908
- Guardians and Wards Act, 1890
- Khyber Pakhtunkhwa Court of Wards Regulations, 1904
- Punjab Court of Wards Act, 1903
- Sindh Court of Wards Act, 1905.

Succession Laws:

- Administration of Estates Regulation, 1827
- Court Fees Act, 1870 (Court Fee on Probates, Letters of Administration and Succession Certificates)
- Legal Representatives' Suits Act, 1855
- Sindh Civil Court Rules (Rules under Succession Act)
- Succession Act, 1925.

Law of Inheritance:

- Hindu Disposition of Property Act, 1916
- Hindu Inheritance (Removal of Disabilities) Act, 1928
- Hindu Law of Inheritance (Amendment) Act, 1929
- Hindu Marriage (Disabilities Removal) Act, 1946

- Hindu Women's Rights to Property (Sindh Extension to Agricultural Land) Act, 1943
- Khoja Disposition of Property Act, 1916
- Married Woman's Property Act, 1874
- The Cutchi Memons Act, 1938
- West Pakistan Hindu Women's Rights to Agricultural Land Ordinance, 1959.

Enforcement of Shariat Law:

- Balochistan Civil Disputes (Shariat Application) Rules, 1977
- Khyber Pakhtunkhwa Muslim Personal Law (Shariat) Application Act, 1935
- Muslim Personal Law (Shariat) Application (Amendment) Act, 1964
- Muslim Personal Law (Shariat) Application (Amendment) Ordinance, 1963
- Muslim Personal Law (Shariat) Application (Sindh Amendment) Act, 1950
- Muslim Personal Law (Shariat) Application Act (Punjab Amendment) Ordinance, 1983
- Muslim Personal Law (Shariat) Application Act, 1937
- Muslim Personal Law (Shariat) Application Act, 1962
- Punjab Muslim Personal Law (Shariat) Application (Amendment) Act, 1951
- Punjab Muslim Personal Law (Shariat) Application (Removal of Difficulties) Act, 1975
- West Pakistan Muslim Personal Law (Shariat) Application Act, 1948.

Juvenile Justice System:

- Indian Juvenile Justice (Care and Protection of Children) Act, 2000
- Juvenile Justice Rules, 2001
- Juvenile Justice System Ordinance (JJSO), 2000
- Khyber Pakhtunkhwa Juvenile Justice System Rules, 2002
- Protection of Breast-Feeding and Child Nutrition Ordinance, 2002
- Punjab Juvenile Justice System Rules, 2002
- Sindh Juvenile Justice System Rules, 2002.

Conciliations:

- Conciliations Courts Ordinance, 1961
- Conciliation Courts Rules, 1962
- Small Claims and Minor Offences Courts Ordinance, 2002.

Marriage Functions Prohibition:

- Marriage Functions (Prohibition of Ostentatious Displays and Wasteful Expenses) Ordinance, 2000
- Punjab Marriage Functions (Prohibition of Ostentatious Displays and Wasteful Expenses)) Act, 2003
- The Punjab Marriage Functions (Prohibition of Ostentatious Displays and Wasteful Expenses (Repeal) Act, 2006.

§4. Court Decisions

70. The various rulings issued by the courts of Pakistan, particularly the Family Courts, High Courts and the Supreme Court have played a crucial role in shaping the country's family laws. These judicial decisions not only provide interpretations of existing legal provisions but also establish important precedents that guide lower courts in resolving family-related disputes. Through landmark judgments, the judiciary has contributed to the evolution of family law by addressing complex legal issues related to marriage, divorce, child custody, inheritance, and other personal matters. These rulings help clarify ambiguities in legislation ensure the protection of fundamental rights and adapt legal principles to contemporary societal needs.

§5. Customs

71. In Islamic or Muhammadan law, customs do not hold legal authority as Muslims adhere strictly to the principles derived from the Holy Quran, Sunnah or Hadith, Ijma, and Qiyas. These primary sources form the foundation of Islamic jurisprudence, ensuring that legal rulings align with divine commandments and scholarly consensus. However, in other religious communities such as Christians, Hindus, and Parsis, customs and traditions play a significant role in shaping legal decisions. Courts often recognize and consider these customs when adjudicating matters related to personal law, such as marriage, inheritance, and succession. This distinction highlights the fundamental difference between Islamic law, which is rooted in divine revelation and other legal systems that incorporate traditional practices alongside religious doctrines.

Chapter 4. The Courts Administering Family Law and Succession Law

§1. Arbitration Council

72. According to section 2(a) of the MFLO, 1961, the term *Arbitration Council* refers to a body composed of a Chairman and one representative from each party involved in a family matter governed by the Ordinance. If a party fails to appoint a representative within the stipulated time, the council will proceed with its functions without that representative, and the remaining members will constitute the Arbitration Council. The primary role of the Arbitration Council is to mediate and resolve family disputes, ensuring that decisions are made in accordance with Islamic principles and legal provisions.

73. Pursuant to Rule 3 of the West Pakistan Rules under MFLO, 1961, the Union Council have jurisdiction in the following matters:

- If a husband seeks permission to contract another marriage, the application must be submitted to the Union Council of the area where his current wife resides. In cases where he has multiple wives, jurisdiction lies with the Union Council of the area where his most recently married wife is residing at the time of application.
- In the event of a divorce notice, the relevant Union Council is the one in the area where the wife was residing at the time the husband pronounced the divorce.
- For maintenance applications, jurisdiction falls under the Union Council of the area where the wife resides at the time of filing. If multiple wives submit maintenance applications, the Union Council where the first application is filed will have jurisdiction.

74. All proceedings conducted before an Arbitration Council are to be held privately unless the Chairman permits otherwise with the agreement of all parties involved. The Chairman is responsible for ensuring that the proceedings are carried out as efficiently and swiftly as possible (as outlined in Rules 4 and 5 of the West Pakistan Rules under the MFLO, 1961). This approach to confidentiality and expediency is designed to protect the privacy of individuals involved in family matters while ensuring that disputes are resolved in a timely manner. The Arbitration Council through these rules aims to foster a fair and impartial process, promoting swift resolutions in family law cases.

75. Decisions of the Arbitration Council are made by majority vote. In situations where the members cannot reach a majority, the Chairman's decision will be regarded as the final ruling of the Arbitration Council. Even in cases of disagreement among the council members, a resolution can still be reached efficiently.

76. A certified copy of the Arbitration Council's decision, signed by the Chairman, is provided at no charge to each party involved in the proceedings. Upon receiving an application for maintenance or a divorce notice, the Chairman is required to issue a written order within seven days, directing each party to appoint a representative. Each party must nominate their representative in writing within seven days of receiving this order and submit the nomination either directly to the Chairman or by registered mail.

77. If a representative appointed by a party is unable to attend the Arbitration Council meetings due to illness or any other reason, wilfully absents themselves, or loses the trust of the party, the party may, with prior written consent from the Chairman, withdraw the nomination. The party can then make a new nomination within the time frame specified by the Chairman. In the event of a new nomination, it will not be necessary to restart the proceedings before the Arbitration Council, unless the Chairman, for reasons stated in writing, instructs otherwise. This provision allows for flexibility in ensuring that each party is adequately represented while maintaining the continuity of the proceedings.

78. If it comes to the attention of the Collector whether through an application by one of the parties or through independent investigation that the Chairman has a personal interest in favour of one party, is biased against any party, or is engaging in misconduct during the proceedings, the Collector may, after notifying all parties involved, appoint another member of the Union Council to serve as Chairman. The Collector has the authority to suspend the proceedings before the Arbitration Council until a decision is made on this matter. Any order issued by the Collector under this rule must be accompanied by a written explanation outlining the reasons for the decision. This ensures transparency and accountability in the process, protecting the fairness of the Arbitration Council's proceedings.

79. An application for the revision of an Arbitration Council's decision must be submitted within thirty days from the date of the decision or the issuance of the certificate, depending on the situation. The application must be submitted in writing, clearly stating the reasons for seeking a revision of the decision or certificate, and it must be signed by the applicant (as per Rules 16(1)(2) of the West Pakistan Rules under the MFLO, 1961). This provision ensures that parties have a specified time frame within which they can challenge a decision while also requiring a clear justification for the request, promoting clarity in the legal process.

80. Once the Arbitration Council has issued its decision under Rule 6, the Chairman must promptly send the record of the proceedings, including the decision, to the Union Council office, where it will be kept on file for a period of five years from the date of the decision. No court shall act on any offence under the Ordinance or these rules unless a written complaint is filed by the Union Council, outlining the facts that constitute the alleged offence. This ensures that legal proceedings are initiated only based on formal complaints and that records are properly maintained for a specified duration.

81. Petitioner, an overseas Pakistani residing in Germany, sought a divorce certificate from the local Union Council in Pakistan after sending divorce notices to his wife. However, the Union Council in Lahore declined to issue the certificate, citing jurisdiction issues, as the wife was residing in Germany. The court referred to the *MFLO, 1961* and relevant S.R.O. notifications, which authorize the *Pakistan Mission abroad* to act as the Chairman of the Arbitration Council in such cases. The court upheld the decision of the Union Council Chairman, emphasizing that jurisdiction for issuing the divorce certificate lay with the Pakistan Mission in Germany, and dismissed the petition, stating that the matter should have been pursued there. The petitioner's lack of transparency regarding legal proceedings in Germany further weakened his case. (2024 LHC 538)

82. Petitioner challenged the orders of the Family Court and Additional District Judge, Sialkot, regarding a complaint under section 6(5) of the *MFLO, 1961*, alleging his second marriage without Arbitration Council's permission. The Family Court declined to accept an oath on the Holy Qur'an as part of the proceedings, as it is not applicable in criminal cases. The petitioner argued that the case should be treated as a family dispute, but the Court ruled that the matter was a criminal offence under section 6(5) of the Ordinance, subject to specific trial procedures. The Court dismissed the petition, finding no jurisdictional error or illegality in the lower court's decisions. (2023 LHC 3363)

83. Petitioner, an overseas Pakistani woman filed a complaint under section 6 of the MFLO, 1961, against her husband for contracting a second marriage without prior permission from the Arbitration Council. The complaint was filed through an attorney, which was dismissed by the Family Court as being procedurally incorrect. The Court ruled that criminal proceedings under the Ordinance cannot be initiated through an attorney, as the complainant must personally appear. The Family Court's jurisdiction, defined by the Family Courts Act, 1964, emphasizes that criminal matters related to family law must be personally pursued by the aggrieved party. Consequently, the petition was dismissed, affirming the trial and revisional court's decisions. (2024 LHC 381)

84. Divorce was pronounced thrice in the presence of witnesses and communicated to the wife at her address and Union Council concerned. Failure of wife to participate in arbitration proceedings initiated by Union Council despite having notice thereof. Application by husband to Union Council for issuance of Divorce Certificate after the expiry of the requisite period of ninety days. Constitutional petition by wife seeking quashment of proceedings before Union Council. Validity: Petitioner herself had chosen not to attend arbitration proceedings initiated by the Union Council. Petitioner had failed to show any lawful reason or justification to quash such proceedings or restrain Union Council from issuing such certificate to husband on expiry of ninety days. High Court dismissed Constitutional petition in the circumstances. LHC (2010 CLC 258)

§2. Family Courts

85. The Family Courts were created under the Family Courts Act, 1964 to ensure the swift resolution of disputes related to marriage and family matters. In line with the provisions of the MFLO and the Conciliation Courts Ordinance, 1961, these courts have exclusive authority to hear, adjudicate, and resolve issues upon following matters:

- Dissolution of marriage
- Dower
- Maintenance
- Restitution of conjugal rights
- Custody of children and the visitation rights of parents
- Guardianship
- Jactitation of marriage
- Dowry
- Personal property and belongings of a wife
- Reconciliation efforts.

86. Appeals from decisions made by the Family Courts are exclusively directed to the High Court. Each town and city typically has a designated Family Court presided over by a Family Judge. In certain regions where there is only one Family Court, the powers and functions of a Family Court Judge may be conferred upon Civil Judges in most other areas. This arrangement ensures that family-related cases are adjudicated efficiently even in jurisdictions where a dedicated Family Court is not available. Moreover, the Family Courts operate with a goal to prioritize the welfare and well-being of family members, particularly in cases involving children and vulnerable spouses. They emphasize mediation and reconciliation efforts before formal legal proceedings aiming to reduce the emotional and financial burdens often associated with protracted family disputes. As family law issues can be complex and sensitive, Family Courts aim to provide a more accessible and compassionate approach to justice in comparison to traditional civil courts. In this system, judges are specially trained to handle the unique challenges of family law cases ensuring both legal expertise and emotional sensitivity.

87. A suit for dissolution of marriage must be resolved within a period of four months from the date it is filed. However, in instances where an appeal is permitted following the dissolution, the appeal must also be concluded within a similar timeframe of four months. This provision makes certain that divorce cases are handled with urgency, minimizing the emotional and financial strain on the parties involved. This time-bound framework aims to expedite the judicial process, allowing individuals to move forward with their lives without unnecessary delays. It also reflects the importance of efficiency in family law matters, where swift resolution is often critical for the well-being of any children or dependents involved. By enforcing such deadlines, the legal system seeks to provide clarity and closure for all parties involved upholding both the principles of justice and the need for a timely resolution in family disputes.

88. Any ruling or decree issued by a Family Court can be appealed to the High Court if the Family Court is presided over by a District Judge, an Additional District Judge, or a person appointed by the government with equivalent authority and status. In all other instances, the appeal is directed to the District Court. This structure ensures that appeals are heard by courts with appropriate judicial authority based on the rank of the presiding judge. By allowing appeals to either the High Court or the District Court, the system ensures that parties have access to a fair process of review, depending on the complexity and importance of the case. The involvement of higher courts in appeals reflects the principle of ensuring that family law decisions are subject to oversight providing an avenue for parties to seek justice in instances of perceived errors in judgment.

89. However, no appeal lies from a decree passed by the Family Court for dissolution of marriage, except in the case of dissolution for reasons specified in clause (*a*) of item (*viii*) of section 2 of the Dissolution of Muslim Marriages Act, 1939, for dower not exceeding PKR 15,000 and for maintenance of PKR 500 or less per month.

90. A person may be deemed in contempt of the Family Court if, without a valid legal excuse, they engage in any behaviour that insults the Family Court, disrupts its proceedings, refuses to answer questions they are legally obligated to respond to or declines to take an oath to testify truthfully or sign a statement they have made in the Family Court. In such cases, the Family Court has the authority to immediately try the individual for contempt and impose a fine not exceeding PKR 200. It is important to note that the Family Court does not possess the authority to issue injunctions or stay proceedings that are ongoing before a Chairman or an Arbitration Council. This ensures that the Family Court's jurisdiction is clearly defined preventing overreach into areas where specialized bodies such as arbitration councils hold exclusive competence.

91. A Family Court shall not question the validity of any marriage registered in accordance with the provisions of MFLO, nor shall any evidence in regard thereto be admissible before such Court.

92. Petitioner filed a suit for the dissolution of marriage and recovery of dowry articles due to alleged cruelty and harsh treatment by the Respondent. The Family Court initially decreed the dissolution of marriage on the grounds of Khula, even though the Petitioner did not specifically request it. The Petitioner challenged this decision, arguing that the dissolution should have been based on the grounds she raised, including cruelty and illegal demands. The Court found that the Family Court acted beyond its jurisdiction by dissolving the marriage on the basis of Khula without the Petitioner's explicit request. As a result, the Court set aside the impugned judgments and remanded the case for retrial, instructing the Family Court to address all the grounds raised by the Petitioner in her suit. SC (2023 SCMR 246)

93. Suit for dissolution of marriage and recovery of maintenance. Petitioner claimed that seven tolas of gold ornaments as dower was fixed between the spouses at the time of engagement which though was tendered to her at the time of nikah but the same was recollected from her on arrival at the house of respondent. Both the parties admitted the amount of PKR 400,000 having been fixed as dower which was paid to the petitioner by the respondent at the time of marriage. No illegality or infirmity was found in the decree and judgment regarding dower passed by the appellate court and the constitutional petition was disposed of accordingly. PHC (2023 MLD 1237).

§3. High Courts

94. Appeals against the decisions of Family Courts can be filed with the respective High Court. Each province has its own High Court, and there is also a High Court for the Federal Capital, Islamabad. These include the LHC in Punjab, the Sindh High Court in Karachi, the PHC in Khyber Pakhtunkhwa, the Baluchistan High Court in Quetta, and the Islamabad High Court. The High Courts serve as the appellate authorities for family, civil, and criminal matters, providing a platform for parties to challenge lower court decisions within their jurisdiction. These courts ensure legal consistency and interpretation across a range of cases within their regions.

§4. Federal Shariat Court

95. The FSC was established by the President's Order No. 1 of 1980 as incorporated in the Constitution of Pakistan, 1973 under Chapter 3A. The Court is a unique institution with no parallel in the entire Muslim world. It is backed by powerful provisions of the Constitution. The preamble to the Constitution explicitly affirms that sovereignty over the entire universe belongs to Almighty Allah alone, and the authority to be exercised by the people of Pakistan within the limits prescribed by Him is a sacred trust. Article 2A lays down that the principles and provisions set out in the Objectives Resolution are a substantive part of the Constitution. Article 227 makes it incumbent that all existing laws shall be brought in conformity with the injunctions of Islam as laid down in the Holy Quran and the Sunnah of the Holy Prophet Muhammad (PBUH), and Chapter 3A which pertains to the functions and organization of FSC, empowers the court and entrusts the court with the responsibility to examine and decide the question whether or not any law or provision of law is repugnant to the injunctions of Islam as laid down in the Holy Quran and the Sunnah of the Holy Prophet Muhammad (PBUH). Law includes any custom or usage having the force of law but does not include the Constitution, Muslim personal law, or any law relating to the procedure of any court or tribunal.[4]

96. Petitioner was aggrieved of distribution of monetary benefits only to widow of deceased officer and not to all relatives entitled to inherit under Islamic law. Court held that declaration of pension, gratuity and other privileges claimed by petitioner was relied on in personam and such relief was beyond the jurisdiction conferred upon FSC under Article 203D of the constitution and could not be granted. Shariat petition was dismissed in circumstances. FSC (2024 PLD 25)

4. https://www.federalshariatcourt.gov.pk/en/establishment/?utm

Part I. Persons

Chapter 1. The Status of a Person

§1. Definition of a Person

97. The term 'Person' can be interpreted in two ways: as a natural human being or as a legal entity. In legal contexts, a 'Person' encompasses not only individuals but also entities such as registered firms, private limited companies, corporations, and other organizations that possess legal recognition. A 'Person' may be either a natural person, referring to an individual, or a juristic person, which is an entity recognized by law as having rights and responsibilities. However, the term does not extend to the State; rather, it is confined to individuals and legally recognized entities with distinct legal standing.

§2. Capacity

I. Minors

98. Under the Succession Act, 1925 'minor' means any person subject to the Majority Act, 1875 who has not attained his majority within the meaning of that Act, and any other person who has not completed the age of 18 years; and 'minority' means the status of any such person. Whereas under section 2(d) of the Child Marriage Restraint Act, 1929, 'minor' means person of either sex who is under 18 years of age.

II. Child

99. Under the Child Marriage Restraint Act, 1929 section 2(a) 'child' means a person who, if a male, is under 18 years of age, and if a female, is under 16 years of age.

III. Lunacy and Idiocy

100. In Pakistan, the term 'lunatic' was historically used to describe individuals with mental illnesses. Recognizing the need for a more respectful and comprehensive approach, the government enacted the Mental Health Ordinance in 2001, replacing the outdated Lunacy Act of 1912. This ordinance aimed to consolidate and amend laws related to the care and treatment of mentally disordered individuals, emphasizing their rights and dignity. It provided guidelines for the management of their properties and affairs, encouraged community-based care, and promoted mental health awareness and prevention strategies. Following the 18th Amendment to the Constitution, health responsibilities were devolved to provincial governments, leading provinces to develop their own mental health legislation. For instance, Sindh province enacted the Sindh Mental Health Act in 2013 further tailoring mental health care to regional needs.

101. The Mental Health Ordinance of 2001 defines 'mental disorder' as any mental illness encompassing conditions such as mental impairment, severe personality disorders, severe mental impairments, and other cognitive disabilities. 'Mentally disordered' individuals are those diagnosed with these conditions. Specifically, 'mental impairment' refers to an incomplete or arrested development of the mind, leading to significant challenges in intelligence and social functioning, often accompanied by notably aggressive or irresponsible behaviour. 'Severe personality disorder' is characterized by persistent mental disturbances that may or may not include significant cognitive impairments but result in markedly aggressive or irresponsible actions. 'Severe mental impairment' denotes a profound developmental halt of the mind causing severe deficits in intelligence and social interactions, coupled with notably aggressive or irresponsible conduct. It's important to note that these definitions exclude conditions arising solely from promiscuity, other immoral behaviours, sexual deviance, or dependencies on substances like alcohol or drugs. In 2013, the Sindh Assembly enacted the Sindh Mental Health Act, replacing the earlier ordinance. This legislation provides a more detailed framework for the treatment and care of individuals with mental disorders, emphasizing community-based care and the protection of patients' rights. The Act defines a 'mental disorder' as a condition necessitating treatment due to any mental dysfunction, explicitly excluding mental impairment and severe personality disorders. This distinction aims to ensure that individuals receive appropriate care tailored to their specific needs. The Sindh Mental Health Act also established the Sindh Mental Health Authority and a Board of Visitors to oversee the implementation of mental health policies and ensure the rights and well-being of mentally disordered individuals are upheld. These bodies are tasked with promoting mental health awareness preventing mental disorders and ensuring that patients receive ethical and effective treatment.

102. If an individual suffering from a mental illness possesses property and their relatives assert that they are incapable of managing their affairs, the Court of Protection has the authority to initiate an inquiry to assess the person's mental competence. The court may appoint two or more assessors, typically medical and legal experts, to evaluate whether the individual can handle their personal, financial, and property-related matters. Under the Sindh Mental Health Act, 2013, and similar legal frameworks in other provinces, if the court determines that the person is incapable of managing their property due to a mental disorder, it may appoint a guardian or manager to oversee their affairs. This guardian is legally responsible for making decisions in the best interest of the individual while ensuring that their property is not misused or unlawfully transferred. The Pakistan Lunacy Act, 1912, previously governed such cases but was replaced by the Mental Health Ordinance, 2001, which later evolved into specific provincial mental health acts. These laws emphasize the protection of mentally disordered individuals' rights, ensuring that any intervention regarding their property and financial affairs is conducted lawfully and ethically. The court may also periodically review the appointed guardian's conduct to prevent exploitation and ensure transparency. If a mentally ill person recovers or shows improvement in their condition, they may petition the court to regain control over their property.

103. Under the Mental Health Ordinance, 2001, if a person is determined to be suffering from a mental illness and is incapable of managing their personal or financial affairs, the Court of Protection has the authority to take necessary legal measures. The court may appoint a responsible and suitable individual as a guardian to oversee the care and well-being of the person. Additionally, the court can order the individual's admission to a recognized mental health care facility for appropriate treatment and ensure provisions for their maintenance and financial support. To safeguard the individual's property and financial interests, the court may designate a manager who will be responsible for handling their assets, ensuring they are protected from misuse, fraud, or unlawful transfers. The appointed guardian and manager must act in the best interest of the mentally ill person, adhering to legal obligations and ethical standards. With the enactment of the Sindh Mental Health Act, 2013, and similar mental health laws in other provinces, these protections have been further strengthened. These emphasize humane treatment, periodic reviews of guardianship and property management, and the right of the affected individual to challenge decisions or regain control if they show signs of recovery. The court may require periodic reports from the appointed guardian or manager to ensure transparency and prevent exploitation. If at any point the individual's condition improves, they may petition the court to reassess their mental capacity and restore their rights to self-management.

104. Under the Mental Health Ordinance, 2001, the appointed manager is required to submit a detailed inventory of all immovable property to the Court within three months of the order. Any significant transactions or dealings involving the property must be carried out only with prior approval from the Court and through a bank authorized by the Court to ensure transparency and accountability. In cases where the Court finds that the individual, initially deemed to be mentally ill, has recovered or regained sufficient mental capacity to manage their own affairs, the Court may order a re-assessment of their mental state. If the re-assessment confirms the individual's recovery, the Court may revoke the previously issued orders for the appointment of a guardian or manager thereby restoring the individual's autonomy over their personal and financial matters.

105. If a public office holder or government employee is diagnosed with a mental illness, they are entitled to continue receiving their salary and other benefits as per their official entitlements, even if they are unable to perform their duties due to their mental health condition under the Mental Health Ordinance, 2001. This provision confirms that individuals who have served in public roles are not deprived of their financial rights during a period of illness. The law emphasizes the importance of safeguarding the dignity and rights of individuals suffering from mental disorders, ensuring that they are supported financially while they recover. This also extends to provisions for reassessing the person's condition periodically, ensuring that they are appropriately supported and that their rights are protected under the law. The continuity of salary and benefits reflects a commitment to the well-being of public servants facing mental health challenges.

Chapter 2. Registration of Civil Status

§1. Muslim Law

106. Under the MFLO, 1961, it is mandatory for every marriage to be officially registered with the designated Registrar. The Union Council is responsible for issuing licenses to individuals who are appointed as Nikah Registrars. These registrars are responsible for recording marriages ensuring that all legal requirements are met. It maintains efficiency and prevents duplication; no more than one Nikah Registrar is permitted to be licensed for any specific ward. The purpose of this registration is to provide legal recognition to the marriage which in turn safeguards the rights of the parties involved. The registration also acts as proof of marriage helping to resolve any future legal disputes related to marital rights, inheritance, and maintenance.

107. The Nikah Registrar is responsible for completing Form 12 in quadruplicate for every marriage solemnized under their supervision. After filling out the form, the necessary parties involved, including the bride, groom, and witnesses, will sign the form. Following this, the Nikah Registrar will affix their own signature and seal, ensuring that the original copy remains in the register for record-keeping purposes. The duplicate and triplicate copies of the Nikahnama (marriage certificate) will be provided to the bride and groom, respectively, upon the payment of a nominal fee. These copies serve as official documentation of the marriage. The quadruplicate copy is then forwarded to the Union Council for formal registration and record-keeping. The procedure for registration of Nikah ensures that marriages are legally recognized and that there is proper documentation for future reference. This process helps in safeguarding the rights of the individuals involved, especially in matters of inheritance, maintenance, and divorce. It also contributes to transparency, preventing any potential disputes or false claims regarding marital status. The marriage registration serves as an essential legal tool in case of any legal proceedings related to the marriage. The Union Council plays a vital role in maintaining the authenticity and integrity of these records, which is why it is crucial that all forms are filled out correctly and the proper procedures are followed for the marriage to be legally valid.

108. Under the Family Laws Amendment Act 2023, if an individual required to sign the marriage register refuses to do so, they may be subject to a fine not exceeding PKR 10,000. This amendment aims to ensure compliance with marriage registration procedures and uphold the integrity of official records.

109. If a marriage in Pakistan is solemnized by someone other than the Nikah Registrar, the officiant must complete Form II, available for purchase at a price set by the Provincial Government. The required signatories must then sign the form, after which the officiant must also sign it and ensure its prompt submission, along with the registration fee, to the Nikah Registrar of the jurisdiction where the marriage took place. Failure of any required signatory to sign the form shall be punishable with simple imprisonment of up to one month, a fine of up to PKR 200, or both.

110. Under the MFLO, 1961, marriage is regarded as a civil contract and section 5 thereof makes it necessary that the marriage shall be registered and the parties can settle their terms and conditions of marriage including dower, through said contract, for which form-II used as nikahnama is prescribed in rule 10 under MFLO, 1961. Relevant entries in such regard can be incorporated by the parties in columns Nos 13 to 16 of nikahnama which relates to dower. LHC (2022 MLD 416)

111. All nikah registrars or other persons who solemnize marriages are under legal obligation to scrutinize credentials at the time of nikah as to whether marriage is solemnized with free will of parties and no child is exposed to marriage. Mere submission of oral entries for the purpose of age should not be accepted unless any proof of age from parties to marriage preferably which should be in the shape of some authentic document either issued by a national database and registration authority in the form of national identity card, B-form, medical certificate based on ossification test issued by competent authority and birth certificate validly issued by Union Council, etc., is produced. LHC (2020 PLD 811)

112. Marriage solemnized under MFLO, 1961 requires its registration but nikah does not become invalid due to its non-registration. If a person does not report marriage to nikah registrar for the purpose of registration, he may be held liable under section 5(4) of MFLO, 1961. LHC (2009 MLD 962)

§2. Minorities Laws

I. Christian Law

113. In Pakistan, Christian marriages are traditionally defined as a voluntary, lifelong union between a man and a woman, excluding all others. Historically, family matters within the Christian community have been governed by the Christian Marriage Act of 1872 and the Divorce Act of 1869. Under the 1872 Act, marriages were required to be registered with Marriage Registrars appointed by the government in each district. In a significant development, the Christian Marriage (Amendment) Act of 2024 was enacted to update these longstanding laws. This amendment raised the legal marriage age for both Christian men and women to 18 years, aligning with broader child protection and human rights frameworks in Pakistan. Previously, the minimum marriageable age was 16 for boys and 13 for girls. The amendment was introduced by Member of the National Assembly Naveed Amir Jeeva and received presidential assent on 23 July 2024. This legislative change has been welcomed by Christian leaders and human rights advocates, as it aims to protect minors from forced marriages and aligns the Christian marriage law with contemporary human rights standards. These reforms reflect Pakistan's commitment to upholding the rights and dignity of its diverse population, ensuring that marriage laws within the Christian community are consistent with modern societal values and international human rights norms.

II. Hindu Law

114. In Pakistan, the Special Marriage Act of 1872 mandates that individuals intending to marry must provide a fourteen-day notice to a Registrar appointed by the Provincial Government. Upon receiving this notice, the Registrar promptly records it in the Marriage Notice Book. Historically, the Hindu community in Pakistan lacked specific codified laws governing family matters, relying instead on customary practices. However, significant legislative advancements have been made to address this gap. The Hindu Marriage Act of 2017 was enacted to provide a formal legal framework for Hindu marriages. This Act outlines conditions for a valid marriage, prescribes ceremonies for solemnization, and establishes procedures for registration. It also addresses matters related to separation and divorce, thereby offering legal recognition and protection to Hindu matrimonial unions. The Sindh province took a pioneering step by passing its own Hindu Marriage Act in 2016, becoming the first province in Pakistan to provide legal mechanisms for the registration of Hindu marriages. This provincial legislation ensures that Hindu marriages within Sindh are legally recognized, facilitating the protection of marital rights and simplifying the resolution of family disputes. These legislative measures have significantly improved the legal standing of the Hindu community in Pakistan, ensuring that family matters are addressed within a structured legal framework rather than solely through customary practices.

III. Parsi Law

115. In Pakistan, the Parsi Marriage and Divorce Act of 1936 governs matrimonial matters for the Parsi community. According to this Act, upon the solemnization of a marriage, the officiating priest is required to certify the union. This certificate must be signed by the priest, the bride and groom (or their fathers or guardians if they are under 21 years of age), and two witnesses present at the ceremony. The priest is then responsible for sending this certificate, along with a prescribed fee paid by the husband, to the Registrar of the area where the marriage took place. Upon receiving the certificate and fee, the Registrar records the details in a designated register and retains the fee. This marriage register is accessible for inspection, and certified extracts can be obtained upon payment of a nominal fee. Additionally, each Registrar is obligated to forward copies of the certificates they issue and record to the Registrar General appointed by the Government. As of now, there have been no significant amendments to the Parsi Marriage and Divorce Act of 1936 in Pakistan. The Act continues to serve as the primary legal framework for marriage and divorce proceedings within the Parsi community. However, it's noteworthy that in India, the corresponding Parsi Marriage and Divorce Act of 1936 has undergone amendments, such as the Amendment Act 5 of 1988, which aimed to update and address evolving matrimonial issues within the Parsi community.

§3. Special Marriage Act, 1872

116. The Special Marriage Act of 1872 was enacted to provide a legal framework for marriages involving individuals who do not adhere to the Christian, Jewish, Hindu, Muslim, Parsi, Buddhist, Sikh, or Jaina religions. It also applies to marriages between individuals who profess the Hindu, Buddhist, Sikh, or Jaina faiths. The Act stipulates that neither party should have a living spouse at the time of marriage, the male must be at least 18 years old, and the female must be at least 14 years old, as per the Gregorian calendar. If either individual is under 21 years of age, they must obtain consent from their father or guardian. Additionally, the parties must not be related to each other in a manner that would render the marriage illegal under any applicable law. However, these age requirements were set in the nineteenth century and may not align with contemporary legal standards. In recent years, there has been a global push to establish the minimum legal age for marriage at 18 to protect the rights and well-being of individuals entering into matrimony. For example, in 2024, Pakistan amended the Christian Marriage Act of 1872, raising the minimum marriage age to 18 for both males and females.

Chapter 3. Personality Rights

§1. Minority Rights

117. In order to protect the minorities in Pakistan, their rights have been envisaged under the Constitution of Pakistan, 1973 and some specific laws protecting minority rights. A full-fledged Ministry of Minorities is working in Pakistan for the betterment and uplift of various religious minorities in Pakistan.

118. Under Article 20 (Chapter 1 Fundamental Rights – Freedom to profess religion and to manage religious institutions) of the Constitution of Pakistan, 1973 subject to law, public order and morality: (a) every citizen has the right to profess, practice and propagate his religion; and (b) every religious denomination and every sect thereof have the right to establish, maintain and manage its religious institutions. This article guarantees the right to every citizen to profess, practice, and propagate their religion. It ensures that every religious community has the right to establish and maintain religious institutions.

119. Under Article 21 (safeguard against taxation for purposes of any particular religion) of the Constitution of Pakistan, no person can be compelled to pay any special tax the proceeds of which are to be spent on the propagation or maintenance of any religion other than his own.

120. Whereas under Article 22 (safeguards as to educational institutions in respect of religion, etc.) of the Constitution of Pakistan, no person attending any educational institution shall be required to receive religious instruction, take part in any religious ceremony, or attend religious worship, if such instruction, ceremony or worship relates to a religion other than his own. In respect of any religious institution, there is no discrimination against any community in the granting of exemption or concession in relation to taxation.

121. Under Article 22(3) of the Constitution of Pakistan, subject to law, no religious community or denomination can be prevented from providing religious instruction for pupils of that community or denomination in any educational institution maintained wholly by that community or denomination; and no citizen can be denied admission to any educational institution receiving aid from public revenues on the ground only of race, religion, caste or place of birth. However, nothing in this Article prevents any public authority from making provision for the Advancement of any socially or educationally backward class of citizens.

122. Under Article 25 of the Constitution of Pakistan, all citizens are equal before law and are entitled to equal protection of law. There is no discrimination on the basis of sex alone. However, nothing in this Article prevents the State from making any special provision for the protection of women and children.

123. Under Article 36 of the Constitution of Pakistan, the Government safeguards the legitimate rights and interests of minorities, including their due representation in the Federal and Provincial services.

124. Section 295 of PPC 1860 criminalizes the act of damaging or defiling places of worship, religious texts, or sacred objects of any religion. The purpose is to prevent acts that could provoke religious unrest. The punishment for violating this section includes imprisonment, a fine, or both.

125. Section 295-A of PPC 1860 targets deliberate and malicious actions intended to insult any religion or religious beliefs which includes speech, written material, or other forms of expression that incite hatred against any religious group. The punishment can extend to ten years of imprisonment, along with a fine.

126. Section 295-B and 295-C of PPC 1860 deals with blasphemy against Prophet Muhammad (PBUH), including derogatory remarks or offensive depictions. The punishment for violating this law is *death penalty or life imprisonment, along with a fine.*

127. Christian Marriage Act, 1872 and Divorce Act, 1869 regulates marriage and divorce for the *Christian* community in Pakistan and requires that marriages be registered with a *Marriage Registrar* appointed by the government. The Divorce Act of 1869 lays down grounds for separation and legal proceedings for dissolution of marriage.

§2. Minors' Responsibility for Crimes

128. To safeguard the rights of children involved in criminal proceedings, the Government of Pakistan enacted the JJSO, 2000, which was later replaced by the Juvenile Justice System Act (JJSA), 2018. This law aims to protect minors in the legal system, ensure their rehabilitation, and establish specialized Juvenile Courts for their trials. Courts have the authority to assess the criminal responsibility of a child based on their age and circumstances.

129. Under this law, a child is defined as any person under the age of 18 years. Section 5 of the JJSO, 2000, retained in the JJSA, 2018, strictly prohibits a child from being charged or tried alongside an adult. If a child is accused of an offence that, under section 239 of the Code of Criminal Procedure (Cr.P.C.) or any other applicable law, would typically be tried alongside an adult, the court must order a separate trial in a designated Juvenile Court.

130. JJSA, 2018, This Act replaced the JJSO of 2000, introducing comprehensive measures for the protection and rehabilitation of juvenile offenders. It defines a child as anyone under 18 years of age and mandates separate trials for minors, ensuring they are not tried alongside adults. The Act also establishes Juvenile Justice Committees to promote diversion and rehabilitation.

131. The National Commission on the Rights of Child Act, 2017, This legislation led to the formation of the National Commission on the Rights of Child tasked with examining and reviewing laws, policies, and practices to ensure they align with child rights principles. The Commission also monitors the implementation of international instruments related to children's rights.

132. The Child Protection & Welfare Act, 2010 is applicable in provinces like Punjab and Khyber Pakhtunkhwa, this Act provides a framework for the protection of children from abuse, neglect, and exploitation. It establishes Child Protection Units and procedures for the care and rehabilitation of vulnerable children.

133. Employment of Children Act, 1991, This Act prohibits the employment of children below the age of 14 in certain hazardous occupations and regulates the working conditions of adolescents aged 14 to 18. It aims to prevent child labour and ensure that children's education and development are not compromised.

§3. JUVENILE RIGHTS

134. Every child who is accused of the commission of an offence or is a victim of an offence shall have the right of legal assistance at the expense of the State. A legal practitioner appointed by the State for providing legal assistance to a child accused of the commission of an offence, or victim of an offence, shall have at least seven years standing at the Bar (section 3 of the JJSA 2018).

135. The Provincial Governments, in consultation with the Chief Justice of High Court, by notification in the Official Gazette, are required to establish one or more Juvenile Courts for any local within its jurisdiction or confer powers of Juvenile Court to other Session Court of Judicial Magistrate of the First Class. The Juvenile Court have exclusive jurisdiction to try cases in which a child is accused of commission of an offence. All cases pending before a Trial Court in which a child is accused of an offence shall stand transferred to the Juvenile Court having jurisdiction (section 4 of the JJSA 2018).

136. The Juvenile Courts are obligated to decide the case within six months of taking cognizance of the offence. A Juvenile Court does not ordinarily take up any other case on a day when the case of a child accused is fixed for evidence on such a day. Where the case is not decided within six months, the Juvenile Court shall seek extension from the High Court concerned explaining the reasons for not being able to decide the case within the prescribed time limit.

137. The arrested juvenile shall be kept in the observation home and the officer-in-charge and the officer in charge of the police station must inform the guardian of the juvenile of such arrest and inform him of the time, date and name of the Juvenile Court and inform the concerned probation officer to enable him to obtain such information about the juvenile which may be of assistance to the Juvenile Court for making inquiry (section 5 of the JJSA 2018).

138. A juvenile accused of bailable offence shall be released by the Juvenile Court on bail with or without surety unless it appears that there are reasonable grounds for believing that the release of such juvenile may bring him in association with criminals or expose him to any other danger. In this situation, the juvenile shall be placed under the custody of a suitable person or Juvenile Rehabilitation Centre under the supervision of a probation officer. The juvenile shall not under any circumstances be kept in a police station under police custody or jail in such cases (section 6 of Juvenile System Ordinance 2018).

139. Where a juvenile is arrested or detained for commission of minor or a major offence, he shall be treated as if he was accused of commission of a bailable offence.

140. Where a juvenile of more than 16 years of age is arrested or detained for a heinous offence, he may not be released on bail if the Juvenile Court is of the opinion that there are reasonable grounds to believe that such juvenile is involved in commission of a heinous crime.

141. A juvenile shall be interrogated by a police officer not below the rank of Sub-inspector under supervision of the Superintendent of Police or Sub-Division Police Officer (SDPO) (section 7 of JJSA 2018).

142. Where a person alleged to have committed an offence physically appears or claims to be a juvenile, the officer-in-charge of the police station or the investigation officer shall make an inquiry to determine the age of such person on the basis of his birth certificate, educational certificates or any other pertinent document. In the absence of such documents, the age of such accused person may be determined on the basis of a medical examination report by a medical officer (section 8 of the JJSA 2018).

143. With the consent of a juvenile or his guardian, the case shall be referred to the Juvenile Justice Committee for disposal of the same through diversion. The diversion can be exercised at any stage during the course of investigation by the police and during trial by the prosecution and the Court in the prescribed manner (section 9 of JJSA 2018).

144. The Juvenile Justice Committee shall dispose of the case with consent of the person against whom the offence was committed by resorting to different modes of diversion including restitution of moveable property, reparation of the damage caused, written or oral apology, participation in the community service, payments of fine and cost of the proceedings, placement in Juvenile Rehabilitation Centre and written and oral reprimand.

145. The Juvenile Justice Committee shall consist of four members namely: (1) serving Judicial Magistrate with powers under section 30 of Code, who shall also head the Committee, (2) district Public Prosecutor, (3) member of local Bar having at least seven years standing at the Bar, appointed by the concerned Sessions Judge for period of two years, (4) serving probation officer or social welfare officer not below the rank of an officer in BPS-17 (section 10 of JJSA 2018).

146. The Juvenile Justice Committee shall perform the following functions which include disposing of the case through diversion upon referral from the police, prosecuting the Juvenile Court within a period of one month from the date of referral, inspecting the observation homes and Juvenile Rehabilitation Centres and may give directions to the officer-in-charge of such places for the measures to be taken for welfare and social reintegration of the juvenile kept under their supervision.

147. No person shall be present at any sitting of the Juvenile Court except staff and officers of the Juvenile Court, parties to the case before the Juvenile Court and such other persons who are directly concerned with the proceedings including the police officers, guardians of the juvenile and such other persons as the Juvenile Court directs to be present. At any stage of proceedings, the Juvenile Court may in the best interest of a juvenile's decency or morality, direct any person to withdraw from the Court for such period as the Court may direct (section 11 of JJSA 2018).

148. When a juvenile who has been brought before the Juvenile Court is found to be suffering from serious illness, whether physical or mental and requires treatment, the Court shall send such juvenile to a hospital or a medical institution where treatment shall be given to the juvenile at the expense of the State.

149. A juvenile may be charged with and tried together with an adult by the Juvenile Court if the Court is satisfied that it is in the interests of justice to hold a joint trial. In case of joint trial, the Juvenile Court may dispense with the physical presence of the juvenile before it without any application in this regard and juvenile may be allowed to join the Court proceedings through audiovisual technology link (section 12 of the JJSA 2018).

150. Whoever prints or publishes the name or any matter which may make known identity of a juvenile shall be punished with imprisonment of either for a term which may extend to three years and shall also be liable to fine (section 13 of Juvenile Justice System 2018).

151. The probation officer shall assist and prepare a report or direction of the Juvenile Court within such time as may be directed to the Court at any stage regarding juvenile's character, educational, social and moral background, juvenile's admission of committing an offence made with free consent and voluntarily, any evidence that juvenile actually committed the offence, all legal and appropriate assistance provides at all levels to juvenile for his understanding, concept and consequences even to the child's family and guardian, steps taken for mediation or compromise with the complainant or victim and possibility of settlement and possibility of sending the juvenile to Juvenile Rehabilitation Centre or release on probation (section 14 of Juvenile Justice System 2018).

152. On receipt of report under section 14 on conclusion of an inquiry, investigation or trial, the Juvenile Court may pass an order for release of the juvenile offender after the victim or complainant, as the case may be, pardons him, pass an order for the community service, fine, compensation to the victim or complainant restitution of property, counselling, direct the juvenile offender to be released on probation for good conduct and place such juvenile offender under care of a guardian or any suitable place or such Juvenile Rehabilitation Centre established for the purpose of this act for any period not extending the period of confinement awarded to such juvenile (section 15 of Juvenile Justice System 2018).

153. No female juvenile shall in any circumstances be apprehended or investigated by a male police officer or released or probation under supervision of a male officer. A female juvenile shall only be kept in a Juvenile Rehabilitation Centre established or certified exclusively for female inmates (section 17 of Juvenile Justice System 2018).

154. In order to report to the Juvenile Court or Juvenile Justice Committee on measures being taken for social reintegration, health, education or other conditions of the inmates a medical officer' a member of the Committee with prior approval of the head of the Committee or an officer authorized by the Government may inspect an observation home or a Juvenile Rehabilitation Centre (section 22 of Juvenile Justice System 2018).

155. A minor child of age about 11 years was reported to have been arrested in a theft case. The court held that at the heart of our criminal justice system, treatment of child offenders should be guided by reformative approach. Young individuals often led astray by difficult circumstances deserve a chance to find their way back to normal life and become valuable members of society. Accused and his siblings having suffered neglect and destitution were sent to embrace Child Protection Bureau and custody of the minor would be regulated by Child Protection Court to undertake all necessary measures to ensure that such vulnerable children were safeguarded from future involvement in any unwanted activities High Court directed investigating agency to dismantle gangs exploiting minors for their nefarious designs, ensuring that such vulnerable youth would no longer be ensnared in criminal activities (section 11 and 14 of JJSA (XXII of 2018), section 5 of Punjab Destitute and Neglected Children Act (XVIII OF 2004), sections 1(k) and 23 of Constitution of Pakistan 1973) LHC (2025 P Cr. L J 1).

156. Qatl-i-amd, abduction for ransom, sodomy and terrorism. Accused was convicted for the offences and was sentenced to death. Plea was raised by the accused that he was juvenile at the time of commission of offence. Plea raised by accused was that Trial Court appointed a defence counsel at State's expense who did not cross-examine the prosecution witnesses and no inquiry regarding accused was conducted before the trial. When controversy regarding age of a person cannot be settled through documentary evidence and medical due to different opinions, preference is always given to medical opinion. High Court set aside conviction and sentence awarded to accused and remanded the matter to Trial Court to give opportunity to accused to engage a counsel of his choice and in case accused was unable to engage any counsel then Trial Court would appoint any senior counsel at state expenses. High Court directed Trial Court to hold inquiry under section 8 of JJSA 2018 and if it was established that the accused at the time of occurrence was a juvenile, the trial of accused would be conducted under the act. Appeal was allowed accordingly (section 302(b), 365 and 377 – Anti Terrorism Act (XXVII of 1997), section 7 JJSA (XXII of 2018), section 340(1) Criminal Procedure Code (V of 1898), Articles 9 and 10A Constitution of Pakistan 1973) (2024 P Cr. L J 772).

157. Accused was convicted by Trial Court for committing Qatl-i-amd and was sentenced to imprisonment for life. Accused contended that he was minor at the time of commission of offence and was not tried under JJSA 2018. Age of accused was recorded as 18–19 years in the card of arrest and investigating officer failed to conduct any inquiry to determine age of accused on the basis of birth certificate, education certificate or any other document. Trial Court granting custody of accused also failed to discharge its functions in light of section 8(2) of JJSA 2018 when accused at the time of arrest was 18–19 years old, while arrest took place one year before his arrest. Non-observance of mandatory provision of law regarding determination of his age deprived accused of special rights and protection available to him as a child/juvenile. High Court set aside conviction and sentence awarded to accused without dilating upon merits and remanded the matter to Child Protection Court. High Court directed Child Protection Court to first determine age of accused and if accused was proved to be minor/juvenile at the time of alleged offence, then to conduct fresh trial under the relevant law. Appeal was allowed accordingly (section 8 Juvenile Justice System (XXII of 2018), sections 7 and 8 Penal Code (XLV of 1860), section 302(b) Code of Criminal Procedure Code (V of 1898)) (2023 P Cr. L J 544).

158. Juvenile offender has a statutory right to be released on bail if his trial is not conducted within six months. Section 6 of JJSA 2018 clearly indicates that like third proviso to section 497 Criminal Procedure Code. It is the statutory duty of the prosecution to complete the trial by all possible means within six months otherwise the juvenile offender shall have the right to be released on bail (section 6 Juvenile Justice System (XXII of 2018), sections 6 and 497 Criminal Procedure Code (V of 1898)) (2023 MLD 777).

159. Juvenile accused detained for a continuous period exceeding six months without conclusion of trial. Period of six months mentioned in section 6(5) of the JJSA 2018 is to be counted from the date of arrest of the juvenile after determination of his age and not from the date of such determination or adjudication by the Court. (section 6(5) JJSA (XXII of 2018)) SC (2022 PLD 551)

160. Accused was alleged to have been found in possession of 3,300 grams of charas and 180 grams of heroin. Age of accused according to the birth registration certificate issued by National Database and Registration Authority (NADRA) was seventeen years, eleven months and twenty-five days on the day of occurrence. Section 6(4) of the JJSA 2018, provided that where the juvenile is of more than sixteen years of age was arrested or detained for a heinous offence, he might not be released on bail if the Juvenile Court was of the opinion that there were reasonable grounds to believe that such juvenile was involved in commission of a heinous offence. Under section 2(g) of JJSA 2018, 'heinous offence' included an offence punishable with death or imprisonment for life or imprisonment for more than seven years. Petition for grant of bail was dismissed in circumstances. (section 497 Khyber Pakhtunkhwa Control of Narcotics Substances Act (XXXI of 2019), sections 9(d) and 11(b) JJSA (XXII of 2018)) (2022 MLD 1123)

Chapter 4. Names

§1. Forename

161. A forename is the personal name given to an individual at birth, commonly known as the first name, and is typically used in daily life to address a person. It is distinct from a surname or family name, which identifies a person's lineage or ancestry. In many cultures, forenames carry significant meaning, often reflecting religious, cultural, or familial heritage, and may include multiple names of historical or spiritual importance. In Islamic tradition, a person will be called by their first and second names on the Day of Judgment, as supported by an authentic narration found in Saheeh al-Bukhari, regardless of whether the name is single or compound. Forenames play a crucial role in identity and are commonly recorded first in legal documents, with their usage varying across cultures, from formal settings to informal or familial contexts.

162. In Islam, giving a good and meaningful name to a newborn child is highly recommended, as names hold significant value in shaping a person's identity and character. The *Holy Prophet Muhammad (PBUH)* emphasized the importance of choosing virtuous names and stated that the best names in the sight of *Allah* are *Abdullah* and *Abdur Rahman*. This is supported by an authentic narration in *Sahih Muslim*, where *Ibn Umar (RA)* reported that the Prophet (PBUH) said, *'The names dearest to Allah are Abdullah and Abdur Rahman.'* In Islamic tradition, names hold great significance as they influence a person's character, identity, and perception in society. The Holy Prophet Muhammad (PBUH) encouraged parents to choose names with good meanings, often recommending the names of prophets, righteous companions, or names that reflect servitude to Allah such as Abdul Malik or Abdul Kareem. He also discouraged names with negative or inappropriate meanings and, in some cases, changed the names of individuals to better ones. Names that convey arrogance, idolatry, or undesirable traits are not encouraged in Islam. Moreover, on the Day of Judgment, people will be called by their names along with their fathers' names, emphasizing the importance of selecting meaningful and righteous names for children.

163. It is narrated by Sunan Abu Dawood that the Holy Prophet Muhammad (PBUH) said: 'Call yourselves by the names of the Prophets. The dearest names to Allah are Abdullah and Abdur Rahman, the truest are Harith (the cultivator) and Hammam (always thinking of initiating something) and the worst are Harb (the war) and Murrah (the bitter)'. The Holy Prophet Muhammad (PBUH) himself gave his sons and daughters good names.

164. Among the most favoured names in Islam are those of Prophets, Angels, righteous companions, and well-known pious individuals, as these names carry deep spiritual and moral significance. For females, the best names are those of the wives of the Holy Prophet Muhammad (PBUH), the pious women mentioned in the Holy Quran, the daughters of the Prophet (PBUH), and the female companions of the

Prophet (PBUH), as well as the names of other virtuous Muslim women known for their faith and righteousness. Islam emphasizes the importance of choosing names with positive meanings, as names can influence a person's character and perception in society. It is discouraged to use names that carry negative or inappropriate meanings, such as those related to fire, war, or suffering, as they do not align with the values of mercy, goodness, and righteousness that Islam promotes.

165. Moreover, Islam forbids names that declare servitude to anyone other than Allah such as 'slave of Jesus … '. Islam also forbids names that are similar to the Names of Allah such as Ar Raheem (The most compassionate) or Al Hakeem (The Wisest). But if the definite article 'Al', 'The' is omitted, then such names become permissible. Naming 'Naa'ilah' is allowed; it was the name of the wife of 'Uthmaan ibn Affaan'. If it were a bad name, he would certainly have changed it to a good one.

166. LHC held that it is difficult to enumerate which was an Islamic name and which was un-Islamic. Any name which did not derogate or offend against any of Islamic principles of faith, could be treated and accepted as an Islamic name. Muslim names differ from place to place and from country to country. Names which though had no similarity with Arabian names or names used by Muslims of other countries, such names could not be treated as un-Islamic and holders of such names could not be held as non-Muslims (LHC – 1999 CLC 1202).

§2. Surname

I. Acquisition of the Surname

167. In Pakistan, it is a common practice for a child to inherit the father's name as a surname. For females, their surname is often changed to that of their husband after marriage, though some Islamic scholars consider this practice impermissible, as Islam emphasizes maintaining one's lineage and identity. According to Islamic teachings, a person should be identified by their father's name, as stated in the Holy Quran: 'Call them by [the names of] their fathers; it is more just in the sight of Allah' (Surah Al-Ahzab 33:5). However, there is no legal requirement in Pakistan that mandates or prohibits adopting or changing a surname, leaving it to the discretion of individuals or their families. Islam places great importance on preserving one's lineage, and altering one's surname in a way that severs the link to one's biological family is discouraged. Instead, maintaining the father's name as a surname is encouraged as a means of upholding one's heritage and family identity. Parents have the freedom to choose a surname for their child, and individuals may also decide on a surname when they grow up, but it is preferable in Islam to retain the father's name to ensure clarity of lineage and identity.

II. Change of the Surname

168. According to Islamic scholars, a surname is traditionally linked to a person's lineage typically derived from the father's name. Therefore, changing one's surname in a way that alters or conceals this lineage is not permissible in Islam. Despite this, it is a common practice in Pakistan for females to adopt their husband's surname after marriage. However, Islamic scholars discourage this practice, as it contradicts the Islamic principle of maintaining one's original family lineage. Islam places great emphasis on preserving one's ancestry and altering a surname to reflect a marital relationship rather than a biological one is considered misleading.

Chapter 5. Nationality

§1. CITIZENSHIP

169. The principal legislation is the Pakistan Citizenship Act 1951, as amended by the Pakistan Citizenship (Amendment) Act 1952, the Pakistan Citizenship (Amendment) Act 1972, the Pakistan Citizenship (Amendment) Act 1973, the Pakistan Citizenship (Second Amendment) Act 1973 and the Pakistan Citizenship (Amendment) Ordinance 2000 regarding citizenship of Pakistan. In December 2024, the federal cabinet mandated that applicants must reside in Pakistan for at least five years to qualify for citizenship. This decision aims to tighten regulations around citizenship eligibility and address ongoing legal and social challenges. Additionally, in November 2024, the National Assembly's Standing Committee on Interior unanimously passed the Citizenship Law Amendment Bill. According to this amendment, children born to foreigners in Pakistan will not be granted Pakistani citizenship. These changes reflect a shift from the previous provision in the Pakistan Citizenship Act of 1951, which granted citizenship to individuals born in Pakistan after the commencement of the Act. The recent amendments emphasize residency requirements and parental nationality in determining citizenship eligibility.

170. Pakistani woman invoked constitutional jurisdiction of the High Court with grievance that the Directorate General of Immigration and Passport declined her husband a Pakistan Origin Card (POC) because he was an Afghan refugee. Although section 10 of the Pakistan Citizenship Act, 1951 gives a Pakistani husband the right to get a citizenship for his wife but denies a Pakistani wife the right to get a citizenship for her foreigner husband. It was held that denial of such right is discriminatory, negates gender equality and violates Articles 2A and 25 of the Constitution. On basis of this, a foreigner husband was entitled to apply and to be considered by the authorities for the issuance of POC in accordance with law. High Court directed the Directorate General of Immigration and passport to consider the case of the husband (Afghan refugee) of the Pakistani woman for issuance of POC. Constitution Petition was disposed of accordingly (PHC 2024 PLD 57).

171. Domicile certificate to be given preference over address on Computerized National Identity Card (CNIC). The domicile of a person is treated as a parent document for recruitment in order to ascertain the permanent abode. Weightage and preference should be given first to the certificate of domicile which cannot be ignored without due consideration. If jobs are given merely considering the Computerized National Identity Card (CNIC) without considering the address on the domicile then it would create various complications and complexities and even in the case of temporary shifting or in case of a rented house, the person will be forced every time to apply for fresh domicile with the address of changed abode and in such eventuality, he will become a rolling stone who would never be able to secure a job due to the alleged discrepancy. High Court petition dismissed. (SC 2023 SCMR 217)

§2. ACQUISITION OF CITIZENSHIP

172. Pakistan Citizenship Act, 1951, is recognized as a Pakistani citizen by birth. For individuals born outside Pakistan before 18 April 2000, citizenship by descent is granted only if the father was a Pakistani citizen, provided he was not a citizen by descent himself. However, exceptions exist where a person born abroad to a father who was a Pakistani citizen by descent may still acquire citizenship, subject to specific conditions. These include registering the birth at a Pakistani Consulate or High Commission abroad or if the father was employed in the service of the Government of Pakistan at the time of birth. Amendments in citizenship laws have sought to address issues related to nationality by descent, ensuring the preservation of Pakistani identity among overseas nationals. Dual nationality agreements with certain countries allow Pakistanis to retain their citizenship while acquiring another nationality, subject to Pakistan's bilateral arrangements. However, individuals seeking Pakistani citizenship through descent must adhere to procedural requirements, including timely registration of birth and verification of lineage.

173. An individual born outside Pakistan on or after 18 April 2000, is eligible for Pakistani citizenship by descent if either parent holds Pakistani nationality at the time of birth. This provision ensures that Pakistani heritage is preserved across generations, even for those born abroad. A Pakistani citizen who has acquired or is in the process of obtaining citizenship of another country has the option to formally renounce their Pakistani nationality. This is done by submitting a declaration of renunciation, subject to approval by the relevant authorities. However, Pakistan allows dual nationality with specific countries under bilateral agreements, enabling individuals to retain their Pakistani citizenship while holding another nationality. Those renouncing their citizenship should be aware that this decision is generally irreversible, and in certain cases, individuals may need to reapply if they wish to regain Pakistani nationality in the future.

174. Pakistan generally does not permit dual nationality, meaning that a citizen of Pakistan who acquires citizenship of another country automatically loses their Pakistani citizenship unless they renounce the foreign nationality. However, the Government of Pakistan has entered into agreements with specific countries that allow Pakistani nationals to retain their citizenship even after obtaining the nationality of those countries. These bilateral agreements aim to facilitate overseas Pakistanis by preserving their connection to their homeland while allowing them to acquire foreign citizenship for professional, educational, or personal reasons. Currently, Pakistan has dual nationality treaties with several countries, including the United Kingdom, Canada, Australia, and the United States, among others. Citizens who hold dual nationality under these agreements retain most of their rights as Pakistani citizens, except for certain restrictions, such as holding high government offices or acquiring sensitive security-related positions. Those seeking foreign citizenship outside these treaty arrangements must formally renounce their Pakistani nationality, as maintaining dual citizenship without legal authorization is not permitted under Pakistani law.

175. If a Pakistani woman marries a foreign national and acquires his nationality, she automatically loses her Pakistani citizenship. However, she may have the option to restore her Pakistani nationality if the marriage is dissolved and she formally renounces her foreign citizenship. This ensures that individuals who wish to reclaim their Pakistani identity after a change in marital status can do so through a legal process. Pakistan's citizenship laws prioritize maintaining national identity and lineage, particularly in cases where individuals acquire foreign nationalities through marriage. While some countries allow dual nationality, Pakistan only permits it with specific nations under bilateral agreements. Women who voluntarily acquire another nationality outside these agreements must undergo the official renunciation and restoration procedures if they later seek to regain Pakistani citizenship.

176. Minors (individuals under 21 years of age) who are eligible for Pakistani citizenship are exempt from the restriction on dual nationality if they acquire a foreign nationality, provided their father retains his Pakistani citizenship. If the father does not lose his Pakistani citizenship – either through automatic revocation upon acquiring another nationality or by formal renunciation – the child may continue to hold dual nationality. However, if the father ceases to be a Pakistani citizen, the minor automatically loses their Pakistani citizenship as well. This ensures that a child's citizenship status remains linked to the father's nationality, reflecting Pakistan's legal framework, which prioritizes lineage-based nationality. In cases where a minor loses Pakistani citizenship due to the father's renunciation, they may have the option to reclaim it upon reaching adulthood by fulfilling the necessary legal requirements. Pakistan's agreements with certain countries on dual nationality may provide further exceptions for minors, depending on the terms of the respective treaties.

Chapter 6. Domicile and Residence

§1. Domicile

177. A domicile certificate is an official document issued by the Government of Pakistan under the Pakistan Citizenship Act, 1951, and its associated rules. This certificate serves as proof of an individual's residence, nationality, citizenship status, place of domicile, and date of arrival in that location. Additionally, it includes details such as the names and ages of the individual's children, occupation or trade, and any distinguishing marks of identification. The issuance of a domicile certificate is subject to specific conditions outlined in section 17 of the Pakistan Citizenship Act, 1951. Applicants must provide valid proof of residence and fulfil legal requirements to establish their permanent connection to a particular region of Pakistan. A domicile certificate is essential for various legal and administrative purposes, including employment, education, property ownership, and government benefits. Under Pakistan's citizenship laws, individuals who migrate to Pakistan and seek citizenship must first obtain domicile status before applying for naturalization. Domicile plays a crucial role in determining eligibility for certain rights and privileges, particularly in cases of nationality by descent or marriage. Pakistan also recognizes dual nationality with select countries, but individuals must comply with legal provisions regarding domicile and citizenship retention.

§2. Domicile of Origin

178. In Pakistan, a domicile certificate serves as official proof of an individual's permanent residence and origin, as stipulated under the Pakistan Citizenship Act of 1951. This document is crucial for various purposes, including employment and education. In the public sector, job vacancies are distributed among the provinces based on a quota system, making it essential for candidates to possess a domicile certificate from their respective province when applying for government positions. Regarding inheritance matters, the Succession Act of 1925 outlines the significance of domicile in determining the applicable laws for succession. Part II of the Act details how an individual's domicile affects the distribution of both movable and immovable property upon death. Notably, the Act specifies that a person can have only one domicile for the purpose of succession to movable property.

179. Under the Succession Act, 1925, an individual can have only one domicile for the purpose of succession to their movable property. The domicile of origin is determined by the country in which the individual's father was domiciled at the time of their birth. In cases where the child is born after the father's death, the domicile of origin is based on the father's domicile at the time of his passing. For example, if a person's father was domiciled in England at the time of birth, the child's domicile of origin remains England, regardless of the actual place of birth. For illegitimate children, the domicile of origin is determined by the mother's domicile at the time of birth. This distinction ensures legal clarity in situations where paternal lineage is not formally recognized. The domicile of origin remains in effect until a new domicile is acquired, which requires both actual residence in a different country and a clear intention to settle there permanently. However, if the acquired domicile is abandoned without establishing a new one, the domicile of origin is automatically reinstated. Domicile plays a significant role in legal matters related to inheritance and succession, particularly when assets are spread across multiple jurisdictions.

180. A man acquires a new domicile by taking up his fixed habitation in a country which is not that of his domicile of origin. A man is not to be deemed to have taken up his fixed habitation in Pakistan merely by reason of his residing therein the civil, military, naval or air force service of Pakistan or in the exercise of any profession or calling. (i) A, whose domicile of origin is in England, proceeds to Pakistan, where he settles as a barrister or a merchant, intending to reside there during the remainder of his life. His domicile is now in Pakistan. (ii) A, whose domicile is in England, goes to Austria, and enters the Austrian service, intending to remain in that service. A has acquired a domicile in Austria. (iii) A, whose domicile of origin is in France, comes to reside in Pakistan under an engagement with the Federal Government for a certain number of years. It is his intention to return to France at the end of that period. He does not acquire a domicile in Pakistan. (iv) A, whose domicile is in England, goes to reside in Pakistan for the purpose of winding up the affairs of a partnership which has been dissolved, and with the intention of returning to England as soon as that purpose is accomplished. He does not by such residence acquire a domicile in Pakistan, however long the residence may last. (v) A, having gone to reside in Pakistan in the circumstances mentioned in the preceding illustration, afterwards alters his intention, and takes up his fixed habitation in Pakistan. A has acquired a domicile in Pakistan. (vi) A, whose domicile is in the French Settlement of Chandernagore, is compelled by political events to take refuge in Peshawar and resides in Peshawar for many years in the hope of such political changes as may enable him to return with safety to Chandernagore. He does not by such residence acquire a domicile in Pakistan. (vii) A, having come to Peshawar in the circumstances stated in the preceding illustration, continues to reside there after such political changes have occurred as would enable him to return with safety to Chandernagore, and he intends that his residence in Peshawar shall be permanent. A has acquired a domicile in Pakistan.

181. An individual may acquire domicile in Pakistan by submitting a formal written declaration expressing their intent to do so. This declaration must be signed and deposited in an office designated by the provincial government for this purpose. To be eligible, the applicant must have continuously resided in Pakistan for at least one year immediately before making the declaration. In addition to fulfilling the residency requirement, the applicant may need to provide supporting documents such as proof of employment, property ownership, or long-term residence to substantiate their claim. Acquiring domicile is a significant legal step as it establishes an individual's permanent residence status, impacting rights related to inheritance, taxation, employment eligibility, and access to government services.

182. An individual appointed by the government of one country as an ambassador, consul, or official representative in another country does not acquire domicile in the host country solely by virtue of residing there for the duration of their appointment. Their legal domicile remains in their home country, as their presence in the foreign nation is considered temporary and tied to diplomatic service. Similarly, family members or domestic staff residing with such a diplomatic representative do not automatically acquire domicile in the host country based solely on their stay. This principle aligns with international diplomatic norms, ensuring that diplomats and their dependents maintain legal ties to their home country despite prolonged residence abroad. Under international law, particularly the Vienna Convention on Diplomatic Relations, diplomats enjoy certain privileges, including immunity from local jurisdiction and taxation, further reinforcing the principle that their residency does not constitute a change in domicile. In Pakistan, the concept of domicile remains crucial for determining legal rights related to citizenship, taxation, and succession, and it is not influenced by temporary diplomatic assignments or government service abroad.

183. A newly acquired domicile remains in effect until an individual either reverts to their previous domicile or establishes another one. For minors, domicile is generally determined by the parent from whom they inherit their domicile of origin. However, there are specific exceptions to this rule. A minor's domicile does not automatically change with that of their parent if the minor is married, holds a government office, is employed in state service, or has independently established a distinct business with parental consent. These exceptions recognize the minor's legal and financial independence, allowing them to maintain a separate domicile under certain circumstances.

184. Upon marriage, a woman generally acquires the domicile of her husband if she did not already share the same domicile prior to the marriage. Throughout the duration of the marriage, the wife's domicile typically follows that of her husband. However, there are legal exceptions to this principle. A wife's domicile ceases to automatically follow that of her husband if they are legally separated by a court order or if the husband is serving a sentence of exile or deportation. In such cases, the wife may retain her existing domicile or establish a new one independently. Additionally, under the law, a minor cannot acquire a new domicile during their minority, except in cases explicitly provided for, such as marriage or state employment. Similarly, an individual who is legally declared insane is unable to establish a new domicile of their own accord. In such instances, their domicile remains linked to the person legally responsible for them, such as a parent or guardian.

185. If a person passes away leaving movable property in Pakistan, and there is no evidence of domicile in another jurisdiction, the succession of the property shall be governed by the laws of Pakistan.

186. If an individual whose domicile is not in Pakistan marries someone domiciled in Pakistan, neither party gains any rights to the other's property by virtue of the marriage, unless such rights were specifically outlined in a prenuptial settlement. In the absence of a pre-marriage agreement, the parties do not acquire any rights to each other's property that they would not otherwise have if both were domiciled in Pakistan at the time of the marriage. This ensures that the legal rights regarding property ownership remain governed by the respective domiciles of the individuals involved. For example, the property rights of the non-Pakistani spouse are determined by the laws of their country of domicile, while the rights of the Pakistani spouse are subject to Pakistani laws. If both parties intend to alter the property rights arising from the marriage, they must do so through a formal marital settlement agreement, which should clearly define the distribution of property in the event of divorce, death, or separation. This could include provisions on *dowries, gifts,* or other financial arrangements agreed upon by both parties prior to the marriage. Legal frameworks like the *MFLO, 1961* and the *Dissolution of Muslim Marriages Act, 1939* are relevant in these matters in Pakistan, particularly when dealing with inheritance and property distribution in matrimonial contexts.

Chapter 7. Mentally Handicapped Persons

§1. Criminal Law

187. Under Islamic law, individuals who are mentally handicapped or insane are not held accountable for their actions in terms of sin, as they are not considered capable of full moral responsibility. The Holy Prophet Muhammad (PBUH) is reported to have said, 'The pen is lifted (i.e., the recording of deeds is suspended) from three types of people: the one who is sleeping until they wake up, the mentally handicapped or insane person until they regain their reasoning, and a child until they reach the age of puberty.' This exemption reflects the Islamic understanding of accountability, where a person's ability to reason and comprehend their actions is a key factor in determining their moral and legal responsibility. The mentally handicapped person, therefore, is not held accountable for sinful actions as they do not possess the capacity to understand the consequences of their deeds in the same way as others. Islam provides a compassionate approach to those with mental disabilities, acknowledging their limitations while ensuring their protection and dignity within society.

188. When the action involves the rights of others, such as stealing, the individual is still required to make restitution, regardless of their mental condition. If the person has taken something unlawfully from another, the stolen property must be returned to its rightful owner, if they are known and available. In the event that the rightful owner has passed away, the object should be returned to their heirs, provided they can be identified. If the rightful heirs cannot be located, or if restitution is not possible, the property should be given in charity as a means of rectifying the wrong.

189. Article 38(d) of the Constitution of Islamic Republic of Pakistan, 1973, stipulates that the State shall provide basic necessities of life, such as food, clothing, housing, education and medical relief, for all such citizens, irrespective of sex, caste, creed or race, as they are permanently or temporarily unable to earn their livelihood on account of infirmity, sickness or unemployment.

§2. Suits By or Against Lunatics

190. Under *Order XXXII* of the *Code of Civil Procedure, 1908*, the legal framework for proceedings involving minors and persons of unsound mind is outlined. Specifically, *Rule 15 of Order XXXII* extends the provisions of *Rules 1 to 14* to individuals who are either adjudicated as of unsound mind by a competent court or are deemed mentally incapacitated by the court following an inquiry. This includes persons who, despite not being officially declared of unsound mind, are found by the court to be incapable of protecting their interests due to mental infirmity or unsoundness of mind, whether in initiating or defending a legal action.

191. Under the *Mental Health Ordinance, 2001* (now the *Mental Health Act, 2017*) provides the legal framework for the treatment and protection of individuals with mental health conditions in Pakistan. It sets the foundation for involuntary admission and treatment, ensuring that individuals suffering from mental disorders are properly cared for while safeguarding their rights. The law defines key terms such as 'mentally ill person', 'guardian', and 'treatment' under section 2. Sections 3 to 8 detail the procedures for admission, discharge, and treatment of mentally ill persons, emphasizing the protection of their rights and preventing unjust detention or treatment. Section 9 focuses on the appointment of legal representatives for individuals with mental illnesses, ensuring they can participate in legal matters. Furthermore, sections 11 and 12 establish the Mental Health Review Board, responsible for overseeing cases related to mental health, ensuring that the rights and interests of mentally ill persons are respected and upheld.

192. In cases involving minors, any legal action must be initiated in the minor's name with a designated representative known as the 'next friend' acting on their behalf. If a suit is filed on behalf of a minor without the appointment of a next friend, the defendant has the right to request that the court remove the plaint from the file, and the costs incurred shall be paid by the individual (whether it be the pleader or any other person) who presented the suit. This ensures that the interests of the minor are properly represented in legal proceedings.

193. If a suit is filed on behalf of a minor without a legally appointed next friend, the defendant has the right to apply for its dismissal. In such cases, the court is required to notify the person who initiated the suit, allowing them an opportunity to present objections before a final decision is made. The court, after considering the circumstances and objections, may pass any order it deems appropriate. Additionally, if the defendant in a case is a minor, the court, upon verifying the minor's status, must appoint a suitable individual as guardian ad litem (guardian for the suit) to represent and safeguard the minor's legal rights and interests throughout the proceedings. This provision aligns with **Order XXXII of the Code of Civil Procedure, 1908**, which ensures that minors and individuals of unsound mind receive adequate legal representation and are not prejudiced in legal matters due to their incapacity. Furthermore, the guardian so appointed must act in the minor's best interest, and any action taken without proper representation can be challenged and set aside by the court.

194. A court may appoint guardian ad litem (legal guardian for the suit) for a minor either upon an application made on behalf of the minor or by the plaintiff. The application for such an appointment must be accompanied by an affidavit confirming that the proposed guardian has no conflicting interest in the subject matter of the suit that could be detrimental to the minor's rights. Additionally, the affidavit must establish that the individual is suitable and competent to act in the minor's best interests.

195. No order on an application concerning a minor shall be passed without prior notice to the minor and their legally appointed guardian, if such a guardian has been designated by a competent authority. In cases where no such guardian exists, notice must be given to the father or any other natural guardian of the minor. If neither a father nor another natural guardian is available, the notice shall be served upon the individual under whose care the minor resides. The court must also provide an opportunity for any objections to be raised by those who receive the notice before making a final decision.

196. A guardian appointed to represent a minor in a legal suit shall continue to serve in that capacity throughout all stages of the legal proceedings unless their appointment is terminated due to retirement, removal by the court, or death. This guardianship extends beyond the trial phase and remains effective in appellate, revisional, and execution proceedings related to the case.

197. Any individual who is of sound mind and has reached the age of majority is eligible to act as the **next friend** or **guardian ad litem** for a minor in legal proceedings, provided that they do not have any conflict of interest that is averse to the minor's rights. A person acting as a **next friend** cannot be a defendant in the case, and a guardian appointed for the suit cannot be a plaintiff.

198. If a minor already has a legally appointed or declared guardian by a competent authority, no other individual shall act as their **next friend** or be appointed as their **guardian ad litem** for legal proceedings unless the court, for recorded reasons, determines that appointing another person would be in the minor's best interest. Furthermore, no individual shall be appointed as a guardian for the suit without their consent. Under **Order XXXII, Rule 4 of the Code of Civil Procedure, 1908**, the court has the discretion to override an existing guardian's authority if it finds that appointing another person would better serve the minor's welfare. This provision ensures that legal representation for minors remains in their best interests and prevents conflicts of interest. The court may also assess the suitability of the proposed guardian, ensuring that they possess the capacity, integrity, and commitment necessary to protect the minor's rights throughout the legal proceedings. If an appointed guardian acts negligently or contrary to the minor's interests, the court has the authority to remove and replace them with a more suitable representative.

199. If no suitable or willing person is available to act as a **guardian ad litem** for a minor in a legal proceeding, the court has the authority to appoint one of its officers to fulfil this role. In such cases, the court may also determine how the expenses incurred by the appointed guardian should be covered. These costs may be assigned to one or more parties involved in the case or paid from any funds held by the court in which the minor has an interest. Additionally, the court may provide directions regarding reimbursement or financial allowances based on the demands of justice and the specific circumstances of the case.

200. All applications made to the court on behalf of a minor, except those that the minor is expressly permitted by law to make, must be submitted through a **next friend** or a **guardian ad litem** appointed for the suit. Any judicial order issued in a case or application that affects a minor in any manner, without proper representation by a next friend or guardian, may be set aside upon review. Furthermore, if the legal representative or pleader responsible for obtaining such an order was aware, or reasonably should have been aware, of the minor's status, the court may impose costs upon the pleader as a corrective measure. Under **Order XXXII, Rules 2 and 3 of the Code of Civil Procedure, 1908**, these provisions ensure the protection of minors in legal proceedings, preventing them from being disadvantaged due to procedural lapses. The law emphasizes that a minor must always be represented by a competent guardian or next friend to safeguard their interests and prevent any unfair or prejudicial outcomes.

201. A next friend or guardian ad litem appointed for a minor in legal proceedings shall not, without the prior approval of the court, receive any monetary payment or other movable property on behalf of the minor, whether: (a) as part of a compromise or settlement reached before a decree or order is issued, or (b) under a decree or order granted in favour of the minor. This restriction is in place to ensure that any financial or material benefit awarded to a minor is safeguarded and used in their best interest. The court exercises oversight to prevent potential mismanagement, undue influence, or exploitation of the minor's rights. These provisions are outlined in Order XXXII, Rule 6 of the Code of Civil Procedure, 1908, which mandates that any agreement involving the minor's assets must be scrutinized and approved by the court.

202. If the next friend or guardian ad litem appointed in a suit has not been designated by a competent authority as the guardian of the minor's property, or if such a guardian has been appointed but is legally incapacitated or otherwise deemed unfit to manage the minor's financial interests, the court shall intervene to ensure the minor's assets are safeguarded. Before granting permission to receive any money or movable property on behalf of the minor, the court will require adequate security and may issue necessary directions to prevent mismanagement, waste, or misuse of the minor's assets. These measures are taken to ensure the property is utilized exclusively for the minor's welfare and benefit. This provision aligns with Order XXXII, Rule 7 of the Code of Civil Procedure, 1908, which stipulates that any transaction involving the minor's property must be carefully regulated by the court to prevent exploitation or financial loss. Additionally, the Guardian and Wards Act, 1890 provides further legal safeguards to protect the minor's property and ensures that only a duly authorized individual, acting in good faith and in the minor's best interest, is permitted to manage such assets.

203. A next friend or guardian ad litem representing a minor in a legal suit cannot, without the express permission of the court, enter into any agreement or compromise on behalf of the minor. Such permission must be formally recorded in the court proceedings to ensure transparency and safeguard the minor's interests. Any agreement or compromise made without obtaining prior approval from the court shall be considered voidable at the discretion of the minor. This means that while the minor retains the right to challenge and nullify the agreement, the other parties involved in the suit will remain bound by its terms.

204. A next friend representing a minor in a legal suit cannot withdraw from their role unless permitted by the court. Before stepping down, the next friend must ensure that a suitable replacement is appointed to protect the minor's legal interests. Additionally, they must provide security for any legal costs already incurred in the proceedings. An application for the appointment of a new next friend must be accompanied by an affidavit verifying the suitability of the proposed individual. This affidavit must confirm that the new appointee is competent to act in the minor's best interests and does not have any conflict of interest or adverse claim against the minor. These provisions are outlined under Order XXXII, Rule 10 of the Code of Civil Procedure, 1908, ensuring that a minor is continuously represented in legal proceedings without any gaps that might jeopardize their rights.

205. If the next friend of a minor has an interest that conflicts with the minor's, or if they have close ties with a defendant whose interests are adverse to the minor, there is a risk that the minor's legal rights may not be adequately safeguarded. If the next friend fails to fulfil their responsibilities, relocates outside Pakistan during the proceedings, or any other sufficient reason arises, an application for their removal may be filed on behalf of the minor or by a defendant. The court, upon being satisfied that the grounds for removal are valid, may order the next friend's dismissal and appoint a replacement who can better serve the minor's interests. Furthermore, the court may issue orders regarding the costs incurred due to such removal.

206. If the next friend of a minor is not the legally appointed or declared guardian under the authority of a competent body, and an application is made by a duly appointed guardian requesting to replace the next friend, the court shall ordinarily remove the existing next friend. However, if the court determines that appointing the guardian as the next friend would not serve the minor's best interests, it must record the reasons for such a decision. In cases where the guardian is deemed suitable, the court shall appoint them as the next friend, ensuring that all prior costs incurred in the suit are appropriately allocated as deemed fit. This process makes certain that a minor is represented by a responsible and legally recognized guardian, minimizing potential conflicts of interest or inadequate representation.

207. If the next friend of a minor retires, is removed, or passes away, all further legal proceedings shall be paused until a new next friend is appointed. In such circumstances, if the legal representative (pleader) of the minor fails to take prompt action to secure a replacement, any person with a legitimate interest in the minor or the subject matter of the case may petition the court for the appointment of a new next friend. The court upon consideration may appoint a suitable individual to act in this capacity ensuring the continued representation and protection of the minor's legal interests.

208. If a guardian appointed for a suit wishes to retire, fails to fulfil their duties, or if any other valid reason arises, the court may permit their retirement or order their removal. The court also has the discretion to impose any necessary cost orders in such cases. In situations where the guardian for the suit retires, passes away, or is removed while the case is still ongoing, the court shall appoint a new guardian to ensure the continued protection of the minor's legal interests.

209. A minor plaintiff, or a minor who is not a party to a suit but for whom an application is pending, upon reaching the age of majority, must decide whether they wish to continue with the suit or application. If they choose to proceed, they must apply for an order to discharge their next friend and seek permission to continue the legal proceedings in their own name. In such cases, the title of the suit or application will be amended to reflect the change, reading: 'A.B., formerly a minor, by C.D., his next friend, but now having attained majority.' This provision is in line with Order XXXII, Rule 13 of the Code of Civil Procedure, 1908, which allows a minor who has reached the age of majority to take control of their legal proceedings, and the role of the next friend is terminated upon their majority.

210. If the minor elects to abandon the suit or application, and they are the sole plaintiff or applicant, they must apply for an order to dismiss the suit or application, while also ensuring repayment of the costs incurred by the defendant or opposing party, or those paid by their next friend. Any application made under this rule may be submitted ex parte; however, no order discharging the next friend and allowing the minor plaintiff to proceed in their own name shall be granted without first providing notice to the next friend. This aligns with the provisions under Order XXXII, Rule 15 of the Code of Civil Procedure, 1908, which outlines the procedures regarding the withdrawal of a suit by a minor and the financial obligations involved. Additionally, it ensures that the minor's legal rights are safeguarded by preventing any undue harm to the interests of the next friend or opposing party.

211. When a minor co-plaintiff reaches the age of majority and wishes to repudiate the suit, they must apply to have their name removed as a co-plaintiff. If the court determines that the minor is not a necessary party, it may dismiss their involvement in the suit, subject to any terms regarding costs or other considerations that it deems appropriate. Notice of this application must be served to the next friend, any co-plaintiffs, and the defendant. The costs of the application, as well as the costs incurred in any proceedings prior to this application, shall be determined by the court and borne by the parties as it deems fit. If the minor is found to be a necessary party to the suit, the court may direct that they be made a defendant instead. This is in accordance with the provisions of Order XXXII, Rule 13 of the Code of Civil Procedure, 1908, which governs the participation of minors in legal actions and their rights to withdraw or be excluded from the suit upon attaining majority.

212. Upon attaining majority, a minor who was the sole plaintiff in a suit may apply to have the suit dismissed if it was instituted in their name by their next friend, on the grounds that the suit was unreasonable or improper. The application must be served on all relevant parties. If the court finds that the suit was indeed unreasonable or improper, it may grant the application and order the next friend to pay the costs incurred by all parties in connection with the application and the proceedings in the suit. Alternatively, the court may issue any other order it deems appropriate.

§3. Marriage

213. In Islam, marriage is regarded as a contract between a man and a woman with the intention of forming a marital union. As with any contract in Islamic law, marriage requires certain essential components or 'pillars' to ensure its validity. These include the offer and acceptance by both parties, the presence of witnesses, and the dowry, which is a legal requirement in Islamic marriage. Additionally, the guardian of the woman plays an essential role in the contract, particularly in the case of a woman who has not yet reached full maturity or understanding. The primary parties to the contract are the man and the woman's guardian, and both must willingly and knowingly agree to the terms.

214. For the marriage contract to be valid, it is crucial that both parties understand the nature of the commitment they are entering into. This includes the capacity to give free and informed consent. In cases where either party, especially the woman, suffers from mental incapacity or is mentally handicapped, the contract cannot be considered valid under both Islamic and Pakistani law. Islamic jurisprudence requires that a person be of sound mind to fully comprehend and consent to the marriage contract.

215. In Pakistan, the legal framework surrounding marriage is governed by both Islamic law and the *MFLO, 1961*. Under this ordinance, if one of the parties is mentally incapacitated, the marriage may be deemed void or voidable, depending on the specific circumstances. The inability to provide informed consent is a critical factor in such cases as a marriage based on lack of understanding or mental incapacity is not legally binding in Pakistan, in line with the principles outlined in Islamic law. Therefore, a marriage involving a mentally handicapped person is not valid under Islamic law and Pakistani legal standards as the essential conditions of informed consent, mental capacity, and the ability to engage in the marriage contract are not met.

216. Under Article 2(vi) of the Dissolution of Muslim Marriages Act, 1939 if husband has been insane for a period of two years or is suffering from leprosy or a virulent venereal disease, the woman married under the Islamic Law is entitled to obtain decree for dissolution of her marriage.

217. Under section 7 of the MFLO, 1961 allows for the wife to seek maintenance or claim divorce under certain conditions, including cases where the husband is unable to perform his marital duties, such as due to mental incapacity.

218. Under section 5 of the Family Courts Act, 1964 outlines the jurisdiction of family courts over matters concerning dissolution of marriage, including cases involving the mental incapacity or serious illness of the husband.

Part II. Family Law

Chapter 1. Marriage

§1. The Nature of Marriage

219. Marriage, under Pakistani law, is viewed as a contract between the husband and wife rather than a sacrament. The SCP has upheld that marriage in Islam is not a sacrament but a civil contract that holds spiritual and moral significance. The contract is based on mutual consent and responsibility and it is not intended to bind the parties in an irreversible or permanent union. This legal understanding reflects the natural principles of Islam (Din al-Fitrah) which acknowledges the human need for both partnership and, when necessary, separation in a just and lawful manner.

220. In Islamic jurisprudence, marriage is viewed as a mutual agreement and both spouses have rights and obligations towards each other. Islamic law permits the dissolution of marriage in cases where there are valid reasons such as the incapacity of a spouse, harm, or other factors that make the continuation of the marriage untenable. This aligns with the principles laid out in the *Dissolution of Muslim Marriages Act, 1939*, which allows for divorce in cases such as mental illness, cruelty, or failure to fulfil marital obligations. The contractual nature of marriage provides both parties with avenues for dissolution when necessary, ensuring that the marriage remains in line with the principles of justice and equity.

221. In Pakistani law, this understanding of marriage as a contract is reflected in statutes such as the *MFLO, 1961*, and the *Family Courts Act, 1964*, which govern the processes for divorce, maintenance, and related family matters. These laws recognize that while marriage carries significant personal and moral implications, it is also a civil contract that can be dissolved under the law for legitimate reasons, including mental incapacity or other substantial causes. This ensures that the rights of both parties are protected while acknowledging the practical realities of marital relationships.

222. In Islam, marriage is designed to fulfil several important purposes with spiritual tranquility, peace, and partnership being central to its objectives. The Holy Quran emphasizes that the primary purpose of marriage is to bring peace and comfort to both partners. In Surah Ar-Rum (30:21), it is mentioned: 'Among His signs is that He created for you spouses of your own kind in order that you may repose to them in tranquility, and He instilled in your hearts love and affection for one another; verily, in these are signs for those who reflect.‘ This verse highlights that the union of husband and wife is meant to bring inner peace and harmony, reflecting the divine wisdom in creating such relationships. Marriage in Islam is not only a personal bond but also a partnership with a shared responsibility towards goodness and the fulfilment of the divine purpose in life. As stated in Surah At-Tawbah (9:71), ‘The believing men and believing women are allies of one another; they enjoin what is right and forbid what is wrong.‘ This verse reflects the idea of mutual cooperation and responsibility between spouses, where both are partners in promoting righteousness, moral conduct, and fulfilling their divine obligations in life.

§2. Marriage Functions

223. Marriage functions in Pakistan are significant cultural and social events that mark the formal union between two individuals and their families. These events are traditionally celebrated with great enthusiasm, involving multiple days of festivities, including customs like *Mehndi*, *Barat*, and *Walima*. While deeply rooted in cultural and religious practices, marriage functions have also become increasingly elaborate, often leading to social pressure and financial strain on families due to excessive spending, dowry demands, and public displays of wealth. In response, provincial governments across Pakistan have introduced the legislative system like Punjab Marriage Functions Act, 2016 and The Khyber Pakhtunkhwa Marriage Functions (Prohibition of Ostentatious Displays and Wasteful Expenses) Act, 2018, to regulate such functions, promote simplicity, discourage wasteful expenditures, and to make certain that marriages are conducted with dignity, fairness, and legal protection for all individuals involved.

224. Marriage functions (including Mehndi, Barat, Walima) shall limit the dishes to one dish only. Serving more than one dish or arranging elaborate meals is strictly prohibited. It also restricts the use of public streets or roads for such events unless permitted (section 3 of Punjab Marriage Functions Act, 2016).

225. Marriage-related functions must **conclude by 10:00 PM**. Holding events beyond this time is a violation of the Act and can result in penalties (section 4 of Punjab Marriage Functions Act, 2016).

226. The Act bans the use of fireworks, aerial firing, and the display or use of arms during marriage ceremonies, considering them dangerous and a public nuisance (section 5 of Punjab Marriage Function Act 2016).

227. Empowers government officers (e.g., Assistant Commissioners) to inspect venues, enforce compliance, and impose fines on those violating the Act. Offenders may face a fine up to PKR 500,000 or imprisonment in case of serious violations (section 7 of Punjab Marriage Function Act 2016).

228. The Khyber Pakhtunkhwa Marriage Functions (Prohibition of Ostentatious Displays and Wasteful Expenses) Act, 2018, was enacted to regulate marriage ceremonies in the province, aiming to curb extravagant displays and reduce financial burdens on families. The Act limits the aggregate value of bridal gifts to PKR 100,000 and restricts the menu for wedding functions to one rice dish, one gravy or salan dish, one dry dish, naan or roti, salad, and a sweet dish. Engagement, mehndi, or nikkah ceremonies are permitted to serve only beverages (section 3 of the Khyber Pakhtunkhwa Marriage Functions (Prohibition of Ostentatious Displays and Wasteful Expenses) Act, 2018).

229. Decorations of houses, streets, or public places with lights or illuminations are prohibited, as is the use of fireworks and aerial firing. All marriage functions must conclude by 11:00 PM (section 5 of the Khyber Pakhtunkhwa Marriage Functions (Prohibition of Ostentatious Displays and Wasteful Expenses) Act, 2018).

230. The Act also penalizes the demand for dowry, with offenders facing imprisonment up to two months and fines not less than PKR 300,000 (section 6 of the Khyber Pakhtunkhwa Marriage Functions (Prohibition of Ostentatious Displays and Wasteful Expenses) Act, 2018).

231. Violations of these provisions can result in fines up to PKR 200,000 or imprisonment for up to three months, or both (section 7 of the Khyber Pakhtunkhwa Marriage Functions (Prohibition of Ostentatious Displays and Wasteful Expenses) Act, 2018).

§3. The Capacity to Marry

232. Under Islamic law, the validity of a marriage primarily hinges on the capacity of the parties involved to marry each other, rather than on the specific customs or formalities followed during the marriage ceremony. The marriage contract must meet the essential requirements, such as the offer (ijab) and acceptance (qabul) from both parties, the presence of witnesses, and the agreement of the woman's guardian, where applicable. These are the fundamental conditions that ensure the marriage is valid according to Islamic principles. Marriage under Islamic law requires the couple to be free from any legal impediments, such as consanguinity, affinity, and other prohibited relationships. The *Family Courts Act, 1964* in Pakistan enforces these requirements and provides a mechanism for the adjudication of marital disputes, ensuring that the validity of the marriage is maintained in accordance with Islamic law. The law also upholds the obligations that arise from the marriage contract, such as the provision of mahr (dowry) and maintenance, which are essential rights of the wife.

I. Different Sex

233. Under both Islamic and Pakistani laws, the recognition of marriage is strictly between a male and a female. Any marriage involving two individuals of the same sex is not only considered impermissible in Islam but is also prohibited by the Pakistani legal system. In Islamic law, marriage is defined as a contract between a man and a woman. Any marriage outside of this framework, particularly same-sex marriages is deemed unlawful. The Quran and the Sunnah explicitly discourage and condemn homosexual relationships emphasizing the natural union between a man and a woman. Homosexuality is regarded as sinful in Islam and is viewed as against the teachings of the religion. The Holy Quran (Surah Al-A'raf 7:80–81) contain references to the prohibition of homosexual behaviour, further establishing its illegitimacy in Islamic law.

234. Section 377 of the PPC 1860 reads: 'Whoever voluntarily has carnal intercourse against the order of nature with any man, woman, or animal, shall be punished with imprisonment of either description for a term which may extend to life or with imprisonment of either description for a term which may extend to ten years, and shall also be liable to a fine.'

II. Consanguinity

235. Under Islamic law, marriage between certain relatives is strictly prohibited to ensure the integrity and stability of the family and social structure. These prohibitions, explicitly outlined in the Shari'ah, safeguard familial bonds by preventing any form of sexual interaction between specific relations. The restrictions apply not only to direct relatives such as parents, siblings, and children but also to extended family members, including aunts, uncles, nieces, nephews, in-laws, and foster relatives. The Qur'an sanctifies these relationships, reinforcing their prohibition in marriage to uphold moral and social harmony.

236. While marriage between immediate family members such as parents, siblings, aunts, uncles, nieces, and nephews are strictly prohibited in Islam, the religion allows marriage between more distant relatives, including cousins. Cousin marriage is considered permissible and is widely practiced in Muslim societies, including Pakistan. However, modern medical research has highlighted potential genetic risks associated with repeated cousin marriages over generations, which can lead to an increased likelihood of hereditary diseases and genetic disorders.

237. Under section 5 of the MFLO, 1961, and the Dissolution of Muslim Marriages Act, 1939, marriages that violate these prohibitions can be legally annulled. Additionally, such marriages may be subject to penal consequences under Pakistani law. Moreover, under **section 375 of the PPC**, any sexual relations with prohibited relations (incestuous relationships) may be considered a punishable offense.

238. In the Holy Quran (Sura Al-Nisa) it is stipulated that:

> And marry not women whom your fathers married – except what has been done in the past: it was shameful and odious – an abominable practice indeed. Prohibited to you [for marriage] are your mothers, daughters, sisters, your maternal and paternal aunts, the daughters of your brothers and sisters; your mothers who have suckled you and your sisters through fosterage, the mothers of your wives, your step-daughters raised under you, born of your wives with whom you have la'in – no offence if you have not la'in with their mothers, and the wives of your begotten sons, and two sisters in wedlock at the same time, except for what has already happened. God indeed is Oft-Forgiving, Most Merciful. Also [prohibited are] women already married, except those whom your right hands possess; this is a written obligation upon you from God (4:22-4).

III. Marriageable Age

239. Under the prevailing laws in Pakistan, a male can legally marry at the age of 18 years with a female who has attained the age of 16 years as stipulated under the Punjab Marriage Restraint (Amendment) Act 2015. Whoever, being a male above 18 years of age, contracts marriage with female below 16 years of age shall be punishable with simple imprisonment which may extend to six month, or with fine which may extend to PKR 50,000, or with both.

240. Whoever performs, conducts or directs any child marriage shall be punishable with simple imprisonment which may extend to six month, or with fine which may extend to PKR 50,000, or with both, unless he proves that he had reason to believe that the marriage was not a child marriage under Punjab Child Marriage Restraint (amendment) Act 2015.

241. Where a minor contracts a child marriage any person having charge of the minor, whether as parent or guardian or in any other capacity, lawful or unlawful, who does any act to promote the marriage or permits it to be solemnized, or negligently fails to prevent it from being solemnized, shall be punishable with simple imprisonment which may extend to six months, or with fine which may extend to fifty thousand rupees, or with both: provided that no woman shall be punishable with imprisonment.

242. Customs like Wanni and marriage in lieu of compromise, or marriage with the Holy Quran are illegal, liable for imprisonment for three to seven years and fine of PKR 500,000 (section 310A, 498-C PPC.

243. Under section 3 of Sindh Child Marriage Restraint Act, 2013, the legal age of marriage at 18 years for both males and females, making any marriage involving a person under this age illegal and punishable by law. It empowers the courts to take legal action against individuals who perform, conduct, or facilitate child marriages, including parents or guardians.

244. Kidnapping, abducting or inducing women to compel for marriage. A Hindu girl below the age of 18 years having contracted marriage with a Muslim boy after embracing Islam was shifted to the shelter home. Mother of the victim girl claimed her custody. Record showed that the court had called victim girl for recording her statement just to ascertain the real facts and to reach at correct conclusion. Statement of the victim girl showed that she had contracted marriage without any inducement after embracing Islam. Said fact showed that she had attain the age of puberty, however in her statement, victim girl wanted to go with her mother, who was Hindu by religion. Perusal of record reflected that in Nikahnama which had not been denied by either party, her age was mentioned as 18 years, whereas, she had been medically examined and report of Medical Board on record showed her age as 15 to 16 years, meaning thereby that she had attained the age of puberty. High Court set at liberty the victim girl to go wherever she wanted and since she wanted to go with her mother, who was presented at the court, therefore, In charge Shelter Home was directed to hand over the custody of victim girl to her mother. Petition was disposed of accordingly. (sections 3 and 4 Penal Code (XLV of 1860), section 365-B Criminal Procedure Code (V of 1898)) Karachi High Court (2021 P Cr. L J 794)

245. Plea of accused that under that section 10 of the Child Marriage Restraint Act, 1929, it was mandatory for the trial court to have conducted a preliminary inquiry under section 202 of the Code of Criminal Procedure but in the present case said requirement was ignored and instead the accused were summoned mechanically without recording statement of the complainant. Purpose of inquiry under section 202 of Criminal Procedure was to see as to whether sufficient material was available to put the accused on trial. Admittedly the Nikahnama in the present case and its veracity had never been disputed at any stage which showed the age of bridegroom as less than 18 years making the complaint sufficiently credible for summoning the accused. Nikahnama sufficiently establish a prima facie case against the accused persons. Petition was disposed of accordingly. (Islamabad (ISB) 2018 PLD 385).

246. Dissolution of Muslim Marriages Act 1939 section 2(vii). Dissolution of marriage. Right of option of puberty exercise of female who was married at the age of 5/6 years, on attaining puberty, exercised her right of option of puberty, repudiated marriage and filed suit for Dissolution of marriage on that ground. Husband had himself stated that age of girl at the time of Rukhsati was below 15 years and that no consummation had taken place after age of 15 years which was, presumptive age of puberty. Suit for Dissolution of marriage was filed by girl well within her right to repudiate her marriage which had taken place during time when she was minor. Court in circumstances had rightly dissolved marriage which was just and fair. LHC (1994 CLC 1046).

247. Every Muslim of sound mind who has attained puberty may enter into a contract of marriage. Puberty is presumed to have been attained on completion of age of 15 years in the absence of evidence. Provision of section 2(vii), Dissolution of Muslim Marriages Act, 1939, does not lay down that female attains puberty at the age of 16 years only; it simply enables a girl to exercise the option of puberty when she attains age of 16 years (MFLO, 1961 section 13. Dissolution of Muslim Marriages Act (VIII of 1939), section 2(vii)). LHC (1988 CLC 113).

248. Violation of the provisions of Child Marriage Restraint Act, 1929 sections 3 and 6 do not render the Marriage invalid though it makes punishable a marriage made in violation of its provisions (LHC 1988 CLC 113).

IV. Prior Marriage

249. Under the MFLO, 1961, section 6 regulates polygamy in Pakistan by requiring a man to obtain prior written permission from the Arbitration Council before contracting a second marriage during the subsistence of an existing one. The husband must apply to the Union Council Chairman, stating valid reasons for the second marriage, after which the existing wife or wives are notified and given an opportunity to present their stance. The Arbitration Council evaluates the case based on factors such as financial capacity, justifiable grounds, and the well-being of the existing wife before granting or denying permission. If a man contracts a second marriage without obtaining approval, he is legally bound to immediately pay the entire dower (Mahr) to his existing wife and may face imprisonment of up to one year, a fine of up to PKR 5,000, or both. While non-compliance with this law does not invalidate the second marriage under Islamic law, it renders the husband liable to legal penalties. Judicial interpretations, including rulings by the SCP, reinforce that the requirement for permission ensures fairness rather than prohibiting polygamy outright. Additionally, under the Dissolution of Muslim Marriages Act, 1939, a wife may seek dissolution of marriage if her husband contracts another marriage without her consent and causes her undue hardship.

250. Islam permits polygamy under certain conditions, as stated in Surah An-Nisa (4:3): 'If you fear that you will not deal justly with the orphans, then marry those that please you of women, two, three, or four. But if you fear that you will not be just, then marry only one.' Islamic scholars emphasize that polygamy is not an unrestricted right but a conditional allowance requiring equal treatment of all wives.

V. Option of Puberty

251. Under the Dissolution of Muslim Marriages Act, 1939, section 2(vii), a woman married under Muslim law is entitled to obtain a decree for the dissolution of her marriage if she was given in marriage by her father or other guardian before attaining the age of sixteen and repudiates the marriage before reaching eighteen, provided the marriage was not consummated. This provision safeguards a woman's right to annul a marriage contracted during her minority without her consent.

252. In Pakistan, the legal framework addressing child marriages is primarily governed by the Child Marriage Restraint Act, 1929. This Act defined a 'child' as a male under eighteen years of age and a female under sixteen. However, recognizing the need for stricter measures against child marriages, the Punjab province enacted the Child Marriage Restraint (Amendment) Act, 2015, which redefined a 'child' as any person below eighteen, irrespective of gender.

253. Petitioner who was a minor, entered into marriage of her choice without consent of her parents. Grievance of petitioner was that police authorities were harassing her on the behest of her parents and other family members. In view of the Articles 9, 14 and 35 of the Constitution, the State was to protect marriage, the family, the mother and the child, as the same was granted. Female has been given a right under Dissolution of Muslim Marriage Act, 1939, to repudiate marriage before attaining age of eighteen years provided that marriage has not been consummated. In case of a male, the right continues until he has ratified marriage either expressly or impliedly as by payment of dower or by cohabitation. High Court directed the authorities to remain within the four corners of law and restrained them from causing any harassment to petitioner in any manner. (LHC – 2020 PLD 811)

254. LHC held that alleged detenue was present in Court and stated that she had married the respondent and was living with him on her own freewill and consent as his wife, and that she was not in illegal detention. *Nikah* had been duly registered. According to the medical report, the alleged detenue was 15 years old and being sui juris she could marry on her own accord and choice even without permission of Wali (Legal guardian) father. Even the child Marriage Restraint Act, 1929, did not invalidate the marriage once it had been performed. Having attained puberty under Islamic Law, the girl could marry. Alleged detenue having not been found in illegal custody, was set at liberty and allowed to accompany her husband (2006 YLR 2936).

255. Legal requirements: (i) performance of marriage during minority with consent of guardian, (ii) non-consummation of marriage and (iii) repudiation between age of 16 and 18 years. Question essentially of fact. Concurrent findings of lower Courts on such points. Cannot be re-examined in second appeal (LHC – 1970 PLD 475).

256. Necessary conditions only two: (i) repudiation before age of 18; and (ii) non-consummation of marriage. Repudiation, though required to be established as fact, can be proved even by conduct of woman. Woman on reaching puberty refusing, despite efforts of husband, to leave parental home. Circumstance furnishes strong corroboration of repudiation. Dissolution of Muslim Marriages Act (VIII of 1939), section 2(vii) (LHC – 1969 PLD 448).

257. Minor girl retains option till age of 18. Right of annulment continues until she expresses her consent or disapprobation in express terms. Mere consummation does not put an end to right consummation, to be effective, must be with wife's consent. Withholding of assent to marriage may be expressed in variety of ways (e.g., remarriage before age of 18 or institution of suit for Dissolution, etc.) Marriage not consummated. Mere institution of suit for Dissolution automatically annuls marriage under Dissolution of Muslim Marriages Act (VIII of 1939), section 2 (vii) (PHC – 1965 PLD 5).

258. The Supreme Court, Azad Kashmir (1962 PLD 7) Minor below 15 years given in marriage before attaining age of 18 provided marriage not consummated. Consummation 'by force' does not disentitle wife to exercise her option of puberty.

259. *Nikah* of minor girl by her step-brother. Consummation took place. Before attaining puberty, marriage repudiated by girl. Marriage held dissolved (LHC – 1952 PLD 548).

260. Dissolution of marriage on ground of '*Khula*' (divorce opted by wife). Trial Court framed issues pertaining to '*Khula*' and option of puberty, but dissolved marriage on basis of '*Khula*' only. High Court also proceeded to uphold judgment and decree of Trial Court without giving any finding on issue pertaining to option of puberty. Marriage on ground of '*Khula*' having been dissolved by Court on the basis of reliable evidence on record, there was no necessity at all under law to have given findings on other issues as marriage could be dissolved on any of the grounds urged by wife. Contention that it was mandatory under law for Court to have decided issue pertaining to option of puberty was repelled. Case having been decided by Courts fairly, justly and in accordance with law on basis of evidence on record and complete justice having been done between the parties, no case whatsoever for interference had been made out in Intra Court Appeal, especially when no violation of law and evidence was apparent from record (MFLO, 1961 (LHC – 1991 MLD 2338)).

VI. Failure to Consent

261. Under the West Pakistan Rules framed under the MFLO, 1961, a standardized Nikahnama is prescribed, requiring the mandatory signatures of both the bride and groom for the marriage to be legally solemnized. According to Islamic law, a valid marriage (Nikah) necessitates the mutual consent of both parties, either expressed personally or through their appointed representatives (Wali or Vakil), in a single sitting. The agreement must also be witnessed by at least two adult Muslim witnesses, ensuring transparency and legal recognition.

262. In cases where the bride has not attained the age of majority, the consent for marriage may be given by her guardian, typically her father. However, under Islamic and Pakistani law, a minor retains the right to either ratify or repudiate the marriage upon reaching puberty, a principle reinforced by the Dissolution of Muslim Marriages Act, 1939. Furthermore, under the Child Marriage Restraint Act, contracting or facilitating a child marriage is a punishable offense, with varying legal stipulations across provinces.

263. For a marriage to be legally valid under Islamic and Pakistani law, the free and informed consent of both the bride and groom is an essential requirement. If a marriage is contracted on behalf of an adult individual of either sex, it is imperative that such a person explicitly consents to the union. A marriage solemnized without the voluntary agreement of either party, their appointed representatives (Wali or Vakil), or legal guardians in cases of minors, is considered invalid and holds no legal standing.

264. A person forcibly marrying a girl against her will is liable to be punished with imprisonment for 3 to 7 years and a fine of PKR 500,000 (section 498-B PPC).

265. Complaint regarding underage marriage can be registered with Police/ Union Council/Judicial Magistrate.

266. Under the MFLO, 1961, mandates that both the bride and groom must sign the Nikahnama, reinforcing the necessity of mutual consent. Section 375 of the PPC considers a marriage void if forced, as it falls under coercion, which is legally punishable. The SCP has also upheld that forced marriages are a violation of fundamental rights under Article 9 of the Constitution, which ensures the security of life and liberty.

267. In the PPC (Act XLV of 1860), in Chapter XV, for section 310A the following shall be substituted, namely: '310-A. Punishment for giving a female in marriage or otherwise in badla-e-sulh, wanni or sawara. – Whoever gives a female in marriage or otherwise compels her to enter into marriage, as badal-e-sulh, wanni, or sawara or any other custom or practice under any name, in consideration of settling a civil dispute or a criminal liability shall be punished with imprisonment of description for a term which may be no less than three years and shall also be liable to fine of 500,000 Rupees.'

268. LHC held that Guardian is allowed in Islam to marry their daughters after getting their consent. However, thrusting or forcing marriage without one's consent is against the Islamic Laws (1980 PLC 386).

269. Sindh High Court held that in a free and democratic country, an adult individual has the right to marry a person of their choice without interference. It directed law enforcement authorities to ensure the couple's protection and prevent any harassment. However, the court acknowledged concerns regarding the bride's age, stating that the matter should be examined by the competent legal forum under the Sindh Child Marriage Restraint Act, 2013 and other relevant laws. It also directed authorities to ensure the couple's protection from harassment while allowing the competent court to determine any claims of underage marriage. The judgment underscores the balance between personal liberty and legal safeguards against coerced or unlawful marriages.

A. Duress

270. If a marriage is solemnized under coercion, undue pressure, or duress from family members, the wife has the legal right to seek dissolution of the marriage through judicial means. Under section 2 of the Dissolution of Muslim Marriages Act, 1939, a woman married under Muslim law is entitled to obtain a decree for the dissolution of her marriage on various grounds specified within the Act. These grounds include cruelty, desertion, failure to provide maintenance, and the husband's prolonged absence, among others.

271. Under Islamic law, a woman can seek Khula if she is unwilling to continue the marriage, even without proving specific wrongdoing by the husband. The Family Courts Act, 1964, facilitates this process, allowing women to petition for Khula by demonstrating irreconcilable differences. Additionally, forced marriages violate fundamental rights as enshrined in Article 9 of the Constitution of Pakistan, which guarantees the right to life and liberty. The Prevention of Forced Marriages Act and PPC also criminalize marriages conducted under duress, ensuring legal protection for women subjected to forced unions. The courts have consistently upheld that marriage must be based on free will, and any marriage conducted through coercion is liable for annulment or dissolution through appropriate legal channels.

272. According to the Islamic Law, the forced or duress marriage is not allowed. Abu Hurayrah (Razi Allaho Unho) reported that the Holy Prophet Muhammad (PBUH) said: 'A non-virgin woman may not be married without her command, and a virgin may not be married without her permission; and enough permission for her is to remain silent (because of her natural shyness).' (Al-Bukhaari, Muslim & Others). Thus, the Holy Prophet Muhammad (PBUH) prohibited forcing a virgin in marriage without her permission, whether by her father or anyone else. Furthermore, Aa'ishah Razi Allaho Unha related that she once asked the Holy Prophet Muhammad (PBUH): 'In the case of a young girl whose parents marry her off, should her permission be sought or not?' HE (PBUH) replied: 'Yes, she must give her permission.' She then said: 'But a virgin would be shy, O Messenger of Allah!' HE (PBUH) replied: 'Her silence is [considered as] her permission.' (Al-Bukhaari, Muslim, & Others).

273. The High Court, Azad Kashmir (2003 PLD 34) held that marriage of a girl by itself would not make her live or reside with her husband, if it was a forced marriage and she was compelled to live with him. Marriage was a civil contract between the spouse solemnized according to social and religious rites of the parties with their free and independent consent. Union had to remain free of coercion and duress, not only at time of marriage but throughout life which was both Islamic and common law/principle. If a woman was forced to a marriage or did not feel convenient to live with spouse at the place where husband wanted, but she felt insecure and was threatened to live, it would amount to illegal custody and detention irrespective of validity or otherwise of the marriage.

274. Man was charged for kidnaping the daughter of complainant for illicit relations. Record shows that daughter of the complainant had married the man out of her own will and in that connection, had appeared before the Court to record her statement that she had allegedly married the man. At that stage a charge under sections 3 and 4 of Sindh Child Marriage Restraint Act, 2013, was also included against the man. Abductee was sent to Darul Aman on the instructions of the court, and it appeared that some days later, she opted to go back home with her parents. Later on, abductee took a somersault on her earlier stance and now alleged that applicant had kidnapped her and all her appearances in court and all earlier statements were obtained from her under duress. Section 376 of PPC for the offence of rape was also added which carried a potential sentence of 10 to 25 years of imprisonment for the remainder period of natural life, thus falling within the non-prohibitory clause of section 497 of Criminal Procedure Code. Bail dismissed. (Karachi High Court 2021 PLD 28)

275. Alleged abductee stated before Investigating Officer that she had not been abducted; had married with her free will and produced documents in support thereof and requested him not to take any action on first information report (FIR). Investigating Officer, however, continued to harass and humiliate her husband. Such facts had not been denied by Investigating Officer. Neither going away of alleged abductee from house of her father without any duress nor her marriage had been denied or challenged. Held, no offence under sections 10 and 11 of Offence of *Zina* (Enforcement of Hudood) Ordinance, 1979 and under section 452, PPC had been made out. FIR was declared to have been lodged malafidely, frivolous and vexatious and the same was quashed in circumstances (SHC 1999 P Cr. L J 638).

B. Insanity

276. According to the consensus of the majority of Muslim scholars, including the four renowned Imams, the presence of mental illness or insanity whether intermittent or permanent is considered a valid ground for the annulment of a marriage. If such a condition arises even periodically, such as once a month, and results in harm or distress to the spouse, the affected party has the right to seek dissolution of the marriage. This ruling applies regardless of whether the condition was pre-existing or developed after the marriage contract was finalized.

277. Islamic jurisprudence recognizes mental instability as a defect that impairs the fundamental objectives of marriage, such as companionship, emotional stability, and mutual well-being. Therefore, many classical and contemporary jurists, based on principles derived from the *Qur'an*, *Hadith*, and *Fiqh*, uphold the right of either spouse to revoke the marriage contract if the mental illness causes undue hardship.

278. In *Hanafi*, *Shafi'i*, *Maliki*, and *Hanbali* legal traditions, the principle of *Faskh* (judicial annulment) is applicable in such cases, allowing a spouse to approach an Islamic court or religious authority for termination of the marriage.

Islamic law emphasizes the importance of fairness, ensuring that the affected individual receives due care and support, while also safeguarding the rights of the healthy spouse from undue suffering.

279. Under the Dissolution of Muslim Marriages Act, 1939 Article 2(vi) if husband has been insane for a period of two years or is suffering from leprosy or a virulent venereal disease, the woman married under the Muslim Law is entitled to obtain decree for dissolution of her marriage.

VII. Failure to Comply with Necessary Formalities

280. Failure to comply with the necessary formalities to solemnize marriage does not make the marriage void. FSC (2000 PLD 63) Non-registration of *Nikah* Effect. Accused had claimed that age of girl according to her own mother was 16/17 years, and that her *Nikah* with him was proved by three witnesses against whom nothing had been said in cross-examination. Contention of prosecution was that as *Nikah* was not registered and was not found in Register of *Nikah*, and also that thumb impression was also not found to be that of girl, *Nikah* was not proved. Validity: Registration of *Nikah* was not necessarily the proof of *Nikah* as, in Muslim Law *Nikah* could be performed by offer and acceptance in presence of witnesses. Non-registration of *Nikah* would only attract a penalty under section 5(4) of MFLO, 1961. In absence of any error in *Nikah* of accused with the girl, conviction and sentence awarded to accused by Trial Court were set aside and he was acquitted (Offence of *Zina* (Enforcement of Hudood) Ordinance 1979. Section 10(3). MFLO (VIII of 1961), section 5).

281. Under the MFLO, 1961, marriage is regarded as a civil contract and section 5 makes it necessary that the marriage shall be registered and the parties can settle their terms and conditions of marriage including dower, through said contract for which form-II used as nikahnama is prescribed in terms of rule 10 of the rules under Muslim Marriage Law Ordinance, 1961. Any entry by way of an amount or an undertaking related to transfer of any property or other valuable such as ornaments, etc., is the dower or part thereof. (LHC-2022 MLD 416)

282. Suit for recovery of maintenance by wife. Plea raised by husband in written statement dated 14 November 2002 was that he had already divorced plaintiff, thus, she was not entitled to maintenance. Passing of ex parte decree by Family Court due to failure of husband to produce evidence. Photocopy of divorce deed filed before High Court did not show its date of execution except purchasing of its stamp paper on 5 April 2002. Plea of husband was that he had announced divorce orally in presence of witnesses in October 2001, which was reduced in writing subsequently; and that oral divorce would become effective despite non-issuance of certificate of Divorce. Wife's plea was that alleged divorce deed was a fake/forged document, which was neither produced before Family Court nor sent to Union Council for issuance of certificate of Divorce, and that husband had manoeuvred the same just to avoid payment of decretal amount. Validity: All such facts would show that husband was only gaining time to avoid payment of amount of decree, which had become final. High Court declined to give finding on such factual issue, which husband might raise before Executing Court, if so advised. Impugned judgment and decree did not suffer from any illegality. High Court dismissed Constitutional petition in circumstances (LHC – 2010 YLR 2061).

283. Marriage solemnized under MFLO, 1961, requires its registration but Nikah does not become invalid due to its non-registration. If a person does not report marriage to Nikah registrar for the purpose of registration, he may be held liable under section 5(4) of MFLO, 1961. (LHC – 2009 MLD 962)

VIII. Formalities of Marriage

284. In Pakistan, marriages are solemnized in accordance with Islamic Law and governed by the MFLO, 1961, which serves as the foundational legal framework for family matters. Every marriage conducted under Islamic Law must be duly registered, ensuring legal recognition and compliance with statutory requirements.

285. For the purpose of marriage registration, the Union Council grants licenses to designated individuals known as Nikah Registrars. These registrars are responsible for maintaining accurate records of marriages within their jurisdiction. As per Rule 7 of the West Pakistan Rules under the MFLO, 1961, any Nikah Registrar who violates the terms and conditions of their license is subject to legal penalties. Such violations may result in penalties prescribed by law, which may include fines, imprisonment, or both, subject to any amendments made to the legislation.

286. Failure to register a marriage as required under section 5 of the MFLO, 1961, may lead to legal consequences. Proper registration is crucial for protecting marital rights, facilitating inheritance claims and ensuring compliance with family laws.

287. Any marriage not solemnized by the *Nikah* Registrar, is reported for registration by the person who has solemnized such marriage as stipulated under section 5(1)(2)(3) of MFLO.

288. Nikah registrar failed to fill each column in nikahnama. He instead of accurately filling the same with specific reply of bride or bridegroom opted to place single vertical line and also left some of the columns blank. Alleged detenue was sui juris and major who contracted marriage with petitioner without blessings of her parents and other siblings. Nikah registrar committed clear violation. High Court referred the matter to district authorities for initiation of penal proceedings against the nikah registrar. Constitutional petition was allowed in circumstances. (LHC-2021 MLD 880)

289. The Union Council, upon payment of a fee determined by the Provincial Government, provides each licensed Nikah Registrar with a bound register containing Nikahnama forms along with an official seal inscribed with 'The Seal of the Nikah Registrar of Ward.' Under the MFLO, 1961, it is the legal duty of the Nikah Registrar to accurately record and maintain marriage details in the prescribed format. The failure to properly document or register a marriage can lead to legal penalties, as stipulated under section 5 of the MFLO, 1961. Any misconduct or negligence in fulfilling the registrar's duties may result in disciplinary action, including fines, suspension, or revocation of the license, as per the applicable provincial regulations.

290. Each register consists of fifty consecutively numbered leaves with each leaf containing a Nikahnama in quadruplicate. The total number of leaves is certified by the Chairman. The register and the official seal remain the property of the Union Council, as per Rule 8 of the West Pakistan Rules under the MFLO, 1961.

291. For the registration of a marriage registered, the *Nikah* Registrar is paid, by the bridegroom or his representative a registration fee of PKR 2, or when the dower exceeds PKR 2,000, a fee calculated at the rate of one rupee for every thousand or part of PKR 1,000 of such dower, subject to a maximum fee of PKR 20 (Rules-9 of the West Pakistan Rules under MFLO, 1961). However, practically the fee is much higher as compared to the prescribed fee, and every *Nikah* Registrar charge the fee according to his will. The *Nikah* Registrar retains 80% fee and remaining 20% deposit with the Union Council.

292. If the dower includes property other than money or a combination of property and money, its valuation for fee purposes shall be determined based on the agreement between the parties to the marriage, as per Rule 9(3) of the West Pakistan Rules under the MFLO, 1961.

293. The Nikahnama is the official document on which marriages are solemnized. Nikah Registrars maintain marriage records, which are preserved by the Union Councils. Upon payment of the prescribed fee, copies of the Nikahnama are provided to the parties. Additionally, any individual may inspect the marriage records at the Union Council office and obtain a copy of any entry or record, as per sections 5 and 6 of the MFLO, 1961.

294. Specimen of *Nikahnama* (Form-2) as prescribed by Rule 8 and Rule 10 of the MFLO, 1961 is appended below:

- *Name of Ward/Moza:______Town/Union:_______Tehsil/Thana:_______ and District:____________ in which the marriage took place.*
- *Name of the bridegroom and his father, with their respective residence and Computerized National Identity Card Number:*
- *Age of bridegroom:*
- *The names of the bride and her father, with their respective residences with Computerized National Identity Card Number:*

- *Whether the bride is a maiden, a widow or a divorce:*
- *5(a).If bride is widow or divorced having children, the number and names of children:*
- *Age of the bride:*
- *Name of Vakil, if any appointed by the bride, father's name and his residence with Computerized National Identity Card Number:*
- *The name of the witnesses to the appointment of the bride's Vakil, with their fathers' names, their residence and their relationship with the bride:*
- *Name of the Vakil, if any, appointed by the bridegroom, his father's name and his residence:*
- *The names of the witnesses to the appointment of the bridegroom's Vakil, with their father's names and their residences :*
- *Names of the witnesses to the marriage, their father's names and their residences:*
- *Date on which the marriage was contracted:*
- *Amount of dower:*
- *How much of the dower is mu'wajjal (prompt) and how much mu'ajjal (deferred):*
- *Whether any portion of the dower was paid at the time of marriage. If so, how much:*
- *Special conditions, if any:*
- *Whether the husband has delegated the power of divorce to the wife, if so, under what conditions?*
- *Whether the husband's right of divorce in any way curtailed?*
- *Whether any document was drawn up at the time of marriage relating to dower, maintenance, etc. If so contents thereof in brief:*
- *Whether the bridegroom has any existing wife, and if so, whether he has secured the permission of the Arbitration Council under the Muslim Family Laws Ordinance, 1961, to contract another marriage:*
  a. *Whether the bridegroom's earlier wife died or he is divorced?*
  b. *Whether the bridegroom has previous wife or wives; if bridegroom is divorced or his wife died, specify number of children and their names:*
- *Number and date of the communication conveying to the bridegroom the permission of the Arbitration Council to contract another marriage:*
- *Name and address of the person by whom the marriage was solemnized and his father:*
- *Date of registration of marriage :*
- *Registration fee paid:*
- *Signature of the bridegroom or his Vakil*
- *Signature of the witness to the appointment of bridge groom's Vakil with Computerized National Identity Card Numbers:*
- *Signature of the bride :*
- *Signature of the wakil of the bride:*
- *Signature of the witness to be appointment of the wakil of the bride with Computerized National Identity Card Numbers:*
- *Signatures of the witnesses to the marriage with Computerized National Identity Card Numbers:*

- *Signature of the person with Computerized National Identity Card Number who solemnize the marriage:*
- *Signature and seal of the Nikah Registrar with Computerized National Identity Card Number:*
- *Seal*

295. If a Pakistani citizen solemnizes a marriage outside Pakistan, they must ensure that the duly completed Nikahnama form, along with the registration fee, is submitted to the Pakistani Consular Officer in the country where the marriage takes place. The Consular Officer will then forward it to the Nikah Registrar of the ward where the bride is a permanent resident. If the bride is not a Pakistani citizen, the form shall be sent to the Nikah Registrar of the ward where the bridegroom is a resident, as per Rule 12(1) of the West Pakistan Rules under the MFLO, 1961.

296. If a marriage is solemnized outside Pakistan by a non-Pakistani citizen, and only the bride is a Pakistani citizen, she shall be considered the person responsible for filling out the Nikahnama for registration purposes, as per Rule 12(2) of the West Pakistan Rules under the MFLO, 1961.

297. Any person who violates marriage registration laws shall be liable to simple imprisonment for up to three months, a fine of up to PKR 1,000, or both, as per section 5(4) of the MFLO.

IX. Christian Marriage

298. Christian Marriage Act of 1872 and the Divorce Act of 1869 have undergone significant amendments to align with contemporary human rights standards and the evolving needs of the community. The Christian Marriage (Amendment) Act of 2024 introduced key changes, including raising the minimum legal age for marriage to 18 years for both men and women, replacing the previous ages of 16 for men and 13 for women. Free and informed consent of both parties is mandatory and the marriage must be solemnized publicly in the presence of at least two witnesses. A notice of intended marriage must be given three consecutive calendar months before the marriage and registration with the appropriate Registrar is required for a marriage certificate to be issued. Marriages are typically solemnized in a church, but with special permission, they can also take place at a private residence. The Divorce Act of 1869, which governs the dissolution of Christian marriages, historically provided limited grounds for divorce, mainly adultery. However, in landmark cases like *Ameen Masih v. Federation of Pakistan* (2016), the LHC restored section 7 of the Divorce Act, allowing courts to apply English matrimonial laws and recognize grounds such as cruelty, desertion, and mutual consent for divorce.

299. The Christian Marriage Act of 1872 governs matrimonial matters within the Christian community in Pakistan. While the Act prohibits marriages between individuals related by blood or affinity, it does not explicitly define the degrees of prohibited relationships. However, it is generally understood that marriages between close relatives, such as siblings or direct ascendants and descendants, are forbidden. Regarding age requirements, the Act stipulates that if either party is below 18 years of age, a marriage certificate will not be issued without the consent of the father, guardian, or mother. Polygamy is strictly prohibited among Christians, mandating monogamy as a fundamental principle of Christian marriages.

300. Those eligible to solemnize Christian marriages include episcopal ordained ministers, provided that the marriage ceremony follows the rules, rites, ceremonies, and customs of their respective churches. Clergy members of the Church of Pakistan are also permitted to conduct marriages in accordance with their denominational practices. Ministers of religion holding a valid license under the Christian Marriage Act, as well as Marriage Registrars appointed under the Act, are authorized to officiate Christian weddings. Furthermore, individuals specifically designated under the Act to grant marriage certificates to native Christians also have the authority to solemnize their marriages.

301. The Christian Marriage Act of 1872, governing matrimonial affairs within Pakistan's Christian community, outlines stringent penalties for violations under Part VII (sections 66 to 75). Offenses include making false declarations or certificates to procure marriage, impersonating another to obstruct a Marriage Registrar's duties, solemnizing marriages without proper authority, conducting ceremonies at unauthorized times or without required witnesses, and tampering with or falsifying marriage register books. Penalties for these violations can be severe, with fines and imprisonment of up to ten years, depending on the nature and gravity of the offense. These provisions are designed to uphold the integrity and sanctity of Christian marriages, ensuring adherence to legal and ethical standards. While there have been amendments to certain sections of the Act, such as the Christian Marriage (Amendment) Act of 2024, which revised the minimum legal age for marriage, the penalties outlined in Part VII remain as originally stipulated.

302. As per section 4 of Part I of the Christian Marriage Act, 1872, any marriage involving one or both Christian individuals must be solemnized in accordance with the provisions of the Act. A marriage conducted in violation of these provisions shall be deemed void.

303. Section 5 of the Christian Marriage Act, 1872 states that the marriage may be solemnized in Pakistan by any person who has received Episcopal ordination, provided that the marriage be solemnized according to the rules, rites, ceremonies and customs of the Church of which he is a minister; or by any Clergyman of the church of Scotland, provided that such marriage be solemnized according to the rules rites, ceremonies customs of the Church of Scotland; or by any Minister of Religion licensed under this Act of solemnize marriage; or by, or in the presence of a Marriage Registrar appointed under Marriage Act; and by any person licensed under this Act to grant certificates of marriage between Native Christians.

304. . Under section 7 of the Christian Marriage Act, 1872, the Provincial Government is empowered to designate one or more Christians, either by name or by virtue of their office to serve as Marriage Registrars within any district under its jurisdiction. In districts with multiple Marriage Registrars, the Provincial Government assigns one as the Senior Marriage Registrar to coordinate activities and ensure uniform application of the law. If a district has only one Marriage Registrar who becomes absent, ill, or if the position is temporarily vacant, the district's Magistrate assumes the role of Marriage Registrar during such periods, ensuring uninterrupted administrative support for marriage proceedings. Section 8 authorizes the Central Government to appoint any Christian, either by name or by their current office, as a Marriage Registrar for any district or area within Acceding States, as announced in the official Gazette.

305. Licensing of persons to grant certificates of marriage between Native Christians is covered under section 9 of the above Act. The Provincial Government or (so far as regards and Acceding State) the Central Government may grant a license to any Christian, either by name or as holding any office for the time being, authorizing him to grant certificate of marriage between Native Christians. Any such license may be revoked by the authority by which it was granted, and every such grant or revocation shall be notified in the Official Gazette.

306. Part II, section 10 of the Act every marriage under Marriage Act shall be solemnized between the hours of six in the morning and seven in the evening: Provided that nothing in this section shall apply to: (1) a Clergyman of the Church of England solemnizing a marriage under a special license permitting him to do so at any hour other than between six in the morning and seven in the evening, under the hand and seal of the Anglican Bishop of the Commissary; or (2) a Clergyman of the Church of Rome solemnizing a marriage between the hours of seven in the evening and six in the morning, when he has received a general or special license in that behalf from the Roman Catholic Bishop of the Diocese or Vicariate in which such marriage is so solemnized, or from such person as the same Bishop has authorized to grant such license; or (3) a Clergyman of the church of Scotland solemnizing a marriage according to the rule, rites, ceremonies and customs of the Church of Scotland.

307. Under section 11 of the Christian Marriage Act, 1872 no clergyman of the Church of England shall solemnize a marriage in any place other than a church, where worship is generally held according to the forms of the church of England: Unless there is no such Church within five miles distance by the shortest road from such place, or unless he has received a special license authorizing him to do so under the hand and seal of the Anglican Bishop of the Diocese or his Commissary. For such special license, the Registrar of the Diocese may charge such additional fee as the said Bishop from time to time authorizes.

308. Whenever a marriage is intended to be solemnized by a Minister of Religion licensed to solemnize marriage under section 12 of Part III of the Christian

Marriage Act, 1872, one of the persons intending marriage shall give notice in writing according to the form contained in the First Schedule hereto annexed, or the like effect, to the Minister of Religion whom he/she desires to solemnize the marriage, and shall state therein: (a) the name and surname, and the profession or condition, of each of the persons intending marriage; (b) The dwelling-place of each of them; (c) The time during which each has dwelt there; and (d) the Church or private dwelling in which the marriage is to be solemnized: Provided that, if either of such persons has dwelt in the place mentioned in the notice during more than one month, it may be stated therein that he/she has dwelt there one month and upwards.

309. If the persons intending marriage desire it to be solemnized in a particular Church and if the Minister of Religion to whom such notice has been delivered be entitled to officiate therein, he shall cause the notice to be affixed in some conspicuous part of such Church vide section 13 of the Christian Marriage Act, 1872. But if he is not entitled to officiate as a Minister in such church, he shall, at his option, either return the notice to the person who delivered it to him, or deliver it to some other Minister entitled to officiate therein who shall thereupon cause the notice to be affixed as aforesaid.

310. If it be intended that the marriage shall be solemnized in a private dwelling, Minister of Religion, on receiving the notice prescribed in section 15 shall forward it to the Marriage Registrar of the district, who shall affix the same to some conspicuous place in his own office, as provided in section 14 of the Christian Marriage Act, 1872.

311. Under section 15 of the Christian Marriage Act, 1872, when one of the persons intending marriage is a minor, every Minister receiving such notice shall, unless within twenty-four hours after its receipt he returns the same under the provisions of section 13, send by the post or otherwise a copy of such notice to the Marriage Registrar of the district, or, if there be more than one Registrar of such district, to the Senior Marriage Registrar.

312. Section 16 of the Christian Marriage Act, 1872 provides that the Marriage Registrar, as the case may be, on receiving any such notice, shall affix it to some conspicuous place in his own office, and the latter shall further cause a copy of the said notice to be sent to each of the other Marriage Registrar in the same district, who shall likewise publish the same in the manner above directed.

313. Section 17 of the Christian Marriage Act, 1872 states that any Minister of Religion consenting or intending to solemnize any such marriage as aforesaid, shall on being required so to do by or on behalf of the person by whom the notice was given, and upon one of the persons intending marriage making the declaration hereinafter required issue under his hand a certificate of such notice having been given and of declaration having been made. Provided: (1) that no such certificate shall be issued until the expiration of four days after the date of the notice by such Minister; (2) that no lawful impediment be shown to his satisfaction why such certificate should not issue; and (3) that the issue of certificate has not been forbidden, in manner hereinafter mentioned, by any person authorized.

314. The Declaration before issue of certificate is discussed in section 18 of the Christian Marriage Act, 1872. It is stated that certificate shall not be issued until one of the persons intending marriage has appeared personally before the Minister and made a solemn declaration: (a) that he/she believes that there is not any impediment of kindred or affinity or other lawful hindrance to the said marriage, and when either or both of the parties is or are minor or minors; and (b) that the consent or consents required by law has or have been obtained there is no person resident in Pakistan having authority to give such consent, as the case may be.

315. Consent of father or guardian or mother has been discussed in section 19 of the Christian Marriage Act, 1872. The father, if living, of any minor, or if, the father be dead, the guardian of such minor, and in case there be no such guardian then the mother of such minor, may give consent to the minor's marriage, and such consent is hereby required for the same marriage unless no person authorized to give such consent be resident in Pakistan. Every person whose consent to a marriage is required under section 19 is hereby authorized to prohibit the issue of the certificate by any Minister, at any time before the issue of the same, by notice in writing to such Minister, subscribed by the person so authorized with his/her name and place of abode and position with respect to either of the persons intending marriage by reason of which he/she is so authorized as aforesaid under section 20 of the Christian Marriage Act, 1872.

316. If any such notice be received by such Minster, he shall not issue his certificate and shall not solemnize the said marriage until he has examined into the matter of the said prohibition, and is satisfied that the person prohibiting the marriage has not lawful authority for such prohibition, or until the said notice is withdrawn by the person who gave it vide section 21, of the Christian Marriage Act, 1872.

317. Section 22 of the Christian Marriage Act, 1872 states that when either of the persons intending marriage is a minor, and the Minister is not satisfied that the consent of the person whose consent to such marriage is required by section 19 has been obtained, such Minister shall not issue such certificate until the expiration of fourteen days after the receipt by him of the notice of marriage.

318. Issue of certificate to Native Christians discussed in section 23 of the Christian Marriage Act, 1872. When any Native Christian about to be married takes notice of marriage to a Minister of Religion, or applies for a certificate from such Minister under section 17, such Minister shall, before issuing the certificate ascertain whether such Native Christian is cognizant of the purport and effect of the said notice or certificate, as the case may be, and, if not, shall translate or cause to be translated the notice or certificate to such Native Christian into some language which he understands.

319. The certificate to be issued by such Minister shall be in the form contained in the Second Schedule, or to the like effect vide section 24 regarding Form of Certificate of the Christian Marriage Act, 1872.

320. Under section 25 of the Christian Marriage Act, 1872, after the issue of the certificate by Minister, marriage may be solemnized between the persons therein described according to such form or ceremony as the Minister thinks fit to adopt: Provided that the marriage be solemnized in the presence of at least two witnesses besides the Minister.

321. Whenever a marriage is not solemnized within two months after the date of the certificate issued by such Minister as aforesaid such certificate and all proceedings (if any), thereon shall be void, and no person shall proceed to solemnize the said marriage until new notice has been given and a certificate thereof issued in the manner aforesaid (section 26 of the Christian Marriage Act, 1872).

322. Quarterly returns to Archdeaconry have been discussed in section 29 of the Christian Marriage Act, 1872. Every Clergyman of the Church of England shall send four times in every year return in duplicate, authenticated by his signature, of the entries in the register of marriages solemnized any place where he has any spiritual charge, to the Registrar of the Archdeaconry to which he is subject, or tithing the limits of which such place is situate. Such quarterly returns shall contain all the entries of marriages contained in the said register from the first day of January to the thirty-first day of March, from the first day of April to the thirtieth day of June, from the first day of July to the thirtieth day of September, and from the first day of October to the thirty-first day of December, of each year respectively, and shall be sent by such Clergyman within two weeks from the expiration of each of the quarters above specified. The said Registrar upon receiving the said returns shall send one copy thereof to the Registrar General of Birth Deaths and Marriages.

323. Under section 30 of the Christian Marriage Act, 1872, every marriage solemnized by a Clergyman of the Church of Rome is to be registered by the person and according to the form directed in that behalf by the Roman Catholic Bishop of the Diocese or Vicariate, in which such marriage is solemnized, and such person shall forward quarterly to the Register General of Births, Deaths and Marriages returns of the entries of all marriages registered by him during the three months next preceding.

324. It is stipulated under section 31 of the Christian Marriage Act, 1872 that every Clergymen of the Church of Scotland shall keep a register of marriages, and shall register therein, according to the tabular form set forth in the Third Schedule hereto annexed, every marriage which he solemnizes under this Act, and shall forward quarterly to the Registrar General of Births, Death and Marriages, through the Senior Chaplain of the Church of Scotland, returns, similar to those prescribed in section 29, of all such marriages.

325. Every marriage solemnized by any person who has received episcopal ordination, but who is not a Clergyman of the Church of England, or of the Church of Rome, or by any Minister of Religion licensed under this Act to solemnize marriages, shall, immediately after the solemnization thereof be registered in duplicated by the same (i.e., to say) in a marriage register-book to be kept by him for that purpose, according to the form contained in the Fourth Schedule hereto annexed and also in a certificate attached to be marriage-register-book as a counterfoil, vide section 32 of the Christian Marriage Act, 1872.

326. The entry of such marriage in both the certificate and marriage-register-book shall be signed by the person solemnizing the marriage, and also by the persons married and shall be attested by two credible witnesses, other than the person solemnizing the marriage, present at its solemnization. Every such entry shall be made in order from the beginning to the end of the book, and the number of the certificate shall correspond with that of the entry in the marriage-register-book (section 33 of Christian Marriage Act, 1872).

327. The person solemnizing the marriage shall forthwith separate the certificate from the marriage-register-book and send it, within one month from the time of the solemnization, to the Marriage Registrar of the district in which the marriage was solemnized, or, if there be more Marriage Registrars than one, to the Senior Marriage Registrar, who shall cause such certificate to be copied into a book to be kept by him for that purpose, and shall send all the certificates which he has received during the month, with such number and signature or initials added thereto as are hereinafter required, to the Registrar General of Births, Deaths and Marriages (section 35 of Christian Marriage Act, 1872). Such copies shall be entered in order from the beginning to the end of the said book and shall bear both the number of the certificate as copied and also a number to be entered by the Marriage Registrar indicating the number of the entry of the said copy in the said book, according to the order in which he receives each certificate.

328. The Marriage Registrar shall also add such last-mentioned number of the entry of the copy in the book to the certificate, with his signature or initials, and shall, at the end of every month send the same to the Registrar General of birth Deaths and Marriages (section 36 of the Christian Marriage Act, 1872).

329. Section 37 of the Christian Marriage Act, 1872 provides that when any marriage between Native Christians is solemnized by any such person, Clergyman or Minister of Religion as is referred to in clause (1) clause (2) or clause (30) of section 5, the person solemnizing the same shall, instead of proceeding in the manner provided by sections 28 to 36, both inclusive, register the marriage in a separate register-book, and shall keep it safely until it is filled, or, if he leaves the district in which he solemnized the marriage before the said book is filled, shall make over the same to the person succeeding to his duties in the said district. Whoever has the control of the book at the time when it is filled, shall send it to the Marriage Registrar of the district, or, if there be more Marriage Registrars than one, to Senior

Marriage Registrar, who shall send it to Registrar General of Birth, Deaths and Marriages, to be kept by him with the records of his office.

330. When a marriage is intended to be solemnized by, or in the presence of, a Marriage Registrar, one, of the parties to such marriage shall give notice in writing, in the form contained in the First Schedule hereto annexed, or to the like effect, to any Marriage Registrar of the District within which the parties have dwelt; or if the parties dwell in different district, shall give the like notice to a Marriage Registrar of each district, and shall state therein the name and surname, and the profession or condition, of each of the parties intending marriage, the dwelling-place of each of them, the time during which each has dwelt therein, and the place at which the marriage is to be solemnized. Provided that, if either party has dwelt in the place stated in the notice for more than one month, it may be stated therein that he/she has dwelt there one month and upwards (section 38 of the Christian Marriage Act, 1872).

331. Every Marriage Registrar shall, on receiving any such notice, cause a copy thereof to be affixed in some conspicuous place in his office. When one of the parties intending marriage is minor, every Marriage Registrar shall, within twenty-four hours after the receipt by him of the notice of such marriage, send, by post or otherwise, a copy of such notice to each of the other Marriage Registrars (if any) in the same district who shall likewise affix the copy in some conspicuous place in his own office (section 39 of the Christian Marriage Act, 1872).

332. The Marriage Registrar shall file all such notices and keep them with the records of his office, and shall also forthwith enter a true copy of all such notices in a book to be furnished to him for that purpose by the Provincial Government and to be called the 'Marriage Notice Book'. And the 'Marriage Notice Book' shall be open at all reasonable times, without fee, to persons desirous of inspecting the same, under section 40 of the Christian Marriage Act, 1872.

333. Section 41 of Christian Marriage Act, 1872 discussed about certificate of notice given and oath made. If the party by whom the notice was given requests the Marriage Registrar to issue the certificate next hereinafter mentioned, and if one of the parties intending marriage has made oath as hereinafter required, the Marriage Register shall issue under his hand a certificate of such notice having been given and of such oath having been made. Proviso provided: (a) that no lawful impediment be shown to his satisfaction why such certificate should not be issued; (b) that the issue of such certificate has not been forbidden in manner hereinafter mentioned, by any person authorized in that behalf by this Act; (c) that four days after the receipt of the notice have expired; and further, (d) that where, by such oath it appears that one of the parties intending marriage is a minor, fourteen days after the entry of such notice have expired.

334. The certificate shall not be issued by any Marriage Registrar, until one of the parties intending marriage appears personally before such Marriage Registrar, and makes oath: (a) that he/she believes that there is not any impediment of kindred or affinity, or other lawful hindrance, to the said Marriage; and (b) that both the parties have, or (where they have dwelt in the district of different Marriage Registrars) that the party making such oath has, had their, his/her usual place of abode within the district of such marriage Registrar, and, where either or each of the parties is a minor; (c) that the consent or consents to such marriage required by law has or have been obtained thereto, or that there is no person resident in Pakistan authorized to give such consent, as the case may be.

335. Consent of father or guardian and protest against issue of certificate has been discussed in section 44 of the Christian Marriage Act, 1872. The provision of section 19 apply to every marriage under this Part, either of the parties to which is a minor; and any person whose consent to such marriage would be required thereunder may enter a protest against the issue of the Marriage Registrar's certificate, by writing, at any time before the issue of such certificate, the word 'forbidden' opposite to the entry of the notice of such intended marriage in the Marriage Notice Book, and by subscribing thereto his/her name and place of abode, and his/her position with respect to either of the parties, by reason of which he/she is so authorized. When such protest has been entered, no certificate shall be issued until the Marriage Registrar has examined into the matter of the protest, and is satisfied that it ought not to obstruct the issue of the certificate for the said marriage, or until the protest be withdrawn by the person who entered it.

336. If any person whose consent is necessary to any marriage under this part is of unsound mind, or if any such person (other than the father) without just cause withholds his consent to the marriage, the parties, intending marriage may apply by petition, to the District Judge, vide section 45 of the Christian Marriage Act, 1872 and the said District Judge may examine the allegations of the petition in a summary way; and, if upon examination such marriage appears proper, such District Judge shall declare the marriage to be a proper marriage. Such declaration shall be as effectual as if the person whose consent was needed had consented to the marriage; and, if he has forbidden the issue of the Marriage Registrar's certificate, such certificate shall be issued and the like proceeding may be had under this Part in relation to the marriage as if the issue of such certificate had not been forbidden.

337. Whenever a Marriage Registrar refuses to issue a certificate under this Part, either of the parties intending marriage may apply by petition to the District Judge. The said District Judge may examine the allegations of the petition in a summary way, and shall decide thereon. The decision of such District Judge shall be final, and the Marriage Registrar to whom the application for the issue of a certificate was originally made shall proceed in accordance therewith (section 46 of the Christian Marriage Act, 1872).

338. Under section 47 of the Christian Marriage Act, 1872, whenever a Marriage Registrar resident in any Acceding State refuses to issue his certificate either of the parties intending marriage may apply by petition to the Central Government, who shall decide thereon. Such decision shall be final, and the Marriage Registrar to whom the application was originally made shall proceed in accordance therewith.

339. Whenever a Marriage Registrar, acting under the provisions of section 44, is not satisfied that the person forbidding the issue of the certificate is authorized by law so to do the said Marriage Registrar shall apply by petition, to the District Judge. The said petition shall state all the circumstances of the case, and pray for the order and direction of the Court concerning the same and the said District Judge shall examine into the allegations of the petition and the said circumstances of the case: And if, upon such examination, it appears that the person forbidding the issue of such certificate is not authorized by law so to do, such District Judge shall declare that the person forbidding the issue of such certificate is not authorized as aforesaid, and thereupon such certificate shall be issued, and the like proceedings may be had in relation to such marriage as if the issue had not been forbidden. Whenever a Marriage Registrar appointed under section 8 to act within any Acceding State is not satisfied that the person forbidding the issue of the certificate is authorized by law so to do, the said Marriage Registrar shall send a statement of all the circumstances of the case, together with all documents relating thereto to the Central Government. If it appears to the Central Government that the person forbidding the issue of such certificate is not authorized by law so to do, the Central Government shall declare that the person forbidding the issue of such certificate is not authorized as aforesaid, and thereupon such certificate shall be issued, and the like proceedings may be had in relation to such marriage as if the issue of the certificate had not been forbidden (section 48 of the Christian Marriage Act, 1872).

340. Every person entering a protest with the Marriage Registrar, under this Part against the issue of any certificate, on grounds which such Marriage Registrar; under section 44 or the District Judge, under section 45 or 46, declares to be frivolous and such as ought not to obstruct the issue of the certificate, shall be liable for the costs of all proceedings in relation thereto and for damages, to be recovered by suit by the person against whose marriage such protest was entered (section 49 of the Christian Marriage Act, 1872).

341. After the issue of the certificate of the Marriage Registrar, or, where notice is required to be given under this Act to the Marriage Registrars for different districts, after the issue of the certificates, of the Marriage Registrars for such districts. Marriage may, if there be no lawful impediment to the marriage of the parties described in such certificate or certificates, be solemnized between them, according to such form and ceremony as they think fit to adopt. But every such marriage shall be solemnized in the presence of some Marriage Registrar (to whom shall be delivered such certificate or certificates as aforesaid), and of two or more credible witnesses besides the Marriage Registrar. And in some part of the ceremony each of the parties declare as follows, or to the like effect: 'I do not solemnly declare that I know not of any lawful impediment why I, A.B., may not be joined in matrimony to C.D.' And each of the parties shall say to the other as follows or to the like effect: 'I call upon these persons here present to witness that I, A.B. do take the, C.D., to be my lawful wedded wife [or husband] (section 51 of the Christian Marriage Act, 1872). When Marriage not had within two months after notice, new notice required, vide section 52 of the Christian Marriage Act, 1872.'

342. After the solemnization of any marriage under section 54 of the Christian Marriage Act, 1872, the Marriage Registrar present at such solemnization shall forthwith register the marriage in duplicate that is to say, in a marriage-register-book, according to the form of the Schedule hereto annexed, and also in a certificate attached to the marriage-book as a counterfoil. The entry of such marriage in both the certificate and the marriage-register-book shall be signed by the person by or before whom the marriage has been solemnized, if there be any such person, and by the Marriage Registrar present at such marriage, whether or not it is solemnized by him, and also by the parties married, and attested by two credible witness other than the Marriage Registrar and person solemnizing the marriage. Every such entry shall be made in order from the beginning to the end of the book, and the number of the certificate shall correspond with that of the entry in the marriage-register-book.

343. The marriage shall forthwith separate the certificate from the marriage-register-book and send it, at the end of every month, to the Registrar General of Births, Deaths and Marriages. The Marriage Registrar shall keep safely the said register-book until it is filled, and shall then send it to the Registrar General of Births, Deaths and Marriages, to be kept by him with the records of his office (section 55 of the Christian Marriage Act, 1872).

344. When any Native Christian about to be married gives a notice of marriage, or applies for a certificate from a Marriage Registrar, such Marriage Registrar shall ascertain whether the said Native Christian understands English language, and, if he does not, the Marriage Registrar shall translate, or cause to be translated, such notice or certificate, or both of them as the case may be, to such Native Christian into a language which he understands; or the Marriage Registrar shall otherwise ascertain whether the Native Christian is cognizant of the purport and effect of the said notice and certificate (section 57 of the Christian Marriage Act, 1872).

345. When any Native Christian is married under the provisions of this Part, the person solemnizing the marriage shall ascertain whether such Native Christian understands English language, and if he does not, the person solemnizing the marriage shall, at the time of the solemnization translate, or cause to be translated, to such Native Christian, into a language which he understands, the declarations made at such marriage in accordance with the provision of this Act (section 58 of the Christian Marriage Act, 1872).

346. Part VI, section 60 of the Christian Marriage Act, 1872 states the conditions of marriages of Native Christian which may be certificated. Every marriage between Native Christians applying for a certificate shall without the preliminary notice required under Part III be certified under this Part, if the following conditions to be fulfilled, and not otherwise: (1) the age of the man intending to be married shall exceed 16 years, and the age of the woman intending to be married shall exceed 13 years; (2) neither of the persons intending to be married shall have a wife or husband still living; and (3) in the presence of a person licensed, and of at least two credible witnesses other than such person, each of the parties shall say to the other. 'I call upon these persons here present to witness that I, A.B. in the presence of Almighty God, and in the name of our Lord Jesus Christ, do take thee, C.D., to be my lawful wedded wife [or husband]' or words to the like effect. Provided that no marriage shall be certified under this Part when either of parties intending to be married has not completed his/her 18th year, unless such consent has been given to the intended marriage, or unless it appears that there is no person living authorized to give such consent.

347. When, in respect to any marriage solemnized and the conditions, prescribed in section 60 of the Act have been fulfilled, the person licensed as aforesaid, in whose presence the said declaration has been made, shall, on the application of either of the parties to such marriage, and on the payment of a fee of four annas, grant a certificate of the marriage. The certificate shall be signed by such licensed person, and shall be received in any suit touching the validity of such marriage as conclusive proof of its having been performed (section 61 of the Christian Marriage Act, 1872).

348. Part VI of the Christian marriage Act, 1872, except so much of sections 62 and 63 as are referred to in section 64, shall not apply to marriages between Roman Catholics. But nothing herein contained shall invalidate any marriage celebrated between Roman Catholics under the provisions of Part invalidate any marriage celebrated between Roman Catholics under the provisions of Part V of Act No. XXV of 1864, previous to the twenty-third day of February, 1865.

349. Whoever, for the purpose of procuring a marriage or license of marriage, intentionally: (a) where an oath or declaration is required by this Act, or by any rule or custom of a Church according to the rites and ceremonies of which a marriage is intended to be solemnized, such Church being the Church of England or of Rome, makes a false oath or declaration, or, (b) where a notice or certificate is required by this Act, signs a false notice or certificate; shall be deemed to have committed the offence punishable under section 193 of the PPC with imprisonment of either description for a term which may extend to three years and, at the discretion of the Court, with fine (Part VII section 66 of the Christian Marriage Act, 1872).

350. Under section 67 of the Christian Marriage Act, 1872, whoever forbids the issue, by a Marriage Registrar, of a certificate, by falsely representing himself to be a person whose consent to the marriage is required by law, knowing or believing such representation to be false or not having reason to believe it to be true, shall be deemed guilty of the offence described in section 205 of the PPC.

351. Solemnizing marriage without due authority has been discussed in section 68 of the Christian Marriage Act, 1872. Whoever, not being authorized by section 5 of the Act to solemnize marriages, solemnizes or professes to be solemnized the absence of a Marriage Registrar of the district in which the ceremony takes place. Marriage between persons one or both of whom is or are a Christian or Christians, shall punished with imprisonment which may extend to ten years, (in lieu of a sentence of imprisonment for seven years or upwards) with transportation for a term of not less than seven years, and not exceeding ten years, and shall also be liable to fine.

352. Whoever knowingly and wilfully solemnizes a marriage between persons one or both of whom is or are a Christian or Christians, at any time other than between the hours of six in the morning and seven in the evening, or in the absence of at least two credible witnesses other than the person solemnizing the marriage, shall be punished with imprisonment for a term which may extend to three years, and shall also be liable to fine, vide section 69 of the Christian Marriage Act, 1872. This section does not apply in marriages solemnized under special licenses granted by the Anglican Bishop of the Diocese or by his Commissary, nor to marriages performed between the hours of seven in the evening and six in the morning by Clergyman of the Church of Rome, when he has received the general or special license in that behalf mentioned in section 10. Nor does this section apply to marriages solemnized by a Clergyman of the Church Scotland according to the rules, rites, ceremonies and customs of the Church of Scotland.

353. Under section 70 of the Christian Marriage Act, 1872, any Minister of Religion licensed to solemnize marriages under this Act, who, without a notice in writing, or, when one of the parties to the marriage is a minor and the required consent of the parents of guardians to such marriage has not been obtained within fourteen days after the receipt by him of notice of such marriage knowingly and wilfully solemnizes a marriage under Part II, shall be punished with imprisonment for a term which may extend to three years, and shall also be liable to fine.

354. Issuing certificate, or marrying without publication of notice; marrying after expiry of notice; solemnizing marriage with minor within fourteen days without authority of Court or without sending copy of notice; issuing certificate against authorized prohibition have been discussed in section 71 of the Christian Marriage Act, 1872. A Marriage Registrar under the Act, who commits any of the following offences: (1) knowingly and wilfully issues any certificate for marriage, or solemnizes any marriage, without publishing the notice of such marriage as directed by this Act; (2) after the expiration of two months after the copy of the notice has been entered as required by section 40 in respect of any marriage, solemnizes such marriage; (3) solemnizes, without any order of a competent Court authorizing him to do so, any marriage, when one of the parties is a minor, before the expiration of fourteen days after the receipt of the notice of such marriage, or without sending, by the post or otherwise, a copy of such marriage, or without sending, by the post or otherwise, a copy of such notice to the Senior Marriage Registrar of the district if there be more Marriage Registrars of the district than one, and if he himself be not the Senior Marriage Registrar; and (4) issue any certificate the issue of which had been prohibited, as in this Act provided, by any person authorized to prohibit the issue thereof shall be punished with imprisonment for a term, which may extend to five years, and shall also be liable to fine.

355. Section 72 of the Christian Marriage Act, 1872 provides about the issuing certificate after expiry of notice, or, in case of minor within fourteen days after notice, or against authorized prohibition. Any Marriage Registrar knowingly and wilfully issuing any certificate for marriage after the expiration of two months after the notice has been entered by him as aforesaid, or knowingly and wilfully issuing, without the order of a competent Court authorizing him to do so, any certificate for marriage, where one of the parties intending marriage is a minor, before the expiration of fourteen days after the entry of such notice, or any certificate the issue of which has been forbidden as aforesaid by any person authorized in his behalf, shall be deemed to have committed an offence under section 166 of the PPC.

356. Persons authorized to solemnize marriage has been discussed in section 73 of the Christian Marriage Act, 1872. (other than Clergy of Churches of England, Scotland or Rome); issuing certificate or marrying, without publishing notice, or other expiry of certificate; issuing certificate for, or solemnizing marriage with minor within fourteen days after notice; issuing certificate authorizedly forbidden; solemnizing marriage authorizedly forbidden. Whoever, being authorized under this Act to solemnize a marriage, and not being a Clergyman of the Church of England, solemnizing a marriage after due publication of bans, or under a license from the Anglican Bishop of the Diocese or a Surrogate duly authorized in that behalf; or not being a Clergyman of the Church of Scotland, solemnizing a marriage according to the rules, rites, ceremonies and customs of that Church; or, not being a Clergyman of the Church of Rome, solemnizing a marriage according to the rites, rules, ceremonies and customs of that Church; knowingly and wilfully issues any certificate for marriage under this Act, or solemnizes any marriage between such persons as aforesaid, without publishing, or causing to be affixed, the notice of such marriage as directed in Part III of this Act, or after the expiration of two months after the certificate has been issued by him; or knowingly and wilfully issues any certificate for marriage, or solemnizes a marriage between such persons when one of the persons intending marriage is a minor, before the expiration of fourteen days after the receipt of notice of such marriage, or without sending, by the post or otherwise, a copy of such notice to the Marriage Registrar, or, if there be more Marriage Registrars than one, to the Senior Marriage Registrar of the district; or knowingly and wilfully issues any certificate the issue of which has been forbidden under this Act, by any person authorized forbid the issue; or knowingly and wilfully solemnizes any marriage forbidden by any person authorized to forbid the same shall be punished with imprisonment for a term which may extend to four years and shall also be liable to fine.

357. Under section 74 of the Christian Marriage Act, 1872, whoever, not being licensed to grant a certificate of marriage under Part VI of this Act, grants such certificate intending thereby to make it appear that he is licensed, shall be punished with imprisonment for a term which may extend to five years, and shall be liable to fine. Whoever, being licensed to grant certificates of marriage under Part VI of this Act, without just cause refuses, or wilfully neglects or omits, to perform any of the duties imposed upon him by that Part shall be punished with fine which may extend to PKR 100.

358. Section 75 of the Christian Marriage Act, 1872 discussed about destroying or falsifying register books. Whoever, by himself or another wilfully destroys or injures any register-book or the counterfoil certificate thereof, or any part thereof, or any authenticated extract therefrom; or falsely makes or counterfeits any part of such register-book or counterfoil certificates; or wilfully inserts any false entry in any such register-book or counterfoil certificate or authenticated extract, shall be punished with imprisonment for a term which may extend to seven years, and shall also be liable to fine. The prosecution for every offence punishable under this Act shall be commenced within two years after the offence is committed, vide section 76 of the Christian Marriage Act, 1872.

359. What matters need not be proved in respect of marriage in accordance with Part VIII, Article 77 of the Christian Marriage Act, 1872. Whenever any marriage has been solemnized in accordance with the provision of sections 4 and 5, it shall not be void merely on account of any irregularity in respect of any of the following matters, namely: (1) any statement made in regard to the dwelling of the persons married, or to the consent of any person whose consent to such marriage is required by law; (2) the notice of the marriage; (3) the certificate or translation thereof; (4) the time and place at which the marriage has been solemnized; and (5) the registration of the marriage.

360. Under section 78 of the Christian Marriage Act, 1872, every person charged with the duty of registering any marriage who discovers any error in the form or substance of any such entry, may, within one month next after the discovery of such error, in the presence of the persons married, correct the error, by entry in the margin, without any alteration of the original entry, and shall sign the marginal entry, and add thereto the date of such correction, and such person shall make the like marginal entry in the certificate thereof. And every entry made under this section shall be attested by the witnesses in whose presence it was made. And in case such certificate has been already sent to the Registrar General of Births, Deaths and Marriages, such person shall make and send in like manner a separate certificate of the original erroneous entry, and of the marginal correction therein made.

361. Searches and copies of entries have been discussed in section 79 if the Christian Marriage Act, 1872. Every person solemnizing a marriage under this Act, and hereby required to register the same; and every Marriage Registrar or Registrar General of Births Deaths and Marriages having the custody for the time being of any register of marriages or of any certificate, or duplicate or copies of certificate, under this Act shall on payment of the proper fees, at all reasonable times, allow searches to be made in such register, or for such certificate, or duplicate, or copies, and give a copy under his hand of an entry in the same.

362. Under section 80 of the Christian Marriage Act, 1872, every certified copy, purporting to be signed by the person entrusted under this Act with the custody of any marriage-register or certificate, or duplicate, required to be kept or delivered under this Act, of an entry of a marriage in such register, or of any such certificate or duplicate shall be received as evidence of the marriage purporting to be so entered, or of the facts purporting to be so certified therein, without further proof of such register or certificate or duplicate, or of any entry therein, respectively or of such copy.

363. Certificates of certain marriages for Central Government have been discussed in section 81 of the Christian Marriage Act, 1872. The Register General of Births, Deaths, and Marriages and the officers appointed under section 56 shall, at the end of every quarter in each year, select, from the certificates of marriages forwarded to them, respectively, during such quarter, the certificates of the marriages of which the Government by whom he was appointed may desire that evidence shall be transmitted to England, and shall send the same certificate, signed by them respectively, to the Central Government.

364. Fees are charged under the Christian Act for: (a) receiving and publishing notices of marriages; (b) issuing certificates for marriage by Marriage Registrars, and registering marriages by the same; (c) entering protests against, or prohibitions of, the issue of certificates for marriage by the said Registrars; and (d) searching register-books or certificates, or duplicates of copies thereof, giving copies of entries in the same under sections 63 and 79.

365. Nothing in the Act applies to any marriage performed by any Minister, Consul or Consular Agent between subjects of the State which he represents and according to the laws of such State, vide section 87 of the Christian Marriage Act, 1872. Nothing in the Act shall be deemed to validate any marriage, which the personal law applicable to either of the parties forbids him/her to enter into, vide section 88 of the Christian Marriage Act, 1872.

X. Hindu Marriages

366. In Pakistan, the Hindu community's family matters were traditionally governed by customary practices, requiring customs to be ancient, certain, reasonable, and not opposed to public policy. However, legislative advancements have introduced codified laws to address these issues. The Sindh Hindu Marriage Act of 2016, applicable within the Sindh province, and the Hindu Marriage Act of 2017, applicable in Islamabad Capital Territory, Balochistan, Khyber-Pakhtunkhwa, and Punjab provinces, provide legal frameworks for the solemnization and registration of Hindu marriages. These acts outline procedures for marriage, divorce, and inheritance rights, aiming to protect the rights of Hindu women and ensure legal recognition of Hindu marriages. Despite these specific laws, members of minority communities, including Hindus, often approach the country's regular Family Courts for various family disputes. The Family Courts Act of 1964 does not restrict its jurisdiction to Muslims alone, allowing individuals from all communities to seek legal redress in family matters.

367. Section 3 of the Protection of the Rights of Religious Minorities Act, 2020 guarantees the right to marriage for members of religious minorities, ensuring they can marry within their faith without facing state-imposed restrictions.

368. Section 5 of Protection of the Rights of Religious Minorities Act, 2020 provides safeguards against forced marriages and coercion which ensures that individuals from religious minority communities can make independent decisions regarding their marriage.

369. Section 7 of Protection of the Rights of Religious Minorities Act, 2020, highlights the registration of marriages within religious minority communities ensuring their legal recognition and protection under the law.

370. Family disputes within the Hindu community in Pakistan are traditionally resolved through community forums with only a limited number of cases being brought before the courts. However, members of scheduled castes in contrast to caste Hindus, are more likely to seek legal recourse through the Family Courts. Historically, Hindu personal law did not recognize the concept of divorce but in certain instances individuals have petitioned the courts citing established customs within their communities as a basis for dissolution of marriage.

371. Under the Hindu Married Women's Right to Separate Residence and Maintenance Act of 1946, a married Hindu woman is entitled to claim a separate residence and maintenance under specific circumstances. These grounds include the husband's affliction with a severe or contagious disease not contracted from the wife, acts of cruelty that make cohabitation unsafe, desertion or abandonment without her consent, the husband's remarriage, conversion to another religion, or maintaining a concubine. Additionally, any other legally justifiable cause may also warrant her right to seek separate living arrangements and financial support.

372. A wife's claim for separate residence and maintenance may be denied under certain circumstances. These include her conversion to another religion, engagement in immoral conduct, or failure to comply with a court decree for the restitution of conjugal rights without valid justification. Additionally, if the wife voluntarily deserts her husband without reasonable cause or enters into a relationship that violates the sanctity of marriage, her entitlement to maintenance may be revoked.

373. Under the Hindu Widow's Remarriage Act of 1856, a Hindu widow has the legal right to remarry. If she is a minor and her previous marriage was not consummated, her remarriage requires the consent of her father or legal guardian. However, if she is an adult or if her previous marriage was consummated, she may remarry based on her own consent. Upon remarriage, a widow forfeits her rights to her deceased husband's property, as her legal status shifts with the new matrimonial alliance. A Hindu widow may serve as the guardian of her minor children if this was explicitly stated in her late husband's will. In the absence of such a provision, she can petition the court for guardianship, particularly if no male guardian has been appointed in the will.

374. The Hindu Widow's Remarriage Act of 1856 remains applicable to the Hindu community in Pakistan, eliminating legal barriers to the remarriage of widows. The Act was originally introduced to reform prevailing customs that deemed Hindu widow's ineligible for remarriage, thereby rendering any subsequent marriage invalid and their offspring illegitimate with no inheritance rights. The preamble acknowledges that while such restrictions were historically upheld by civil courts under British colonial rule, many Hindus believed these legal constraints were inconsistent with the true principles of their faith. Recognizing the need for legal reform, the Act was enacted to grant Hindu widows the right to remarry freely, ensuring that those who wished to adopt this practice in accordance with their conscience could do so without legal hindrance. By removing obstacles to widow remarriage, the legislation aimed to uphold social justice, promote moral well-being, and contribute to the broader public welfare. Today, while Hindu personal laws in Pakistan continue to evolve, the Act remains a foundational legal instrument ensuring the rights and dignity of Hindu widows. It is enacted as follows:

375. Under Article 1 of the Hindu Widow's Remarriage Act, 1856, no marriage contracted between Hindus shall be invalid, and the issue of no such marriage shall be illegitimate, by reason of the woman having been previously married or betrothed to another person who was dead at the time of such marriage, any custom and any interpretation of Hindu Law to the contrary notwithstanding.

376. It is stipulated under Article 2 of the Hindu Widow's Remarriage Act, 1856 all rights and interests which any widow may have in her deceased husband's property by way of maintenance, or by inheritance to her husband or to his lineal successors, or by virtue of any will or testamentary disposition conferring upon her, without express permission to remarry, only a limited interest in such property, with no power of alienating the same, shall upon her remarriage, cease and determine as if she had then died; and the next heirs of her deceased husband, or other persons entitled to the property on her death, shall thereupon succeed to the same.

377. Under Article 3 of the Hindu Widow's Remarriage Act, 1856, it is stated that on the remarriage of a Hindu widow, if neither the widow nor any other person has been expressly constituted by the will or testamentary disposition of the deceased husband the guardian of his children, the father of paternal grandfather or paternal grandmother, of the deceased husband, or any male relative of the deceased husband, may petition the highest Court having original jurisdiction in civil cases in the place where the deceased husband was domiciled at the time of his death for the appointment of some proper person to be guardian of the said children, and thereupon it shall be lawful for the said Court, if it shall think fit, to appoint such guardian, who when appointed shall be entitled to have care and custody of the said children, or of any of them during their minority, in the place of their mother; and in making such appointment the Court shall be guide, so far as may be, by the laws and rules in force touching the guardianship of children who have neither father nor mother: Provided that when the said children have no property of their own sufficient for their support and proper education while minors, no such appointment shall be made otherwise than with the consent of the mother unless the proposed guardian shall have given security for the support and proper education of the children while minors.

378. It is stipulated nothing in this Act contained shall be construed to render any widow who, at the time of the death of any person leaving any property, is a childless widow, capable of inheriting the whole or any share of such property, if before the passing of this Act, she would have been incapable of inheriting the same by reason of her being a childless widow.

379. Under Article 5 of the Hindu Widow's Remarriage Act, 1856 except as provided in the Act, a widow shall not, by reason of her remarriage forfeit any property or any right to which she would otherwise be entitled; and every widow who has remarried shall have the same rights of inheritance as she would have had such marriage been her first marriage.

380. It is also stated under Article 6 of the Act that whatever words spoken, ceremonies performed or engagements made on the marriage of a Hindu female who has not been previously married, are sufficient to constitute a valid marriage, shall have the same effect if spoken, performed or made on the marriage of a Hindu widow, and no marriage shall be declared invalid on the ground that such words, ceremonies or engagements are inapplicable to the case of a widow.

381. Under Article 7 of the said Act, if the widow remarrying is a minor whose marriage has not been consummated, she shall not remarry without the consent of her father, or if she has no father, of her paternal grandfather, or if she has no such grandfather, of her mother, or, failing all these, of her elder brother, or failing also brothers, of her next male relative.

382. All persons knowingly abetting a marriage made contrary to the provisions of the Hindu Widow's Remarriage Act, 1856 shall be liable to imprisonment for term not exceeding one year or to fine or to both. And all marriages made contrary to the provisions of this section may be declared void by a Court of law: Provided that in any question regarding the validity of marriage made contrary to the provisions of this section, such consent as is aforesaid shall be presumed until the contrary is proved, and that no such marriage shall be declared void after it had been consummated.

383. Under the Act, in the case of a widow who is of full age, or whose marriage has been consummated, her own consent shall be sufficient consent to constitute her remarriage lawful and valid.

384. In order to remove certain disabilities and doubts under the Hindu Law in respect of marriages between Hindus, the Hindu Marriage Disabilities Removal Act, 1946 (Act No. XXVII of 1946) was enacted on 22 November 1946. It is stated under the Act that notwithstanding any text, rule or interpretation of the Hindu Law or any custom or usage, a marriage between Hindus, which is otherwise valid, shall not be invalid by reason only of the fact that the parties thereto belong to the same gotra or gravara, or belong to different sub-divisions of the same caste.

XI. Parsi Marriages

385. The **Parsi Marriage and Divorce Act, 1936** governs the family matters of the Parsi community in Pakistan, establishing legal requirements for a valid marriage. Under this Act, a marriage is considered invalid if it violates any of the following conditions: (a) the couple is related within the prohibited degrees of consanguinity or affinity as outlined in **Schedule I** of the Act; (b) the marriage is not solemnized in accordance with the traditional **Parsi Ashirvad** ceremony, which must be conducted by a duly authorized Parsi priest in the presence of at least two Parsi witnesses, excluding the officiating priest; or (c) either party to the marriage, if below the age of **21 years**, has failed to obtain prior consent from their father or legal guardian, irrespective of any change in religion or domicile. Additionally, the Act provides a legal framework for marriage registration, divorce, and other matrimonial rights, ensuring that the personal laws of the Parsi community are upheld within the jurisdiction of Pakistan.

386. Under section 4 of the Parsi Marriage and Divorce Act, 1936 no Parsi (whether such Parsi has changed his/her religion or domicile or not) shall contract any marriage under this Act or any other law in the lifetime of his/her wife or husband, whether a Parsi or not, except after his/her lawful divorce from such wife or husband or after his/her marriage with such wife or husband has lawfully been declared null and void or dissolved, and, if the marriage was contracted with such wife or husband under the Parsi Marriage and Divorce Act, 1865 (Rep. by this Act.), or under this Act, except after a divorce, declaration or dissolution as aforesaid under either of the said Acts, XV of 1865. Every marriage contracted contrary to these provisions shall be void. Under section 11 of the Act, any priest knowingly and wilfully solemnizing any marriage contrary to and in violation of this section shall, on conviction thereof, be punished with simple imprisonment for a term which may extend to six months, or with fine which may extend to PKR 200, or with both.

387. It is stipulated under section 5 of the Parsi Marriage and Divorce Act, 1865 that every Parsi who during the lifetime of his/her wife or husband, whether a Parsi or not, contracts a marriage without having been lawfully divorced from such wife or husband, or without his/her marriage with such wife or husband having legally been declared null and void or dissolved, shall be subject to the penalties provided in sections 494 and 495 of the PPC for the offence of marrying again during the lifetime of a husband or wife.

388. Under section 6, every Parsi marriage contracted shall, immediately on the solemnization thereof, be certified by the officiating priest in the form contained in Schedule II. The certificate shall be signed by the said priest, the contracting parties, or their fathers or guardians when they shall not have completed the age of 21 years, and two witnesses present at the marriage; and the said priest shall thereupon send such certificate together with a fee to be paid by the husband to the Registrar of the place at which such marriage is solemnized. The Registrar on receipt of the certificate and fee shall enter the certificate in a register to be kept by him for that purpose and shall be entitled to retain the fee. The register of marriages can be inspected by making payment of prescribed fee. It is stipulated under section 12 that if any priest neglecting to comply with any of the requisitions affecting him contained in this section shall, on conviction thereof, be punished for every such offence with simple imprisonment for a term which may extend to three months, or with fine which may extend to PKR 100, or with both. Under section 13 every other person required by section 6 to subscribe or attest the said certificate who shall wilfully omit or neglect to do so, shall, on conviction thereof, be punished for every such offence with a fine not exceeding PKR 100. Similarly, under section 15 if any Registrar fails to enter the certificate, he shall be punished with simple imprisonment for a term which may extend to one year, or with fine which may extend to PKR 1,000, or with both.

389. Under section 10 of the Parsi Marriage and Divorce Act, 1865, when a Court passes a decree for divorce, nullity or dissolution, the Court shall send a copy of the decree for registration to the Registrar of Marriages within its jurisdiction.

390. It is prescribed under section 14 of the Act, that any person making or signing or attesting any such certificate containing a statement which is false, and which he either knows or believes to be false, shall be punished with simple imprisonment for a term which may extend to three months, or with fine which may extend to PKR 100, or with both; and if the act amounts to forgery as defined in the PPC, then such person shall also be liable, on conviction thereof, to the penalties provided in section 466 of the said Code, XLV of 1860.

391. Under section 16 of the above Act, any person secreting, destroying, or dishonestly or fraudulently altering the said register in any part thereof, shall be punished with imprisonment of either description as defined in the PPC for a term which may extend to two years, or if he be a Registrar, for a term which may extend to five years and shall also be liable to fine which may extend to PKR 500, XLV of 1860. The Districts Courts established under the Act are entitled to hear the suits relating to Parsi community.

392. Under section 38 of the Parsi Marriage and Divorce Act, 1865 no suit shall be brought in any Court to enforce any marriage or any contract connected with or arising out of any marriage, if, at the date of the institution of the suit, the husband shall not have completed the age of 16 years, or the wife shall not have completed the age of 14 years.

393. Under section 39 of the Parsi Marriage and Divorce Act, 1865 in any suit under this Act if the wife shall not have an independent income sufficient for her support and the necessary expenses of the suit, the Court, on the application of the wife, may order the husband to pay her monthly or weekly during the suit such sum not exceeding one-fifth of her husband's net income as the Court, considering the circumstances of the parties, shall think reasonable.

394. As stipulated under section 40 of the Parsi Marriage and Divorce Act, 1865, the court may, if it shall think fit at the time of passing any decree under this Act or subsequently thereto on application made to it for the purpose, order that the husband shall, while the wife remains chaste and unmarried, (a) to the satisfaction of the Court, secure to the wife such gross sum or such monthly or periodical payment of money for a term not exceeding her life as, having regard to her own property, if any, her husband's ability and the conduct of the parties, shall be deemed just, and for that purpose may require a proper instrument to be executed by all necessary parties and suspend the pronouncing of its decree until such instruments shall have been duly executed, or (b) make such monthly payments to the wife for her maintenance and support as the Court may think reasonable.

395. If a husband fails to comply with such an order, it may be enforced in accordance with the provisions for executing decrees and orders under the Code of Civil Procedure, 1908. Furthermore, during the period of non-compliance, any third party providing the wife with essential necessities may initiate legal action against the husband to recover the cost of those necessities, as stipulated under section V of 1908. Additionally, the court retains the authority to review the order based on a change in circumstances affecting either party. At the request of either spouse, the court may vary, modify, or rescind the order in a manner it deems just and appropriate, ensuring fairness and adaptability to evolving situations.

396. If an order for alimony or maintenance has been granted to a wife under the provisions of the Parsi Marriage and Divorce Act, 1865, the court holds the authority to modify or revoke the order if it is established that the wife has remarried or has not maintained chastity. In such cases, upon sufficient proof presented before the court, the financial obligation of the husband may be reconsidered, ensuring that maintenance is only provided where legally and morally justified. The court may also consider other relevant circumstances such as changes in the financial standing of either party, while deciding on the continuation, modification, or termination of the order.

397. Under section 41 of the Parsi Marriage and Divorce Act, 1865, in all cases in which the Court shall make any decree or order for alimony it may direct the same to be paid either to the wife herself, or to any trustee on her behalf to be approved by the Court, and may impose any terms or restrictions which to the Court may seem expedient, and may from time to time appoint a new trustee, if for any reason it shall appear to the Court expedient so to do.

398. Under section 42 of the Parsi Marriage and Divorce Act, 1865 it is stipulated that in any suit under this Act the Court may make such provisions in the final decree as it may deem just and proper with respect to property presented at or about the time of marriage which may belong jointly to both the husband and wife.

399. Under the Parsi Marriage and Divorce Act, 1865, any suit shall be conducted in a closed courtroom if either party requests it. Additionally, in a trial before a Parsi Matrimonial Court, the proceedings shall remain valid as long as at least five delegates have attended throughout, even if some delegates are absent during certain parts of the trial.

400. An appeal shall lie to the High Court from (a) the decision of any Court established under the Parsi Marriage and Divorce Act, 1865 on the ground of the decision being contrary to some law or usage having the force of law, or of a substantial error or defect in the procedure or investigation of the case which may have produced error or defect in the decision of the case upon the merits, and on no other ground; and (b) the granting of leave by any such Court: Provided that such appeal shall be instituted within three calendar months after the decision appealed from shall have been pronounced.

401. Under section 48 of the Act, when the time hereby limited for appealing against any decree granting a divorce or annulling or dissolving a marriage shall have expired, and no appeal shall have been presented against such decree, or when any such appeal shall have been dismissed, or when in the result of any appeal a divorce has been granted or a marriage has been declared to be annulled or dissolved, but not sooner, it shall be lawful for the respective parties thereto to marry again, as if the prior marriage had been terminated by death.

402. The section 49 of the Parsi Marriage and Divorce Act, 1865 deals regarding children of the Parties. The Court may from time to time pass such interim orders and make such provisions in the final decree as it may deem just and proper with respect to the custody, maintenance and education of the children under the age of 16 years, the marriage of whose parents is the subject of such suit, and may, after the final decree upon application, by petition for this purpose, make, revoke, suspend or vary from time to time all such orders and provisions with respect to the custody, maintenance and education of such children as might have been made by such final decree or by interim orders in case the suit for obtaining such decree were still pending.

403. Section 50 of the Parsi Marriage and Divorce Act, 1865 provide settlement of wife's property for benefit of children. In any case in which the Court shall pronounce a decree of divorce or judicial separation for adultery of the wife, if it shall be made to appear to the Court that the wife is entitled to any property either in possession or reversion, the Court may order such settlement as it shall think reasonable to be made of any part of such property, not exceeding one-half thereof, for the benefit of the children of the marriage or any of them.

404. Under Schedule-I of the Parsi Marriage and Divorce Act, 1865 a man cannot marry his paternal grand-father's mother; paternal grand-mother's mother; maternal grand-father's mother; maternal grand-mother's mother; paternal grand-mother; paternal grand-father's wife; maternal grand-mother; maternal grand-father's wife; mother or step-mother; father's sister or step-sister; mother's sister or step-sister; sister or step-sister; brother's daughter or step-brother's daughter, or any direct lineal descendant of a brother or step-brother; sister's daughter or step-sister's daughter, or any direct lineal descendant of a sister, or step-sister; daughter or step-daughter, or any direct lineal descendant of either; son's daughter or step-son's daughter, or any direct lineal descendant of a son or step-son; wife of son or step-son, or of any direct lineal descendant of a son or step-son; wife of daughter's son or of step-daughter's son, or of any direct lineal descendant of a daughter or step-daughter; mother of daughter's husband; mother of son's wife; mother of wife's paternal grand-father; mother of wife's paternal grand-mother; mother of wife's maternal grand-father; mother of wife's maternal grand-mother; wife's paternal grand-mother; wife's maternal grand-mother; wife's mother or step-mother; wife's father's sister; wife's mother's sister; father's brother's wife; mother's brother's wife; brother's son's wife and sister's son's wife.

405. Under Schedule-I of the Parsi Marriage and Divorce Act, 1865 a woman is allowed to marry her paternal grand-father's father; paternal grand-mother's father; maternal grand-father's father; maternal grand-mother's father; paternal grand-father; paternal grand-mother's husband; maternal grand-father; maternal grand-mother's husband; father or step-father; father's brother or step-brother; mother's brother or step-brother; brother or step-brother; brother's son or step-brother's son, or any direct lineal descendant of a brother or step-brother; sister's son or step-sister's son, or any direct lineal descendant of a sister or step-sister; son or step-son, or any direct lineal descendant of either; daughter's son or step-daughter's son, or any direct lineal descendant of a daughter or step-daughter; husband of daughter or of step-daughter, or of any direct lineal descendant of a daughter or step-daughter; husband of son's daughter or of step-son's daughter, or of any direct lineal descendant of a son or step-son; father of daughter's husband; father of son's wife; father of husband's paternal grand-father; father of husband's paternal grand-mother; father of husband's maternal grand-father; father of husband's maternal grand-mother; husband's paternal grand-father; husband's maternal grand-father; husband's father or step-father; brother of husband's father; brother of husband's mother; husband's brother's son, or his direct lineal descendant; husband's sister's son, or his direct lineal descendant; brother's daughter's husband; sister's daughter's husband;

§4. Dower (Haq Mehr)

406. In pre-Islamic Arabia, it was common for men to abandon their wives after taking advantage of them, leaving them without support or resources. To protect women's rights and ensure financial security, Islamic law established the concept of dower (mahr), which became an essential condition for the validity of marriage. The dower is the exclusive property of the wife, serving as a financial safeguard in case of separation. Unlike a fixed amount, the payment of dower varies based on mutual agreement, social customs, and financial capacity. The Holy Quran emphasizes the ethical treatment of women in marriage and divorce, stating, *'If you separate from your wives, do so with generosity'*, and further declares, *'It is not lawful for you to take back what you have given them.'* These principles reinforce the husband's obligation to honour his financial commitments and ensure that women are treated with dignity and fairness in marital relationships.

407. Under Islamic jurisprudence, the primary purpose of mehr (dower) is to provide financial security and protection to the wife, particularly as a safeguard against the unilateral exercise of talaq (divorce) by the husband. In Islamic law, a husband traditionally holds the right to dissolve the marriage without requiring specific justification. However, the obligation to pay mehr acts as a deterrent against impulsive or unjustified divorces, ensuring that the wife is not left in a vulnerable financial position. Mehr serves as a legal and moral check on the husband's authority, reinforcing his responsibility toward his spouse. It also symbolizes the husband's commitment and respect toward his wife, providing her with an independent financial right that she can claim at any time. Islamic scholars emphasize that while the husband possesses the right to talaq, it must be exercised with justice, fairness, and adherence to Quranic principles, rather than as an arbitrary act. The Holy Quran promotes reconciliation and fairness in marital relations, underscoring the importance of treating wives with dignity and ensuring their well-being, even in cases of separation.

408. Under Islamic law, the dower (mehr) stipulated in the nikahnama is generally divided into two categories based on the timing of payment. The first part, known as prompt dower (mu'ajjal mehr), becomes payable immediately upon demand by the wife at any time after the marriage contract is finalized. It serves as her immediate financial right and symbolizes the husband's commitment. The second part, referred to as deferred dower (muwajjal mehr), is payable at a later stage, either after a specified period agreed upon at the time of marriage or, in the absence of such a stipulation, upon the husband's death or the dissolution of the marriage. The deferred dower acts as a form of financial security for the wife, ensuring she has a claim to financial support in the future. Islamic scholars emphasize that both forms of dower are legally binding and must be honoured, as they serve to uphold the wife's financial independence and dignity within the marriage.

409. Prompt dower is payable immediately upon the wife's demand, regardless of whether the marriage has been consummated. Once the Nikah is solemnized, the wife gains the legal right to claim the full amount of the prompt dower at any time. She also has the right to refuse consummation of the marriage until the payment is made. In cases where the husband divorces the wife before consummation, he is obligated to pay only half of the agreed dower amount. However, during the subsistence of the marriage, the wife can claim the full prompt dower, and consummation is not a prerequisite for its payment. If the husband refuses to fulfil this obligation, the wife has the legal right to live separately while still being entitled to maintenance. The prompt dower serves as an essential financial safeguard for the wife, reinforcing her legal and economic security within the marriage.

410. If the amount of dower is not specified or fixed in the marriage contract, the wife is still entitled to receive what is known as 'proper dower' (Mahr al-Mithl). Even if the marriage was solemnized with an explicit agreement that she would not claim any dower, such a condition holds no legal validity under Islamic law. Proper dower is determined by considering the customary dower amount given to other female members of her paternal family, particularly her sisters, aunts, or women of similar social and economic status. The wife has the right to refuse cohabitation and deny conjugal relations until her prompt dower is paid.

411. According to section 10 of the MFLO, if the Nikahnama or marriage contract does not specify the mode of payment for the dower, it shall be legally presumed that the entire amount is payable on demand. This provision ensures that the wife has the right to claim the full dower at any time during the marriage.

412. SC (2024 SCMR 142): Failure of husband to pay dower. Trial Court directed the husband to pay to the wife the mehr of PKR 500,000 mentioned in the Nikahnama and maintenance with annual increase of 10%. Mehr has to be paid whenever demanded by the wife. Mehr can be demanded during the subsistence of the marriage, and the husband is under obligation to pay it. In present case, the husband had two wives but he did not fulfil his obligations towards one of them when he failed to pay the mehr demanded by her. Wife had to file a suit for recovery of the mehr and maintenance, and the husband unnecessarily involved the wife in litigation which reached the Supreme Court after six and half years. Supreme Court directed that in addition to imposing costs throughout it was imposing compensatory costs to the extent of PKR 100,000 on the husband considering the decrease in the value of money, and if the mehr and the said costs were not paid the Family Court shall execute present order, which may include attachment of the properties of the husband. Leave to appeal was declined and the petition was dismissed (section 5 and Schedule. MFLO (VIII of 1961), section 10).

413. LHC (2022 MLD 416): husband claimed that although the transfer of house was promised in the Nikahnama but the same was deferred dower and the marriage between the parties was still intact, therefore, the wife was not entitled to receive the same during the subsistence of marriage. Reading of entry 16 pf nikahnama of the parties revealed that neither mode of transfer was provided for nor the time for transfer of house promised under column no. 16 was incorporated indicating the same to be part of deferred dower, hence, there was failure to classify the house under column no. 16 as deferred dower coupled with the omission to specify mode and time of payment thereof. By virtue of section 10, the wife was entitled to claim for the discharge of obligation, which the husband undertook in terms of entry under column no. 16. Court held that the wife is rightly entitled to the house. Constitutional petition dismissed (sections 5 and 10 MFLO (VIII of 1961), section 5. Constitution of Pakistan (1973), Article 199).

414. The Shariat Court, Azad Kashmir (1999 YLR 2303) Suit for recovery of dower. Claim of plaintiff wife was that the whole amount of dower was payable to her on demand, whereas defendant husband contended that he had paid full amount of dower and nothing was against him. Burden to prove payment of amount of dower was on defendant, but he failed to discharge that burden through evidence. In absence of anything to the contrary regarding nature of dower fixed at time of *Nikah*, whole dower amount was payable to plaintiff by defendant as he had failed to prove that he had already paid said amount. Trial Court was not justified to dismiss suit for recovery of dower amount (MFLO, 1961 section 10. West Pakistan Family Courts Act (XXXV of 1964), section 5 and Schedule).

415. Leave to appeal was granted by Supreme Court to consider the correct import of 'deferred dower' and whether it could become prompt if and when demanded; whether Family Court could not grant maintenance which instead could be granted by Arbitration Council as mentioned in section 9 of MFLO, 1961; whether amount of maintenance decree commensurated with status and income of husband; whether restitution of conjugal rights could be allowed subject to condition of separate living of wife with husband abroad; and whether restitution of conjugal rights could be subjected to payment of maintenance (section 5. MFLO (VIII of 1961), section 9. Constitution of Pakistan (1973), Article 185(3)) SCP (2009 SCMR 1458).

416. Wife sough recovery of deferred dower during subsistence of marriage. Prompt dower was payable on demand during subsistence of marriage tie whereas the deferred dower was payable on time stipulated between the parties but where no time was stipulated, it was payable on dissolution of marriage either by death or divorce. High Court observed that the wife was not entitled to recover her dower at this stage and her suit was premature. Constitutional petition was allowed in circumstances. (section 10. MFLO Ordinance (VIII of 1961)) LHC (2020 MLD 1008).

417. Dower: Factum of gift of property by husband to wife in lieu of dower as recorded in Column No. 13 of *Nikahnama.* Validity: Presumption of truth was attached to *Nikahnama*, which could not be rebutted. Husband after having gifted property to wife in lieu of dower would have no title to dispose of the same (section 5. West Pakistan Rules under MFLO, 1961, Rr. 8, 10, 11, 12 and Form II, Column 13 *Nikahnama*) SCP (2004 PLD 10).

418. Property given in lieu of dower. Execution of dower deed separately. Validity: If marriage was registered under the provisions of section 5 of MFLO, 1961, any property transferred to the bride by her father-in-law in lieu of dower would have been mentioned in *Nikahnama* prescribed in form II of West Pakistan Rules under MFLO, and in such case there was no need to execute a dower deed separately. Property mentioned in *Nikahnama* would stand transferred in the name of the bride (MFLO 1961. Section 5 West Pakistan Rules under MFLO, R. 10, Form II) PHC (2003 YLR 250)

419. Transfer of land by way of dower. Husband of the petitioner at the time of marriage transferred land in name of the petitioner by way of dower. Husband submitted declaration under section 7 of Land Reforms Act, 1977, excluding land transferred to the petitioner but Authority included the said land in his holding and after calculating total produce index units ordered him to surrender excess land in favour of the Government. Validity: Nothing was on record to prove that *Nikahnama* whereby land in question was given/transferred to the petitioner by her husband by way of dower was a fabricated document. Authority considered *Nikahnama* as forged and fabricated one on the ground that columns therein dealing with amount and nature of dower were left blank. Question as to whether leaving blank said columns could lead to an inference that the *Nikahnama* was forged and fabricated, needed consideration, but no opportunity was given to the petitioner to prove that in relevant column of *Nikahnama* it was clearly mentioned that the bridegroom had given said land to his wife/petitioner as dower, and said *Nikahnama* was written long prior to the enforcement of Land Reforms Act, 1977. *Nikahnama* was admissible to prove factum of alienation of property in lieu of dower. Authority which had not seen the matter in its true perspective, had committed material irregularity and illegality while rendering order which had resulted in grave miscarriage of justice. Order passed by the Authority was set aside and case was remanded to be decided afresh on merits (Land Reforms Act, 1977. Section 7 MFLO (VIII of 1961), section 10, Constitution of Pakistan (1973), Article 199) LHC (2002 MLD 31)

420. Dissolution of marriage on ground of '*Khula*'. Repeated attempts for reconciliation made by Court had failed, and wife had openly stated that she would prefer death to live with her husband as his wife. Trial Court concluded that it was not possible for the parties to live together as husband and wife within limits ordained by God and passed decree for divorce subject to return of ornaments or value thereof to the husband as '*Khula*' amount. Wife had herself admitted that she had received ornaments from the husband at the time of *Nikah* as dower. Trial Court, in circumstances, had rightly dissolved marriage directing wife to return ornaments received by her from husband as dower or to pay amount thereof as she had herself gone to Court seeking dissolution of marriage on ground of '*Khula*' (MFLO, 1961. Section 8 West Pakistan Family Courts Act (XXXV of 1964), sections 5, 14 and Schedule) The Shariat Court, Azad Kashmir (2000 YLR 1857):

421. Suit for maintenance and dower. Dower and dowery. Distinction. Wife in her suit for maintenance and dower had claimed gold ornaments and a house as dower. Family Court decreed the suit, but Appellate Court in appeal dismissed the claim of wife. Claim of wife qua ornaments and house was specifically mentioned in dower/deed/*Nikahnama*. Wife who admittedly had received gold ornaments at the time of marriage had contended that gold ornaments which were given at the time of *Nikah* were part of dowery but were snatched and kept into possession by the husband. Contention was devoid of force because dowery were those articles which were given to wife by parents at the time of 'Rukhsati' whereas dower was a right of wife which was always paid or to be paid in lieu of marriage by husband. Dower once paid, liability of same would be satisfied. Taking away of dower by husband after marriage could be considered as loan/credit, return of which could only be sought through civil suit. Wife was entitled to payment of dower in shape of house which had been given to her in dower by husband as per dower deed (MFLO, 1961 sections 9 and 10 West Pakistan Family Courts Act (XXXV of 1964), sections 5 and Schedule 14. Constitution of Pakistan (1973), Article 199) PHC (2000 MLD 1638)).

422. Recovery of deferred dower. Contracting of second marriage without the permission of Arbitration Council. Petitioner/wife filed a suit for recovery and the same was decreed by the Trial Court whereas in appeal the Lower Appellate Court reversed the finding of the Trial Court and dismissed the suit. Validity: Where a man had contracted another marriage without permission of the Arbitration Council such person under the provisions of section 6(5) of MFLO, 1961 was liable to pay immediately the entire amount of dower whether prompt or deferred due, to the existing wife, and such amount if not so paid would be recoverable as arrears of land revenue. Where it was not pleaded that the subsequent *Nikah* had been contracted with the permission of the Arbitration Council, the husband had become liable to pay the entire amount of dower forthwith. Judgment and decree of the Lower Appellate Court was without lawful authority and the same was set aside (MFLO, 1961, section 6(5). West Pakistan Family Courts Act (XXXV of 1964), section 5 and Schedule Constitution of Pakistan (1973), Article 199) LHC (2000 YLR 537)

423. Suit for recovery of dower and maintenance. Kinds and mode of payment of dower. Dower fixed with the agreement of the parties to the marriage, could be prompt or deferred or partly deferred. Prompt dower was payable immediately on demand and deferred dower would be payable on a date or time agreed between the parties and it was more appropriate that date and time agreed for payment of deferred dower by certain. Parties could agree that deferred dower would be payable on the happening of a certain event like divorce or death. (section 10 of MFLO (VIII of 1961),sections 5 and 14 of West Pakistan Family Court Act (XXXV of 1964), Constitution of Pakistan (1973), Article 199) ISB (2010 YLR 1539)

424. Transfer of immoveable property by husband to wife through *Nikahnama* which had not been registered under Registration Act, 1908. Validity: *Nikah* of parties was in the form prescribed under MFLO, 1961 and the rules framed thereunder and same was registered with the *Nikah* Registrar in accordance with prescribed mode, and thus, *Nikahnama* had a different status than any other unregistered document through which some immoveable property had purportedly been transferred. *Nikahnama* was a public document executed by a Public Officer, certified copy whereof, was sufficient for proof of its contents unless its rebuttal was effected through cogent evidence. Dower deed by which immoveable property was purported to be transferred was, thus, not considered to be compulsorily registerable under Registration Act, 1908, and wife was entitled to claim immoveable property on basis of *Nikahnama* wherein same was incorporated in lieu of dower (Registration Act 1908 section 5. West Pakistan Family Courts Act (XXXV of 1964), section 5. Registration Act (XVI of 1908), sections 17 and 49. Constitution of Pakistan (1973), Article 199) PHC (1996 PLD 64).

425. Defendant female, contended that house sought to be partitioned by plaintiff, had been gifted to her by her deceased husband in lieu of her dower debt. Defendant lady failed to produce any documentary evidence in proof of her claim. Matters like dower debt or its satisfaction through transferring house in favour of lady deserved more pragmatic approach than mere words of mouth before a witness or two and more substantial evidence like transfer deed was expected. Existence of such deed was even affirmed by the lady, but she failed to produce it or prove it by secondary evidence. Finding of Courts below that house was not transferred to lady by way of *hibabilewaz* was unexceptionable in circumstances (MFLO, 1961 section 10) LHC (1991 CLC 1620)

426. Recovery of Dower: Husband himself fixed amount of dower at the time of marriage. Marriage was consummated, and a child was born out of the wedlock. Husband, held, neither could resile from his liability to pay dower amount nor disown his responsibility on technicality that since his person and property was under superintendence of Court of Wards, he being under wardship could not fix any dower as consideration for his marriage (MFLO, 1961, section 10) LHC (1989 MLD 989).

427. Haq mahr received by the wife in consideration of marriage at the time marriage were of considerable importance. Words received would mean that the payment of dower had either been established or its payment had been admitted by the wife at the time of granting decree. Only in that case, the Family Court had to simultaneously direct the restoration of dower to the husband. Dower was a consideration of marriage contract, on its dissolution, the contract would stand rescind, and the consideration paid would remain un-discharged debt liability, but would be subject to proof, the burden of which was undeniably on the husband to discharge by adducing evidence to that effect, unless it was shown to have been paid either in the dower deed or in the nikahnama. If the Family Court would defer the ground of decree, because the payment of dower was a point of contest, it had to revert back to the old fashion of trail where both the parties would lead evidence, such process in all probabilities, would consume sufficient time sufficient time and the purpose intended to be achieved through section 10(4) of West Pakistan Family Court Act, 1964, would be defeated. Time frame fixed by legislature for disposal of cases would lend iron clad support to that view. Ambiguity in the section 10(4) of West Pakistan Family Court, 1964, as to how to deal with the present eventuality needed to be clarified and efforts had to be made to make the same effective and meaningful so that the object of the legislature was achieved fairly and squarely (section 10(4). West Pakistan Family Court Act) PHC (2009 PLD 92).

§5. Dowry and Bridal Gifts

428. In Pakistan, the institution of marriage carries not only spiritual and emotional significance but also profound legal and financial implications. Among the central components of a Muslim marriage contract (*nikah*) are **dower (mahr)** and **bridal gifts**, which, while often intertwined in practice, serve distinct purposes in

Islamic jurisprudence and local customs. **Dower**, in particular, is a compulsory financial obligation upon the husband, payable to the wife as a token of respect, responsibility, and security. Bridal gifts, although traditionally voluntary and symbolic of goodwill have over time become a culturally entrenched expectation, frequently influenced by social status, regional customs, and material display. This trend has unfortunately led to situations where the distinction between **gifts** and **dowry demands** becomes blurred, often placing undue financial burden on the bride's family and contradicting the very principles of simplicity and equity emphasized in both Islam and Pakistani law.

429. Dower in Islamic law serves multiple purposes, primarily ensuring the economic security of the wife, compensating her for the husband's right to marital relations, and acting as a safeguard against unjust divorce. Under the provisions of Islamic jurisprudence, dower is classified into two categories: prompt dower (Mu'ajjal Mahr), which is payable immediately upon demand, and deferred dower (Muwajjal Mahr), which is payable after a specified period, typically at the time of divorce.

430. Pakistani family law recognizes the significance of dower and provides legal recourse for women to claim their rightful dues in case of disputes. The MFLO, 1961, which governs various aspects of Muslim marriages in Pakistan, upholds the obligation of dower and stipulates that if the mode of payment is not specified in the Nikahnama, the entire amount shall be presumed to be payable on demand under section 10 of the ordinance. This provision strengthens the wife's position by ensuring that she can demand her dower at any time and seek legal enforcement if the husband fails to fulfil his obligation. If a husband refuses to pay the prompt dower, the wife has the right to refuse cohabitation and may even live separately while retaining her claim to maintenance.

431. While dower is an obligatory component of an Islamic marriage, bridal gifts (Jahez) are a cultural practice that has persisted in South Asian societies for centuries. The tradition of giving dowry, which includes household items, cash, and jewellery, is primarily driven by societal expectations rather than religious doctrine. Unlike dower, which is a legal right of the wife, dowry is often considered an expectation placed upon the bride's family, sometimes leading to undue financial strain. In many cases, excessive dowry demands have resulted in social injustices, including domestic abuse, financial exploitation, and even dowry-related violence. To curb the adverse effects of this practice, the Pakistani government enacted the Dowry and Bridal Gifts (Restriction) Act, 1976, which sets limits on the value of dowry and prohibits forced demands by the groom or his family.

432. Under section 2(b) of the Dowry and Bridal Gifts (Restriction) Act, 1976, 'Dowry' means any property given before, at or after the marriage either directly or indirectly, to the bride by her parents in connection with the marriage, but it does not include property which the bride may inherit under the laws of inheritance and succession applicable to her; whereas under section 2(a) of the Dowry and Bridal Gifts (Restriction) Act, 1976 'Bridal gift' means any property given as a gift before, at or after the marriage, either directly, by the bridegroom or his parents to the bride in connection with the marriage but does not include Mehr.

433. Under section 2(e) of the Dowry and Bridal Gifts (Restriction) Act, 1976, 'Present' means a gift of any property, not being bridal gift or dowry, given before, at or after the marriage, either directly in connection with the marriage, or to the relatives of the bride or bridegroom but does not include 'neundra' and 'salami'. Neither the aggregate value of the dowry and presents given to the bride by her parents nor the aggregate value of the bridal gifts or the presents given to the bridegroom shall exceed PKR 5,000. Explanation: The ceiling of PKR 5,000 specified in this sub-section does not in any way imply that the dowry, bridal gifts and presents of a lesser amount may not be given.

434. No dowry, bridal gifts or presents may be given before or after six months of *Nikah* and if rukhsati takes place sometime after *Nikah*, after six months of such rukhsati (section 3 of the Dowry and Bridal Gifts (Restriction) Act, 1976).

435. No person gives to either party to the marriage any present, the value of which exceeds PKR 100, provided that the limit of PKR 100 shall not apply to the presents given to the bridegroom by the parents of the bride under sub-section (1) of section 3: Provided further that the President, the Prime Minister, Federal Minister, Chief Minister of State, Adviser, Governor, Speaker, Deputy Speaker, the Chairman or the Deputy Chairman of the Senate, Parliamentary Secretary, Member of the Senate, National Assembly or Provincial Assembly, Government servant or an official serving in any corporation, industry or establishment owned, controlled or managed by Government shall not receive any present in connection with his marriage or the marriage of his son or daughter except from his relations (khandan): Provided further that this restriction shall not apply to a Government servant or official serving in the scale below National Pay Scale 17 not exercising in any manner judicial, revenue or executive authority (section 4 of the Dowry and Bridal Gifts (Restriction) Act, 1976).

436. All property given as dowry or bridal gifts and all property given to the bride as a present shall vest absolutely in the bride and her interest in property however derived shall hereafter not be restrictive, conditional or limited (section 5 of the Dowry and Bridal Gifts (Restriction) Act, 1976).

437. The total expenditure on a marriage, excluding the value of dowry, bridal gifts and presents, but including the expenses on mehndi, baarat and walima, incurred by or on behalf of either party to the marriage shall not exceed PKR 2,500 (section 6 of the Dowry and Bridal Gifts (Restriction) Act, 1976).

438. The parents of each party to a marriage, at the time of rukhsati, display all items of dowry, bridal gifts and presents given or received in connection with the marriage so as to be visible to the persons attending the rukhsati (marriage ceremony) (section 7 of the Dowry and Bridal Gifts (Restriction) Act, 1976).

439. The parents of each party to a marriage shall furnish to the Registrar lists of dowry, bridal gifts and presents given or received in connection with the marriage. The lists shall be furnished in the case of property given or accepted before or at the time of the marriage; and in the case or property given or accepted after the marriage, within fifteen days of its being given or accepted.

440. The lists referred to shall contain details of the property along with the value thereof, and be signed or thumb-marked by the person furnishing them to the Registrar and attested by at least two witnesses.

441. The parents of each party to a marriage shall furnish to the Registrar the details of expenditure incurred on the marriage, duly signed or thumb-marked by them within one week. The Registrar shall forward the lists furnished and the details of expenditure submitted to the Deputy Commissioner within fifteen days of receipt of such list or details of expenditure (section 8 of the Dowry and Bridal Gifts (Restriction) Act, 1976).

442. Whoever, contravenes, or fails to comply with, any provision of Dowry and Bridal Gifts (Restriction) Act, 1976 shall be punishable with imprisonment of either description for a term which may extend to six months, or with fine which may extend to PKR 10,000, or with both, and the dowry, bridal gifts or presents given or accepted in contravention of the provisions of this Act shall be forfeited to the Federal Government to be utilized for the marriage of poor girls: Provided that if both the parents of a party to the marriage contravene, or fail to comply with, any provision of Act, action shall be taken only against the father: Provided further that if the parent who contravenes, or fails to comply with, any provisions of this Act or the rules made thereunder, is a female, shall be punishable with fine only.

443. An offence punishable under Dowry and Bridal Gifts (Restrictions) Act, 1976 shall be triable only by a Family Court established under the West Pakistan Family Courts Act, 1964 (W.P. Act No. XXXV of 1964). No Family Court takes cognizance of an offence punishable under this Act except upon a complaint in writing made by, or under the authority of the Deputy Commissioner within nine months from the date of *Nikah*, and if rukhsati takes place sometime after *Nikah*, from the date of such rukhsati.

444. While trying an offence punishable under this Act, a Family Court follows the procedure prescribed by the Code of Criminal Procedure, 1898 (Act V of 1898), for the trial of offences by Magistrates (section 9 of the Dowry and Bridal Gifts (Restriction) Act, 1976).

445. Where marriage was dissolved on various grounds including '*Khula*' then wife would be entitled to recover dower and dowry, but where it was dissolved solely on the ground of '*Khula*' then her offer made for getting marriage dissolved on '*Khula*' would be examined. Wife filed suit for dissolution of marriage on various grounds viz. cruelty, non-payment of maintenance, non-performance of marital obligations, impotency of husband and '*Khula*'. Wife also filed suit for recovery of dowry amount. Family Court decreed the suit for dissolution of marriage on all such grounds holding that wife in lieu of '*Khula*' would not be entitled to claim dower, dowry and maintenance. Husband, in view of such findings, filed in latter suit an application for rejection of the plaint. Wife filed application for clarification of judgment and decree, but it was dismissed by Family Court and its order was maintained by the Appellate Court. High Court accepted Constitutional petition filed by wife and set aside the conditions regarding relinquishment of dower, dowry and maintenance. Contention of husband was that High Court in exercise of Constitutional jurisdiction could not change judgment and decree passed by Family Court, especially when the wife had not challenged same and her petition for clarification had been dismissed by Courts below. 'Held' wife in her deposition recorded before Family Court had forgiven only her claim for remaining amount of dower in lieu of '*Khula*' and had not given up her claim of dowry. Marriage was dissolved on various rounds including '*Khula*'. Where marriage was dissolved on other grounds also, then wife would be entitled to recover amount of dower and dowry, but where it was dissolved solely on ground of '*Khula*' then situation would be different, and it would be examined keeping in view the offer she had made for getting marriage dissolved on '*Khula*'. Findings of High Court were correct and not open to any exception. Supreme Court dismissed the appeal of husband while making it clear that suit filed by wife for recovery of dowry amount would be decided on its own merits (reference West Pakistan Family Court Act 1964. Section 5 and Schedule. Dissolution of Muslim Marriages Act (VIII of 1939), section 2) (SCP – 2002 PLD 273).

446. Bridal Gifts, presents or all the other moveable properties are the belongings of bride and the husband if deprives her of the same, she has the right to recover all these articles even though the same were given in contradiction of provisions of section 3 of the Dowry and Bridal Gifts (Restriction) Act, 1976. Bride can always recover the articles of Dowry and Wari given to her by the bridegroom or the bridegroom side at the time of marriage. Bridal gift given by the husband is the absolute property of the wife, and it could not be snatched away from her (LHC – 2004 PLD 290).

447. In Islam, the payment of dower to bride at marriage is an obligation that is imposed by Allah Almighty, and is thus an intrinsic and integral part of a Muslim marriage. Dower is considered an obligatory bridal gift offered by the bridegroom to the bride graciously as a manifestation of his love and respect for her. Some Muslim men compliment the obligatory bridal gift, dower, with other gifts and presents as per their financial capacity. (SC-2022 PLD 686).

448. Husband had no right to bridal gifts even if it is a property given to her at the time of marriage. Woman also did not need permission to dispose of her property or to acquire property. Unless a married woman elected to gift, sell or otherwise dispose of her property neither her husband nor any male relative had any right over it. These bridal gifts could be added to but not subtracted by the husband. (SC-2020 PLD 269).

§6. EFFECTS OF MARRIAGE

I. General

449. Marriage is a sacred and legally binding contract that establishes a relationship between a husband and wife granting them certain rights and responsibilities toward each other. Under Islamic jurisprudence, marriage (Nikah) is not just a social institution but a contract (aqd) that ensures mutual obligations and privileges for both spouses. Upon marriage, several rights and privileges arise, particularly concerning companionship, support, inheritance, and sexual relations each with specific legal and religious stipulations.

450. One of the fundamental effects of marriage is the right to companionship. According to Islamic teachings, marriage is intended to provide emotional, psychological, and physical companionship to both spouses. The Holy Quran describes marriage as a means of tranquility, love, and mercy, stating in Surah Ar-Rum (30:21): '*And among His signs is that He created for you mates from among yourselves that you may find tranquility in them, and He placed between your affection and mercy.*' This companionship is not only spiritual but also legal, as both spouses have a right to live together in a harmonious environment. Under Pakistani law, a husband cannot arbitrarily abandon his wife, nor can he deprive her of her right to marital cohabitation without valid justification. The Dissolution of Muslim Marriages Act, 1939, allows a wife to seek divorce if her husband fails to fulfil his duty of companionship for a prolonged period.

451. Another major right and obligation arising from marriage is mutual financial support and maintenance (nafqah). According to Islamic law, it is the husband's duty to provide for his wife's needs, including food, clothing, shelter, and medical care, regardless of her financial status. This responsibility continues as long as the wife remains obedient and fulfils her marital obligations. If the husband fails to provide maintenance, the wife has the legal right to seek redress through Pakistani courts. The Family Courts Act, 1964, empowers the courts to enforce maintenance orders, ensuring that a husband fulfils his financial obligations. In cases where a husband refuses to maintain his wife without justification, she may seek separation or even dissolution of marriage under the MFLO, 1961.

452. Sexual rights and obligations also emerge upon marriage. Under Islamic teachings, both spouses have the right to intimacy and marital relations. The Quran emphasizes the lawful fulfilment of desires within marriage, stating in Surah Al-Baqarah (2:187): '*They are your garments and you are their garments.*' This verse signifies mutual comfort and protection between spouses. Islamic law mandates that neither spouse may deny the other their marital rights without valid reasons. However, Pakistani law also recognizes that consent is essential in a marital relationship, and any act of coercion or force in intimate matters is prohibited.

453. Marriage also establishes inheritance rights under Islamic law. A wife is entitled to inherit from her husband's estate upon his death, and vice versa, as stipulated in Surah An-Nisa (4:7-14). Pakistani inheritance laws, governed by the Muslim Personal Law (Shariat) Application Act, 1937, ensure that spouses receive their rightful share of inheritance. A wife is entitled to one-eighth of her deceased husband's estate if they have children, and one-fourth if they do not. Similarly, a husband inherits one-fourth of his deceased wife's estate if they have children, and one-half if they do not.

454. Marriage also impacts the legal status of children. Under the law, children born within a valid marriage are considered legitimate and entitled to full legal rights, including inheritance, financial support, and protection. The legitimacy of a child is crucial in Islamic law, as illegitimate children do not inherit from their biological fathers. The West Pakistan Muslim Personal Law (Shariat) Act, 1962, upholds these principles, ensuring that children born within wedlock are legally recognized and protected.

II. Rights and Duties of Husband

455. There is no specific law in Pakistan which clearly defines the rights and duties of a husband after marriage. However under the Islamic Law, the husband has the right for the following:

- The husband has the right to intimacy with his wife and she is obligated to fulfil this marital duty, considering health and decency. This right is fundamental to the marriage contract and cannot be annulled.
- The husband has the discretion to decide the place of residence for the couple. A stipulation that the wife must live separately at her parents' home while the husband only visits her is considered void under Islamic law. The husband has the right to expect modest behaviour from his wife. While he may restrict her interaction with unrelated males, this does not extend to her immediate family members (such as parents, siblings, and children from a previous marriage). However, a husband is not obligated to impose such restrictions and may waive this right in the marriage contract.
- If the husband cannot afford a wet nurse, or if no wet nurse is available, the wife is bound to suckle her own children. That the duty of suckling is not one of the essentials of marriage as is clear from the fact that an agreement by the wife to suckle her own children and thereby relieve the husband from pecuniary liability may be sufficient consideration for a '*Khula*' divorce.
- The wife is bound to general conformity with the husband's wishes, but the management of house is not necessarily part of her duties, as is obvious from the possibility of more than one wife, and cannot be compelled to perform menial duties if unbefitting either her rank or his means.
- . Islamic law permits a husband to correct his wife if she is persistently disobedient. However, physical discipline must be a last resort, after verbal warnings and other corrective measures have failed. It must not cause any injury, wound,

or severe bruising. Modern interpretations discourage any form of physical discipline, advocating for mutual respect and dialogue instead.
- In Islamic law, it is an undisputed right of the husband that his wife shall not have any other spouse during the subsistence of their marriage. Polyandry (a woman having multiple husbands) is strictly prohibited in Islam, and a married woman is not permitted to enter into another marital relationship as long as her marriage remains valid.
- The husband is solely responsible to maintain his wife, pay her dower, arrange accommodation for her, provide food and cloth and pay pocket money to her for personal usage. In addition, he is also responsible to arrange medical treatment of her wife as and when required and deal with her politely.
- If a man has more than one wife, he is obligated to treat them with fairness and justice in all aspects of marital life. One of the key obligations in this regard is the equal division of time among his wives. The requirement to allocate time equitably is essential to maintaining harmony and balance in a polygamous marriage.

The Quran, in Surah An-Nisa (4:3), states: *'If you fear that you will not be able to deal justly [with multiple wives], then [marry] only one ... '*

A husband is commanded by divine law to treat his wife with equity, respect her emotions, and demonstrate kindness and consideration at all times.

The Quran explicitly commands husbands to be just and considerate in their marital relationships. In Surah An-Nisa (4:19), Allah instructs: *'O you who have believed, it is not lawful for you to inherit women by compulsion. And do not make difficulties for them ... And live with them in kindness. For if you dislike them – perhaps you dislike a thing and Allah makes therein much good.'*

The Holy Prophet Muhammad (PBUH) also emphasized kindness towards women in numerous teachings and actions. His Last Sermon, delivered during his farewell pilgrimage, contains a powerful message on the fair treatment of women. He declared: *'O people, fear Allah concerning women! Verily, you have taken them on the security of Allah, and intercourse with them has been made lawful to you by the words of Allah. You too have rights over them, and they have rights over you.'*

III. Rights and Duties of Wife

456. After the marriage, it is right of wife that husband pay her dower, arrange accommodation, perform conjugal rights, meet her requirements, deal with her politely and respectable manner, provide medical treatment, provide food and cloth and pay pocket money for her daily use. The husband must provide a suitable matrimonial residence for his wife. If he has more than one wife, he must provide each of them with a separate apartment, according to his means, a separate room with a separate bathroom at least or in case of a wealthy man, a separate suit or house.

457. Under customary practices and court rulings, the duties of a wife extend beyond mere cohabitation and include several responsibilities essential for a harmonious marital life. Among the primary duties is maintaining conjugal relations with her husband in accordance with his wishes, provided there is no harm or undue hardship. A wife is also expected to conceive and bear children, thereby fulfilling one of the fundamental objectives of marriage in Islam, the continuation of family lineage.

458. One of the fundamental duties of a wife in marriage is to contribute to the success, harmony, and happiness of the relationship. She is expected to be a source of comfort, support, and tranquility for her husband, just as he is for her. A strong marital bond is built upon mutual love, understanding, and cooperation, where both spouses work together to create a peaceful and fulfilling life. This principle is beautifully expressed in the Quran: *'Our Lord, grant us from among our wives and offspring comfort to our eyes and make us an example for the righteous.'* (Surah Al-Furqan 25:74). A wife plays a vital role in maintaining a positive and loving atmosphere within the home. She is encouraged to be attentive to her husband's needs, offering emotional and moral support in times of hardship and sharing in his joys and successes. A respectful and caring attitude fosters a deep emotional connection, strengthening the foundation of the marriage.

459. A wife should uphold trust and honesty in her marriage. She should not intentionally prevent conception without mutual understanding with her husband. Faithfulness is essential, and she must remain committed to her spouse. To maintain harmony and avoid misunderstandings, she should not entertain unfamiliar men at home without her husband's knowledge or accept gifts from them without his consent. Additionally, she should respect his belongings and seek his permission before disposing of them.

460. A wife should make herself attractive to her husband and be responsive to his advances. The wife should not refuse her husband without reason as this may lead to marital problems and worse still – tempt the man to adultery. The husband, of course, should consider the wife's health and consideration of circumstances. In Islam, intimacy between spouses is regarded as a sacred aspect of marriage, strengthening the bond and ensuring emotional fulfilment. A wife should be attentive to her husband's needs and be responsive to his advances, as long as there are no valid reasons to refrain, such as health issues, emotional distress, or other genuine concerns. The Prophet Muhammad (PBUH) emphasized the importance of maintaining marital harmony, stating: *'When a husband calls his wife to his bed and she refuses, and he spends the night angry with her, the angels curse her until morning.'* (Bukhari, Muslim). However, this does not mean that a wife should comply without regard to her own physical and emotional well-being.

461. A wife is encouraged to be cooperative and respectful toward her husband as mutual understanding and harmony are essential for a successful marriage. The concept of obedience is not about blind submission but rather about maintaining balance, structure, and stability within the family unity. The obedience of a wife to her husband is conditional and does not mean unquestioning submission to unreasonable or unjust demands. It is expected only in matters that align with Islamic teachings, ethical principles, and the well-being of the family. A wife is not obligated to obey her husband if he asks her to do something that contradicts Islamic principles, harms her, or violates her personal rights. The Prophet Muhammad (PBUH) clearly stated, *'There is no obedience in matters involving disobedience to Allah.'* (Sunan an-Nasa'i). This means that a wife's obedience is within the limits of what is permissible, reasonable, and beneficial for both partners and their family.

462. Marriage is a legal contract through which both parties agree to live a harmonious life by honouring their respective obligations and duties towards each other. Islam, also nowhere forces the spouses to live a life devoid of harmony and happiness rather allows the parties to part, it they cannot live together, as they should. Man has a unilateral right to give talaq but the women has also been provided a right to seek separation by way of khula. This prima facie, is a way out for woman to come out of such bond of marriage and foe such claim, she even not supposed to give details for such move but her disliking is sufficient for exercise of such right. In such event, she would only be required to return the benefits, if any, she received from husband, Karachi High Court (2022 CLC 709).

IV. Maintenance of Wife

463. The husband is obligated to provide for his wife's maintenance, a responsibility firmly established in Islamic teachings through the Holy Quran and Sunnah. This duty applies regardless of the wife's religion, financial status, or physical condition whether she is Muslim or non-Muslim, wealthy or poor, healthy or ill. The obligation of *nafaqah* (maintenance) is a fundamental right of the wife and includes providing her with food, clothing, shelter, and other necessities in a manner befitting her status and the husband's means. Islamic law places great emphasis on the financial security and well-being of the wife. The Quran explicitly states: *'Men are the protectors and maintainers of women because Allah has made one of them excel over the other, and because they spend (to support them) from their wealth.'* (Surah An-Nisa 4:34).

464. A wife's right to maintenance in Islamic law includes lodging, clothing, food, and medical care, all of which the husband must provide according to his means. The Quran commands husbands to ensure their wives' security and well-being, granting them a dignified standard of living. Accommodation must be private and comfortable, and if the husband has multiple wives, fairness requires separate housing for each. The Prophet (PBUH) emphasized treating wives with kindness, ensuring they receive proper sustenance and clothing. Healthcare is also a husband's responsibility, covering medical treatment and hospital expenses. Neglecting these obligations can be grounds for legal action, allowing the wife to seek separation if necessary.

465. The husband is obligated to provide for his wife's maintenance, regardless of her financial status. Even if she is wealthy and he is poor, she has the absolute right to be supported at his expense in accordance with his financial capacity. This includes essential provisions such as food, clothing, housing, medical expenses, and other necessities. If the wife belongs to a social class that requires domestic assistance, the husband must also provide for servants. She is under no obligation to spend her own money on these essentials. If the husband persistently fails to provide for her, she may seek dissolution of marriage under Islamic laws, though in Hanafi jurisprudence, financial inability alone is not a valid ground for divorce. In contrast, other schools of thought, such as Maliki and Shafi'i, allow for dissolution if the husband is unable to support his wife.

466. Under section 9 of MFLO if any husband fails to maintain his wife adequately, or where there are more wives than one, fails to maintain them equitably, the wife, or all or any of the wives, may in addition to seeking any other legal remedy available apply to the Chairman of Union Council, who shall constitute an Arbitration Council to determine the matter, and the Arbitration Council may issue a certificate specifying the amount which shall be paid as maintenance by the husband. Any amount payable by Husband, not paid in the due time, shall be recoverable as arrears of land revenue. However, a husband or wife may, prefer an application for revision of the certificate, to the Collector and his decision shall be final and shall not be called in question in any Court.

467. Under sections 488–490 of the Criminal Procedure Code of Pakistan, if any person having sufficient means neglects or refuses to maintain his wife or his legitimate or illegitimate child unable to maintain itself, a Magistrate of the first class may, upon proof of such neglect or refusal, order such person to make a monthly allowance for the maintenance of his wife or such child, at such monthly rate, not exceeding PKR 400 in the whole, as the Magistrate thinks fit, and to pay the same to such persons as the Magistrate from time to time direct. If any persons fails without sufficient cause to comply with the orders of the Magistrate, the Magistrate may issue a warrant for levying of fine and sentence for the whole or any part of each month's allowance remaining unpaid after the execution of the warrant, to imprisonment for a term which may extend to one month or until payment if sooner made. However, no wife shall be entitled to receive an allowance from her husband under these sections if she is living in adultery or if without any sufficient reasons, she refused to live with her husband or if they are living separately by mutual consent.

468. Petitioner had failed to pay the maintenance allowance to his wife and children by the fourteenth day of each month during the pendency of the proceedings. In view of the callous disregard of the petitioner for the court order to pay interim maintenance and his attempts to delay the payment of decreed maintenance allowance for his minor children, the Supreme Court imposed costs in the sum of PKR 100,000 to deter such conduct in the future with the discretion that the costs shall be recovered by the executing court as part of the decree for maintenance. Petition was accordingly dismissed. (SC-2024 SCMR 1292).

469. Controlling Authority set aside order of Arbitration Council according to which past maintenance was granted to wife for a period of eleven years and four months prior to filing of application for grant of past and future maintenance by wife. Controlling Authority after setting aside order of Arbitration Council, granted past maintenance only for three years prior to riling of application for grant of maintenance. High Court found both orders of Authorities below as illegal and found wife entitled to past maintenance for a period of six years prior to filing of application for grant of maintenance as provided under Article 120, Limitation Act, 1908 (LHC – 1993 CLC 2063).

470. Maintenance allowance granted to wife for a period of three years by Arbitration Council reversed by Collector to the period of *Iddat*. Collector had based his finding on the judgment of Family Court whereby children of spouses were granted maintenance allowance from specified date and no past maintenance was allowed to them. Validity: Provisions of section 9, MFLO, 1961, provides maintenance to wife only, on entirely different grounds while Family Court is guided by the law laid down in West Pakistan Family Courts Act, 1964, where wife or the children can invoke their right of maintenance allowance which could not exceed period of six months retrospectively. District Collector had thus, erroneously based his judgment on the basis of decree of Family Court which was granted for maintenance of children of spouses. Judgment passed by District Collector was also devoid of all considerations that husband was bound to maintain his wife who had not demanded divorce and was mother of two children. Order passed by District Collector was completely devoid of reasons and application of mind to the facts, law and circumstances relevant to the case of wife. Order of Collector whereby he had reduced period of maintenance to wife was set aside and that of Arbitration Council which was completely legal and based upon true appraisal of evidence, was restored (LHC – 1995 CLC 914).

471. Petitioner filed suit for recovery of maintenance for herself and her daughters. Family Court and Lower Appellate Court fixed maintenance allowance to the extent of daughters only. Petitioner failed to discharge her part of obligation because factum of leaving house of respondent (husband) at her own was established on record. Petitioner was not entitled to past and future maintenance. High Court declined to interfere in concurrent finding of fact by two Courts below. Constitutional petition was dismissed, in circumstances. (Quetta High Court – 2024 MLD 1349).

472. Husband is under legal, moral and religious obligation to maintain his legally wedded wife. Under section 272 of Mohammdan law provides obligation of a husband to maintain his wife, if he fails to do so, wife may sue for maintenance. Hence, it is the obligation of husband to pay maintenance, if construed in accordance with the principles as laid down in 'HIDAYA' translated by Charles Hamilton in chapter XV such as 'Nafqa' in the language of law, signifies all those things which are necessary to support life, such as food, clothes and lodging. In present case, the Courts below had held the husband under obligation to pay maintenance allowance of the wife, which by no means was in deviation to law and Sharia. Father's obligation to maintain his children has reportedly been recognized and emphasized in law and Holy Quran. (LHC-2024 CLC 1580).

473. Chairman, Arbitration Council had jurisdiction to decide application of ex-wife for grant of maintenance for period during which marriage subsisted. Findings of Collector that Chairman Arbitration Council could not entertain application for maintenance by a wife who had already been divorced, were not valid. Past maintenance could be awarded by Arbitration Council for a period up to six years and the wife who had been divorced by husband, was also entitled to claim maintenance through application to Chairman, Arbitration Council. Husband, in the present case had not been able to, show that wife was divorced at the time when she filed application for maintenance. Order of Collector to the extent that Arbitration Council had no jurisdiction to award maintenance to wife, was illegal. Chairman, Arbitration Council was competent to, award different quantum of maintenance for different periods (reference MFLO 1961 section 9) (LHC – 2002 MLD 1716).

474. Petitioner was a British national who had divorced the respondent. Proceedings for recovery of past maintenance and that of the period of *Iddat* were initiated under section 9 of MFLO, 1961. Both the Courts below granted past maintenance along with period of *Iddat* for ninety days. Grievance of petitioner was that the Courts below had wrongly assumed jurisdiction in the matter as the petitioner was not a Muslim citizen of Pakistan and period of *Iddat* was thirty-nine days which was wrongly fixed as ninety days. Validity: Petitioner did not raise point of jurisdiction in the contents of the revision petition filed below; therefore, he was not permitted to argue the same before High Court in exercise of Constitutional jurisdiction. Judgments of both the Tribunals below to the extent of period of *Iddat* were not in accordance with the dictum laid down by Supreme Court in case titled *Allah Dad v. Mukhtar* reported as 1992 SCMR 1273. High Court modified judgments passed by both the Tribunals below to the extent that instead of granting maintenance of *Iddat* period consisting of ninety days, the same was reduced to thirty-nine days. Petition was disposed of accordingly (LHC – 2002 CLC 1964).

475. Wife of the petitioner/ respondent had approached Chairman, Union Council/respondent with application for maintenance on 9 January 1993. Two notices had been sent to the petitioner by the Chairman, Union Council which had returned undelivered and he had observed in the order sheet that neither of the notices had been received by the petitioner. Petitioner, thereafter was proceeded ex parte and after recording the evidence of the wife of the petitioner, the Chairman, Union Council ordered the petitioner to pay PKR 84,000 as past maintenance for seven years to his wife and minor daughter. Wife of the petitioner had filed the execution petition 6½ years after the order of the Chairman, Union Council while the period of limitation was clearly six years. If first application for execution had been filed within three years, the execution proceedings were patently time-barred. Petitioner had filed a revision petition when he received notice of the execution proceedings and the Deputy Commissioner without taking into consideration contentions of the petitioner that he had been condemned unheard had proceeded to dismiss his revision petition as being time-barred and also dismissed the review petition on merits. Order of the Chairman, Union Council suffered from three legal lacunas; first, Chairman Union Council had not effected service on the petitioner through citation published in some daily of the area where the petitioner resided as the notices had returned unserved and as required under MFLO; second the Chairman had awarded maintenance for seven years to the petitioner while under Article 120 of the Limitation Act, 1908, maximum period for which maintenance could be awarded was six years; and third, application of the wife of the petitioner for execution of decree of Chairman, Union Council had been filed after 6½ years, and therefore, it was time-barred. Orders of the Chairman Union Council and of Deputy Commissioner were declared to be of no legal effect and were set aside by the High Court (LHC – 2003 YLR 2445).

476. Mother invoked constitutional jurisdiction of the High Court to seek enhancement of maintenance allowance on the ground of daily growing requirements of minor. Held that the Family Court had exclusive jurisdiction to pass an order on the application under section 151 of Civil Procedure Code, 1908 for enhancement of the maintenance allowance even after the passing the final judgment. Constitutional petition was disposed of accordingly. (LHC-2024 MLD 145)

477. Maintenance: Wife specifically claimed maintenance for herself as also for three minor children. Though minors were not impleaded as parties in suit, but it was specifically averred that they were living with plaintiff's wife and that defendant husband was bound to maintain them. In written statement filed by defendant husband, there was no objection that minors should have been impleaded as parties. Both Courts below in circumstances had erred in non-suiting minors. Reference MFLO 1961, section 9 (LHC – 1991 CLC 784).

478. Application for maintenance has to be filed before Union Council where wife was residing at the time of making her application. Reference MFLO 1961. Section 9. West Pakistan Rules under MFLO, Rule 3. (LHC – 1989 MLD 905).

479. Husband assailed award of maintenance allowance to the wife on the ground that she herself had left the house of her own volition. Respondent levelled allegations of bad and disrespectful behaviour on part of the husband towards her and she deposed in her evidence that on account of torture inflicted by the husband upon asking for maintenance. Defence witnesses had admitted the date of desertion as well as the fact that the husband had not paid any amount of maintenance from the said date till dissolution of the marriage. Decree for maintenance was rightly passed in favour of the wife. (LHC-2022 CLC 634)

480. Record showed that father of the husband had undertaken, during the proceedings, that if his son will take any step which may give mental torture or cruel treatment to his wife or the husband will not perform matrimonial relationship, he will pay PKR 400,000 to the wife. Effect. Held, even the equity and natural justice demanded that the wife, who was neglected throughout by her husband and who was divorced by him at his whims and caprice, and she was left alone at the mercy of cruel circumstances in a male-dominated society, without any source of income, should be maintained by the divorcing husband who had acted without justification. High Court observed that Legislature, in Pakistan having the supreme power to enact and legislate law, may, if so, deemed fit, look into this aspect of the matrimonial life and make amendment in section 9, MFLO, 1961 enabling the Chairman, Arbitration. Council to grant maintenance to a destitute divorced wife and may enact separate provisions of law in the same Ordinance (LHC – 2004 CLC 473).

481. When Court had come to the conclusion that wife had developed such aversion for her husband as to justify dissolution of marriage on basis of '*Khula*', then wife was not entitled to either past or future maintenance on dissolution of marriage on basis of '*Khula*' (PHC – 1991 MLD 1732).

V. Maintenance of Children

482. Under Islamic law, the financial responsibility for the maintenance of children primarily rests on the father, even if their custody remains with the mother. A father is obligated to provide for his sons until they reach puberty and for his daughters until they get married. This includes their food, clothing, education, medical care, and other essential needs. If the father is unable to fulfil this duty, the responsibility then falls upon the paternal grandfather. The Quran emphasizes this duty in Surah Al-Baqarah (2:233), stating, '*But the father of the child shall bear the cost of the mother's food and clothing on a reasonable basis.*'

483. The father is required to support his children whether or not he remains married to their mother. Generally, maintenance is obligatory until the children reach the age of 15 or exhibit signs of maturity, making them capable of earning their livelihood. However, if a child is unable to support themselves due to disability or other circumstances, the father's obligation continues.

484. If the father lacks financial means and the mother is capable, she may voluntarily bear the expenses for her children. However, under Islamic law, she cannot demand compensation from the father for doing so. In the event that neither parent can provide for the children, other financially stable male relatives may be responsible. Islamic teachings emphasize that ensuring the well-being of children is a fundamental duty, reinforcing the importance of family support, fairness, and financial justice in society.

485. Islamic law establishes clear guidelines regarding a father's financial responsibility for his children. If custody (ḥaḍānah) of the children is granted to the father, he cannot relinquish this responsibility in exchange for not spending on them. A father is obligated to provide for his children under two primary conditions: (a) when they are unable to support themselves financially due to age, disability, or other reasons, and (b) when he possesses financial means beyond his own essential expenses and those of his wife. If the father has no surplus income after covering his necessary expenditures, he is not legally bound to provide for his children, and in such cases, other capable family members may assume responsibility. Islamic teachings strongly emphasize the fair and just distribution of financial responsibilities within the family. The Holy Prophet Muhammad (PBUH) stated,

'Start with yourself and spend on yourself first; if anything remains, spend it on your family, and if anything is left after that, spend it on your relatives.' (Reported by Imam Muslim). In another narration, he instructed, *'And begin spending on the members of your household.'* This highlights the importance of prioritizing financial obligations in an organized manner, first ensuring one's own sustenance, then fulfilling the needs of immediate family and finally extending assistance to other relatives when possible.

486. The Muslim man has to spend on his wife as long as she is his wife and also his children by providing food, shelter and proper education for them until the children become adults and become able to satisfy their own needs by themselves. He should also spend on his poor mother and his poor sisters (although there is a disagreement over spending on sisters) according to his own ability as Allah Says: (Let the rich man spend according to his means, and the man whose resources are restricted, let him spend according to what Allâh has given him … .) (65:7) He also has the right to save for the future and to invest from his own property. But he is not asked to do the same thing for his mother, sisters and children unless he has some money that belongs to them. In this case, he takes all appropriate steps that increase this money and protect it. The Pakistani Courts have categorically held in different cases that father of children is responsible for the maintenance of his children.

487. Maintenance allowance awarded to minor daughter. Father's suit for restitution of conjugal rights decreed but not put in execution. Wife along with minor daughter staying back from father and filing suit for maintenance. Maintenance allowance awarded to minor daughter, affirmed in appeal. Contention that minor daughter was unauthorizedly being kept away from father's custody not tenable in circumstances. Mother was entitled to retain custody of minor girl till she reaches age of puberty, unless mother was deprived of her custody through proceedings before competent forum. Child entitled to separate maintenance till mother was lawfully deprived of minor's custody. Minor could not be made to suffer because of rift between parents. Absolute duty of father to provide maintenance to his minor children regardless of fact where the Stay Order awarding maintenance allowance to child, held, well warranted both on facts and in law and not open to interference. Petition being devoid of merits, dismissed (LHC – 1985 CLC 487).

488. Maintenance allowance of the minor is legal and moral responsibility of the father coupled with the fact that it is an indispensable right of the minor, which is why an interim order for grant of maintenance allowance has to be passed at the convenient stage of the proceeding and the Family Court has to consider the interest and protection of the minor at the earliest. A father is not only legally but also morally under an obligation to meet the expenses of his minor regardless of the fact that the minor resides with him or his mother. Family Court has to take into consideration the subject interest of the minor at the earliest. Family Court has to adopt a pragmatic approach while fixing the interim maintenance under section 17-A of the Family Courts Act, 1964. (PHC – 2024 YLR 2841).

489. Respondent was the unmarried daughter of the petitioner (father), and she was studying in the university, thus, in order to meet her educational expenses, she required a sufficient amount. In Trial as well as Appellate Court the mother had sufficiently established with cogent evidence that besides receiving pension, the petitioner had other sufficient sources of income. Although the petitioner was not bound to provide the maintenance for education at higher levels, however, he was duty bound to provide maintenance to his daughter till she completed her graduation studies and gained an employment to support herself. The Appellate Court duly undertook expenses analysis and conducted that sum of PKR 25,000 per month was required to ensure the continuation of the studies of the daughter. Therefore, the amount of maintenance so granted was neither excessive nor unjustified. Petition was dismissed and leave was refused. (SC – 2024 PLD 581)

490. Custody of child retained voluntarily or against wishes of father by a person not entitled to custody. Liability of father to maintain such child. Scope. Father not liable to maintain a child separately, if latter keeps away or is kept away by someone not entitled to custody from his house without his consent. Father is bound to maintain an indigent child himself, but not through another, unless so directed by the Qazi or Court. Child already being voluntarily maintained by another does not stand in need of food, cloth or lodging, thus, cannot require father to pay maintenance. Person maintaining child of another voluntarily without reference to his father is not entitled to claim his maintenance from father. Where father is entitled to custody of minor son under personal law, then he cannot be forced to pay maintenance for him, if his wife/ex-wife retains his custody against his wishes. If father establishes that he had all along been anxious and made bona fide demands for custody of minor child, whose legal guardianship under personal law vested in him, then he can well defeat application for grant of maintenance of his child (LHC – 2004 YLR 768).

491. Petitioner five years old daughter was suffering from the Autism Spectrum Disorder. Interim maintenance allowance had been raised from PKR 20,000 to PKR 50,000 per month. Petitioner had served at eminent positions as neurosurgeon in Pakistan and abroad. Held, that reason for excessive interim maintenance was manifestly reflected in the impugned order that the child whose maintenance was in issue was an autistic child whose needs/requirements were indeed over and above and in excess of what were generally associated with typical five years old children. In the present days of massive inflation, especially in the case of an autistic child, could not be said to be unreasonable or even harsh. Amount fixed had a rational nexus with the requirements/needs of a differently abled child and therefore, was quite proportionate. Constitutional petition was dismissed in circumstances. (LHC – 2022 CLC 89)

492. Two courts below having changed the custody of minor from the petitioner/father to respondent/mother, petitioner had impugned said concurrent judgments in the Constitutional petition. Father had an obligation under law to provide maintenance to his minor children. Argument that mother had weak financial position as compared to the father, was misconceived. Father had contracted a second marriage, and he would have to remain out of his house for considerable time in connection with his daily pursuits. Minor could not be left to the surveillance of stepmother who could never be substitute for the real mother. Real mother had inherent right to keep her minor children close to her bosom. Intelligent preference of the minor while considering comparative rights of the real mother vis-a-vis the father, who had already contracted a second marriage, could be legitimately pushed to oblivion and that was what the two courts below had done. Well-reasoned findings of facts recorded by the two courts below, could not be interfered within Constitutional petition (LHC – 2009 CLC 1010).

493. Mother was capable of earning the good amount of money and provide for a child but to maintain the child is the obligation of father and his responsibility could not be absolved merely on the basis that the mother was an earning hand. Trial Court granted annual enhancement in maintenance allowance at the rate of 30%. Petitioner challenged annual enhancement being against statutory provisions. Keeping in view the increase in day to day needs of a minor, there existed strong factual basis for grant of annual increase in the maintenance of the child. (LHC – 2015 MLD 11)

VI. Sexual Intercourse

494. In Pakistan, sexual intercourse outside of marriage is strictly prohibited under both Islamic law and the country's legal framework. However, within the bounds of marriage, certain rights and responsibilities arise between spouses, including companionship, mutual support, and lawful intimacy. While consummation of marriage is an essential aspect of marital life, it is not obligatory immediately after the marriage ceremony and may take place when both spouses are ready. Under the **Dissolution of Muslim Marriages Act, 1939**, a wife has the legal right to seek divorce under specific circumstances, ensuring her protection and well-being. Grounds for divorce include the husband's absence for a continuous period of four years, his conviction and imprisonment for a term of seven years or more, or his failure to fulfil marital obligations without reasonable cause for a period of three years. Additionally, a wife may seek dissolution if the husband has been impotent since the time of marriage, treats her with cruelty, or suffers from an incurable mental or physical illness that makes cohabitation unbearable.

495. Islamic principles emphasize that marriage is built upon love, kindness, and mutual respect, ensuring that both spouses fulfil their roles responsibly. If a husband persistently neglects his duties, including providing emotional, financial, and physical support, the wife is granted the right to seek legal recourse for the protection of her rights. These provisions reflect the balance in Islamic law between upholding marital commitments and providing an avenue for relief in cases of injustice or hardship.

496. There are several court decision according to which impotency has been admitted to be ground for the annulment of marriage. However, the right of cancellation by the wife will not be allowed, if the incapacity supervened after the marriage had been consummated or if she had the knowledge of the fact of impotency of the man.

497. In Islamic jurisprudence, all four major schools of thought – Hanafi, Maliki, Shafi'i, and Hanbali – identify certain physical and mental defects that provide a legal basis for either spouse to annul the marriage if these conditions were undisclosed prior to the contract. These defects are broadly categorized into three groups: those applicable to both spouses, those exclusive to men, and those specific to women. Among the defects common to both men and women are insanity, leprosy, and vitiligo. Insanity can be either temporary or permanent, but in both cases, if it significantly affects the mental stability of a spouse and hinders the ability to fulfil marital duties, it constitutes valid grounds for dissolution. Leprosy, historically a highly contagious disease, and vitiligo, which causes noticeable skin depigmentation, may also serve as justifications for annulment, particularly if they cause social isolation or psychological distress.

498. For men, two specific conditions allow the wife to seek annulment. The first is permanent impotency, where the husband is physically incapable of consummating the marriage. In such cases, Islamic legal tradition allows the husband a grace period typically one year to seek treatment. If no improvement occurs, the wife has the right to dissolve the marriage. The second condition is the complete or partial removal of the reproductive organ, rendering marital relations impossible. If the wife was unaware of this before marriage, she may seek legal recourse to terminate the marriage.

499. For women, there are four recognized conditions that justify annulment. The first is a congenital or developed bony obstruction in the vaginal canal that prevents penetration. The second is a condition where the vaginal passage is completely sealed, making sexual relations impossible. The third is the presence of an abnormal opening between the urinary tract and the vaginal passage, which leads to continuous leakage and prevents normal marital intimacy. The fourth is excessive flesh growth or abnormal wetness in the vaginal area, which severely impairs intercourse.

500. Modern legal interpretations have expanded the scope of marital defects to include severe psychological disorders, genetic disorders that may affect offspring, and undisclosed chronic illnesses that impact the ability to maintain a marital relationship. In Pakistani legal practice, courts often require medical examinations to verify claims before granting annulments. Deception or concealment of such defects at the time of marriage may be considered fraud, further strengthening the affected spouse's right to seek dissolution.

§7. Polygamy (Second Marriage)

501. In Islam, polygamy is permitted, allowing a Muslim man to marry up to four women simultaneously, provided he upholds justice and fairness among them. However, in Pakistan, legal reforms under the *MFLO, 1961* have introduced regulatory measures to prevent the misuse of this provision. Under these laws, a husband intending to contract a second marriage must first seek permission from the local Union Council. He is required to submit a formal application along with a prescribed fee, explaining the necessity of the proposed marriage.

502. Upon receiving the application, the Chairman of the Union Council convenes an *Arbitration Council*, comprising representatives from both the husband and his existing wife or wives. The Council evaluates whether the additional marriage is justified based on reasonable grounds, such as infertility, chronic illness, or other compelling reasons. The husband's application must also specify whether he has obtained consent from his current wife or wives.

503. If a husband contracts a second marriage without prior approval from the Union Council, he is subject to penalties, which may include a fine and imprisonment. He becomes legally bound to make immediate payment of the dower (mehr) to his existing wife or wives. Despite these legal consequences, the second marriage remains valid under Islamic law, even if the formal permission was not obtained. However, failure to comply with the legal process can lead to civil and criminal proceedings, affecting the husband's legal standing.

504. Under the *MFLO, 1961*, a man is legally required to obtain prior written permission from the *Arbitration Council* before contracting a second marriage while his first marriage is still in effect. Any marriage entered into without such authorization cannot be officially registered. To seek approval, the husband must submit a formal application to the *Chairman of the Union Council*, outlining the reasons for the proposed marriage and indicating whether he has secured the consent of his existing wife or wives. The *Arbitration Council* will then review the application and assess the necessity and justification for the additional marriage.

505. Upon receiving the application, the Chairman of the Union Council shall require both the applicant and his existing wife or wives to nominate their respective representatives. These representatives along with the Chairman, will form the Arbitration Council, which will carefully examine the merits of the request. If the Arbitration Council is satisfied that the proposed marriage is both necessary and just, it may grant permission, subject to any conditions it deems appropriate.

506. When deciding an application, the Arbitration Council shall provide a recorded explanation for its decision. Any party may file a revision application with the Collector, whose decision shall be final and not subject to challenge in any court, as per section 6 of the MFLO.

507. When determining whether a proposed marriage is just and necessary during the subsistence of an existing marriage, the Arbitration Council may consider various factors, including but not limited to sterility, physical infirmity, inability to fulfil conjugal obligations, wilful non-compliance with a decree for restitution of conjugal rights, or insanity of the existing wife. This is in accordance with section 14 of the West Pakistan Rules under the MFLO, 1961.

508. An application for permission to contract another marriage while an existing marriage is in effect must be submitted in writing. It should indicate whether the consent of the current wife or wives has been obtained, include a brief statement of the reasons justifying the new marriage, bear the applicant's signature, and be accompanied by a fee of PKR 100, as per section 15 of the West Pakistan Rules under the MFLO, 1961.

509. Any man who contracts another marriage without obtaining permission from the Arbitration Council shall be required to immediately pay the full amount of dower, whether prompt or deferred, owed to his existing wife or wives. If unpaid, this amount shall be recoverable as arrears of land revenue. Upon conviction following a complaint, he shall be liable to simple imprisonment for up to one year, a fine of up to PKR 5,000, or both, as per section 6(5) of the MFLO.

510. Polygamy is a subject matter covered by section 6 of the MFLO, 1961, postulates that no man, during the subsistence of marriage, shall, except with the previous permission in writing of the Arbitration Council, contract another marriage, nor shall any such marriage contracted without such permission be registered under the MFLO, 1961. Sub section (5) of MFLO, 1961, stipulates consequences for contracting another marriage without permission of the Arbitration Council in terms of making him liable to pay immediately the entire amount to dower, whether prompt or deferred, due to existing wife or wives, if not so paid, to be recovered as arrears of land revenue and prescribes it to be an offence triable upon complaint and punishable on conviction with simple imprisonment which may extend to one year and with fine of PKR 5000. (LHC – 2023 YLR 2140)

511. Accused petitioners had been summoned by the Magistrate to face the trial in the private complaint filed by the respondent under section 6(5)(b) of MFLO, 1961. Validity: Provisions of section 6(5)(b) of MFLO, 1961, were meant for the prosecution and punishment of a person who had contracted second marriage without observing the legal formalities as provided in section 6 of the said Ordinance, and the same did not entail any punishment for a person who had abetted or facilitated the commission of the offence. MFLO, 1961, is a special law and unless the special law itself indicates about the application of certain penal provisions, the same cannot be applied or set into motion. Provisions of section 109, PPC, therefore, would not be attracted in the case, and only husband could be prosecuted or punished for the violation of the aforementioned provision. Simply signing of *Nikahnama* being a brother or friend of the bridegroom or to participate in his second marriage would not be an offence within the meaning of section 6 of the Ordinance, as one could be a witness of the *Nikah* between the spouses having taken place in his presence. Accused petitioners could not be saddled for the responsibility of anything wherein they were not a party, and similarly they could not be made responsible for any condition written in the *Nikahnama*. Summoning of the petitioners in the complaint filed under section 6(5)(b) of MFLO, 1961, was illegal and without jurisdiction. Proceedings pending before the Magistrate qua the petitioners were quashed accordingly (LHC – 2009 P Cr. L J 1189).

512. The petitioner challenged the orders of the Family Court and Additional Sessions Judge, Lahore, regarding her complaint under section 6(5) of the MFLO, 1961 against her husband for contracting a second marriage without the permission of the Arbitration Council. The complaint also accused other respondents of facilitating the marriage. The Family Court only summoned the husband and dismissed the complaint against the remaining respondents. The revision petition was also dismissed. The LHC upheld the lower courts' decisions, ruling that section 6 of MFLO only penalizes the husband for contracting a second marriage without permission and does not create an offense for facilitators. The Court held that abetment provisions under the PPC cannot be applied to expand the scope of MFLO. Consequently, the complaint against other respondents was rightly dismissed, and the petition was rejected in limine. (LHC-2023 MLD 6888)

513. The petitioner had instituted a private complaint under the section 6(5) of MFLO, 1961, with the allegation that he had contracted second marriage without her permission and thus, committed an offence. In complaint proceedings, an application under section 249-A of the Criminal Procedure Code, 1989 (CrPC), filed by the respondent was allowed on the assertion that he had already divorce the complainant. Held that while providing appeal in case of acquittal under section 417 of Cr.P.C. which stipulates that if such an order of acquittal is passed in any case instituted upon complaint and the High Court on an application made to it by the complainant in this behalf, grants special leave to appeal from the order of acquittal, the complainant may present such an appeal to the High Court. Acquittal order passed under section 249-A Cr.P.C., is not amenable to revisional jurisdiction as enriched in section 439-A Cr.P.C.. Criminal petition was dismissed in limine, in circumstances. (LHC-2024 P Cr. L J 1081)

514. Plea of husband that the court could not take cognizance of the offence on the complaint of the first wife since the Union Council had not itself complained to the court. Plea of husband that at the time of second marriage term of elected councillors had expired and local government elections had not been held, therefore, there was no Chairman of the Arbitration Council before whom he could apply for second marriage. Said plea was not sustainable because in the absence of elected representatives the administrator or another designated officer elected as the Chairman. Petition was leave to appeal was dismissed accordingly. (SC – 2017 PLD 187)

515. Suit for specific performance of agreement. Wife had granted permission to the husband to contract a second marriage on the condition that husband will continue to pay PKR 500 per month as maintenance and also transfer one residential room and one shop part of the house, belonging to husband and his father. Parties entered into an agreement incorporating the said conditions. Husband, on the basis of permission from the wife obtained a certificate from the Arbitration Council entitling him to have a second wife and thereafter he entered into second marriage. Husband did not fulfil the promise and instead divorced the first wife. Father of the husband, in divorce proceedings, affirmed that he had transferred the residential room in favour of the first wife of his son and volunteered that whenever she wanted he will execute the sale deed. Such promise was also not fulfilled. Wife filed suit for specific performance of their agreement which was tried and dismissed up to Appellate Court on the ground that the agreement between husband and wife was not enforceable as there was no consideration, and further the same was violative of section 27, Contract Act, 1872. High Court, in revision took the view that grant of permission to marry was a valid consideration for the agreement to transfer the specified property. Validity: Agreement was not without consideration in the facts and circumstances of the case. Provision of section 27, Contract Act, 1872 which otherwise was not attracted to the facts and circumstances of the case, gave way to the provision of section 3, MFLO, 1961 which provides that the Ordinance shall have overriding effect, notwithstanding the provision of any law to the contrary. Provision of section 6, MFLO, 1961 which placed a restraint on the right of the husband to enter into an additional marriage during the subsistence of the earlier marriage, except with the permission of the existing wife or in case of her refusal, with the permission of Arbitration Council, section 6 of the Ordinance, therefore, could not be said to be in conflict with the provision of section 27, Contract Act, 1872. Mandate of section 3, MFLO, 1961 had to prevail in any case. High Court, in circumstances, had rightly interfered in the exercise of revisional jurisdiction conferred by section 115, CPC as the Trial Court, and the Appellate Court had dismissed the suit on the wrong understanding of law that the agreement was without consideration or was violative of section 27 of the Contract Act, 1872 (SCP – 2003 PLD 128).

§8. Re-marriage

516. Under section 7(6) of the MFLO, 1961, if a divorce has not been pronounced three times, the wife may remarry the same husband without the requirement of an intervening marriage. However, if the husband has pronounced divorce three times (Talaq-e-Mughallazah), the wife is prohibited from remarrying him unless she enters into a valid marriage with another man and that marriage is consummated and subsequently dissolved through divorce or the husband's death (a process known as Halala).

517. Under Islamic law, if a husband irrevocably divorces his wife (Talaq-e-Mughallazah) by pronouncing divorce three times, he is prohibited from remarrying her unless she lawfully marries another man, the marriage is consummated, and is subsequently dissolved either through divorce or the husband's death (a process known as Halala). Any attempt to remarry without fulfilling this requirement renders the marriage void. This rule serves to discourage impulsive divorces and arbitrary reconciliations, ensuring that divorce is exercised with serious deliberation. It upholds the integrity of the marital bond, prevents the exploitation of women through cyclical divorces and remarriages, and reinforces public morality within the framework of Islamic principles.

518. According to Sharia, Khula operates as a single irrevocable divorce, which means that both the spouses can contract a fresh marriage with mutual consent, of course if they want to, without any intermediary marriage of the wife with another person, which is known as 'halala'. Iddat shall be incumbent upon the wife if she wants to contract marriage with someone else after khula. However, when a husband pronounces divorce to his wife for the third time and that attains finality, then if he wants to remarry that lady, a halala is required, i.e., the lady marries someone else and that marriage is dissolve in normal course either by divorce or due to the death of her second husband and she becomes a widow. (FSC – 2023 PLD 286)

519. Family Court decreed suit filed by wife for dissolution of marriage on ground of '*Khula*' and dissolved marriage between the parties in lieu of dower amount. Husband had challenged the decree in Constitutional petition. During pendency of Constitutional petition, application was filed praying therein to dispose of Constitutional petition in the light of settlement arrived at between the parties. Terms and conditions of said settlement were: that husband had undertaken to maintain wife and to provide her necessities and luxuries according to his status; that wife was ready to join husband as his wife; and that decree for dissolution of marriage by way of '*Khula*' be recalled and parties be allowed to remarry. Dissolution of marriage by way of '*Khula*' was pronounced by Family Court subject to return of dower amount by wife, but said amount of dower neither was returned by wife nor was the same accepted by husband. Pronouncement of '*Khula*' by Family Court, in circumstances, would amount to single divorce and until third divorce would take place, husband would be at liberty to remarry his wife again, and parties could join as husband and wife on solemnization of *Nikah* without intervention of third person (SHC – 2000 MLD 447).

520. As khula is a special and exclusive right given to a woman, which is not available to a man. She must out her offer before the court that she seeks release from the marriage by waiving her dower and only then court can grant her khula. Fundamentally, the principle is that khula cannot be granted, if has not been explicitly sought for by the woman. She can remarry the same man if she wants. (SC-2024 PLD 645)

§9. Void and Voidable Marriages

I. Impotency

521. Under the *Dissolution of Muslim Marriages Act, 1939*, a married woman has the legal right to seek the dissolution of her marriage if her husband was impotent at the time of marriage and remains so. The Court, upon satisfaction of this condition, may declare the marriage void. However, as per section 2(ii)(c) of the Act, before passing such a decree, the Court is required, upon the husband's application, to grant him a period of one year to prove that he has overcome his impotence. If the husband successfully demonstrates his potency within this period, no decree for dissolution shall be granted on this ground.

522. Under *Shariah (Islamic Law)*, the ruling on divorce in cases of a husband's impotence depends on the circumstances of the marriage. If the wife's rights are adversely affected due to her husband's impotence and she seeks dissolution, the husband is obligated to grant a divorce unless she willingly chooses to forgo this right. This is because marital intimacy is considered one of the fundamental rights of a wife. However, if the wife does not experience harm or willingly accepts her husband's condition, then there is no obligation upon the husband to divorce her. In such a case, divorce is generally discouraged, as there is no compelling reason for the dissolution of the marriage.

523. In cases where a husband is unable to consummate the marriage due to impotence, the wife has two options under *Islamic law*: she may either choose to remain in the marriage or seek a dissolution. According to *Māliki jurisprudence*, as stated by the scholar *An-Nafraawi*, if a wife discovers that her husband is incapable of fulfilling marital relations whether due to illness, magic, or any other cause, the court may grant the husband a one-year period to seek treatment and demonstrate his ability to perform marital duties. If he remains impotent after this period, the wife has the right to seek a divorce. However, if she was aware of his condition before marriage and consented to the union despite his impotence, she forfeits the right to dissolution on this ground.

524. If husband does not apply under Article 2(ii)(c) of the Dissolution of Muslim Marriage Act, 1939 for one-year period to satisfy the Court regarding his impotency, the dissolution of marriage would become effective after expiration of ninety days of the decision of Court (PHC – 1995 CLC 731).

525. Impotency means that husband is not in a position to perform sexual intercourse. Physical weakness does not reflect on potency. Physical weakness is not provided anywhere in Dissolution of Muslim Marriages Act, 1939 as ground for dissolution or marriage (LHC – 2003 CLC 1954).

526. Suit for dissolution of marriage on ground of impotency, non-payment of maintenance and cruelty. Husband in his written statement denied all the allegations including that of impotency and annexed his medical report as to prove potency. Held that for passing a decree on the ground of impotency of husband, the Family Court was not required to send the husband to appear before a medical board for its report. Family Court had to require the husband to satisfy within a period of one year from the date of his order that he had ceased to be impotent. If the husband would satisfy the court, the decree of dissolution of marriage should not be passed on the ground of impotency. Petitioner had not been treated by Family Court in accordance with law had been compelled to do which the law did not require him to do and had been deprived of the protection of law. Constitution petition was allowed accordingly. (PHC – 2022 CLC 1821)

527. Suit was filed by Hindu wife against her husband on grounds of impotency, imbalance of mind, cruelty, harshness and danger to her life from his hands. Trial Court, after hearing parties, decreed the suit. Judgment of Trial Court, though was not a reasonable and/or a detailed judgment, but when allegations of danger to life, ground of impotency and unsound mind of defendant husband had been raised by plaintiff, then defendant should have volunteered for examination as provided under Order XXXII, Rule-7, Code of Civil Procedure (CPC) whereby he could be referred to for medical examination (SHC – 2004 YLR 1666).

528. Decree for Dissolution of marriage was granted to wife by Family Court on ground of impotency of husband on only evidence furnished by lady doctor to the effect that hymen of the wife being intact, she was a virgin. According to settled medical and scientific phenomenon, fact of hymen being intact was not a conclusive proof of virginity, because hymen in certain cases is so flexible that it is not ruptured and at times was ruptured by incidence of first delivery. Evidence on record indicated that husband and wife had tried to produce their own medical certificates by consulting doctors themselves, but Court had not referred same for examination which had shown touch of personal involvement of Court. Better approach would have been to get the parties medically examined through Court. Application filed by husband under the Dissolution of Muslim Marriages Act, 1939, was also not considered by Family Court before passing decree for Dissolution of marriage on ground of impotency of husband. Family Court had acted without jurisdiction and also had exercised jurisdiction not vested in it as Family Court could not pass decree for Dissolution of marriage on the ground of impotency of husband, unless, on application of husband, he was required to satisfy the Court within one year from the date of such order that he had ceased to be impotent. If husband so satisfies the Court within such period qua the same woman involved, no decree for Dissolution of marriage would be passed on ground of impotency. Judgment of Family Court was set aside, and case was remanded to be decided afresh after complying with provisions of proviso (e) of section 2(v) of Dissolution of Muslim Marriages Act, 1939 (PHC – 1998 MLD 1216).

II. Cruelty

529. The courts have the authority to declare a marriage void if the husband subjects his wife to cruelty, as outlined under the Dissolution of Muslim Marriage Act, 1939. Cruelty is not limited to physical violence but extends to various forms of mistreatment, including habitual assault, emotional and psychological abuse, and conduct that makes the wife's life intolerable through verbal humiliation, coercion, or persistent neglect. Moral misconduct, such as associating with women of ill repute, leading an infamous life, or attempting to force the wife into immoral activities, also falls within the ambit of cruelty. Additionally, financial exploitation, including depriving the wife of her property, misappropriating her assets, or obstructing her from exercising her financial rights, can be grounds for dissolution of marriage. Religious oppression, where a husband prevents his wife from practicing her faith or interferes with her religious observances, is another form of mistreatment recognized under the law. In cases of polygamy, if the husband fails to treat co-wives equitably as mandated by Islamic injunctions, it may also constitute cruelty. Contemporary legal interpretations consider other forms of cruelty, such as abandonment, refusal to provide financial maintenance, imposing unjustified restrictions on the wife's movement, severing her communication with family, and making false accusations, all of which may cause severe mental distress and serve as valid grounds for seeking dissolution of marriage.

530. Cruelty by husband was asserted by wife. Wife claimed that after four months of marriage she was diagnosed with breast cancer which strained the relationship between the spouses and the attitude of the husband kept worsening and he subject her to mental, physical and psychological torture. Family Court decreed the dissolution of marriage on the basis of cruelty. Record revealed that the defendant had never inquired about the mental health of his wife and not have given a single penny for her maintenance or medical treatment. High Court dissolved the marriage on the basis of cruelty and allowed the past maintenance to the extent that the ex-wife was entitled to the same from the date of institution of the suit till her iddat period. Constitutional petition of the wife was allowed, in circumstances. (PHC – 2023 MLD 1237)

531. Plaintiff in her suit had alleged that behaviour and treatment of defendant husband towards her, had become cruel, and he started beating and abusing her and had resorted to ill and inhuman treatment against her. Wife had alleged that in view of said inhuman and cruel treatment of husband, she had suffered from severe spiritual and mental torture and had developed extreme disliking against the husband with whom she could not live in any case within the limits ordained by Allah. Family Court dismissed suit holding that allegation against husband had not been proved. Wife had contended that when it was made clear before the Family Court that spouses could not live within the limits ordained by Allah, it was obligatory for Family Court to have dissolved the marriage on basis of '*Khula*' even if cruelty or other grounds as alleged by her were not proved. Validity: Wife had throughout maintained that she could not live with the husband against whom she had developed severe hatred and disliking. Said state of affairs itself had made out a case for '*Khula*' even if her pleas of torture, beating, etc., were not proved. Wife was at liberty to take up plea of '*Khula*' before High Court in appeal, even if said plea was not specifically taken before Family Court. Dissolution of marriage on ground of '*Khula*' was a pure question of law and could be raised even before the highest Court of Appeal. Such plea would not require any evidence as it was the statement of plaintiff/wife alone which was the determining factor in case of '*Khula*'. Aversion, disliking, hatred, incompatibility of temperaments, mental, intellectual, social, cultural or ideological disparity or conflict, which had the apprehension of disturbing the family life and happiness, were sufficient grounds for wife to seek '*Khula*'. Wife was empowered to get marriage cancelled on any reason whatsoever, whether husband was at fault or not. Unfettered powers of husband were counter balanced by right of wife to obtain dissolution of marriage through Court subject to condition that if husband was not at fault, she was to compensate him and if he was found at fault, she was not to pay anything. Said right of wife could not be made hostage to husband's pleasure. When relations between the spouses had become so strained that they could not live together in accordance with limits ordained by Allah, Family Court should have dissolved marriage on ground of '*Khula*'. High Court accepting appeal, set aside judgment and decree of Family Court, and decree of dissolution of marriage was passed in favour of wife on '*Khula*' subject to payment of dower amount to the husband (Shariat Court, Azad Kashmir – 2004 CLC 17).

532. Wife alleged that due to the cruelty of her husband she was compelled to leave his place and live with her parents where minor daughter was born. Petitioners suit was partially decreed entitling the wife to receive maintenance for her iddat period only and delivery expenses and minor was awarded past and future maintenance allowance since her birth. Held that for proving herself entitled to the recovery of past maintenance, petitioner could not prove the fact that she had been compelled to leave the house on account of cruelty. High Court partially allowed the Constitutional petition and deemed the question of return of dowry articles pending before Family Court and directed that the same to be decided in view of evidence on record and not on the basis of said presumptions. (LHC-2023 MLD 51)

533. Cruelty in matrimonial life is considered to be of founded variety, which may be an act violent or non-violent act, gestures, or mere silence. Term 'cruelty' with reference to matrimonial matter is to be judged within the parameters of statutory provision of section 2 of Dissolution of Marriage Act, 1939, which speaks of different kinds and natures of cruelty. The term 'cruelty' not only confined to physical assault or infliction of physical injuries rather it, being a comprehensive term as elaborated in the statutory provision which includes all types of cruelty which may be classified as legal, mental and physical. Non-providing of maintenance itself is a form of cruelty which serves as one of the grounds on which the decree for dissolution of marriage can be passed. (SC Azad Kashmir – 2022 PLD 1)

534. Petitioner assailed the judgements and decrees passed by courts below. Bone of contention between the parties was an iqrarnama whereby the wife had returned the gold ornaments which were earlier handed over to her. Husband had failed to rebut that he had treated his wife with cruelty and that she had left his house of her own volition. Husband had not produced even a single witness to support his stance or for that matter to say a word in rebuttal to that story put forward by the wife and her witnesses. Constitutional petition being devoid of merits was dismissed, in circumstances. (PHC – 2021 MLD 288)

III. Idiocy or Lunacy

535. Under the Dissolution of Muslim Marriage Act, 1939, a wife has the right to seek a decree for the dissolution of her marriage if her husband has been suffering from insanity for a continuous period of at least two years, or if he is afflicted with a severe and incurable disease such as leprosy or a virulent venereal infection. The rationale behind this provision is to protect the wife from enduring undue hardship, emotional distress, and the risk of contagion. Insanity, in this context, refers to a mental condition that renders the husband incapable of fulfilling his marital obligations, including providing companionship, financial support, and a stable environment. Courts also consider whether the mental illness is treatable or if it has reached an advanced stage where recovery is improbable. Similarly, diseases such as leprosy or severe venereal infections, which are highly contagious and can pose a significant health risk to the wife, are valid grounds for dissolution of marriage. The law recognizes that a wife should not be compelled to remain in a marriage where her well-being, dignity, and physical health are compromised. However, before granting a decree, courts may assess medical evidence to determine the severity and incurability of the condition, ensuring that the decision aligns with principles of fairness and justice.

IV. Consent Obtained by Force or Fraud

536. . If a woman's consent to marriage is obtained through coercion, undue influence, or fraud, such a marriage is considered voidable, and the court has the authority to annul it. Under Islamic law and the Dissolution of Muslim Marriage Act, 1939, a woman has the right to seek dissolution of marriage if she was married off by her father or guardian before reaching the age of 16 and subsequently repudiates the marriage before turning 18, provided that the marriage has not been consummated. This provision is aimed at protecting young girls from forced or child marriages, ensuring that they have the autonomy to decide their future once they attain maturity. Additionally, fraudulent consent may include misrepresentation about the husband's identity, concealment of critical facts such as a pre-existing marriage, criminal record, or serious medical condition. In such cases, the wife has legal grounds to seek annulment of the marriage. Courts carefully assess evidence to determine whether coercion or fraud was involved, ensuring that a woman's right to enter into marriage with free will and informed consent is upheld.

537. Under section 4 of The Prohibition of Forced Religious Conversion Act, 2019 addresses the issue of **forced marriages linked to forced conversions**, declaring that any marriage that occurs as a result of forced conversion is **invalid**. Legal action will be taken against those who engage in or facilitate such marriages.

538. Lady, in her pleadings categorically contended that she was abducted by the man with the help of his companions and thereafter, without her freewill and accord entered into a marriage contract with her and eventually on the intervention of the respectables of the area she was restored to her parents, and during this period the man started claiming her as his legally wedded wife. Claim of the lady, being in negative form and nature, obviously she could not have been burdened to substantiate the same by producing further evidence that she did not, in the exercise of her own free will and accord, entered into a contract of marriage. Record also showed that the alleged *Nikah* was not performed even in the District where the lady was ordinarily residing rather, hundreds of miles away from her place of ordinary abode. Stated *Nikah* was registered and performed in a mosque, where no relative, friend or any other acquaintance of the bride was present, therefore, in such a situation, the evidence of lady which withstood the test of cross-examination was sufficient to convince that she did not enter into contract of marriage out of her own freewill in exercise of her right of option. Lady, therefore, succeeded in discharging the onus of the issue and thereupon the burden shifted to the man to rebut the same through evidence that *Nikah* between the parties was validly and lawfully performed by the lady in exercise of her free will being the persona majora, who consented for the same and thereby entered into the contract of marriage by performance of *Nikah.* Man, in peculiar facts and circumstances of the case, was obliged to have proved the factum of performance of a valid *Nikah,* and such onus on him could not have been successfully discharged unless the witnesses of *Nikah* and other witnesses in whose presence lady allegedly appointed the cited witness in the *Nikahnama* to act as her Wakil for *Nikah,* was produced, which in the present case was completely wanting. Material evidence in the case having been misread, misconstrued and misapplied by the lower forums that is, Family Court and the Appellate Court, by upholding the marriage as valid one, interference of High Court in exercise of its Constitutional jurisdiction, was very much called for to rectify the manifest error committed by them in the exercise of their jurisdiction (SCP – 2006 PLD 489).

539. Kidnapping, abducting or inducing woman to compel for marriage , cohabitation caused by a man deceitfully inducing a belief of lawful marriage. FIR was registered against the accused with the allegation that he along with another had abducted complainants' younger daughter. Held that the accused had contracted second marriage and committed Zina. The marriage according to the given record is irregular but the same could not be treated as void. Petitioner for cancellation of bails were dismissed, in circumstances. (ISB-2020 PLD 443)

V. Prohibited Marriages

540. Under Islamic law, marriage between certain relatives is strictly prohibited, as outlined in the Shari'ah. These prohibitions serve to preserve the sanctity of family ties and maintain a morally and socially stable society. The primary rationale behind these restrictions is to prevent potential conflicts, protect genetic integrity, and uphold the natural bonds of respect and care among close relatives. The Qur'an explicitly forbids marriage with direct blood relatives, including parents, children, siblings, and their descendants. Additionally, prohibitions extend to close kin such as paternal and maternal aunts and uncles, nieces and nephews, as well as in-laws under specific circumstances. Foster relationships established through breastfeeding (raḍā'ah) are also subject to marital prohibitions, ensuring that milk kinship holds the same sanctity as biological ties. These restrictions not only safeguard the fundamental structure of family life but also prevent potential exploitation and moral corruption within households.

541. In the Holy Quran (Sura Al-Nisa) it is stipulated that:

> And marry not women whom your fathers married – except what has been done in the past: it was shameful and odious – an abominable practice indeed. Prohibited to you [for marriage] are your mothers, daughters, sisters, your maternal and paternal aunts, the daughters of your brothers and sisters; your mothers who have suckled you and your sisters through fosterage, the mothers of your wives, your step-daughters raised under you born of your wives with whom you have lain – no offence if you have not lain with their mothers, and the wives of your begotten sons, and two sisters in wedlock at the same time, except for what has already happened. God indeed is Oft-Forgiving, Most Merciful. Also [prohibited are] women already married, except those whom your right hands possess; this is a written obligation upon you from God. (4:22-4).

542. According to *Surah Al-Nisaa* 4: 23, the relations prohibited for marriage are as follows:

Relations by Birth (or Direct Relations):

- Mothers;
- Daughters;
- Sisters.

Indirect Relations:

- Father's sisters;
- Mother's sisters;
- Sisters' daughters; and
- Brothers' daughters.

Relations by Fosterage:

- Foster Mothers; and
- Sisters on the basis of fosterage.

Relations by Marriage:

- Wives' mothers;
- Wives' daughters, if conjugal relation has been established with the wife;
- Wives of real sons; and
- Wives' sisters, while the wife is still in marriage.

Chapter 2. Divorce

§1. Grounds of Muslim Divorce

543. In Islamic law, a Muslim man of sound mind who has attained puberty has the right to divorce his wife at any time without providing a specific reason. In Pakistan, the dissolution of marriage can occur in the following ways: (i) by the husband's unilateral pronouncement of divorce (Talaq) without court intervention; (ii) by mutual consent of the husband and wife, without requiring court involvement, known as Khula or Mubarat, depending on the nature of the agreement; and (iii) through a judicial decree initiated by either spouse. While a wife does not have the unilateral right to divorce her husband without his consent, she may obtain a judicial divorce under the Dissolution of Muslim Marriage Act, 1939, if she meets specific legal grounds, such as cruelty, desertion, or failure to provide maintenance. Additionally, if the husband has granted her the right of delegated divorce (Talaq-e-Tafweez) in the Nikahnama (marriage contract), she can dissolve the marriage without requiring his further consent. Talaq must be pronounced in accordance with Islamic principles, and under the MFLO, 1961, the husband is required to notify the relevant Arbitration Council for the divorce to be legally effective. In the case of Khula, the wife must return the dower (Mahr) or any agreed compensation to the husband in exchange for the dissolution of marriage.

544. According to the four major schools of Islamic jurisprudence, Hanafi, Maliki, Shafi'i, and Hanbali, there are specific defects that may grant a spouse the right to either continue the marriage or seek its annulment. These defects are categorized into those common to both men and women, those specific to men and those specific to women. The defects common to both spouses include insanity, leprosy, and vitiligo, as these conditions can severely impact marital life. For men, specific defects include impotence and the complete loss of the male organ which would render marital intimacy impossible. In the case of women, defects that may justify annulment include congenital or acquired physical conditions that obstruct intercourse, such as a bone or flesh growth inside the vagina, an imperforate hymen (a closed vaginal passage), an abnormal connection between the vaginal and urinary tracts, or excessive vaginal wetness that prevents sexual fulfilment.

545. If one spouse is aware of the other's defect at the time of marriage and consents to the union despite it, the marriage remains valid. However, if a spouse discovers such a defect only after the marriage and it significantly impairs the ability to fulfil marital obligations, he or she has the right to seek annulment through the proper judicial process. In Islamic law, the purpose of allowing annulment on these grounds is to ensure fairness and protect the well-being of both spouses, recognizing that physical and psychological factors play a crucial role in a successful marital relationship.

I. Divorce by Mutual Consent

546. Both the husband and wife have the legal and religious right to dissolve a marriage by mutual consent. In Islamic law, marriage is considered a civil contract, and like any other contract, it can be terminated by the agreement of both parties. This form of dissolution, known as *Mubarat*, allows both spouses to part ways amicably without the need for judicial intervention. Additionally, the wife may seek *Khula*, a form of dissolution initiated by her, which requires her to return the *Mahr* (dower) or other agreed compensation if the husband consents. On the other hand, the husband retains the unilateral right to pronounce *Talaq*, subject to the conditions set forth in Islamic law and the MFLO, 1961. A marriage is automatically dissolved upon the death of either spouse, bringing an immediate and natural termination to the marital bond. In such cases, the widow must observe *Iddah*, a prescribed waiting period of four months and ten days, as mandated by Islamic teachings, before she can remarry. If the wife is pregnant at the time of her husband's death, the *Iddah* extends until childbirth.

547. Islam permits dissolution of marriage between Muslims spouses in three ways, i.e., Talaq, Mubarat, and Khula. Mubarat is a form of dissolution of marriage whereunder spouses may agree to part their ways through mutual consent. In present case despite the efforts, parties did not arrive at any reconciliation and the wife was not willing to reconcile with her husband at any cost and both decided to part ways from each other. Constitutional petition was dismissed in circumstances. (LHC-2024 CLC 1648)

548. If spouses decide to separate with mutual consent and a document in the shape of divorce is prepared and is signed by the husband, divorce becomes final for all intents and purposes, and the husband thereafter cannot withdraw the divorce, and the Chairman, Union Council is bound to register the same under section 8 of MFLO, 1961 (LHC – 1995 P Cr. L J 1247 Islamic Law).

549. Detenue admitting her marriage with petitioner and wishing to go with him. Detenue's previous marriage with one 'B' allegedly subsisting as no Divorce from 'B' effected. Offence of Bigamy and *Zina* allegedly committed. Court on enquiry, finding performance of marriage of detenue with 'B' as Vatta in lieu of which sister of 'B' married to brother of detenue. Later relations between 'B' and detenue becoming strained, and both marriages were decided to be mutually dissolved. Divorce deed executed. 'B' admitting execution of divorce deed. Detenue believing to be divorced under mutual agreement, contracting second marriage with petitioner. Divorce by mutual agreement, held, was in nature of Mubarat and had become irrevocable from date of its execution and provision of revocation in section 7 of Family Laws Ordinance was inapplicable in circumstances (LHC – 1987 CLC 1496).

550. Parties had handed over and taken over articles of dowry, therefore, parties case was not covered by section 7, but under section 8, MFLO, 1961. No special procedure having been prescribed under section 8 of the Ordinance, provisions of section 7, MFLO, 1961, have been made applicable, subject, however, to conditions of 'so far as applicable'. Provision of section 7 of the Ordinance deals only with divorce by husband and cases of other forms of divorce recognized by Islam would not be covered by it. Divorce having been effected by parties through mutual agreement, same was 'Talaq Mubaraat' and irrevocable. Divorce deed having been executed between parties of free will and benefits taken thereof, such course would disentitle husband of any relief against issue of divorce certificate in Constitutional jurisdiction (LHC – 1997 CLC 1985).

II. Divorce by Husband

551. Under Muhammadan Law and the MFLO, 1961, a husband retains the inherent right to unilaterally pronounce divorce (Talaq), a prerogative that cannot be revoked. However, this right may be regulated or restricted through specific stipulations in the Nikahnama, allowing for certain conditions to be imposed to ensure procedural safeguards and fairness in the dissolution of marriage.

552. Under the MFLO, 1961, a husband who pronounces divorce, irrespective of its form, is legally required to provide written notice to the Chairman of the Union Council at the earliest opportunity. The Chairman is then responsible for delivering a copy of this notice to the wife. Failure to comply with this requirement is a punishable offense, carrying the possibility of imprisonment and/or a monetary fine. Upon receiving the notice, the Chairman must, within thirty days, establish an Arbitration Council to facilitate reconciliation efforts between the spouses. If these efforts do not result in a resolution and the divorce remains unrevoked either explicitly or implicitly, the dissolution of marriage becomes effective after ninety days from the date the notice was initially served. However, if the wife is pregnant at the time of divorce pronouncement, the divorce does not take legal effect until the later of either ninety days or the conclusion of the pregnancy.

553. The complainant (husband) alleged that the accused, including the woman's father, maternal uncle, close relative, and second husband, had forged a divorce deed and used it as genuine. However, the accused contended that the complainant had already divorced the woman, and she later married her second husband, as reflected in the marriage registration certificate. During legal proceedings under section 491, Cr.P.C., the woman denied her relationship with the complainant. She later recorded a statement under section 164, Cr.P.C., affirming the accused's innocence. Additionally, she filed a harassment petition against the complainant. The prosecution admitted that the complainant was avoiding the legal process by not producing the woman for her statement under section 161, Cr.P.C., which indicated mala fide intent. The case is based on documentary evidence, and the petitioners had already joined the investigation. None of the alleged offenses fell within the prohibitory clause of section 497, Cr.P.C.; sections 468 and 471, PPC were non-cognizable, while section 420, PPC was bailable. The court accepted the petition for pre-arrest bail and confirmed the ad-interim bail. The petitioners were required to furnish fresh bail bonds of PKR 100,000 each with one surety in the like amount to the satisfaction of the trial court. (LHC-2020 P Cr. L J Note 182)

554. Divorce pronounced thrice in one sitting becomes effective immediately and, in such eventuality, the question of its revocation does not arise under MFLO section 7(3) (LHC – 1990 CLC 1683).

555. Divorce pronounced by the husband upon the wife having not been revoked, had become effective after the expiry of ninety days from the date of receipt of notice by the *Nazim*/Chairman, Arbitration Council in view of MFLO sections 7(3) and (5) (LHC – 2004 PLD 316).

556. The petitioner challenged the judgments of the Family Court and the Appellate Court, which dissolved her marriage through Khula and dismissed her claims for dower, dowry articles, and increased maintenance allowance. She argued that her marriage should be considered dissolved through her husband's subsequent pronouncement of talaq rather than by the court's Khula decree. However, the court held that once the Family Court had granted Khula, the husband's later pronouncement of talaq had no legal effect. The court emphasized that Khula is irrevocable and not subject to appeal, and since the petitioner had already invoked this right, her husband's subsequent talaq did not alter the legal standing of the case. Consequently, the court dismissed the petition, affirming the lower courts' decisions. (ISB-2021 YLR 1753)

557. Provisions of section 7 of MFLO, 1961 had stipulated three steps to pronounce divorce: first, it had to be verbally pronounced; as mandated by Shariat; second, the same be pronounced in any form whatsoever, which would mean that in any prevalent mode that is, one's own language or in Arabic as some sects prescribed in that behalf; third, verbal pronouncement of divorce had to be reduced into writing and had to be conveyed to the Chairman of Union Council with a copy to the wife. Failure to strictly comply with said procedure would not, invalidate divorce. Necessary requirement or ingredients of divorce was a conscious and wilful pronouncement of divorce with intention to release wife from marriage bond. Failure to follow said procedure could entail or be followed by punishment prescribed under succeeding sub-section (2) of section 7 of MFLO, 1961, but validity of divorce or separation of spouses from the marriage bond would not be affected (FSC – 2004 YLR 619).

558. SCP, Azad Kashmir (2004 CLC 984) held that divorce deed was not the requirement of law to be written on a stamp paper under MFLO.

III. Divorce by Wife

559. A wife may unilaterally dissolve her marriage only if the husband has explicitly and unconditionally granted her the right to divorce through Clause 18 of the Nikahnama (marriage contract) at the time of the marriage ceremony. This delegation of authority must be clearly stated in the contract to ensure the wife's legal ability to exercise this right without requiring further consent or approval from the husband.

560. Under Islamic law, the authority to dissolve a marriage primarily rests with the husband as he holds the unilateral right to pronounce divorce (Talaq). A wife, on the other hand does not have the independent right to divorce unless the husband grants her this authority, either at the time of the marriage contract or afterward. This authorization, known as *Talaq-e-Tafweez*, allows the wife to initiate divorce under agreed-upon conditions. The majority of Islamic scholars recognize this delegation as legally valid and enforceable. A woman can seek dissolution of marriage through *Khula*, a judicial divorce granted by the court, if she has valid grounds, such as mistreatment, financial neglect, or irreconcilable differences.

561. The petitioner filed a writ petition challenging the judgments of the Additional District Judge-IV and the Family Court-XI, Abbottabad, seeking the restitution of conjugal rights, recovery of a car, and modification of the decree for dower and maintenance allowances. The case originated when respondent filed a suit for recovery of past and future maintenance for their daughter and dower. She claimed that she was subjected to physical and mental abuse, leading her to exercise her right of *Talaq-e-Tafweez* as granted in Column No. 18 of the *Nikah Nama*. The trial court ruled in her favour, granting the dower and maintenance for the child while awarding the petitioner the recovery of a car. On appeal, the court modified the decree, adjusting the maintenance and reversing the car recovery decision. The petitioner argued that *Talaq-e-Tafweez* should be equated with *Khula*, making the dower claim invalid, and contested the financial assessment for maintenance. The respondent countered that her delegated right of divorce was lawfully exercised and effective after ninety days. The court upheld the validity of *Talaq-e-Tafweez*, citing Islamic and legal precedents, affirming that a husband can delegate divorce rights, and once exercised, it is irrevocable. Held that the respondent was rightfully entitled to her dower and maintenance, dismissing the petitioner's claims. (PHC – 2013 CLC 1625)

562. Delegated right of divorce given to wife was exercised by her, but no notice was sent to Chairman Arbitration Council. Subsequently husband divorced his wife; sent notice to Chairman Arbitration Council and divorce became effective. Wife filed suit for recovery of dower amount, which was dismissed by Family Court being barred by limitation on the ground that divorce had already been effected when she had exercised her right. Appeal filed by wife was also dismissed by Appellate Court. Plea raised by wife in the Constitutional petition was that divorce did not become effective, after her exercise of such right, as no notice to the Chairman was given by her. Validity: No notice was served in terms of section 7 read with section 8 of MFLO, 1961, and result was that prescribed period of ninety days never started running so as to make divorce effective at any time after exercise of such right by wife. Divorce pronounced by wife in exercise of her delegated right of divorce never took effect and divorce pronounced by husband did take effect on expiry of ninety days, when notice was delivered to Chairman Arbitration Council. Suit brought by wife was within the period of three years as prescribed in Articles 103 and 104 of Limitation Act, 1908. Judgments and decrees dismissing suit of wife for recovery of dower amount on the sole ground that the claim was barred by time, were declared to be without lawful authority and were set aside. Suit filed by wife for recovery of dower amount against husband was decreed by High Court in exercise of Constitutional jurisdiction. Petition was allowed accordingly (LHC – 2007 CLC 1009).

563. Power to give divorce, though belonged to husband, but he could delegate said power to wife or to third person, either absolutely or conditionally and either for a particular period or permanently. Section 7 of MFLO, 1961 had specifically provided such divorce which was known as 'Talaq-e-Tafweez'. Person, to whom power was so delegated, could then pronounce same accordingly. Temporary delegation of power was irrevocable, but a permanent delegation could be revoked. Such delegation of option called 'Tafweez' by husband to his wife would confer on her power of divorcing herself. Said 'Tafweez' was of three kinds viz., Ikhtiar, giving her authority to Talak herself; AmrbaYed, leaving the matter in her own hand; and Mashiat, giving her the option to do what she liked. All these factors when analysed would resolve themselves into one, viz., leaving it on her or somebody else's option to do what she/he liked. Wife could not sue to enforce authority alleged to have been given to her, but she would sue after she had given effect to it to make husband liable for dower or to restrain him from seeking conjugal relations. Wife was entitled to exercise her right of 'Tafweez of Talaq', and she was entitled to be separated from her husband (LHC – 2006 YLR 335).

564. One of the conditions of the marriage between parties was that husband had delegated the right to divorce wife and entry to that effect was made in Column No. 18 of *Nikahnama*. Wife in exercise of said right pronounced divorce upon herself for her husband, and a notice was sent to *Nazim* Union Council concerned. *Nazim* had intimated wife that husband being not ready to pronounce divorce, wife could approach the Court as he could not grant '*Khula*', and *Nazim* sent the case to the Family Court. *Nazim* was oblivious of legal position as right of divorce could be lawfully delegated by husband to wife, and that had happened in the present case and notice was sent by wife in compliance with the terms of sections 7 and 8 of MFLO, 1961. Ninety days prescribed period having expired after receipt of notice issued by wife and reconciliation being not possible between the parties, law as prescribed in sections 7(3) and 8 of MFLO, 1961 would have its course. *Nazim* would issue requisite document regarding receipt of notice and failure of reconciliation within prescribed time (LHC – 2004 PLD 77).

IV. Divorce Through Judicial Process ('*Khula*')

565. . A wife has the legal right to seek the dissolution of marriage through a judicial process by approaching the Family Courts. The primary legal mechanisms available to her include *Khula* and judicial divorce, which also encompasses the *option of puberty*. *Khula* refers to the wife's right to unilaterally dissolve the marriage by returning the dower or any agreed-upon compensation, whereas judicial divorce is granted on specific legal grounds, such as cruelty, desertion, or failure to provide maintenance. Notably, *Khula* may be granted by the court without the husband's consent if the wife voluntarily relinquishes her financial claims, including dower. In contrast, a judicial divorce requires the wife to establish valid reasons as per the law. Both forms of dissolution ensure that the wife can lawfully exit an irreparable marriage while adhering to legal and procedural requirements.

566. Under the Dissolution of Marriage Act, 1939 a married woman is entitled to obtain a decree for dissolution of her marriage on any one or more of the following grounds, namely:

- that the whereabouts of the husband have not been known for a period of four years;
- that the husband has neglected or has failed to provide for her maintenance for a period of two years;
- that the husband has taken an additional wife in contravention of the provisions of MFLO;
- that the husband has been sentenced to imprisonment for a period of seven years or upwards;
- that the husband has failed to perform, without reasonable cause, his marital obligations for a period of three years;
- that the husband was impotent at the time of the marriage and continues to be so;
- that the husband has been insane for a period of two years or is suffering from leprosy or a virulent venereal disease;
- that she, having been given in marriage by her father or other guardian before she attained the age of 16 years, repudiated the marriage before attaining the age of 18 years; provided that marriage has not been consummated;
- that the husband treats her with cruelty, that is to say: habitually assaults her or makes her life miserable by cruelty of conduct even if such conduct does not amount to physical ill-treatment; or associates with women of evil repute or leads an infamous life; or attempts to force her to lead an immoral life; or disposes of her property or prevents her from exercising her legal rights over it; or obstructs her in the observance of her religious profession or practice; or if he has more wives than one, does not treat her equitably in accordance with the Injunctions of the Holy Quran; and
- on any other ground which is recognized as valid for the dissolution of marriage under Muslim Law; provided that: (a) no decree shall be passed on ground until the sentence has become final; (b) a decree passed on ground shall not take effect for a period of six months from the date of such decree, and if the husband appears either in person or through an authorized agent within that period and satisfies the Court that he is prepared to perform his conjugal duties; the Court shall set aside the said decree; and (c) before passing a decree on ground that the Court shall, on application by the husband, make an order requiring the husband to satisfy the Court within a period of one year from the date of such order that he has

ceased to be impotent, and if the husband so satisfies the Court within such period no decree shall be passed on the said ground.

567. The mere renunciation of Islam or conversion to another faith by a married Muslim woman does not automatically dissolve her marriage. However, following such renunciation or conversion, she has the legal right to seek a decree for the dissolution of marriage under any of the grounds specified in the Dissolution of Muslim Marriages Act, 1939. This provision does not apply to a woman who had previously converted to Islam from another religion and subsequently reverts to her former faith. In such cases, the marital bond remains intact unless the woman initiates legal proceedings for dissolution based on recognized legal grounds.

568. Applicant filed a transfer application under section 25-A of the West Pakistan Family Courts Act, 1964, seeking to transfer Family Suit filed by his wife for Khula, dowry articles, and medical expenses, to another court. The Family Judge granted Khula in exchange for the remaining dower amount and directed the defendant to pay maintenance for the Iddat period and return the dowry articles or pay compensation. The appellate court set aside the judgment regarding dowry articles and medical expenses and remanded the case for further evidence. Applicant alleged bias and claimed he was not allowed to present evidence. The court dismissed the transfer application, finding no substantial proof of bias and emphasizing that the wife's convenience takes precedence. It upheld the dissolution of marriage by Khula, affirming the wife's right to maintenance during Iddat and reinforcing Khula as a valid ground for divorce. (Sindh High Court-2023 YLR 530)

569. The petitioner filed a writ petition under Article 199 of the Constitution of Pakistan, 1973, challenging the judgments of the Family and Appellate Courts, which granted dissolution of marriage on the basis of Khula, maintenance for the Iddat period, and child custody to the respondent, Mst. Tehseen Bibi. The petitioner initially sought restitution of conjugal rights and contested the decree of Khula, claiming that the court erred in granting it without ordering the return of dower (Zar-e-Khula). The trial court found that the wife had received 16 tolas of gold as dower, but the Appellate Court concluded that the petitioner had taken it back. Since the dower had already been retrieved, the court ruled that no further return was required. The High Court upheld this decision, affirming that when a marriage becomes irreconcilable, Khula can be granted, and the return of dower is subject to the facts of the case. Additionally, the court upheld the custody of the minors with the mother, citing the petitioner's lack of financial stability and past criminal record. Consequently, the writ petition was dismissed. (PHC – 2023 CLC 916)

570. Suits for dissolution of marriage by wife and for conjugal rights by husband. Constitutional petition by wife. Wife had expressed her hatred by saying that she wanted to spit on her husband. Wife maintained her such aversion and deposed the same on all the occasions including in her plaint, her written statement in the suit for conjugal rights by her husband, in her statement before Family Court, in appeal filed before District Judge and her statement in person in Constitutional petition before the High Court. Held, Courts could otherwise in case of wife's failure to prove the grounds for dissolution of marriage see that she had a right of '*Khula*'. Courts were under a duty of law to pass a judgment on said factum. Failure of Court to do so would tantamount to misapplication of their mind to the Injunctions of Islam in respect of right of '*Khula*' and being not in conformity with law. High Court set aside the order of Family Court and that of Appellate Court having been passed without lawful authority and jurisdiction, accepted the wife's Constitutional petition and decreed the wife's suit for dissolution of marriage on the basis of her right of '*Khula*' and dismissed the suit of husband for restitution of conjugal rights (LHC – 1995 PLD 19).

571. Suit for dissolution of marriage dissolution suit filed by the respondent (wife) on the basis of Khula, which was decreed on 8 December 2010, subject to the return of dower (4 tolas of gold ornaments). The petitioner (husband) sought the execution of this decree for the return of dower. Initially, the Executing Court directed the respondent to return the gold or its market value, but this was overturned by the Additional District Judge, Rawalpindi, on the ground that an execution petition for the recovery of dower in a Khula case was not maintainable. The court reaffirmed that a decree of Khula is validly subject to the return of dower if so ordered by the Family Court. Since the Family Court's judgment had explicitly mandated the return of dower, it was legally enforceable through execution proceedings. The High Court clarified that a decree for Khula with conditions, such as returning the dower, is binding and can be executed like any other decree under the Family Courts Act, 1964. The revision order denying execution was deemed erroneous, and the petition was allowed. (LHC-2023 CLC 1285)

572. Wife, seeking dissolution of marriage insisted on divorce and was not prepared under any circumstances to live with her husband as his wife, and there were no prospects for reconciliation between them as hatred between spouses was deep rooted. Case, held, was fit for grant of '*Khula*' divorce to wife (LHC – 1990 CLC 917).

573. Dissolution of marriage on ground of '*Khula*'. Record showed that parties were at daggers drawn and husband levelled ugly allegations against wife and at one stage matter went before Police. Parties, during the spell of four to five months of marriage, had become rivals to each other, and it was beyond their control to live a happy married life. Family Court, thus was justified in dissolving the marriage of parties on the ground of '*Khula*'. Reference Islamic Law, MFLO, 1961 section 8, West Pakistan Family Courts Act (XXXV of 1964, section 7 (SHC – 1990 MLD 1151)).

574. The petitioner filed a Shariat Petition challenging the validity of section 10(4) of the West Pakistan Family Courts Act, 1964, arguing that granting Khula without the husband's consent is un-Islamic. The petitioner contended that the wife's unilateral right to obtain Khula from a court violates Islamic injunctions and should be declared void. The petition also referenced a personal case where the petitioner's wife was granted Khula by a Family Court without his consent. The court examined the matter in light of Islamic principles, citing relevant Quranic verses and Ahadith, as well as previous legal precedents. The court referred to the Full Bench judgment in *Saleem Ahmad and others v. Government of Pakistan and others (PLD 2014 FSC 43)*, which upheld the Family Court's authority to grant Khula when reconciliation efforts fail. The ruling emphasized that Khula is a right granted to women in Islam, distinct from Talaq, which is exercised by the husband, courts have the jurisdiction to dissolve a marriage through Khula if reconciliation fails, even if the husband does not consent., Khula operates as a single irrevocable divorce, allowing the couple to remarry without an intermediary marriage (Halala), unlike in the case of a triple Talaq. And the wife must observe *Iddat* after obtaining Khula before marrying another person. Based on these principles, the court reaffirmed the legality of section 10(4) and dismissed the petition as having no merit. (FSC-2023 PLD 286)

575. Dissolution of marriage on ground of '*Khula*'. Where Court after taking into consideration over all circumstances, came to the conclusion that it was not possible for parties to live together as husband and wife and perform their marital obligations within limits prescribed by God, marriage, could be dissolved on basis of '*Khula*'. Parties were not to be forced into a hateful union, if reconciliation had become impossible between them (LHC – 1989 MLD 5005).

576. The petitioner filed a writ petition under Article 199 of the Constitution of Pakistan, challenging the order in Family Suit. The order had granted dissolution of marriage (Khula) to Respondent No. 2, the petitioner's wife, after reconciliation efforts failed during pre-trial proceedings. The petitioner argued that he was not given an opportunity to be heard as he was unable to attend the pre-trial hearing due to COVID-19 lockdown restrictions. He claimed that the decision was made without considering the oral and documentary evidence on record. It noted that the Family Court had made multiple attempts to facilitate reconciliation, but the petitioner repeatedly failed to appear. The Family Judge declared the reconciliation efforts unsuccessful and granted Khula after the respondent-wife expressed extreme hatred and an unwillingness to continue the marriage. The court dismissed the petition, holding that the Family Court had jurisdiction to grant Khula when reconciliation failed, even if the husband was absent. The court also stated that the dissolution of marriage had attained finality and could not be reopened under section 14(2) of the Family Courts Act, 1964, except in specific circumstances under the Dissolution of Muslim Marriages Act, 1939. It concluded that the constitutional petition was not maintainable, as there was no illegality or jurisdictional defect in the Family Court's decision. The court upheld the validity of the Khula decree and dismissed the petition as meritless. (Sindh High Court-2022 CLC 1447)

577. Dissolution of marriage only ground of '*Khula*'. Where wife had categorically averred in her plaint that she had developed irretrievable hatred against husband, and her aversion had duly been substantiated by evidence, omission on part of Trial Court to specifically frame issue on ground of '*Khula*', held would not invalidate decree for '*Khula*' (LHC – 1989 MLD 3349).

578. The petitioner challenged the appellate court's decision affirming the dissolution of marriage (Khula) and maintenance for minors. The trial court granted Khula after reconciliation failed and initially ordered the wife to return 10 tolas of gold, but the appellate court ruled she was not required to do so. The court found that the dower was legally sold, and its proceeds went to the petitioner. It held that the gold ornaments were a gift and could not be reclaimed. The court upheld the Khula decree, modified the maintenance order by reducing the annual increase from 20% to 10%, and dismissed the petition with this minor adjustment. (LHC-2021 YLR 570)

579. Court granted dissolution of marriage (Khula) to wife under section 10(5) of the Family Courts Act, 1964. The petitioner argued that the decree was issued without the wife's consent, without sufficient time for reconciliation, and without valid grounds. The court found that multiple opportunities were given for reconciliation, but the petitioner repeatedly avoided recording his statement. The court also noted allegations of cruelty and mental and physical abuse against the petitioner, which justified the dissolution. The court reaffirmed that under Islamic injunctions and the Family Courts Act, 1964, a wife cannot be compelled to stay in a marriage against her wishes. It cited precedents, including *Khurshid Bibi v. Muhammad Amin (PLD 1967 SC 97)* and *Abid Hussain v. Additional District Judge (2006 SCMR 100)*, emphasizing that Khula is a right when the marriage becomes strained beyond reconciliation. The court held that the Family Court's decision was legally sound and that a decree for Khula is non-appealable under section 14(2) of the Family Courts Act, 1964, to protect women from prolonged litigation. Finding no jurisdictional defect or legal infirmity, the petition was dismissed. (LHC-2021 MLD 1506)

580. Suit for dissolution of marriage filed by the petitioner. The original suit was filed for dissolution of marriage on the basis of cruelty, recovery of dower amount, dowry articles, and maintenance. The petitioner/defendant contested the amendment application, but the trial court allowed it and directed the parties to appear for reconciliation. The court held that the Family Court has exclusive jurisdiction over family disputes and that the amendment was made in the best interest of both parties to avoid further litigation. The trial court did not exceed its jurisdiction by allowing the amendment, as the law does not prohibit such modifications. The court emphasized that the Family Court has the power to facilitate reconciliation efforts at multiple stages of the proceedings, even after evidence has been recorded. The objective of the Family Courts Act is to encourage compromise and resolve disputes efficiently. Since the plaintiff/respondent initially sought dissolution based on cruelty and later amended it to khula, the court upheld the trial court's decision, stating that there was no illegality or irregularity in the order. The petition was dismissed in limine, reinforcing the principle that the Family Court has broad authority to grant khula and regulate its own procedures for the expeditious resolution of family matters. (LHC-2021 MLD 420)

581. Statements made by plaintiff wife and her witnesses had shown that even after seven years of marital relations parties could not lead a happy life, and even birth of two children could not develop some love and affection between them.

Plaintiff wife had categorically deposed before Trial Court that because of defendant husband's attitude and his bad character and habits, she would not live with him at any cost, and that she wanted dissolution of marriage. Parties could not live together and lead a happy life within limits ordained by God. When hatred and disrespect developed between spouses and while wife refused to stay with her husband and expressed view that she did not like her husband, Court had the only option to pass a decree on basis of '*Khula*' (Shariat Court, Azad Kashmir 1999 YLR 1725).

582. The respondent (wife) filed a suit for dissolution of marriage, recovery of dower, maintenance, gold, and dowry articles in the Family Court, Attock. The petitioner contested the suit, but after reconciliation efforts failed, the Family Court granted a decree of khula under section 10(5) of the Family Courts Act, 1964, subject to the relinquishment of dower. The petitioner challenged this decision under Article 199 of the Constitution, arguing that as the spouses followed Fiqah-e-Jafria, the marriage could only be dissolved if the husband pronounced the necessary seeghas without coercion. During the proceedings, the petitioner relied on various case laws to assert that khula without the husband's consent is not valid in Shia jurisprudence. The court held that khula is a recognized form of marital dissolution in Islam, supported by Quranic injunctions and ahadith. It emphasized that all Muslims are governed by Quranic principles and cited Surah Al-Baqarah (2:229) and the precedent of Habibah bint Sahl, who was granted khula by the Prophet Muhammad (PBUH) upon returning her dower. The court dismissed the petition, ruling that the Family Court had lawfully exercised its powers under section 10(5) of the Family Courts Act, 1964, to grant khula without the husband's consent. The petition was dismissed with no order as to costs. (LHC-2025 PLD 18)

583. Question of '*Khula*' was to be considered on its own merits. Even if wife was unable to prove grounds available for dissolution of marriage as contained in Dissolution of Muslim Marriages Act, 1939, marriage could be dissolved on '*Khula*'. Wife was entitled to dissolution of marriage on '*Khula*' on restoration of what she had received in consideration of marriage, in case Court apprehended that parties would not observe limits of God (Shariat Court, Azad Kashmir – 1999 MLD 1763).

584. Petitioner filed a family suit seeking dissolution of marriage due to her husband's cruelty, non-payment of maintenance, and his second marriage without her consent, along with claims for dower, gold ornaments, and dowry articles. The trial court dissolved the marriage on the basis of Khula and dismissed her other claims. The petitioner argued that she did not seek Khula but rather a dissolution based on cruelty and other grounds recognized under section 2 of the Dissolution of Muslim Marriages Act, 1939. The High Court found that the trial court had mis appreciated the evidence, as cruelty by the husband was established. Since a wife forfeits her dower only when seeking dissolution solely on the basis of Khula, the court ruled that the marriage should not have been dissolved on this ground when cruelty was proved. The High Court held that Khula should not have been the basis for dissolving the marriage when the petitioner had successfully proven cruelty and other valid grounds under the Dissolution of Muslim Marriages Act, 1939. It emphasized that a woman can seek dissolution on multiple grounds and if cruelty is established, she retains her right to dower. The court allowed the petition, setting aside the trial court's decision to dissolve the marriage on the basis of Khula. (PHC – 2020 CLC 1874)

585. Petitioner filed a suit against her husband seeking dissolution of marriage based on maltreatment, cruelty, and his second marriage. She also sought the recovery of 13-1/2 tolas of golden ornaments as dower and maintenance allowance. The Family Court granted dissolution of marriage on the basis of Khula, ordering petitioner to return 1-1/2 tolas of gold while waiving the claim to the remaining 13-1/2 tolas, as she had never received them. The court awarded her PKR 3,82,000 for dowry articles but denied past maintenance, reasoning that she had refused to fulfil conjugal obligations. However, she was granted maintenance until the completion of her Iddat period. Ex-husband later filed a writ petition challenging the decision, contending that since the marriage was dissolved through Khula, he was entitled to recover the 13-1/2 tolas of gold. The High Court dismissed his petition ruling that Khula is irrevocable and cannot be appealed except regarding dower matters. The court also emphasized that the burden of proving the payment of dower was on the husband, which he failed to do. Since his ex-wife never received the 13-1/2 tolas of gold, she was not required to return them. The court reaffirmed that Khula is a financial settlement where the wife seeks divorce by returning what she had received, and in this case, there was no evidence that she had received the full dower. Therefore, the court upheld the Family Court's decision and dismissed the petition. (PHC-- 2018 YLR 2663)

586. Wife having developed hatred against husband on account of fact that he compelled her to convert her sect. Held, spouses could not lead their matrimonial life within limits prescribed by Allah. Dissolution of marriage on ground of '*Khula*' not interfered with in exercise of Constitutional jurisdiction (LHC – 1987 MLD 2549).

587. Relations between parties becoming strained within a period of four years of marital life to the extent that they could not live happily together. Wife not only was beaten and thrown out from house of husband on one or two occasions but also character of her husband was bad and insisting on her to lead immoral life. Observations of Appellate Court that such fact could be hardly termed as habitual cruelty or would not be taken into consideration for purpose of '*Khula*', held, were not proper. Case remanded to Appellate Court for disposal after considering plea of '*Khula*' and satisfying its conscience that wife, if forced to live with husband would not be observing limits prescribed by God, and after fixing benefits, if any, to be returned by wife to her husband as consideration of '*Khula*' (LHC – 1987 MLD 2486).

588. Mental torture to wife established. Parties could not live within limits of God as wife had developed internal disliking to husband. Court. held, rightly dissolved marriage on 'principle of '*Khula*' (SHC – 1985 MLD 225).

589. The petitioner filed a constitutional petition challenging the order passed by the Judge Family Court, Lahore, which dismissed his suit for restitution of conjugal rights and granted dissolution of marriage in favour of respondent. The petitioner argued that he was not given an opportunity for reconciliation and the statement of respondent was recorded in his absence. He claimed that the order was unlawful and void. The court noted that respondent had categorically refused to reconcile due to the petitioner's alleged cruel treatment. Under Islamic principles, if a wife develops hatred toward her husband and cannot continue the marriage, she is entitled to Khula. The court cited the Quran and Hadith, emphasizing that Islam does not force a woman to remain in a hateful marriage. The court further held that no appeal is provided against a Khula decree under the West Pakistan Family Courts Act, 1964 and where an appeal is barred, writ jurisdiction is also not available. It concluded that the Judge Family Court exercised its jurisdiction lawfully and dismissed the writ petition in limine, finding no illegality in the impugned order. (LHC-2019 PLD 160)

§2. Procedure of Divorce

590. The MFLO outlines a clear procedure for divorce. According to section 7(1), a husband who intends to divorce his wife must provide a written notice to the Chairman of the Union Council immediately after pronouncing divorce in any form. A copy of this notice must also be supplied to the wife. Failure to comply with this requirement is a legal offense. Under section 7(2), if a husband does not issue a written notice to the Chairman, he may face penalties, including simple imprisonment for up to one year, a fine of up to PKR 5,000, or both. After the notice is given, a mandatory period of ninety days (or until the completion of pregnancy if the wife is expecting) is observed for reconciliation efforts. During this period, the Union Council constitutes an Arbitration Council to attempt a settlement between the spouses. If reconciliation is not achieved within the stipulated time, the divorce takes effect.

591. If the whereabouts of the wife who is to be supplied a copy of the notice of divorce are not known to the husband, or cannot, with due diligence, be ascertained by him, he may, if so permitted by the Chairman, give notice of the divorce to the wife through her father, mother, adult brother or adult sister, or if their whereabouts are not known to the husband or cannot, with due diligence, be ascertained by him, he may, with the permission of the Chairman serve the notice of divorce on her by publication in a newspaper, approved by the Chairman, having circulation in the locality where he last resided with the wife (section 3-A of the West Pakistan Rules under MFLO).

592. If the right to divorce (Talaq-e-Tafweez) has been delegated to the wife in the Nikahnama, and she chooses to exercise this right, she must follow the same legal procedure outlined in the MFLO. Likewise, if either spouse seeks to dissolve the marriage through means other than divorce, such as through Khula or Mubarat, the prescribed procedure under MFLO will apply with necessary modifications. In cases where the wife exercises her delegated right to divorce, she must issue a written notice to the Chairman of the Union Council, similar to the procedure required for a husband pronouncing divorce. The Arbitration Council is then formed to facilitate reconciliation efforts within a mandatory 90-day period. If no reconciliation is reached, the divorce takes effect after the completion of this period. For dissolutions initiated by the wife through Khula, a petition is filed in the Family Court. If the court is satisfied that reconciliation is not possible and the wife is firm in her decision, a decree of dissolution is granted. Unlike a delegated divorce, Khula may require the wife to return the dower or other benefits received during the marriage, as determined by the court.

593. Petitioner divorced his wife and ninety days period after the pronouncement/ sending of notice to the Chairman Arbitration having elapsed, Chairman Arbitration Council, Union Council concerned issued a certificate of effectiveness of Divorce as required under section 7 of MFLO. After more than two years of effectiveness of Divorce, *Naib Nazim* Union Council cancelled certificate of effectiveness of Divorce. Petitioner had challenged cancellation of certificate of effectiveness of Divorce contending that *Naib Nazim* Union Council had no authority to revoke the earlier order of effectiveness of Divorce. On Court Notice, *Nazim* of Union Council concerned appeared in court along with relevant record and appraised the court that *Naib Nazim*, who had cancelled certificate of effectiveness of Divorce, had died and that he did not own the documents allegedly having been issued by deceased *Naib Nazim*. Petition was disposed of with the observation that as no record was available with the Union Council regarding certificate cancelling effectiveness of Divorce, it appeared that it had been manipulated. Even otherwise after a lapse of more than two years, *Naib Nazim* Union Council had no authority to revoke the certificate of Divorce (LHC – 2009 YLR 1879).

594. The petitioner challenged the decision of the Chairman, Arbitration Council, Islamabad, which refused to issue a divorce certificate on the ground that both parties were residents of Azad Jammu & Kashmir (AJK) and currently residing in the United States, where their marriage had already been dissolved by the Superior Court of California. The petitioner argued that since the marriage was solemnized and registered in Islamabad, the Arbitration Council had the jurisdiction to issue the divorce certificate. The respondent contended that jurisdiction lay where the wife was residing at the time of divorce pronouncement, which was California. The court held that the Arbitration Council in Islamabad had jurisdiction since the Nikah Nama was registered there. It ruled that a foreign divorce decree, if not challenged and meeting legal requirements, is valid and should be recognized under Pakistani law. The Arbitration Council does not have adjudicatory power and must issue the divorce certificate as per its administrative role. Consequently, the petition was allowed, and the Arbitration Council was directed to issue the divorce certificate. (ISB-2025 CLC 22)

595. '*Khula*' Dissolution of marriage under right of '*Khula*' Judge, Family Court coming to conclusion on basis of material on record that spouses could not live together within limits prescribed by Allah. Court, held, justified in dissolving marriage on ground of '*Khula*' on terms and conditions appropriate to facts of case. Husband and wife in litigation, civil, criminal for six years. Wife stating that she was not prepared to live with her husband at any cost, and that no formal Rukhsati had yet taken place. Held, this long drawn out litigation between parties by itself was a circumstance to indicate that relations were severely strained, and that it would be futile to expect that they can live happily together as husband and wife. Finding of Trial Court that case for '*Khula*' was made out, held, called for no interference in exercise of Constitutional jurisdiction Provisional Constitution Order (1 of 1981), Article 9 (SHC – 1984 CLC 3147).

§3. Different Modes of Divorce

596. Muslim jurists categorize divorce into two types based on the number of pronouncements. The first type is *Rajei Talaq* (revocable divorce), where the husband retains the right to reconcile with his wife without requiring a new marriage contract, provided he does so within the *Iddat* (waiting period). If he does not revoke the divorce within this time, it becomes final. The second type is *Bain Talaq* (irrevocable divorce), which is further divided into *Minor Bain Talaq* and *Major Bain Talaq*. In *Minor Bain Talaq*, if the husband pronounces one or two divorces and does not reconcile before the *Iddat* period ends, they can remarry, but only through a new *Nikah* with fresh terms and conditions. In contrast, *Major Bain Talaq* occurs when a husband pronounces divorce three times, permanently severing the marital bond. The wife cannot remarry her former husband unless she lawfully marries another man, consummates the marriage, and is subsequently divorced or widowed. This ruling is based on the Quranic injunction in Surah Al-Baqarah (2:230).

597. Islamic law recognizes various modes of effecting divorce. A husband can pronounce *Talaq* verbally or in writing, ensuring clarity in intent. Divorce can also be classified based on the manner of pronouncement, such as *Talaq-e-Sunnah*, which follows the prescribed method in accordance with the teachings of the Prophet Muhammad, and *Talaq-e-Bid'ah*, an instant and irrevocable divorce discouraged in Islamic jurisprudence. Divorce can occur through mutual agreement (*Mubarat*), or at the wife's request through *Khula*, where she seeks dissolution by returning her *Mehr* (dower) or any agreed compensation. If a husband refuses to grant divorce, a wife may petition a court under *Faskh*, a judicial annulment granted for valid reasons like cruelty, abandonment, or failure to fulfil marital obligations. Islam emphasizes reconciliation before divorce, encouraging mediation between spouses and intervention by elders. If disputes persist, Islam allows for divorce as a last resort while ensuring fairness and the protection of rights for both parties.

A. Talak Ahsan *(Most Approved Way for Divorce)*

598. The *Ahsan* form of divorce consists of a single pronouncement of *Talaq* made during a *Tuhr* (the period between two menstrual cycles), followed by complete abstinence from sexual relations for the entire duration of the *Iddat* period. If the marriage has not been consummated, the husband may pronounce *Talaq* in the *Ahsan* form at any time, including during the wife's menstruation, since the waiting period does not apply in such cases. Additionally, if the wife has reached menopause and no longer experiences menstrual cycles, the requirement of pronouncing divorce during *Tuhr* is irrelevant. It is important to note that this condition applies only to verbal divorces, whereas a written declaration of *Talaq* in the *Ahsan* mode remains valid regardless of the wife's menstrual state. A divorce in the *Ahsan* mode remains revocable during the *Iddat* period, allowing the husband an opportunity to reconcile with his wife. Revocation can be done explicitly through a clear statement or implicitly through actions, such as resuming conjugal relations. However, if the *Iddat* period expires without reconciliation, the divorce becomes irrevocable and final, permanently dissolving the marital bond. The *Ahsan* form is regarded as the most appropriate and Islamically recommended method of divorce, as it allows time for reflection and possible reconciliation before final separation.

599. Effect of enactment of MFLO, 1961. Legislature had, to a great extent, trammelled and curtailed the arbitrary power of husband to divorce his wife. MFLO, 1961 had abolished the practice of disapproved form of 'divorce' and mode prescribed in the Ordinance was that of a *'Talaq-e-ahsan'* and by the Ordinance it had been made mandatory that the notice of 'divorce' should be given in writing to the Chairman of Union Council. 'Divorce' would be effected only if efforts of reconciliation would fail. Law prevailing previous to the enforcement of MFLO, 1961, had made it obligatory for the couples divorced by any mode of 'divorce' other than *'Talaq-e-ahsan'* not to remarry each other again, unless wife married another man who died or divorced her after actual consummation, and she married her first husband after period of '*Iddat*'. Before re-marriage parties had to prove that bar to their marriage was removed by intermediate marriage, consummation and dissolution; otherwise, their marriage was not considered. Validity: Mode of 'divorce' effected under provisions of MFLO, 1961 being almost that of *'Talaq-e-ahsan'*, the couples could remarry without any intervening marriage except where they had been divorced thrice, and the third divorce had become effective, and in that case they could not remarry without an intervening marriage. Plain reading of section 7 of MFLO, 1961 though had implied that all kinds of 'divorces' had been made revocable without an intervening marriage and could be that its repugnancy to such extent could validly be agitated on the touchstone of Quranic behest and the traditions of Holy Prophet Muhammad (PBUH), but neither vires of said section 7 had been challenged nor matter raised in case pertained to all kinds of 'divorces'. Matter, in the present case, pertained, to 'divorce' obtained by wife through Court decree in shape of '*Khula*' (PHC – 2003 PLD 169).

B. Talaq Hasan *(Approved Way for Divorce)*

600. The *Hasan* mode of *Talaq* is a recognized and systematic form of divorce in Islamic law, adhering to the principles outlined in *Talaq al-Sunnah.* It is considered a more structured approach to divorce, allowing time for contemplation and possible reconciliation before final dissolution. In this form, the husband pronounces *Talaq* three times over successive periods of *Tuhr*, which is the state of purity between a woman's menstrual cycles. The first pronouncement of *Talaq* must be made during a *Tuhr* in which no conjugal relations have taken place. If the husband does not revoke it, the second pronouncement occurs during the next *Tuhr* under the same conditions. The third and final pronouncement is made in the third successive *Tuhr*, at which point the *Talaq* becomes irrevocable, regardless of whether the *Iddat* period has concluded. Once the third pronouncement is given, the marital bond is completely severed, and the wife is required to observe the *Iddat* period before she is free to remarry.

C. Talaq-ul-Bidaat or Talaq-i-Badai

601. Under Islamic law, Talaq-ul-Bidaat, also known as Talaq-i-Badai, refers to an irregular and instantaneous form of divorce that is not in accordance with the principles of Shari'ah. This form of divorce occurs when a husband either pronounces Talaq three times in a single sitting, whether in one continuous statement such as 'I divorce you thrice' or in separate successive statements within the same Tuhr, such as 'I divorce you, I divorce you, I divorce you.' Alternatively, it can also take the form of a single pronouncement that explicitly conveys an irrevocable intention to dissolve the marriage, for instance, 'I divorce you irrevocably.' In both cases, the divorce becomes immediately binding and irreversible, earning the classification of Talaq-i-Bain, meaning an irrevocable divorce. Despite being legally recognized by the majority of classical jurists, Talaq-ul-Bidaat is widely regarded as contrary to the fundamental tenets of Islamic law. It is considered an innovation (Bidaah) and is strongly discouraged as it bypasses the principles of restraint, reflection, and reconciliation that Islam prescribes in matters of divorce. Jurists across various Islamic schools of thought acknowledge that while such a divorce may technically be valid, it is morally and religiously reprehensible. It contravenes the ideal process of divorce, which encourages patience, deliberation, and the possibility of reconciliation before final separation.

602. The majority of classical jurists, including Imam Abu Hanifah, Imam Malik, Imam Shafi'i, and Imam Ahmad, along with most traditional Islamic scholars, consider the pronouncement of triple Talaq in a single sitting as constituting an irrevocable divorce. According to this view, the woman is immediately separated from her husband and cannot lawfully return to him unless she enters into a valid marriage with another man, consummates that marriage, and subsequently obtains a legitimate divorce from him. This process, known as Halala, is considered a necessary condition for her to remarry her former husband. However, a dissenting opinion exists among some scholars, including Imam Tawoos, certain jurists from the

Ahle-e-Zahir school, Sheikh-ul-Islam Ibn Taimiyah, and several contemporary Islamic thinkers. They argue that a triple pronouncement of divorce in a single sitting should not be treated as three separate divorces but rather as a single revocable divorce (Talaq-e-Raj'i). According to this interpretation, the husband retains the right to reconcile with his wife during the Iddah period without requiring her to undergo Halala. This perspective is rooted in the argument that the Prophet Muhammad disapproved of instantaneous triple Talaq and that the Quran prescribes a gradual and deliberate process of divorce, emphasizing reflection and reconciliation.

603. It is narrated in *Bukhari* and Muslim that during the life of Allah's Apostle. Abdullah Ibn Umar had divorced his wife while she was menstruating. Umar bin al-Khattab asked Allah's apostle about that. Allah's Apostle said, 'Order him (your Son) to take her back and keep her till she is clean and then to wait till she gets her next period and becomes clean again, whereupon, if he wishes to keep her, he can do so, and if he wishes to divorce her he can divorce her before having sexual intercourse with her, and that is the prescribed period which Allah has fixed for the women meant to be divorced'.

604. An-Nasaaee, in his Sunan, narrates on the authority of Mahmood bin Labeed (Radiya Allahu Anhu) that a man once divorced his wife three times in a single sitting. Upon hearing this, the Prophet Muhammad (PBUH) stood up in intense anger and said, *'Will the Book of Allah be played with while I am still in your midst?'* His anger was so apparent that one of the companions even asked, *'O Messenger of Allah! Shall I kill him?'* This Hadith strongly indicates that pronouncing triple Talaq in one instance is an act of grave disobedience and contradicts the proper process outlined in the Quran and Sunnah. Despite the Prophet's evident displeasure, the juristic ruling on the validity of such a divorce remains a subject of scholarly debate. The majority of classical Islamic jurists, including those from the Hanafi, Maliki, Shafi'i, and Hanbali schools, maintain that even though the act is sinful, the pronouncement of triple Talaq in one sitting is legally binding and results in an irrevocable divorce. As a result, the wife immediately becomes unlawful for her husband, and she cannot return to him unless she marries another man, consummates the marriage, and then lawfully obtains a divorce (Halala).

605. The case revolves around the validity and effectiveness of the divorce (Talaq) pronounced by the deceased, upon his second wife. The plaintiff contended that she remained legally married to the deceased at the time of his death, thereby entitling her to inheritance rights and a deferred dower amount. The defendants, particularly the first wife and children of the deceased, argued that the plaintiff had been divorced through an irrevocable Talaq (Talaq-e-Bain), which legally severed the marital relationship prior to her husband's death. Under Islamic law, different forms of Talaq exist, including Talaq-e-Ahsan, Talaq-e-Hasan, and Talaq-e-Bain. The first two allow for the possibility of revocation and reconciliation, whereas Talaq-e-Bain is immediate and final upon pronouncement. The defendants presented a Talaqnama (divorce deed) claiming it was executed and sent to the plaintiff, making the divorce effective. The plaintiff, however, contested this, arguing that the Talaq did not comply with section 7 of the MFLO, 1961, which requires a ninety-day period before a divorce becomes effective and provides room for reconciliation. The court analysed whether Talaq-e-Bain being an irrevocable form of divorce was subject to the procedural requirements of section 7. It concluded that since Talaq-e-Bain takes effect immediately upon pronouncement, the legislative mechanism for reconciliation under section 7 does not apply. The court further ruled that the divorce had already taken effect before the deceased's death, meaning the plaintiff ceased to be his legal wife and thus had no inheritance. The Court held that while the plaintiff's claim to inheritance was dismissed due to the finality of Talaq-e-Bain, her right to the deferred dower amount was upheld as a financial obligation on the deceased's estate. (Sindh High Court – 2013 CLC 584)

D. Divorce under Compulsion

606. Under Islamic law, when a husband pronounces divorce using express (sarih) words, the Talaq is considered valid and binding regardless of his intention or the circumstances surrounding its declaration. This means that even if the husband utters the words of divorce under compulsion, such as being forced by family or external pressure, the divorce still takes effect. Similarly, if he pronounces it while voluntarily intoxicated, he is held accountable for his actions, and the divorce remains legally valid. Even if he issues Talaq merely to satisfy his father or another person without genuinely intending to dissolve the marriage, the divorce is still considered effective because express words leave no room for ambiguity. Islamic jurisprudence, particularly under the Hanafi school, maintains that once Talaq is pronounced in clear terms, it cannot be revoked based on claims of coercion, intoxication, or external influence. However, some jurists, particularly in the Maliki and Shafi'i schools, acknowledge exceptions in cases of extreme coercion, but the general principle remains that an explicitly pronounced divorce is legally binding.

607. Some Islamic jurists hold the view that a divorce pronounced under coercion is invalid and does not take effect. This is based on the saying of the Holy Prophet Muhammad (PBUH): 'There is no divorce under coercion' (Abu Dawood, authenticated by Al-Suyuti). According to this interpretation, if a person is forced to divorce his wife due to threats or pressure that endangers his life, wealth, or the well-being of his family, the divorce is not considered valid. Coercion is defined as a situation where a person faces serious harm or unbearable consequences if he does not comply with the demand to divorce. For example, if a husband is threatened with severe bodily harm or financial ruin unless he divorces his wife, the divorce is deemed invalid in some schools of thought. Similarly, if a wife threatens to take her own life unless her husband divorces her, and he issues the divorce only to prevent her from doing so, it is not a valid divorce provided that he genuinely believes she would act on her threat. Some scholars differentiate between physical and psychological coercion, arguing that true coercion must involve an immediate and tangible danger rather than emotional pressure. While the Hanafi school generally holds that even a coerced divorce is valid, the Maliki, Shafi'i, and Hanbali schools largely agree that a divorce pronounced under genuine and extreme duress does not take effect. This interpretation aligns with the principle that consent is a fundamental aspect of legal transactions in Islam, including marriage and divorce. However, the burden of proof lies on the person claiming coercion, and courts or religious authorities may assess the circumstances to determine whether the coercion was legitimate enough to nullify the divorce.

E. Divorce by Ila (Vow of Continence)

608. In Islamic jurisprudence, **Ila** is a form of conditional divorce that occurs when a husband, who is of sound mind and has reached puberty, swears an oath to abstain from sexual relations with his wife for a period of at least four months. If he persists in his vow and does not resume marital relations within this time frame, the marriage is automatically dissolved with a single irrevocable divorce (**talaq bain**). This ruling is based on **Surah Al-Baqarah (2:226–227)**, where Allah states that husbands who swear an oath of abstinence have a waiting period of four months, after which they must either reconcile or proceed with divorce.

609. If the husband breaks his vow within the four-month period and resumes intimacy with his wife, he must offer expiation (**kaffarah**) for breaking an oath, which usually involves feeding or clothing the needy or fasting for three days. However, if the four-month period lapses without reconciliation, the wife is granted the right to seek judicial intervention for separation, even if she does not initiate divorce herself. Some Islamic schools of thought, such as the **Hanafi** and **Hanbali** schools, consider Ila to result in automatic divorce after four months, while the **Maliki** and **Shafi'i** schools hold that judicial decree is required for its finalization. Ila is seen as a severe form of estrangement, and its purpose in Islamic law is to prevent prolonged neglect of a wife without formally ending the marriage.

F. Zihar (Injurious Assimilation)

610. Zihar is a pre-Islamic form of divorce that was later reformed under Islamic law. It occurs when a husband likens his wife to his mother or any other woman within the prohibited degrees of marriage, such as his sister or aunt, with the intention of making her unlawful for himself. Though this statement does not constitute an immediate and effective divorce, it places a severe restriction on marital relations, making the wife unlawful for the husband until he performs the required expiation. The Quran explicitly addresses Zihar in Surah Al-Mujadila (58:2–4), where Allah condemns this practice and mandates a form of penance for those who commit it. The prescribed expiation involves either freeing a slave, fasting for two consecutive months, or feeding sixty poor people before the husband can resume conjugal relations with his wife. Until the expiation is completed, the wife has the right to refuse intimacy, and if the husband persistently avoids fulfilling the penance, she can seek judicial intervention to dissolve the marriage. Unlike other forms of divorce, Zihar does not automatically dissolve the marriage but acts as a suspended state of separation, emphasizing the importance of atonement and the sanctity of marital bonds in Islam.

G. 'Khula' *(Redemption) and* Mubarat *(Mutual Freeing)*

611. A marriage may be dissolved not only by divorce, which is the arbitrary act of the husband, but also by agreement between the husband and wife. Dissolution of marriage by agreement may take the form of '*Khula*' or *Mubarat.* A divorce by '*Khula*' is a divorce with the consent, and at the instance of the wife, in which she gives or agrees to give a consideration of the husband for her release from the marriage tie. In such a case, the terms of the bargain are matters of arrangement between the husband and wife, and the wife may, as the consideration, release her dower and other rights, or make any other agreement for the benefit of the husband. Failure on the part of the wife to pay the consideration for the divorce does not invalidate the divorce through the husband may sue the wife for it.

612. 'Khula' is a form of divorce in Islamic law initiated by the wife, whereby she offers compensation to the husband in exchange for her release from the marital bond. This compensation can be in the form of returning the dower (Mahr) or any other agreed-upon financial settlement. Once the husband accepts the offer, the divorce becomes final and takes the form of Talaq-i-Bain (an irrevocable divorce), meaning the couple cannot reconcile unless they remarry with a new contract and fresh Mahr. Unlike Talaq, which is at the discretion of the husband, Khula grants the wife the right to seek dissolution of the marriage when living together becomes unbearable for her. The validity of Khula is not dependent on the execution of a formal document (Khulanama); rather, the moment the husband consents to the offer, the divorce is effective. In cases where the husband refuses to grant Khula despite valid reasons, the wife has the right to approach an Islamic court or religious authority to intervene. The Quran in Surah Al-Baqarah (2:229) recognizes the concept of Khula, emphasizing that it is preferable for a woman to part ways with dignity rather than remain in a distressing marriage.

613. Mubarat is a form of divorce in Islamic law that occurs through mutual agreement between the husband and wife when both parties wish to end the marriage. While it shares similarities with Khula, the primary distinction lies in its origin, Khula is initiated by the wife due to her aversion to the marriage, whereas Mubarat is based on a mutual desire to separate. In a Mubarat divorce, the offer can be made by either spouse, and once the other party accepts it, the dissolution of marriage is finalized. Like Khula, Mubarat results in Talaq-i-Bain (an irrevocable divorce), meaning the couple cannot reunite unless they enter into a new marriage contract with fresh Mahr. Unlike Khula, where compensation is typically offered by the wife to the husband, in Mubarat, there is no obligation for compensation unless specifically agreed upon. This form of divorce is considered a peaceful means of separation, ensuring that both parties part ways amicably without the need for judicial intervention. Once the agreement is reached, the divorce is effective immediately, and neither spouse has the right to revoke it unilaterally. Islamic scholars emphasize that Mubarat, like all forms of divorce, should be pursued only when reconciliation is not possible, in keeping with the Quranic principles of justice and fairness in marital relations.

614. Court held that there is a difference between '*Khula*' and mubarat and the main distinction between a '*Khula*' and *mubarat* is that in the former the aversion is on the side of the wife and she desires a separation but in the latter the aversion is mutual and both sides desire separation. Second, in a divorce by '*Khula*' some consideration must be given by the wife to the husband for her release from the marital tie. It is in effect an offer from the wife for her release on payment of compensation. Where a suit filed by the husband for restitution of conjugal rights had been decreed but as against that the wife's suit claiming dissolution of marriage had been dismissed by the Trial Court, it was held that it was the wife who sought severance of the marital tie and not the husband and, therefore, in the circumstances the divorce ultimately agreed upon by the parties was only a *mubarat* and not '*Khula*' (SCP – 1964 PLD 456).

§4. Effects of Divorce

615. After a divorce, if the marriage was consummated, the wife must observe a mandatory waiting period known as Iddat before she can remarry. The duration of Iddat varies depending on the circumstances: for a divorced woman who is not pregnant, it lasts for three menstrual cycles (or three lunar months if she does not menstruate), while for a pregnant woman, it continues until she gives birth. This period is intended to determine whether she is carrying her former husband's child and to allow for emotional and legal closure before entering a new marriage. However, if the marriage was not consummated, there is no requirement for Iddat, and the woman is free to remarry immediately.

616. If the marriage was consummated and the husband had four wives at the time of divorce, he is not permitted to marry another woman until the Iddat period of the divorced wife is completed. This restriction ensures that he does not exceed the maximum limit of four wives allowed in Islamic law at any given time. Once the Iddat is completed, the marital bond with the divorced wife is fully dissolved, creating space for him to lawfully marry another woman if he chooses. The Iddat period serves multiple purposes, including confirming the absence of pregnancy and allowing for the proper transition of marital responsibilities. Additionally, if the divorce was revocable (Talaq-e-Raj'i), the husband has the option to reconcile with his wife within the Iddat period without requiring a new marriage contract. However, if the divorce was irrevocable (Talaq-i-Bain), any reconciliation would necessitate a fresh Nikah with new terms and consent from both parties.

617. If the marriage was consummated, the wife has the absolute right to receive the entire unpaid dower, including both the prompt and deferred portions, immediately upon divorce. This financial obligation is binding on the husband and serves as a form of financial security for the wife. However, if the marriage was not consummated but the dower amount was specified in the marriage contract, she is entitled to receive only half of the agreed sum. In cases where no dower amount was stipulated, she is entitled to receive three articles of dress as a minimum provision. If the marriage is dissolved due to the apostasy of the wife after consummation, she is still entitled to the full dower amount.

618. Until a divorce becomes irrevocable, both the husband and wife retain their mutual rights of inheritance. However, once the divorce attains irrevocability, these rights are immediately extinguished, meaning neither spouse can inherit from the other. An exception to this rule applies when the husband pronounces divorce while suffering from a death-illness (marad-ul-maut). In such cases, the wife's right to inherit continues until the completion of her Iddat period, ensuring that she is not unjustly deprived of her rightful share. However, if the wife sought the divorce of her own volition, such as through Khula or Mubarat, she forfeits her claim to inheritance upon the finalization of the divorce.

619. Once a divorce becomes irrevocable, any sexual relations between the former spouses are strictly prohibited under Islamic law. If such intercourse takes place after the divorce has attained finality, it is considered unlawful, and any child born as a result is deemed illegitimate. Such a child cannot be legitimized through mere acknowledgment by the father, as legitimacy in Islamic law is strictly tied to a valid marital relationship. However, if the couple wishes to reconcile, they must enter into a new marital contract with a fresh dower and fulfil all legal and religious requirements. In the case of a triple Talaq, the wife must lawfully marry another man, consummate that marriage, and undergo a valid separation (Halala) before she can remarry her former husband.

620. If a husband divorces his wife through three pronouncements of talaq, he cannot remarry her unless she first marries another man, and that marriage is consummated, followed by a valid divorce or the husband's death. The presumption of marriage based on an acknowledgment of legitimacy does not apply to remarriage between divorced spouses unless it is proven that the legal bar to remarriage has been removed through consummation and subsequent divorce. Even if a remarriage is established, it remains invalid unless compliance with these conditions is confirmed. However, in other cases, the divorced couple may remarry whether during the Iddat period or after its completion, as if no divorce had taken place.

621. Divorce, unless revoked earlier, expressly or otherwise, shall not be effective until the expiration of ninety days from the day on which notice is delivered to the Chairman (section 7(3) of MFLO).

622. If the wife is pregnant at the time divorce is pronounced, divorce shall not be effect until the period of ninety days or the pregnancy, whichever later, ends (section 7(5) of MFLO).

623. Within thirty days of the receipt of divorce notice, the Chairman shall constitute an Arbitration Council for the purpose of bringing about conciliation between the parties, and the Arbitration Council shall take all steps necessary to bring about such reconciliation (section 7(4) of MFLO).

624. Unless divorce has not been conveyed three times, nothing debars a wife to remarry the same husband without an intervening marriage with a third person (section 7(6) of MFLO). However, if husband has conveyed divorce three times, a woman cannot remarry with the ex-husband unless and until she has been married to another person and that person divorce the woman.

§5. Iddat (Time Limitation for Woman to Remarry)

625. When a woman is divorced by her husband, she must observe a waiting period known as Iddat before she can remarry. For a woman who menstruates, this period lasts for three complete menstrual cycles. However, if she does not menstruate due to reasons other than pregnancy, such as age or medical conditions, her Iddat is three lunar months. In the case of pregnancy, the Iddat continues until she gives birth, regardless of whether this period is shorter or longer than three months. The purpose of Iddat is to ascertain whether the woman is carrying the husband's child, to allow for emotional and legal closure, and to maintain the sanctity of lineage in Islamic law. During this period, the woman is entitled to maintenance from her former husband unless the divorce was initiated due to her misconduct. If the husband dies during her Iddat, the period extends to four lunar months and ten days, reinforcing the significance of mourning and legal considerations in Islamic jurisprudence.

626. Iddat is a legally prescribed waiting period that a woman must observe after the termination of her marriage before she can lawfully enter into a new marriage. This period serves multiple purposes, primarily ensuring the certainty of paternity in case of pregnancy and allowing time for emotional and legal transition. In the case of divorce, the duration of Iddat varies based on the woman's physical condition – three menstrual cycles for a menstruating woman, three lunar months for one who does not menstruate, and until childbirth if she is pregnant. However, in the event of the husband's death, Iddat is obligatory for four lunar months and ten days, regardless of whether the marriage was consummated. If a woman remarries before the completion of her Iddat, such a marriage is considered irregular (Fasid) rather than void (Batil) under Pakistani law, meaning it can be rectified but remains legally flawed until the waiting period is properly observed.

627. Marriage of a woman before completion of her *Iddat*, was irregular and not void. Irregular marriage could have its own consequences under personal law, but same could not be treated as void and could not be regarded as un-Islamic or against the *Shariah* (FSC – 2004 YLR 619).

628. Revision petition filed by the petitioners against the judgment which recognized Mst. Zaib-un-Nisa as the third wife of the deceased Hussain Ali and entitled her to a share in his inheritance. The petitioners challenged this decision, arguing that Zaib-un-Nisa's marriage with Hussain Ali was irregular because it allegedly took place during her Iddat period. The court discussed the legal standing of marriages contracted during the Iddat period. It held that such marriages, under Islamic law, are not void (Batil) but are considered irregular (Fasid). The court cited Allah Dad v. Mukhtar Ahmed (1992 SCMR 1273) to support this view, clarifying that an irregular marriage does not invalidate a woman's entitlement to inheritance or succession rights. The court further ruled that the procedure under section 373 of the Succession Act, 1925, is summary in nature and does not conclusively determine property rights. Instead, it merely grants authority to collect debts of the deceased. If any party wishes to contest the legitimacy of a marriage or inheritance entitlement, the proper course is to file a separate civil suit. Petition was dismissed. (Balochistan-2021 PLD 28)

629. The court dismissed the bail cancellation petitions filed by the petitioner against the bail granted to the respondents. The case involved allegations of abduction, unlawful marriage, and zina after Shahid Mehmood, who was previously married to the petitioner's elder daughter, contracted a second marriage with the petitioner's younger daughter. The petitioner contended that Shahid Mehmood had not legally divorced his first wife before marrying the second, rendering his second marriage invalid and amounting to zina. The court ruled that an irregular marriage is not unlawful in itself, but unlawful due to temporary circumstances (such as during the iddat period). The court found that Shahid Mehmood had pronounced talaaq to his first wife before marrying her sister. The court noted that under Hanafi law, marriage with the wife's sister during the subsistence of the first marriage is not void (batil) but merely irregular (fasid). Additionally, it was observed that even if the second marriage occurred during the iddat period, it would still be considered an irregular marriage, not void, and would become valid once the iddat period expired. Thus, the petitions were dismissed, and the court upheld the respondents' bail while stating that these findings would not affect the merits of the trial. (ISB-2020 PLD 443)

630. Petitioner sought dissolution of marriage and maintenance, while her husband sought restitution of conjugal rights. The trial court dissolved the marriage on the ground of non-maintenance but denied petitioner's claim for past maintenance, granting only her minor daughter's maintenance. On appeal, the High Court modified the decision, holding that while petitioner failed to prove two years of non-maintenance before filing the suit, she established cruelty as a valid ground for divorce. The court found that she was forced to leave due to her husband's conduct, including his second marriage, and was entitled to maintenance, including the *Iddat* period. The court emphasized that under Sharia law, a husband is bound to provide maintenance during *Iddat*. It also increased the minor daughter's maintenance with a 10% annual increment. The husband's appeal was dismissed, and the decree of dissolution was based on cruelty rather than non-maintenance. (AJ&K High Court – 2020 PLD 1)

§6. Christian Marriage Dissolution

631. In Christian law, marriage is considered a sacred and lifelong union. The dissolution of marriage is primarily recognized through the death of a spouse, while divorce during their lifetime is permitted only on limited grounds. The legal framework governing Christian marriage and divorce in India is established under the *Christian Marriage Act of 1872* and the *Divorce Act of 1869*. Unlike some other personal laws, Christian law does not recognize unilateral divorce; instead, the dissolution of marriage requires judicial intervention. Either spouse seeking a divorce must file a civil petition before the appropriate Civil Court. Additionally, while civil courts have the primary authority to grant divorces, in practice, the Church also plays a role in the annulment or dissolution of marriage within the religious domain.

632. The *Divorce Act of 1869* (Act No. IV of 1869) governs the dissolution of marriage for individuals professing the Christian faith. It grants court's jurisdiction over matrimonial matters, allowing them to issue decrees for dissolution or nullity of marriage under specific conditions. Under this Act, courts can provide relief to Christian petitioners and respondents by granting divorce or nullity of marriage. However, a decree of dissolution of marriage can only be granted if the parties were domiciled in Pakistan at the time of filing the petition. Similarly, a decree of nullity can be issued only if the marriage was solemnized before 15 August 1947, in India, or after that date in Pakistan, with the petitioner residing in Pakistan when filing the petition. Furthermore, other forms of relief under this Act, apart from dissolution or nullity of marriage, can only be granted if the petitioner is a resident of Pakistan at the time of filing.

633. Under the Divorce Act, 1869 'Minor Children' means, in the case of sons of Pakistan fathers, boys who have not completed the age of 16 years, and, in case of daughters of Pakistan fathers, girls who have not completed the age of 13 years; in other cases, it means unmarried children who have not completed the age of 18 years; 'Incestuous adultery' means adultery committed by a husband with a woman with whom, if his wife were dead, he could not lawful contract marriage by reason of her being within the prohibited degrees of consanguinity (whether natural or legal) or affinity; 'Bigamy with adultery' means adultery with the same woman with whom the bigamy was committed; 'Marriage with another woman' means marriage of any person, being married, to any other person, during the life of the former wife, whether the second marriage shall have taken place within Pakistan or elsewhere; 'Desertion' implies an abandonment against the wish of the person charging it; and 'Property' includes, in the case of a wife, any property to which she is entitled for an estate in remainder or reversion, or as a trustee, executrix or administratrix; and the date of the death of the testator or intestate shall be deemed to be the time at which any such wife becomes entitled as executrix or administratrix.

634. Part III (sections 10–17) of the *Divorce Act, 1869* governs the dissolution of marriage for Christians. Under **section 10**, a husband may file a petition before the Civil Court seeking dissolution of marriage on the grounds that his wife has committed adultery after the solemnization of their marriage. The petition must explicitly state the facts supporting the claim in as much detail as possible. According to **section 11**, when a husband files such a petition, he is required to name the alleged adulterer as a co-respondent unless the court allows an exception based on one of the following grounds:

- that the respondent is leading the life of a prostitute, and that the petitioner knows of no person with whom the adultery has been committed;
- that the name of the alleged adulterer is unknown to the petitioner although he has made due efforts of discover it; and
- that the alleged adulterer is dead.

635. Under section 10, a wife may file a petition in the District Court or High Court seeking the dissolution of her marriage on specific grounds. These include her husband's conversion from Christianity to another religion and subsequent remarriage; incestuous adultery; bigamy with adultery; marriage to another woman with adultery; rape, sodomy, or bestiality; adultery accompanied by cruelty that would independently justify a divorce a mensa et toro; or adultery coupled with desertion for at least two years without reasonable cause. The petition must clearly state the facts supporting the claim for dissolution, as precisely as the case allows.

636. Upon receiving a petition for the dissolution of marriage, the Court must thoroughly examine not only the facts presented but also assess whether the petitioner has been complicit in or has condoned the alleged adultery or the marriage itself. The Court must also determine if the petitioner has, in any way, facilitated or connived in the commission of adultery. Additionally, the Court is required to consider any counterclaims made against the petitioner before proceeding with the case.

637. If, after examining the evidence, the Court determines that the petitioner has failed to substantiate the claims or is not convinced that the alleged adultery occurred, the petition shall be dismissed. Additionally, the Court will reject the petition if it finds that the petitioner, at any point during the marriage, was complicit in, encouraged, or condoned the alleged adultery. Furthermore, if there is evidence that the petition was filed or pursued in collusion with the respondent, the Court will dismiss the case to prevent misuse of legal provisions. The judicial process ensures that petitions for divorce are based on genuine grievances rather than being a means to manipulate legal proceedings for personal gain.

638. If the Court, based on the evidence presented, is satisfied that the petitioner has successfully proven the case and does not find that the petitioner has, in any way, been accessory to, or conniving at, the solemnization of the marriage or the adultery of the other party, or has condoned the adultery, or that the petition was filed or pursued in collusion with the respondent, the Court shall issue a decree declaring the marriage dissolved. However, the Court is not bound to grant such a decree if it finds that the petitioner has committed adultery during the marriage, has unreasonably delayed filing or pursuing the petition, has subjected the respondent to cruelty, has deserted or wilfully separated from the respondent before the alleged adultery without reasonable justification, or has engaged in neglect or misconduct that contributed to the adultery. Under this Act, adultery is not considered condoned unless there has been a resumption or continuation of conjugal cohabitation.

639. In any suit filed for the dissolution of marriage, if the respondent contests the relief sought by the petitioner, the Court has the authority to grant appropriate relief to the respondent under certain circumstances. If a husband files for divorce, the wife may oppose it on the grounds of his adultery, cruelty, or desertion without reasonable cause. Similarly, if a wife files for divorce, the husband may contest it on the grounds of her adultery or cruelty. In such cases, upon the respondent's application, the Court may grant the same relief that the respondent would have been entitled to if they had filed a separate petition for dissolution of marriage. The respondent is also permitted to present evidence related to cruelty or desertion in support of their defence. This provision ensures that both parties have an equal opportunity to seek justice and that the Court considers all relevant factors before deciding. It also prevents wrongful dissolution of marriage based solely on one party's claims and provides a fair legal framework for addressing matrimonial disputes.

640. Section IV of the Divorce Act, 1869 (sections 18~21) deals with the nullity of marriage. Any husband or wife can present a petition to the Court of Civil Judge, praying that his/her marriage may be declared null and void. However, such decree may be made on any of the following grounds:

- that the respondent was impotent at the time of the marriage and at the time of the institution of the suit;
- that the parties are within the prohibited degrees of consanguinity whether natural or legal or affinity;
- that either party was a lunatic or idiot at the time of marriage; and
- that the former husband or wife or either party was living at the time of marriage, and the marriage with such former husband or wife was then in force.

641. However, nothing in this section of the Act limits the Court's authority to declare a marriage null and void if it is proven that the consent of either party was obtained through force, coercion, or fraud. A marriage is considered legally valid only when both parties enter into it voluntarily and with full understanding of its implications. If it is established that one spouse was compelled or deceived into marriage, the Court retains the jurisdiction to annul the marriage, irrespective of any other claims or defences raised in a divorce petition.

642. Under section 21 of the Act, when a marriage is annulled on the ground that former husband or wife was living, and it is adjudged that the subsequent marriage was contracted in good faith with the full belief of the parties that the former husband or wife was dead, or when a marriage is annulled on the ground of insanity children begotten before the decree is made shall be specified in the decree, and shall be entitled to succeed, in the same manner as legitimate children, to the estate of the parent who at the time of the marriage was competent to contract.

643. Section IV of the Divorce Act, 1869 (sections 22~25) deals with the judicial separation. It is stated that no decree shall be made for a divorce a *mensa et thoro*, but the husband or wife may obtain a decree of judicial separation, on the ground of adultery, or cruelty, or desertion without reasonable excuse for two years or upwards, and such decree shall have the effect of a divorce a *mensa et thoro,* under the existing law, and such other legal effect. Application for judicial separation on any one of the grounds aforesaid shall be made by either husband or wife by petition to the Court of Civil Judge; and the Court, on being satisfied of the truth of the statements made in such petition and that there is no legal ground why the application should not be granted, may decree judicial separation accordingly.

644. Upon judicial separation under the Divorce Act, the wife shall, from the date of the decree and throughout the separation, be legally regarded as an unmarried woman concerning any property she acquires, inherits, or otherwise becomes entitled to. She shall have full ownership and control over such property, with the right to manage, use, or dispose of it independently, as if she were single. In the event of her death without a will, the property shall be distributed as though her husband had predeceased her. However, if she resumes cohabitation with her husband, any property in her possession at that time shall remain her separate property, unless otherwise agreed upon in writing during the separation. This provision safeguards her financial autonomy while allowing for legally binding agreements upon reconciliation.

645. During a judicial separation, the wife shall be deemed an unmarried woman concerning contracts, civil liabilities, and legal proceedings. She shall have full legal capacity to enter into agreements, initiate or defend lawsuits, and be solely responsible for any obligations incurred during the separation. The husband shall not be held liable for any debts, actions, or omissions undertaken by her during this period. However, if the court has granted or ordered alimony and the husband fails to make the required payments, he shall remain responsible for the cost of essential provisions provided for her sustenance. The wife retains the right to participate in the exercise of any joint legal power granted to both her and her husband at any time during the separation.

646. Under section 26 of the Divorce Act, any husband or wife, upon the application of whose wife or husband, as the case may be, a decree of judicial separation has been pronounced, may, at any time thereafter, present a petition to the Court by which the decree was pronounced, praying for a reversal of such decree on the ground that it was obtained in his/her absence, and that there was reasonable excuse for the alleged desertion, where desertion was the ground of such decree. The Court may, on being satisfied of the truth of the allegations of such petition, reverse the decree accordingly, but such reversal shall not prejudice or affect the rights or remedies which any other person would have had, in case it had not been decreed, in respect of any debts, contracts or acts of the wife incurred, entered into are done between the times of the sentence of separation and of the reversal thereof.

647. Section 27 of the Divorce Act, 1869 stipulated that any wife to whom section 4 of the Indian Succession Act, 1865 does not apply, may, when deserted by her husband, present a petition to the Court of Civil Judge at any time after such desertion, for an order to protect any property which she may have acquired or may acquire, and property of which she may become possessed after such desertion, against her husband or his creditors, or any person claiming under him. Under section 28, if Court is satisfied of the fact of such desertion, and that the same was without reasonable excuse, and that the wife is maintaining herself by her own industry or property, may make and give to the wife an order protecting her earnings and other property from her husband and all creditors and persons claiming under him. Every such order shall state the time at which the desertion commenced, and shall, as regards all persons dealing with the wife in reliance thereon, be conclusive as to such time.

648. The husband or any creditor of, or person claiming under him, may apply to the Court by which such order was made for the discharge or variation thereof and the Court, if the desertion has ceased, or if for any other reason it thinks fit so to do, may discharge or vary the order accordingly. If the husband, or any creditor of, or person claiming under, the husband seizes or continues to hold any property of the wife after notice any such order, her shall be liable, at the suit of the wife (which she is hereby empowered to bring), to return or deliver to her the specific property, and also to pay her sum equal to double its value So long as any such order of protection remains in force, the wife shall be and be deemed to have been, during such desertion of her, in the like position all respects, with regard to property and contracts and suing and being sued, as she would be under this Act if she obtained a decree of judicial separation (sections 29~31 of the Divorce Act, 1869).

649. Under section 32 of the Divorce Act, 1869, when either the husband or the wife has, either reasonable excuse, withdrawn from the society of the other wife or husband may apply a petition to the High Court or Civil Judge for restitution of conjugal rights, and the Courts, on being satisfied of the truth of the statements made in such petition, and that there is no legal ground why the application should not be granted, may decree restitution of conjugal rights accordingly. However, nothing shall be pleaded in answer to a petition for restitution of conjugal rights which would not be ground for a suit for a judicial separation or for a decree of nullity of marriage.

650. Part VIII (section 34) of the Divorce Act, 1869, any husband may, either in a petition for dissolution of marriage or for judicial separation, or in a petition to the Court of Civil Judge limited to such object only, claim damages from any person on the ground of his having committed adultery with the wife of such petitioner. Such petition shall be served on the alleged adulterer, and the wife unless the Court dispenses with such service or directs some other service to be substituted. The damages to be recovered on any such petition shall be ascertained by the said Court, although the respondents or either of them may not appear. After the decision has been given, the Court may direct in what manner such damages shall be paid or applied.

651. Section 35 of the Divorce Act, 1869 stipulates that whenever in any petition resented by a husband, the alleged adulterer has been made a co-respondent, and the adultery has been established, the Court may order the co-respondent to pay the whole or any part of the proceedings: Provided that the co-respondent shall not be ordered to pay the petitioner's costs. If the respondent was, at the time of the adultery, living apart from her husband and leading the life of a prostitute, or if the co-respondent had not, at the time of the adultery, reason to believe the respondent to be a married woman.

652. Part IX (sections 36~38) deals with the alimony. In any suit, whether it be instituted by a husband or a wife, and whether or not she has obtained an order of protection, the wife may present a petition for alimony pending the suit. Such petition shall be served on the husband, and the Court, on being satisfied of the truth of the statements therein contained, may make such order on the husband for payment to the wife of alimony pending the suit as it may deem just: Provided that alimony pending the suit shall in no case exceed one-fifth of the husband's average net income for the three years next preceding the date of the order, and shall continue, in case of a decree for dissolution of marriage or of nullity of marriage, until the decree is made absolute or is confirmed, as the case may be. The Court may, if it thinks fit on any decree declaring a marriage to be dissolved, or on any decree of judicial separation obtained by the wife, order.

653. The Court may issue an order requiring the husband to pay the wife a reasonable monthly or weekly sum for her maintenance and support. However, if the husband later becomes unable to make such payments due to any reason, the Court shall have the authority to modify, suspend, or discharge the order, either in whole or in part. The Court may reinstate the order, fully or partially, as it deems appropriate.

654. In all cases in which the Court makes any decree or order for alimony it may direct the same to be paid either to the wife herself, or to any trustee on her behalf to be approved by the Court, and may impose any terms or restriction which the Court seem expedient, and may from time to time appoint a new trustee, if it appears to the Court expedient so to do.

655. Part X (sections 39~44) of the Divorce Act, 1869 deals with the Settlements. Whenever the Court pronounces a decree of dissolution of marriage or judicial separation for adultery of the wife if it is made to appear to the Court that the wife is entitled to any property, the Court may, if it thinks fit, order such settlement as it thinks reasonable to be made of such property of any part thereof, for the benefit of the husband, or of the children of the marriage, or of both. Any instrument executed pursuant to any order of the Court at the time of or after the pronouncing of a decree of dissolution of marriage or judicial separation shall be deemed valid notwithstanding the existence of the disability of coverture at the time of the execution thereof. The Court may direct that the whole or any part of the damages recovered under section 34 shall be settled for the benefit of the children of the marriage, or as a provision for the maintenance of the wife.

656. Upon granting a decree of dissolution or nullity of marriage, the Court may inquire into the existence of any ante-nuptial or post-nuptial settlements between the parties. The Court shall have the authority to issue such orders as it deems just and proper regarding the application or distribution of the whole or any portion of the settled property. Such orders may be made for the benefit of either spouse, the children of the marriage (if any), or both the children and the parents. However, that no order shall be made for the benefit of either parent if it is to the detriment of the children, ensuring that their welfare and financial security remain paramount in all property-related determinations.

657. In any proceedings for judicial separation, the Court may, at its discretion and at any stage before rendering its final decree, issue interim orders as it deems appropriate concerning the custody, maintenance, and education of any minor children of the marriage in question. The Court may incorporate such provisions into its final decree as it considers just and equitable. Additionally, if deemed necessary, the Court may direct that appropriate legal proceedings be initiated to place such children under its protection, ensuring their welfare and best interests remain paramount.

658. Following the issuance of a decree of judicial separation, the Court may, upon petition, issue such orders and provisions as it deems necessary concerning the custody, maintenance, and education of any minor children of the marriage. The Court may also take measures to place such children under its protection, as it could have done through interim orders or within the decree itself had the proceedings for judicial separation still been pending. The Court retains the authority to modify or issue further orders from time to time, ensuring the continued welfare and best interests of the children remain safeguarded.

659. In any proceedings for the dissolution or nullity of marriage, the Court may, at its discretion and at any stage before issuing its final decree, make such interim orders or incorporate such provisions in the decree as it deems just and appropriate concerning the custody, maintenance, and education of any minor children of the marriage. If the Court considers it necessary, it may direct that proceedings be initiated to place such children under its protection, ensuring their welfare and best interests remain paramount.

660. Upon granting a decree of dissolution or nullity of marriage, the Court may, upon application by petition, issue such orders and make such provisions as it deems necessary, from time to time, regarding the custody, maintenance, and education of any minor children of the marriage. The Court may also take appropriate measures to place such children under its protection, as it could have done within the decree itself or through interim orders issued during the proceedings.

661. Section 48 of the Divorce Act, 1869 stipulates that when the husband or wife is a lunatic or idiot, any suit (other than a suit for restitution of conjugal rights) may be brought on his/her behalf by the committee or other person entitled to his/her custody.

662. Under section 49 where the petitioner is a minor, he/she shall sue by his/her next friend to be approved by the Court; and no petition presented by a minor under this Act shall be filed until the next friends has undertaken in writing to be answerable for costs. Such undertaking shall be filed in Court, and the next friend shall thereupon be liable in the same manner and to the same extent as if he/she were a plaintiff in an ordinary suit.

663. Part XIII (sections 57~59) stipulates provisions relating to re-marriage. After the expiry of six months from the date of decree for the dissolution of a marriage, or, where an appeal has been presented against any such decree, after the dismissal of such appeal or the declaration of the marriage is dissolved as a result of such appeal, but not sooner, it shall be lawful for the parties to the marriage to marry again as if the prior marriage had been dissolved by death. No clergyman in Holy Orders of the Church shall be compelled to solemnize the marriage of any person whose former marriage has been dissolved on the ground of his/her adultery, or shall be liable to any suit, penalty or censure for solemnizing or refusing to solemnize the marriage of any such person. When any minister of any Church or chapel of the said Church refuses to perform such marriage service between any persons who, but for such refusal would be entitled to have same service performed in such Church or chapel, such minister shall permit any other minister in Holy Orders of fee paid Church entitled to officiate within the diocese in which such Church or chapel is situate to perform such marriage service in such Church or chapel.

664. Suit for dissolution of marriage. This case, brought under section 20 of the Divorce Act, 1869, involved a petition for nullity of marriage between two first cousins, both Christians by birth. The petitioner filed a case in the District Court, Karachi, seeking a declaration that the marriage was null and void, along with a decree for divorce or judicial separation. The grounds for the petition were that their marriage was within the prohibited degrees of consanguinity under Christian law, that she had been coerced and fraudulently induced into marriage, and that she had never lived with the respondent. The respondent contested the petition, admitting they were first cousins but denying any prohibition under Christianity and asserting that they had lived together for ten days. The trial court ruled in favour of the petitioner, holding that Christianity prohibits cousin marriages and that Hindu converts to Christianity remain subject to Hindu laws on consanguinity. However, the appellate court found serious flaws in the judgment, noting the lack of proper reasoning and inconsistencies in the evidence, particularly letters from the petitioner that contradicted her claim of never having lived with the respondent. The court also noted that her allegations of coercion were abandoned during testimony, suggesting they were false and an abuse of the legal process. The appellate court refused to confirm the trial court's decree of nullity, criticizing its reliance on weak and contradictory evidence. (Karachi High Court-1974 PLD 185)

665. Judicial separation of husband and wife. The petitioner filed a case for judicial separation under section 23 of the Divorce Act, 1869, in a Civil Court at Lahore, while the respondent filed a suit for restitution of conjugal rights in the Civil Court at Shakargarh. The petitioner then moved an application under section 24 of the Civil Procedure Code to transfer the respondent's suit to Lahore, arguing that common legal and factual issues existed in both cases, and it would be in the interest of justice to have them decided by the same court to avoid conflicting decisions. The respondent opposed the request, contending that the Lahore court lacked jurisdiction, as the couple had never resided within its territorial limits, and under section 23 of the Divorce Act, only the court where the couple last resided together had jurisdiction. The court observed that transferring the case to Lahore would not serve the intended purpose if the jurisdictional objection raised by the respondent was upheld, as it would result in the petitioner's application being returned for filing in the appropriate court, leaving the respondent's suit pending in Shakargarh. Therefore, the court directed that the Lahore court first decide the jurisdictional objection raised by the respondent, and until then, proceedings in the Shakargarh court would remain stayed. If the Lahore court rejects the objection, the petitioner may then seek the transfer of the respondent's suit to Lahore. The application for transfer was thus disposed of accordingly. (LHC – 1985 CLC 1907)

§7. Parsi Marriage Dissolution

666. The Parsi Marriage and Divorce Act, 1936 regulates the divorce matters of Parsi community in Pakistan. Under section 31 of the Parsi Marriage and Divorce Act, 1936, a marriage solemnized under the Act may be dissolved if either spouse has been continuously absent for a period of seven years and has not been heard of as being alive by those who would naturally have received such information had they been alive. In such circumstances, the aggrieved spouse may file a petition for dissolution of marriage before a court of competent jurisdiction. Upon due inquiry and satisfaction that the conditions prescribed under the law are met, the court may grant a decree of divorce, thereby legally dissolving the marriage. Additionally, the petitioner must provide sufficient evidence to establish the prolonged absence and lack of communication from the missing spouse. If the decree is granted, it shall have the same legal effect as any other decree of divorce under the Act, severing all marital obligations and rights between the parties.

667. Under section 32 of the Act, any married person may sue for divorce on any one or more of the following grounds, namely (a) that the marriage has not been consummated within one year after its solemnization owing to the wilful refusal of the defendant to consummate it; (b) that the defendant at the time of the marriage was of unsound mind and has been habitually so up to the date of the suit: Provided that divorce shall not be granted on this ground, unless the plaintiff (1) was ignorant of the fact at the time of the marriage, and (2) has filed the suit within three years from the date of the marriage; (c) that the defendant was at the time of marriage pregnant by some person other than the plaintiff: Provided that divorce shall not be granted on this ground, unless (1) the plaintiff was at the time of the marriage ignorant of the fact alleged, (2) the suit has been filed within two years of the date of marriage, and (3) marital intercourse has not taken place after the plaintiff came to know of the fact; (d) that the defendant has since the marriage committed adultery or fornication or bigamy or rape or an un-natural offence: Provided that divorce shall not be granted on this ground if the suit has been filed more than two years after the plaintiff came to know of the fact; (e) that the defendant has since the marriage voluntarily caused grievous hurt to the plaintiff or has infected the plaintiff with venereal disease or, where the defendant is the husband, has compelled the wife to submit herself to prostitution; Provided that divorce shall not be granted on this ground if the suit has been filed more than two years (i) after the infliction of the grievous hurt, or (ii) after the plaintiff came to know of the infection, or (iii) after the last act of compulsory prostitution; (f) that the defendant is undergoing a sentence of imprisonment for seven years or more for an offence as defined in the PPC, XLV of 1860: Provided that divorce shall not be granted on this ground, unless the defendant has prior to the filing of the suit undergone at least one year's imprisonment out of the said period; (g) that the defendant has deserted the plaintiff for at least three years; (h) that a decree or order for judicial separation has been passed against the defendant, or an order has been passed against the defendant by a Magistrate awarding separate maintenance to the plaintiff, and the parties have not had marital intercourse for three years or more since such decree or order; (i) that the defendant has failed to comply with a decree for restitution of conjugal rights for a year or more; and (j) that the defendant has ceased to be a Parsi: Provided that divorce shall not be granted on this ground if the suit has been filed more than two years after the plaintiff came to know of the fact. Under section 33 of the Act, in every such suit for divorce on the ground of adultery, the plaintiff shall, unless the Court shall otherwise order, make the person with whom the adultery is alleged to have been committed a co-defendant, and in any such suit by the husband the Court may order the adulterer to pay the whole or any part of the costs of the proceedings.

668. Under section 34 of Parsi Marriage and Divorce Act, 1936, any married person may sue for judicial separation on any of the grounds for which such person could have filed a suit for divorce, or on the ground that the defendant has been guilty of such cruelty to him/her or their children, or has used such personal violence, or has behaved in such a way as to render it in the judgment of the Court improper to compel him/her to live with the defendant.

669. If the Court is satisfied that any of the grounds set forth in any suit under sections 30, 31, 32 or 34 of Parsi Marriage and Divorce Act, 1936 whether defended or not, those sections for granting relief exist, that none of the grounds therein set forth for withholding relief exist and that (a) the act or omission set forth in the plaint has not been condoned; (b) the husband and wife are not colluding together; (c) the plaintiff has not connived at or been accessory to the said act or omission; (d) (save where a definite period of limitation is provided by this Act) there has been no unnecessary or improper delay in instituting the suit; and (e) there is no other legal ground why relief should not be granted; then and in such case, but not otherwise, the Court shall decree such relief accordingly.

670. Under section 36 of the Parsi Marriage and Divorce Act, 1936 where a husband shall have deserted or without lawful cause ceased to cohabit with his wife, or where a wife shall have deserted or without lawful cause ceased to cohabit with her husband, the party so deserted or with whom cohabitation shall have so ceased may sue for the restitution of his/her conjugal rights and the Court, if satisfied of the truth of the allegations contained in the plaint, and that there is no just ground why relief should not be granted, may proceed to decree such restitution of conjugal rights accordingly. In any suit under this Act, the defendant may make a counter-claim for any relief he/she may be entitled to under this Act.

671. Under section 30 of the said Act, any case in which consummation of the marriage is from natural causes impossible, such marriage may, at the instance of either party thereto, be declared to be null and void.

Chapter 3. Cohabitation Outside Marriage

672. Under Pakistani law, in accordance with Islamic principles, extramarital sexual relations referred to as *Zina* are considered a grave offense and a major sin in Islam. The Offence of Zina (Enforcement of Hudood) Ordinance, 1979, promulgated on 9 February 1979, criminalizes such acts and prescribes strict punishments in line with Islamic jurisprudence. Under the ordinance, *Zina* includes voluntary sexual intercourse between individuals who are not lawfully married to each other. The prescribed punishments vary depending on the nature of the offense and the evidence available. If *Zina* is proven through the testimony of four adult male Muslim witnesses of unimpeachable character, the punishment under *Hadd* includes stoning to death for married offenders and public flogging (100 lashes) for unmarried individuals. In the absence of such evidence, the offense may be prosecuted under *Tazir*, where punishments include imprisonment, fines, or corporal punishment as determined by the court. The ordinance has been subject to legal and human rights debates, particularly regarding its evidentiary requirements and its impact on women's rights. The Protection of Women (Criminal Laws Amendment) Act, 2006, introduced significant reforms by shifting certain cases of *Zina* from the Hudood Ordinances to the PPC, thereby providing safeguards against misuse of the law.

673. Under the Office of *Zina* (Enforcement of Hadood) Ordinance, 1979 'Adult' means a person who has attained, being a male, the age of 18 years or, being a female, the age of 16 years, or has attained puberty; and 'Muhsan' means a Muslim adult man who is not insane and has had sexual intercourse with a Muslim adult woman who, at the time he had sexual intercourse with her, was married to him and was not insane; or a Muslim adult woman who is not insane and has had sexual intercourse with a Muslim adult man who, at the time she had sexual intercourse with him, was married to him and was not insane; '*Zina*' means a man and a woman are said to commit '*Zina*' if they wilfully have sexual intercourse without being married to each other. Penetration is sufficient to constitute the sexual intercourse necessary to the offence of *Zina*.

674. *Zina* is considered liable to *Hadd* under Islamic law and the Offence of Zina (Enforcement of Hudood) Ordinance, 1979, if it is committed by an adult, sane man with a woman to whom he is neither lawfully married nor under the genuine misconception of being married, or by an adult, sane woman with a man to whom she is neither lawfully married nor under the mistaken belief of marriage. To establish *Zina-bil-Jabr* (rape) or *Zina* liable to *Hadd*, the law requires the testimony of four adult Muslim male witnesses of good character who have directly observed the act, making the evidentiary standard extremely stringent. If such evidence is not available, the offense may be prosecuted under *Tazir*, where lesser punishments, including imprisonment, flogging, or fines, may be imposed at the discretion of the court. The stringent evidentiary requirements for *Hadd* often result in cases being dealt with under *Tazir*, where convictions can be based on circumstantial evidence or confession.

675. A person found guilty of *Zina* liable to *Hadd* shall face severe punishments in accordance with Islamic law. If the offender is a *Muhsan* (a legally married Muslim adult who has consummated the marriage), the prescribed punishment is *Rajm* (stoning to death) at a public place. If the offender is not a *Muhsan* (i.e., unmarried), the punishment consists of one hundred lashes of whipping in a public setting. The execution of *Hadd* punishments requires an exceptionally high standard of proof, including the testimony of four adult Muslim male witnesses of unimpeachable character who have directly observed the act of penetration or a voluntary, repeated confession by the accused.

676. No punishment for *Zina* liable to *Hadd* shall be carried out unless it has been duly confirmed by the appellate court authorized to hear appeals against the conviction. In cases where the prescribed punishment is whipping, the sentence shall not be executed until it has been formally upheld by the relevant court. Until such confirmation and execution take place, the convict shall be treated in accordance with the provisions applicable to individuals sentenced to simple imprisonment.

677. The proof of *Zina* liable to *Hadd* is established under Islamic law and the *Offence of Zina (Enforcement of Hudood) Ordinance, 1979*. A conviction requires either a voluntary and unequivocal confession made by the accused before a court of competent jurisdiction or the testimony of at least four adult Muslim male witnesses who fulfil the criteria of *Tazkiyah al-Shuhood* – meaning they are deemed truthful, credible, and abstain from major sins (*Kabair*). These witnesses must provide direct and unequivocal testimony as eye-witnesses to the act of penetration, which is an essential element of the offense. However, if the accused is a non-Muslim, the law permits non-Muslim witnesses to testify. The stringent evidentiary requirements for *Hadd* punishment reflect the gravity of the offense and serve as a safeguard against false accusations, ensuring that convictions are based on irrefutable and reliable evidence.

678. In cases where the offense of *Zina* is established solely through the confession of the accused, the *Hadd* punishment, or any portion of it yet to be executed, shall not be enforced if the accused retracts their confession before its execution. Similarly, if the conviction is based exclusively on witness testimony, the *Hadd* punishment, or any remaining part of it, shall not be carried out if any witness withdraws their testimony before enforcement, thereby reducing the number of required eyewitnesses below four. This principle aligns with the stringent evidentiary standards in Islamic law, ensuring that *Hadd* punishments are not imposed in cases where doubt arises. The requirement for four credible eyewitnesses or an uncoerced confession emphasizes the high threshold of proof necessary to administer *Hadd* penalties, reflecting the fundamental Islamic legal principle that severe punishments should only be enforced when guilt is proven beyond any reasonable doubt.

679. The punishment of stoning to death, once awarded, shall be carried out by the available witnesses who testified against the convict. They shall initiate the stoning and if during the process the convict is shot and succumbs to the gunfire, the execution shall be halted immediately.

Chapter 4. Filiation

§1. Children Born in Wedlock

680. Under Islamic law, the principle of *'child of the bed'* (i.e., the presumption that a child born in lawful wedlock is attributed to the husband of the mother) is well recognized. A child born within a valid marriage is deemed legitimate and follows the legal status of the father. However, unlike English law, which presumes legitimacy for any child born in wedlock without further conditions, Islamic law mandates that both conception and birth must occur within the bounds of marriage. Consequently, a child conceived before marriage, even if born after a valid marriage, is considered illegitimate under Islamic law, whereas English law upholds such legitimacy. Additionally, Islamic law does not recognize the doctrine of *legitimation per subsequent matrimonium*, meaning a child conceived through *Zina* (illicit sexual relations) cannot become legitimate by the subsequent marriage of the parents. However, Islamic jurisprudence does acknowledge a strong presumption of legitimacy if a man accepts a child as his own and does not publicly repudiate its parentage. This presumption is not merely a rule of evidence but a fundamental principle in Islamic law aimed at protecting the child's status and lineage.

§2. Legitimacy of Child

681. Under Islamic law, the paternity of a child can only be legally established through a valid or irregular (*fasid*) marriage between its parents, but not from a void (*batil*) marriage or an illicit relationship. A valid (*sahih*) marriage confers full legitimacy, while an irregular marriage, though defective in certain respects, may still establish paternity if the marriage is recognized as such under Islamic jurisprudence. However, a child born from an entirely void marriage or *Zina* (illicit relations) is not granted legitimate status. Once paternity is established through a valid or irregular marriage, legitimacy is automatically conferred upon the child, ensuring inheritance rights and social recognition. Islamic law strongly upholds the sanctity of lineage, and any claim of paternity must adhere to strict evidentiary standards, such as acknowledgment by the father, birth within lawful wedlock, or a legal presumption based on the husband's silence regarding repudiation

682. Before the advent of Islam, the customary laws regarding parentage in pre-Islamic Arabia were flexible and largely influenced by tribal power dynamics, much like the prevailing customs on marriage and divorce. Lineage and kinship were often determined by social and political considerations rather than strict biological ties. Adoption was common, and a man could declare someone his son, granting them full rights of inheritance and social status without a formalized legal framework. This practice provided tribal leaders with additional warriors and supporters, strengthening their position in an era marked by frequent conflict and instability. However, there were few reciprocal obligations imposed upon the adopted individuals, as kinship ties were often based on strategic alliances rather than family responsibilities. Islam, however, introduced strict regulations regarding lineage and paternity, abolishing formal adoption (*tabanni*) in favour of *Kafalah* (guardianship), ensuring that inheritance rights and family lineage remained clearly defined.

683. A child born at least six months after the commencement of a valid marriage is presumed to be legitimate unless the putative father formally disclaims paternity through *Li'an*, a legal process involving mutual oaths and curses before a court. Similarly, if a child is born within 280 days of the dissolution of a marriage, such as through divorce or the husband's death, the presumption of legitimacy remains intact unless *Li'an* is invoked. This legal principle ensures the protection of the child's lineage and inheritance rights, preventing arbitrary claims of illegitimacy. In Islamic jurisprudence, legitimacy is a fundamental concept, and a child born within wedlock cannot be declared illegitimate except through undeniable proof of non-access, meaning that the husband could not have possibly fathered the child.

684. Under the Mohamedan Law, the paternity of a child is established through the existence of a valid or irregular (*Fasid*) marriage between the parents at the time of conception or birth. If no such marriage can be proven, the child is considered illegitimate and does not inherit from the father. Islamic jurisprudence recognizes certain legal presumptions that favour legitimacy when a man acknowledges the child as his own, provided such acknowledgment is not contradicted by clear evidence. While the doctrine of *istilhaq* (acknowledgment of paternity) can grant the child social and legal recognition, it does not confer full inheritance rights unless supported by proof of lawful wedlock.

685. Petitioner challenged the legitimacy of his deceased brother's children, asserting they were not entitled to inherit his property. Petitioner claimed that his brother was in Libya during the time of their births and had disowned one of the children in a past legal proceeding. However, both lower courts dismissed his suit, finding no credible evidence against the children's legitimacy. The High Court upheld these decisions, emphasizing that under Islamic law, a child born in wedlock is presumed legitimate unless disproven through *Li'an*. The court noted that petitioner never challenged their parentage during his lifetime and ruled that the children had lawful inheritance rights. It also criticized petitioner actions as an attempt to deprive them of their rightful legacy, imposing a cost of PKR 25,000 on him for bringing a frivolous claim. Consequently, the revision petition was dismissed. (LHC – 2009 CLC 137)

686. Suit for dissolution of marriage, recovery of dowry articles, and maintenance for the wife (respondent No. 1) and minor son (respondent No. 2). The trial court dissolved the marriage, granted dowry articles except for gold ornaments, and awarded maintenance to the wife for the Iddat period and to the child at PKR 800 per month. The appellate court upheld the trial court's decision, modifying the dowry articles' recovery. The petitioner challenged the decrees, arguing that the child was illegitimate due to the period of desertion and that dowry articles could not be claimed in Khula. The court dismissed the petition, emphasizing that legitimacy follows wedlock unless disproven through Liyan proceedings. It held that the child was legitimate and entitled to maintenance, and dowry articles under lock and key at the petitioner's house rightfully belonged to the wife. The petition lacked merit and was dismissed. (LHC-2007 CLC 1145)

§3. Ex-nupital Children

687. Under Islamic law, a child born less than six months after marriage or outside of wedlock is considered illegitimate. However, Islam emphasizes that every human being is born with dignity and is not responsible for the actions of their parents. Illegitimate children and foundlings are integral members of the Muslim community and are entitled to the same rights and protections as others. They cannot be discriminated against based on their birth status, as stated in the Quran: *'No soul shall bear the burden of another'* (Surah Al-An'am 6:164). Islam upholds the principle of justice and compassion, ensuring that such children have the right to care, education, and a dignified life. The responsibility for their welfare falls upon the Muslim society and government, which must provide for their upbringing, protection, and integration. Classical Islamic scholars, including those from the Hanafi, Maliki, Shafi'i, and Hanbali schools of thought, agree that an illegitimate child cannot be deprived of fundamental rights such as sustenance, education, and social acceptance. Furthermore, while an illegitimate child does not inherit from their biological father under Islamic inheritance laws, scholars have encouraged alternative means of financial security, such as bequests (wasiyyah) and general societal support.

688. The illegitimate child is, like other people, competent person obligated to observe religious duties (if he is sane and adult), and he will be held accountable for his own deeds. If he does righteous deeds, he will be rewarded; otherwise, he will deserve punishment. Allah The Almighty Says (what means): (And no bearer of burdens will bear the burden of another.) (Holy Quran 17:15).

689. According to Imam Abu Hanifa, if a man commits *zina* (fornication) with a woman and she becomes pregnant, he may marry her to safeguard her dignity and protect the child from social stigma. In such a case, the child will be traced back to him, ensuring legitimacy and social acceptance. This opinion is rooted in the principle of concealing sins and preventing harm in society. However, Islamic scholars have held differing views regarding the permissibility of marrying a fornicatress before confirming whether she is pregnant. Some scholars, particularly from the Hanafi and Maliki schools, allow such a marriage if it meets all the valid conditions of a *nikah* (marriage contract), including the consent of both parties, the presence of the guardian (*wali*), and two witnesses. Others, including scholars from the Shafi'i and Hanbali schools, argue that marriage should be postponed until it is confirmed that the woman is not pregnant to avoid lineage confusion. If the marriage contract is performed without verifying pregnancy but fulfils all necessary conditions, the majority of jurists who permit it consider the marriage valid. However, in cases where a woman is pregnant due to *zina*, some scholars require waiting until childbirth before marriage to ensure clear lineage. This ruling aligns with the broader Islamic principles of preserving lineage (*nasab*), preventing disputes over paternity, and maintaining social stability.

I. Name

690. According to Muslim scholars, an illegitimate child whether a boy or a girl should be given a neutral second name that reflects their status without falsely attributing lineage to a specific individual. Common names such as *Abdullah* (slave of Allah) or *Abdur-Rahman* (slave of the Most Merciful) are recommended, as these names signify servitude to Allah, which applies to all human beings regardless of their background. This practice upholds the Islamic principle that lineage should not be falsely assigned, as Islamic law strictly prohibits attributing a child to a man who is not their biological father. Islam emphasizes justice and fairness, ensuring that an innocent child is not held accountable for the circumstances of their birth. While an illegitimate child does not inherit from the biological father under traditional *Shariah* rulings, the child still holds the same dignity, rights, and responsibilities as any other member of society. Scholars stress that such children should be raised with care and provided with opportunities for education and personal growth.

691. A child born out of an illicit relationship (*Zina* – fornication/adultery) is not legally attributed to the biological father in Islamic law. Instead, the child is traced back to the mother, as per the dominant opinion of Islamic scholars and the majority of jurists. This ruling is based on the principle that lineage in such cases cannot be established through unlawful relations, and the father has no legal or inheritance rights over the child. Despite this, Islam emphasizes that the child is not to be blamed or treated unjustly for the actions of their parents. The child retains full human dignity and has the right to be cared for, educated, and supported by the mother and the wider Muslim community. While the child does not inherit from the biological father, scholars have debated whether the father may provide financial support voluntarily. Some contemporary scholars and legal systems allow for acknowledgment of paternity if the father voluntarily accepts responsibility, especially in cases where there is no dispute. However, the classical stance remains that lineage is established only through lawful marriage.

II. Maintenance

692. According to Islamic scholars, an illegitimate child is legally attributed to the mother, who bears full responsibility for the child's care, protection, and financial support. She is obligated to nurture and provide for the child, ensuring their well-being and upbringing. Abandoning the child without a valid reason is considered a grave sin in Islam, regardless of whether the mother is a Muslim or non-Muslim. However, a Muslim woman may be held to a higher moral and religious standard, as she is expected to be fully aware of the prohibition against neglecting or endangering a child. Islamic teachings emphasize the sanctity of human life and the duty to protect the vulnerable, including children born out of wedlock. The child, being innocent, should not be penalized for the actions of the parents. If a mother is unable to care for the child due to extreme circumstances, she is encouraged to seek help from the community, charitable organizations, or responsible individuals rather than abandoning the child. In Islamic societies, ensuring the welfare of such children is a collective duty (*Fard Kifayah*), meaning that the community must step in to support and protect them.

693. If the mother of an illegitimate child disappears or is unable to care for the child, the responsibility falls upon the Muslim community to provide for and protect them. Caring for such children is considered a noble act of worship (*Ibadah*) and a means of drawing closer to Allah. The child should be raised with love, faith, and strong moral values, ensuring that they grow up as a righteous and contributing member of society. It is strictly prohibited in Islam to hold resentment or treat the child unfairly due to the circumstances of their birth, as they bear no responsibility for the actions of their parents. Islamic history offers examples of such care and responsibility. During the caliphate of Umar ibn al-Khattab, a foundling (an abandoned child who could potentially be the offspring of an illegitimate relationship) was discovered. Umar, known for his justice and compassion, instructed: *'Take the child with you, for you have the right of guardianship (Wali), and we will provide for his maintenance.' In another narration, he added: 'We will bear the expenses of his feeding.'* This precedent highlights the duty of the Muslim community to support and safeguard such vulnerable children. In Islamic law, blood relatives from the mother's side remain *Maharim* (unmarriageable kin) for an illegitimate child, just as in the case of a child born within a lawful marriage. Additionally, relationships established through *Rada'ah* (breastfeeding) are also recognized, meaning that the same restrictions on marriage apply to those who share a foster relationship. Furthermore, such children are entitled to all basic rights, including education, inheritance in some cases (through bequests or discretionary allowances), and societal inclusion. The Sharia strictly prohibits any form of discrimination against them, emphasizing that each person is accountable only for their own deeds, as stated in the Quran: *'No soul shall bear the burden of another.'* (Surah Al-An'am, 6:164)

III. Guardianship, Custody and Access

694. The mother of a child born out of *Zina* (fornication or adultery) holds primary responsibility for the child's guardianship, care, and upbringing. If she neglects this duty without a valid reason, she is accountable for her negligence in addition to the sin of *Zina*. However, Islam unequivocally asserts that the child is completely innocent and bears no responsibility for the circumstances of their birth. It is strictly forbidden to hold or treat them with blame or discrimination. Every individual is accountable for their own deeds, and no soul shall bear the burden of another, as emphasized in the Quran.

695. A child born from adultery or fornication is traced back to the mother, as she is responsible for nurturing and financially supporting the child. Since the child is a direct result of her actions, she must bear the consequences of her choices, though both parents share the sin of *Zina*. However, the child himself is completely innocent and must not be held accountable for the circumstances of his birth. While some jurists hold the view that the child may be attributed to the biological father if he marries the mother, the dominant opinion is that lineage follows only a legitimate marriage. This is because family lineage (*nasab*) is considered an honour and a legal right that is granted through lawful wedlock, not through illicit relationships. The Prophet Muhammad (PBUH) stated: 'The child is to be attributed to the mother [in the absence of a valid marriage], and the male fornicator has no claim.' (Al-Bukhari and Muslim). Therefore, Islamic law protects the child from any social or legal discrimination while upholding the sanctity of legitimate lineage.

696. As for the Maharim of illegitimate children (unmarriageable relatives) they are their brothers, sisters, their children from mother side only, and maternal uncles, maternal aunts. Only the relatives of the mother are considered, not of the father because an illegitimate child does not trace back to his father. All the relatives who are forbidden from the mother's side include those forbidden through suckling. Allah Says (interpretation of meaning): (… , your foster mother who gave you suck, your foster milk suckling sisters, …) (4:23). The Holy Prophet Muhammad (Sallallahu Alaihi wa Sallam) said: 'What is made Haram by reason of blood is made Haram by reason of the relations based on suckling'. (Reported by Imams al-Bukhari and Muslim).

697. Holy Prophet Muhammad (PBUH), said: 'A child is traced to the owner of the bed (i.e., the legitimate husband).' (Al-Bukhaari and Muslim) Since there is no marriage here, so the child is attributed to his mother, who must look after him and support him financially, and she inherits him and he inherits her.

IV. Nationality and Citizenship

698. Since an illegitimate child is traced back to the mother, the child's nationality and citizenship are generally determined by the mother's nationality, regardless of the country of birth. This principle aligns with Islamic jurisprudence, which attributes lineage to the mother in the absence of a legally recognized father. However, nationality laws vary across different countries, and some may grant citizenship based on birthplace (*jus soli*) or through the biological father under specific legal provisions. In cases where the mother's nationality does not automatically confer citizenship to the child, the legal framework of the country where the child is born or resides may play a role in determining their status. Nevertheless, in an Islamic context, the child should not be deprived of fundamental rights due to circumstances beyond their control.

V. Inheritance

699. According to the majority of Muslim scholars, a child born outside wedlock (from *Zina* – fornication or adultery) is legally attributed to the mother and her family. This means that the child's lineage follows the mother, and he or she is considered part of her kin. The laws of *Mahram* (unmarriageable relatives) apply only to the maternal side, and the legal *Wali* (guardian) is also from the mother's family. In terms of inheritance, the child can inherit only from the mother's side, and vice versa; there are no legal inheritance rights between the child and the biological father in the absence of a valid marriage. However, some scholars hold the view that if the biological father acknowledges the child as his own, the child can be attributed to him. This opinion is supported by scholars such as *Is'haq Ibn Rahawahi, Urwa, Sulaiman Ibn Yasar,* and *Imam Abu Hanifa*. Imam Abu Hanifa stated that if a man commits *Zina* with a woman and she conceives, he may marry her to protect her honour, and in such a case, the child may be traced back to him. While this view exists, the dominant opinion among Islamic jurists remains that legal paternity is established only through a valid marriage contract, ensuring that the child's lineage is clear and protected.

700. There is sound evidence backing the opinion of the majority of scholars which is the judgment reported from the Holy Prophet Muhammad (Sallallahu Alaihi wa Sallam) about the child of *Zina*:

> The Holy Prophet Muhammad (PBUH) decided regarding one who was treated as a member of a family after the death of his father, to whom he was attributed when the heirs said he was one of them, that if he was the child of a slave-woman whom the father owned when he had intercourse with her, he was included among those who sought his inclusion, but received none of the inheritance which was previously divided; he, however, received his portion of the inheritance which had not already been divided; but if the father to whom he was attributed had disowned him, he was not joined to the heirs. If he was a child of a slave-woman whom the father did not possess or of a free woman with whom he had illicit intercourse, he was not joined to the heirs and did not inherit even if the one to whom he was attributed is the one who claimed paternity, since he was a child of fornication whether his mother was free or a slave. [Reported by Imams Ahmad, Abu Dawood, Ibn Majah and al-Darimi].

Chapter 5. Adoption and Foster Care

§1. Adoption

701. According to the Mohamedan Law, there is no legal adoption. It is prohibited for a person to legally adopt a son or a daughter of whom he is not the biological father. If a person adopts a son or daughter, the Sharee'ah will not confer on the adopted person the status or rights of a biological son or daughter. According to the Holy Quran, one cannot become a person's real son merely by virtue of a declaration; Allah Says (what means):

> And He [i.e., Allaah] has not made your claimed [i.e., adopted] sons your [true] sons. That is [merely] your saying by your mouths, but Allaah says the truth, and He guides to the [right] way. Call them [i.e., the adopted children] by [the names of] their fathers; it is more just in the sight of Allaah. But if you do not know their fathers, they are your brothers in religion … [Holy Quran 33: 4–5].

702. This demonstrates that adoption in itself does not alter biological realities, nor does it create a genuine blood relationship between the adoptive parents and the child. A verbal declaration or legal formality cannot transform an unrelated individual into a biological son or daughter, nor can it establish the natural lineage that comes through birth. An adopted child does not share the genetic makeup, inherited traits, or physical, mental, and psychological characteristics of the adoptive parents. In Islam, while adoption as a form of care and guardianship (*Kafala*) is encouraged and highly rewarded, it does not grant the child the same legal status as a biological offspring. The child retains their original lineage, surname, and inheritance rights as per Islamic law. The adoptive parents have the responsibility to nurture, educate, and support the child, but the child is not considered a *Mahram* (unmarriageable kin) and does not inherit automatically unless designated through a will (which can cover up to one-third of the estate).

703. In Islam, a child is considered an extension of their father, inheriting their lineage and carrying forward their name. The child strengthens the family lineage and contributes to its continuity. Islam places great emphasis on the right of every child to legitimacy, ensuring that their paternity is clearly established and undisputed. This is why Islam has ordained marriage as the legitimate framework for procreation and has strictly prohibited adultery (*Zina*), as it leads to confusion regarding lineage and parentage. The principle of legitimacy in Islam dictates that every child must have one recognized father, and no child should be falsely attributed to a man who is not his biological parent. This principle is deeply rooted in the preservation of social order and individual rights. Allah commands in the Quran: *'Call them by (the names of) their fathers; it is more just in the sight of Allah...'* (Surah Al-Ahzab 33:5).

704. Taking a stranger into the family as one of its members and allowing him to be in privacy with women who are non-mahram (i.e., non-marriageable relatives) to him is a deception, for the adopter's wife is not the adopted son's real mother, nor is his daughter the boy's sister, nor is his sister the boy's aunt, since all of them are non-mahram to him and vice-versa for an adopted daughter. The Holy Quran has, thus, declared that only the wives of one's real sons, and not the wives of any sons under one's care, are permanently forbidden in marriage. This is according to the verse (which means): '… The wives of your sons who are from your (own) loins …' (Holy Quran 4:23). Accordingly, it is permissible for a man to marry the divorced wife of any son under his care, since, in actuality; she has been the wife of a 'stranger' who was not related by blood. Also, when the adopted child's lineal identity or paternity is changed, it is quite possible that the adopted child may, unknowingly, enter into incestuous relationships by marrying close relatives of his natural parents; also, his marital chances may, in general, become subject to confusion.

705. The petitioner filed a petition under Article 199 of the Constitution of Pakistan, 1973, seeking custody of her minor son who had been adopted by respondent The court ordered a DNA test, which confirmed that Mst. Arzu was the biological mother of the child. The court examined the Islamic and legal perspectives on adoption, concluding that while adoption is encouraged for the welfare of children, it does not create legal parentage under Islamic law. The court held that custody must prioritize the child's welfare and, as the biological mother was entitled to custody. However, Rasheed Ahmad was given the right to file an application under the Guardians and Wards Act, 1890, for guardianship, which the competent forum must decide on its own merits without being influenced by this order. The adopted father was also directed to produce the child before the competent forum if required, ensuring petitioner could meet the minor but not take him away from the premises. Accordingly, the petition was allowed, and custody was granted to petitioner. (LHC – 2024 YLR 1973)

706. The appellants challenged the judgment and decree dated 21.09.2021, which dismissed their suit seeking a declaration that Malik Mohammad Rafique and Tehmina Rafique were the adoptive parents of Osman. Osman, and was allegedly adopted by adoptive parents in Islamabad, though no formal adoption deed was executed at that time. In 2021, the parties executed an adoption deed and sought a legal declaration, but the Civil Court dismissed the suit due to inordinate delay and possible collusion. The Court considered whether adoption is permissible under Pakistani law, what rights adopted children and adoptive parents have, and whether a declaration could be granted after such a long delay. The amici curiae submitted that adoption is not prohibited under Islamic law but does not create inheritance rights, while courts in Pakistan have recognized the legal character of adoption. The Court held that adoption is legally recognized and declarations can be sought under section 42 of the Specific Relief Act, 1877. It found that limitation starts when a right is denied, not from the date of adoption, and that Pakistani case law supports adoptive parents in matters of custody, maintenance, and identity registration. However, the appellants' request for a mere declaration without further relief was problematic under legal principles. (ISB-2023 CLC 1916)

707. SCP held that adoption does not confer any legal right on adoptee under Muslim Law of any provision of settlement law (1978 SCMR 214). LHC held (2000 YLR 2317) that there is no concept of adoption in Islam.

§2. Adoptees

708. Islam highly encourages the care and upbringing of orphans, emphasizing compassion, love, and responsibility without altering their lineage or inheritance rights. When a person takes in an orphan, providing them with shelter, education, and love while ensuring they retain their biological identity, it is considered a noble and rewarding act in Islam. The Holy Prophet Muhammad (PBUH) said, *'The one who cares for an orphan and I will be together in Paradise like this'*, and he gestured by bringing his index and middle fingers close together (Sahih al-Bukhari). The Quran repeatedly highlights the importance of protecting orphans' rights, treating them with justice, and ensuring their well-being, as seen in verses such as (Surah Al-Baqarah 2:220), (Surah An-Nisa 4:2, 4:6, 4:10, 4:127), and (Surah Al-Isra 17:34). Islam strictly forbids attributing an orphan to anyone other than their biological parents (Surah Al-Ahzab 33:4–5) but allows them to be raised with love and dignity, ensuring they receive financial and emotional support. Unlike formal adoption in Western legal systems, where an adopted child may acquire inheritance rights, Islamic law maintains clear distinctions while still encouraging the highest level of care and generosity toward orphans.

709. A foundling or abandoned child is also regarded as an orphan, and one may apply the term 'wayfarer' to him as well. In this case too, as in that of orphans, the child's lineal identity must be unchanged and parenthood to the natural parents should not be denied. When the parents of such children are unknown, the children must be made brethren in faith; *see* (Holy Quran: 33:4–5).

710. Islam upholds a just and balanced inheritance system, ensuring that rightful heirs receive their designated shares without deprivation. Adopting a child as one's own and granting them inheritance rights equivalent to natural heirs is not permissible, as it disrupts the divinely ordained distribution of wealth. The Quran clearly states that inheritance is strictly based on blood and marital relationships, as mentioned in (Surah Al-Anfal 8:75): *'But those of (blood) relationship are more entitled (to inheritance) in the decree of Allah. Indeed, Allah is knowing of all things.'* This prevents any injustice toward natural heirs, maintaining fairness and social harmony. Islam encourages generosity and care toward orphans and foundlings. A man who wishes to support an adopted child financially may gift them any amount during his lifetime or allocate up to one-third of his wealth for them in his will (wasiyyah) after death, as per Islamic inheritance laws. This allows for both kindness and justice, ensuring that orphans receive care and support without violating the rights of legitimate heirs.

§3. FOREIGN ADOPTION

711. Foreigners can adopt a child from Pakistan, provided they fulfil the necessary legal procedures and obtain approval from the relevant court. Organizations like the Edhi Foundation facilitate adoptions, but prospective adoptive parents must also meet the adoption requirements of their home country. Since Pakistan does not have formal adoption laws, foreigners must apply for legal guardianship through a Family Court under the Guardians and Wards Act of 1890. Guardianship grants legal responsibility for the child, allowing the guardian to provide care and protection under the supervision of the court. Once granted, the guardian may seek permission from the court to take the child abroad, ensuring compliance with local and international laws. Additionally, some foreign countries require prospective adoptive parents to meet specific immigration and residency conditions before granting citizenship or entry rights to the child.

712. Once a guardianship decree is obtained from the court, the next step is to register the child with NADRA by applying for a Child Registration Certificate (B-Form). This document assigns a national identity number to the child, which later enables them to obtain a Computerized National Identity Card (CNIC) upon reaching 18 years of age. After securing the B-Form, the guardian can apply for a Pakistani passport for the child. For overseas Pakistani residents, a NICOP (National Identity Card for Overseas Pakistanis) can also be obtained, facilitating international travel and legal documentation. Most foreign embassies require a valid Pakistani passport before issuing an immigration visa for the child. Additionally, depending on the adoptive parents' home country, further steps such as consular registration, legal authentication of adoption/guardianship and compliance with international adoption laws may be required.

Chapter 6. Guardianship and Custody

§1. Introduction

713. Under the Guardian and Wards Act, 1890 'Guardian' means a person having the care of the person of a minor or his property, or of both his person and property; and 'Ward' means a minor for whose person or property, or both, there is a guardian. Whereas 'minor' means a person who, under the provisions of the Majority Act, 1875, is to be deemed not to have attained his Majority.

714. A guardian for a minor can be appointed upon receiving an application from one of the following: (a) an individual who wishes to become or claims to be the guardian of the minor, (b) a relative or close friend of the minor, (c) the District Collector or any other local authority in the area where the minor resides or possesses property, or (d) a Collector who holds jurisdiction over the class or community to which the minor belongs. The appointment of a guardian is governed by the Guardians and Wards Act, 1890, and the primary consideration in such cases is always the welfare of the child. The court assesses factors such as the minor's age, religion, financial security, emotional well-being, and overall best interests before deciding. If the minor has property, the appointed guardian may also be responsible for managing the minor's assets under the supervision of the court.

715. An application for guardianship is filed under the provisions of the Guardians and Wards Act, 1890 (No. VIII) in the appropriate court that has jurisdiction over the area where the minor ordinarily resides. If the application pertains specifically to the guardianship of the minor's property, it may be submitted either to the court in the jurisdiction where the minor resides or to a court with jurisdiction over the location where the minor's property is situated. The court carefully evaluates such applications, prioritizing the minor's welfare, security, and best interests. In deciding, the court considers factors such as the applicant's financial stability, moral character, previous relationship with the child, and overall ability to provide proper care. Additionally, if the minor is of an age where they can express their preference, the court may take their opinion into account.

716. A guardian can either be de facto or de jure. A de jure guardian is legally appointed, either by the court or under statutory provisions, whereas a de facto guardian is someone who has voluntarily assumed the care and responsibility of a minor without formal legal recognition. Under the Guardians and Wards Act, 1890, the father is considered the natural guardian of a child under the age of 18 years. In the absence of the father, the mother may assume guardianship, and if both parents are deceased or incapable, the court may appoint a suitable guardian in the best interests of the child.

717. Unlike a de jure guardian, who is legally appointed by the court or under statutory provisions, a de facto guardian is someone who voluntarily assumes the care of a minor without formal legal recognition. This could be the mother, a sibling, an uncle, other relatives, or even an institution such as an orphanage. Although the father is the natural guardian of a child, the mother is the next eligible guardian if the father is absent, deceased, or incapable of fulfilling his responsibilities. If the father has appointed another guardian through a will, that person may take precedence. Under certain circumstances, a mother may also appoint a guardian by will, either during her husband's lifetime if he is unable to act or after his death. A de facto guardian primarily acts as a custodian responsible for the child's well-being and property but does not possess legal authority over inheritance matters unless granted by the court.

718. A charitable society is not a person within the meaning of section 4(2) of the Guardian and Wards Act, 1890 and thus cannot be appointed as the guardian of the person, or property, of the minor. It is due to the fact that anyone having an interest adverse to that of a minor cannot be appointed as a guardian. However, it has been held by courts that a manager of a registered society can be appointed as the guardian of a child. In the latter context, it has also been stated that the meaning of person in the context of being appointed a guardian should not be confined to an individual, despite section 3(39) of the General Clauses Act as would then conflict with Guardian and Wards Act sections 43(4) and 45.

719. Under the Majority Act 1875 (No. IX), minority ceases upon the completion of 18 years, unless a guardian of the person, or property, or both, of the minor has been, or shall be appointed before the minor has attained the age of 18 years, or the property of the minor is under the superintendence of a court of wards, in which case the age of minority is prolonged, until the minor has completed the age of 21 years. Accordingly, notwithstanding Shariah, minority of a child continues until the completion of 18 years. Until then, the court has the power to appoint a guardian for the child and her/his property or both under the provisions of the Guardian and Wards Act. The relevant provision in this respect is section 3 of the Majority Act 1875, which reads as follows:

> Subject as aforesaid, every minor, of whose person or property or both a guardian, other than for a suit within the meaning of Order XXXII of the First Schedule to the Code of Civil Procedure 1908 (No V), has been or shall be appointed or declared by any Court of Justice before the minor has attained the age of 18 years, and every minor of whose property the superintendence has been or shall be assumed by any Court of Wards before the minor has attained that age shall, notwithstanding anything contained in the Succession Act 1925 (No XXXIX) or in any other enactment, be deemed to have attained his majority when he shall have completed his age of 21 years and not before.
>
> Subject as aforesaid, every other person domiciled in Pakistan shall be deemed to have attained his majority when he shall complete his age of 18 years and not before.

720. A court may not have the authority to appoint a guardian under certain circumstances. For instance, if the minor is a married female and her husband is deemed capable of fulfilling his responsibilities as a guardian, the court will not intervene. Similarly, if the minor's father is alive and considered competent to act as the child's guardian, the court will not appoint another person. Additionally, if the minor's property is under the supervision of a court of wards, a separate guardian may not be appointed. A minor is legally incapable of acting as a guardian for another minor, except in the case of his own child or wife.

721. Any individual, whether a relative, friend, or concerned party, who wishes to assume the role of a guardian must formally apply to the court under the provisions of the Guardian and Wards Act. There is no requirement to wait until their legal title or eligibility to act as a guardian is challenged by another person. The application procedure is outlined in section 10 of the Act, ensuring that due process is followed. The court requires that prior notice of the application be given to all relevant parties who have an interest in the welfare of the minor. This step is essential to allow any objections or concerns to be raised before the final decision is made.

722. During court proceedings, the court exercises parental jurisdiction over the minor, ensuring their welfare and best interests are prioritized. The court is authorized to grant temporary custody to a suitable individual or institution if necessary and can issue protective orders regarding the child's safety and property until a final decision on guardianship is made. The court may impose specific conditions on the guardian to safeguard the child's rights and well-being. If there is a dispute over custody or guardianship, the court may conduct inquiries, seek expert opinions, or involve child welfare agencies to make an informed judgment.

723. When appointing a guardian, the court prioritizes the welfare of the minor, taking into account various factors such as the child's age, gender, and religion. The court also evaluates the character, financial stability, and overall capacity of the proposed guardian, along with their proximity to the child and any previous or existing relationship with the minor or their property. The court considers the wishes of the deceased parents, if known, and any legal provisions outlined in their will. If the child is of an age where they can express a reasonable and informed preference, their opinion may also be considered.

724. A guardian is entrusted with the responsibility of ensuring the minor's overall well-being, which includes providing proper support, nutrition, shelter, clothing, healthcare, and education in accordance with the child's social standing and future prospects. The guardian must manage the minor's upbringing in a manner that safeguards their physical, emotional, and intellectual development. If the guardian is appointed by the court, they may be entitled to a reasonable allowance as deemed appropriate by the court for fulfilling their duties. This allowance may be drawn from the minor's property or financial assets, ensuring that the guardian is fairly compensated for the time, effort, and resources they invest in the child's welfare.

§2. Custody of Children

725. The matter of child custody is governed by the Guardians and Wards Act of 1890, which firmly establishes that the child's welfare is the highest priority. When deciding custody, the Guardian Court considers multiple factors to ensure the child's best interests, including the child's age, gender, religion, emotional and physical well-being, and the character and financial stability of the prospective guardian. The court also considers the child's comfort, security, education, and overall development, as well as the wishes of the deceased parents if applicable. If the child is mature enough to express a reasoned preference, their opinion may also influence the decision.

§3. Adopted Children

726. There is no concept of child adoption in Islam or in Pakistani laws. However, a guardian can be appointed under the Guardian and Wards Act, 1890 to look after the child and property.

727. Suit for the recovery of maintenance allowance filed under Article 199 of the Constitution of Pakistan, 1973. The minor petitioner's claim was initially accepted by the Family Court, which directed the adoptive father (respondent No. 1) to pay PKR 800 per month with a 5% annual increase. However, the Additional District Judge overturned this decision, citing that Islam does not recognize adoption, and thus the petitioner was not entitled to maintenance. The High Court examined whether an adopted child could claim maintenance from an adoptive parent and concluded that while adoption does not create a legal parent-child relationship in Islamic law, a fiduciary obligation arises when adoptive parents voluntarily take responsibility for a minor. The court held that respondent No. 1 had publicly presented the minor as his daughter, thereby assuming a constructive guardianship role, which imposed a duty to provide maintenance. The court reinstated the Family Court's judgment, restoring the petitioner's right to maintenance, and also emphasized Islam's directive to protect orphans and vulnerable children. Consequently, the appellate decision was set aside, and the respondent was ordered to fulfil his maintenance obligation. (LHC – 2015 PLD 336)

728. Custody of minor, who was in the care of her paternal aunt since she was five days old. Her mother filed an application for custody under section 25 of the Guardians and Wards Act, 1890, while the petitioner sought guardianship under sections 7 and 17. Both the Guardian Court and the Additional District Judge ruled in favour of the mother, ordering the return of the minor. However, upon writ petition, the High Court considered the minor's preference, as she was 12 years old and wished to remain with her aunt. The Court noted that the mother had delayed legal action and that the minor had developed emotional attachment with her aunt. It was held that overall welfare of the minor should be prioritized, allowing her to stay with the petitioner while ensuring regular contact with her parents. The Court directed both parties to maintain cordial relations, facilitate visitation, and jointly participate in the child's upbringing, including decisions about her future. (LHC – 2015 PLD 401)

§4. Interim Orders

729. Under section 12 of the *Guardians and Wards Act, 1890*, the Court has the authority to issue directions requiring the person having custody of a minor to produce them at a specified place and time before a designated individual. Additionally, the Court may issue appropriate orders concerning the minor's temporary custody and protection, considering the best interests and welfare of the child. In cases involving a female minor who should not be compelled to appear in public, the Court must ensure that her production aligns with the customs and traditions of the country. However, the Court is not empowered under this section to grant temporary custody to a person claiming to be the minor's guardian based on a marital relationship unless she is already in his custody with the explicit consent of her parents or lawful guardians. Furthermore, if the Court entrusts the temporary custody or protection of a minor's property to an individual, that person cannot dispossess anyone already in possession of the property except through legal means. Additionally, the overarching principle governing custody matters is the *welfare of the minor*, which takes precedence over all other considerations. Courts must ensure that any interim custody arrangement does not compromise the minor's physical, emotional, or psychological well-being.

730. In a case where the mother of a minor girl passed away at the time of childbirth, the maternal grandmother obtained custody of the minor through a habeas corpus petition. During proceedings before the Guardian Judge, the parties reached a compromise, agreeing that the minor's custody would be transferred to her father upon attaining the age of seven. However, the father later remarried and had a child from his second marriage. The deceased mother was a government employee, and the minor's rightful share in the financial benefits left by her was deposited by the father into his own account. This amount was subsequently recovered through a court decree after his arrest warrants were issued. While a separate suit was pending regarding the father's appointment as the minor's guardian for both her person and property, he filed an application seeking enforcement of the prior compromise, demanding custody of the child. The Guardian Judge ruled in favour of the father, directing the grandmother to transfer custody. The grandmother's appeals before the Appellate Court and High Court were dismissed. The Supreme Court, however, emphasized that the *welfare of the minor* is the paramount consideration in such matters. Despite the earlier compromise, the substantial change in circumstances necessitated a fresh assessment of the minor's best interests. Given that the minor had been in the continuous care of her maternal grandmother since birth, a sudden shift in custody could cause emotional and psychological distress. Recognizing this, the Supreme Court allowed the appeal, set aside the impugned orders, and permitted the minor to remain with her grandmother until the pending petition before the

Guardian Judge was decided on its merits based on recorded evidence. The judgment reinforced the principle that *compromises in custody matters are not absolute* and must always be subject to re-evaluation in light of the minor's welfare. Courts are duty-bound to consider not just legal agreements but also the emotional stability, environment, and well-being of the child. The ruling also highlighted the importance of financial accountability, ensuring that a minor's inheritance or financial entitlements are safeguarded against misuse by legal guardians.

731. Under section 14 of the Guardian and Wards Act, 1890 if proceedings for the appointment or declaration of a guardian of a minor are taken in more Courts than one, each of those Courts shall, on being apprised of the proceedings in the other Courts, stay the proceedings before itself. If the Courts are both or all subordinate to the same High Court, they shall report the case to the High Court, and the High Court shall determine in which of the Courts the proceedings with respect to the appointment or declaration of a guardian of the minor shall be had. In any other case in which proceedings are stayed under this section, the Courts shall report the case to, and be guided by such orders as they may receive from their respective Provincial Governments.

732. The petitioner challenged the order of the Guardian Judge-II, Lahore, which dismissed her application for rejecting the custody petition filed by respondent No. 2 (grandmother) under section 5 of the Family Courts Act, 1964, read with section 8 of the Guardians and Wards Act, 1890. The minor and after her parents' divorce, she remained in her mother's custody. The petitioner argued that only parents could seek visitation rights, excluding grandparents, and that granting interim custody to the grandmother would not be in the minor's welfare. However, the Guardian Court ruled that the term 'parents' should be interpreted broadly, especially since the minor is entitled to inheritance from her grandmother. The court relied on legal precedents to establish that grandparents could seek visitation rights. The LHC dismissed the writ petition as not maintainable, stating that the grandmother's petition was competent, and the matter should be decided by the Guardian Court based on evidence. It further directed that the case be concluded expeditiously, preferably within six months, without prejudice to any party. (LHC – 2021 YLR 1989)

733. The petitioner filed a petition under section 278 of the Succession Act, 1925, for the estate of her late husband who was murdered in 1998. The deceased left behind his widow (petitioner), his minor son (living in the USA), and his mother (objector). The dispute primarily concerns a double-story bungalow in Karachi, which the objector claims was gifted by the deceased to his father before his death. The court appointed the petitioner as the guardian ad litem of her son, noting she had cared for him for ten years without support from the grandmother. The petitioner also sought the appointment of a receiver to collect rental income from the property. The objector opposed, citing an alleged oral gift of the property, but the court found the claim doubtful due to inconsistencies in the documents. The case revolves around determining the rightful heirs and ownership of the contested property. (Karachi High Court – 2008 CLC 741)

734. The petitioner filed a constitutional petition challenging the judgments which granted custody of an 11-year-old minor girl to the respondent under section 25 of the *Guardians and Wards Act, 1890.* The respondent claimed that the minor initially lived with him, but the petitioner wrongfully obtained custody through a court order. The petitioner argued that, as the biological mother, she was better suited to care for the minor, especially considering her growing age. The courts below had ruled in favour of the respondent, primarily relying on a prior agreement between the parties, under which the petitioner had relinquished her right to custody. However, the petitioner contended that the courts failed to prioritize the welfare of the minor. The minor girl, during court proceedings, expressed her desire to live with her mother, who ensured her education and well-being, whereas the respondent's minor son was working at a tea stall instead of attending school. The court ultimately held that the paramount consideration in custody matters is the *welfare of the minor*, which outweighs any prior agreement between the parents. It observed that the minor girl was receiving proper education and care under the petitioner's custody, whereas the respondent's other child was deprived of education. Given the age and developmental needs of the minor girl, it was deemed more appropriate for her to live with her mother. Consequently, the court set aside the previous judgments, dismissed the respondent's custody application, and ruled that the petitioner was entitled to retain custody of the minor girl. However, the respondent was granted visitation rights and required to provide maintenance. (LHC – 2009 YLR 991)

735. The petitioner, a mother and academic, sought to be appointed as the guardian of her minor son under sections 7 and 17 of the Guardians and Wards Act, 1890, after being granted custody by the Supreme Court following a dispute with her ex-husband, the natural guardian. The trial and appellate courts dismissed her petition, citing section 19, which restricts guardian appointment if the father is alive and not deemed unfit. The petitioner argued that the father's alleged abduction of the child and his disqualification as a guardian warranted her appointment. The respondent countered that he had cared for the child in the petitioner's absence and had been acquitted of criminal charges. The court emphasized that guardianship and custody differ, with guardianship primarily linked to financial responsibility and legal oversight. Case law established that a father remains a natural guardian unless proven unfit, and a lack of financial support could disqualify him. Ultimately, the law prioritizes the child's welfare, assuming the father is the best guardian unless compelling reasons suggest otherwise. (ISB – 2021 MLD 817)

736. Petitioner filed two petitions under Article 199 of the Constitution of Pakistan, 1973, seeking custody of his son, Minor A, born in 2014. His marriage with Respondent No. 4 ended, and she moved to Karachi while pregnant, allegedly without informing him. Due to her medical condition and the petitioner's lack of involvement, she handed over Minor A's custody to Respondents No. 2 and 3, who have raised him since birth. The petitioner's applications for custody were dismissed by the Family Judge and the 3rd Additional District Judge Karachi (South) due to delays and lack of evidence, leading to further appeals. The courts prioritized Minor A's welfare, ruling that his long-term caregivers provided stability, especially given his medical needs. Legal arguments highlighted that while the father is the natural guardian under Islamic law, custody decisions must consider the child's welfare. The courts found the petitioner had abandoned Minor A and ruled in favour of Respondents Nos 2 and 3. Consequently, the petitioner's requests for custody and guardianship were denied. (Karachi High Court – 2024 CLC 1033)

737. The petitioner filed a Habeas Corpus petition under Article 199 of the Constitution of Pakistan, 1973, seeking custody of her minor children's. She married in 2007, but their marriage ended in 2019 when he divorced her. After the divorce, mother took the children to Karachi and retained their custody. The petitioner attempted to recover them through various courts in Karachi, Rawalpindi, and Mansehra but faced jurisdictional challenges and misleading information from the respondent. The court found that the children were unlawfully detained by their paternal grandmother and uncle in Karachi, without legal authority. It observed that the children had been alienated from their mother and needed reformation under her care. The court granted custody to the petitioner until a final decision by the Guardian Court in Karachi. It also ordered safe escort for the petitioner and her children and emphasized the need for a supportive environment for their education and well-being. The court further criticized the conduct of the respondent's counsel for inappropriate behaviour. The petition was accepted. (PHC – 2023 YLR 34)

§5. Guardians Court

738. Guardian courts in Pakistan handle matters related to the custody and guardianship of minors under the Guardians and Wards Act, 1890, and the West Pakistan Family Courts Act, 1964. These courts prioritize the welfare of the child when deciding custody disputes between parents or other claimants. According to section 25 of the West Pakistan Family Courts Act, 1964, the jurisdiction of family courts extends to all matters related to the guardianship of minors, including custody and visitation rights. If a parent seeks custody of a child, they must file a case in the guardian court, which is usually the family court of the district where the child resides. While the father is traditionally considered the natural guardian, the mother is often granted custody of young children under the principle of Hizanat. However, the court ultimately decides based on the best interests of the child, considering factors such as the child's age, emotional well-being, and parental financial stability. Sections 7, 17 and 19 of the Guardians and Wards Act empower the court to appoint or restrict guardianship based on these considerations.

739. Constitutional petition filed by a mother, seeking guardianship of her minor sons (7 years old) and (4 years old), after the murder of their father. Initially, the Guardian Judge, Peshawar, appointed her as the guardian of their person and property under section 7 of the Guardians and Wards Act, 1890. However, her father-in-law challenged the decision before the Additional District Judge-XVII, Peshawar, who set aside the lower court's judgment and remanded the case, directing the family court to implead the paternal grandfather as a respondent and decide the case afresh on merits. Aggrieved by this, the mother filed a constitutional petition under Article 199 of the Constitution before the High Court. The High Court observed that the respondent's repeated adjournments delayed the proceedings unnecessarily. It ruled that the welfare of the minors lies with the mother, as she provides emotional security and care, which the grandfather or other relatives cannot match. It also emphasized that there were no allegations against the mother's moral character, and the minors had been living with her since birth. The court held that the Additional District Judge erred in setting aside the Family Court's order and restored the earlier judgment, allowing the mother to retain guardianship of her children without any costs. (PHC – 2025 CLC 145)

§6. Restriction on Removal of Children from Pakistan

740. A guardian appointed by the court with the court's permission, cannot remove the ward from the limits of the court's jurisdiction. The permission could be special or general and could be specified in the court order. Illegal removal of a ward from the court's jurisdiction is punishable with a fine not exceeding PKR 1,000 or a jail term extending to six months.

741. Custody dispute between a mother and father following their divorce. The father filed an application under section 25 of the Guardians and Wards Act for permanent custody of their daughter, born in 2006. The Family Judge dismissed his request for permanent custody but granted him visitation rights, including alternate weekends, Eid, summer and winter vacations, and birthdays. The mother, a doctor by profession, later sought permission to take the child to Dubai for her job, offering guarantees for the father's visitation. The trial and appellate courts maintained the child's custody with the mother but required court permission for international travel. The father opposed, citing concerns about access to the child. The High Court ruled in favour of the mother, recognizing her right to pursue a career while ensuring the father retained visitation. The court emphasized that both parents should have a role in the child's upbringing and upheld gender equality in professional opportunities. (Sindh High Court – 2012 PLD 166)

742. The petitioner challenged the Family Court's order which required him to submit two surety bonds of PKR 1,000,000 each for visitation rights with his minor children. The petitioner had earlier agreed to the dissolution of marriage and custody of the minors with their mother, provided he was granted visitation rights. The Family Court allowed his visitation but imposed the condition of surety bonds, despite there being no apprehension of the petitioner removing the minors from the court's jurisdiction. The petitioner contended that this condition was excessive, violated his fundamental rights, and was beyond the scope of the parties' request. The respondent's counsel argued that the petitioner should have filed an appeal instead of invoking constitutional jurisdiction. The High Court ruled that the Family Court's order was arbitrary and an unjustified restriction on the petitioner's rights, as there was no evidence suggesting any risk of abduction. The court set aside the condition of surety bonds and modified the order, allowing the petitioner to meet his children twice a month with seventy-two hours' prior notice. However, if he misused this concession, he would face contempt proceedings and could lose his visitation rights. (LHC – 2014 CLC 1168)

743. The applicant filed an application under section 491, CrPC, seeking custody of her three minor children, allegedly taken away forcibly by her husband and his brother. She claimed that as their real mother, she had the right of Hizanat, especially since two of the children were girls. The learned 1st Additional Sessions Judge, Larkana, dismissed her application, citing lack of jurisdiction and the absence of exceptional circumstances to invoke section 491, Cr.P.C. The respondent argued that the children had been residing with their father in Karachi since birth and were not forcibly removed. The Additional Prosecutor General supported this view, stating that the proper forum for custody matters is the Guardian Court. The court observed that section 491, Cr.P.C., can only be invoked in exceptional cases, such as illegal removal of minors from lawful custody or situations of immediate harm. Since no such urgency was established, and the children were residing with their father in Karachi, the application was dismissed for lack of jurisdiction. The applicant was advised to seek relief from the relevant Family/Guardian Court. (Sindh High Court – 2022 YLR 1125)

§7. Principles on Guardianship Custody and Access Awards

744. No matter what customs or personal law rules the parents' community or sect follows regarding custody, any parent who wants custody and does not presently have custody has to seek custody from the Guardian Court. In other words, there is never any automatic transfer of a child's custody to a particular parent. Normally following factors are considered by the Courts when granting custody of children:

- the welfare of the minor is very broadly defined and includes many diverse factors, notably;
- the age, sex and religion of the minor: Courts take into account the personal law of the father. The welfare of younger children is generally regarded as being in the mother's custody;
- the character and capacity of the proposed guardian: Courts usually reject baseless allegations against mothers;
- the wishes, if any, of a deceased parent, for example specified in a will;
- any existing or previous relations of the proposed guardian with the minor's;
- property: Courts do not look on guardians seeking custody just in order to have control over the minor's property. But if, for example, the minor's property is shared with the mother and she is otherwise a suitable guardian, the court will regard the property relationship as an additional factor in the mother's favour;
- the minor's preference if she/he is old enough to form an intelligent preference, usually accepted as about 9 years old;

- whether siblings would be divided: courts prefer to keep children united and award custody of both to either the mother or the father;
- whether either/both parents have remarried and there are step-children: Although the mother's remarriage to someone who is not the children's close blood-relative often means the court will not grant her custody, this rule is not strictly followed. Although the father's remarriage usually denies him custody, sometimes the courts agree to grant him custody especially when the children's step-mother cannot or will not have her own children;
- whether the parents live far apart: Courts sometimes do not give the mother custody because she lives very far away from the father who is the 'natural' guardian. But in 1994, an Uzbek woman living in Uzbekistan was given custody; the judge said modern transport had shortened distances and meant that the father could depart from his home in the morning and return by evening;
- the child's comfort, health, material, intellectual, moral and spiritual welfare: This very broad category includes the adequate and undisturbed education of the child. However, the mere fact that the mother is economically less secure than the father, or that she suffers from ill-health or a disability is not usually reason enough to deny her custody because maintenance is the father's responsibility irrespective of who holds custody; and
- the mental and psychological development of the minor should not be upset by a reversal of the existing status quo: Courts will take into account the likely impact of a change in guardians and the child's reaction to this change.

745. The petitioner, who had married respondent No. 1, later divorced her but continued residing in her house. The respondent left with their two minor children and the petitioner unable to trace them lodged a FIR suspecting illegal confinement. Later, it was revealed that respondent No. 1 had remarried and moved to Saudi Arabia. The petitioner sought cancellation of certain documents through a civil suit, which was initially allowed by the Family Court. However, the Additional District Judge ruled that family disputes fall under the exclusive jurisdiction of the Family Court under section 5 of the Family Courts Act. Consequently, the High Court upheld the decision, dismissed the constitutional petition, and concluded that the matter should be resolved within the Family Court's domain. (Sindh High Court – 2016 MLD 854)

746. The court granted dissolution based on khula and allowed dowry recovery but dismissed maintenance and guardianship claims. Petitioner contested the khula decision, arguing he had paid dower, including 8-1/2 tolas of gold, but failed to prove it. The court upheld the khula decree, noting irreparable differences, including a FIR lodged by the husband against the wife. It also ruled in favour of the mother for child custody, emphasizing their welfare, particularly as she was more educated and the father had remarried. The father was directed to pay PKR 2,000 per month for each child. Consequently, the petitioners appeal was dismissed, while the respondent(mother) appeal for guardianship was accepted. (Shariat Court (AJ&K) – 2017 MLD 1677)

747. Minor son of 8 years age, custody. Contest between mother and father of minor both having remarried. Father of minor employed as school teacher and owning agricultural land. Mother and step father of minor being illiterate and having no permanent source of income as step father was a labourer. Order of Guardian Judge handing over custody of minor to his mother set aside by Appellate Court. Validity: While determining question of custody of a minor, prime consideration would be his welfare. Record showed that father was financially stable, thus, he was in a better position to meet material needs of minor. Father having no child from second wife could keep minor with him in school, supervise his activities and directly take care of his educational, financial, psychological and emotional needs. Present environment at which minor was living and role models which he had were of paramount importance, and this was a stage for laying foundation of his career. Keeping minor in environment of uncertainty and having flaws in his educational foundation and upbringing would affect entire structure of his responsibility and future career. Obligation of father was to provide adequate funds to mother to meet needs of minor, which was likely to be misapplied by her for not having source of income. Depriving minor of opportunity of growing up with support, in company and under direct supervision of his real father would not be in his welfare. All stepmothers were not Cinderella's stepmothers. Possibility of ill-treatment by stepmother in present case was quite remote as minor would spend most part of day and week in school in academic environment under supervision of his father. Record showed that mother could not cater educational needs of minor, who being about 8 years old was still in Class-1. Need of minor for maternal love and affection could be met by providing adequate visitation time to mother. Mother was allowed to meet minor on first Sunday of every month from 11 am to 2 pm, the one week during winter vacations and two weeks during summer vacations. High Court partly accepted Constitutional petition in circumstances (LHC – 2010 MLD 340).

748. Respondent/mother of the minor after the death of her husband continued residing with her in-laws along with minor, but later on she was expelled by the grandmother of the minor retaining the custody of minor. After being turned out of her home, she being mother of the minor filed petition under section 491, Criminal Procedure Code for recovery of the minor, which on the statement of minor that he would prefer living with his paternal grandmother/the petitioner, petition was dismissed. Mother of the minor later on filed petition under section 7 of Guardians and Wards Act, 1890 to appoint her as guardian of person and property of the minor, which again was dismissed on the statement of minor in favour of his paternal grandmother. Appeal filed by the mother of the minor against judgment and decree, however having been accepted, judgment and decree of the Guardian Judge, was set aside with direction to the Guardian Judge, to hand over custody of minor to the mother. Grandmother had impugned said order in Constitutional petition. Minor was brainwashed to the extent that he abhorred his real mother and was making up stories of her having inflicted physical violence on him even in the court, which was abnormal. Petitioner/grandmother of the minor had not adhered to the visitation schedule as determined by the Guardian Court and was teaching the child how to lie and hate. Danger to a child's life was not only physical, but it was also mental. Extent of the mother's sacrifice for her minor son was that despite being a young woman she had not remarried after the death of minor's father; she was educated, holding a job and seemed to be intelligent woman. Initially the minor may not be happy in his mother's custody, but the tie of the umbilical cord was too strong to be severed. Lady was mother of minor and knew the best of her child. No one can take place of real mother. Moreover under Islamic Law, the custody of paternal grandmother was subservient to the custody of the mother. What had to be taken into consideration at each and every stage of litigation involving minors and their custody was the welfare of the minor. Welfare of the minor in the case lay with his real mother. Constitutional petition dismissed (LHC – 2010 MLD 42).

749. The petitioner challenged the orders passed by the XII Civil Judge and VI Additional District Judge, Karachi, Central, regarding the interim custody of minor. Respondent No. 1 filed for custody of the minor, and the Family Court granted her interim custody for ten days. The petitioner contested this, arguing it was against the minor's welfare and that the appellate court wrongly dismissed his appeal. The court ruled that the interim custody order was not illegal, as it was a temporary arrangement and did not affect the petitioner's rights. It emphasized that the child's welfare was paramount and upheld the decision, dismissing the petition. The court also noted that factual disputes could not be settled without a full trial and that the mother, being a natural guardian, could not be considered an outsider in custody matters. (Sindh High Court – 2018 CLC 50)

750. Marriage between the parties was dissolved by way of divorce through written deed. Dissolution of marriage was with mutual consent. Compromise was entered into between the parties with regard to custody of minor on application filed by the petitioner under section 491, Criminal Procedure Code custody of minor was with maternal grandfather of the minor by compromise as well as under the orders of two courts below. Family Court would exercise parental jurisdiction and must consider all aspects relevant to custody of minor; and decide as to what would be in the best interest of the minor. Any previous compromise or any previous order of the court, could not bind hands of the Family Court. Court could recall its previous order, provided sufficient grounds were made that after previous order, what were new and evolving circumstances keeping in view interest of minor. Compromise between the parties, must be looked at by the Family Court, but was not conclusive and binding, as far as Family Court was concerned. Court in appropriate circumstances could pass an order, even setting at nought the compromise. Prime responsibility and obligation of Family Court was welfare of the minor, which was supreme and should not, in any circumstances be lost sight of. In the present case, there were factors which had been considered by the courts below which clearly emerged; first, petitioner mother of minor had no source of income; second, she had remarried and had been blessed with three children after her remarriage; third, her second husband was a stranger as far as minor was concerned; fourth, her second husband had not come in witness box to depose about his income and whether he was willing to shoulder responsibilities of minor; fifth. maternal grandfather was a retired servant and received pension; sixth, the maternal grandfather had his own house, whereas mother and stepfather of minor lived in a rented house; seventh, real father of minor had no objection if child would remain with his maternal grandfather; and eighth, child had been receiving education while living with maternal grandfather. Two courts below, in circumstances, had rightly observed that for welfare of child, he should be under custody of his maternal grandfather with consent of father of the child (SHC – 2010 YLR 513).

751. The petition challenges the Family Judge-XXI Karachi South's order allowing the respondent (father) interim custody of the minors during summer vacations. The petitioner (mother) opposed this, citing concerns over the children's welfare and alleging procedural irregularities. The respondent argued the petition's non-maintainability, asserting that the order was interlocutory and appealable before the District Court. The court ruled that since guardianship matters fall under the Family Courts Act, an appeal against an interim custody order under section 12 of the Guardians and Wards Act is maintainable before the District Judge. Consequently, the petition was dismissed, reaffirming that interim custody orders are subject to modification based on changing circumstances to ensure the minors' welfare. (Sindh High Court – 2018 MLD 727)

752. Custody of minor: Right to life not only included one's own life, but also life, liberty and happiness of one's children. Denying a person right of company of his children was as severe a penalty and curse on him than denying him life altogether. Strongest bond that nature had created was bond between the mother and the child, and it was not restricted only for the period when the child was within the body of the mother, but would continue thereafter. First food of the child, after all, would come from the body of the mother itself, therefore, if a mother was denied her right of company of her child, it would amount to violation of her fundamental right to life. Petition thus, was maintainable both under section 491, Criminal Procedure Code as well as under Article 199(1)(c) of the Constitution. Elder child was already with the mother, for the custody of which application had been filed by his father under the Guardians and Wards Act, 1890. Mother petitioner had right of *Hizant* of her younger child which was only 3 years old. Bringing up of the two children together would be more appropriate. Custody of the minor was, consequently given to the mother. Family Court, however, would finally determine the custody of minors after a proper trial. Constitutional petition was allowed accordingly (SHC – 2010 PLD 119).

753. The petitioner challenged the appellate court's order which dismissed his appeal as rejecting his application for interim custody of the minor. The petitioner argued that the appellate court should have prioritized the welfare of the minor over procedural technicalities. The respondent maintained that the petitioner should await the decision on permanent custody. The court observed that strict adherence to technicalities should not overshadow the welfare of the minor in guardianship matters. Since the appellate court did not consider this aspect, the constitutional petition was allowed, and the matter was remanded for a fresh decision, with the appeal and application for condonation of delay deemed pending for rehearing. (LHC – 2019 CLC Note 88)

754. The petitions challenged FIR registered under section 364-A, PPC, regarding the alleged abduction of a minor by her father. The petitioner contended that, as the natural guardian, no offence of kidnapping was made out against him, especially since the mother had voluntarily allowed visitation. The respondent mother confirmed that the FIR resulted from a misunderstanding and did not oppose its quashment. The court observed that the petitioner's actions fell within the exception to section 361, PPC, as he had lawful custody rights. Since the parties had reconciled and were living together, the court quashed the FIR, allowing both writ petitions. (ISB-2022 P Cr. L J Note 130)

755. Mother of minors (an Austrian national), accompanied by her children was arrested at the Airport; on search of luggage, 20 kilograms and 875 grams heroin was recovered, on which FIR under sections 9(c) and 15, Control of Narcotic Substances Act, 1997 was registered against her and since then she was confined in jail as an under-trial prisoner; the minors were also so confined with their mother, especially for the reason that at the time of her remand before the Magistrate she requested that 'I want to keep my children along with myself in judicial lockup, because I am foreigner and has no relation or friend in Pakistan at this time who will take care of my children'. Mother of minors wrote a letter to the Austrian Embassy for sending the minors to Austria so that they could live with her parents (the petitioners). Austrian Embassy could not succeed to get the minors released without the court's order for custody. Maternal grandparents of the minors through their counsel, moved the High Court with reference to Article 199(1)(b)(i) of the Constitution and section 491, Criminal Procedure Code contending that the minors were in an improper and illegal custody , therefore, they should be released and given in the custody of their grandparents and that their mother herself having made a request that the minors be sent to her parents abroad, it was in the welfare of the minors to live with their grandparents and elder brother and to have proper education as the parents of minors were involved in drug trafficking and had blatant track record. Grandparents had obtained a custody order by Austrian Courts for the said minors. Visa of minors for visit to Pakistan had expired. Father of minors whose whereabouts were not known, had moved a superficial custody petition before the Guardian Judge for the minors, and it seemed that the mother and father were in league on the custody issue. Held, it prima facie seemed in the welfare of the minors that they should be sent back to their home country, which, undoubtedly, was a welfare State and capable of taking care of even those children whose parents were not there. High Court observed that there was apprehension that the minors may not be used as a shield or carrier for any sordid business and if it so happened, the life of the minors shall be ruined, therefore, it was in the best interest of the minors that their custody be given to the grandparents as requested, particularly when elder brother of the minors, was there and was old enough to look after them. Deputy Head of Mission, Austrian Embassy, was allowed to take the custody of the minors from the jail authorities and was directed to make arrangements for sending them to Austria to enable the petitioners to take their custody. Constitutional petition was, allowed accordingly (LHC – 2009 PLD 393).

756. The petitioner filed two constitutional petitions challenging the orders by the Civil Appellate Court which dismissed his appeals and upheld the orders. The trial court had returned the petitioner's applications for guardianship and custody under sections 7 and 25 of the Guardians and Wards Act, 1890, based on a lack of territorial jurisdiction, stating that the minor was not residing within its jurisdiction. The petitioner married respondent and they had a son. In 2018, respondent left for the USA with the minor to continue her education at Johns Hopkins University. The petitioner claimed they had agreed the minor would return to Pakistan after two years and continue travelling between the two countries. The respondent later refused to send the minor back. The petitioner argued that the minor's ordinary residence was Karachi, as he had spent most of his life there. Respondent No. 3, through her attorney, filed an application under section 9 of the Guardians and Wards Act, 1890, challenging the jurisdiction of Pakistani courts, citing the minor's current residence in the USA. The trial and appellate courts ruled in favour of respondent determining that jurisdiction was governed by the Guardians and Wards Act, rather than the West Pakistan Family Courts Act, 1964. The petitioner contended that the courts had erred in their interpretation and failed to consider the minor's residence before 2018. He also asserted that the respondent's absence due to her work left the minor unattended. The courts' reasoning was based on the minor's stay in the USA from 2018 onwards, disregarding the mutual agreement between the parents. The petitioner argued that since there was no written objection from respondent denying the agreement, it should be considered admitted. He cited case law supporting that 'ordinary residence' implies more than just factual residence and should include the minor's long-term living arrangements. The courts failed to properly evaluate these factors and incorrectly applied the Guardians and Wards Act instead of the Family Courts Act. Consequently, the petitioner sought relief through these constitutional petitions, arguing that Karachi should be deemed the minor's ordinary residence and that he should be granted custody. (Sindh High Court – 2022 PLD 171)

757. The petitioners filed an instant writ petition under Article 199 of the Constitution of Pakistan, 1973, challenging the orders passed by the Guardian Judge-1, Lahore, and the judgment by the Additional District Judge, Lahore. Respondent filed a petition under section 25 of the Guardians and Wards Act for custody of the minors which was granted ex-parte. They argued that no proper notices were served, violating sections 7(2)(3) and 8(3) of the West Pakistan Family Courts Act, 1964. The petitioners alleged misreading of evidence, procedural irregularities, and violations of fundamental rights under Article 4 of the Constitution. They contended that the mother, as the natural guardian, should have custody of the minors and that the courts below erred in their findings. Respondent countered that the mother had concealed facts, disrespected court proceedings, and kept the minors away from their father. He argued that the mother had remarried and the minors were living with a stranger whereas he remained unmarried for their welfare. The court emphasized that child custody decisions prioritize the minors' welfare, citing various judicial precedents. It also noted that at the time of the decision, the minors had reached an age where their preference should be considered. The judgment underscored that while parental conduct is relevant, the children's best interests remain paramount under section 17 of the Guardians and Wards Act, 1890. (LHC – 2022 CLC 762)

758. Petitioner had challenged only the schedule of meeting with the minor given by the Appellate Court. Schedule given in the impugned judgment was being complied with by both the parties. Submission of the petitioner, however, was that because of the schedule given in the impugned judgment, education of the minor was being disturbed so a new schedule to meet the child with his father be given. Petitioner had suggested that it was appropriate to allow the father to meet the minor after six weeks. Suggestion was repelled on the ground that it was also part of the education that the minor should meet his father; and even otherwise no ground was urged in the petition or in the argument of the counsel for the petitioner that father should be deprived to meet his son. Appellate Court had given schedule in its judgment keeping in view the welfare of the minor. No reason was at all available to disturb the same or to give new schedule. Constitutional petition was dismissed in circumstances (LHC 2009 YLR 222).

759. The petitioner has challenged the order by the Guardian Judge (IV), Lahore, which returned her application under section 12 of the Guardians and Wards Act, 1890, regarding her mentally disabled minor daughter citing the jurisdiction of the Court of Protection under the Mental Health Ordinance, 2001. Her request for interim custody of her other daughters who are in their father's custody, was denied, though she was granted visitation rights. The petitioner argues that the Guardian Judge erroneously declined jurisdiction over her disabled daughter custody and that the Family Courts Act, 1964, grants exclusive authority to family courts over custody and guardianship matters, irrespective of a child's mental or physical condition. She maintains that the Mental Health Ordinance, 2001, does not confer exclusive jurisdiction regarding guardianship of mentally disabled minors and that a harmonious interpretation of statutes is necessary. As for her other daughters she contends that their education under the father's custody was insufficient grounds to deny her interim custody, emphasizing the importance of a nurturing environment and reasonable visitation rights. The respondent's counsel defends the order, asserting that the Mental Health Ordinance, 2001, governs mentally disordered individuals, including minors, and vests authority in the Court of Protection. The court acknowledges that family law distinguishes between custody and guardianship, emphasizing that the father as a natural guardian must provide financial support, while the mother retains primary custody rights unless disqualified. The court finds the impugned order legally deficient particularly regarding the denial of the mother's custody of her minor daughters and highlights the necessity of a mother's care especially for young girls. The judgment clarifies that the Guardians and Wards Act, 1890 along with the Family Courts Act, 1964, confers exclusive jurisdiction upon family courts regarding custody matters. Regarding disabled daughter the court notes that the lower court failed to determine whether her condition falls under the definition of mental disorder in the Mental Health Ordinance, 2001. The ruling suggests that legislative provisions must be harmonized to avoid contradictions and that the jurisdiction of family courts over minor custody remains exclusive under the Family Courts Act, 1964. (LHC – 2023 PLD 433)

760. Applicant/mother of a minor girl had alleged that respondent who had divorced the applicant and had driven her out of his house along with her two daughters, had snatched away one of the daughters aged 14 months from the custody of the applicant, though she had right of *Hizant* till the minor attained majority. Applicant had prayed for restoration of the custody of minor girl to her. Validity: Minor of such a tender age would need constant care of mother, and it was a universal truth that there could not be any substitute for a mother; and that the lap of mother was God's own cradle for child. Custody of minor girl with respondent/father was improper, if not illegal. Application was allowed with the direction that minor girl would be handed over by respondent to the applicant/mother forthwith (SHC – 2009 PLD 325).

761. Both petitioner/father of minor and respondent/mother of minor filed respective applications for custody of minor girl. Guardian Judge dismissed application of respondent/mother and allowed that of petitioner/father, but Appellate Court below on filing appeal, reversed judgment of Guardian Judge. Judgment passed by Appellate Court below confirmed and found respondent/mother of minor entitled to get the custody of minor, holding that minor was about 10 years of age and was not getting education in any school under the custody of petitioner/father; that petitioner/father was spending most of his time away from the house for earning his livelihood, and his mother who was residing with him was aged about 75 years and could not look after the minor girl; that according to Islamic Law, mother was entitled to the custody of her female child until she would obtain puberty; that respondent/mother of minor had not contracted second marriage, and no evidence was available that she was leading an immoral life. Petitioner was directed to hand over the custody of minor to respondent mother. Held, welfare of minor was that minor to remain with her mother and she was entitled to custody of the minor girl in circumstances, Constitutional petitions were dismissed (LHC – 2008 CLC 1317).

762. The applicant seeks pre-arrest bail under sections 363 and 365 of the PPC. The applicant claims he is falsely implicated due to enmity, arguing that as the lawful guardian of his daughters, no FIR can be registered against him under section 361 PPC. The daughters have sworn affidavits stating they were not abducted but living happily with their father. The prosecution contends that the FIR was filed on court directions, and the mother was notified but failed to appear. The case arises from a dispute between the parents over custody. The court noted that section 361 PPC protects lawful guardians from kidnapping charges and that a father removing his children from their mother's custody does not constitute kidnapping. The investigating officer admitted that statements under sections 161 and 164 of the Criminal Procedure Code (Cr.P.C.) were not recorded, further raising doubts about the prosecution's claims. The court observed that the dispute appeared to be a custody battle rather than a criminal offense and that deeper appreciation of the case was not required at the bail stage. Finding mala fide intent on the complainant's part, the court granted bail under section 497(2) Cr.P.C. The pre-arrest bail granted was confirmed, subject to the applicant attending the trial. The court clarified that any misuse of bail would lead to revocation and that its observations were only tentative, not affecting the trial's final decision. (Sindh High Court – 2024 MLD 1309)

763. Courts below concurrently gave custody of minor to mother and the father who had divorced her had challenged said concurrent judgments of the courts below in Constitutional petition. Validity: Minor was patient of imperforated disease and had been operated thrice, in such circumstances when minor had attachment with his mother, in case he was given in the custody of his father who was stranger for him, it would deteriorate his health. Father, who had contracted second marriage, when he would leave for his job, child would be at the mercy of step mother. In presence of real mother, who was living in a combined family having sisters and mother, it would not be proper to deprive the child from the natural love and affection of the mother particularly when nothing substantial had come on record to prove that the mother had failed to properly look after her son. Scope of powers of High Court while dealing with the concurrent findings of the two courts below, in exercise of Constitutional jurisdiction, was very limited. Burden of proving that findings recorded by courts below were vitiated by evidence on record or suffered from non-reading of material evidence or there was jurisdictional defect, lay on the petitioner, which the petitioner in the present case had failed to point out. Both courts below had very carefully examined all the aspects of the matter in regard to the welfare of the minor. Concurrent judgments of the courts below could not be interfered with by the High Court in exercise of its Constitutional jurisdiction (SHC – 2008 PLD 132).

764. Application by petitioner/father for custody of minor son under section 25 of Guardians and Wards Act, 1890 was accepted by the Trial Court, but on appeal same was dismissed by Appellate Court. Petitioner had contracted second marriage and mother of minor had also contracted second marriage. Minor, who was aged about 12 years was happily living with his maternal grandfather for the last many years. Appellate Court below interviewed the minor who was not willing to live in the house of his father/petitioner with his stepmother. Minor at the relevant time was student of class-V. Maternal grandfather of minor was looking after minor and was attending to his educational requirements. Petitioner/father who had contracted second marriage had children from his second wife, and it was not safe to remove minor from his present family set up. Welfare of the minor demanded that he should be permitted to continue to live with his maternal grandfather. Appellate Court, in circumstances had rightly accepted appeal against judgment of the Trial Court. Paramount consideration in determining the question of custody of minor was welfare of the minor, and in the present case, welfare of the minor was that he should remain with his maternal grandfather. In absence of any illegality or infirmity in the impugned order of Appellate Court, same could not be interfered with by the High Court in exercise of its Constitutional jurisdiction (LHC – 2007 MLD 1089).

765. In presence of the parents claiming the custody of child, grandfather or other legal guardians, could not be considered for handing over the custody to them under any law including Islamic Law and Guardians and Wards Act, 1890. Rule that welfare of the minor, would be presumed with person who was entitled, to the custody under Islamic Law, was not absolute and matter of custody would always remain subject to the welfare of the minor. Guidelines provided by Islamic Law were not absolute in nature and while appointing a guardian of the person of a minor, her (minor's) choice could not be overlooked. Paramount consideration which had to weigh with the court was welfare of the minor which also included not only her well-being, but also had to be determined keeping in view the surroundings in and outside the house where her father or mother lived. Despite disqualification incurred by the mother, she could be handed over the custody of her minor child if welfare of the minor so warranted. Prime consideration for appointment of guardian was the welfare of the minor which must weigh with the court irrespective of the provisions of Personal Law. Conduct of the father or mother must also be considered and choice of minor could not be taken lightly and must be given weight (Supreme Court, Azad Kashmir – 2007 CLC 474).

766. Under section 19 of the Guardian and Wards Act, 1890, the court does not appoint a guardian in the following cases:

- When the minor is a married female and her husband is deemed fit by the court to act as her guardian.
- When the minor's father is alive and the court does not consider him unfit to be the guardian of the minor.
- When the minor's property is under the supervision of a Court of Wards, which has the authority to appoint a guardian for the minor.
- When both parents of the minor are alive and competent to take care of the child, unless exceptional circumstances necessitate intervention.
- When the minor has attained an age where they can make an informed preference regarding guardianship, and their welfare does not require a court-appointed guardian.
- When an existing legal guardian is already fulfilling their responsibilities in the best interest of the minor.
- When appointing a guardian would contradict the religious or personal laws applicable to the minor, unless justified for their welfare.

§8. Wishes of the Child

767. Under section 17(3) of the Guardian and Wards Act, 1890 (VIII of 1890), if a minor is capable of forming an intelligent preference, the court may take their wishes into account while deciding matters of guardianship and custody. The court gives considerable weight to the minor's preference, provided it aligns with their welfare and best interests. The child's age, maturity, and ability to make a reasoned decision are key factors in determining how much importance their preference holds. The court has the authority to assess the child's emotional, psychological, and physical well-being before deciding. It may also consider factors such as the minor's comfort, relationship with the parents or guardians, educational stability, and any history of neglect, abuse, or undue influence. The child's preference is particularly significant in cases where they have reached an age where they can express a well-reasoned choice. However, the court ensures that the decision is made free from coercion or external pressure. While the child's preference is important, it is not the sole determining factor, as the court's ultimate objective is to secure the minor's welfare. In cases of conflicting parental claims, the court balances the minor's wishes with legal and moral considerations, ensuring that the final decision promotes the minor's overall development and well-being.

768. The petitioner (father) challenged the Appellate Court's judgment which modified the visitation schedule of his three minor children with their mother (respondent No. 2). Initially, the parents had agreed on shared custody but after a second guardian petition, the father was granted interim custody with the mother allowed visitation rights. The petitioner argued that the minors were unwilling to meet their mother, making the visitation schedule unsustainable. However, the Court emphasized that children's preferences are not absolute in custody matters, as they may be influenced by the custodial parent. The Court ruled that depriving the mother of visitation would be harsh and detrimental to the minors' welfare, potentially causing permanent estrangement. The Court upheld the Appellate Court's decision stating that a mother's presence is irreplaceable in a child's life and that parental alienation must be avoided. It dismissed the father's petition, ruling that the visitation schedule was fair and in the best interest of the children. (LHC – 2021 YLR 1299)

769. Children's capability of making intelligent preference about which of the parents they choose to live with. Minor's opinion was never obtained by District Judge while deciding question of their custody. Children being present in Court, High Court obtained their opinion and they were intelligent enough to express their opinion as they have been studying in good schools. Minors stated that they would prefer to live with their mother. Petitioner mother would not be disentitled and disqualified to retain custody of minors on the ground that she has contracted second marriage with a person who was not related to minors and is stranger. Courts would preserve to the mother custody of children if interest and welfare of minor so demanded. Impugned order of District Judge whereby he had declared father (respondent) to be the guardian of person and property of minors was set aside. Order of Guardian Judge was modified to the extent that father (respondent) was allowed to see his children once in a month provided their educational programme was not disturbed. Minor children can stay with father once in a month preferably on weekends and also stay for full day on their birthday and for two days on every Eid. (PLJ 2000 Peshawar 175 and PLD 2000 Peshawar 23)

770. Family Court allowed application for custody of minors in favour of mother but Lower Appellate Court, relying upon preference of minors to live with their father, set aside the order passed by Family Court. Validity: Court was authorized under section 17(3) of Guardians and Wards Act, 1890, to consider an intelligent preference of minor in the matter of custody. Lower Appellate Court recorded statements of minors on the date of judgment, when parties had already been in Court for the last two years, and minors had come along with their father. High Court only relied upon statement of the eldest son who was of the age and had grown a beard as well, but statements of remaining two children were not intelligent preference in the matter. Mother of minors had not remarried after divorce and was constantly fighting for custody of her children, while father of minors had contracted marriage and had three children from new wedlock. Daughter and younger son were of tender age and required care which only a mother could provide. High Court in exercise of Constitutional jurisdiction declared judgment passed by Lower Appellate Court to be without lawful authority and set aside the same to the extent of daughter and younger son, who would remain with their mother. Petition was allowed accordingly (LHC – 2009 MLD 33).

771. The petitioner (father) challenged the LHC's order which restored the Senior Civil Judge's decision granting custody of four children to the respondent (mother) and set aside the Appellate Court's ruling that had awarded custody to the father. The petitioner argued that the mother's second marriage disqualified her from custody, citing Islamic law. However, the court emphasized that the welfare of the children is the paramount consideration in custody matters, not rigid legal provisions. Relying on precedents, the court held that a mother's remarriage does not automatically disqualify her from custody, particularly when the children's well-being and preference favour living with her. The court also considered the financial independence, stable living conditions, and willingness of the children to stay with their mother. Given that all four children expressed their desire to live with their mother, the court found no illegality in the High Court's decision and dismissed the father's petition, affirming the custody arrangement in the children's best interest. (SC – 2022 SCMR 2123)

I. Performance in Court

772. Under section 17 of the Guardians and Wards Act, 1890, while appointing or declaring a guardian for a minor, the court must prioritize the minor's welfare, taking into account the personal law applicable to the child. The court assesses various factors, including the minor's age, sex, religion, the character and capacity of the proposed guardian, and any existing ties of affection. Additionally, the court may consider the child's preference if they are of sufficient age and maturity to express an intelligent opinion. The principle of welfare is not limited to financial stability but extends to the emotional, psychological, educational, and moral well-being of the minor. Courts have consistently held that the mere legal entitlement of a parent or relative is not decisive; rather, the child's overall best interest remains the paramount consideration in determining guardianship.

773. In determining the welfare of a minor under section 17 of the Guardians and Wards Act, 1890, the court takes into account multiple factors, including the minor's age, gender, and religion, as well as the character, financial stability, and overall capacity of the proposed guardian. The court also considers the guardian's relationship with the minor, any wishes expressed by a deceased parent, and any previous interactions between the proposed guardian and the minor or their property. If the minor has reached an age where they can express an intelligent and independent preference, the court may take their wishes into consideration. However, the court cannot appoint or declare a guardian against the minor's will if they are capable of making an informed decision. Additionally, the principle of welfare is paramount, encompassing not only financial security but also the emotional, moral, and psychological well-being of the child. The courts have emphasized that no rigid rule applies in determining guardianship; instead, each case is decided on its own facts to ensure that the minor's best interests are protected.

774. The custody was granted to the maternal grandfather through a compromise recorded in court in 2003. However, in 2006, the mother filed a petition under the Guardians and Wards Act, 1890, seeking custody. The trial court dismissed her application in 2007, stating that the child was well-settled with his grandfather, and the mother, having remarried and lacking independent financial means, was not a suitable guardian. An appeal was also dismissed in 2008. The court considered multiple factors, including the grandfather's financial stability, the father's consent to the arrangement, and the lack of evidence regarding the mother's husband's willingness to support the minor. The court reiterated that while compromises in such matters are not binding, the welfare of the minor is paramount. It also noted that character judgments against the mother were unnecessary and unwarranted. Ultimately, the petition was dismissed, and the mother was directed to return the child to the maternal grandfather. (Karachi High Court – 2010 YLR 513)

II. Preference for Natural Parents

775. When appointing or declaring a guardian or determining the custody of a minor, the primary consideration is always the welfare and best interests of the child. Courts generally give preference to the natural parents, as they are presumed to be the most suitable guardians unless proven otherwise. The Supreme Court of Islamabad affirmed that a mother has an inherent right to custody of her minor son until he reaches the age of seven. However, this right is not absolute, and she may only be deprived of custody if compelling and substantial reasons are established, demonstrating that her care would be detrimental to the child's welfare. Such reasons may include neglect, immorality, inability to provide proper care, or any circumstance that could harm the physical or emotional well-being of the minor. Additionally, the court considers factors such as the child's emotional attachment, stability of the environment, financial security, and the moral and ethical upbringing provided by the custodial parent before making a final determination on custody.

776. The petitioner challenged the orders passed by the Vth Additional District Judge, Karachi (East) and the Family Court, respectively, seeking to retain custody of his two minor sons. The respondent (mother) had initially filed for permanent custody under section 25 of the Guardians and Wards Act, 1890, claiming that the petitioner was irresponsible, jobless, and an alcoholic. She obtained *Khula* and later sought custody, which was granted by the Family Court and upheld on appeal. The petitioner contended that he had informed the respondent about his previous marriage, was financially stable, and had been the sole caregiver for the minors since 2015. He also argued that Islamic law grants a mother custody of male children only until the age of seven, and since both minors had crossed that age, their preference should be considered. The court examined the circumstances, recorded the statements of the minors, and found them happy and well-settled with their father. Since there was no evidence of any disqualification on the father's part and the minors preferred to stay with him, the court ruled in his favour. The orders granting custody to the mother were set aside, and she was granted visitation rights, including meetings on alternate Saturdays, specific holidays, and extended time during school vacations, subject to a surety bond for the safe return of the minors. The petition was allowed. (Sindh High Court – 2018 YLR 649)

777. Whether mother has preferential right of *Hizant*. Mother of minors, having contracted second marriage with person not related to minors within prohibited degrees has lost her right of *Hizant*. Petition dismissed. (PLJ 1998 Lahore 146 = 1998 CLC 846).

778. The case involves two writ petitions concerning the custody and maintenance of minors. Mother challenged the appellate court's decision granting custody of her three male children to their father while he sought to terminate maintenance payments, claiming the children had reached the age of majority. The court noted that the paramount consideration in custody matters is the welfare of minors, not merely the father's financial capability or his right to custody after the age of seven. Given that the children had lived with their mother since birth and were at an age where a change in custody could cause psychological harm, the court set aside the appellate court's decision and ruled in favour of the mother. Regarding maintenance, the court determined that the minor children, including the child who had not yet married, were still entitled to maintenance, dismissing father's petition while allowing him to seek termination only if a male child attained majority. The execution proceedings for maintenance were directed to continue. (2015 PLD Balochistan 18)

779. Father of minors after divorcing their mother had contracted second marriage. Father, who was a driver of the truck, by virtue of his profession had to remain away from his house, as such the minors if given to his custody, they would ultimately remain at the mercy of their stepmother, who could not be a substitute of real mother having a natural love and affection for her children. Trial Court rejected application filed by father of minors for their' custody on the basis of welfare of the minors. Trial Court, after appreciating evidence, had rightly concluded that as father had contracted second marriage and being a driver of the truck could not look after his minor children himself, they could not be left at the mercy of a stepmother. Father had contended that as mother of minors had also contracted second marriage; that male child being 8 years of age, she had lost the right of custody. Contention of father was repelled because the question was not of the age or of second marriage of mother of the minors, but main focus was on the welfare of the minors. If both claimants for custody of the minors had contracted second marriage, then the matter of custody of the minors had to be decided with more care and caution; and that was what in the interest of the minors and more importance had to be given to welfare of the minors. Female child, who was 13 months of age, naturally would need the company and association of mother, while male child who was 2-1/2 years of age, would also need the same atmosphere, especially when throughout the period they had been living with their mother. Impugned order rightly passed by the Trial Court could not be interfered with in appeal by the Shariat Court (Shariat Court, Azad Kashmir 2008 YLR 1446).

780. The petitioner challenged the judgment of the III-Additional District Judge, Karachi-Central, which upheld the trial court's decision granting custody of two minors to their mother, respondent No. 1. The petitioner contended that he was the natural guardian, providing proper education and care for the children and that their consent to stay with him was ignored. However, the court emphasized that the primary consideration in custody matters is the welfare of minors. The evidence showed that the petitioner being a businessman was often away and the minors were living in a joint family setup without their mother's care. The court held that the mother as the natural guardian could better look after them with love and affection. It rejected the argument that changing custody would disrupt their education stating that the father remains responsible for their maintenance. The court also dismissed reliance on the case of Sughra Bibi, distinguishing it on factual grounds. Finding no legal infirmity in the lower courts' judgments, the petition was dismissed in limine. (Karachi High Court – 2008 CLC 652)

781. LHC held that it would be harsh to hand over the custody of the minor son to the father leaving him at the mercy of stepmother in presence of real mother, who otherwise was maintaining her child properly (2008 CLC 1595).

782. LHC held that dual control of minor children by father and mother has been recognized under Islamic Law. Father is a legal and natural guardian of minor, whereas right of *Hizant* (custody of minor) vests in the mother of minor. Mother, under the Sunni law, is entitled to custody of male child until he has completed age of 7 years and of her female child until she has attained puberty. Such right of *Hizant* (custody of minor) of mother continues though she is divorced by the father of minor children (LHC – 2008 PLD 533).

783. Respondent has no woman in his house that can look after children if given to his custody. Respondent claimed that he has a sister in his house that could look after children. Sister of respondent could not be a substitute of mother, and she could not provide love and affection to children which mother can, as lap of mother is God's own cradle for children. Mother was, thus, entitled to custody other minor children (PLJ 2000 Peshawar 175 = PLD 2000 Peshawar 23).

784. Minors remaining in custody of their step-mother after death of their real mother with whom their father contracted second marriage. After death of their father, their paternal uncle applied for their custody which was granted. Petitioner's appeal was dismissed. Constitutional Petition. Welfare of minors. By now it is well settled that while disposing of applications under sections 17 and 25 of Guardian and Wards Act, supreme consideration should be welfare of minors, coupled with their own wishes. Petitioner is undoubtedly step mother of female minors, but they are living with her for last more than eight years, when their real mother expired away. All minors were examined thrice by trial and Appellate Court, who on every occasion, insisted to stay with their step-mother, instead of preferring to live with their real uncle (Respondent). It is noteworthy that in his statement, he has given his age to be of 90 years. Moreover, minors have developed intimacy with petitioner (step mother) and even otherwise, being female minors, it is necessary that they should stay with female instead of male. Findings of Courts below are not based on correct application of law, as well as appreciation of evidence on record (PLJ 1998 Quetta 137 = 1998 MLD 1697).

III. Economic Factors

785. While determining the custody of a child, the court primarily considers the welfare and best interests of the child, which includes various factors such as love, care, emotional well-being, and stability. Although financial stability is an important consideration, it is not the sole determining factor. The ability of a parent to provide a nurturing environment, emotional support, and moral upbringing is often given greater weight. A mother's financial status alone cannot be a reason to deny her custody, as the father remains legally responsible for the maintenance of the child under Islamic and statutory law. Additionally, courts assess the living conditions, education opportunities, and overall well-being the guardian can provide while ensuring that the child maintains a healthy relationship with both parents.

786. The Supreme Court set aside the LHC's order that transferred the custody of a minor from her mother to the paternal grandmother. The Court held that the High Court had overstepped its constitutional jurisdiction by deciding a custody matter through a writ of habeas corpus when an alternative remedy under the Guardians and Wards Act, 1890, was available. It emphasized that a mother's remarriage does not automatically disqualify her from custody, citing established legal precedents. The Court reiterated that custody matters should be decided by the Guardian Court, which is the competent forum for such issues, and that habeas corpus petitions in custody cases should only be entertained in exceptional circumstances, such as abduction or unlawful confinement. The judgment also referenced Pakistan's obligations under international conventions like the Convention on the Rights of the Child (CRC) and Convention on the Elimination of All Forms of Discrimination Against Women (CEDAW), affirming that separating a mother from her child solely due to remarriage is unjustified. Consequently, the Court restored the child's custody to the mother and directed the Guardian Court to decide the case on its merits. (SC – 2024 SCMR 486)

787. Custody dispute between a US citizen father and a Pakistani mother over their minor child, who was born in the US and brought to Pakistan by the mother without the father's consent. The father, holding full custody as per a US court order, sought the child's return under the Hague Convention, arguing that the mother had illegally abducted the minor. The US court had previously determined that the father was the more suitable guardian, citing concerns over the mother's fitness and her alleged attempts to keep the child hidden. The Pakistani Family Court had already dismissed the mother's guardianship plea and ordered the child's return to the US. The Sindh High Court, after considering international legal obligations, precedents, and the best interests of the minor, directed the mother to hand over the child to the father or US authorities. The court also instructed Pakistani authorities to facilitate the child's return to the US, ensuring compliance with both Pakistani and US court decisions. The father undertook to withdraw contempt proceedings against the mother in the US, allowing her to retain her parental rights as per US law. (Sindh High Court – 2024 YLR 1330)

§9. Cessation of Guardianship

788. In different court cases, the Court removed the guardian appointed or declared by it, or even a guardian appointed by will, on the application of any interested person or on its own motion, for the following reasons:

- for abuse of trust;
- for continued failure to perform the duties of his trust;
- for incapacity to perform the duties of his trust;
- for ill-treatment, or neglect to take proper care of the ward;
- for contumacious disregard of any of the Guardians and Wards Act's provisions or of any of the court orders;
- for conviction of an offence implying a defect of character;
- for having an interest adverse to the faithful performance of his duties;
- for ceasing to reside within the local limits of the court's jurisdiction; and
- for bankruptcy or insolvency in the case of a guardian of property.

789. A guardian may petition the court for relief from their duties if they are unable to continue fulfilling their responsibilities. Guardianship also terminates under several circumstances, including the death, removal, or discharge of the guardian; when the minor reaches the age of majority; when a female ward marries and her husband is deemed fit to act as her guardian; or when the court assumes direct supervision over the minor. Additionally, a guardian may be removed by the court if they are found negligent, incompetent, or involved in misconduct that jeopardizes the minor's welfare. The court's primary consideration in such matters is always the best interest and well-being of the minor.

Part III. Matrimonial Property Law

Chapter 1. Matrimonial Property

§1. Introduction

790. Under Islamic inheritance laws, spouses are entitled to a share of each other's property upon death. If a wife passes away without children, her husband is entitled to one-half of her estate; however, if she has children, his share is reduced to one-fourth. Conversely, if a husband dies without children, his wife inherits one-fourth of his estate, but if he has children, her share is reduced to one-eighth. These shares are determined after settling any debts and funeral expenses of the deceased. Additionally, Islamic law ensures that the remaining estate is distributed among other heirs, such as parents, siblings, and children, in accordance with prescribed shares under *Faraid* (Islamic rules of inheritance).

§2. Property Regime During Marriage and Cohabitation

791. Under PART III (Marriage) of the Succession Act, 1925 no person shall, by marriage, acquire any interest in the property of the person whom he/she marries or becomes incapable of doing any act in respect of his/her own property which he/she could have done if unmarried. However, this (a) shall not apply to any marriage contracted before the first day of January, 1866; (b) shall not apply, and shall be deemed never to have applied, to any marriage one or both of the parties to which professed at the time of the marriage the Hindu, Muslim, Buddhist, Sikh or Jaina religion.

792. Under section 21 of the Succession Act, 1925 if a person whose domicile is not in Pakistan marries in Pakistan a person whose domicile is in Pakistan neither party acquires by the marriage any right in respect of any property of the other party not comprised in a settlement made previous to the marriage, which he/she would not be acquired thereby if by where domiciled in Pakistan at the time of the marriage.

793. Under section 22 of the Succession Act, 1925 the property of a minor may be settled in contemplation of marriage, provided the settlement is made by the minor with the approbation of the minors father, or, if the father is dead or absent from Pakistan, with the approbation of the High Court.

794. However, this shall not apply to any will made or intestacy occurring before the first day of January, 1866, or to intestate or testamentary succession to the property of any Hindu, Muslim, Buddhist, Sikh or Jaina.

§3. Adjudication of Property Disputes

795. Petitioners challenged the inheritance mutation of respondent estate, arguing that his daughters should be excluded since he had given them gifts and dowries during his lifetime. Their claim was initially dismissed by the trial court in and subsequent appeals were also rejected by the appellate court and the civil revision court. The Supreme Court noted that the petitioners who were in possession of the daughters' share, sought to unjustly deprive their sisters of their inheritance, which was against both Islamic Shariah and Pakistani law. The Court condemned the frivolous litigation that prolonged the daughters' deprivation for decades, emphasizing that inheritance rights must be protected. Consequently, the Supreme Court dismissed the petition with a penalty of PKR 500,000, ordering the revenue authorities to ensure fair distribution of the estate and report compliance. (SC – 2024 PLD 1273)

796. The appellants filed a suit for declaration and injunction, claiming their father was given a share in the property by his father during his lifetime. However, since he passed away before the grandfather the inheritance mutation was attested in favour of the surviving three sons, excluding the father's heirs. The trial court dismissed the suit and the first appellate court upheld this decision. The appellants then filed a second appeal, arguing that they were entitled to their father's share. The court held that since the private partition of property was not legally confirmed under section 147 of the West Pakistan Land Revenue Act, 1967, it had no legal validity. Additionally, the court noted that second appeals are only entertained in cases of misreading or non-reading of evidence, which was not established. The court also clarified that the 2021 amendment to the Transfer of Property Act, which grants inheritance rights to the children of a deceased son, does not apply retrospectively. Consequently, the second appeal was dismissed for lack of merit. (High Court (AJ&K) – 2025 MLD 309)

Part IV. Succession Law

Chapter 1. Intestate Succession

§1. The Open of the Succession

797. Under the Succession Act, 1925, the succession of immovable property located in Pakistan is governed by Pakistani law, regardless of the deceased's domicile at the time of death. However, the succession of movable property is determined by the law of the country where the deceased was domiciled at the time of death. This ensures that real estate remains subject to the laws of the jurisdiction where it is situated, while personal assets are distributed according to the legal system of the deceased's permanent residence. For instance, if a Pakistani national domiciled in Pakistan dies while in France, leaving movable property in France, England, and Pakistan, along with immovable property in Pakistan, Pakistani law governs the succession of all his assets, whether movable or immovable, regardless of their location. On the other hand, if an English national domiciled in France dies in Pakistan, leaving both movable and immovable property in Pakistan, the movable property will be inherited according to French law, specifically the rules that apply to an Englishman domiciled in France, while the immovable property in Pakistan will be governed strictly by Pakistani law. Additionally, under conflict of laws principles, Pakistani courts generally recognize foreign legal determinations regarding movable property unless they contradict local laws or public policy. However, any immovable property within Pakistan remains under the exclusive jurisdiction of Pakistani inheritance laws.

§2. Death

798. The Succession Act, 1925, along with Islamic inheritance laws, governs the distribution of movable and immovable property in Pakistan after an individual's death. For Muslims, inheritance is primarily regulated by Islamic laws which provide a detailed framework for the distribution of assets among heirs. A will (wasiyat) plays a significant role in succession but is subject to limitations under Islamic law, as a Muslim can only bequeath up to one-third of their estate to non-heirs, with the remaining two-thirds distributed among legal heirs according to prescribed shares. If a will exists, it must comply with legal requirements, including proper execution and attestation, to be considered valid. In cases where no will is present, the estate is distributed strictly according to Islamic principles. Non-Muslims in Pakistan, however, follow the succession laws outlined in the Succession Act, 1925, which vary based on their respective personal laws and religious practices. The courts oversee inheritance matters to ensure rightful distribution and prevent unlawful deprivation of heirs, especially in cases of disputes.

§3. The Heir and Other Beneficiaries

799. The Succession Act, 1925 Part V deals with the intestate succession. This Part shall not apply to any intestacy occurring before the first day of January 1866, or to the property of any Hindu Muslim, Buddhist, Sikh or Jaina. (2) Save as provided in sub-section (1) or by any other law for the time being in force, the provisions of this Part shall constitute the law of Pakistan in all cases of intestacy.

800. A person is deemed to die intestate in respect of all property of which he has not made a testamentary disposition which is capable of taking effect. Illustrations: (i) A has left no will. He has died intestate in respect of the whole of his property. (ii) A has left a will, whereby he has appointed B his executor; but the will contains no other provisions. A has died intestate in respect of the distribution of his property. (iii) A has bequeathed his whole property for an illegal purpose. A has died intestate in respect of the distribution of his property. (iv) A has bequeathed PKR 1,000 to B and PKR 1,000 to the eldest son of C, and has made no other bequest; and has died leaving the sum of PKR 2,000 and no other property. C died before A without having ever had a son. A has died intestate in respect of the distribution of PKR 1,000.

801. In the case of intestate succession, the property of a deceased individual is distributed among the surviving spouse and kindred (blood relatives) in accordance with the rules set forth in the applicable inheritance laws. Under Islamic law, inheritance is strictly governed by prescribed shares, ensuring that legal heirs receive their rightful portions. A widow is generally entitled to her share of her husband's estate; however, if she has been excluded from inheritance through a legally valid contract made before marriage, she may not be entitled to claim her distributive share. Such agreements must comply with legal requirements to be enforceable. The distribution of an intestate's property follows a specific hierarchy, prioritizing immediate family members such as spouses, children, parents, and siblings. If no direct heirs are present, the property may pass to extended relatives according to the legal framework. Courts play a crucial role in adjudicating inheritance disputes, ensuring that the estate is distributed fairly and in accordance with the law.

802. Where the intestate has left a widow (a) if he has also left any lineal descendants, one-third of his property shall belong to his widow, and the remaining two-thirds shall go to his lineal descendants, according to the rules hereinafter contained; (b) save as provided by section 33A, if he has left no lineal descendant, but has left persons who are of kindred to him, one-half of his property shall belong to his widow, and the other half shall go to those who are of kindred to him, in the order and according to the rules hereinafter contained (c) if he has left none who are of kindred to him the whole of his property shall belong to his widow.

803. Where the intestate has left a widow but no lineal descendants and the net value of his property does not exceed PKR 5,000, the whole of his property shall belong to the widow.

804. Where the net value of the property exceeds the sum of PKR 5,000, the widow shall be entitled to PKR 5,000 thereof and shall have a charge upon the whole of such property for such sum of PKR 5,000, with interest thereon from the date of the death of the intestate at 4% per annum until payment. The provision for the widow made by this section shall be in addition and without prejudice to her interest and share in the residue of the estate of such intestate remaining after payment of the said sum of PKR 5,000, with interest as aforesaid, and such residue shall be distributed in accordance with the provisions of section 33 as if it were the whole of such intestates property.

805. The net value of an intestate's property is determined by deducting all outstanding debts, funeral expenses, administrative costs, and any other lawful liabilities from the total gross value of the estate. Only after these deductions is the remaining estate distributed among the legal heirs. However, this provision does not apply in certain cases, including the property of Pakistan Christians, the descendants of a male Pakistan Christian, or individuals belonging to Hindu, Buddhist, Sikh, or Jaina religions whose succession is governed by the provisions of the Special Marriage Act, 1872. Additionally, these rules only come into effect if the deceased has died intestate (without leaving a valid will) concerning all of their property. In cases where part of the estate is governed by a will, the distribution of that portion will follow the terms set out in the will, while the remaining estate (if any) will be distributed according to the applicable intestacy laws.

806. If a person dies intestate (without a will) and has no surviving widow, their property is inherited by their lineal descendants, such as children and grandchildren, or by other relatives according to the prescribed legal rules. If no direct descendants or other kindred relatives exist, the estate ultimately escheats to the Government. The law ensures that inheritance follows a structured order, prioritizing close family members before more distant relatives. In cases where no eligible heirs are found, the property is taken over by the state, preventing it from remaining unclaimed.

807. A surviving husband has the same inheritance rights over his deceased wife's property, in cases where she dies intestate (without a will), as a widow has over her deceased husband's estate under the law. The distribution of property follows the legal framework that ensures fairness and equality in inheritance matters. However, the specific share of the husband in his wife's estate is determined by personal laws applicable to the deceased, such as Islamic law for Muslims, which grants the husband a fixed share based on the presence of other heirs. In the absence of any direct heirs, the surviving spouse may receive a larger portion or full ownership of the estate, ensuring financial security and legal protection.

808. If a person dies intestate, leaving behind one or more surviving children but no grandchildren or other more remote descendants through a deceased child, the entire estate is inherited by the surviving child if there is only one. If multiple children survive, the property is divided equally among them.

809. If a person dies intestate without leaving behind any surviving children but is survived by one or more grandchildren, and there are no great-grandchildren or more remote descendants through a deceased grandchild, the estate is inherited by the surviving grandchild if there is only one. If multiple grandchildren survive, the property is divided equally among them. Inheritance laws, such as the Succession Act, 1925, or Islamic laws for Muslims, determine the exact distribution. Under Islamic inheritance principles, grandchildren may inherit only if their parent (the deceased's child) is not alive at the time of succession, and their share is subject to the presence of other heirs. For instance, if an intestate had three children John, Mary, and Henry who all predeceased him, leaving behind two, three, and four children, respectively, his estate would be equally divided among his nine grandchildren. However, if one of the deceased children, such as Henry, had no surviving offspring, the inheritance would be divided equally among the remaining five grandchildren, the children of John and Mary.

810. If a person dies intestate and is not survived by children or grandchildren, the inheritance passes to the closest surviving lineal descendants, such as great-grandchildren or more remote descendants, following the principles of succession law. If all surviving heirs belong to the same degree of descent – such as all being great-grandchildren – they inherit the property equally. However, if there are multiple generations of descendants, inheritance laws determine the division. Under Islamic inheritance principles, great-grandchildren generally inherit only if their parent (the grandchild of the deceased) is not alive at the time of succession, and their share is subject to the presence of other heirs. In cases where there are no direct lineal descendants, the estate may pass to collateral relatives or, in the absence of eligible heirs, to the state.

811. If an intestate has left lineal descendants who are not all in the same degree of kinship and the ancestors through whom the more remote descendants inherit have already passed away, the estate is divided according to the principle of representation. The property is divided into equal shares corresponding to the number of direct descendants in the nearest degree of kinship who were alive at the time of the intestate's death, or who had predeceased the intestate but left surviving descendants. Under Islamic inheritance law, the concept of 'Tanzil' (representation) applies in certain cases, ensuring that grandchildren or great-grandchildren inherit only if their parent (the intestate's child) has passed away before the intestate. In non-Islamic inheritance laws, the estate is typically distributed per stirpes (by branch) rather than per capita (by headcount), ensuring that each family line receives an appropriate share of the inheritance.

812. One of such shares shall be allotted to each of the lineal descendants who stood in the nearest degree of kindred to the intestate at his decease; and one of such shares shall be allotted in respect of each of such deceased lineal descendants; and the share allotted in respect of each of such deceased lineal descendants shall belong to his surviving child or children or more remote lineal descendants, as the case may be; such surviving child or children or more remote lineal descendants always taking the share which his or their parent or parents would have been entitled to respectively if such parent or parents had survived the intestate. Illustrations: (i) A had three children, John, Mary and Henry. John died, leaving four children, and Mary died, leaving one, and Henry alone survived the father. On the death of A, intestate, one-third is allotted to Henry, one-third to John's four children and the remaining one-third to Mary's one child. (ii) A left no child, but left eight grandchildren, and two children of a deceased grandchild. The property is divided into nine parts, one of which is allotted to each grandchild, and the remaining one-ninth is equally divided between the two great-grandchildren. (iii) A has three children, John, Mary and Henry; John dies leaving four children, and one of John's children dies leaving two children. Mary dies leaving one child. A afterwards dies intestate. One-third of his property is allotted to Henry, one-third to Mary's child, and one-third is divided into four parts, one of which is allotted to each of John's three surviving children, and the remaining part is equally divided between John's two great-children. (iv) A has two children, and no more; John and Mary. John dies before his father, leaving his wife pregnant. Then A dies leaving Mary surviving him, and in due time a child of John is born. A's property is, to be equally divided between Mary and the posthumous child.

813. If an intestate has left no lineal descendants, the distribution of his estate, after deducting the widow's share (if applicable), shall follow the provisions outlined in sections 42 to 48 of the Succession Act, 1925. In such cases, the father of the deceased, if alive, has the primary right to inherit the property. If the father is not alive, the estate is distributed among other heirs according to the prescribed order of succession. Under Islamic inheritance law, if the deceased has no children, the father is entitled to a fixed share, typically one-sixth, and may inherit the remainder as a residuary if no other residuary heir exists. If the father is also deceased, inheritance typically passes to the mother, siblings, or more distant relatives in a hierarchical manner. In cases where there are no heirs at all, the property may ultimately escheat to the state.

814. If an intestate's father has passed away but their mother is still alive, along with surviving brothers and sisters, and there are no surviving children of any deceased siblings, the estate shall be divided equally among the mother and each living sibling. Under this arrangement, the mother receives a share equal to that of each surviving sibling. For example, if A dies intestate and is survived by his mother, two full-blood brothers (John and Henry), and a half-blood sister (Mary, who shares the same mother but not the same father), the estate is distributed as follows: the mother receives one-fourth, each full-blood brother receives one-fourth, and the half-blood sister also receives one-fourth. In Islamic inheritance law, however, the distribution follows a different structure. The mother is entitled to a fixed share, usually one-sixth if there are other heirs. Brothers and sisters inherit as residuary heirs, with full-blood siblings having a stronger claim than half-blood siblings. If there are multiple siblings, the male heirs generally receive twice the share of female heirs, following the Islamic principle of inheritance distribution. If the deceased has no direct heirs or close kindred, the estate is passed on to more distant relatives in accordance with established legal and religious principles.

815. If an intestate's father has passed away but their mother is still alive, and there are surviving siblings along with the children of any deceased siblings, the estate shall be divided equally among the mother, the living siblings, and the surviving children of any deceased siblings. The children of a deceased sibling collectively inherit only the share their parent would have received had they been alive at the time of the intestate's death, and they divide this share equally among themselves. For example, if A, the intestate, is survived by his mother, his brothers John and Henry, one child of his deceased sister Mary, and two children of his deceased half-blood brother George (who shared the same father but not the same mother), the estate will be distributed as follows: the mother receives one-fifth, John and Henry each receive one-fifth, Mary's child inherits one-fifth, and George's two children equally share the remaining one-fifth. In Islamic inheritance law, however, distribution follows specific fixed shares, with the mother entitled to one-sixth if there are other heirs. Siblings and the children of deceased siblings inherit as residuary heirs, but males typically receive twice the share of females. The presence of full-blood and half-blood relations can further affect the distribution, with full siblings having a stronger claim than half-blood siblings. If there are no other heirs, the estate is passed on to more distant relatives or ultimately reverts to the state in accordance with legal and religious principles.

816. If the intestates father is dead, but the intestates mother is living, and the brothers and sisters are all dead, but all or any of them have left children who survived the intestate, the mother and the child or children of each deceased brother or sister shall be entitled to the property in equal share, such children (if more than one) taking in equal shares only the shares which their respective parents would have taken if living at the intestates death. Illustration: A, the intestate, leaves no brother or sister, but leaves his mother and one child of a deceased sister, Mary, and two children of a deceased brother, George. The mother takes one-third, the child of Mary takes one-third, and the children of George divide the remaining one-third equally between them.

817. If an intestate's father has passed away but their mother is still alive, and there are no surviving siblings or children of any deceased siblings, the entire estate shall be inherited by the mother. In the absence of other heirs, she becomes the sole beneficiary of the intestate's property. However, under Islamic inheritance law, the mother's share is generally one-third if the deceased has no surviving spouse or children. If there are no other legal heirs, the remainder of the estate may be distributed among more distant relatives, such as paternal or maternal uncles, aunts, or cousins, following the principles of Islamic succession. If no eligible heirs are found, the estate ultimately reverts to the state.

818. If an intestate has not left behind any lineal descendants, father, or mother, the estate shall be distributed equally among the surviving brothers. If any brothers have passed away before the intestate, their children shall inherit their respective parent's share in equal proportions. This ensures that the share of a predeceased brother is not extinguished but is instead transferred to his children. Under Islamic inheritance law, male and female heirs are generally entitled to specific shares based on their relationship to the deceased. If there are no siblings or their descendants, the property may pass to more distant relatives such as uncles, aunts, or cousins, and in the absence of any legal heirs, the estate may ultimately revert to the state.

819. Where the intestate has left neither lineal descendant, nor parent, nor brother, nor sister, his property shall be divided equally among those of his relatives who are in the nearest degree of kindred to him. Illustrations: (i) A, the intestate, has left a grandfather, and a grandmother and no other relative standing in the same or a nearer degree of kindred to him. They, being in the second degree, will be entitled to the property in equal shares exclusive of any uncle or aunt of the intestate, uncles and aunts being only in the third degree. (ii) A, the intestate, has left a great-grandfather, or a great-grandmother, and uncles and aunts, and no other relative standing in the same or a nearer degree of kindred to him. All of these being in the third degree will take equal shares. (iii) A, the intestate, left a great-grandfather, an uncle and a nephew, but no relative standing in a nearer degree of kindred to him. All of these being in the third degree will take equal shares. (iv) Ten children of one brother or sister of the intestate, and one child of another brother or sister of the intestate, constitute the class of relatives of the nearest degree of kindred to him. They will each take one-eleventh of the property.

820. When a child or a descendant of a child claims a share in the property of a person who has died intestate, any financial support, gifts, or property settlements made by the deceased during their lifetime for the benefit or advancement of that child will not be deducted from their share of inheritance. This means that prior financial assistance or gifts given by the deceased do not reduce the rightful portion of the heir under the laws of succession. However, this principle does not apply to Parsis, as their inheritance and succession matters are governed by separate legal provisions. In Islamic inheritance law, any gifts or property transfers made during the deceased's lifetime are considered separate from the fixed shares of heirs, ensuring that each legal heir receives their rightful portion as prescribed by Shariah.

§4. Islamic Law of Inheritance and Succession

821. Muslims in Pakistan primarily belong to two major sects: Sunni and Shia, with the Sunni population being the majority. Within the Sunni sect, there are four main schools of thought: Hanafi, Maliki, Shafi'i, and Hanbali, each following distinct interpretations of Islamic jurisprudence (Fiqh). The Hanafi school is the most widely followed in Pakistan, influencing legal and religious practices, including matters of inheritance, marriage, and contracts. The Shia community, though smaller in number, follows the Jafari school of thought, which has its own interpretations of Islamic laws, particularly in personal and family matters. These sectarian differences impact legal proceedings, especially in matters of succession and inheritance, as Pakistan's legal system considers the specific jurisprudential school to which an individual belongs when determining applicable laws.

I. Sunni Laws

822. Under the Islamic Law Sunni sect following the following law of inheritance:

> 1.**Father:** Father gets 1/6 when there is child or child of a son besides other heirs; or when there is no child or child of a son, but there are husband, mother and son's daughter. Father gets 1/3 when there is no child or child of son, or son's daughter, but there are husband and mother; then there is no child or child of a son or sons' daughter but there are husband and maternal true grandmother; when there is no son, but there are more than one daughter; when there is no son, no daughter or son's son, but there is son's daughter or son's daughter.

823. The father is entitled to one-half of the deceased's estate in several scenarios under Islamic inheritance law. These include situations where there is no surviving child, grandchild (through a son), or great-grandchild (through a son's son), but a husband is present. Similarly, if the deceased has a daughter but no son, the father still retains a share. Additionally, if there are no direct male descendants (such as a son, grandson, or great-grandson), but the deceased is survived by a wife and mother, the father is entitled to a portion of the inheritance. Likewise, if there is a grandson (son's son) or granddaughter (son's daughter) but also a wife and a maternal true grandmother, the father's share remains significant. The exact distribution of shares follows the principles of Islamic inheritance law, ensuring the fair division of assets while prioritizing closer heirs according to prescribed shares (Faraid).

824. The father's share in inheritance varies depending on the presence of other heirs, as determined by Islamic inheritance laws. He is entitled to two-thirds of the estate when there are no surviving children, grandchildren (through a son), or great-grandchildren (through a son's daughter), but the deceased is survived by a mother or a maternal true grandmother. If there are no direct descendants but a widow is present, the father receives two-fourths (or one-half). In cases where there are no sons, daughters, grandsons, or granddaughters, and no surviving husband or wife, but the deceased is survived by a mother and multiple sibling, the father's share increases to five-sixths. If none of the primary heirs, such as children, grandchildren, spouse, mother, or maternal true grandmother, exist, the father inherits the entire estate. These rules ensure that the inheritance is distributed according to prescribed shares (Faraid), giving precedence to closer male and female relatives while maintaining a structured division of assets.

825. When the father is alive, certain relatives are excluded from inheritance under Islamic law, meaning they do not receive any share of the estate. These include the uterine brother, uterine sister, full sister, consanguine sister, and the true grandfather. Additionally, residuaries from Classes III and IV (which typically include more distant paternal relatives) do not inherit in the presence of the father. This rule ensures that closer male ascendants, such as the father, take precedence over other relatives, maintaining the structured hierarchy of inheritance as prescribed in Islamic law. The exclusion of these heirs helps preserve the father's legal share without dilution from more distant relatives.

826. The true grandfather does not inherit if the father is alive, as the father holds a closer degree of kinship to the deceased. However, if the father has passed away, the true grandfather assumes the role of the father in inheritance matters and is entitled to the same share that the father would have received. This principle ensures that in the absence of the father, the paternal lineage continues to have a rightful claim over the deceased's estate, following the established rules of Islamic inheritance. The true grandfather's entitlement depends on the presence of other heirs, and his share may vary accordingly.

827. **Mother:** The mother gets one-sixth, when there is a child or child of a son, or when there are two or more brothers or sisters, or even one brother and one sister, whether full, consanguine or uterine. She gets one-third, when there is no child or child of a son, and not more than one brother or sister if any. She gets one-fourth, when there are also wife and father plus one-third as above. She gets one-sixth, when there are also husband and father plus one-third as above.

828. **Maternal true grand-mother**: She gets one-sixth, when, is no mother, father no nearer true grand-mother; either parental or maternal, and no near true grand-mother, either paternal or maternal.

829. **Paternal true grand-mother:** She gets one-sixth, when there is no mother, father no nearer true grand-mother, either paternal or maternal, and no intermediate true grand-father.

830. **Husband:** He gets one-fourth, when there is child or child of a son. He gets one-half, when there is no child or a son.

831. **Wife:** She gets one-eighth, when there is child or child of a son. If the number of wives is more than one, they jointly get four-eighth. When no child and the wife is one or more, she or they get one-fourth.

832. **Daughter:** She gets one-half, when one and no son. When the number is more than one, they get two-third, provided there is no son. If there is son, she becomes residuary with the son, and takes one-half share than that of the son. In caner words the son takes a double portion. For instance if twenty-three remains after ducting the sharers of the shares, a son will get nine and daughter will get two-ninth. If sharers are three sons and two daughters, each son will get one-sixth and each daughter will get one-twelfth.

833. **Son's Daughter:** Son's daughter. She inherits only where there is no son, no daughter, or no son's son. She will get one-half if only one, and it more than one they will get two-third jointly. She or they will get one-sixth, if there is only one daughter, and there is no son or son's son. If there is son's son and no heirs as mentioned above she will inherit with him as residuary and her share will be like a daughter. If there is no equal son's son, but there is a lower son's son, she takes as a residuary with him, provided she cannot inherit as a sharer. In either case, each son son's son takes double the shares of each son's daughter. When the son's daughter becomes a residuary with a lower son's son, and there are son's daughter equal in degree with the lower son's son she shares equally with them as if they were all of the same grade.

834. **Son's son's daughter:** If one she will get one-half, provided there is no (1) son (2) daughter (3) son's son (4) son's daughter, or (5) son's son. If more than two they will get two-third jointly. Whether one or inure will get one-sixth, when there is only one daughter or son's daughter, provided there is no son, no son's son, nor son's son's son. If there is son's sons, she will inherit with them as residuary and her share will be like a sons s daughter.

835. **Uterine brother/sister:** When one, will get one-sixth, provided there is 'no child, no child of a son, no father, no true grand-father. When more than one, they will get one-third jointly. If there is uterine sister also the uterine brother will get half of his share that is instead one-sixth, he will get one-twelfth. In other words uterine brother and uterine sister inherit equally. The same share as given under uterine brother. Both inherit jointly.

836. **Full sister:** When only one and no (1) child (2) child of son (3) father (4) true grand-father or (5) full brother, she will get one-half, but if the number of sisters exceeds one, they get two-third jointly. In the circumstances given above, but when there is also brother, she does not inherit as barer. However, she will then inherit as residuary with the full brother. But the brother will take a double portion. In default of full brother, son, son's son, son's daughter, daughter, father and true grand-father, the full sister takes the residue if any, if there by (1) a daughter or daughters or to (2) a son's daughter or daughters or even if there he (3) one daughter and son's daughter or daughters.

837. **Consanguine brother:** He does not inherit as a sharer. He inherits as residuary with the Consanguine sister. He gets double portion. He gets share only, when there is no (1) son (2) son's in (3) daughter (4) son's daughter (5) father (6) true grand-father (7) full brother, (8) full sister.

838. **Consanguine sister:** When only one, she will get one-half, provided there is no (1) child to other. When more than one, they will get three jointly sharing equally. Whether one or more will get one-sixth, provided there is only one full sister and she succeeds sharer, provided further she is not otherwise excluded from inheritance. With the consanguine brother she inherits as a residuary. But the consanguine brother taking a double portion. She also inherits as residuary, if there be no heirs as mentioned under consanguine brother.

839. **Son:** The son is not a sharer. He inherits with the daughter as residuary. The son will get a double portion. Supposing two-third remains after allotting shares of the shares and there is one son and one daughter. The son will get four-ninth, and the daughter will get two-ninth. But if there are two sons and three daughters, then in such case each son will get 4/21, while each daughter will get 2/21. The son and daughter belong to Class-I of residuaries, and the son or the daughter and son together exclude all other residuaries and get the whole residue. Daughter alone inherits as sharer only.

840. **Son's son:** He does not inherit as sharer. He inherits as residuary, provided there is no son or no son's son nearer is degree. If there is son's daughter also, he inherits as residuary with the son's daughter. The son's son will get a double portion.

841. **Full brother:** Full brother does not inherit as sharer. He can however, inherit as residuary, if there is no residuary of classes I and II. He gets a double portion with the full sister.

842. **Full brother's son:** He inherits as residuary, if there be no heirs as already mentioned above. In their absence he gets the residue. Consanguine brother's son: In absence of heirs as already mentioned above, he gets the residue.

843. **Full brother's son's son:** In absence of heirs mentioned above, he gets the residue. Consanguine brother's son's son. In absence of heirs mentioned above, he gets the residue.

844. Then come remoter male descendants of full brother's son's son and consanguine brother's son's son, that is, the son of hill brother's son's son then the son of consanguine brother's son's son, then the son's son of full brother's son, then the son's son, of consanguine brother's son's son and so on in like order.

845. **Full paternal uncle:** In absence of above heirs, he will get, the residue, if any. Consanguine paternal uncle. In absence of above heirs, he will get the residue, if any. Full paternal uncle's son. In absence of above heirs, he will get the residue, if any. Consanguine paternal uncle's son. In absence of above heirs, he will get the residue, if any. Full paternal uncle's son's son. In absence of above heirs, he will get the residue, if any. Consanguine paternal uncle's son's son. In absence of above heirs, he will get the residue, if any.

846. Next in the line of inheritance are the more distant male descendants, specifically the sons of a full paternal uncle's son and the sons of a consanguine paternal uncle's son. Their inheritance follows the same order and pattern as the descendants of a full brother's son's son. The closer male relatives within the paternal lineage are given precedence, ensuring that inheritance remains within the direct bloodline before passing to more distant relatives.

847. After the nearer paternal relatives, the inheritance extends to the male descendants of more remote true grandfathers. These descendants inherit in the same order and manner as the deceased's paternal uncles, their sons, and their grandsons. The principle follows the hierarchy of male lineage, ensuring that closer paternal relatives inherit first before the estate passes to more distant branches of the family.

848. **Distant kindred:** If there be no sharers or residuaries, the inheritance is divided among Distant Kindred. If the only sharer be a husband or wife, and there be no relation belonging to the class of residuaries, the husband or wife will take his or her full share and the remainder of the estate will be divided among Distant Kindred.

849. The Distant Kindred are divided in four classes, Class-I succeeds in priority to Class-II, Class-II succeeds in priority to Class-III and Class-III succeeds in priority to Class-IV.

850. The order of succession in the first class is to be determined by applying the following two rules:

- the nearer in degree excludes the more remote. For instance daughter's son is preferred to a son's daughter's daughter; and
- among claimants in the same degree of relationship, the children of sharers and residuaries are preferred to those of Distant Kindred. For instance, a son's daughter's son succeeds in preference to a daughter's daughter's son.

851. The following is the order of succession among Distant Kindred of the first class: (1) daughter's children; (2) son's daughter's children; (3) daughter's grandchildren; (4) son's son's daughter's children; (5) daughter's great grand-children and son's daughters' grand-children; (6) other descendants of the deceased in like order. Of the above groups, each in turn must be exhausted before any member of the next group can succeed.

852. After ascertaining, which of the descendants of the deceased are entitled to succeed, the next step is to distribute the estate among them. The distribution in this case is governed by the rules, which are as follows:

- If the intermediate ancestors do not differ in their sexes, the estate is to be divided among the claimants per capita according to the rule of the double share of the male.

- If the intermediate ancestors differ in their sexes, the estate is to be distributed according to the following rules:
  a. The simplest case is where there are only two claimants, the one claiming through one line of ancestors, and the other, claiming through another line. In such a case, the rule is to stop at the first line of descendant in which the sexes of the intermediate ancestors differ and to assign to the male ancestor a portion double that of the female ancestor. The share of the male ancestor will descend to the claimant who claims through him, and the share of the female ancestor will descend to the claimant who claims through her, irrespective of the sexes of the claimants.
  b. The next case is where there are three or more claimants, each claiming through a different line of ancestors. Here again the rule is to stop at the first line in which the sexes of the intermediate ancestors differ, and assign to each male ancestor a portion double that of each female ancestor. But in this case, the individual share of each ancestor does not descend to his/her descendants as in the preceding case, but the collective share of all the male ancestors is to be divided among all the descendants claiming through them, and the collective share of all the female ancestors is to be divided among their descendants, according to the rule as between claimants in the same group of a double portion the male.
  c. The last case is where there are two or more claimants claiming through, the same intermediate ancestor. In such a case, there is this further rule to be applied, namely, to count for each such ancestor, if male, as many males as there are claimants claiming through him, and if females as there are claimants claiming through her, irrespective of the sexes of the claimants.

853. If there are no distant kindred from the first class, the entire estate will pass to the maternal grandfather, as he is the closest relative among the distant kindred of the second class. In Islamic inheritance law, priority is given to the closest eligible relatives, and if no immediate heirs or first-class distant kindred exist, the inheritance moves to the next closest category.

854. If the maternal grandfather is not alive, the estate will pass to the nearest false ancestors in the third degree who are connected to the deceased through shares, specifically the paternal grandmother's father and the maternal grandmother's father. Among these, the paternal side holds a greater right, with the paternal grandmother's father receiving two-thirds of the estate, while the maternal grandmother's father receives one-third. This division follows the principle of prioritizing paternal lineage in inheritance distribution, ensuring that closer male ancestors from the father's side inherit a larger portion than those from the maternal side.

855. If none of the previously mentioned false ancestors are alive, the estate will pass to the remaining false ancestors in the third degree, specifically the maternal great-grandfather (mother's father's father) and the maternal great-grandmother (mother's father's mother). Since both belong to the maternal lineage and are of the same generational level, the division follows the principle of male preference in inheritance. The maternal great-grandfather, being male, will receive two-thirds of the estate, while the maternal great-grandmother, being female, will receive one-third. This distribution aligns with the general rule that closer male relatives inherit a larger portion than female relatives, and the nearer in degree of kinship excludes more remote relations from inheritance.

856. If there be no Distant Kindred of the first or second class, the estate devolves upon Distant Kindred of the third class. This comprises such of the descendants of brothers and sisters as are neither shares nor residuaries. The order in succession in this class is to be determined by applying the following three rules on order:

- the nearer in degree excludes the more remote;
- among claimants in the same degree of relationship, the children or residuaries are preferred to these of Distant Kindred; and
- among claimants in the same degree of relationship, and not excluded by reason of rule (2), above, the descendants of full brothers exclude those of consanguine brothers and sisters. But the descendants of full sisters do not exclude the descendants of consanguine brothers or sisters, and the latter take the residue, if there be any, after allotting sharers to the descendant of full sisters and of uterine brothers and sisters. The descendants of uterine brothers and sisters are not excluded by descendants either of full or consanguine brothers or sisters but they inherit with them. The above rules lead to the following order of succession among Distant Kindred of the third class. Of the below groups, each in turn must be exhausted before any member of the next group can succeed:
- Full brother's daughters, full sister's children and children of uterine brothers and sisters;
- Full sister's children, children of uterine brothers and sisters, consanguine brother's daughters and consanguine sister's children, the consanguine group taking the residue, if any;
- Consanguine brother's daughters, consanguine sister's children, and children of uterine brothers and sisters;
- Full brothers' sons' daughters (children of residuaries);
- Consanguine brothers' sons' daughters (children of residuaries);
- Full brothers' daughters' children, full sister's grand-children, and grand-children of uterine brothers and sisters;
- Full sister's grand-children, grand-children of uterine brothers and sisters, consanguine brother's daughter's children and consanguine sister's grand-children the consanguine group taking the residue if any;
- Consanguine brother's daughters' children, consanguine sisters' grand-children, and grand-children of uterine brothers and sisters; and
- Remoter descendants of brothers and sisters in like order.

857. After ascertaining which of the descendants of brothers and sisters are entitled to succeed, the next step is to distribute the estate among them, and this is to be done by applying the following rules in order.

858. Rule-1: First, divided the estate among the Roots, that is to say, among the brothers and sisters (as if they were living) and in doing so, treat each brother who has two or more claimants descended from him as so many brothers and each sister who has two or more claimants descended from her as so many sisters. If there is a residue left after assigning their shares to the Roots, but there are no residuaries among the Roots (i.e., neither a full nor consanguine brother), apply the doctrine of return as described in section 5. The hypothetical claimants being brothers and sisters, no case of increase is possible at all.

859. Rule-2: After determining the hypothetical shares of the Roots, the next step is to assign its share to the uterine group. If there be only one claimant in that group, assign one-sixth to him, that being the hypothetical share of his parents. But if there be two more claimants in that group, whether descended from a single uterine brother, or a single uterine sister, or two or more uterine brothers or sisters, assign one-third to them, that being the hypothetical share of their parent or parents, and divide it equally among them without distinction of sex.

860. Rule-3: Lastly, divided the hypothetical shares of the full and consanguine brothers and sisters among their respective descendants as among Distant Kindred of the first case.

861. If there are no Distant Kindred of the first, second or third class, the estate will devolve upon distend kindred of the fourth class in the other given below:

- paternal and maternal uncles and aunts of the deceased, other than his full and consanguine paternal uncles who are residuaries;
- the descendants of all the paternal and maternal uncles and aunts of the deceased, other than sons of his full and consanguine paternal uncles (they being residuaries), the nearer excluding the more remote;
- paternal and maternal uncles and aunts of the parents, other than the full and consanguine paternal uncles of the father who are residuaries;
- the descendants of all the paternal and maternal uncles and aunts of the parents, their sons, of the full and consanguine paternal uncles of the father (they being residuaries), the nearer excluding the more remote;
- paternal and maternal uncles and aunts of the grand-parents, other than the full and consanguine paternal uncles of the father's father who are residuaries;
- the descendants of all the paternal and maternal uncles and aunts of the grand-parents, other than the sons of the full and consanguine paternal uncles of the father's father (they being residuaries), the nearer excluding the more remote;
- remoter uncles and aunts and their descendants in like manner and order; and
- of the above groups each in turn must be exhausted before any member of the next group can succeed.

862. To distribute the estate among uncles and aunts of the deceased, proceed as follows:

- First, assign two-third to the paternal side, that is, to paternal uncles and aunts, even if there be only one such, and one-third to the maternal side, that is, to maternal uncles and aunts, even in there be only one such.
- Next, divide the portion assigned to the paternal side, that is, two-third of the estate, among:
  - full paternal aunts in equal shares: failing them, among;
  - consanguine paternal aunts in equal shares: and failing them, among; and
  - uterine paternal uncles and aunts, according to the rule of the double share to the male.
- Lastly divide the portion assigned to the maternal side, that is, one-third of the estate, among:
  - full maternal uncles and aunts, failing them, among;
  - consanguine maternal uncles and aunts, and failing them, among; and
  - uterine maternal uncles and aunts, according to the rule, in each case, of the double share, to the male.

863. If there are no uncles or aunts from the paternal side, the entire estate will pass to the maternal side. Conversely, if there are no uncles or aunts from the maternal side, the paternal side will inherit the entire estate. In cases where both paternal and maternal sides have surviving relatives, the distribution follows the established inheritance rules, ensuring that closer relatives inherit before more distant ones.

864. **Descendants of uncles and aunts:** If there are no uncles or aunts of the deceased, the estate will devolve upon the descendants of uncles and aunts, other than sons howsoever of full paternal uncles and consanguine paternal uncles who are residuaries. To distribute the estate among these relations, proceed as follows:

- First, assign two-third to the paternal side, that is, to descendants of paternal uncles and aunts, even if there be only one such, and one-third to the maternal side that is, to descendants of maternal uncles and aunts, even if there be only one such.
- Next, divide the portion assigned to the paternal side, that is, two-third of the estate, among:
  - full paternal aunt's children, failing them, among;
  - full paternal aunt's children, failing them, among;
  - consanguine paternal uncle's daughters, failing them, among;
  - consanguine paternal aunt's children, and failing them, among; and
  - children to uterine paternal uncles and aunts, the division among the members of each of the five groups above to be made as among Distant Kindred of the first class.
- Lastly, divide the portion assigned to the maternal side, that is, one-third of the estate among:
  - children of full maternal uncles and aunts, failing them, among;
  - children of consanguine maternal uncles and aunts, failing them, among; and

  - children of uterine maternal uncles and aunts, the division among the members of each of the three groups above to be made among Distant Kindred of the first class.
- If there be no children of paternal uncles and aunts, the children of maternal uncles and aunts will take the whole. Similarly, if there be no children of maternal uncle and aunts, the children of paternal uncles and aunts will take the whole.
- If there be no children either of paternal uncles and aunts or maternal uncles and aunts, the estate will be divided among their grand-children on the same principles. Failing grand-children, it will be divided among remoter descendants, the nearer decree excluding the more remote.

865. **Other Distant Kindred of the fourth class**: If there are no descendants of uncles and aunts, the estate will devolve upon other Distant Kindred of the fourth class in the order of succession given on pages above the distribution among higher uncle and aunts being governed by the principles stated above and that among their descendants by those stated above.

866. In absence of Distant Kindred inheritance devolves on Successor by Contract, 'and in his absence on' 'Acknowledged Kindred' and in his absence on 'Universal Legatee' and in absence of all, the property escheats to the State.

Table of Shares: Sunni Law

(1)	*(2)*		*(3)*	*(4)*
Shares	*Normal Share*		*Conditions under which the normal share is inherited*	*This columns sets out:-(A)Shares of Sharers Nos 3, 4, 5, 8 and 12 as varied by special circumstances;(B)Conditions under which Shares Nos 1, 2, 7, 8, 11 and 12 succeed as Residuaries.*
	of one	*of two or more collectively (b)*		
FATHER 1.	1/6	–	When there is a child or child of a son h.l.s.	(When there is no child or child of a son h.l.s, the father inherits as a residuary: *see* Tab. of Res., No. 3.)
(a)). (sec. 62 cl. GRANDFATHER TRUE 2.	1/6	–	When there is a child or child of a son h.l.s. and no father or nearer true grandfather.	(When there is no child or child of a son h.l.s., the Tr. G.F. inherits as a residuary, provided there is no father or nearer Tr. G.F.: *see* Tab. of Res., No. 4).
HUSBAND 3.	1/4	–	When there is a child or child of a son h.l.s.	1/2 when no child or child of a son h.l.s.
WIFE (c) 4.	1/8	1/8	When there is a child or child of a son h.l.s.	1/4 when no child or child of a son h.l.s.
MOTHER 5.	1/6	–	(a)When there is a child or child of a son h.l.s., or(b)When there are two or more brothers or sisters, or even one brother and one sister, whether full consanguine or uterine.	1/3 when no child or child of a son h.l.s., and not more than one brother or sister (if any); but if there is also a wife or husband and the father, then only 1/3 of what remains after deducting the wife's or husband's share.

(1)	*(2)*		*(3)*	*(4)*
(section 62, cl. (c)). GRANDMOTHER TRUE 6.	1/6	1/6	A. Maternal – when no mother, and no nearer true grandmother either paternal or maternal. B. Paternal – when no mother, no father, no nearer true grandmother either paternal or maternal, and no intermediate true grandfather.	
DAUGHTER 7.	1/2	2/3	When no son.	(When the son she becomes a residuary: sec Tab. of Res., No. 1.)
h.l.s. (sec. 62, cl. (f)). SON'S DAUGHTER 8.	1/2	2/3	When no (1) son, (2), daughter, (3) higher sons son, (4) higher son's daughter, or (5) equal son's son (d).	When there is only one daughter, or higher son's daughter but no (1) son, (2) higher son's son, or (3) equal son's son, the daughter will take ½ and the son's daughter h.l.s. (whether one or more) will take 1/6, i.e., 2/3 – 1/2)(With an equal son's son she becomes a residuary: *see* Tab. of Res. No. 2).
Son's Daughter (i) e.g.	1/2	2/3	When no (1) son, (2), daughter, or (3) son's son.	When there is only one daughter, the son's daughter (whether one or more) will take 1/6, if there be no son or son's son. (With the son's son she becomes a residuary: *see* Tab of Res. No. 2).

(1)	*(2)*		*(3)*	*(4)*
Son's Son's Daughter (ii)	1/2	2/3	When no (1) son, (2), daughter, (3) son's son, (4) son's daughter, or (5) son's son's son.	When there is only one daughter or son's daughter, the son's son's daughter (whether one or more) will take 1/6, if there be no (1) son (2) son's son or (3) son's son's son. (With the son's son's son she become: residuary: *see* Tab of Res. No. 2).
UTERINE BROTHER 9.	1/6	1/3	When no (1) child, (2) child of a son h.l.s., (3) father or (4) true grandfather.	
or SISTER 10.				
FULL SISTER 11.	1/2	2/3	When no (1) child, (2) child of a son h.l.s., (3) father (4) true grandfather, or (5) full brother.	(When the full brother she becomes a residuary: *see* Tab. of Res. No. 5.)
SISTER CONSANGUINE 12.	1/2	2/3	When no (1) child, (2) child of a son h.l.s., (3) father (4) true grandfather, (5) full brother, (6) full sister, or (7) consanguine brother.	But if there is only one full sister and she succeeds as a sharer, the consanguine sister (whether one or more) will take 1/6, provided she is not otherwise excluded from inheritance. (With the consanguine brother she becomes a residuary: *see* Tab. of Res., No. 7.)

a. The collective share is always divided equally among those to whom it is allotted.
b. A Mahomedan can have as many as four wives at a time.
c. If there be a son's son and a son's son's daughter, the former is a higher son's son in relation to the latter. If there be a son's son and a son's daughter the former is a lower son's son in relation to the latter. And if there be a son's son and son's daughter or a son's son's daughter, the former is in equal son's son in relation to the latter, both being equally removed from the deceased.

A. Shia Laws

867. The Shias divide heirs to two groups namely, (1) heirs by consanguinity, that is, blood relations, and (2) heirs by marriage, that is, husband and wife. Heirs by consanguinity are divided into three classes, and each class is sub-divided into two sections. These classes are respectively composed as follows:

1. i. Parents;
   ii. Children and other lineal descendants h.l.s.
2. i. Grand-parents h.h.s. (true as well as false);
   ii. Brothers and sisters and their descendants h.l.s.
3. i. Paternal, and
   ii. maternal, uncles and aunts, of the deceased, and of his parents and grand-parents h.h.s., and their descendants h.l.s.

868. Among the three classes of heirs, the first class takes precedence and excludes the second from inheritance, while the second class, in turn, excludes the third. However, within each class, heirs from both sections inherit together, with those in a closer degree of kinship excluding those more distantly related within the same section. This hierarchical structure ensures that inheritance follows a clear order, prioritizing the closest relatives before extending to more remote kin.

869. **Husband and wife:** The husband or wife is always entitled to a share in the inheritance and is never excluded from succession. They inherit alongside the closest blood relatives. The husband's share is either one-fourth or one-half, while the wife's share is either one-eighth or one-fourth, depending on the presence of other heirs. These shares are determined based on specific conditions outlined in the table of sharers. In cases where there are no other legal heirs, the spouse may inherit the entire estate or a portion of it, with the remainder distributed according to the applicable inheritance laws.

870. **Table of Sharer Shia Law:** For the purpose of determining the shares of heirs; the Shias divide heirs into two classes, namely, shares and residuaries. There is no separate class of heirs corresponding to the 'Distant Kindred' of Sunni Law.

871. There are nine primary Sharers in inheritance under Islamic law. The table of shares outlines the specific portions allocated to each Sharer, particularly under

Shia law. In addition to these primary Sharers, their direct descendants may also qualify as Sharers, inheriting in accordance with the established rules of succession. The distribution of shares is determined by the presence or absence of other heirs, ensuring that the estate is divided fairly among the eligible beneficiaries.

872. **Residuaries:** All heirs other than Sharers and Residuaries. The descendants h.l.s. of Residuaries are also Residuaries.

873. **Distribution of property:** If the deceased left only one heir, the whole property would devolve upon that heir, except in case of a wife. If the only heir be a wife, the older view is that she is entitled to not more than her Quranic share (one-fourth) and the residue (three-fourths) escheats to the Government.

874. When a deceased person leaves behind multiple heirs, the first step in the distribution of the estate is to allocate the rightful share to the surviving spouse, whether husband or wife. Once this share is assigned, the next step is to determine which of the remaining relatives are entitled to inherit. This process follows the prescribed rules of inheritance, ensuring that the rightful heirs are identified based on their relationship to the deceased. After deducting the spouse's share, the remaining estate is distributed among the eligible heirs according to the established principles governing their respective classes of inheritance.

875. **Representation:** The principle of representation has more than one meaning. It may be applied for the purpose of deciding:

a. what persons are entitled to inherits, or
b. the quantum of the share given to person on the footing that he is entitled to inherit.

876. In both Sunni and Shia inheritance laws, the rule of exclusion applies, meaning that a nearer heir in degree excludes a more remote one. The principle of representation, which allows a descendant to inherit in place of a deceased parent, is not recognized in a way that overrides this rule. For instance, if a person (A) dies leaving behind a son and grandsons from a predeceased son, the surviving son will exclude the grandsons from inheritance. The grandsons do not inherit in their father's place, even though their father would have been an heir if he had survived. However, if both sons of A have already passed away before him, leaving grandsons from each, all the grandsons will inherit. The next question that arises is how their shares are determined. If the principle of representation is applied at this stage, the grandsons will inherit based on their respective branches – meaning that the grandsons from one deceased son will divide their father's share among themselves, while those from the other deceased son will do the same.

877. In Shia inheritance law, while the rule of exclusion applies in determining the heirs, the principle of representation is recognized for the purpose of calculating individual shares. This means that if a deceased son's descendants are entitled to inherit, they will collectively receive the share that their father would have taken had he been alive, effectively representing him in succession. Similarly, the descendants of a deceased daughter inherit in her place, receiving the share she would have been entitled to if she were alive. This principle extends to other relatives as well, including the descendants of a deceased brother, sister, or aunt, ensuring that inheritance is distributed in a manner that maintains the rightful succession of property across generations.

878. The principle of representation in Shia inheritance law is not limited to descendants alone but extends to both ascending and descending lines. This means that great-grandparents inherit the share that would have belonged to the grandparents if they were alive. Similarly, the father's uncles and aunts receive the portion that the deceased's uncles and aunts would have taken had they survived. This principle ensures a structured and equitable distribution of inheritance, maintaining the rightful succession of property within the family across multiple generations. It applies universally to all eligible heirs, reinforcing the continuity of inheritance rights beyond immediate descendants.

Table of Sharers – Shia Law

Sl. No.	*Shares*	*Normal Share*		*Condition under which the share is inherited*	*Share as varied by special circumstances*
		of one	*of two of more collectively*		
1.	Husband	1/4	–	When there is a lineal descendant.	1/2 when no such descendant.
2.	Wife	1/8	1/8	When there is a lineal descendant.	1/4 when no such descendant.
3.	Father	1/6	–	When there is a lineal descendant.	(If there be no lineal descendant, father inherits as a residuary.)
4.	Mother	1/6	–	When there is a lineal descendant: or When there are two or more full or consanguine brothers. Or one such brother and two such sisters. Or four such sisters, with the father.	1/3 in other cases.
5.	Daughter	1/2	2/3	When no son –	(With the son she takes as a residuary.)

Sl. No.	*Shares*	*Normal Share*		*Condition under which the share is inherited*	*Share as varied by special circumstances*
		of one	*of two of more collectively*		
6.	Uterine Brother	1/6	1/3	When no parent. or lineal descendant. (*see* section 88)	
7.	or sister				
8.	Full sister	1/2	2/3	When no parent, or lineal descendant, or full brother, or father's father(*see* sections 88, 101.)	(The full sister takes as a residuary with the full brother and also with the father's father: *see* section 101.)
9.	Consanguine sister	1/2	2/3	When no parent or lineal descendant, or full brother, or sister, or consanguine brother, or father's father (*see* sections 99, 101.)	(The consanguine sister takes as a residuary with the consanguine brother and also with the father's father: *see* section 101.)

Note – The descendants h.l.s. of sharers are also sharers.

879. **Stirpital succession:** Succession among descendants in each of three classes of heirs is per stripes and not per capita.

880. **Succession among descendants:** The descendants of a person who, if living, would have taken as Sharers, succeed as Sharers. The descendants of a person who, if living, would have taken as a Residuaries.

881. **Distribution among Heirs of the First Class:** Rules of succession among heirs of the first class. The persons who are entitled to succeed to the estate of a deceased Shia Muslim are the heirs of the first class along with the husband or wife, if any. The first class of heirs comprises parents, children, grand-children, and remoter lineal descendants of the deceased. The parents inherit together with children named, failing children, with grand-children, and, failing grand-children, with remoter lineal descendants of the deceased, the nearer excluding the more remote (section 88). Succession in this class is governed by the following rules:

1. **Father:** The father takes one-sixth as a Sharer if there is a lineal descendant; as a Residuary, it there be no lineal descendant (*see* Tab. of Sh. No. 3).
2. **Mother:** The mother is always a Sharer, and her share is one-sixth or one-third (*see* Tab. of Sh. No. 4).

3. **Son:** The son always takes as a Residuary.
4. **Daughter:** The daughter inherits as a Sharer, unless there is a son in which case she takes as a Residuary with him according to the rules of the double share to the male (*see* Tab. of Sh. No. 5).
5. **Grand-children:** On failure of children, the grand-children stand in the place of their respective parents, and they inherit according to the principle of representation described in sections 93, 94 and 95, that is to say:
   i. The children of each son take the portion which their father, if living, would have taken as a Residuary, and divide it among them according to the rule of the double share to the male.
   ii. the children of each daughter take the portion which their mother, if living would have taken either as a Sharer or as a Residuary and divide it among them also according to the double share to the male.
6. **Remoter lineal descendants:** Succession among remoter lineal descendants is governed by the same principle of representation, that is to say, great-grandchildren take the portion which their respective parents, if living, would have taken, and divide it among them according to the rule of the double share to the male, and great great-grandchildren take the protection which their respective parents, if living, would have taken, and divide it among them also according to the same rule.

882. **Distribution among Heirs of the Second Class:** Rules of succession among heirs of the second class. If there are no heirs of the first class, the estate (minus the share of the husband or wife, if any) devolves upon the heirs of the second class. The second class of heirs comprises grand-parents h.h.s. and brothers and sisters and their descendants h.l.s. (section 88). The rules of succession among the heirs of their class are different accordingly as the surviving relations are:

1. grand-parents h.h.s. without brothers or sisters or their descendants;
2. brothers and sisters or their descendant, without grand-parents or remoter ancestors;
3. grand-parents h.h.s. with brothers and sisters or their descendants.

883. **Grand-parent h.h.s., without brothers of sisters of their descendants:** If there are no brothers of sisters, or descendants of brothers of sisters, the estate (minus the share of the husband or wife, if any) is to be distributed among grand-parents according to the following rules:

1. if the deceased left all his four grand-parents surviving, the paternal grand-parents take two-thirds, and divide it between them according to the rule of the double share to the male, and the maternal grand-parents take one-third, and divide it equality between them;
2. if there is only one grand-parent on the paternal side, he/she takes the entire two-third. Similarly, if there is only one grand-parent on the maternal side, he/she takes the entire one-third; and

3. if there are no grand-parents the property will devolve according to the same rules upon remoter ancestors of the deceased, the nearer excluding the more remote.

884. **Brothers and sisters, without any ancestor:** If the deceased left no ancestors, but brothers, of various kind, the estate (minus the share of the husband or wife, if any) will be distributed among them according to the same rules as those in Hanafi Law.

885. **Descendants of brothers and sisters, without any ancestor:** If there are no brothers of sisters of any kind, and no ancestors, but there are children of brothers and of sisters, the estate (minus the share of the husband or wife, if any) will devolve upon them according to the principle of representation described in sections 93, 94, 95, that is to say:

1. the children of each full or consanguine brother will take the portion which their father, if living, would have taken as a Residuary, and they will divide it among them according to the rule of the double share to the male; and the children of each full or consanguine sister will take the portion which their mother, if living, would have taken either as a Sharer or as a Residuary, and they will divide it among them accordingly also to the rule of the double share to the male;
2. the children of each uterine brother will take the portion which their father, if living, would have taken as a Sharer, and they will divide it equally among them and so will the children of each uterine sister; and
3. if there are no children of brothers or sisters, the estate will, devolve upon the grand-children of brothers and sisters according to the principle of representation, that is to say the grand-children of full or consanguine brothers and sisters take the portion which their respective parents, if living, would have taken and divide it among them according to the rule of the double, share in male, he and the grand-children of uterine brothers and sisters take the portion which their respective parents, if living, would have taken, and divide it equally among them without distinction of sex.

886. **Grand-parents and remoter ancestor with brothers and sisters of their descendants:** If the deceased left grand-parents, and also brother or sisters, the estate (minus the share of the husband or wife, if any) is to be distributed among grand-parents and brothers and sisters, according to the following rules:

a. a paternal grand-father counts as a full or consanguine brother, and a paternal grand-mother counts as a full or consanguine sister; and
b. a maternal grand-father counts as a uterine brother and a maternal grandmother counts as a uterine sister.

887. If the deceased has no surviving grandparents, the more distant ancestors take their place, inheriting in accordance with their connection to the deceased.

Likewise, if there are no surviving brothers or sisters, their children (nieces and nephews of the deceased) inherit in place of their parents. This makes certain that inheritance remains within the family lineage preserving the rightful shares of those who would have inherited if their immediate ancestors had been alive.

888. **Distribution among Heirs of the Third class:** Order of succession among heirs of the third class. If there are no heirs of the first or second class, the estate (minus the share of the husband or wife, if any) devolves upon the heirs of the class in the order given below:

- paternal and maternal uncles and aunts of the deceased;
- their descendants h.l.s. nearer in degree excluding the more remote;
- paternal and maternal uncles and aunts of the parents;
- their descendants h.l.s. the nearer in degree excluding the more remote;
- paternal and maternal uncles and aunts of the grand-parents;
- their descendants h.l.s., the nearer in degree excluding the more remote;
- remoter uncles and aunts and their descendants in like order; and
- of the above groups each in turn must be exhausted before any member of the next group can succeed.

889. Exception: If the only claimants be the son of a full paternal uncle and consanguine paternal uncle, the former, though he belongs to group (2), excludes the latter who is nearer though he belongs to group (1).

890. Uncles and Aunts: To distribute the estate among uncles and aunts proceed as follows:

1. First, assign two-third of the estate to the paternal side, that is, to paternal uncles and aunts, even if there be only one such, and one-third to the maternal side, that is, to maternal uncles and aunts, even if there be only one such.
2. Next, divide the portion assigned to the paternal side (i.e., two-third of the estate) among the paternal uncles and aunts exactly as if they were brothers and sisters of the deceased, that is to say:
   i. assign to uterine paternal uncles and aunts:
      a. if there be two or more of them, one-third to be equally divided among them; and
      b. if there be only one of them, one-sixth.
   ii. divide the remainder among full paternal uncles and aunts according to the rule of the double share to the male, and, failing them, among consanguine paternal uncles and aunts according to same rule.
3. Lastly, divide the portion assigned to the maternal side, among the maternal uncles and aunts as follows:
   i. assign to uterine maternal uncles and aunts:
      a. if there be two or more of them, one-third to be equally divided among them; and
      b. if there be only one of them, one-sixth.

ii. divide the remainder equally among full maternal uncles and aunts, and, failing them among consanguine maternal uncles and aunts.

4. If there be no uncle or aunt on the maternal side paternal side takes the whole. Similarly if there be no uncle or aunt on the paternal side, the maternal side takes the whole.

891. **Descendants of uncles and aunts.** If there are no uncles or aunts of any kind, children of deceased uncles and aunts take the portion of their respective parents according to the principle of representation described in sections 80, 81 and 82, the children of each full or consanguine paternal uncle or aunt dividing their parents share among them according to the rule of the double share to the male, and the children of each of the remaining uncles, and aunts, that is, of uterine paternal uncles and of maternal uncles and aunts, whether full, consanguine or uterine, dividing their parents share equally among them.

892. If there are no surviving children of the deceased's uncles or aunts, their grandchildren inherit in their place, receiving the share their respective parents would have taken. This follows the established principle of representation, ensuring that inheritance is passed down within the family lineage in an orderly manner.

893. **Other heirs of the third class:** If there are no descendants of uncles or aunts, the estate will devolve upon the other heirs of the third class in the order of succession the distribution among higher uncles and aunts being governed by the principles and that among their descendants being governed by the principles, the 'Return' and the 'Increase'.

894. The Doctrine of 'Return' (Radd) applies when, after distributing the estate among the entitled Sharers, there is a remaining residue, and no Residuaries exist in the class to which the Sharers belong. In such cases, the leftover portion is redistributed among the Sharers in proportion to their respective shares, ensuring that no part of the inheritance remains undistributed. However, this rule is subject to specific exceptions outlined in sections 107, 108, and 109, which may alter the distribution in particular circumstances.

895. Doctrine of 'Return' (Radd), neither the husband nor the wife is entitled to receive the surplus inheritance if there are other heirs present. However, if a deceased individual leaves behind only a husband and no other heir, the remaining estate, after assigning the husband's legal share, will revert to him. Conversely, if the deceased leaves only a wife with no other heirs, earlier interpretations held that she would receive her rightful one-fourth share, while the remaining estate would escheat to the state, as the surplus was not traditionally considered to revert to a wife. However, modern interpretations in certain jurisdictions have evolved to grant the wife the surplus through Return, aligning inheritance distribution more equitably.

896. Mother when excluded from 'Return': If the deceased left a mother, a father, and one daughter, and also:

a. two or more full or consanguine brothers, or
b. one such brother and two such sisters, or
c. four such sisters,

the brothers and sisters, though they themselves excluded from inheritance as being heirs of the second class, prevent the mother from participating in the Return, and the surplus reverts to the father and the daughter in the proportion of their respective shares. This is the only case in which the mother is excluded from the Return.

897. **Uterine brothers and sisters when excluded from 'Return':** If an estate has remaining assets after distributing the prescribed shares (Return or Radd), uterine brothers and sisters do not share in the surplus if there are full sisters present. In such a case, the entire residue goes to the full sisters. However, this rule does not apply to consanguine sisters. When consanguine sisters are present along with uterine brothers and sisters, the surplus is divided among them in proportion to their respective shares, ensuring a more equitable distribution in accordance with inheritance principles.

898. **Doctrine of 'Increase':** The Sunni doctrine of increase is not recognized in the Shia Law. According to the Shia Law, if the sum total of the sharers exceeds unity, the fraction in excess of the unity is deducted invariably from the share of:

a. the daughter or daughters; or
b. full or consanguine sister or sisters.

899. **Escheat:** On failure of all natural heirs, the estate of a deceased Shia Islamic escheats to the Government.

900. **Miscellaneous** he eldest son, if mentally sound, has an exclusive right to inherit the personal belongings of his father, including his wearing apparel, the Holy Quran, sword, and ring, provided that the deceased has left other property in addition to these items. A childless widow is not entitled to any share in her husband's agricultural land; however, she retains the right to one-fourth of the value of trees and buildings on the land, as well as a share in his movable property, including outstanding debts, even if they are secured by a usufructuary mortgage or other means. An illegitimate child is not entitled to inherit from either parent or their relatives, and likewise, the parents and relatives do not inherit from the illegitimate child.

901. The consanguine sister of the deceased and his real mother over his estate in Muzaffargarh. Petitioner claimed a share in the inheritance asserting that the respondent was a Sunni Muslim, while the mother contended that he belonged to the Shia sect and that she was his sole legal heir. Initially, an inheritance mutation was sanctioned in favour of the mother but it was later challenged by the petitioner leading to a remand for an inquiry into the sect of the deceased. Subsequently, petitioner filed a suit seeking her and her sisters' legal recognition as heirs. The Trial

Court ruled in favour of the mother, concluding that the deceased was a Shia Muslim. However, the District Court reversed this decision on appeal, holding that the deceased was a Sunni Muslim, thus granting inheritance rights to the consanguine sister and her sisters. The case was brought before the Supreme Court, which analysed the burden of proof regarding a deceased Muslim's sect and the period of limitation for filing an inheritance claim. The Court reaffirmed the principle established in *Pathana v. Mst. Wasai*, stating that, in the Indo-Pak subcontinent, a Muslim is presumed to follow Sunni Hanafi law unless proven otherwise with strong evidence. The Court found that the Appellate Court had correctly evaluated the evidence and concluded that the petitioner was a Sunni Muslim, whereas the mother failed to rebut the initial presumption or provide substantial evidence to prove his adherence to Shia law. Furthermore, the Supreme Court held that the suit was filed within the six-year limitation period, as the right to sue accrues when a co-heir denies the inheritance rights of another, not merely upon the entry of an inheritance mutation in the revenue record. The revisional court's decision to dismiss the case as time-barred was deemed legally incorrect. Consequently, the Supreme Court allowed the appeal, restored the judgment of the Appellate Court, and decreed the suit in favour of the consanguine sister. (SC – 2022 SCMR 399)

902. Islamic Law. Inheritance. Shia law. Issueless widow of a deceased who belonged to Fiqah Jafaria was excluded from the estate of the deceased. Validity: Mutation of inheritance suffering front no legal or jurisdictional defects, Court declined interference (LHC – 2000 YLR 2580).

903. Islamic Law Inheritance. Shia sect. Original owner of house in question admittedly being Shia by faith, plaintiff being his sister, was his sole heir (he having died issueless). Ownership of house in question, would automatically vest in plaintiff sister by way of inheritance (LHC – 1993 CLC 2152).

904. Inheritance of deceased where the petitioners, his brother and sister, challenged the validity of a mutation of inheritance sanctioned in favour of his wife and daughter (respondents Nos 1 and 2) on the basis that the deceased was of Sunni faith, whereas the impugned mutation recorded him as a follower of Shia faith. The trial court dismissed the suit, and the appellate court upheld the decision. The petitioners contended that there is a presumption that every Muslim is Sunni unless proven otherwise and argued that the burden of proof was on the respondents to establish that the deceased was Shia. However, the court, after examining various legal precedents, held that no legal provision explicitly supports this presumption. It ruled that since the petitioners alleged fraud and claimed the deceased was Sunni, the burden of proof was on them under Article 119 of the Qanun-e-Shahadat Order, 1984. The court found that the petitioners failed to provide cogent evidence to support their claim, as arguments based on the Nikah solemnized by a Sunni Maulana, the deceased's payment of Zakat, and the respondent's lack of knowledge about Shia faith were insufficient to establish that the deceased was a Sunni. The court also emphasized that inheritance is governed by the faith of the deceased, not the successors, and noted that a certificate from Jafria Trust confirming the deceased's Shia faith was not challenged by the petitioners. Since the petitioners could not prove any jurisdictional defect or procedural impropriety in the concurrent findings of the lower courts, the court dismissed the revision petition, affirming the validity of the impugned mutation. (LHC – 2022 CLC 675)

905. Islamic Law Inheritance (Shia Law). Childless widow of an 'Asna Asharia' Muslim could not inherit any portion of the lands left behind by him (SCP – 1972 PLD 346).

906. The dispute arose when the petitioner, one of his sons, initially agreed to have the inherited property evaluated and to pay the legal heirs their respective shares according to Shariah but later reneged on this commitment and challenged his signed 'Consent/Joint Statement' before the High Court. The court noted that the petitioner was literate, had retired from a government position and was represented by counsel at the time of signing, making his claim that he did not understand what he was signing unjustified. The petitioner also filed a suit for partition, declaration, specific performance, and injunction two months after his sisters sought their inheritance, despite the fact that the property of a deceased Muslim vests in legal heirs immediately upon death. The court emphasized the importance of protecting inheritance rights, particularly of vulnerable members like female heirs, and condemned the practice of using litigation tactics to deprive legal heirs of their rightful shares. Given the petitioner's dishonest tactics, the court dismissed the petition with costs of PKR 300,000, to be equally distributed among the deprived heirs. Additionally, the respondents were entitled to claim mesne profits for the delay caused by the petitioner in fulfilling his obligations under the 'Consent/Joint Statement'. (SC – 2025 SCMR 98)

907. Widow and brother. Plea of brother was that he to the exclusion of childless widow was entitled to inherit whole land left by deceased belonging to Shia Sect. Proof. Burden to prove such plea was lying on brother. Widow was still receiving family pension of deceased as supported by an entry made in Pension Book. Mutation of land sanctioned in accordance with Sunni Personal Law had not been challenged by brother in Revenue hierarchy. Widow had applied for partition of land and notice had been issued to brother. Brother had not produced any convincing evidence that deceased belonged to Fiqa Jafria. Brother and his witness in their statements in Court had shown ignorance about the manner in which funeral ceremonies of deceased had been conducted (SCP – 2004 SCMR 1783).

908. Islamic Law Inheritance. The petitioners filed a civil revision petition against the judgment and decree of the First Appellate Court Skardu, which had upheld the trial court's decision dismissing their claim for declaration and possession of the disputed land. The petitioners, as legal heirs of their great-grandfather sought a 2/5 share of the land in possession of respondent No. 1, his daughter. The trial court had framed 14 issues, examined evidence, and dismissed the suit, a decision later affirmed by the First Appellate Court. The dispute had a prior history of litigation where respondent No. 1 had successfully obtained a court decree in her favour. The petitioners also previously filed an application under section 12(2) CPC challenging a judgment from 1991 but were directed to file an independent suit instead, leading to the present proceedings. The court found that great grandfather had four children – one son and three daughters – and that under Shia inheritance law, the closer legal heir excludes more distant ones. Since two daughters had pre-deceased his son inherited the estate, which later passed to his son who died issue-less. Consequently, respondent No. 1, being the sole surviving legal heir, was entitled to the land. The court found no legal or factual errors in the decisions of the lower courts and held that there was no misreading or non-reading of evidence to warrant interference. Therefore, the civil revision petition was dismissed as merit-less, and the judgments of the lower courts were upheld. (Gilgit-Baltistan Chief Court – 2021 MLD 1759)

III. Case Laws Inheritance and Succession

909. Inheritance. The court held that the oral gift made by defendant No. 1 in favour of his mother was valid under Muhammadan law, as it fulfilled the essential requirements of offer, acceptance, and delivery of possession. The gift, initially made and later confirmed in writing was acknowledged by the defendant himself, who admitted to executing and handing over the gift deed out of love and gratitude. The court rejected the argument that the donee had refused the gift, emphasizing that her retention of the document indicated acceptance. It also ruled that the fact that the property was mortgaged at the time did not affect the validity of the gift, as Muhammadan law permits the transfer of mortgaged property. Additionally, the defendant continued to recognize the gift even after his mother's death and never sought its revocation. Based on these findings, the court upheld the validity of the gift and held that after the death, the property was to be inherited by all legal heirs according to Hanafi Muslim law. (Sindh High Court – 2024 CLC 468)

910. Amount of Benevolent Fund and Group Insurance would devolve upon the heirs, of the deceased being his 'Tarka'. Mother of the deceased, who was nominee, would not be entitled exclusively to claim such amounts except to the extent of her share as per Shariat with other legal heirs of the deceased (SCP – 2005 SCMR 512).

911. Inheritance. Estoppel. Under Islamic Law of Inheritance as soon as owner dies succession to his property opens. Due share of inheritance vests in the heirs. Any entry in mutation contrary to law did not operate as estoppels (LHC – 2005 MLD 1).

912. Inheritance: The petitioner filed a suit for declaration, claiming his rightful share in the inheritance of his maternal uncle through his deceased mother, and challenged it. The petitioner argued that the judgments were based on misreading of evidence and misapplication of law, particularly regarding the principle that no limitation applies to inheritance matters. The court reviewed the evidence, noting that the petitioner's name appeared in the succession certificate and revenue records, affirming his entitlement. It reiterated that inheritance rights are not extinguished by the passage of time, as misrepresentation cannot override a legal heir's claim. The court found that the lower courts had overlooked crucial aspects and decided the case on technical grounds. Consequently, the revision petition was allowed, the impugned judgments were set aside, and the petitioner's suit was decreed in his favour. (LHC – 2024 CLC 106)

913. Distant Kindred. Distant Kindred inherit only when there are no sharers or residuaries. If a sharer or residuary exists, the Distant Kindred are completely ousted from the inheritance. Principles (SCP – 2004 PLD 768).

914. Limitation would not apply to enforcement of right of inheritance in estate of deceased predecessor (LHC – 2004 PLD 1).

915. The respondents being the widow and daughters of the deceased claimed their inheritance rights and challenged the mutations of gift alleging fraud and impersonation. The appellants contended that the deceased had the right to gift the property and that the suit was time-barred. However, the courts found that the power of attorney used for the gift was fraudulent and lacked authority to transfer property through a gift. The appellants failed to prove the three essential elements of a valid gift – declaration, acceptance, and transfer of possession nor did they produce the original power of attorney or any direct witnesses to support their claim. The courts held that the property rightfully devolved upon the deceased legal heirs as per Islamic law and the claim was within time as the respondents acted promptly upon discovering the fraud. The courts concluded that the alleged gift was a device to deprive female heirs of their rightful inheritance, which is impermissible. Since no valid gift was proven and the mutations were fraudulent, the appeal was dismissed. (LHC – 2024 YLR 1238)

916. Deceased not owning property at time of death, but only his claim, according to which allotment was to be made was pending. Such claim would go to entire family on death of deceased before allotment (SCP – 2004 SCMR 94).

917. The petitioners challenged the judgment of the Additional District Judge, which upheld the trial court's decision dismissing their suit regarding inheritance and possession of property. They had sought a declaration, permanent injunction, and possession, claiming joint ownership of the property inherited from their predecessor and alleging an unfair private division. The respondents argued that a partition deed had been executed in 1963, which was acknowledged by the petitioners' own witnesses. The courts found that the petitioners failed to challenge the partition deed during their predecessor's lifetime and could not prove their claims. Legal precedents established that a plaintiff must prove their case with solid evidence and cannot benefit from the weaknesses in the defendant's case. The court ruled that the lower courts had correctly assessed the evidence, and there was no misreading or illegality warranting interference under section 115, CPC. Consequently, the revision petition was dismissed. (Peshawar (Mingora Bench) – 2024 YLR 1227)

918. Opening of succession. Inheritance under Muslim Personal Law takes place automatically, and each legal heir is entitled to get his respective share irrespective of any claim or demand therefore (SCP – 2004 SCMR 1391).

919. Existence of custom depriving females from inheritance at time of opening of succession. Proof. Once such custom was not proved, then property would devolve in accordance with normal principles of Islamic inheritance (SCP – 2004 SCMR 1524).

920. The plaintiffs, legal heirs of the deceased filed a suit seeking their Shari shares in the ancestral property, possession through partition and cancellation of sale deeds executed without their consent. The trial court ruled in their favour, holding that their right to inheritance could not be extinguished by limitation. The petitioners, who contested the claim, argued that their grandfather had gifted the property to their father, and later changed their stance, stating that the property was obtained through a compromise. The appellate court upheld the trial court's decision, dismissing the appeal. The High Court in revisional jurisdiction refused to interfere with the concurrent findings, emphasizing that inheritance rights are fundamental under Islamic law and cannot be denied based on technicalities or delay. The petitioners' inconsistent stance weakened their case and the courts found no jurisdictional defect, material irregularity, or misreading of evidence to justify reversal. Consequently, the revision petition was dismissed. (PHC – 2024 YLR 1342)

921. Court, in the cases which involved inheritance inter se among legal heirs, should make efforts to ensure that no legal heir was denied his legal share in the estate of deceased on a technical ground (PHC – 2004 YLR 340).

922. Islamic Law Inheritance. Opening of. Inheritance of Muslim deceased opens at the time of death of Muslim owner of the property (LHC – 2003 PLD 186).

923. Inheritance dispute concerning the estate of the deceased whose great-grandchildren, the appellants, claimed a share in his property after a significant lapse of time. The courts found that neither the deceased son nor his granddaughter had asserted their rights during their lifetimes. The respondents argued that the appellants' claim was barred by limitation, as third-party interests had already been established decades ago through property sales. The appellants contended that inheritance rights under Islamic law are not subject to limitation and alleged fraud in omitting granddaughter name from the pedigree table. The Court, however, distinguished between cases where heirs are directly deprived of their share and those where third-party interests have been created. Since the appellants' claim emerged long after such interests were established, they failed to justify the delay under section 18 of the Limitation Act. The Court upheld the decisions of the lower courts, emphasizing that inheritance claims must be asserted in a timely manner to prevent legal complications and third-party entanglements. Consequently, the appeal was dismissed. (SC – 2024 PLD 600)

924. The appellant, filed a civil appeal challenging the High Court of Balochistan's judgment, which granted her a one-third share in the sale proceeds of her late father agricultural land instead of a one-third share in the actual property. Her father passed away leaving behind his son and daughter as legal heirs. However, his son fraudulently mutated the entire property in his name through an oral gift mutation excluding his sister from her rightful inheritance. The trial and appellate courts dismissed appellant claims, but the High Court set aside their decisions and ordered her compensation from the sale proceeds. The Supreme Court, upon reviewing the case held that inheritance rights vest immediately upon the death of the predecessor and cannot be denied based on fraudulent mutations. It ruled in favour of the appellant granting her a one-third share in the entire inherited property rather than just the sale proceeds. The court cancelled the fraudulent mutation and all subsequent transactions, directing revenue authorities to redistribute the estate accordingly while ensuring the sold portion is adjusted from the son's share. Consequently, the appeal was allowed. (SC-2024 SCMR 938)

925. The petitioner challenged the LHC's order dismissing his revision application regarding the inheritance mutation which was and granted a 7/72 share of the property to Respondent No. 4, the son of the petitioner's predeceased sister. The petitioner argued that his father who passed away owned the land and Respondent No. 4 was not entitled to any share. Initially, the trial court ruled in the petitioner's favour but on appeal the district court set aside the judgment and remanded the case for consideration of the limitation issue. The suit was later dismissed as time-barred, a decision upheld by the appellate court and the High Court. The petitioner contended that he was unaware of the mutation due to residing in Canada, but the courts rejected this argument, noting that he never pleaded this fact in his plaint. The Supreme Court reaffirmed that limitation laws apply even in inheritance cases, especially when claims are delayed without justification. The petitioner's inaction for 27 years was deemed a failure to exercise his legal rights in a timely manner, and since no other legal heirs contested the mutation, the court found no grounds for interference. Consequently, the petition was dismissed. (SC – 2024 PLD 1269)

926. Devolution of property would take place through inheritance immediately without any other intervention irrespective of the fact whether mutation of inheritance was recorded or not or was incorrectly recorded. Wrong mutation would confer no right in property as Revenue Record was maintained only for the purposes of ensuring realization of land revenue. No question of limitation in inheritance suits. Co-heirs-co-sharer who was in possession, would be deemed to hold possession on behalf of other co-sharers. Persons in possession of land being in constructive possession on behalf of other co-sharers, mere omission by them to pay their share of produce would not constitute their ouster (LHC – 2003 CLC 1593).

927. Islamic Law Inheritance. Relationship of husband and daughter with deceased woman. Proof. Last male owner was survived by his mother and sister. Petitioners as collateral of last male owner claimed to be exclusive owner of suit land. Respondents claimed to be entitled to one-half share in suit land being husband and daughter of the deceased sister of last male owner. Trial Court declared petitioners to be entitled to one-half share in suit land, while remaining half would vest in respondents as husband and daughter of deceased sister of last male owner. Appellate Court in appeal by petitioners accepted their claim to be exclusive owners of suit land. High Court in revision set aside such findings of Appellate Court.

Contention of petitioners was that respondents had not proved their such relationship with deceased sister of last male owner, thus, her half share would revert back to petitioners as collateral of last male owner. Validity: Copy of judgment of Family Court placed on record showed that deceased sister of last male owner while appearing as defence-witness in a suit for restitution of conjugal rights filed against her by another person had stated that she was married to respondent husband and that respondent-daughter was born as a result of such wedlock, and that she was never married to plaintiff in that suit. Such statement was supported by another witness, who stated that she had been living with respondent-husband for the last thirty-two years. Such other person while appearing as witness in a suit filed against him by deceased sister of last male owner claiming damages for defamation had stated on oath that respondent-daughter was born as result of her wedlock with respondent-husband. Findings of Appellate Court were based on gross misreading of such overwhelming evidence and same were perverse, which had rightly been reversed by High Court in exercise of its jurisdiction under section 115, CPC. Impugned judgment was based on proper appreciation of evidence and material available on record, wherein no misreading or non-reading of evidence or misconstruction of facts and law was found. Supreme Court dismissed the petition for leave to appeal in circumstances. Constitution of Pakistan (1973), Article 185(3). Civil Procedure Code (V of 1908), section 115 (SCP – 2003 SCMR 125).

928. Inheritance Law. Respondent No. 1 who was falsely reported as deceased leading to the property's transfer to respondents Nos 2 and 3 through inheritance mutation. They later sold it to respondent No. 8, who then transferred it to the petitioner. The petitioner mortgaged the property with respondent No. 6 but defaulted on loan payments, prompting the bank to file a recovery suit, which was decreed. During execution proceedings, objections arose including one claiming that Respondent No. 1 had not actually died in 1985 but was alive until 2003. A civil court declared the inheritance mutation fraudulent, restoring ownership to her, after which she transferred the property to respondents Nos 3 and 4. However, subsequent litigation questioned the legitimacy of the decree, particularly since her actual date of death remained unclear. The petitioner filed an application under section 12(2) of CPC to challenge the decree but was dismissed on limitation grounds, despite the Banking Court and High Court questioning the validity of the inheritance claim. The case remains unresolved, pending before the Supreme Court, with the core issue being whether the inheritance mutation and subsequent property transfers were fraudulent due to misrepresentation of the original owner's death. (LHC – 2021 PLD 533)

929. Islamic Law Inheritance. Daughter of predeceased son of original owner was only entitled to her Quranic share from estate of her deceased father. Other successors-in-interest of original owner would get their shares according to principles of inheritance (LHC – 2003 MLD 484).

930. The petitioners challenged the inheritance mutation through a suit for declaration, claiming ownership of property as legal heirs of petitioner, daughter of deceased. They alleged that the revenue entries transferring the property to the respondents were fraudulent and sought possession through partition. The respondents contested the claim, asserting that the mutation was legally attested and that Mst. Bibi Roshan had predeceased her father. The trial court dismissed the suit due to insufficient evidence proving that petitioner was alive at the time of her father's death. The appellate court upheld this decision emphasizing that the petitioners failed to provide credible records of death dates and that the mutation had been attested in an open assembly in 1973. Furthermore, the petition was barred by limitation as the claim was brought nearly three decades later. The court also rejected the petitioners' reliance on section 4 of the MFLO, 1961, since the deaths in question occurred before its enactment, and the law was not retroactive. The High Court, exercising its limited revisional jurisdiction, found no illegality or jurisdictional defect in the lower courts' judgments and dismissed the petition (PHC – 2021 CLC 383).

931. Islamic Law Inheritance. In absence of residuaries, entire property left by the owner would revert to real sister of owner on account of principle of return, if owner died issueless (Supreme Court Azad Kashmir – 2003 YLR 389).

932. Inheritance Law. The case arose from the murder of wife by her husband, the appellant, who inflicted axe blows on her leading to his conviction and life imprisonment under section 302(b) PPC along with six months' rigorous imprisonment under the Khyber Pakhtunkhwa Arms Act. Initially, the complainant deceased father, accused the appellant of habitual drug use and domestic violence but during trial, a compromise was reached between the appellant and the deceased's parents, who were her only legal heirs under Hanafi inheritance law. The court verified the compromise and confirmed that it was made voluntarily, without coercion. However, upon reviewing the record, the court considered whether the murder fell under the category of honour killing, which would prohibit compounding under section 311 PPC and section 345(7) CrPC. The court distinguished between premeditated honour killings and killings committed due to grave and sudden provocation. Since the appellant confessed to killing his wife after finding her in a compromising position, the court ruled it was an act of grave and sudden provocation rather than an honour killing, making it compoundable. Given that only the deceased's parents could inherit from her directly, they had the exclusive right to pardon the appellant. The court accepted the compromise, setting aside the murder conviction while maintaining the sentence under the Arms Act. Consequently, the appellant was acquitted of murder and ordered to be released unless required in another case. (PHC – 2021 P Cr. L J 469)

933. Inheritance Opening. When a person demises, his succession opens at the same moment and according to the Sharia, all the persons who are entitled to inherit his estate, immediately and automatically become co-sharers of the estate left by the deceased (LHC – 2002 YLR 3247).

934. Occupancy tenant died leaving behind four sons and two daughters, but mutation in respect of property comprising in occupancy tenancy left by deceased was attested in favour of four sons of deceased and names of his daughters of deceased were omitted. Legal heirs of deceased daughters had filed suit to the effect that their deceased mothers being daughters of deceased occupancy tenant were entitled to inherit property comprising in occupancy tenancy of the deceased. Omission of names of daughters of deceased was without any legal or moral justification when at the relevant time rule of inheritance was Islamic Law. Even if mothers of plaintiffs were not in possession of suit property, sons of deceased who happened to be sharers, would be deemed to be in possession on their behalf as well. Heir in possession of property of his predecessor, had to be considered to be in constructive possession of property on behalf of other heirs in spite of his exclusive possession. Possession of brothers in circumstances would be taken to be possession of their sisters as well. Dispute being among legal heirs of deceased same could be taken to Civil Court without having recourse to any other proceedings. Trial Court, in circumstances, had rightly decreed the suit, and Appellate Court was not justified to set aside judgment and decree of Trial Court. High Court set aside judgment and decree passed by Appellate Court and restored those of Trial Court (PHC – 2002 YLR 608).

935. Inheritance rights under Islamic law. The respondent, a daughter of the deceased challenged a gift mutation executed by her brothers, the petitioners, who claimed that their father had gifted them the property in his lifetime. However, the respondent argued that the deceased had already passed away before the alleged gift was made. The LHC overturned the lower courts' decisions, finding that the petitioners failed to establish the validity of the gift. The Supreme Court upheld this ruling, emphasizing that inheritance rights under Islamic law vest immediately upon a person's death, and any subsequent claims to property must align with this principle. The Court also criticized the persistent practice of depriving female heirs of their rightful inheritance and stressed the need for proactive state measures to prevent such injustices. The Court directed the revenue authorities to cancel the fraudulent gift mutation, prepare the correct inheritance record, and ensure the respondent receives her rightful share. The petition was dismissed with costs payable by the petitioners. (SC – 2021 PLD 812)

936. Deceased having died issueless was survived by progeny of his two brothers. Question of inheritance was to be resolved by keeping in view the position/status of the progeny of such two brothers that is, as residuaries being at equal distances from the deceased, and they will inherit not as representing their respective fathers as a group but equally being placed in scenario for the purposes of inheritance to the estate of the deceased (SCP – 2000 SCMR 1574).

937. Islamic Law Inheritance This civil revision challenges the judgments and decrees of the lower courts, which dismissed the petitioner suit for declaration with consequential relief against mutations No. 528 and No. 539 allegedly executed through an oral gift in favour of her brothers. The petitioner claimed these mutations were fraudulent and deprived her of her rightful inheritance. The respondents failed to provide essential details in their pleadings and evidence, such as the time, place, and witnesses of the alleged gift, nor did they establish the mandatory legal requirements of offer, acceptance, and possession transfer. The courts below erred in assuming that the mere attestation of mutations was sufficient to validate the gift, ignoring settled legal principles that require strict proof, especially when female heirs are being disinherited. Moreover, key revenue officials and witnesses were not produced and no valid explanation was provided for their absence. The objection of limitation was also misplaced, as the right of inheritance does not extinguish with time, and the claim was filed promptly after discovering the fraud. The objection regarding the co-plaintiff's absence in appeal was dismissed under procedural rules allowing one plaintiff to challenge a decree affecting all co-owners. Lastly, the argument that concurrent findings of fact could not be disturbed in revision was rejected, as higher courts can intervene where lower courts fail to consider material evidence or misinterpret the law. Consequently, the revision is allowed and the judgments and decrees of the lower courts are set aside. (LHC – 2022 CLC 890)

938. Islamic Law Gift. Death-bed gift and acknowledgment. Alienation of property. Only restraint imposed by Muslim Laws upon a Muslim relates to will and gifts on death-bed (LHC – 2000 YLR 242).

939. Requirement of mutation. Necessity. When a Muslim owner dies, his estate passes on to the legal heirs in accordance with the Quranic Injunctions. No mutation or any other act of the State or individual is required for acquisition of the proprietary rights by inheritance (LHC – 2000 YLR 621).

940. Devolution of estate of a Muslim deceased. Scope. Estate of the last male owner comes to vest in his heirs, the moment he breaths his last. Under the Islamic jurisprudence no State or individual intervention is required or is necessary for such devolution upon the heirs of the deceased defined in the Holy Quran in accordance with the shares allocated to them (LHC – 2000 YLR 633).

941. Appellants asserted that respondent was not daughter of the deceased and had been wrongly included in the legal heirs of the deceased. Validity: Evidence led by parties preponderantly showed that respondent, although daughter of the widow yet was not daughter of the deceased. Judgment and decree passed by Court, in favour of the respondent were set aside (LHC – 2000 YLR 1496).

942. Inheritance Law. This civil revision challenges the legality of orders which dismissed the petitioners' application for setting aside an ex-parte judgment and decree. The dispute concerns the inheritance mutation of deceased whose estate was initially mutated in favour of his sons, excluding his widow and daughters under customary law but was later corrected to include all heirs under Islamic law. The plaintiffs, his sons, challenged this correction and obtained an ex-parte decree without recording any evidence. The petitioner's legal heirs of the excluded daughters, only became aware of the decree when the respondents sought its implementation in prompting them to file for its annulment. The lower courts dismissed their application, but the revision court found that the summons for the original suit were improperly served, violating mandatory legal provisions. The process server's report lacked essential verification, and the trial court failed to ensure due service before proceeding ex-parte. Furthermore, the decree was not based on verified pleadings or recorded evidence, making it legally defective. Given the respondents' unexplained 34-year delay in enforcing the decree and the petitioners' lack of awareness, the application was deemed within limitation. The court emphasized principles of natural justice, particularly the right to a fair hearing, and recognized the petitioners' disadvantaged position as illiterate, Parda-observing village women. Consequently, the revision was allowed, the lower court orders and the 1976 decree were set aside, and the case was remanded for a fresh trial on merits. (LHC – 2022 MLD 250)

943. Limitation. No principle of limitation could be used to defeat visible right of inheritance (LHC – 1999 MLD 1140).

944. Sect of deceased person. Reliance was placed on the death certificate of the deceased to prove the sect of the deceased. Validity: Person who reported the death of the deceased appeared as a 'witness' in the Trial Court and denied the assertion that the deceased was Shia by sect. Presumption was that every Muslim citizen was a Sunni sinless otherwise proved (LHC – 1999 YLR 2692).

945. Specific Relief Act (I of 1877), section 42. Constitution of Pakistan (1973), Article 185(3). Inheritance. Adverse possession. Limitation. Last male owner having died in 1936, his inheritance mutation was attested in 1937, whereby his daughters and widow were deprived of their share of inheritance while his nephews got his whole property claiming that their tribe was governed by custom whereby females were excluded from inheritance. Trial Court dismissed plaintiff's claim while Appellate Court and High Court decreed their suit on the ground that tribe of plaintiffs was governed by Islamic Law and not by custom, and that two daughters and widow were entitled to succeed to their respective shares of inheritance. Validity: Land in question, admittedly, belonged to predecessor-in-interest of plaintiffs who died sometime in 1935–1936, and his inheritance mutation was attested in 1937 wherefrom plaintiffs were excluded from inheritance whose relationship with deceased male owner was not denied. Main question, however, for determination was that of limitation and adverse possession for more than twelve years. Leave to appeal was, thus, granted to determine legal question relating to limitation and adverse possession (SCP – 1998 PLD 1512).

946. The appeal was filed with a delay of 183 days, citing the COVID-19 lockdown as the reason but even after considering the excluded period per the Court's Circular, it remained time-barred. Despite this, the Court examined the merits due to the respondents' absence. The appellant claimed that his father had gifted land to him through a mutation. However, the mutation lacked acceptance of the gift and evidence showed that the father had allegedly gifted the land on the very day of his death, making the claim highly suspect. The burden of proof lay on the appellant, which he failed to fulfil. Islamic law dictates that upon a Muslim's death, legal heirs inherit the estate, and possession by one is deemed possession by all. The appellant's sisters had filed a suit in their lifetime which was valid and the appellate court's decision favouring the appellant was rightly set aside. The appeal was dismissed both on merits and as time-barred with costs throughout. The Court expressed regret over the appellant's fraudulent attempt to deprive legal heirs of their rightful shares and directed the District Collector to implement the Trial Court's decision ensuring the legal heirs receive their shares and possession within three months. (SC – 2022 SCMR 346)

947. Co-heirs. Co-sharer claiming title through adverse possession. Presumption relating to possession of joint property. Defendant being co-heirs claimed to have matured their title through adverse possession. Validity: Parties to suit being co-heirs/co-sharers, possession of one co-sharer/co-heir was presumed to be possession of others. Male co-heir could not allege adverse possession against female co-heir (PHC – 1998 MLD 1857).

948. Issueless widow. Full brothers sons. Entitlement to inherit widows share on her death. Widow had inherited estate left by her husband as sharer to the extent of one-fourth whereas remaining three-fourth share had gone to legal descendants of deceased male landowner. Respondents who were sons of her brothers on widow's death, were entitled to inherit estate left by the widow as being full brothers sons. Courts below had committed no error in law while declining claims of appellants that is, descendants of male landowner. Azad Jammu and Kashmir Interim Constitution Act (VIII of 1974), section 42 (Supreme Court, Azad Kashmir – 1998 MLD 411).

949. Islamic Law Inheritance. Duty of Court. In cases which involve inheritance inter se among the legal heirs, Court should make efforts to ensure that no legal heir is denied of his legal share in the estate of the deceased concerned on a technical ground. Such an approach will also be in consonance with the Injunctions of Islam (SCP – 1997 SCMR 281).

950. The petitioner filed a suit for declaration, asserting her right to inherit her deceased father estate which had been denied due to a fraudulent gift mutation (No. 1943, dated 21.03.1972) in favour of her brothers. She contended that the gift was never made with her knowledge or consent and that she had been deprived of her rightful share. The respondents, her brothers claimed that the gift was voluntarily executed by their father but they failed to substantiate their claim by proving the three essential elements of a valid oral gift offer, acceptance, and delivery of possession through credible evidence. The court observed that they neither provided clear details about the transaction nor produced key witnesses, such as the Patwari and Tehsildar, who were responsible for attesting the mutation. Moreover, the court highlighted that under Islamic law, inheritance rights particularly of female heirs, are protected and cannot be nullified through fabricated transactions. The principle that claims of inheritance are not subject to limitation unless explicitly repudiated was also reaffirmed. the court ruled that mere entry of a mutation does not establish ownership unless the underlying transaction is proven through lawful means. Since the respondents failed to meet this burden of proof, the court determined that the alleged gift mutation was fraudulent and intended to deprive the petitioner of her lawful inheritance. As a result, the findings of the lower courts were set aside, and the case was decided in favour of the petitioner restoring her rightful share in her father's estate. (LHC – 2023 CLC 1171)

951. Articles 64 and 114(g). Islamic Law. Inheritance. Withholding the best evidence. Effect. Defendant not producing those witnesses who were presumed to have knowledge of relationship of plaintiff with deceased land owner. Where any party withholds best evidence, presumption would be that if such evidence had been produced, it would have gone against that party. Two Courts below, on material available on record had concurrently found that plaintiff was the real sister of deceased. There being no other heirs of such deceased, she was entitled to inherit legal estate of deceased to the extent of two-third of his estate. Concurrent findings of two Courts below on basis of evidence on record on relationship of parties being correct, no interference with such finding was called for. Judgment and decree of First Appellate Court, although holding plaintiff to be sister of deceased land owner, yet deprived her of inheritance on grounds extraneous to legal proposition (LHC – 1997 MLD 67).

952. Islamic Law Inheritance. Person committing homicide is excluded from inheriting the property of the victim (BHC – 1997 P Cr. L J 247).

953. Inheritance Law. Petitions arising from inheritance disputes among the legal heirs of deceased. The plaintiffs, who are descendants of deceased brother contested several inheritance mutations asserting their legal rights over the property originally owned by deceased and subsequently transferred through various mutations. They argued that after the death of deceased son, his mother who inherited the property as a limited owner under customary law should have had her share revert to deceased heirs upon her demise. The trial court ruled partially in favour of the plaintiffs, particularly regarding mutation which dealt with the deceased inheritance, while dismissing their claims concerning other mutations. The appellate court largely upheld the trial court's findings but modified its decision on mutation stating that deceased uterine brothers were not entitled to inherit. Upon further revision, the present court affirmed the previous courts' rulings regarding most mutations but made a crucial correction concerning mutation. It ruled that after satisfying the inheritance shares of deceased widow and daughter, the remaining property should pass to deceased paternal cousins as residuary rather than to his uterine brothers. The court also concluded that the plaintiffs lacked the legal standing to challenge the other mutations, dismissing their claims accordingly. Thus, the judgment clarified the rightful heirs of the disputed property, reinforcing the principles of Islamic inheritance law and the doctrine of legal heirship while rectifying errors in the prior inheritance records. (LHC – 2023 MLD 1357)

954. Islamic Law Inheritance. Share of daughters sold by brothers without their consent. Effect. Land devolved on two daughters of deceased landowner was alienated by their brothers. Two Courts below decreed plaintiffs' (daughters') suit. High Court remanding case for fresh decision. Validity: Leave to appeal was granted to consider the contention that defendants had not denied factum of plaintiff and one of the defendants being daughters of deceased land owner; that property in question to the extent of one-third share devolved on daughters could not have been alienated by brothers in favour of vendees without their (daughters') consent; and whether observations of High Court to the effect that vendees of land in question, appeared to be bona fide purchasers without notice was untenable and contrary to evidence on record. Constitution of Pakistan (1973), Article 185(3) (SCP – 1996 SCMR 1213).

955. Dispute relating to inheritance. Parties' common ancestor had two wives. Deceased land-owner and respondents were from one wife of common ancestor while petitioners were born from the other wife. Respondents being real brothers of deceased were thus, entitled to his inheritance to the exclusion of their step-brothers. Both parties being in joint possession of land in question, mere wrong entry in Revenue Record would not deprive respondents from ownership in respect of land left by deceased, their real brother. High Court had effectively and correctly dealt with question of inheritance. Leave to appeal was refused in circumstances (SCP – 1996 SCMR 1964).

956. Inheritance Law. Dispute over inheritance concerning the legal heirs of deceased whose property was initially distributed under customary law (riwaj). The plaintiffs challenged the inheritance mutations arguing that they should have been distributed equally among all five sons under the North West Frontier Province Muslim Personal Law (Shariat) Application Act, 1935. The trial and appellate courts ruled in favour of the plaintiffs, applying Islamic inheritance principles retroactively. However, the court in revision addressed two key issues: the applicability of the 1935 Act and the limitation period for filing the suit. It was established that the 1935 Act did not have retrospective effect, and subsequent amendments, including the 1962 and 1983 Acts, did not apply to past and closed transactions. Additionally, the court held that inheritance rights are immediately vested upon the ancestor's death, and if legal heirs fail to challenge their deprivation in a timely manner, their successors lack the legal standing to do so later. Since the deceased immediate heirs did not contest the mutations during their lifetimes, the plaintiffs' suit filed in 2006 was time-barred. Consequently, the revision was allowed and the judgments of the lower courts were set aside dismissing the plaintiffs' claims. (PHC – 2023 PLD 12)

957. Islamic Law. Inheritance. The petitioners/defendants challenged the judgment and decree passed by Majlis-e-Shoora Kalat at Mastung, which reversed the trial court's decision and decreed the plaintiffs' suit regarding the inheritance of late. The plaintiffs being legal heirs claimed that the defendants fraudulently transferred the entire inherited land to their names, depriving them of their rightful share. They asserted that the land in question belonged to their predecessor, and the defendants unlawfully mutated it in their names. The defendants on the other hand argued that their grandfather had gifted the land to them through an oral gift which was duly mutated. The trial court dismissed the plaintiffs' suit but the appellate court allowed the appeal. The High Court examined the case and emphasized that in matters of gift, the burden of proof lies on the beneficiary (donee) to establish the three essential conditions of a valid gift: offer, acceptance, and delivery of possession. The defendants failed to produce any credible witnesses to prove the alleged oral gift, and no close relatives of the donor were present at the time of the transaction. The court noted that depriving legal heirs especially female heirs without valid justification is suspicious and requires strict scrutiny. The court held that mere mutation entries do not constitute a valid gift and that the defendants had failed to establish their claim. Since no independent witnesses could confirm the gift and the key identifiers were not produced in court, the claim appeared dubious. The court also pointed out that the alleged donor was of old age and no reasonable explanation was provided for why he would deprive his daughters of their inheritance. Court put pressure on protecting inheritance rights especially of female heirs, the court concluded that the defendants' claim of oral gift was not legally sustainable. Therefore, the revision petition was dismissed, and the judgment of the appellate court was upheld, restoring the plaintiffs' right to their inherited property. (Balochistan High Court – 2023 CLC 1391)

958. Islamic Law. Inheritance. Where personal actions have matured into a decree, they become part of the estate of the deceased and can be inherited. Maxim '*actio personalis moritur cum persona*'. Exception. (Maxim) (LHC – 1995 PLD 381).

959. Islamic Law. Inheritance. Exclusion. Heir of deceased who was disobedient and involved in criminal litigation could not be deprived of legal right of inheritance on that account (LHC – 1995 MLD 1841).

960. Estate of deceased male owner opening up for succession after the death of his widow who was holding it as a limited owner. Sister of deceased and his collateral alone coming forward to claim inheritance. No other person claiming to be the heir of deceased coming forward to claim inheritance over the period of years when litigation was going on nor coming forward thereafter. Except heirs of deceased and those of widow (to the extent of her share), no one including donee whose gift was declared to be invalid was entitled to inherit the estate of deceased. Judgment of High Court to that extent was valid. Leave was refused in circumstances (SCP – 1994 SCMR 2044).

961. Islamic Law. Inheritance. Entitlement to property in question, as an heir of deceased. Leave to appeal was granted to consider, whether from the evidence on record, purported grandmother (maternal) of respondent was proved to be the sister of deceased land owner and respondent her grandson that is, 'Nawasa' and was thus entitled to inherit and if so, to what extent, from the estate of deceased land owner. Constitution of Pakistan (1973), Article 185(3) (SCP – 1994 SCMR 2292).

962. Islamic Law. Inheritance. Property of deceased full owner held by his wife as limited owner, would revert to full owner after death of limited owner and would devolve upon heirs of full owner (LHC – 1994 CLC 976).

963. Appellants who were legal heirs of deceased daughter of original owner of land in dispute had claimed that said daughter of original owner died after death of original owner whereas claim of respondents was that she died much earlier than the death of original owner, and thus heirs of predeceased daughter could not inherit property of original owner under Islamic Law. Courts below on basis of evidence on record had concluded that daughter had died much earlier to death of original owner. Concurrent findings of fact of Courts below based on evidence on record and not suffering from any illegality such as misreading or non-reading or misconstruction of any material piece of evidence, could not be interfered with (LHC – 1994 CLC 1964).

964. Inheritance of deceased property whose son fraudulently mutated the land in his favour excluding his sisters. The petitioners, being legal heirs of the sisters challenged the inheritance mutation claiming their rightful share. The trial court decreed the suit ruling that inheritance claims are not time-barred. However, the appellate court reversed the decision, citing that the sisters were aware of the exclusion when the son received compensation for acquired land, yet they did not challenge it. The High Court upheld this view, relying on precedents emphasizing that limitation applies to inheritance claims once rights are denied through overt acts. The Supreme Court analysed the principles governing limitation in inheritance cases and concluded that the petitioners' claim was time-barred as the six-year limitation period had expired in the lifetime of their predecessors. Since their right to sue derived from their predecessors, they could not revive a lapsed claim. Consequently, the petition for leave to appeal was dismissed. (SC – 2023 PLD 362)

965. Death of deceased employee during course of his employment. Social insurance death compensation amount awarded to defendants of deceased by employer whether to be treated as 'Tarka' of deceased so as to devolve upon his legal heirs. Social insurance death compensation was a type of group insurance and a sort of Benevolent Fund or grant from employer, which was not realizable in the lifetime, thus, it could not be treated as 'Tarka' of deceased and would not devolve upon the legal heirs of deceased but would go to dependents of deceased as compensation. Widow and children of deceased would be entitled to such amount but not the other heirs of deceased. Deceased having nominated his father to recover debt, such nomination was simply due to the fact that deceased keeping in view local culture and traditions had nominated his father to recover debt. Father of deceased was although not entitled to inherit anything out of compensation amount, yet, keeping in view his nomination by deceased, he was allowed his 'Sharai share' out of the said amount. Share given to mother of deceased was, however, directed to be refunded for depositing the same in Trial Court which had to be disbursed among the widow and children of deceased according to their 'Sharai shares' (PHC – 1994 PLD 1).

966. Heir loses the right to inherit, if found guilty of having murdered the person who was the source of inheritance (SCP – 1993 SCMR 1073).

967. Petitioner, the sole legal heir of the deceased challenged a fraudulent inheritance mutation sanctioned in 1955, which deprived her of her rightful share. After multiple legal proceedings, the trial court awarded her half of the inheritance. Her appeal for full inheritance was dismissed. The central issue was determining the petitioner's faith as inheritance rules differ for Sunni and Shia sects. The petitioners failed to provide credible evidence proving that the petitioner was Shia, leading courts to presume he was Sunni. The fraudulent concealment of the deceased legal heirship was evident and courts upheld her entitlement to half petitioner property. Fraud nullifies limitation defences, and possession of the disputed property favoured in the deceased heirs. No illegality or mis appreciation of evidence was found in the lower courts' judgments, and under section 115 of the CPC, revisional jurisdiction does not allow interference unless a gross error is present. Hence, both revision petitions were dismissed. (LHC – 2024 CLC 895)

968. Inheritance: As soon as a Muslim owner dies, succession of estate left by him immediately opens and title passes to the heirs without any intervention by State functionaries or clergy. Theory of representation of estate by intermediary is unknown to Islamic Law of Inheritance. Inheritance. Limitation. No principle of limitation can be used to defeat the visible right of inheritance. (LHC – 1993 PLD 575).

969. Widow of deceased son would not inherit his due share. Remainder would revert to collaterals. Inheritance. Evidence on record was insufficient for a final determination of all the true heirs to the deceased land owner and their actual shares in the estate left by him. Case was remanded to the limited extent for determining true heirs and their actual shares in the property left by the deceased (LHC – 1993 CLC 133).

970. The Supreme Court dismissed the civil appeals challenging the LHC's judgments which granted succession rights in tenancy to the daughters of the deceased under Sharia law. The dispute arose from the exclusion of female heirs from inheriting tenancy rights after the death whose tenancy was inherited by his male descendants under section 20 of the Colonization of Government Lands (Punjab) Act, 1912. The appellants argued that succession should be governed by this provision as he died before the amendment introducing section 19-A which mandated succession under Sharia law. However, the court held that Sharia law applied to Muslims in Bahawalpur due to the West Punjab Muslim Personal Law (Shariat) Application Act, 1948. The court also rejected the appellants' claim of being original tenants based on their payment for the tenancy, emphasizing that they were treated as legal heirs under earlier inheritance mutations. Additionally, the limitation argument was dismissed, as the sisters had been receiving tenancy proceeds until they were abruptly denied, making their suits timely. Concluding that the High Court's judgments were legally sound, the Supreme Court upheld them and dismissed the appeals without costs. (SC – 2023 SCMR 1901)

971. Dispute relating to inheritance of deceased who was the real brother of plaintiffs. Defendants claiming share in inheritance, were stepbrothers and sisters of deceased. Inheritance of deceased would, thus, devolve on plaintiffs alone being his direct heirs; defendants being step-brothers and sisters could not inherit property in question, in presence of real brothers of deceased (LHC – 1993 CLC 2539).

972. Islamic Law. Inheritance. Co-heirs. Bar of limitation would not stand among co-heirs and their successors. Suit filed by a co-heir inheriting under Islamic Law, would not be barred by limitation. Limitation Act (IX of 1908), section 3. (Co-sharer) (LHC – 1993 MLD 1207).

973. Gift: Essentials. Declaration of gift by the donor; acceptance of subject-matter of gift by the donee expressly or impliedly; and handing over possession by donor to donee of the subject-matter of gift are the essential ingredients of a gift. Where any of the three ingredients was lacking, gift would not be deemed to have been proved (SHC – 1993 MLD 1542).

974. The trial and appellate courts decreed the suit in favour of respondents Nos 1 to 3, declaring them as legal heirs of the deceased and invalidating the mutations of Gift. The respondents, being the widow and daughters of deceased claimed that the property was fraudulently transferred to the predecessor of the appellants, through impersonation and deceit. The appellants contended that the deceased had the right to gift his property and that the findings on issues Nos 1 and 2 were based on misreading of evidence. However, after examining the entire record, the courts concluded that no valid gift was made as the essential ingredients of a valid gift declaration, acceptance, and delivery of possession were not proven. The alleged power of attorney did not grant authority for a gift and the appellants failed to produce key witnesses or documentary proof. Additionally, Supreme Court precedents established that gifts intended to deprive female heirs are invalid and constitute fraud. The court also dismissed the limitation objection holding that the respondents filed the suit within time upon discovering the fraudulent mutations. Consequently, the appeal was dismissed for lack of merit. (LHC – 2024 YLR 1238)

975. The petitioners challenged the judgments of the Additional District Judge and Civil Judge which dismissed their suit regarding the inheritance of a property. They claimed the property was the legacy of their predecessor and that no official partition had taken place whereas the respondents contended that a private partition had occurred supported by a partition deed. The courts found that the petitioners failed to prove their claims as the partition deed was acknowledged and their predecessor never challenged it during his lifetime. The court ruled that belated inheritance claims cannot be entertained when earlier legal heirs did not contest them. Furthermore, the burden of proof lay on the petitioners which they failed to discharge. Given that the trial and appellate courts had properly evaluated the facts and evidence, no interference was warranted in the revision petition, which was accordingly dismissed. (PHC – 2024 YLR 1227)

976. Inheritance Law. The appellant challenged the order whereby the II-Additional District Judge, dismissed their Succession Miscellaneous Petition (SMA) seeking probate under section 272 of the Succession Act, 1925, for a Will allegedly made by the deceased regarding his flat. The trial court found that the Will was not executed by the deceased himself but by a third party four months after his death, making it legally ineffective. The appellant lacked locus standi since they were neither the executor nor had sufficient evidence to support their claim. Additionally, no proof of the deceased's death or burial was provided. Given the risk of misappropriation, the High Court appointed its Nazir as Curator to take possession of the property, protect it from loss, and attempt to locate the legal heirs through NADRA. If no heirs come forward within six months, the property will be considered escheated and dealt with under Article 24 and Article 172 of the Constitution of Pakistan. The appeal was dismissed, and the Nazir was directed to report on progress monthly. (Sindh High Court – 2020 PLD 563)

977. Inheritance. Heirs of deceased Muslim. Shares in inheritance. Plaintiffs 1 and 2 were sons and plaintiffs 3 and 4 were daughters while defendant was 'the widow of deceased'. Shares of parties would be that each son's share would be to the extent of 29 paisa, while each daughter would inherit to the extent of 14.5 paisa. Defendant wife's share would be 13 paisa in the property left by deceased (SHC – 1992 PLD 234).

978. Islamic Law. Inheritance. The plaintiff filed a suit for declaration and injunction, claiming that his father had constructed the disputed house with the plaintiff's funds and later orally gifted it to him. Meanwhile, the respondent daughter filed a suit for possession through partition. Both suits were consolidated, and after considering the evidence, the trial court dismissed the plaintiff's suit and decreed the respondent's suit. The appellate court upheld this decision. The plaintiff failed to prove the essential elements of a valid oral gift, including declaration, acceptance, and possession. No family member was produced as a witness, and the evidence presented was deemed unconvincing and contradictory. The court observed that the alleged gift aimed to deprive female heirs of their rightful inheritance. Since no legal or factual irregularity was found in the judgments of the lower courts, and no substantial grounds for interference were established, the civil revision petitions were dismissed in limine. (LHC – 2020 YLR Note 26)

979. Co-sharer. Rights of females. Islamic Law affords special protection to Muslim females. Relinquishment deed from inheritance executed by a female while she was living under roof of her father, brother, husband or any other male relative had no value whatsoever, and she could not be deprived of her property on basis of such relinquishment deed. Relinquishment deed in question, was, however, executed in such circumstances that it tended to violate protection afforded by Islam to females (SHC – 1992 MLD 1598).

980. The petitioners claimed ownership of inherited property and contested the entries in favour of defendants, arguing that their ancestor's estate was wrongly distributed. They alleged that a descendant from a second wife improperly inherited land belonging to the petitioner. However, the court found that the estate had been recorded in revenue documents with no evidence proving the alleged wrongful inheritance. The court also noted that the plaintiffs failed to challenge inheritance mutations for over a century and had themselves excluded female heirs from their shares, thus lacking clean hands in their claim. Additionally, two registered sale deeds which the plaintiffs disputed were never legally challenged. Given the presumption of truth attached to old revenue records and the lack of evidence supporting the petitioners' claims, the court found no irregularity in the lower courts' decisions. The suit was deemed time-barred, and the revision was dismissed. (PHC – 2020 YLR 2645)

981. Inheritance. Constitution of Pakistan (1973), Article 185(3). Leave to appeal was granted on contention that there was a difference of opinion among the Muslim Jurists and Aima on the question whether the heirs of the murderer would also be excluded from inheritance and that this was a case of first impression as far as Supreme Court was concerned (SCP – 1991 PLD 724).

982. The case pertains to the inheritance of 600 kanals of agricultural land left by the deceased leaving behind his son and daughter. At the time of his death, the land was mutated in his son's name under the prevalent customary law. His daughter later married but returned to her paternal home after her husband's death and gave birth to a daughter. Upon her daughter's death and sister's. Daughter's heirs filed a suit seeking their share in the inheritance. Son argued that since the land had been mutated in his name under customary law, the claim was not valid. The trial court, however, ruled in favour of daughter's heirs, applying the North-West Frontier Province (NWFP) Muslim Personal Law (Shariat) Application Act, 1935 which superseded customary law and mandated the distribution of inheritance per Islamic principles. On appeal, the Additional District Judge ruled in favour of son but the High Court reversed this holding that Muslim Personal Law applied retrospectively, entitling daughter to a 1/3rd share in her father's estate. Upon her death, this share passed to her daughter and after her death, it devolved upon her heirs. The Supreme Court, while upholding this ruling modified the division of the inheritance stating that daughter was entitled to only half of her mother's 1/3rd share (100 kanals), while the remaining 100 kanals would revert to the son giving him a total of 500 kanals. The appeal was thus partly allowed, modifying the inheritance distribution accordingly. (SC – 2020 SCMR 346)

983. Articles 30 and 133. Islamic Law. Inheritance. Appellant in previous suit, as a defendant had taken a definite plea that he was heir of deceased and had led evidence in support of such plea. In present suit, he had produced evidence to the effect that he was the son of deceased and entitled to her property. No attempt was made in cross-examination to show that he had made a wrong statement. One of the co-heirs/respondent had admitted that appellant was his brother. Such admission by one of the respondents could be examined in two different contexts; one, that insofar as his own share in inheritance was concerned respondent could not prevent sharing the same with appellant; and second, that as a witness he had deposed in favour of appellant stating that he was the son of deceased, which statement not only was against his own interest but also against the interest of other respondent that is, his real sister. Respondent's statement was thus, a strong piece of evidence in favour of appellant. Appellant as a son of deceased was a co-heir of respondents and thus, entitled to inherit his share in property in question (SCP – 1991 SCMR 1381).

984. Petitioner while still a minor, inherited 2722-Kanal 12-Marla of land from her father but later discovered, upon returning from the United States that the land had been mutated in favour of her nephew orchestrated by her brother. At the time of the mutation the nephew was only 1.5 years old, making the transaction highly questionable. The trial court initially dismissed her suit but the appellate court and the LHC later ruled in her favour, prompting the current appeal. The appellants argued that they were bona fide purchasers and that the suit was time-barred since the petitioner was not in possession of the land. However, the court ruled that the fraudulent mutation was void ab initio and could not be validated by the passage of time. It emphasized that a minor female's right to inheritance under Islamic and Pakistani law could not be unlawfully alienated, and any fraud concerning such rights did not fall under the limitation period. The court also rejected the appellants' defence under the doctrine of bona fide purchase, stating that they should have exercised due diligence. Furthermore, it reaffirmed that a co-sharer in undivided property remains in possession until formal partition. Finding no legal basis for interference, the Supreme Court dismissed the appeals and upheld the High Court's ruling (SC – 2020 SCMR 352).

985. Petitioner lady was deprived of inheritance of deceased on the ground that she was not his real sister. Petitioner's claim to be the real sister of deceased failed up to the High Court. Leave to appeal. Petitioner had produced copies of entries from Death Register and Birth Register of her predecessors to prove that she was real sister of deceased. Contentions raised by petitioner required examination. Leave to appeal was granted in circumstances (SCP – 1991 SCMR 1839).

986. Plaintiffs/petitioners' suit was decreed, and a finding was recorded that deceased was a Shia. Such finding was, however, reversed in appeal and revision, wherein deceased was treated to be a Sunni, and his property was divided according to law of inheritance applicable to that sect. Findings of fact rendered against plaintiffs/petitioners by the two higher Courts, notwithstanding acceptance of their plea by Trial Court, were unexceptionable. No infirmity, legal or of principle, having been discovered, nor there being any misreading or non-reading of evidence, no justification was found for interference. Leave to appeal was refused in circumstances (SCP – 1991 SCMR 2049).

987. Islamic Law. Inheritance. The dispute revolved around a fraudulent gift mutation executed by the petitioner and his brothers, depriving their sisters of their rightful inheritance from their father. The trial court ruled in favour of the sisters, cancelling the mutation. The first appellate court modified this decision by protecting the purchase of land and others from one of the sons. The High Court, however, reinstated the trial court's full decision leading to the present appeals. The Supreme Court dismissed the petition of the petitioner and others affirming that they failed to prove the validity of the oral gift, as key details such as time, place, and witnesses were missing from their evidence. The court also noted that the deceased remained the owner of the property until his death, further invalidating the alleged gift. However, the court found merit in the appeal by the purchaser and others, who were bona fide purchasers without knowledge of the fraudulent mutation. Since the other son was still entitled to a share in his father's estate exceeding the disputed land, the court ruled that bona fide purchaser and others should retain ownership of the land they purchased. Accordingly, the Supreme Court restored the first appellate court's decision to this extent, ensuring that the bona fide purchasers were not unfairly penalized. The appeal was allowed in part, with no order as to costs. (SC – 2020 SCMR 1021)

988. Inheritance. Muslim male owner died without leaving male issue. Deceased's wife and three daughters got their share respectively as one-eighth and two-third. Remainder 5/24th share was claimed by two rival residuaries. Trial Court found plaintiff to be a descendant in the fifth degree in the male line of descent from common ancestor. Court in appeal reversed the finding of the Trial Court and found that the defendant was a nearer residuary. Held, plaintiff and defendant both being descendants of a common ancestor, defendant was found to be a remoter residuary as compared to plaintiff. Plaintiff was thus, entitled to take the residue to the extent of 5/24th share of estate left by deceased (LHC – 1991 PLD 330).

989. Islamic Law. Inheritance The petitioner filed a suit for declaration, perpetual injunction and cancellation of mutation alleging that the defendants fraudulently cancelled a previous mutation and claimed inheritance under Shia law, excluding him and other pro forma respondents. The trial court dismissed the suit for lack of proof and subsequent appeals before the District Judge and the High Court met the same fate. The appellant's counsel argued misreading of witness statements and procedural unfairness in the mutation review, but the court found no substantial misreading or non-reading of evidence. The concurrent findings of fact by lower courts were upheld as no significant legal error was demonstrated. The court noted that the appellant failed to summon relevant records or implead the necessary revenue officials for challenging the mutation on technical grounds. It concluded that since an alternative legal remedy was available, discretionary relief could not be granted. Consequently, the appeal was dismissed with no order as to costs. (Supreme Court (AJ&K) – 2020 CLC Note 7)

990. Islamic Law. Inheritance. Deceased had left alive two brothers and one sister. Plaintiff (brother) was entitled to two-fifth share out of property of deceased while two-fifth share would go to other brother who was in India and not a party in suit and one-fifth would be inherited by the sister (SHC – 1991 CLC 1580).

991. Islamic Law. Inheritance. The Shariat Petition filed by Messrs Najaat Welfare Foundation sought to declare certain paragraphs of D.F. Mulla's *Principles of Muhammadan Law* as repugnant to Islamic injunctions, arguing that it is not a statutory law but is widely applied in inheritance matters. The petitioners also contended that there is no codified inheritance law in Pakistan and emphasized the need for legislation. The federal and provincial governments responded by asserting that Mulla's book is merely a reference and not statutory law, citing Article 203-D of the Constitution, which limits the FSC's jurisdiction to actual laws. The court dismissed the petition, referencing past rulings that established the book's status as a guide rather than law. It reiterated that Islamic jurisprudence, developed by Pakistan's judiciary, ensures inheritance laws align with the Quran and Sunnah. The court also noted that other Islamic texts on inheritance exist and that legislative matters fall under the Parliament's purview. Ultimately, it emphasized that Mulla's book should neither be discarded outright nor treated as binding law and dismissed the petition as misconceived. (FSC – 2021 PLD 1)

992. Islamic Law. Inheritance. Courts below had found that divorce of lady was not proved as original document of divorce had not been produced before Trial Court. Only marginal witnesses could not be believed in absence of divorce deed. Lady was thus rightly held to be a widow and as such was entitled to the inheritance of her husband as co-sharer (SCP – 1990 SCMR 629). Person, entitled to inheritance, becomes a vested holder of due rights the moment succession opens (SHC – 1990 MLD 164).

993. Inheritance. Will. Leave to appeal arising out of inheritance suit was granted to examine the question that even if the Will made in favour of plaintiff/ respondent by deceased was proved as alleged what would be its effect vis-a-vis rights of petitioners/defendants and their predecessor-in-interest to inherit property of deceased (SCP – 1989 SCMR 755) Constitution of Pakistan (1973), Article 185(3).

994. Inheritance. Mere fact that the owner of the property is living in Dar-ul-Harab while heirs are living in Dar-ul-Islam does not have the effect of depriving the heirs from inheriting the property of their predecessor-in-interest if both the parties are believers. Such heirs are not prevented from inheriting the property (SCP – 1989 SCMR 828).

995. Inheritance. The appellant challenged the judgments of the Senior Civil Judge and Additional District Judge which upheld the dismissal of his suit for declaration-cum-permanent injunction and possession regarding a disputed property. He claimed ownership of 3/4th of the land and alleged that the defendants fraudulently procured gift deed. The trial court after evaluating the evidence found no proof of fraud or undue influence and dismissed the suit, a decision later upheld by the appellate court. The appellant argued that the donee was not a close relative of the deceased donor and the gift deeds were improperly executed but failed to provide legal grounds or medical evidence supporting his claims. The court reaffirmed that an owner can gift property to anyone of their choice and inheritance laws do not apply to gifted property. As the appellant did not demonstrate any misreading or non-reading of evidence, the court dismissed the second appeal with costs. (High Court (AJ&K) – 2021 Y L R 1155) Islamic Law. Civil Procedure Code (V of 1908).

996. Islamic Law. Inheritance Law. The petition seeks a writ directing authorities to ensure that the names of female legal heirs are included in inheritance records during the transfer of movable and immovable properties. The petitioner highlighted that women particularly in Balochistan are often deprived of their inheritance rights due to tribal customs forced waivers and revenue authorities' negligence.

The court acknowledged that women's inheritance rights are protected under Islamic law and the Constitution of Pakistan but are frequently denied in practice. The Board of Revenue admitted these issues and proposed procedural reforms though the court found them insufficient. The judgment emphasized that revenue officials must ensure women's names are recorded in inheritance documents involve NADRA for verification and establish a complaint mechanism to prevent corruption. Courts were directed to prioritize inheritance cases for swift resolution. The ruling called for a fundamental shift in societal attitudes and legal enforcement to uphold women's inheritance rights effectively. (Balochistan High Court – 2021 PLD 172)

997. Islamic Law. Inheritance, opening of Inheritance, under Islamic Law opens immediately on death of ancestor. Sanction of mutation was only an executive step to give effect to law of inheritance. Person becomes owner in the estate immediately on death of his father (LHC – 1989 CLC 795).

998. Islamic Law. Inheritance, The appellants' predecessor had filed a suit claiming ownership of the disputed land and alleged that the respondents fraudulently obtained his thumb impression on blank papers under the pretence of acquiring a tractor, later using it to fabricate a registered gift deed. The respondents, legal heirs of the predecessor's deceased son argued that the gift was made in their favour and was lawfully registered. The trial court ruled in favour of the appellants but the appellate court reversed the decision, accepting the respondents' appeal. The appellants contended that the respondents failed to prove the gift deed as required under Article 79 of the Qanun-e-Shahadat Order, 1984, which mandates two attesting witnesses while the respondents presented only one. The appellate court's findings were deemed legally flawed, as it dismissed the requirement of two attesting witnesses as a mere technicality. The court also noted that the appellants' predecessor was an illiterate elderly man who had denied executing the gift and was allegedly deceived. Given the failure to meet the legal standard of proof and the apparent fraud, the court allowed the second appeal, setting aside the appellate court's judgment and restoring the trial court's decree in favour of the appellants. (LHC – 2017 MLD 1586)

999. Inheritance. Child in womb. Right to inherit. Foetus, viz. the child in womb is an heir along with other heirs, provided such child was present in the womb of the mother at the time of death of his ancestor and was born alive within six months from his death. Such child if born after a period of more than six months would not be entitled to inherit. Period of six months is the minimum period of gestation (SHC – 1989 PLD 85).

1000. Inheritance. The petitioner challenged the legality of multiple judicial orders that set aside a decree obtained in her favour through an arbitration award. The case involved inherited property originally owned which was claimed by his son based on an alleged oral gift. During litigation the petitioner claimed ownership of the property through an arbitration award which was made a rule of court based on conceding statements. However, sisters who were legal heirs were neither parties to the arbitration nor the court proceedings. Upon learning of the decree, they filed an application under section 12(2) of the CPC, which was allowed by the trial court, followed by the dismissal of the petitioner's revision and review petitions. The High Court dismissed the constitutional petition, holding that the decree was obtained through fraud and misrepresentation to deprive female heirs of their rightful inheritance. It emphasized that fraud vitiates all proceedings and criticized the judicial officer who had issued the flawed decree, directing an inquiry into his conduct. (LHC – 2017 CLC 1601) Islamic Law. Civil Procedure Code (V of 1908).

1001. Initial presumption where parties were Muslims. Custom as a rule of inheritance. Mode of proof. Muslims in AJK were governed vis-a-vis inheritance by personal law. Rule was, however, subject to exception of Custom. Where a particular tribe or family was governed by Custom vis-a-vis inheritance of estate, it could prove Custom to the exclusion of personal law. Where exception of Custom was alleged, same had to be proved by very cogent and convincing evidence. Initial presumption would always be in favour of personal law. (Presumption) (Supreme Court, Azad Kashmir – 1989 CLC 407).

1002. Islamic Law. Inheritance. This revision petition challenges the judgement which dismissed the petitioner's suit for declaration, cancellation of a gift deed, and permanent injunction. The case revolves around a disputed oral gift mutation allegedly made by the petitioner and her sisters in favour of their brothers. The trial and appellate courts dismissed the suit but upon review, it was found that the respondents failed to prove the validity of the oral gift as their witnesses could not specify the time, date, place, or witnesses of the transaction. Furthermore, no revenue official or scribe of the gift mutation was produced, making the transaction dubious. The court highlighted that the petitioner, an illiterate and parda-nasheen woman was unaware of the gift and likely deceived. Supreme Court emphasizing the protection of women's inheritance rights, the court found that the lower courts misread the evidence and ignored material facts. Consequently, the revision petition was allowed, the lower court judgments were set aside and the petitioner's suit was decreed in her favour. No order was made as to costs. (LHC – 2017 YLR 1020)

1003. Inheritance. Deceased at time of her death was living in India while plaintiff as heir of deceased was living in Pakistan. Impediment to succession on account of deceased living in Darul-Harab not applicable to plaintiff. At the time of death of deceased, Pakistan was not at war with India. Place of residence of deceased, therefore, could not be treated as Darul-Harab. Held, even if deceased had been living in Darul-Harab her heirs living in Pakistan could not have been deprived of her inheritance because both parties were believers. Impediments to successions were applicable only to non-believers (LHC – 1988 PLD 588).

1004. Islamic Law. Inheritance. The petitioner challenged the judgments of the lower courts which had dismissed her suit for declaration and permanent injunction regarding her Shari share in a house inherited from her mother. The respondents claimed ownership based on a sale deed from their grandfather, and alleged that the petitioner had relinquished her share through a deed after receiving compensation. The trial and appellate courts ruled against the petitioner but upon revision, the High Court found that the relinquishment deed was not proven as per Article 79 of the Qanun-e-Shahadat, 1984, and that the respondents failed to establish payment of consideration. It was further established that the suit house originally belonged to her mother entitling the petitioner to her rightful share. The court, therefore, set aside the lower court judgments and issued a preliminary decree for partition of the property, ensuring the petitioner's entitlement to her Shari share (PHC – 2017 YLR Note 124).

1005. Islamic Law. Inheritance. Entitlement to inheritance. Right to inherit as daughters of propositus, proof of. Cause of action for petitioners, arose on demise of propositus, to prove themselves to be his daughters. Concurrent findings of Courts below on such point of fact that respondents were daughters of deceased would remain decisive (LHC – 1988 MLD 1015).

1006. Islamic Law. Inheritance. The petitioners challenged the concurrent judgments of the Additional District Judge-I which had dismissed their suit and appeal regarding a disputed gift mutation attested. The petitioners, step-siblings of the donee argued that the mutation was fraudulent and deprived them of their inheritance rights. The trial court dismissed the suit and the appellate court upheld this decision. However, upon revision, the court found that the donee failed to prove the essential elements of a valid gift, including offer, acceptance, and delivery of possession. Additionally, the supporting documents lacked necessary signatures, thumb impressions, and verification from relevant authorities. The court also noted inconsistencies in the defendant's stance and relied on precedents establishing that gifts resulting in disinheritance must be strictly proven by the beneficiary. Concluding that the lower courts had misread and mis appreciated the evidence, the revision was allowed and the petitioners' suit was decreed in their favour (PHC – 2017 MLD 1488).

1007. Constitution of Pakistan (1973), 185(3). Inheritance. Leave to appeal, grant of. Progeny of murder, whether to inherit property of his victim. Case of first impression. Leave to appeal granted to consider *inter alia* that petitioner having ultimately been found guilty only of culpable homicide not amounting to murder, whether rule of Islamic Law pressed in service against petitioner/his progeny would be attracted (SCP – 1987 SCMR 976).

1008. Hanafi Law. Inheritance. Heirs connected with deceased divided into three classes: Sharers, agnates and uterine relations. Agnates are called residuaries and uterine relations Distant Kindred. When neither 'sharer' nor 'agnate' present only then is the estate divided among uterine relations. Distant Kindred related to deceased through intervention of female cannot inherit in presence of agnate (SCP – 1987 SCMR 1560).

1009. Islamic Law. Inheritance. Land of original owner taken over by his widow as limited owner, held, would devolve upon heirs of such original owner in accordance with Muslim Laws after death of widow. Where any person entitled to inherit such land died prior to death of widow, heirs of such person at time of death of widow, would inherit his share according to Islamic Law. (LHC – 1987 CLC 579).

1010. The appellants daughters had challenged a gift-deed executed by their father in favour of only one daughter, defendant No. 2, alleging fraud and exclusion from their rightful inheritance. The trial court dismissed their suit for lack of proof and subsequent appeals before the District Judge Kotli and the High Court were also dismissed. The appellants argued that the burden of proving the validity of the gift-deed lay on defendant No. 2, who failed to appear as a witness, raising doubts about the transaction. They cited precedents emphasizing the necessity of proving a valid gift transaction, particularly when it results in the disinheritance of legal heirs. The respondents countered that the lower courts' concurrent findings should not be disturbed but the Supreme Court found that the gift-deed was executed fraudulently especially since it was not entered into the revenue record until after the donor's death. It ruled that the lower courts had mis appreciated the evidence and that the exclusion of other legal heirs violated Muslim inheritance principles. Consequently, the appeal was accepted, the previous judgments were overturned, and the gift-deed was declared illegal and inoperative. No costs were awarded. (Supreme Court (AJ&K) – 2017 M L D 2051)

1011. Article 185(3) Islamic Law. Inheritance. Parties allowed shares in accordance with law applicable to evacuee land under laws of. Rehabilitation and Settlement. Petitioner admitting that there would be no defect in distribution of inheritance. Otherwise too, he was unable to satisfy that principles of Muslim law relied upon by him had in any way been contravened. Leave to appeal refused. (SCP – 1986 SCMR 1369)

1012. Islamic Law. Inheritance. The appeal filed by the petitioner against his conviction for the murder of his wife as per the judgment of the Additional Sessions Judge. The prosecution's case was based on eyewitness accounts from the wife brother and brother-in-law who claimed to have witnessed attacking her with a hatchet and strangling her. However, the court found several inconsistencies and doubts in the prosecution's version, including unexplained delays in reporting the incident, the questionable presence of witnesses at the scene, contradictions between the medical evidence and the alleged weapon used and the absence of a proven motive. Furthermore, the appellant's defence, supported by his son's testimony suggested that the complainant himself was responsible for the murder due to a dispute over inheritance. The court also noted that petitioner was present at the crime scene when the police arrived, contradicting the prosecution's claim that he fled. Given these substantial doubts, the court ruled that the prosecution failed to prove its case beyond a reasonable doubt and thus accepted the appeal, acquitting petitioner of the charges and ordering his immediate release. (LHC – 2018 P Cr. L J 537). Inheritance. Doctrine of inheritance not governed by rule of necessity (SHC – 1986 PLD 269).

1013. Inheritance. Sunni Law. Residuaries. Inheritance devolves from descendants of true grand-father how highs ever on full paternal uncle, then on full paternal uncle's son and thereafter on full paternal uncle's son's son. Plea that remoteness or closeness of relationship of residuaries with last male holder of property is of no consequence, repelled (SCP – 1985 SCMR 947).

1014. Article 98. West Pakistan Muslim Personal Law (Shariat Application) Act (V of 1962), section 2. Civil Procedure Code (V of 1908), section 9. Islamic Law. Inheritance. Question as to who among parties entitled to inherit property in dispute and to which extent, held, basically a question of title which could only be decided by civil Courts. (Islamic Law. Jurisdiction) (LHC – 1985 CLC 89).

1015. Islamic Law. Inheritance. The appellants challenged the trial court's decision which dismissed their suit for partition of a property inherited from their father. They claimed entitlement to half of the property, while the respondent (their brother) asserted ownership based on a Will Deed and an oral gift. The court found that the respondent failed to prove the oral gift, as essential details such as date, time, witnesses, and proper execution were missing. Moreover, the court ruled that Ahmadis, being declared non-Muslims under the Constitution, could not rely on Muhammadan Law but had to follow the Transfer of Property Act, under which the oral gift was legally invalid due to non-compliance with registration and attestation requirements. The court also observed that the respondent's reliance on both a Will Deed and an oral gift was contradictory. Additionally, it rejected the trial court's ruling on limitation, affirming that inheritance claims among co-sharers do not lapse over time. The appeal was allowed, the trial court's decision was set aside, and the appellants were declared entitled to half of the property. (LHC – 2018 PLD 819).

1016. Inheritance Law. Appeal arose from a judgment of the Balochistan High Court which had set aside the revocation of a succession certificate granted to Respondent No. 1 who had initially obtained the certificate fraudulently by claiming to be the sole legal heir of the deceased. The appellants, two daughters from one of the deceased's wives filed for revocation after learning of the fraud and the trial court ruled in their favour. However, the High Court overturned this decision on technical grounds including the delay in filing the revocation application and procedural deficiencies. The Supreme Court upon review found that the High Court had ignored substantive justice in favour of technicalities, emphasizing that inheritance rights vest immediately upon death and that fraud nullifies any time limitations. It was held that the appellants as legal heirs were entitled to their Shari shares, and Respondent No. 1 had failed to prove that he had distributed their inheritance. The Supreme Court reinstated the trial court's decision, ordered the recovery of the misappropriated amount within two months, and directed legal action against Respondent No. 1 under section 198 of the PPC for fraudulently obtaining the succession certificate. The appeal was allowed with costs imposed on Respondent No. 1. (SC – 2018 SCMR 762).

1017. Islamic Law. Inheritance. The petitioners challenged the judgment of the Additional District Judge which upheld the trial court's decision dismissing their suit for declaration, permanent injunction, and possession regarding inherited property. They claimed that no formal partition had taken place, while the respondents asserted that a private partition occurred supported by a partition deed. The courts found that the petitioners failed to challenge this deed during their predecessor's lifetime, making their claim legally weak. The courts also held that the petitioners could not rely on deficiencies in the defendants' case but had to prove their own claim. High Court ruled that there was no misreading of evidence or legal errors warranting interference under section 115, CPC. Consequently, the revision petition was dismissed. (PHC – 2024 YLR 1227).

1018. Inheritance. Appeals under Article 185(2) of the Constitution of Pakistan stem from a suit for declaration filed by the petitioner claiming a 1/3rd share in the estate of her deceased brother. The trial court dismissed the suit as time-barred, but the District Judge reversed this decision granting her share. The High Court modified this ruling recognizing her entitlement but upholding the validity of land transfers made by the deceased brother to third parties. The appellants in Civil Appeal argued that abolishing customary inheritance was not in effect when the deceased died and the suit was time-barred. However, the Supreme Court held that the Act came into force upon the Governor's assent before the deceased died making the sister a rightful heir under Shariah. Regarding limitation, the Court ruled that a co-heir cannot be deprived of inheritance and that the sister's exclusion justified relief under section 18 of the Limitation Act, 1908. While declining to annul transactions made by the respondent, the Court apportioned all such transfers to his share, ensuring the sister's 1/3rd entitlement from the remaining estate. Civil Appeal was partially allowed with modifications to the High Court's judgment. (SC – 2013 SCMR 1540)

1019. Inheritance. F deceased leaving behind widow and two daughters Widow marrying another man M and after death leaving behind two more daughters from second husband M. Entitlement of four daughters to shares in land left by widow out of share inherited by her from deceased husband F. worked out (Supreme Court, Azad Kashmir – 1982 CLC 1709).

1020. Inheritance. Succession certificate. District Judge dismissed the appellants' succession application for lack of jurisdiction. The appellants' predecessor, a permanent resident of Turbat, was working as a farmer in Sharjah (UAE) when he died in an accident and they sought a succession certificate to claim his dues. The trial court held that the deceased was domiciled in Sharjah at the time of his death, thus lacking jurisdiction. However, the appellate court found that the deceased had not abandoned his domicile in Pakistan, as he was only temporarily residing in Sharjah for work. Referring to section 5(2) of the Succession Act, 1925, the court emphasized that domicile at the time of death determines jurisdiction. Concluding that the trial court had misinterpreted 'domicile', the appellate court set aside the order and directed the trial court to decide the case on its merits. The appeal was accepted. (Balochistan High Court – 2015 PLD 132)

1021. Inheritance. Objection that without amending plaint share of plaintiff could not be determined though specious, held, has no force. Parties being aware of substance of controversy and contesting matter on merits. Too late to raise hyper-technical objection of procedure. Share in inheritance to be determined in accordance with law. Applicable (LHC – 1980 CLC 937).

1022. Inheritance. This constitutional petition which dismissed the landlord's application for ejectment of a tenant from a shop. However, the appellate court allowed the appeal overturning the trial court's findings on default, sub-letting, alteration, and bona fide personal use. The tenant challenged this decision, arguing that after the landlord's death, his legal heirs (who were all female) could not claim personal bona fide need. The court rejected this argument, emphasizing that under the Sindh Rented Premises Ordinance, 1979, a landlord's spouse, son, or daughter is treated as part of a single unit for determining bona fide need. It is a right to sue survives legal heirs, irrespective of gender, citing constitutional principles of equality and historical examples of women in commerce. The court upheld that bona fide need persists after the landlord's death. Concluding that there was no misapplication of law or miscarriage of justice, the court dismissed the petition cautioning the petitioner's counsel against making discriminatory remarks contrary to Article 25(2) of the Constitution. (Sindh High Court – 2017 PLD 409).

1023. Inheritance. Succession. The petitioner filed a petition seeking custody of her children and recovery of compensation and salary benefits allegedly misappropriated by her brother-in-law. She claimed that her brother-in-law fraudulently obtained a succession certificate, received PKR 2 million compensation and took her children's custody while depriving her of financial support. During proceedings, two minors were handed over to her while the others remained with relatives. It was found that the succession certificate was legally issued, but her brother-in-law acting as an attorney failed to safeguard the minors' financial interests as required by law. The court, converting the petition into an appeal remanded the matter to the trial court to recover the minors' inheritance from brother-in-law and his surety ensuring deposit into National Savings Certificates. The trial court was also tasked with verifying whether the petitioner received her rightful share. Additionally, the Deputy Commissioner was directed to manage the deceased's salary for the benefit of both the widow and the minors. The petitioner was advised to seek custody through the Family Court and the court urged the provincial government to implement measures protecting minors' rights in similar cases. (Balochistan High Court – 2017 PLD 22)

1024. Islamic Law. Inheritance. Marazul Maut. Divorce. Person under fear of death divorcing his wife. Such woman, held, not deprived of inheritance if person dies within period of *Iddat*. Marazul Maut a question of fact (LHC – 1976 PLD 119).

1025. Divorce. Inheritance. Husband paralytic and on his death-bed. Woman entitled to inheritance from his estate if he dies prior to expiration of her period of *Iddat* (SCP – 1974 PLD 22).

1026. Inheritance. Criminal Procedure Code (V of 1898). The petitioner sought bail in FIR registered under sections 419, 420, 468, 471 PPC, and section 5(2) of the Prevention of Corruption Act at Police Station Anti-Corruption, Nowshera, after being denied relief by the lower court. He was accused of fabricating a false death certificate for his father who had died, falsely recording his death to manipulate inheritance mutation thereby attempting to deprive his late brother's legal heirs. Upon a complaint by the respondent an inquiry by the Anti-Corruption Establishment found the petitioner responsible. The court, while refraining from detailed discussion at the bail stage, determined that the petitioner was prima facie linked to the fraudulent act. His argument that the alleged offenses did not fall within the prohibitory clause of section 497 CrPC was rejected, as bail decisions depend on case-specific facts. Consequently, the bail application was dismissed, with a directive that these findings remain tentative and not prejudice the trial court's proceedings. (PHC – 2016 YLR Note 142).

1027. Islamic Law. Conversion to Islam Hindu having wife and children embracing Islam and marrying a Muslim lady. Muslim wife and children by her inherit, on his death, entire property to exclusion of Hindu wife and children (LHC – 1971 PLD 1020).

1028. Islamic Law. Inheritance. Property dispute where Respondents Nos 1 to 11, as heirs of the deceased claimed ownership of the suit property against the petitioners who contended that their predecessor solely owned the property. The case had a prolonged history with multiple suits, appeals, and revisions, including proceedings before the Supreme Court which allowed the respondents to file a fresh suit. The appellate court ruled in favour of the respondents, finding that their predecessor had a legitimate share in the disputed property and that petitioner's dominant position had led to their wrongful dispossession. The petitioners' claims of sole ownership, waiver by respondent and time-barred litigation were rejected due to lack of conclusive evidence. The court upheld the appellate court's findings, concluding they were based on a proper appraisal of evidence and dismissed the revision petition, maintaining the respondents' entitlement to their share in the property. (PHC – 2016 YLR 1532)

1029. Islamic Law. Inheritance. Residuaries. Female children of grandfather, how-high-soever, are not included in category of residuaries in their own right. The female children of the grand-father how-high-soever are not included in the category of 'residuaries in their own right' (LHC – 1967 PLD 1214).

1030. Islamic Law. Inheritance. The petitioner filed a suit seeking a declaration with possession of 16 kanals of land, claiming inheritance as the son of the deceased. The defendant contested, stating that their father had already partitioned the land among his three sons during his lifetime. The courts below ruled in favour of the Provincial Government regarding a portion of the land but failed to address key legal and Shariah-based aspects of inheritance, including the rights of daughters. Additionally, no issue was framed regarding the alleged partition by the father. The High Court, noting these irregularities and the consensus of parties, remanded the case to the trial court for a fresh decision, directing it to consider all legal heirs' shares and ensure compliance with Shariah laws. (Gilgit-Baltistan Chief Court – 2018 YLR Note 137)

1031. Islamic Law. Inheritance. Murderer or his progeny cannot be allowed to benefit by crime of murder. Principles of justice, equity and good conscience (LHC – 1964 PLD 451). Ascertainment of shares of co-heirs is not tantamount to partition of estate. Shares can be separated only by an actual partition (Dhaka High Court – 1958 PLD 68). Estate of deceased Muslim devolves on his heirs at the moment of his death (Supreme Court, Azad Kashmir – 1958 PLD 19).

1032. Succession. 'Nomination' and 'gift'. Distinction. Unless a nomination could amount to a valid gift *inter vivos*, same could not pass title to nominee in respect of immoveable property. Making of a nomination could not give right to nominator at his choice to change Law of Succession, which otherwise would be applicable in case of his death. Nomination could not operate as a valid gift under Islamic Law as gift in order to confer title on donee must be accompanied by delivery of possession of property gifted (SCP – 2004 SCMR 1219).

1033. Succession. Gift. Making nomination in respect of property. Validity: Nomination, unless amounted to a valid gift *inter vivos*, cannot pass title in property to nominee nor can give right to nominator to change Law of Succession, which would be applicable in case of his death. Nomination cannot operate as a valid gift under Islamic Law as gift, in order to confer title on donee, must be accompanied by delivery of possession of the property gifted. Nomination does not stop succession of estate of deceased to his legal heirs as per succession law applicable to him (SHC – 2003 CLC 1521).

1034. Succession. Gift. Will. Nomination by member of a Cooperative Society. Such nomination does not operate as a gift or will, thus cannot deprive other heirs, who may be entitled thereto under law of succession. Nominee is merely a trustee of allottee, and he cannot become owner of property after demise of original allottee. Nominee remains accountable to legal heirs of original allottee for all benefits derived out of such property. As nomination does not confer any title in favour of nominee, mutation and transfer of title on basis of nomination would not be legal. Nominee by virtue of nomination simpliciter is not seized or possessed of any right, title or interest in property (SHC – 2003 MLD 1095).

1035. Islamic Law. Inheritance. This civil revision challenges the judgments and decrees of the lower courts which declared the respondents as rightful heirs to the suit land. Inheritance of the deceased leaving behind two daughters. The petitioners, however, manipulated the inheritance mutation by falsely as issueless and excluding his daughters from their rightful share. The petitioners argued that, according to customary law at the time, daughters were not entitled to inherit, and that the suit was time-barred. However, the respondents contended that the deceased daughters were alive at the time of his death, and their exclusion was fraudulent. The court examined witness statements and documentary evidence, concluding that the daughters were indeed legal heirs and that the petitioners had committed fraud by omitting their names from the inheritance record. The court held that Islamic law prevails over customary practices, affirming the respondents' inheritance rights. Consequently, the civil revision was dismissed, and the judgments of the lower courts were upheld. (LHC – 2017 YLR 372)

1036. Islamic Law. Constitution of Pakistan (1973), Article 185(3). Succession. Deceased land owner's property was divided between his widow to the extent of one-fourth and his brother to the extent of three-fourth. Petitioner's predecessor was excluded being the consanguine brother. Petitioner on the death of his father brought a suit claiming that his father was the real brother of deceased and thus was entitled to three-eighth of the land in question. Trial Court dismissed suit but First Appellate Court decreed the suit. High Court in second appeal set aside decision of First Appellate Court and restored that of Trial Court. Leave to appeal. Two documents having been referred to in judgments of Courts below having been withheld by the petitioners, petition for leave to appeal was not properly documented, and same had to be dismissed on that ground alone. Leave to appeal was refused in circumstances (SCP – 1991 SCMR 309).

1037. Islamic Law. Inheritance. Gift. The dispute arose after the deceased son claimed the entire inheritance through an alleged oral gift. While his sisters contested this, his wife, the petitioner, filed a separate arbitration case claiming ownership of the property through an award. The court found that the arbitration and subsequent decree were fraudulent as the female heirs were neither involved nor consented to the arbitration. The judgment highlighted the persistent issue of women being deprived of their inheritance rights and condemned the misuse of legal processes to deprive female heirs of their rightful shares. The petition was dismissed, and the court emphasized the responsibility of the judiciary in preventing such injustices. (LHC-2017 CLC 219)

1038. Succession. Administration of the estate of a deceased person. Locus standi of each heir. Estate of a deceased person vests in predetermined proportions in the legal heirs. All such heirs, on opening of succession, become tenants-in-common in such estate. All the heirs have equal rights and none of them has precedence over the other (SHC – 1989 PLD 350).

1039. Sections 7 to 11. Islamic Law. Talaq. Special Oath. Connotation. Special oath relates to offer by one party to be bound by such oath made by other party or by any witness in proceedings. Court is, however, not bound to take notice of such offer. Discretionary with Court to ask the other party or witness that if such offer was accepted and special oath was administered, statement made thereon, would be conclusive proof of matter stated in it. To propose and take special oath though permissible, yet oath administered under section 8, Oaths Act, 1873, held, could not be repugnant to justice or decency and should not a fact third party. Taking oath on Talaq to one's wife, and that too without fault on her part was not an approved action in Islam to which parties belonged. Oath proposed and accepted by parties on divorce to wife for decision of civil suit was in contravention of section 8 of

Oaths Act, 1873 and could neither be proposed nor taken because of being opposed to rule of decency and also affecting the third party (LHC – 1987 CLC 1602).

1040. Islamic Law. Inheritance. Petitioners filed the case over their heir late father's property which was transferred to the brothers through mutation. The sisters challenged the mutation, claiming it was obtained through fraud and misrepresentation depriving them of their rightful share. The trial court ruled in favour of one sister granting her inheritance rights, while two other sisters were initially proceeded against ex parte. The appellate court upheld the decision, but a revision was filed, arguing procedural errors and the deprivation of the sisters' rights. The court ultimately ruled that the female heirs were unlawfully excluded and reaffirmed their entitlement to inherit their father's property, emphasizing the legal duty of courts to protect women's inheritance rights as per Islamic and statutory law. (LHC – 2018 YLR Note 138)

1041. Succession. Interpretation by Courts. Contention that since deceased disowned her affiliation to any particular sect of Islam and claimed to be a simple Muslim she had to be governed by Islamic Law interpreted by Courts on basis of Holy Qur'an (Sura Nissa referred) free from jurisprudential theories of two sects. Held: Legal relevance of question whether deceased belonged to Shia or Sunni sect arising by virtue of operation of provisions of West Pakistan Muslim Personal Law (Shariat) Application Act, 1962 and each sect having to be governed according to law applicable to such sect as already prevalent and applied; and Shariat Act not allowing interpretation by Courts by process of reasoning in their own light, contention fallacious Acceptance of contention tantamount, to creation of a new system of personal law applicable to cases of Muslims not belonging to any sect. New theories cannot be propounded independent of rival theories of great antiquity and authority propounded by two sects of Shias and Sunnis (SHC – 1977 PLD 320).

1042. Succession. Widow succeeding to estate-of her deceased husband as limited owner and later transferring property to her daughter M (petitioner) by way of gift. Widow's share of one-eighth on her death, held, devolved upon all her heirs including daughter (SCP – 1976 SCMR 382).

1043. Islamic Law. Succession. Distinction between immovables and movables. Islamic Law as administered in Pakistan does not accept any such distinction. Principle of scission not recognized by Islamic Law in matters of succession (SHC – 1968 PLD 480). Distant Kindred cannot succeed in presence of sharer (LHC – 1960 PLD 261).

1044. Islamic Law. Succession. Punjab Rehabilitation Re-settlement Scheme, Part II, paragraph 46. Grandson whose father has pre-deceased his own father. Inherits grandfather only in cases of allotment simpliciter and not where grandfather has filed his claim or allotment is on quasi-permanent basis. Genesis of rule (LHC – 1960 PLD 265).

§5. Parsi Intestates

1045. Under the Succession Act, 1925 Chapter-III provides the special rules for Parsi intestates. For the purpose of intestate succession among Parsis: (a) there is no distinction between those who were actually born in the lifetime of a person deceased and those who at the date of his death were only conceived in the womb, but who have been subsequently born alive; (b) a lineal descendant of an intestate who has died in the lifetime of the intestate without leaving a widow or widower or any lineal descendant or a widow of any lineal descendant shall not be taken into account in determining the manner in which the property of which the intestate has died intestate shall be divided; and (c) where a widow of any relative of an intestate has married again in the lifetime of the intestate, she shall not be entitled to receive any share of the property of which the intestate has died intestate, and she shall be deemed not to be existing at the intestates death.

1046. In the event of the intestate death of a male Parsi, the distribution of his estate shall be governed as follows: (a) If the deceased is survived by a widow and children, the estate shall be divided among them, with the widow and each son receiving a share equal to twice that of each daughter. (b) If the deceased is survived by children but leaves no widow, the estate shall be distributed among the children, with each son receiving a share equal to twice that of each daughter. Furthermore, where the deceased is survived by one or both parents in addition to children or a widow and children, the father shall be entitled to a share equivalent to half the share of a son, while the mother shall be entitled to a share equivalent to half the share of a daughter.

1047. In the event of the intestate death of a female Parsi, the distribution of her estate shall be governed as follows: (a) If the deceased is survived by a widower and children, the estate shall be distributed equally among them, with the widower and each child receiving an equal share or (b) If the deceased is survived by children but leaves no widower, the estate shall be divided equally among the children, with each child inheriting an equal portion. The distribution of the estate shall be carried out in accordance with the applicable personal laws governing Parsi intestate succession, ensuring the equitable allocation of assets among the legal heirs. The principles of succession shall be subject to statutory provisions, safeguarding the rights of all beneficiaries while upholding the intent of uniform distribution among eligible heirs.

1048. In all instances where a Parsi dies intestate leaving behind any lineal descendant, the estate shall be distributed in accordance with the following principles in cases where a child of the deceased has predeceased the intestate. If the predeceased child was a son, his widow and children shall inherit his share as if he had survived the intestate and died immediately thereafter. However, if such a son left behind a widow or a widow of a lineal descendant but no direct lineal descendant, the remaining portion of his share, after the initial distribution, shall revert to the general estate of the intestate and be divided among the heirs as per the applicable provisions, disregarding the predeceased son in the computation of shares. If the predeceased child was a daughter, her share shall be distributed equally among her surviving children. In cases where a grandchild of the intestate, who would have been entitled to a share, has also predeceased the intestate, their share shall be divided in accordance with the rules applicable to the distribution of their parent's share whether through the provisions applicable to sons or daughters, as the case may be. In situations where a more remote lineal descendant of the intestate has died before the intestate, the same principles shall apply with necessary modifications ensuring that the share such a descendant would have inherited, had they survived the intestate is distributed among their eligible successors in accordance with the established rules of Parsi intestate succession.

1049. Where a Parsi dies without leaving any lineal descendant but leaving a widow or widower or a widow of a lineal descendant, the property of which the intestate dies intestate shall be divided in accordance with the following rules, namely:

a. if the intestate leaves a widow or widower but no widow of a lineal descendant, the widow or widower shall take half the said property;
b. if the intestate leaves a widow or widower and also a widow of any lineal descendant, his widow or her widower shall receive one-third of the said property, and the widow of any lineal descendant shall receive another one-third, or if there is more than one such widow, the last mentioned one-third shall be divided equally among them;
c. if the intestate leaves no widow or widower but one widow of a lineal descendant, she shall receive one-third of the said property or, if the intestate leaves no widow or widower but more than one widow of a lineal descendant, two-thirds of the said property shall be divided among such widows in equal shares;
d. the residue after the division specified in clause (a), (b) or (c) has been made shall be distributed among the relatives of the intestate in the order specified in Part I of Schedule II. The next-of-kin standing first in Part I of the Schedule shall be preferred to those standing second, the second to the third, and so on in succession, provided that the property shall be so distributed that each male shall take double the share of each female standing in the same degree of propinquity; and
e. if there are no relatives entitled to the residue under cause (d), the whole of the residue shall be distributed in proportion to the share specified among the persons entitled to receive shares under this section.

1050. In the event that a Parsi dies intestate without leaving behind any lineal descendants, a surviving spouse, or a widow of any lineal descendant, the entirety of the deceased's estate shall devolve upon the next-of-kin in the order of priority specified in Part II of Schedule II. Among the eligible heirs, those standing in a higher category within the prescribed order shall have precedence over those in the subsequent categories, with succession proceeding sequentially in accordance with the designated hierarchy. The distribution of the estate shall be carried out in a manner that ensures each male heir receives double the share of each female heir who stands in the same degree of kinship to the deceased.

1051. In the absence of any relative entitled to inherit under the provisions of Chapter III of the Succession Act, 1925, the estate of a Parsi who dies intestate shall devolve equally among the nearest surviving relatives of the deceased, determined by the closest degree of kinship. In such cases, no distinction shall be made between male and female heirs, and all relatives standing in the same degree of kindred shall inherit in equal proportions.

Chapter 2. Testamentary Succession

§1. Introduction

1052. Testamentary succession in Pakistan is governed by personal laws applicable to individuals based on their religion, along with the provisions of the Succession Act, 1925. Under Islamic law, which applies to Muslim citizens, a person of sound mind and who has attained majority may dispose of their property through a will (wasiyat). However, such a will cannot exceed one-third of the net estate after deducting funeral expenses and outstanding debts, unless the legal heirs provide their consent after the testator's death. This restriction ensures the protection of the statutory heirs' rights under Islamic inheritance principles, which are derived from the Quran and Hadith and enforced under Pakistani law. For non-Muslims, testamentary succession is primarily regulated by the Succession Act, 1925, which allows individuals to dispose of their entire estate through a will, subject to legal formalities. Procedural requirements for a valid will, including execution, attestation, probate, and letters of administration, ensuring that the testator's intentions are honoured while protecting the interests of potential beneficiaries. Additionally, wills made under this Act must comply with specific formalities, such as being in writing and properly witnessed, to prevent disputes over their validity. In cases where a person dies intestate (without making a will), the estate is distributed according to the applicable succession laws, ensuring legal heirs inherit as per their respective entitlements.

§2. Capacity to Make a Will

1053. Part VI of the Succession Act, 1925, governs the execution of wills and codicils made by Hindus, Buddhists, Sikhs, and Jainas in Pakistan. According to the Act, any person of sound mind, who is not a minor, has the legal capacity to dispose of their property through a will. A married woman is also entitled to execute a will concerning any property that she has the right to alienate during her lifetime. Individuals who are deaf, mute, or blind are not disqualified from making a will, provided they comprehend the nature and consequences of their actions. A person who is ordinarily of unsound mind may execute a will during lucid intervals when they are of sound judgment. However, no individual can create a valid will while in a state of mental incapacity due to intoxication, illness, or any other cause that impairs their ability to understand their actions. The validity of a will depends on the testator's cognitive ability to understand the nature of their property, the legal implications of their decisions, and the rightful heirs to whom the estate should be bequeathed. If a testator lacks such understanding, the will shall be deemed invalid. Similarly, if a person executes a will without comprehending its contents and effects, such an instrument will not be recognized as a legally valid testament. Conversely, a will executed by a person who, despite physical weakness or old age, retains the capacity to make reasoned decisions regarding the distribution of their property remains legally enforceable. A father, regardless of his age holds the right to appoint a guardian for his minor child through his will, ensuring the child's welfare and protection until the age of majority. The provisions under the Act serve to ensure that wills are executed with free will, full comprehension, and legal certainty, thereby preventing disputes and safeguarding the rightful claims of heirs and beneficiaries.

§3. Different Types of Will

1054. **Unprivileged Wills:** Under the Succession Act, 1925, every testator, except for soldiers engaged in an expedition or active warfare, airmen similarly employed, or mariners at sea, must execute a will in accordance with specific legal formalities to ensure its validity. The execution of a will must adhere to the following requirements: (a) The testator must either sign the will personally or affix a mark as a substitute for a signature. Alternatively, another individual may sign the will on behalf of the testator, provided it is done in the testator's presence and under their explicit direction. (b) The signature, mark, or authorized signature by another person must be positioned in a manner that clearly indicates the testator's intent to authenticate the document as their last will and testament. (c) The will must be attested by a minimum of two witnesses, each of whom must either witness the testator signing or affixing their mark, observe another person signing in the presence and at the direction of the testator, or personally receive an acknowledgment from the testator confirming the authenticity of the signature, mark, or signature made on their behalf. Each witness must sign the will in the presence of the testator; however, it is not necessary for all witnesses to be present simultaneously, and no specific form of attestation is mandated. If a duly attested will or codicil makes reference to another document that is not physically incorporated within the will but is intended to express part of the testator's wishes, such a document shall be deemed to form an integral part of the will or codicil. This provision ensures that external references included in a will, if properly acknowledged, retain legal validity and effect.

1055. **Privileged wills:** Under the Succession Act, 1925, certain categories of individuals are granted the ability to make privileged wills, allowing them to dispose of their property with fewer formalities due to the exigencies of their profession. Any soldier actively engaged in an expedition or actual warfare, any airman similarly employed, or any mariner at sea, provided they have attained the age of 18 years, may execute a privileged will as prescribed under section 66 of the Act. Unlike ordinary wills, privileged wills may be made orally or in writing without strict adherence to the formal execution requirements applicable to standard testamentary instruments. Illustratively, a medical officer attached to a regiment participating in an expedition qualifies as a soldier actively engaged in an expedition and is therefore entitled to make a privileged will. Similarly, a purser serving aboard a merchant ship at sea qualifies as a mariner and may execute a privileged will. A soldier engaged in combat against insurgents is deemed to be in actual warfare and is entitled to the same privilege. Likewise, a mariner who is temporarily ashore while his ship is anchored in a harbour remains, for legal purposes, a mariner at sea and can make a privileged will. However, an admiral who commands a naval force but resides onshore and only occasionally boards his ship is not considered 'at sea' and is therefore ineligible to make a privileged will. In contrast, a mariner serving on a military expedition, though not at sea, is regarded as a soldier for the purposes of this provision and may validly execute a privileged will.

1056. Privileged wills may be executed either in writing or orally, providing greater flexibility to individuals engaged in military or maritime service. A privileged will may be entirely handwritten by the testator, in which case it does not require a signature or attestation. Alternatively, it may be written wholly or partially by another person and signed by the testator, in which case attestation is not mandatory. If a will is written, either wholly or in part, by another person without the testator's signature, it shall still be deemed valid if it is established that the testator directed its preparation or acknowledged it as his will. However, if the document appears incomplete on its face and it is evident that the testator intended to execute it in a specific manner, the will shall not be considered invalid merely due to non-execution, provided there is reasonable justification to conclude that the testator's failure to complete the execution was due to circumstances beyond his control rather than an abandonment of his testamentary intentions. In instances where a soldier, airman, or mariner has provided written instructions for the preparation of a will but has died before its formal execution, such instructions shall be considered as constituting his will. Similarly, if verbal instructions for a will have been given in the presence of two witnesses and subsequently reduced into writing during the testator's lifetime, but the testator passes away before the will is formally prepared and executed, those written instructions shall be treated as his will, even if they were neither written in his presence nor read over to him. Moreover, a privileged will may be made orally by the testator declaring his testamentary intentions before two witnesses present at the same time. However, such an oral will shall become null and void if the testator, remaining alive, ceases to be in a position to make a privileged will for a continuous period of one month.

1057. A will shall not be considered inadequately attested solely on the grounds that it confers a benefit, either by way of bequest or appointment, upon any individual serving as an attesting witness, or upon the spouse of such a witness. However, any such bequest or appointment shall be deemed void with respect to the attesting witness, their spouse, or any individual deriving a claim through them. This provision safeguards the integrity of testamentary dispositions while preventing conflicts of interest that may arise from attesting witnesses receiving benefits under the will. Explanation: A beneficiary named in a will does not forfeit their legacy by acting as an attesting witness to a codicil that merely confirms the original will. This ensures that codicils intended to affirm or clarify testamentary provisions do not inadvertently disqualify legatees who act as witnesses to such codicils.

1058. No individual shall be deemed disqualified from serving as a witness to establish the execution, validity, or invalidity of a will merely by virtue of having a vested interest in the will or being named as its executor. The mere fact that a person stands to benefit under the will or holds fiduciary responsibilities as an executor does not impair their competency as a witness in legal proceedings concerning the testamentary document.

1059. No obliteration, interlineation, or any other alteration made in an unprivileged will after its execution shall have any legal effect unless it renders the words or meaning of the will illegible or indiscernible. Any such modification shall only be valid if executed in the same manner as required for the original execution of the will. However, an altered will shall be considered duly executed if the testator's signature, along with the attestation of the witnesses, appears in the margin, near the alteration, at the foot or end of the document or opposite a memorandum that refers to the alteration and is inscribed at the end or on another part of the will.

1060. The payment and apportionment of annuities has been prescribed under sections 338–340 of the Succession Act, 1925. Where an annuity is given by a will and no time is fixed for its commencement, it shall commence from the testators death, and the first payment shall be made at the expiration of a year next after that event.

1061. When a will includes a directive for an annuity to be paid on a quarterly or monthly basis, the first instalment shall become due at the end of the first quarter or first month following the testator's death, as applicable. However, the executor or administrator, at their discretion, may make the payment when it becomes due but is not legally obligated to do so until the completion of one year from the testator's death. This provision ensures that the executor or administrator has sufficient time to manage and settle the estate's financial affairs before being required to disburse annuity payments, thereby preventing undue financial strain on the estate's administration.

1062. When a will specifies that the initial payment of an annuity is to be made within a specified period, such as one month or any other designated time frame from the testator's death, or on a fixed date, all subsequent annuity payments shall be made annually on the corresponding anniversary of the earliest authorized payment date. In the event that the annuitant passes away between scheduled payment intervals, a proportionate share of the annuity, calculated up to the date of their death, shall be payable to their legal representative.

§4. Revocation of Will

1063. A will is generally revoked upon the marriage of the testator, except in cases where the will is made in the exercise of a power of appointment over property that, in the absence of such an appointment, would not devolve upon the testator's executor, administrator, or heirs in accordance with intestate succession laws. This exception ensures that the disposition of property subject to a power of appointment remains valid despite the testator's subsequent marriage. Explanation:

A person is deemed to have a power of appointment when they possess the authority to determine the distribution of property they do not personally own.

1064. No unprivileged will or codicil, nor any part thereof, shall be revoked otherwise than by marriage, or by another will or codicil, or by some writing declaring an intention to revoke the same and executed in the manner in which an unprivileged will is hereinbefore required to be executed, or by the burning, tearing or otherwise destroying the same by the testator or by some person in his presence and by his direction with the intention of revoking the same. Illustrations: (i) A has made an unprivileged will. Afterwards, A makes another unprivileged will which purports to revoke the first. This is a revocation. (ii) A has made an unprivileged will. Afterwards, A, being entitled to make a privileged will, makes a privileged will, which purports to revoke his unprivileged will. This is a revocation.

1065. A privileged will or codicil can be revoked by the testator through an unprivileged will or codicil, or by any act that demonstrates an intention to revoke it, provided it is carried out with the formalities required for the validity of a privileged will. Additionally, it may be revoked by burning, tearing, or otherwise destroying it, either by the testator or by another person in their presence and under their direction, with the clear intent of revocation. Explanation: For a privileged will or codicil to be revoked through an act requiring the formalities of a privileged will, the testator does not need to be in a situation that qualifies them to create a privileged will at the time of performing the act.

1066. An unprivileged will or codicil, once revoked in any manner, cannot be reinstated except through its formal re-execution or by a duly executed codicil that expressly indicates an intention to revive it. In cases where a will or codicil has been partially revoked and subsequently revoked in its entirety, any subsequent revival shall not extend to the portions that were revoked prior to the complete revocation, unless a clear intention to restore such portions is explicitly expressed in the will or codicil. This ensures that a previously revoked testamentary document does not regain legal effect unless the testator unequivocally reaffirms it in accordance with the formal execution requirements.

§5. Void Will

1067. A will or any part of a will, the making of which has been caused by fraud or coercion, or by such importunity that takes away the free agency of the testator, is void. Illustrations: (i) A, falsely and knowingly represents to the testator that the testator's only child is dead, or that he has done some undutiful act and thereby induces the testator to make a will in his A's favour; such will has been obtained by fraud, and is invalid. (ii) A, by fraud and deception, prevails upon the testator to bequeath a legacy to him. The bequest is void. (iii) A, being a prisoner by lawful authority, makes his will. The will is not invalid by reason of the imprisonment. (iv) A threatens to shoot B, or to burn his house or to cause him to be arrested on a criminal charge, unless he makes a bequest in favour of C. B, in consequence, makes a bequest in favour of C. The bequest is void, the making of it having been caused by coercion. (v) A, being of sufficient intellect, if undisturbed by the influence of others, to make a will yet being so much under the control of B that he is not a free agent, makes a will, dictated by B. It appears that he would not have executed the will but for fear of B. The will is invalid. (vi) A, being in so feeble a state of health as to be unable to resist importunity, is pressed by B to make a will of a certain purport and does so merely to purchase peace and in submission to B. The will is invalid. (vii) A being in such a state of health as to be capable of exercising his own judgment and volition, B uses urgent intercession and persuasion with him to induce him to make a will of a certain purport. A, in consequence of the intercession and persuasion, but in the free exercise of his judgment and volition, makes his will in the manner recommended by B. The will is not rendered invalid by the intercession and persuasion of B. (viii) A, with a view to obtaining a legacy from B, pays him attention and flatters him and thereby produces in him a capricious partiality to A. B, in consequence of such attention and flattery, makes his will, by which he leaves a legacy to A. The bequest is not rendered invalid by the attention and flattery of A. A will is liable to be revoked or altered by the maker of it at any time when he is competent to dispose of his property by will.

§6. Provisions and Interpretation of Will

1068. The Succession Act, 1925 (Chapter VI) deals with the preparation of wills. It is not necessary that any technical words or terms of art be used in a will, but only that the wording be such that the intentions of the testator can be known therefrom.

1069. For the purpose of determining questions as to what person or what property is denoted by any words used in a will, a Court shall inquire into every material fact relating to the persons who claim to be interested under such will, the property which is claimed as the subject of disposition, the circumstances of the testator and of his family, and into every fact a knowledge of which may conduce to the right application of the words which the testator has used. Illustrations: (i) A, by his will, bequeaths PKR 1,000 to his eldest son or to his youngest grandchild, or to his cousin, Mary. A Court may make inquiry in order to ascertain to what person the description in the will applies. (ii) A, by his will, leaves to B 'my estate called Black Acre'. It may be necessary to take evidence in order to ascertain what is the subject-matter of the bequest; that is to say, what estate of the testators is called Black Acre. (iii) A, by his will, leaves to B 'the estate which purchased of C'. It may be necessary to take evidence in order to ascertain what estate the testator purchased of C.

1070. Where the words used in a will to designate or describe a legatee or a class of legatees sufficiently shows what is meant, an error in the name or description shall not prevent the legacy from taking effect. A mistake in the name of a legatee may be corrected by a description of him, and a mistake in the description of a legatee may be corrected by the name. Illustrations: (i) A bequeaths a legacy 'to Thomas, the second son of my brother John'. The testator has an only brother named John, who has no son named Thomas, but has a second son whose name is William. William will have the legacy. (ii) A bequeaths a legacy 'to Thomas, the second son of my brother John'. The testator has an only brother, named John, whose first son is named Thomas, and whose second son is named William. Thomas will have the legacy. (iii) The testator bequeaths his property 'to A and B, the legitimate children of C'. C has no legitimate child, but has two illegitimate children, A and B. The bequest to A and B takes effect, although they are illegitimate. (iv) The testator gives his residuary estate to be divided among 'my seven children and, proceeding to enumerate them, mentions six names only. This omission will not prevent the seventh child from taking a share with the others'. (v) The testator, having six grandchildren, makes a bequest to 'my six grandchildren' and, proceeding to mention them by their Christian names, mentions one twice over omitting another altogether. The one whose name is not mentioned will take a share with the others. (vi) The testator bequeaths 'PKR 1,000 to each of the three children of A'. At the date of the will, A has four children. Each of these four children will, if he survives the testator, receive a legacy of PKR 1,000.

1071. Where any word material to the full expression of the meaning has been omitted, it may be supplied by the context. Illustration: The testator gives a legacy of 'PKR 500' to his daughter A and a legacy of 'PKR 500' to his daughter B. A will take a legacy of PKR 500.

1072. If the thing which the testator intended to bequeath can be sufficiently identified from the description of it given in the will but some parts of the description do not apply, such parts of the description shall be rejected as erroneous, and the bequest shall take effect. Illustration (i) A bequeaths to B 'my marsh-lands lying in L and in the occupation of X'. The testator had marsh-lands lying in L but had no marsh-lands in the occupation of X. 'The words in the occupation of X' shall be rejected as erroneous, and the marsh-lands of the testator lying in L will pass by the bequest. (ii) The testator bequeaths to A 'my zamindari of Rampur'. He had an estate at Rampur, but it was a Talaq and not a zamindari. The Talaq passes by this bequest.

1073. If a will mentions several circumstances as descriptive of the thing which the testator intends to bequeath, and there is any property of his in respect of which all those circumstances exist, the bequest shall be considered as limited to such property, and it shall not be lawful to reject any part of the description as erroneous, because the testator had other property to which such part of the description does not apply. Explanation: In judging whether a case falls within the meaning of this section, any words which would be liable to rejection under section 78 shall be deemed to have been struck out of the will. Illustrations: (i) A bequeaths to B 'my marsh-lands lying in L and in the occupation of X'. The testator had marsh-lands lying in L, some of which were in the occupation of X, and some not in the occupation of X. The bequest will be considered as limited to such of the testators marsh-lands lying in L as were in the occupation of X. (ii) A bequeaths to B 'my marsh-lands lying in L and in the occupation of X, comprising 1,000 "bighas" of lands'. The testator had marah-lands lying in L some of which were in the occupation of X and some not in the occupation of X. The measurement is wholly in applicable to the marsh-lands of either class, or to the whole taken together. The measurement will be considered as struck out of the will, and such of the testators marsh-lands lying in L as were in the occupation of X shall alone pass by the bequest.

1074. Where the words of a will are unambiguous, but it is found by extrinsic evidence that they admit of applications, one only of which can have been intended by the testator, extrinsic evidence may be taken to show which of these applications was intended. Illustrations: (i) A man, having two cousins of the name of Mary, bequeaths a sum of money to 'my cousin Mary'. It appears that there are two persons, each answering the description in the will. That description, therefore, admits of two applications, only one of which can have been intended by the testator. Evidence is admissible to show which of the two applications was intended. (ii) A, by his will, leaves to B 'my estate called Sultanpur Kliurd'. It turns out that he had two estates called Sultanpur Kliurd. Evidence is admissible to show which estate was intended.

1075. Where there is an ambiguity or deficiency on the face of a will, no extrinsic evidence as to the intentions of the testator shall be admitted. Illustrations: (i) A man has an aunt, Caroline, and a cousin, Mary, and has no aunt of the name of Mary. By his will he bequeaths PKR 1,000 to 'my aunt. Caroline' and PKR 1,000 to 'my cousin, Mary' and afterwards bequeaths PKR 2,000 to 'my before-mentioned aunt, Mary'. There is no person to whom the description given in the will can apply, and evidence is not admissible to show who was meant by 'my before-mentioned aunt, Mary'. The bequest is therefore void for uncertainty. (ii) A bequeaths PKR 1,000 to leaving a blank for the name of the legatee. Evidence is not admissible to show what name the testator intended to insert. (iii) A bequeath to B rupees, or 'my estate of'. Evidence is not admissible to show what sum or what estate the testator Intended to insert.

1076. The meaning of any clause in a will is to be collected from the entire instrument, and all its parts are to be construed with reference to each other. Illustration: (i) The testator gives to B a specific fund or property at the death of A, and by a subsequent clause gives the whole of his property to A. The effect of the several clauses taken together is to vest the specific fund or property in A for life, and after his decease in B; it appearing from the bequest to B that the testator meant to use in a restricted sense the words in which he describes what he gives to A. (ii) Where a testator having an estate, one part of which is called Black Acre, bequeaths the whole of his estate to A, and in another part of his will bequeaths Black Acre to B, the latter bequest is to be read as an exception out of the first as if he had said 'I give Black Acre to B, and all the rest of any estate to A'.

1077. General words may be understood in a restricted sense where it may be collected from the will that the testator meant to use them in a restricted sense; and words may be understood in a wider sense than that which they usually bear, where it may be collected from the other words of the will that the testator meant to use them in such wider sense. Illustrations: (i) A testator gives to A 'my farm in the occupation of B', and to C 'all my marshland in L'. Part of the farm in the occupation of B consists of marsh-lands in L, and the testator also has other marsh-lands in L. The general words, 'all my marsh-lands in L', are restricted by the gift to A. A takes the whole of the farm in the occupation of B, including that portion of the farm which consists of marsh-lands in L. (ii) The testator (a sailor on ship-board) bequeathed to his mother his gold ring, buttons and chest of clothes and to his friend, A (a shipmate), his red box, clasp-knife and all things not before bequeathed. The testators share in a house does not pass to A under this bequest. (iii) A, by his will, bequeathed to B all his household furniture, plate, linen, china, books, pictures and all other goods of whatever kind; and afterwards bequeathed to B a specked part of his property. Under the first bequest, B is entitled only to such articles of the testators as are of the same nature with the articles therein enumerated.

1078. Where a clause is susceptible of two meanings according to one of which it has some effect, and according to the other of which it can have none, the former shall be preferred. No part of a will shall be rejected as destitute of meaning if it is possible to put a reasonable construction upon it. If the same words occur in different parts of the same will, they shall be taken to have been used everywhere in the same sense, unless a contrary intention appears.

1079. The intention of the testator shall not be set aside because it cannot take effect to the full extent, but effect is to be given to it as far as possible. Illustration: The testator by a will made on his death-bed bequeathed all his property to CD for life and after his decease to a certain hospital. The intention of the testator cannot take effect to its full extent, because the gift to the hospital is void, but it will take effect so far as regards the gift to CD.

1080. Where two clauses or gifts in a will are irreconcilable, so that they cannot possibly stand together, the last shall prevail. Illustration: (i) The testator by the first clause of his will leaves his estate of Gujrat 'to A', and by the last clause of his will leaves it 'to B and not to A'. B will have it. (ii) If a man at the commencement, of his will gives his house to A, and at the close of it directs that his house shall be sold and the proceeds invested for the benefit of B, the latter disposition will prevail.

1081. A will or bequest not expressive of any definite intention is void for uncertainty. Illustration: If a testator says 'I bequeath goods to A', or 'I bequeath to A', or 'I leave to A all the goods mentioned in the Schedule' and no Schedule is found, or 'I bequeath money, wheat, oil', or the like, without saying how much, this is void.

1082. The description contained in a will of property, the subject of gift, shall, unless a contrary intention appears by the will, be deemed to refer to and comprise the property answering that description at the death of the testator.

1083. Unless a contrary intention appears by the will, a bequest of the testator shall be construed to include any property which he may have power to appoint by will to any object he may think proper, and shall, operate as an execution of such power; and a bequest of property described in a general manner shall be construed to include any property to which such description may extend, which he may have power to appoint by will to any object he may think proper, and shall operate as an execution of such power.

1084. Where property is bequeathed to or for the benefit of certain objects as a specified person may appoint or for the benefit of certain objects in such proportions as a specified person may appoint, and the will does not provide for the event of no appointment being made; if the power given by the will is not exercised, the property belongs to all the objects of the power in equal shares. Illustration: A, by his will, bequeaths a fund to his wife, for her life, and directs that at her death it shall be divided among his children in such proportions as she shall appoint. The widow dies without having made any appointment. The fund will be divided equally among the children.

1085. Where a bequest is made to the 'heirs' or 'right heirs' or 'relations' or 'nearest relations' or 'family' or 'kindred' or 'nearest of kin' or 'next-of-kin' of a particular person without any qualifying terms, and the class so designation forms the direct and independent object of the bequest, the property bequeathed shall be distributed as if it had belonged to such person, and he had died intestate in respect of it, leaving assets for the payment of his debts independently of such property. Illustration: (i) A leaves his property 'In my own nearest relations'. The property goes to those who would be entitled to it if A had died intestate, leaving assets for the payment of his debts independently of such property (ii) A bequeaths PKR 10,000 'to B for his life, and, after the death of B, to my own right heirs'. The legacy after B's death belongs to those who would be entitled to it if it had formed part of A's un-bequeathed property. (iii) A leaves his property to B; but if B dies before him, to B's next-of-kin; B dies before A; the property devolves as if it had belonged to B, and he had died intestate, leaving assets for the payment of his debts independently of such property. (iv) A leaves PKR 10,000 'to B for his life, and after his decease to the hairs of C'. The legacy goes as if it had belonged to C, and he had died intestate, leaving assets for the payment of his debts independently of the legacy.

1086. Where a bequest is made to the 'representatives' or 'legal representatives' or 'personal representatives' or 'executors or administrators' of a particular person, and the class so designated forms the direct and independent object of the bequest, the property bequeathed shall be distributed as if it had belonged to such person and he had died intestate in respect of it. Illustration: A bequest is made to the 'legal representatives' of A. A has died intestate and insolvent. B is his administrator. B is entitled to receive the legacy, and will apply it in the first place to the discharge of such part of A's debts as may remain unpaid: if there be any surplus, B will pay it to those persons who at A's death would have been entitled to receive any property of A's which might remain after payment of his debts, or to the representatives of such persons.

1087. Where property is bequeathed to any person, he is entitled to the whole interest of the testator therein, unless it appears from the will that only a restricted interest was intended for him.

1088. Where property is bequeathed to a person with a bequest in the alternative to another person or to a class of persons, then, if a contrary intention does not appear by the will, the legatee first named shall be entitled to the legacy if he is alive at the time when it takes effect; but if he is then dead, the person or class of persons named in the second branch of the alternative shall take the legacy. Illustrations: (i) A bequest is made to A or to B. A survives the testator. B takes nothing. (ii) A bequest is made to A or to B. A dies after the date of the will, and before the testator. The legacy goes to B. (iii) A bequest is made to A or to B. A is dead at the date of the will. The legacy goes to B. (iv) Property is bequeathed to A or his heirs. A survives the testator. A takes the property absolutely. (v) Property is bequeathed to A or his nearest of kin. A dies in the lifetime of the testator. Upon the death of the testator, the bequest to A's nearest of kin takes effect. (vi) Property is bequeathed to A for life, and after his death to B or his heirs. A and B survive the testator. B dies in A's lifetime. Upon A's death the bequest to the heirs of B takes effect. (vii) Property is bequeathed to A for life, and after his death to B or his heir; B dies in the testators lifetime. A survives the testator. Upon A's death, the bequest to the heirs of B takes effect.

1089. Where property is bequeathed to a person, and words are added which describe a class of persons but do not denote them as direct objects of a distinct and independent gift, such person is entitled to the whole interest of the testator therein, unless a contrary intention appears by the will. Illustration (i) A bequest is made to A and his children, to A and his children by his present wife, to A and his heirs, to A and the heirs of his body, to A and the heirs male of his body, to A and the heirs female of his body, to A and his issue, to A and his family, to A and his descendants, to A and his representatives, to A and his personal representatives, to A, his executors and administrators. In each of these cases, A takes the whole interest which the testator had in the property. (ii) A bequest is made to A and his brothers. A and his brothers are jointly entitled to the legacy. (iii) A bequest is made to A for life and after his death to his issue. At the death of A, the property belongs in equal shares to all persons who then answer the description of issue of A.

1090. Where a bequest is made to a class of persons under a general description only, no one to whom the words of the description are not in their ordinary sense applicable shall take the legacy. In a will (a) the word 'children' applies only to lineal descendants in the first degree of the person whose 'children are spoken of'; (b) the word 'grandchildren' applies only to lineal descendants in the second degree of the person whose 'grandchildren' are spoken of; (c) the words 'nephews' and 'nieces' apply only to children of brothers or sisters; (d) the words 'cousins', or 'first cousins', or 'cousins-german', apply only to children of brothers or of sisters of the father or mother of the person whose 'cousins', or 'first cousins', or 'cousins-german', are spoken of; (e) the words 'First cousins once removed' apply only to children of cousins-german, or to cousins-german of a parent of the person whose 'first cousins once removed' are spoken of; (f) the words 'second cousins' apply only to grandchildren of brothers or of sisters of the grandfather or grandmother of the person whose 'second cousins' are spoken of; (g) the words 'issue' and 'descendants' apply to all lineal descendants whatever of the parson whose 'issue' or 'descendants' are spoken of; (h) words expressive of collateral relationship apply alike to relatives of full and of half-blood; and (i) all words expressive of relationship apply to a child in the womb who is afterwards born alive.

1091. In the absence of any intimation to the contrary in a will, the word 'child', the word 'son', the word 'daughter', or any word which expresses relationship, is to be understood as denoting only a legitimate relative, or, where there is no such legitimate relative, a person who has acquired, at the date of the will, the reputation of being such relative. Illustration: (i) A having three children, B, C and D, of whom B and C are legitimate and D is illegitimate, leaves his property to be equally divided among 'my children'. The property belongs to B, and C in equal shares, to the exclusion of D. (ii) A, having a niece of illegitimate birth, who has acquired the reputation of being his niece, and having no legitimate niece bequeaths a sum of money to his niece. The illegitimate niece is entitled to the legacy. (iii) A, having in his will enumerated his children, and named as one of them B, who is illegitimate, leaves a legacy to 'my said children'. B will take a share in the legacy along with the legitimate children. (iv) A leaves a legacy to 'the children of B'. B is dead and has left none but illegitimate children. All those who had at the dale of the will acquired the reputation of being the children of B are objects of the gift. (v) A bequeaths a legacy to 'the children of E'. B never had any legitimate child. C and D had, at the date of the will, acquired the reputation of being children of B. After the date of the will and before the death of the testator, E and F were born, and acquired the reputation of being children of B. Only C and D are objects of the bequest. (vi) A makes a bequest in favour of his child by a certain woman, not his wife, B had acquired at the date of the will the reputation of being the child of A by the woman designated. B takes the legacy. (vii) A makes a bequest in favour of his child to be born of a woman who never becomes his wife. The bequest is void. (viii) A makes a bequest in favour of the child of which a certain woman, not married to him, is pregnant. The bequest is void.

§7. Consanguinity

1092. Sections 23 to 28 of the Succession Act, 1925 (Part IV) govern matters related to consanguinity. In Pakistan, the succession to both movable and immovable property of an intestate is regulated by the applicable laws as per section 5 of the Succession Act, 1925. In cases of Christian succession, the estate of the deceased devolves upon the surviving spouse or, in the absence thereof, upon the nearest kin in the ascending or descending line, in accordance with the principles of intestate succession (CLC 2020 Lahore 151).

1093. Kindred or consanguinity in the connection or relation of persons descended from the same stock or common ancestor. Property in case of Christian succession devolves upon surviving spouses or upon those who are kindred in ascending or descending order to the intestate (PLD 2003 Kar. 270).

1094. Lineal consanguinity refers to the direct blood relationship between individuals, where one is a direct descendant of the other. This relationship exists in both ascending and descending lines. In the ascending line, it includes a person's father, grandfather, great-grandfather, and so forth. In the descending line, it extends to a person's children, grandchildren, great-grandchildren, and beyond. Each generation represents a degree of kinship, a father and son are related in the first degree, a grandfather and grandson in the second degree, and a great-grandfather and great-grandson in the third degree. This pattern continues indefinitely, with each successive generation constituting a new degree of relationship. Lineal consanguinity is a fundamental concept in inheritance laws, determining the order of succession and distribution of an intestate's estate.

1095. Collateral consanguinity refers to the blood relationship between individuals who share a common ancestor but are not directly descended from one another. This includes siblings, cousins, uncles, aunts, and other relatives who originate from the same ancestral line but branch off in different directions. To determine the degree of kinship between a deceased person and a collateral relative, one must trace the lineage upward to the nearest common ancestor and then downward to the collateral relative, counting each generational step as a degree of relationship. For example, siblings share a second-degree collateral relationship as they have a common parent, while first cousins are related in the fourth degree, as they descend from the same grandparent but through different parental lines.

1096. For the purposes of succession, no distinction is made between relatives based on the following factors: (a) whether they are connected to the deceased through the paternal or maternal lineage, as both lines are considered equally for inheritance purposes; (b) whether they are related by full blood (same father and mother) or half-blood (sharing only one parent), as both are entitled to succession rights without any legal differentiation; and (c) whether they were born during the deceased's lifetime or were conceived before the deceased's death but born alive afterward, as posthumous children are also recognized as legal heirs. The degrees of kinship are determined according to the Table of Kindred specified in Schedule I of the Succession Act, 1925, which provides a structured approach for computing relationships and inheritance entitlements. These principles ensure that inheritance rights are fairly distributed among heirs, irrespective of the nature of their relation to the deceased.

1097. Illustrations: (i) The person whose relatives are to be reckoned, and his cousin-german, or first cousin, are, related in the fourth degree; there being one degree of ascent to the father and another to the common ancestor, the grandfather; and from him one of descent to the uncle, and another to the cousin-german, making in all four degrees. (ii) A grandson of the brother and a son of the uncle, that is, a great nephew and a cousin-german, are in equal degree being each four degrees removed. (iii) A grandson of a cousin-german is in the same degree as the grandson of a great-uncle, for they are both in the sixth degree of kindred.

1098. Under section 138 of the Succession Act, 1925 if a fund is bequeathed absolutely to or for the benefit of any person, but the will contains a direction that it shall be applied or enjoyed in a particular manner, the legatee shall be entitled to receive the fund as if the will had contained no such direction. Illustration: A sum of money is bequeathed towards purchasing a country residence for A, or to purchase an annuity for A, or to place A in any business. A chooses to receive the legacy in money. He is entitled to do so.

1099. When a testator makes an absolute bequest of a fund, effectively separating it from his estate, but imposes restrictions on how the legatee may utilize it to secure a particular benefit, such restrictions will only be enforceable if the intended benefit can be achieved. If it becomes impossible to fulfil the specified purpose, the legatee shall be entitled to the fund as if no such restrictive conditions had been imposed in the will. For instance, if a testator bequeaths the remainder of his estate to be divided equally among his daughters, stipulating that their respective shares be held in trust for their lifetime and then transferred to their children after their death, but the daughters pass away unmarried and childless, their respective shares shall devolve upon their legal representatives. Similarly, if a testator instructs his trustees to set aside a sum of money for his daughter, directing them to invest it and provide her with the income generated during her lifetime, with the principal to be distributed among her children after her death, but she dies without having any children, then her legal representatives will be entitled to inherit the fund. Such provisions ensure that a legatee's rightful inheritance is not unduly restricted when the intended benefit cannot materialize.

1100. When a testator bequeaths a fund without absolutely severing it from his estate but instead assigns it for specific purposes, any portion of the fund that remains unutilized due to the impossibility of fulfilling those purposes shall revert to the testator's estate. This ensures that the unallocated portion does not pass arbitrarily but remains part of the testator's residual assets. For example, if a testator instructs his trustees to invest a sum of money in a designated manner and directs them to pay the interest to his son for life, with the principal to be distributed among the son's children upon his death, but the son passes away without having any children, the principal amount reverts to the testator's estate. Similarly, if a testator bequeaths the residue of his estate to be equally divided among his daughters, specifying that they shall receive only the interest during their lifetime and that the principal shall pass to their children upon their death, but the daughters die without leaving any children, the entire fund shall remain a part of the testator's estate.

1101. If a legacy is bequeathed to a person who is named an executor of the will, he shall not take the legacy, unless he proves the will or otherwise manifests an intention to act as executor. Illustration: A legacy is given to A, who is named an executor. A orders the funeral according to the directions contained in the will, and dies a few days after the testator, without having proved the will. A has manifested an intention to act as executor.

1102. Under the Succession Act, 1925 (sections 180-190), where a person, by his will, professes to dispose of something which he has no right to dispose of, the person to whom the thing belongs shall elect either to confirm such disposition or to dissent from it, and, in the latter case, he shall give up any benefits which may have been provided for him by the will.

1103. An interest relinquished in the circumstances stated in section 180 shall devolve as if it had not been disposed of by the will in favour of the legatee, subject, nevertheless, to the charge of making good to the disappointed legatee the amount or value of the gift attempted to be given to him by the will.

1104. The provisions of sections 180 and 181 apply whether the testator does or does not believe that which he professes to dispose of by his will to be his own. Illustrations: (i) The farm of Sultanpur was the property of C. A bequeathed it to B, giving a legacy of PKR 1,000 to C. C has elected to retain his farm of Sultanpur, which is worth PKR 800. C forfeits his legacy of PKR 1,000, of which PKR 800 goes to B, and the remaining PKR 200 falls into the residuary bequest, or devolves according to the rules of intestate succession, as the case may be. (ii) A bequeaths an estate to B in case B's elder brother (who is married and has children) shall leave no issue living at his death. A also bequeaths to C a jewel, which belongs to B. B must elect to give up the jewel or to lose the estate. (iii) A bequeaths to B PKR 1,000, and to C an estate which will under a settlement, belong to B is his elder brother (who is married and has children) shall leave no issue living at his death. B must elect to give up the estate or to lose the legacy. (iv) A, a person of the age of 18, domiciled in Pakistan but owning real property in England, to which C is heir at law, bequeaths a legacy to C and, subject thereto, devises and bequeaths to B 'all my property whatsoever and wheresoever', and dies under 21. The real property in England does not pass by the will. C may claim his legacy without giving up the real property in England.

1105. A bequest for a person's benefit is, for the purpose of election, the same thing as a bequest made to himself. Illustration: The farm of Sultanpur Khurd being the property of B, A bequeathed it to C: and bequeathed another farm called Sultanpur Buzurg to his own executors with a direction that it should be sold and the proceeds applied in payment of B's debts. B must elect whether he will abide by the will, or keep his farm of Sultanpur Khurd in opposition to it.

1106. A person taking no benefit directly under a will, but deriving a benefit under it indirectly, is not put to his election. Illustration: The lands of Sultanpur are settled upon C for life, and after his death upon D, his only child. A bequeaths the lands of Sultanpur to B, and PKR 1,000 to C. C dies intestate shortly after the testator, and without having made any election. D takes out administration to C, and as administrator; elects on behalf of C's estate to take under the will. In that capacity, he receives the legacy of PKR 1,000 and accounts to B for the rents of the lands of Sultanpur which accrued after the death of the testator and before the death of C. In his individual character, he retains the lands of Sultanpur in opposition to the will.

1107. A person who in his individual capacity takes a benefit under a will may, in another character, elect to take in opposition to the will. Illustration: The estate of Sultanpur is settled upon A for life, and after his death, upon B. A leaves the estate of Sultanpur to D, and PKR 2,000 to B, and PKR 1,000 to C, who is B's only child. B dies intestate, shortly after the testator, without having made an election. C takes out administration to B, and as administrator elects to keep the estate of Sultanpur in opposition to the will, and to relinquish the legacy of PKR 2,000. C may do this, and yet claim his legacy of PKR 1,000 under the will.

1108. Notwithstanding anything contained in sections 180 to 185, where a particular gift is expressed in the will to be in lieu of something belonging to the legatee which is also in terms disposed of by the will, then, if the legatee claims that thing, he must relinquish the particular gift, but he is not bound to relinquish any other benefit given to him by the will. Illustration: Under A's marriage-settlement his wife is entitled, if she survives him, to the enjoyment of the estate of Sultanpur during her life. A by his will bequeaths to his wife an annuity of PKR 200 during her life, in lieu of her interest in the estate of Sultanpur, which estate he bequeaths to his son. He also gives his wife a legacy of PKR 1,000. The widow elects to take what she is entitled to under the settlement. She is bound to relinquish the annuity but not the legacy of PKR 1,000.

1109. Acceptance of a benefit given by a will constitutes an election by the legatee to take under the will, if he had knowledge of his right to elect and of those circumstances which would influence the judgment of a reasonable man in making an election, or if he waives inquiry into the circumstances. Illustrations: (i) A is owner of an estate called Sultanpur Khurd, and has a life interest in another estate called Sultanpur Buzurg to which upon his death his son B will be absolutely entitled. The will of A gives the estate of Sultanpur Khurd to B, and the estate of Sultanpur Buzurg to C. B, in ignorance of his own right to the estate of Sultanpur Buzurg, allows C to take possession of it, and enters into possession of the estate of Sultanpur Khurd. B has not con-finned the bequest of Sultanpur Buzurg to C. (ii) B, the eldest son of A, is the possessor of an estate called Sultanpur. A bequeaths Sultanpur to C, and to B the residue of A's property. B having been informed by A's executors that the residue will amount to PKR 5,000, allows C to take possession of Sultanpur. He afterwards discovers that the residue does not amount to more than PKR 500. B has not confirmed the bequest of the estate of Sultanpur to C.

1110. In the absence of evidence to the contrary, a legatee's knowledge of a bequest or waiver of the right to inquire into its validity shall be presumed if the legatee has accepted and enjoyed its benefits for a continuous period of two years without expressing any form of dissent. Moreover, such knowledge or waiver may also be inferred from any action taken by the legatee that irrevocably alters the subject matter of the bequest, making it impossible to restore the interests of other concerned parties to their original state.

For instance, if a testator bequeaths an estate to B, despite C being its rightful owner, and simultaneously grants C a coal mine, and C proceeds to take possession of the mine and depletes its resources, C's actions constitute an implicit confirmation of the bequest of the estate to B. This principle ensures that a legatee cannot selectively benefit from a will while later challenging its provisions, thereby promoting fairness and certainty in testamentary dispositions.

1111. If a legatee fails to indicate, within one year following the testator's death, whether they accept or reject the provisions of the will, the legal representatives of the testator shall, upon the expiration of this period, formally require the legatee to make an election. Should the legatee fail to respond within a reasonable time after receiving such a request, it shall be presumed that they have chosen to accept and confirm the terms of the will. This rule ensures that estate administration is not indefinitely delayed due to a legatee's inaction. By imposing a clear timeframe and procedural obligation, it prevents uncertainty in the distribution of assets and safeguards the interests of other beneficiaries and stakeholders in the estate.

1112. If a legatee is under a legal disability at the time an election is required, the decision shall be deferred until such disability ceases, or until a legally competent authority makes the election on their behalf. This provision ensures that individuals who are unable to act due to legal incapacity such as minors, persons with mental disabilities, or those otherwise unable to make an informed decision are not unfairly prejudiced. The delay in election protects their rights and interests, allowing for a fair determination once they regain capacity or a legally designated representative acts in their best interest.

§8. The Joint Will

1113. A **Joint Will** is a single testamentary document executed by two individuals, typically spouses, outlining the distribution of their assets upon the death of either party. Such a Will specifies that upon the death of one testator, the surviving testator shall inherit the entire estate, and it further dictates how the estate will be distributed upon the death of the survivor. Essentially, a Joint Will functions as a binding contract between the testators and cannot be revoked unilaterally after the death of one party, as both parties must consent to its modification or revocation during their lifetimes. One of the primary advantages of a Joint Will is that it ensures the wishes of both testators are honoured, even after the first testator's passing. It serves as a safeguard to prevent the surviving testator from altering the distribution of assets, which can be particularly useful in cases where there are concerns about remarriage or potential disinheritance of intended beneficiaries. For instance, if a husband fears that his wife might remarry and subsequently change her Will to leave assets to her new spouse or stepchildren, a Joint Will ensures that the original testamentary intentions remain intact. However, there are notable drawbacks. A Joint Will can significantly limit the surviving testator's ability to respond to changing circumstances. The survivor is bound by the original terms and may be unable to adapt the distribution of assets in response to unforeseen events, such as a beneficiary becoming financially independent or suffering from financial hardship. Additionally, the surviving testator may face legal challenges if they wish to modify or revoke the Joint Will, often requiring extensive legal proceedings to navigate the complexities of invalidating the original contractual obligations. For example, if a wife inherits all assets after her husband's passing and later wishes to redistribute them due to changes in her family's financial situation, she may be unable to do so without breaching the terms of the Joint Will. This rigidity can lead to complications, making it essential for individuals considering a Joint Will to weigh both its protective benefits and potential restrictions before executing such a document.

1114. Under section 106 of the Succession Act, 1925, when a legacy is bequeathed to two individuals jointly and one of them predeceases the testator, the surviving legatee is entitled to inherit the entire legacy. This principle applies unless the will explicitly states otherwise or a different intention can be inferred from its terms. For instance, if a testator bequeaths a legacy simply to A and B, and A passes away before the testator, then B will inherit the entire legacy by right of survivorship. This rule ensures that the surviving legatee receives the benefit of the bequest in cases where no alternative arrangement is specified in the will. However, if the testator has expressly mentioned that the deceased legatee's share should pass to another person or should lapse upon their death, then such instructions would take precedence.

§9. Bequests

1115. The Bequests in Pakistan are regulated under Chapter-VI of the Succession Act, 1925. The bequest means receiving of property through will. Under the Succession Act, 1925 if a will purports to make two bequests to the same person, and a question arises whether the testator intended to make the second bequest instead of or in addition to the first; if there is nothing in the will to show what he intended, the following rules shall have effect in, determining the construction to be put upon the will: (a) If the same specific thing is bequeathed twice to the same legatee in the same will or in the will and again in the codicil, he is entitled to receive that specific thing only. (b) Where one and the same will or one and the same codicil purports to make, in two places, a bequest to the same person of the same quantity or amount of anything, he shall be entitled to one such legacy only. (c) If two legacies of unequal amount are given to the same person in the same will, or in the same codicil, the legatee is entitled to both. (d) If two legacies, whether equal or unequal in amount, are given to the same legatee, one by a will and the other by a codicil, or each by a different codicil, the legatee is entitled to both legacies. Explanation**:** In clauses (a) to (d) of this section, the word 'will' does not include a codicil. Illustrations: (i) A, having ten shares, and no more, in this Imperial Bank of

India, made his will, which contain near its commencement the word 'I bequeath my ten shares in the Imperial Bank of India to B'. After other bequests, the will concludes with the words 'and I bequeath my ten shares in the Imperial Bank of India to B'. B is entitled simply to receive A's ten shares in the Imperial Bank of India. (ii) A, having one diamond ring, which was given to him by B, bequeaths to C the diamond ring which was given by B. A afterwards made a codicil to his will, and thereby, after giving other legacies, he bequeathed to C the diamond ring which was given to him by B. C can claim nothing except the diamond ring which was given to A by B. (iii) A, by his will, bequeaths to B the sum of PKR 5,000 and afterwards in the same will repeats the bequest in the same words. B is entitled to one legacy of PKR 5,090 only. (iv) A by, his will bequeaths to B the sum of PKR 5,000 and afterwards in the same will bequeaths to B the sum of PKR 6,000. B is entitled to receive PKR 11,000. (v) A, by his will, bequeaths to B PKR 5,000 and by a codicil to the will he bequeaths to him PKR 5,000. B is entitled to receive PKR 10,000. (vi) A, by one codicil to his will, bequeaths to B PKR 5,000 and by another codicil bequeaths to him PKR 6,000. B is entitled to receive PKR 11,000. (vii) A, by his will, bequeaths 'PKR 500 to B because she was my nurse', and in another part of the will bequeaths PKR 500 to B 'because she went to England with my children'. B is entitled to receive, PKR 1,000, (viii) A, by his will, bequeaths to B the sum of PKR 5,000 and also, in another part of the will, an annuity of PKR 400. B is entitled to both legacies. (ix) A, by his will, bequeaths to B the sum of PKR 5,000 and also bequeaths to him the sum of PKR 5,000 if he shall attain the age of 18. B is, entitled absolutely to one sum of PKR 5,000, and takes a contingent interest in another sum of PKR 5,000.

1116. A residuary legatee may be constituted by any words that show an intention on the part of testator that the person designated shall take the surplus or residue of his property. Illustrations: (i) A makes her will, consisting of several testamentary papers, in one of which are contained the following words: 'I think there will be something left, after all funeral expenses, etc., to give to B, now at school, towards equipping him to any profession he may hereafter be appointed to.' B is constituted residuary legatee. (ii) A makes his will, with the following passage at the end of it: 'l believe there will be found sufficient in my bankers hands to defray and discharge my debts, which I hereby desire B to do and keep the residue for her own use and pleasure.' E is constituted of the residuary legates, (iii) A bequeaths all his property to B, except certain stocks and funds which he bequeaths to C. B is the residuary legatee.

1117. Under a residuary bequest, the legatee is entitled to all assets owned by the testator at the time of death, except those that have been specifically disposed of through a valid testamentary provision. If any part of the testator's estate remains undisposed of due to a lapse, failure, or invalidity of a specific bequest, such property automatically forms part of the residuary estate and passes to the residuary legatee. For example, if a testator bequeaths several specific legacies, but one becomes void under legal provisions and another lapses due to the legatee's predeceasing the testator, the undistributed portions will fall into the residue of the estate. If the testator has designated a residuary beneficiary, that beneficiary will inherit not only the remaining assets specified in the will but also any property acquired by the testator after making the will, provided no other provision has been made for it. If the testator, after executing the will, purchases a zamindari (estate) and does not make a separate bequest for it, the residuary legatee will be entitled to inherit it as part of the residual estate.

1118. If a legacy is given in general terms, without specifying the time when it is to be paid, the legatee has a vested interest in it from the day of the death of the testator, and, if he dies without having received it, it shall pass to his representatives. If the legatee does not survive the testator, the legacy cannot take effect, but shall lapse and form part of the residue of the testators property, unless it appears by the will that the testator intended that it should go to some other person. In order to entitle the representatives of the legatee to receive the legacy, it must be proved that he survived the testator. Illustrations: (i) The testator bequeaths to B 'PKR 500 which B owes me'. B dies before the testator; the legacy lapses. (ii) A bequest is made to A and his children. A dies before the testator, or happens to be dead when the will is made. The legacy to A and his children lapses. (iii) A legacy is given to A, and, in case of his dying before the testator, to B. A dies before the testator. The legacy goes to B. (iv) A sum of money is bequeathed to A for life, and after his death to B. A dies in the lifetime of the testator; B survives the testator. The request to B takes effect. (v) A sum of money is bequeathed to A on his completing his 18th year, and in case he should die before he completes his 18th year, to B. A completes his 18th year, and dies in the lifetime of the testator. The legacy to A lapses, and the bequest to B does not take effect. (vi) The testator and the legatee perished in the same ship-wreck. There is no evidence to show who died first; the legacy lapses.

1119. If a legacy is given to two persons jointly, and one of them dies before the testator, the other legatee takes the whole. Illustration: The legacy is simply to A and B. A dies before the testator. B takes the legacy. If a legacy is given to legatees in words which show that the testator intended to give them distinct shares of it, then, if any legatee dies before the testator, so much of the legacy as was intended for him shall fall into the residue of the testators property. Illustration: A sum of money is bequeathed to A, B and C, to be equally divided among them. A dies before the testator. B and C will only take so much as they would have had if A had survived the testator. Where a share which lapses is a part of the general residue bequeathed by the will, that share shall go as undisposed of. Illustration: The testator bequeaths the residue of his estate to A, B and C, to be equally divided between them. A dies before the testator. His one-third of the residue goes as undisposed of.

1120. If a bequest has been made to any child or other lineal descendant of the testator, and the legatee dies in the lifetime of the testator, but any lineal descendant of his survives the testator, the bequest shall not lapse, but shall take effect as if the death of the legatee had happened immediately after the death of the testator, unless a contrary intention appears by the will. Illustration: A makes his will, by which he bequeaths a sum of money to his son, B, for his own absolute use and benefit. B dies before A, leaving a son, C, who survives A, and having made his will whereby he bequeaths all his property to his widow, D, The money goes to D.

1121. If a bequest is made to one person for the benefit of another, the legacy does not lapse by the death, in the testators lifetime, of the person to whom the bequest is made.

1122. If a bequest is made simply to a described class of persons, the thing bequeathed shall go only to such as are alive at the testators death. Exception: If property is bequeathed to a class of persons described as standing in a particular degree of kindred to a specified individual, but their possession of it is deferred until a time later than the death of the testator by reason of a prior bequest or otherwise, the property shall at that time go to such of them as are then alive, and to the representatives of any of them who have died since the death of the testator. Illustrations: (i) A bequeaths PKR 1,000 to 'the children of B' without saying when it is to be distributed among them. B had died previous to the date of the will, leaving three children, C, D and E. E died after the date of the will, but before the death of A. C and D survive A. The legacy will belong to C and D, to the exclusion of the representatives of E. (ii) A lease for years of a house was bequeathed to A for his life, and after his decease to the children of B. At the death of the testator, B had two children living, C and D, and he never had any other child. Afterwards, during the lifetime of A, C died, leaving P, his executor. D has survived A. D and E arc jointly entitled to so much of the lease-hold term as remains expired. (iii) A sum of money was bequeathed to A for her life, and after her decease, to the children of B. At the death of the testator, B had two children, living, C and D, and, after that event, two children, E and F, were born to B. C and E died in the lifetime of A, C having made a will, E having made no will. A has died, leaving D and F surviving her. The legacy is to be divided into four equal parts, one of which is to be paid to the executor of C, one to D, one to the administrator of E and one to P. (iv) A bequeaths one-third of his lands to B for his life, and after his decease to the sisters of B. At the death of the testator, B had two sisters living, C and D, and after that event another sister E was born. C died during the life of B, D and E have survived B. One-third of A's lands belong to D, E and the representatives of C, in equal shares. (v) A bequeaths PKR 1,000 to B for life and after his death equally among the children of C. Up to the death of B, C had not had any child. The bequest after the death of B is void. (vi) A bequeaths PKR 1,000 to 'all the children born or to be born' of B to be divided among them at the death of C. At the death of the testator, B has two children living, D and E. After the death of the testator, but in the lifetime of C, two other children, F and G, are born to B. After the death of C, another child is born to B. The legacy belongs to D, E, F and G, to the exclusion of the after-born child of B. (vii) A bequeaths a fund to the children of B, to be divided among them when the eldest shall attain majority. At the testators death, B had one child living, named C. He afterwards had two other children, named D and E. E died, but C and D were living when C attained majority. The final belongs to C, D and the representatives of E, to the exclusion of any child who may be born to B after C's attaining majority.

1123. Under sections 167~170 of the Succession Act, 1925 payment of liabilities in respect of the bequest has been covered. Where property specifically bequeathed is subject at the death of the testator to any pledge, lien or encumbrance created by the testator himself or by any person under whom he claims, then, unless a contrary intention appears by the will, the legatee, if he accepts the bequest, shall accept it subject to such pledge or incumbrance, and shall as between himself and the testators estate be liable to make good the amount of such pledge or incumbrance. A contrary intention shall not be inferred from any direction which the will may contain for the payment of the testators debts generally. Explanation: A periodical payment in the nature of land-revenue or in the nature of rent is not such an incumbrance. Illustrations: (i) A bequeaths to B the diamond ring given to him by C. At A's death, the ring is held in pawn by D, to whom it has been pledged by A. It is the duty of A's executors, if the state of the testators assets will allow them, to allow B to redeem the ring. (ii) A bequeaths to B a zamindari which at A's death is subject to a mortgage for PKR 10,000; and the whole of the principal sum, together with interest to the amount of PKR 1,000, is due at A's death. B, if he accepts the bequest, accepts it subject to this charge, and is liable, as between himself and A's estate, to pay the sum of PKR 11,000 thus due.

1124. Where anything is to be done to complete the testators title to the thing bequeathed, it is to be done at the cost of the testators estate. Illustrations: (i) A, having contracted in general terms for the purchase of a piece of land at a certain price, bequeaths to B, and dies before he has paid the purchase-money. The purchase-money must be made good out of A's assets. (ii) A, having contracted for the purchase of a piece of land for a certain sum of money, one-half of which is to be paid down and the other half secured by mortgage of the land, bequeaths it to B, and dies before he has paid or secured any part of the purchase-money. One-half of the purchase-money must be paid out of A's assets.

1125. Where there is a bequest of any interest in immoveable property in respect of which payment in the nature of land-revenue or in the nature of rent has to be made periodically, the estate of the testator shall (as between such estate and the legatee) make good such payments or a proportion of them, as the case may be, up to the day of his death. Illustration: A bequeaths to B a house, in respect of which PKR 365 are payable annually by way of rent. A pays his rent at the usual time, and dies twenty-five days after. A's estate will make good PKR 25 in respect of the rent.

1126. In the absence of any direction in the will, where there is a specific bequest of stock in a joint stock company, if any call or other payment is due from the testator at the time of his death in respect of the stock, such call or payment shall, as between the testators estate and the legatee, be borne by the estate; but, if any call or other payment becomes due in respect of such stock after the testators death, the same shall, as between the testators estate and the legatee, be borne by the legatee, if he accepts the bequest. Illustrations: (i) A bequeaths to B his shares in a certain railway. At A's death, there was due from him the sum of PKR 100 in respect of each share, being the amount of a call which had been duly made, and the sum of live rupees in respect of each share, being the amount of interest which had accrued due in respect of the call. These payments must be borne by A's estate. (ii) A has agreed to take fifty shares in an intended joint stock company, and has contracted to pay up PKR 100 in respect of each share, which sum must be paid before his title to the shares can be completed. A bequeaths these shares to B. The estate of A must make good the payments which were necessary to complete A's title. (iii) A bequeaths to B his shares in a certain railway. B accepts the legacy. After A's death, a call is made in respect of the shares. B must pay the call. (iv) A bequeaths to B his shares in a joint stock company. B accepts the bequest. Afterwards the affairs of the company are wound up, and each shareholder is called upon for contribution. The amount of the contribution must be borne by the legatee. (v) A is the owner of ten shares in a railway company. At a meeting held during his lifetime a call is made of PKR 50 per share, payable by three instalments. A bequeaths his shares to B, and dies between the day fixed for the payment of the first and the day fixed for the payment of the second instalment, and without having paid the first instalment. A's estate must pay the first instalment and B, if he accepts the legacy, must pay the remaining instalments.

1127. Under the Succession Act, 1925, section 171, if there is a bequest of something described in general terms, the executor must purchase for the legatee what may reasonably be considered to answer the description. Illustrations: (i) A bequeaths to B a pair of carriage-horses or a diamond ring. The executor must provide the legatee with such articles if the state of the assets will allow it. (ii) A bequeaths to B 'my pair of carriage-horses'. A had no carriage-horses at the time of his death. The legacy fails.

1128. Under the Succession Act, 1925 (section 172) where the interest or produce of a fund is bequeathed to any person, and the will affords no indication of an intention that the enjoyment of the bequest should be of limited duration, the principal, as well as the interest, shall belong to the legatee. Illustrations: (i) A bequeaths to B the interest of his 5% promissory notes of the Federal Government. There is no other clause in the will affecting those securities. B is entitled to A's 5% promissory notes of the Federal Government. (ii) A bequeaths the interest of his 5½% promissory notes of the Federal Government to B for his life, and after his death to C. B is entitled to the interest of the notes during his life, and C is entitled to the notes upon B's death. (iii) A bequeaths to B the rents of his lands at X. B, is entitled to the lands.

1129. The Succession Act, 1925 (sections 173~176) describes about bequests annuities. It is stated that where an annuity is created by will, the legatee is entitled to receive it for his life only, unless a contrary intention appears by the will, notwithstanding that the annuity is directed to be paid out of the property generally, or that a sum of money is bequeathed to be invested in the purchase of it. Illustrations: (i) A bequeaths to B PKR 500 a year. B is entitled during his life to receive the annual sum of PKR 500. (ii) A bequeaths to B the sum of PKR 500 monthly. B is entitled during his life to receive the sum of PKR 500 every month. (iii) A bequeaths an annuity of PKR 500 to B for life, and on B's death to C. B is entitled to an annuity of PKR 500 during his life. C, if he survives B, is entitled to an annuity of PKR 500 from B's death until his own death.

1130. Where the will directs that an annuity shall be provided for any person out of the proceeds of property, or out of property generally, or where money is bequeathed to be invested in the purchase of any annuity for any person, on the testators death, the legacy vests in interest in the legatee, and he is entitled at his option to have an annuity purchased for him or to receive the money appropriated for that purpose by the will. Illustrations: (i) A by his will directs that his executors shall, out of his property, purchase an annuity of PKR 1,000 for B. B is entitled at his option to have an annuity of PKR 1,000 for his life purchased for him or to receive such a sum as will be sufficient for the purchase of such an annuity. (ii) A bequeaths a fund to B for his life, and directs that after B's death, it shall be laid out in the purchase of an annuity for C. B and C survive the testator. C dies in B's lifetime. On B's death, the fund belongs to the representative of C.

1131. When an annuity is bequeathed under a will, but the available assets of the testator are insufficient to satisfy all the legacies provided therein, the annuity shall be subject to abatement in proportion to the reduction imposed on other pecuniary legacies. This ensures an equitable distribution among all beneficiaries when the estate lacks sufficient funds to fulfil the testator's intended bequests. In such cases, no particular legatee, including an annuitant, is given preference over others unless explicitly stated in the will. Instead, all pecuniary legacies, including fixed sums and annuities, will be reduced proportionately to accommodate the shortfall in the testator's estate.

1132. Where there is a gift of an annuity and a residuary gift, the whole of the annuity is to be satisfied before any part of the residue is paid to the residuary legatee, and, if necessary, the capital of the testators estate shall be applied for that purpose.

1133. Under sections 177-179 of the Succession Act, 1925 where a debtor bequeaths a legacy to his creditor, and it does not appear from the will that the legacy is meant as a satisfaction of the debt, the creditor shall be entitled to the legacy, as well as to the amount of the debt.

1134. Where a parent, who is under obligation by contract to provide a portion for a child, fails to do so, and afterwards bequeaths a legacy to the child, and does not intimate by his will that the legacy is meant as a satisfaction of the portion, the child shall be entitled to receive the legacy, as well as the portion. Illustration: A, by articles entered into in contemplation of his marriage with B, covenanted that he would pay to each of the daughters of the intended marriage a portion of PKR 20,000 on her marriage. This covenant having been broken, A bequeaths PKR 20,000 to each of the married daughters of himself and B. The legatee are entitled to the benefit of this bequest in addition to their portions.

1135. No bequest shall be wholly or partially a deemed by a subsequent provision made by settlement or otherwise for the legatee. Illustrations: (i) A bequeaths PKR 20,000 to his son B. He afterwards gives to B the sum of PKR 20,000. The legacy is not thereby a deemed. (ii) A bequeaths PKR 40,000 to B, his orphan niece whom he had brought up from her infancy. Afterwards, on the occasion of B's marriage, A settles upon her the sum of PKR 30,000. The legacy is not thereby diminished.

§10. Void Bequests

1136. Under the sections 112~118 of the Succession Act, 1925 identifies the bequests which are void under the law. It is stated that if a bequest is made to a person by a particular description, and there is no person in existence at the testators death who answers the description, the bequest is void. Exception: If property is bequeathed to a person described as standing in a particular degree of kindred to a specified individual, but his possession of it is deferred until a time later than the death of the testator, by reason of a prior bequest or otherwise; and if a person answering the description is alive at the death of the testator, or comes into existence between that event and such later time, the property shall, at such later time, go to that person, or, if he is dead, to his representatives. Illustrations: (i) A bequeaths PKR 1,000 to the eldest son of B. At the death of the testator, B has no son. The bequest is void. (ii) A bequeaths PKR 1,000 to B for life, and after his death to the eldest son of C. At the death of the testator, C had no son. Afterwards, during the life of B, a son is born to C. Upon B's death, the legacy goes to C's son. (iii) A bequeaths PKR 1,000 to B for life, and after his death to the eldest son of C. At the death of the testator, C had no son. Afterwards during the life of B, a son, named D, is born to C. D dies, then B dies. The legacy goes to the representative of D. (iv) A bequeaths his estate of Green Acre to B for life, and at his decease, to the eldest son of C. Up to the death of B, C has had no son. The bequest to C's eldest son is void. (v) A bequeaths PKR 1,000 to the eldest son of C, to be paid to him after the death of B. At the death of the testator, C has no son, but a son is afterwards born to him during the life of B and is alive at B's death. C's son is entitled to the PKR 1,000.

1137. Similarly if a bequest is made to a person not in existence at the time of the testators death, subject to a prior bequest contained in the will, the later bequest shall be void, unless it comprises the whole of the remaining interest of the testator in the thing bequeathed. Illustrations: (i) Property is bequeathed to A for his life, and after his death to his eldest son for life, and after the death of the latter to his eldest son. At the time of the testators death, A has no son. Here the bequest to A's eldest son is a bequest to a person not in existence at the testators death. It is not a bequest of the whole interest that remains to the testator. The bequest to A's eldest son for his life is void. (ii) A fund is bequeathed to A for his life, and after his death to his daughters. A survives the testator. A has daughters some of whom were not in existence at the testator's death. The bequest to A's daughters comprises the whole interest that remains to the testator in the thing bequeathed. The bequest to A's daughters is valid. (iii) A fund is bequeathed to A for his life, and after his death to his daughters, with a direction that, if any of them marries under the age of 18, her portion shall be settled so that it may belong to herself for life and may be divisible among her children after her death. A has no daughters living at the time of the testators death, but has daughters born afterwards who survive him. Here the direction for a settlement has the effect in the case of each daughter who marries under 18 of substituting for the absolute bequest to her merely for her life; that is to say, a bequest to person not in existence at the time of the testators death of something which is less than the whole interest that remains to the testator in the thing bequeathed. The direction to settle the fund is void. (iv) A bequeaths a sum of money to B for life, and directs that upon the death of B the fund shall be settled upon his daughters, so that the portion of each daughter may belong to herself for life, and may be divided among her children after her death. B has no daughter living at the time of the testators death. In this case the only bequest to the daughters of B is contained in the direction to settle the fund, and this direction amounts to a bequest to person not yet born, of a life-interest in the fund, that is to say, of something which is less than the whole interest that remains to the testator in the thing bequeathed. The direction to settle the fund upon the daughters of B is void.

1138. However, no bequest is valid whereby the vesting of the thing bequeathed may be deleted beyond the lifetime of one or more persons living at the testators death and the minority of some person who shall be in existence at the expiration of that period, and to whom, if he attains full age, the thing bequeathed is to belong. Illustrations: (i) A fund is bequeathed to A for his life and after his death to B for his life; and after B's death to such of the sons of B as shall first attain the age of 25. A and B survive the testator. Here the son of B who shall first attain the age of 25 may be a son born after the death of the testator; such son may not attain 25 until more than 18 years have elapsed from the death of the longer liver of A and B; and the vesting of the fund may thus be delayed beyond the lifetime of A and B and the minority of the sons of B. The bequest after B's death is void. (ii) A fund is bequeathed to A for his life, and after his death to B for the life, and after B's death to such of B's sons as shall first attain the age of 25. B dies in the lifetime of the testator, leaving one or more sons. In this case the sons of B are persons living at the time of the testators decease, and the time when either of them will attain 25 necessarily falls within his own lifetime. The bequest is valid. (iii) A fund is bequeathed to A for his life, and after his death to B for his life, with a direction that after B's death it shall be divided among such of B's children as shall attain the age of 18, but that, if no child of B shall attain that age, the fund shall go to C. Here the time for the division of the fund must arrive at the latest at the expiration of eighteen years from the death of B, a person living at the testators decease. All the bequests are valid. (iv) A fund is bequeathed to trustees for the benefit of the testators daughters, with a direction that, if any of them marry under age, her share of the fund shall be settled so as to devolve after her death upon such of her children as shall attain the age of 18. Any daughter of the testator to whom the direction applies must be in existence at his decease, and any portion of the fund which may eventually be settled as directed must vest not later than eighteen years from the death of the daughters whose share it was. All these provisions are valid.

1139. If a bequest is made to a class of persons with regard to some of whom it is inoperative by reason of the provisions of section 113, or section 114, such bequest shall be void in regard to those persons only and not in regard to the whole class. Illustrations: (i) A fund is bequeathed to A for life, and after his death to all his children who shall attain the age of 25. A survives the testator, and has some children living at the testators death. Each child of A's living at the testators death must attain the age of 25 (if at all) within the limits allowed for a bequest. But A may have children after the testators decease, some of whom may not attain the age of 25 until more than 18 years have elapsed after the decease of A. The bequest to A's children, therefore, is inoperative as to any child born after the testators death and in regard to those who do not attain the age of 25 within 18 years after A's death, but is operative in regard to the other children of A. (ii) A fund is bequeathed to A for his life, and after his death to B, C, D and all other children of A who shall attain the age of 25. B, C, D arc children of A living at the testators decease. In all other respects the case is the same as that supposed in illustration (i). Although the mention of B, C and D does not prevent the bequest from being regarded as a bequest to a class, it is not wholly void. It is operative as regards any of the children B, C or D, who attains the age of 25 within 18 years after A's death.

1140. If any bequest in favour of a person or of a class of persons is void in regard to such person or the whole of such class, any bequest contained in the same will and intended to take effect after or upon failure of such prior bequest is also void. Illustrations: (i) A fund bequeathed to A for his life, and after his death to such of his sons as shall first attain the age of 25, for his life, and after the decease of such son to B. A and B survive the testator. The bequest to B is intended to take effect after the bequest to such of the sons of A as shall first attain the age of 25, which bequest is void under section 114. The bequest to B is void. (ii) A fund is bequeathed to A for his life, and after his death to such of his sons as shall first attain the age of 25, and, if no son of A shall attain that age, to B. A and B survive the testator. The bequest to B is intended to take effect upon failure of the bequest to such of A's sons as shall first attain the age of 25, which bequest is void under section 114. The bequest to B is void.

1141. If a will includes a provision directing that the income generated from any property be accumulated, either wholly or partially, for a period exceeding eighteen years from the testator's death, such a directive shall be deemed void to the extent that it surpasses the prescribed eighteen-year limit. Upon the expiration of this period, the property and any accumulated income shall be disposed of as if the accumulation period had elapsed in accordance with the terms of the will. However, this limitation does not apply to certain specified purposes, where accumulation may be legally directed. These exceptions include: (i) the settlement of debts owed by the testator or any beneficiary under the will, ensuring financial obligations are met before distribution, (ii) the allocation of portions for the children or more remote descendants of the testator or any other beneficiary, securing financial provisions for future generations, and (iii) the preservation, maintenance, or enhancement of any bequeathed property to ensure its value and integrity are upheld. In these instances, accumulation beyond the general limitation may be permitted, as such provisions serve legitimate purposes recognized under succession law.

1142. A person who has a nephew, niece, or any closer relative is restricted from bequeathing property for religious or charitable purposes unless the will containing such a bequest is executed at least twelve months prior to the testator's death. Furthermore, the will must be deposited in a legally designated place for the safe custody of wills within six months of its execution. If these formalities are not complied with, any such bequest shall be rendered void. For instance, if a person with a nephew attempts to leave property for purposes such as aiding the poor, supporting hospitals, providing for sick soldiers, funding orphan education, maintaining schools, constructing bridges or roads, financing religious institutions, or establishing public gardens, the bequests shall have no legal effect due to non-compliance with the prescribed requirements.

1143. Where by the terms of a bequest the legatee is not entitled to immediate possession of the thing bequeathed, a right to receive it at the proper time shall, unless a contrary intention appear by the will, become vested in the legatee on the testators death, and shall pass to the legatees representatives if he dies before that time and without having received the legacy, and in such cases the legacy is from the testators death said to be vested in interest. Explanation: An intention that a legacy to any person shall not become vested in interest in him is not to be inferred merely from a provision whereby the payment or possession of the thing bequeathed is postponed, or whereby a prior interest therein is bequeathed to some other person, or whereby the income arising from the fund bequeathed is directed to be accumulated until the time of payment arrives, or from a provision that, if a particular event shall happen, the legacy shall go over to another person. Illustrations: (i) A bequeaths to B PKR 100, to be paid to him at the death of C. On A's death, the legacy becomes vested in interest in B, and if he dies before C, his representatives are entitled to the legacy. (ii) A bequeaths to B PKR 100, to be paid to him upon his attaining the age of 18. On A's death, the legacy becomes vested in interest in B. (iii) A fund is bequeathed to A for life, and after his death to B. On the testators death, the legacy to B becomes vested in interest in B. (iv) A fund is bequeathed to A until B attains the age of 18 and then to B. The legacy to B is vested in interest from the testators death. (v) A bequeaths the whole of his property to B upon trust to pay certain debts out of the income, and then to make over the fund to C. At A's death, the gift to C becomes vested in interest in him. (vi) A fund is bequeathed to A, B and C in equal shares to be paid to them on their attaining the age of 18, respectively, with a proviso that, if all of them die under the age of 18, the legacy shall devolve upon D. On the death of the testator, the shares vested in interest in A, B and C, subject to be divested in case A, B and C shall all die under 18, and, upon the death of any of them (except the last survivor) under the age of 18, his vested interest passes, so subject, to his representatives.

1144. A legacy bequeathed in case a specified uncertain event shall happen does not vest until that event happens. A legacy bequeathed in case a specified uncertain event shall not happen does not vest until the happening of that event becomes impossible. In either case, until the condition has been fulfilled, the interest of the legatee is called contingent. Exception: Where a fund is bequeathed to any person upon his attaining a particular age, and the will also gives to him absolutely the income to arise from the fund before he reaches that age, or directs the income, or so much of it as may be necessary, to be applied for his benefit, the bequest of the fund is not contingent, Illustrations: (i) A legacy is bequeathed to D in case A, B and C shall all die under the age of 18. D has a contingent interest in the legacy until A, B and C all die under 18, or one of them attains that age. (ii) A sum of money is bequeathed to A 'in case he shall attain the age of 18', or 'when he shall attain the age of 18'. A's interest in the legacy is contingent until the condition is fulfilled by his attaining that age. (iii) An estate is bequeathed to A for life, and after his death to B if B shall then be living; but if B shall not be then living to C. A, B and C survive the testator. B and C each take a contingent interest in the estate until the event which is to vest it in one or in the other has happened. (iv) An estate is bequeathed as in the case last supposed. B dies in the lifetime of A and C. Upon the death of B, C acquires a vested right to obtain possession of the estate upon A's death. (v) A legacy is bequeathed to A when she shall attain the age of 18, or shall marry under that age with the consent of B, with a proviso that, if she neither attains 18 nor marries under that age with B's consent, the legacy shall go to C. A and C each take a contingent interest in the legacy. A attains the age of 18. A becomes absolutely entitled to the legacy although she may have married under 18 without the consent of B. (vi) An estate is bequeathed to A until he shall marry and after that event B. B's interest in the bequest is contingent until the condition is fulfilled by A's marrying. (vii) An estate is bequeathed to A until he shall take advantage of any law for the relief of insolvent debtors, and after that event to B. B's interest in the bequest is contingent until A takes advantage of such a law. (viii) An estate is bequeathed to A if he shall pay PKR 500 to B. A's interest in the bequest is contingent until he has paid PKR 500 to B. (ix) A leaves his farm of Sultanpur Khurd to B, if B shall convey his own farm of Sultanpur Buzurg to C. B's interest in the bequest is contingent until he has conveyed the latter farm to C. (x) A fund is bequeathed to A if B shall not marry C within five years after the testators death; A's interest in the legacy is contingent until the condition is fulfilled by the expiration of the five years without B's having married C, or by the occurrence within that period of an event which makes the fulfilment of the condition impossible. (xi) A fund is bequeathed to A if B shall not make any provision for him by will. The legacy is contingent until B's death. (xii) A bequeaths to B PKR 500 a year upon his attaining the age of 18, and directs that the interest, or a competent part thereof, shall be applied for his benefit until he reaches that age. The legacy is vested. (xiii) A bequeaths to B PKR 500 when he shall attain the age of 18, and directs that a certain sum, out of another fund, shall be applied for his maintenance until he arrives at that age. The legacy is contingent.

1145. When a bequest is made in favour of a specific class of individuals, subject to the condition that only those who attain a particular age shall be entitled to it, no person who has not yet reached the specified age can claim a vested interest in the legacy. For example, if a fund is bequeathed to such children of A who reach the age of 18, and there is a stipulation that while any child remains under 18, the income from their presumptive share shall be utilized for their maintenance and education, no child below the age of 18 acquires a vested interest in the bequest. Their entitlement remains contingent upon fulfilling the age requirement.

1146. If a bequest imposes an obligation on the legatee, he can take nothing by it unless he accepts it fully. Illustration: A, having shares in (X), a prosperous joint stock company and also shares in (Y), a joint stock company in difficulties, in respect of which shares heavy calls are expected to be made, bequeaths to B all his shares in joint stock companies; B refuses to accept the shares in (Y). He forfeits the shares in (X).

1147. If a will contains two separate and independent bequests to the same person, the legatee is at liberty to accept one of them and refuse the other, although the former may be beneficial and the latter onerous. Illustration: A, having a lease for a term of years of a house at a rent which he and his representatives are bound to pay during the term, and which is higher than the house can be let for, bequeaths to B the case and a sum of money. B refuses to accept the lease. He will not by this refusal forfeit the money.

1148. Where a legacy is given if a specified uncertain event shall happen and no time is mentioned in the will for the occurrence of that event, the legacy cannot take effect, unless such event happens before the period when the fund bequeathed is payable or distributable. Illustrations: (i) A legacy is bequeathed to A, and, in case of his death, to B. If A survives the testator, the legacy to B does not take effect. (ii) A legacy is bequeathed to A, and, in case of his death without children, to B. If A survives the testator or dies in his lifetime leaving a child, the legacy to B does not take effect. (iii) A legacy is bequeathed to A when and if he attains the age of 18, and, in case of his death, to B. A attains the age of 18. The legacy to B does not take effect. (iv) A legacy is bequeathed to A for life, and, after his death to B, and, 'in case of B's death without children', to C. The words 'in case of B's death without children' are to be understood as meaning 'in case B dies without children during the lifetime of A'. (v) A legacy is bequeathed to A for life, and, after his death to B, and, 'in case of B. death', to C. The words 'in case of B's death' are to be considered as meaning 'in case B dies in the lifetime of A'.

1149. Where a bequest is made to such of certain persons as shall be surviving at some period, but the exact period is not specified, the legacy shall go to such of them as are alive at the time of payment or distribution, unless a contrary intention appears by the will. Illustrations: (i) Property is bequeathed to A and B to be equally divided between them, or to the survivor of them. If both A and B survive the testator, the legacy is equally divided between them. If A dies before the testator, and B survives the testator, it goes to B. (ii) Property is bequeathed to A for life, and, after his death, to B and C, to be equally divided between them, or to the survivor of them. B dies during the life of A; C survives A. At A's death the legacy goes to C. (iii) Property is bequeathed to A for life, and after his death to B and C, or the survivor, with a direction that, if B should not survive the testator, his children are to stand in his place. C dies during the life of the testator; B survives the testator, but dies in the life time of A. The legacy goes to the representative of B. (iv) Property is bequeathed to A for life, and, after his death, to B and C, with a direction that, in case either of them dies in the lifetime of A, the whole-shall go to the survivor. B dies in the lifetime of A. Afterwards C dies in the lifetime of A. The legacy goes to the representative of C.

1150. A bequest upon an impossible condition is void. Illustrations: (i) An estate is bequeathed to A on condition that he shall walk 100 miles in an hour. The bequest is void. (ii) A bequeaths PKR 500 to B on condition that he shall marry A's daughter. A's daughter was dead at the date of the will. The bequest is void. A bequest upon a condition, the fulfilment of which would be contrary to law or to morality, is void. Illustrations: (i) A bequeaths PKR 500 to B on condition that he shall murder C. The bequest is void. (ii) A bequeaths PKR 5,000 to his niece if she will desert her husband. The bequest is void.

1151. Where a will imposes a condition to be fulfilled before the legatee can take a vested interest in the tiling bequeathed, the condition shall be considered to have been fulfilled if it has been substantially complied with. Illustrations: (i) A legacy is bequeathed to A on condition that he shall marry with the consent of B, C, D and E. A marries with the written consent of B, C is present at the marriage. D sends a present to A previous to the marriage. E has been personally informed by A of his intentions, and has made no objection. A has fulfilled the condition. (ii) A legacy is bequeathed to A on condition that he shall marry with the consent of B, C and D. D dies. A marries with the consent of B and C. A has fulfilled the condition. (iii) A legacy is bequeathed to A on condition that he shall marry with the consent of B, C and D. A marries in the lifetime of B, C and D, with the consent of B and C only. A has not fulfilled the condition. (iv) A legacy is bequeathed to A on condition that he shall marry with the consent of B, C and D. A obtains the unconditional assent of B, C and D to his marriage with E. Afterwards B, C and D capriciously retract their consent. A marries E. A has fulfilled the condition. (v) A legacy is bequeathed to A on condition that he shall marry with the consent of B, C and D. A marries without the consent of B, C and D but obtains their consent after the marriage. A has not fulfilled the condition. (vi) A makes his will whereby he bequeaths a sum of money to B if B shall marry with the consent of A's executors. B marries during the lifetime of A, and A afterwards expresses his approbation of the marriage. A dies. The bequest to B takes effect. (vii) A legacy is bequeathed to A if he executes a certain document within a time specified in the will. The document is executed by A within a reasonable time, but not within the time specified in the will. A has not performed the condition, and is not entitled to receive the legacy.

1152. If there is a bequest to one person and a bequest of the same thing to another, if the prior bequest shall fail, the second bequest shall take effect upon the failure of the prior bequest although the failure may not have occurred in the manner contemplated by the testator. Illustrations: (i) A bequeaths a sum of money to his own children surviving him, and, they all die under 18, to B. A dies without having sever had a child. The bequest to B takes effect. (ii) A bequeaths a sum of money to B, on condition that he shall execute a certain document within three months after A's death, and, if he should neglect to do so, to C. B dies in the testators lifetime. The bequest to C takes effect.

1153. If a will explicitly states that a subsequent bequest shall only take effect upon the failure of a prior bequest in a specified manner, the subsequent bequest will not be valid unless the prior bequest fails in that exact manner. For instance, if A bequeaths his property to his wife but provides that, in the event of her predeceasing him, the same property shall pass to B, the effectiveness of B's bequest depends strictly on the wife dying before A. If A and his wife die simultaneously under circumstances where it cannot be determined who passed away first, the bequest to B does not take effect.

1154. A bequest may be made to any person with the condition super added that, in case a specified uncertain event shall happen, the thing bequeathed shall go to another person, or that in case a specified uncertain event shall not happen, the thing bequeathed shall go over to another person. In each case the ulterior bequest is subject to the rules contained. Illustrations: (i) A sum of money is bequeathed to A, to be paid to him at the age of 18, and if he shall die before he attains that age, to B. A takes a vested interest in the legacy subject to be divested and to go to B in case A dies under 18. (ii) An estate is bequeathed to A with a proviso that if A shall dispute the competency of the testator to make a will, the estate shall go to B. A disputes the competency of the testator to make a will. The estate goes to B. (iii) A sum of money is bequeathed to A for life, and, after his death, to B; but if B shall then be dead, leaving a son, such son is to stand in the place of B. B takes a vested interest in the legacy, subject to be divested if he dies leaving a son in A's lifetime. (iv) A sum of money is bequeathed to A and B, and if either should die during the life of C, then to the survivor living at the death of C. A and B die before C. The gift over cannot take effect, but the representative of A takes one-half of the money, and the representative of B takes the other half. (v) A bequeaths to B the interest of a fund for life, and directs the fund to be divided at her death equally among her three children, or such of them as shall be living at her death. All the children of B die in B's lifetime. The bequest over cannot take effect, but the interests of the children pass to their representatives.

1155. An ulterior bequest of the kind contemplated cannot take effect, unless the condition is strictly fulfilled. Illustrations: (i) A legacy is bequeathed to A, with a proviso that, if he marries without the consent of B, C and D, the legacy shall go to E. D dies. Even if A marries without the consent of B and C, the gift to E does not take effect. (ii) A legacy is bequeathed to A, with a proviso that, if he marries without the consent of B, the legacy shall go to C. A marries with the consent of B. He afterwards becomes a widower and marries again without the consent of B. The bequest to C does not take effect. (iii) A legacy is bequeathed to A, to be paid at 18; or marriage, with a proviso that, if A dies under 18 or marries without the consent of B, the legacy shall go to C. A marries under 18, without the consent of B. The bequest to C takes effect.

1156. If the ulterior bequest be not valid, the original bequest is not affected by it. Illustrations: (i) An estate is bequeathed to A for his life with condition super added that, if he shall not on a given day walk 100 miles in an hour, the estate shall go to B. The condition being void, A retains his estate as if no condition had been inserted in the will. (ii) An estate is bequeathed to A for her life and, if she does not desert her husband, to D. A is entitled to the estate during her life as if no condition had been inserted in the will. (iii) An estate is bequeathed to A for life, and, if he marries, to the eldest son of B for life. B, at the date of the testators death had not had a son. The bequest over is void under section 105, and A is entitled to the estate during his life.

1157. A bequest may be made with the condition super added that it shall cease to have effect in case a specified uncertain event shall happen, or in case a specified uncertain event shall not happen. Illustrations: (i) An estate is bequeathed to A for his life, with a proviso that, in case he shall cut down a certain wood, the bequest shall cease to have any effect. A cuts down the wood. He loses his life interest in the estate. (ii) An estate is bequeathed to A, provided that, if he marries under the age of 25 without the consent of the executors named in the will, the estate shall cease to belong to him. A marries under 25 without the consent of the executors. The estate ceases to belong to him. (iii) An estate is bequeathed to A, provided that, if he shall not go to England within three years after the testators death, his interest in the estate shall cease. A does not go to England within the time prescribed. His interest in the estate ceases. (iv) An estate is bequeathed to A, with a proviso that, if she becomes a nun, she shall cease to have any interest in the estate. A becomes a nun. She loses her interest under the will. (v) A fund is bequeathed to A for life, and, after his death, to B, if B shall be then living, with a proviso that, if B shall become a nun, the bequest to her shall cease to have any effect. B becomes a nun in the life time of A. She thereby loses her contingent interest in the fund.

1158. For a condition leading to the termination of a bequest to be legally valid, it must be based on an event that can lawfully serve as a condition for a bequest. The condition must be clear, possible, and legally enforceable; otherwise, it will have no effect on the bequest. Any condition that is vague, impossible, or contrary to law will not be recognized as a valid ground for the bequest to cease.

1159. Where a bequest is made with a condition superadded that, unless the legatee shall perform a certain act, the subject matter of the bequest shall go to another person, or the bequest shall cease to have effect but no time is specified for the performance of the act; if the legatee takes any step which renders impossible or indefinitely postpones the performance of the act required, the legacy shall go as if the legatee had died without performing such act. Illustrations: (i) A bequest is made to A, with a proviso that, unless he enters the Army, the legacy shall go over to B. A takes Holy Orders, and thereby renders it impossible that he should fulfil the condition. B is entitled to receive the legacy. (ii) A bequest is made to A, with a proviso that it shall cease to have any effect if he does not marry B's daughter. A marries a stranger and thereby indefinitely postpones the fulfilment of the conditions. The bequest ceases to have effect.

1160. Where the will requires an act to be performed by the legatee within a specified time, either as a condition to be fulfilled before the legacy is enjoyed, or as a condition upon the non-fulfilment of which the subject-matter of the bequest is to go over to another person or the bequest is to cease to have effect, the act must be performed within the time specified, unless the performance of it be prevented by fraud, in which case such further time shall be allowed as shall be requisite to make up for the delay caused by such fraud.

§11. Legacies

1161. The Succession Act, 1925, sections 142~149 (Chapter XIV) deals with the specific legacies. If a testator bequeaths to any person a specified part of his property, which is distinguished from all other parts of his property, the legacy is said to be specific. Illustrations: (i) A bequeaths to B 'the diamond ring presented to me by C': 'my gold chain': 'a certain bale of wool': 'a certain piece of cloth': 'all my household goods which shall be in or about my dwelling-house in M Street, in Karachi, at time of my death': 'the sum of PKR 1,000 in a certain chest': 'the debt which B owes me': 'all my bills, bonds and securities belonging to me lying in my lodgings in Karachi': 'all my furniture in my house in Karachi': 'all my goods on board a certain ship now lying in the river Indus': 'PKR 2,000 which I have in the hands of C': 'the money due to me on the bond of D': 'my mortgage on the Rahimyarkhan factory': 'one-half of the money owing to me on my mortgage of Rahimyarkhan factory': 'PKR 1,000, being part of a debt due to me from C': 'my capital stock of PKR 1,000 in East India Stock': 'my promissory notes of the Federal Government for PKR 10,000 in their 4% loan': 'all such sums of money as my executors may, after my death, receive in respect of the debt due to me from the insolvent firm of D and Company': 'all the wine which I may have in my cellar at the time of my death': 'such of my horses as B may select': 'all my shares in the National Bank of Pakistan': 'all my shares in the National Bank of Pakistan which I may possess at the time of my death': 'all the money which I have in the 5½% loan of the federal Government': 'all the Government securities I shall be entitled to at the time of my decease'. Each of these legacies is specific. (ii) A, having Government promissory notes for PKR 10,000, bequeaths to his executors 'Government promissory notes for PKR 10,000 in trust to sell' for the benefit of B. The legacy is specific. (iii) A, having property at Peshawar, and also in other places, bequeaths to B all his property at Peshawar. The legacy is specific. (iv) A bequeaths to B his house in Karachi: his zamindari of Rahimyarkhan: his Talaq of Nawabshah: his lease of the indigo-factory of Salkya: an annuity of PKR 500 out of the rents of his zamindari of W. A directs his zamindari of X to be sold, and the proceeds to be invested for the benefit of B. Each of these bequests is specific. (v) A by his will charges his zamindari of Y with an annuity of PKR 1,000 to C during his life, and subject to this charge he bequeaths the zamindari to D. Each of these bequests is specific. (vi) A bequeaths a sum of money – to buy a house in Karachi for B: to buy an estate in Zila Peshawar for B: to buy a diamond ring for B: to buy a horse for B: to be invested in shares in the National Bank of Pakistan for B: to be invested in Government securities for B. 'A bequeaths to B a diamond ring: a horse': 'PKR 10,000 worth of Government securities': an 'annuity of PKR 500': 'PKR 2,000 to be paid in cash': 'so much money as will produce PKR 5,000 4% Government securities'. These bequests are not specific. (vii) A, having property in England and property in

Pakistan, bequeaths a legacy to B, and directs that it shall be paid out of the property which he may leave in Pakistan. He also bequeaths a legacy to C, and directs that it shall be paid out of property which he may leave in England. No one of these legacies is specific.

1162. If a certain sum is bequeathed, the legacy is not specific merely because the stock, funds or securities in which it is invested are described in the will. Illustration: A bequeaths to B 'PKR 10,000 of my funded property': 'PKR 10,000 of my property now invested in shares of the National Bank of Pakistan': 'PKR 10,000, at present secured by mortgage of Rahimyarkhan factory'. No one of these legacies is specific.

1163. If a bequest is made in general terms of a certain amount of any kind of stock, the legacy is not specific merely because the testator was at the date of his will, possessed of stock of the specified kind, to an equal or greater amount than the amount bequeathed. Illustration: A bequeaths to B PKR 5,000, 4% Government securities. A had at the date of the will 5% Government securities for PKR 5,000. The legacy is not specific.

1164. A money legacy is not specific merely because the will directs its payment to be postponed until some part of the property of the testator has been reduced to a certain form, or remitted to a certain place. Illustration: A bequeaths to B PKR 10,000 and directs that this legacy shall be paid as soon as A's property in India shall be realized in England. The legacy is not specific.

1165. If a will includes a residuary bequest of the testator's estate while also listing certain items of property that were not previously disposed of, those enumerated items shall not be considered as specifically bequeathed. Instead, they shall be treated as part of the general residue of the estate, unless a contrary intention is clearly expressed in the will.

1166. Where property is specifically bequeathed to two or more persons in succession, it shall be retained in the form in which the testator left it, although it may be of such a nature that its value is continually decreasing. Illustrations: (i) A, having lease of a house for a term of years, fifteen of which were unexpired at the time of his death, has bequeathed the lease to B for his life, and after B's death to C. B is to enjoy the property as A left it, although, if B lives for fifteen years. C can take nothing under the bequest. (ii) A, having an annuity during the life of B, bequeaths it to C, for his life, and, after C's death, to D. C is to enjoy the annuity as A left it, although, if B dies before D, D can take nothing under the bequest.

1167. If property comprised in a bequest to two or more persons in succession is not specifically bequeathed, it shall, in the absence of any direction to the contrary, be sold, and the proceeds of the sale shall be invested in such securities as the High Court may by any general rule authorize or direct, and the fund thus constituted shall be enjoyed by the successive legatees according to the terms of the will. Illustration: A, having a lease for a term of years, bequeaths ail his property to B for life, and, after B's death, to C. The lease must be sold, the proceeds invested as stated in this Motion and the annual income arising from the fund is to be paid to B for life. At B's death the capital of the fund is to be paid to C. If there is a deficiency of assets to pay legacies, a specific legacy is not liable to abate with the general legacies.

1168. The Succession Act, 1925 (sections 150 and 151) deals with demonstrative legacy. Where a testator bequeaths a certain sum of money, or a certain quantity of any other commodity, and refers to a particular fund or stock so as to constitute the same the primary fund or stock out of which payment is to be made, the legacy is said to be demonstrative. Explanation: The distinction between a specific legacy and a demonstrative legacy consists in this, that where specified property is given to the legatee, the legacy is specific; where the legacy is directed to be paid out of specified property, it is demonstrative. Illustrations: (i) A bequeaths to B PKR 1,000, being part of a debt due to him from W. He also bequeaths to C PKR 1,000 to be paid out of the debt due to him from W. The legacy to B is specific, the legacy to C is demonstrative. (ii) A bequeaths to B 'ten bushels of the corn which shall grow in my field of Green Acre': '80 chests of the indigo which shall be made at my factory of Rahimyarkhan': 'PKR 10,000 out of my 5% promissory notes of the Federal Government': 'an annuity of PKR 500' 'from my funded property': 'PKR 1,000 out of the sum of PKR 2,000 due to me by C': an annuity, and directs it to be paid 'out of the rents arising from my Taluqa of Nawabshah'. (iii) A bequeaths to B: 'PKR 10,000 out of my estate at Nawabshah', or charges it on his estate at Nawabshah: 'PKR 10,000, being my share of the capital embarked in a certain business', Each of these bequests is demonstrative.

1169. Where a portion of a fund is specifically bequeathed and a legacy is directed to be paid out of the same fund, the portion specifically bequeathed shall first be paid to the legatee and the demonstrative legacy shall be paid out of the residue of the fund and, so far as the residue shall be deficient, out of the general assets of the testator. Illustration: A bequeaths to B PKR 1,000, being part of a debt due to him from W. He also bequeaths to C PKR 1,000 to be paid out of the debt due to him from W. The debt due to A from W is only PKR 1,500 of these PKR 1,500, PKR 1,000 belong to B, and PKR 500 are to be paid to C. C is also to receive PKR 500 out of the general assets of the testator.

1170. The sections 152~166 of the Succession Act, 1925 deals with the redemption of legacies. If anything which has been specifically bequeathed does not belong to the testator at the time of his death, or has been converted into property of a different kind, the legacy is a deemed: that is, it cannot take effect, by reason of the subject-matter having been withdrawn from the operation of the will. Illustrations: (i) 'A bequeaths to B – the diamond ring presented to me by C': 'my gold chain': 'a certain bale of wool': 'a certain piece of cloth': 'all my household goods which shall be in or about my dwelling-house in M Street in Sahiwal, at the time of my death': A in his lifetime, – sells or gives away the ring: converts the chain into a cup: converts the wool into cloth: makes the cloth into a garment: takes another house into which he removes all his goods.

Each of these legacies is a deemed. (ii) A bequeaths to B – 'the sum of PKR 1,000 in a certain chest': 'all the horses in my stable'. At the death of A, no money is found in the chest, and no horses in the stable. The legacies are a deemed. (iii) A bequeaths to B certain bales of goods. A takes the goods with him on a voyage. The ship and goods are lost at sea, and A is drowned. The legacy is a deemed.

1171. A demonstrative legacy does not lose its character merely because the specific property designated for its payment under the will is no longer in existence at the time of the testator's death or has been transformed into a different form of property. In such cases, the legacy shall be satisfied from the general assets of the testator's estate.

1172. Where the thing specifically bequeathed is the right to receive something of value from a third party, and the testator himself receives it, the bequest is a deemed. Illustrations: (i) A bequeaths to B 'the debt which C owes me'; 'PKR 2,000 which I have in the hands of D': 'the money due to me on the bond of E': 'my mortgage on the Rahimyarkhan factory'. All these debts arc extinguished in A's lifetime, some with and some without his consent. All the legacies are a deemed. (ii) A bequeaths to B his interest in certain policies of life assurance. A in his lifetime receives the amount of the policies. The legacy is a deemed.

1173. The receipt by the testator of a part of an entire thing specifically bequeathed shall operate as a redemption of the legacy to the extent of the sum so received. Illustration: A bequeaths to B 'the debt due to me by C'. The debt amounts to PKR 10,000. C pays to A PKR 5,000 the one-half of the debt. The legacy is revoked by redemption, so far as regards the PKR 5,000 received by A.

1174. If a portion of an entire fund or stock is specifically bequeathed, the receipt by the testator of a portion of the fund or stock shall operate as a redemption only to the extent of the amount so received; and the residue of the fund or stock shall be applicable to the discharge of the specific legacy. Illustration: A bequeaths to B one-half of the sum of PKR 10,000 due to him from W. A in his lifetime receives PKR 6,000, part of the PKR 10,000. The PKR 4,000 which are due from W to A at the time of his death belong to B under the specific bequest.

1175. Where a portion of a fund is specifically bequeathed to one legatee, and a legacy charged on the same fund is bequeathed to another legatee, then, if the testator receives a portion of that fund, and the remainder of the fund is insufficient to pay both the specific and the demonstrative legacy, the specific legacy shall be paid first, and the residue (if any) of the fund shall be applied so far as it will extend in payment of the demonstrative legacy, and the rest of the demonstrative legacy shall be paid out of the general assets of the testator. Illustration: A bequeaths to B PKR 1,000, part of the debt of PKR 2,000 due to him from W. He also bequeaths to C PKR 1,000 to be paid out of the debt due to him from W. A afterwards receives PKR 500, part of that debt, and dies leaving only PKR 1,500 due to him from W. Of these PKR 1,500, PKR 1,000 belong to B, and PKR 500 are to be paid to C. C is also to receive PKR 500 out of the general assets of the testator.

1176. Where stock which has been specifically bequeathed does not exist at the testator's death, the legacy is a deemed. Illustration: A bequeaths to B 'my capital stock of 1,000 in East India Stock': 'my promissory notes of the Federal Government for PKR 10,000 in their 4% loan'. A sells the stock and the notes. The legacy is a deemed.

1177. Where stock which has been specifically bequeathed exists only in part at the testator's death, the legacy is a deemed so far as regards that part of the stock – which has ceased to exist. Illustration: A bequeaths to B his PKR 10,000 in the 5½% loan of the Federal Government, A sells one-half of his PKR 10,000 in the loan in question. One-half of the legacy is a deemed.

1178. A specific bequest of goods under a description connecting them with a certain place is not a deemed by reason that they have been removed from such place from any temporary cause, or by fraud, or without the knowledge or sanction of the testator. Illustrations: (i) A bequeaths to B 'all my household goods which shall be in or about my dwelling-house in Faisalabad at the time of my death'. The goods are removed from the house to save them from fire. A dies before they are brought back. (ii) A bequeaths to B 'all my household goods which shall be in or about my dwelling-house in Faisalabad at the time of my death'. During A's absence upon a journey, the whole of title goods are removed from the house. A dies without having sanctioned their removal. Neither of these legacies is a deemed.

1179. The removal of the thing bequeathed from the place in which it is stated in the will to be situated does not constitute redemption, where the place is only referred to in order to complete the description of what the testator meant to bequeath. Illustrations: (i) A bequeaths to B 'all the bills, bonds and other securities for money belonging to me now lying in my lodgings in Karachi'. At the time of his death, these effects had been removed from his lodgings in Karachi. (ii) A bequeaths to B all his furniture then in his house in Karachi. The testator has a house at Karachi and another at Quetta, in which he lives alternately, being possessed of one set of furniture only which he removes with himself to each house. At the time of his death, the furniture is in the house at Quetta. (iii) A bequeaths to B all his goods on board a certain ship then lying in the river Indus. The goods are removed by A's directions to a warehouse, in which they remain at the time of A's death. No one of these legacies is revoked by redemption.

1180. Where the thing bequeathed is not the right to receive something of value from a third person, but the money or other commodity which may be received from the third person by the testator himself or by his representatives, the receipt of such sum of money or other commodity by the testator shall not constitute an redemption; but if he mixes it up with the general mass of his property, the legacy is a deemed. Illustration: A bequeaths to B whatever sum may be received from his claim on C. A receives the whole of his claim on C, and sets it apart from the general mass of his property. The legacy is not a deemed.

1181. Where a thing specifically bequeathed undergoes a change between the date of the will and the testators death, and the change takes place by operation of law, or in the course of execution of the provisions of any legal instrument under which the thing bequeathed was held, the legacy is not a deemed by reason of such change. Illustrations: (i) A bequeaths to B 'all the money which I have in the 5½% loan' of the 'Federal Government'. The securities for the 5½% loan are converted during A's lifetime into 5% stock. (ii) A bequeaths to B the sum of 2,000 invested in Consoles in the names of trustees for A. The sum of 2,000 is transferred by the trustees into A's own name. (iii) A bequeaths to B the sum of PKR 10,000 in promissory notes of the Federal Government which he has power under his marriage settlement to dispose of by will. Afterwards, in A's lifetime, the fund is converted into Consoles by virtue of an authority contained in the settlement. No one of these legacies has been a deemed.

1182. Where a thing specifically bequeathed undergoes a change between the date of the will and the testators death, and the change takes place without the knowledge or sanction of the testator, the legacy is not a deemed. Illustrations: A bequeaths to B 'all my 3% Consoles'. The Consoles arc, without A's knowledge, sold by his agent, and the proceeds converted into East India Stock. This legacy is not a deemed.

1183. If stock that has been specifically bequeathed is lent to a third party with the stipulation that it must be replaced, and it is indeed replaced, the bequest remains valid and is not considered to have failed. Similarly, if stock that was specifically bequeathed is sold but an equivalent quantity of the same stock is later acquired and remains part of the testator's estate at the time of death, the bequest continues to hold effect.

1184. Under sections 332~337 of the Succession Act, 1925, the assent of the executor or administrator is necessary to complete a legatees title to his legacy. Illustrations: (i) A by his will bequeaths to B his Government paper which is in deposit with the National Bank of Pakistan. The Bank has no authority to deliver the securities, nor B a right to take possession of them, without the assent of the executor. (ii) A by his will has bequeathed to C his house in Quetta in the tenancy of B. C is not entitled to receive the rents without the assent of the executor or administrator.

1185. The assent of the executor or administrator to a specific bequest shall be sufficient to divest his interest as executor or administrator therein, and to transfer the subject of the bequest of the legatee, unless the nature or the circumstances of the property require that it shall be transferred in a particular way. This assent may be verbal, and it may be either express or implied from the conduct of the executor or administrator. Illustrations: (i) A horse is bequeathed. The executor requests the legatee to dispose of it, or a third party proposes to purchase the horse from the executor, and he directs him to apply to the legatee. Assent to the legacy is implied. (ii) The interest of a fund is directed by the will to be applied for the maintenance of the legatee during his minority. The executor commences so to apply it. This is an assent to the whole of the bequest. (iii) A bequest is made of a fund to A and after him to B. The executor pays the interest of the fund to A. This is an implied assent to the bequest to B. (iv) Executors die after paying all the debts of the testator, but before satisfaction of specific legacies. Assent to the legacies may be presumed. (v) A person to whom a specific article has been bequeathed takes possession of it and retains it without any objection on the part of the executor. His assent may be presumed.

1186. The assent of an executor or administrator to a legacy may be conditional, and if the condition is one which he has a right to enforce, and it is not performed, there is no assent. Illustrations: (i) A bequeaths to B his lands of Sultanpur, which at the date of the will, and at the death of A, were subject to a mortgage for PKR 10,000. The executor assents to the bequest, on condition that B shall within a limited time pay the amount due on the mortgage at the testators death. The amount is not paid. There is no assent. (ii) The executor assents to a bequest on condition that the legatee shall pay him a sum of money. The payment is not made. The assent is nevertheless valid.

1187. When an executor or administrator is also a legatee, their assent to their own legacy is required to establish their entitlement to it, just as it would be for any other beneficiary. This assent may be either expressly stated or implied through their actions. Assent shall be presumed if, in the course of administering the estate, the executor or administrator performs an act that aligns with their role as a legatee rather than solely as an executor or administrator. For instance, if an executor collects rent from a property or interest from government securities that have been bequeathed to them and uses the proceeds for their own benefit, such conduct constitutes an implied assent to the legacy.

1188. The assent of the executor or administrator to a legacy gives effect to it from the death of the testator. Illustrations: (i) A legatee sells his legacy before it is assented to by the executor. The executor's subsequent assent operates for the benefit of the purchaser and completes his title to the legacy. (ii) A bequeaths PKR 1,000 to B with interest from his death. The executor does not assent to his legacy until the expiration of a year from A's death. B is entitled to interest from the death of A.

1189. An executor or administrator is not obligated to distribute or settle any legacy until one year has passed since the testator's death, regardless of any contrary provision in the will. For example, if a testator stipulates in their will that legacies must be paid within six months of their passing, the executor is not legally required to comply with this timeline and retains the right to withhold payment until the completion of the one-year period.

1190. The Succession Act, 1925 (sections 349~355) provide detail of legacies. The legatee of a specific legacy is entitled to the clear produce thereof, if any, from the testator's death. Exception: A specific bequest, contingent in its term; does not comprise the produce of the legacy between the death of the testator and the vesting of the legacy. The clear produce of it forms part of the residue of the testator's estate. Illustrations: (i) A bequeaths his flock of sheep to B. Between the death of A and delivery by his executor, the sheep are shorn or some of the ewes produce lambs. The wool and lambs are the property of B. (ii) A bequeaths his Government securities to B, but postpones the delivery of them till the death of C. The interest which falls due between the death of A and the death of C belongs to B, and must, unless he is a minor, be paid to him as it is received. (iii) The testator bequeaths all his 4% Government promissory notes to A when he shall complete the age of 18. A, if he completes that age, is entitled to receive the notes, but the interest which accrues in respect of them between the testator's death and A's completing 18, form part of the residue.

1191. A legatee receiving a general residuary bequest is entitled to the income generated by the residuary estate from the date of the testator's death. However, an exception applies when the bequest is contingent in nature. In such cases, any income that accrues on the residuary fund between the testator's death and the vesting of the legacy does not automatically form part of the legacy. Instead, such income remains undisposed of and is treated separately. Illustrations (i) If a testator leaves the residue of his estate to A, a minor, with instructions that it shall be paid to him upon reaching the age of 18, A is entitled to the income generated from the estate from the testator's death. (ii) If a testator bequeaths the residue of his estate to A, contingent upon A reaching the age of 18, A will only receive the residue upon fulfilling this condition. The income accrued from the time of the testator's death until A reaches the specified age does not automatically form part of A's legacy and remains un disposed of.

1192. Where no time has been fixed for the payment of a general legacy, interest begins to run from expiration of one year from the testator's death. Exception: (1) Where the legacy is bequeathed in satisfaction of a debt, interest runs from the death of the testator. (2) Where the testator was a parent or a more remote ancestor of the legatee, or has put himself in the place of a parent of the legatee, the legacy shall bear interest from the death of the testator. (3) Where a sum is bequeathed to a minor with a direction to pay for his maintenance out of it, interest is payable from the death of the testator.

1193. When a specific time is set for the payment of a general legacy, interest on that legacy begins to accrue from the designated time. The interest accumulated before the legacy is transferred becomes part of the testator's residuary estate. Exception: If the legatee is a minor and the testator is their parent, a more distant ancestor, or has assumed a parental role, the legacy will accrue interest from the date of the testator's death. However, this does not apply if the will either provides a separate sum for the minor's maintenance or explicitly states otherwise.

1194. The applicable rate of interest on a legacy is generally 4% per annum. However, if the testator was a Hindu, Muslim, Buddhist, Sikh, Jaina, or classified as an exempted person, the rate increases to 6% per annum. Additionally, no interest shall be paid on any outstanding annuity within the first year following the testator's death, even if the will specifies an earlier date for the first annuity payment.

1195. When a will instructs that a certain sum of money be invested to generate an annuity, interest on that sum shall accrue from the date of the testator's death.

1196. Sections 356~367 of the Succession Act, 1925 deals with the refunding of legacies. It is provided that when an executor or administrator has paid a legacy under the order of a Court, he is entitled to call upon the legatee to refund in the event of the assets proving insufficient to pay all the legacies.

1197. f an executor or administrator willingly disburses a legacy, they cannot later demand reimbursement from the legatee if the estate's assets turn out to be inadequate to cover all the legacies.

1198. If the period specified in the will for fulfilling a condition has passed without its fulfilment, and the executor or administrator has lawfully distributed the estate without fraud, they are not liable to return the legacy if additional time for compliance is later granted under section 137 and the condition is subsequently met. Instead, the individuals who received the distributed assets must refund the amount.

1199. If an executor or administrator has already distributed the estate through legacies and later becomes aware of an outstanding debt that must be settled, they have the right to require each legatee to return a proportionate share to cover the debt.

1200. If an executor or administrator issues notices, as required by the High Court's general rules or in accordance with the procedure followed in an administration suit, inviting creditors and claimants to submit their claims against the deceased's estate within a specified period, they may, upon the expiration of that period, proceed to distribute the assets in settlement of known valid claims. The executor or administrator will not be held liable for any assets distributed to claimants they were unaware of at the time. However, this does not affect the rights of creditors or claimants to trace and recover assets from those who have received them.

1201. A creditor who has not been paid may demand repayment from a legatee who has already received their legacy, regardless of whether the deceased's estate had sufficient assets at the time of death to cover both debts and legacies. This right applies irrespective of whether the executor or administrator made the legacy payment voluntarily or under the belief that all obligations had been met.

1202. If, at the time of the testator's death, the estate had enough assets to cover all legacies, a legatee who has not received their share, or who was required to refund under section 361, cannot compel another legatee – who has already received full payment to return any portion, regardless of whether the payment was made voluntarily or through legal proceedings. This holds true even if the estate later becomes insufficient due to mismanagement by the executor.

1203. If the estate was insufficient to cover all legacies at the time of the testator's death, a legatee who has not received their share must first seek payment from the executor or administrator, provided they are financially capable. However, if the executor or administrator is insolvent or not legally responsible for the shortfall, the unpaid legatee may require those who have already received their legacies to refund a proportional amount.

1204. The refunding of one legatee to another shall not exceed the sum by which the satisfied legacy ought to have been reduced if the estate had been properly administered. Illustration: A has bequeathed PKR 240 to B, PKR 480 to C, and PKR 720 to D. The assets are only PKR 1,200 and, if properly administered, would give PKR 200 to B, PKR 400 to C, and PKR 600 to D. C and D have been paid their legacies in full, leaving nothing to B. B can oblige C to refund PKR 80, and D to refund PKR 120. The refunding shall in all cases be without interest.

1205. After settling all debts and legacies, any remaining portion of the deceased's estate shall be handed over to the residuary legatee if one has been designated in the will. In cases where a person who was not domiciled in Pakistan passes away, leaving assets both within Pakistan and in their country of domicile, and where probate or letters of administration have been granted separately in each jurisdiction, the executor or administrator in Pakistan after issuing the required notices under section 360 and settling known lawful claims may, instead of directly distributing the surplus to beneficiaries residing outside Pakistan, transfer the remaining assets to the executor or administrator in the country of domicile, provided they consent, for further distribution in accordance with the will.

1206. Sections 341~348 details with the investment of funds to provide for legacies. It is stated that where a legacy, not being a specific legacy, is given for life, the sum bequeathed shall at the end of the year be invested in such securities as the High Court may by any general rule authorize or direct, and the proceeds thereof shall be paid to the legatee as the same Investment of sum bequeathed, where legacy, not specific given for life shall accrue due.

1207. When a general legacy is directed to be paid at a future date, the executor or administrator must allocate and invest an adequate sum in securities as specified under section 341 to ensure its fulfilment. Any interest or income generated from such an investment in the interim shall be considered part of the residuary estate of the testator.

1208. If an annuity is bequeathed without any specific fund being designated for its payment or set aside under the terms of the will, a Government annuity of the specified amount shall be acquired. In cases where such an annuity is unavailable, an equivalent sum sufficient to generate the required annuity shall be invested in securities as prescribed under section 341 to ensure its fulfilment.

1209. When a bequest is conditional upon a future event, the executor or administrator is not obligated to set aside and invest the amount of the legacy. Instead, the entire remaining estate may be handed over to the residuary legatee, provided that the legatee furnishes adequate security to ensure payment of the legacy should the contingency occur.

1210. If a testator has left the residue of their estate to a beneficiary for life without specifying any particular securities for investment, any portion of the estate that is not already invested in securities mentioned in section 341 at the time of the testator's death shall be liquidated and invested accordingly. However, this provision does not apply in cases where the deceased was a Hindu, Muslim, Buddhist, Sikh, Jaina, or any other exempted person.

1211. If a testator has left the residue of their estate to a beneficiary for life with instructions that it be invested in specific securities, any portion of the estate not already invested in those designated securities at the time of the testator's death shall be converted into cash and allocated accordingly to fulfil the testator's directive.

1212. The conversion and investment required under sections 345 and 346 shall be carried out at such times and in such a manner as the executor or administrator deems appropriate. Until the process is completed, the individual entitled to receive income from the invested fund shall instead receive interest at a rate of 4% per annum, based on the market value of the uninvested portion of the fund as assessed at the testator's death. However, if the testator was a Hindu, Muslim, Buddhist, Sikh, Jaina, or an exempted person, the applicable interest rate prior to investment completion shall be 6% per annum.

1213. (1) Where, by the terms of a bequest, the legatee is entitled to the immediate payment or possession of the money or thing bequeathed, but is a minor, and there is no direction in the will to pay it to any person on his behalf, the executor or administrator shall pay or deliver the same into the Court of the District Judge, by whom or by whose District Delegate the probate was, or letters of administration with the will annexed were, granted, to the account of the legatee, unless the legatee is a ward of the Court of Wards. (2) If the legatee is a ward of the Court of Wards, the legacy shall be paid to the Court of Wards to his account. (3) Such payment into the Court of the District Judge, or to the Court of Wards, as the case may be, shall be a sufficient discharge for the money so paid. (4) Money when paid in under this section shall be invested in the purchase of Government securities, which, with the interest thereon, shall be transferred or paid to the person entitled thereto or otherwise applied for his benefit, as the Judge or the Court of Wards, as the case may be may direct.

§12. GRANTS

1214. Sections 237 to 260 of the Succession Act, 1925, pertain to limited grants. According to section 237, if a will has been lost or misplaced after the testator's death, or has been accidentally or wrongfully destroyed without any intentional act by the testator, and a copy or draft of the will is available, probate may be issued based on that copy or draft. However, this grant remains limited until the original will or an authenticated copy is presented.

1215. As per section 238 of the Succession Act, 1925, if a will has been lost or destroyed without any copy or draft being preserved, probate may still be granted, provided that its contents can be proven through credible evidence.

1216. If the original will is in the possession of someone residing outside the province where the probate application is filed, and that person refuses or neglects to surrender it, but a copy has been forwarded to the executor, probate may be issued based on the transmitted copy. This provisional grant ensures the administration of the estate is not unduly delayed. However, such probate remains subject to revocation or confirmation upon the production of the original will or an authenticated copy, ensuring the rightful execution of the testator's intentions.

1217. If the will of the deceased cannot be located, but there is sufficient reason to believe that a valid will exists, the court may issue letters of administration on a temporary basis. This grant remains in effect until the original will or a duly authenticated copy is presented, ensuring that the estate is managed appropriately in the meantime.

1218. If an executor is not present in the province where the probate application is filed and no other executor within the province is willing to assume responsibility, the court may grant letters of administration with the will annexed. In such cases, the grant may be issued to an attorney or authorized agent acting on behalf of the absent executor. This arrangement allows for the management of the estate in the executor's absence and remains valid until the executor himself obtains probate or letters of administration. This ensures that the estate's administration is not unduly delayed due to the executor's unavailability.

1219. If an individual who would be entitled to receive letters of administration with the will annexed is not present in the province, the court may grant such letters to an appointed attorney or agent on their behalf. However, this grant shall be subject to the limitations outlined in section 241, ensuring that it remains in effect only until the rightful person obtains probate or letters of administration personally. This provision facilitates the timely administration of the estate despite the temporary absence of the entitled individual.

1220. If an individual who is entitled to administer an intestate estate is not present in the province and no other equally entitled person is willing to take on the responsibility, the court may grant letters of administration to a duly appointed attorney or agent of the absent person. However, such a grant shall be subject to the limitations specified in section 241, remaining valid only until the rightful person obtains the necessary probate or letters of administration in their own capacity.

1221. If a minor is the sole executor or the sole residuary legatee of a will, the court may grant letters of administration, with the will annexed, to the minor's legal guardian or any other suitable person deemed appropriate by the court. This arrangement shall remain in effect until the minor reaches the age of majority, at which point, and not before, probate of the will may be granted directly to them.

1222. If there are multiple executors who are minors and no executor has reached the age of majority, or if there are multiple residuary legatees and none of them has attained majority, the grant of letters of administration shall be limited until at least one of them comes of age.

1223. If the sole executor, sole universal or residuary legatee, or the individual solely entitled to the intestate's estate under applicable succession laws is a minor or of unsound mind, letters of administration, with or without the will annexed, may be granted to the person lawfully entrusted with the care of their estate. In the absence of such an appointed guardian, the Court may designate another suitable person to manage the estate for the benefit of the minor or the person of unsound mind until they reach the age of majority or regain mental capacity.

1224. While a suit is pending regarding the validity of a deceased person's will or the issuance or revocation of probate or letters of administration, the Court may appoint an administrator to manage the deceased's estate. This appointed administrator shall possess all the rights and authority of a general administrator, except the power to distribute the estate. Such an administrator shall remain under the direct supervision of the Court and act in accordance with its instructions.

1225. When an executor is designated for a specific purpose outlined in the will, the probate granted shall be restricted to fulfilling that purpose. If the executor appoints an attorney or agent to administer the estate on his behalf, the letters of administration, with the will annexed, shall also be confined to the scope of that appointment.

1226. If a generally appointed executor grants authority to an attorney or agent to probate a will on his behalf, and such authority is restricted to a specific purpose, the letters of administration, with the will annexed, shall be confined to that particular purpose.

1227. When an individual passes away, leaving behind property in which they held only a trustee's interest and had no personal beneficial claim, and there is no general representative available or willing to act, letters of administration, restricted to that property, may be issued to the beneficiary or another suitable person acting on their behalf.

1228. When it becomes necessary to appoint a representative of a deceased person in an ongoing legal proceeding, and the executor or individual entitled to administration is either unwilling or unable to act, the Court may grant letters of administration to a nominee of one of the parties in the case. This grant shall be limited to representing the deceased in that specific suit, as well as any related legal proceedings in the same or another Court, until a final decree is issued and fully executed.

1229. If an executor or administrator, who has been granted probate or letters of administration, remains absent from the relevant Province for a period of twelve months from the date of such grant, the Court may appoint another person, as it deems appropriate, to receive limited letters of administration. This grant shall be restricted to enabling the appointed person to become a party to any legal proceedings initiated against the executor or administrator and to ensure the enforcement of any decree issued in the matter.

1230. If it becomes essential to safeguard the property of a deceased individual, the Court having jurisdiction over the location of such property may issue limited letters of administration. These may be granted to a person deemed suitable by the Court, specifically for the purpose of collecting and preserving the deceased's assets and settling any outstanding debts owed to the estate, all under the Court's supervision and directives.

1231. When a person has died intestate or has left a will but no executor is willing or competent to act, or where the appointed executor resides outside the Province at the time of the testator's death, the Court may, if it deems necessary or expedient, appoint an administrator for the estate or any portion thereof. Such appointment may be made in favour of a person other than the one who would ordinarily be entitled to a grant of administration. In exercising its discretion, the Court shall take into consideration factors such as the degree of kinship, the extent of the applicant's interest, the security of the estate, and the likelihood of its proper administration. The grant of letters of administration in such cases may be either general or limited, as the Court deems appropriate.

1232. Where the circumstances of a case necessitate an exception, probate of a will or letters of administration with the will annexed shall be granted subject to such exception. Likewise, where the nature of the case so demands, letters of administration shall be issued with the requisite exception, as determined by the Court.

1233. When a grant of probate or letters of administration, with or without the will annexed, has been issued with exceptions, the individual entitled to administer the remaining portion of the deceased's estate may obtain a subsequent grant of probate or letters of administration for the un-administered estate, as deemed appropriate.

1234. If an executor to whom probate was granted passes away, leaving a portion of the testator's estate un-administered, the Court may appoint a new representative to administer the remaining estate.

1235. In the issuance of letters of administration for an estate that remains partially un-administered, the Court shall adhere to the same principles governing original grants and shall confer such letters only upon those individuals who would have been eligible for the initial grant.

1236. Upon the expiration of a limited grant, whether by the passage of time or the occurrence of the specified event or contingency, if any portion of the deceased's estate remains un-administered, letters of administration shall be issued to those individuals who would have been eligible for the original grant.

1237. Sections 261 to 263 of the Succession Act, 1925, govern the alteration and revocation of grants. Under section 261, if any inaccuracies arise concerning names, descriptions, the date and place of the deceased's death, or the purpose specified in a limited grant, the Court possesses the authority to rectify such errors. Consequently, the grant of probate or letters of administration may be modified or amended as deemed appropriate.

1238. If, subsequent to the issuance of letters of administration with the will annexed, a codicil is discovered, the Court may, upon proper verification and proof of its authenticity, incorporate the codicil into the grant. Accordingly, the grant may be modified or amended to reflect the inclusion of the codicil.

1239. The grant of probate or letters of administration may be revoked or annulled for just cause. Explanation: Just cause shall be deemed to exist where (a) the proceedings to obtain the grant were defective in substance; or (b) the grant was obtained fraudulently by making a false suggestion, or by concealing from the Court something material to the care; or (c) the grant was obtained by means of an untrue allegation, of a fact essential in point of law to justify the grant, though such allegation was made in ignorance or inadvertently; or (d) the grant has become useless and inoperative through circumstances; or (e) the person to whom the grant was made has wilfully and without reasonable cause omitted to exhibit an inventory or account in accordance with the provisions of Chapter VII of the Succession Act, 1925, or has exhibited under that Chapter an inventory or account which is untrue in a material respect. Illustrations: (i) The Court by which the grant was made had no jurisdiction. (ii) The grant was made without citing parties who ought to have been cited. (iii) The will of which probate was obtained was forged or revoked. (iv) A obtained letters of administration to the estate of B, as his widow, but it has since transpired that she was never married to him. (v) A has taken administration to the (intestate) of B as if he had died intestate, but a will has since been discovered. (vi) Since probate was granted, a later will has been discovered. (vii) Since probate was granted, a codicil has been discovered which revokes or adds to the appointment of executors under the will. (viii) The person to whom probate was, or letters of administration were, granted has subsequently become of unsound mind.

§13. PROTECTION OF PROPERTY OF DECEASED

1240. Sections 192 to 210 of the Succession Act, 1925, provide safeguards for the property of a deceased person. In the event of a person's death leaving behind movable or immovable property, any individual asserting a right to such property, whether in whole or in part, by way of succession, may seek relief by filing an application before the District Judge of the district where any portion of the property is located. Such relief may be sought either after possession has been unlawfully acquired by another or when there exists a reasonable apprehension of forcible dispossession.

1241. In cases where a minor, a disqualified individual, or an absentee is entitled to inherit property by succession, an application for relief may likewise be made by an agent, a relative, or a near friend on their behalf. In matters falling within its jurisdiction, the Court of Wards may also initiate such an application to safeguard the interests of the entitled person.

1242. Upon receiving such an application, the District Judge shall first examine the applicant under oath and may conduct any further inquiries deemed necessary to ascertain whether there exist sufficient grounds to believe that the party currently in possession, or seeking to seize possession through forcible means, lacks a lawful title. The Judge shall also determine whether the applicant, or the person on whose behalf the application is made, holds a legitimate claim to the property and is likely to suffer substantial prejudice if left to pursue the ordinary course of legal proceedings. The Judge shall ensure that the application has been made in good faith.

1243. If the District Judge is satisfied that there are sufficient grounds to support the claims set forth in the application, he shall proceed to summon the party against whom the complaint has been made. Additionally, the Judge shall issue a notice by publication regarding any vacant or disputed possession. After allowing a reasonable period to elapse, the Judge shall summarily adjudicate the right to possession, subject to any subsequent legal proceedings, and shall accordingly direct the delivery of possession. The Judge shall have the authority, upon application, to appoint an officer to prepare an inventory of the property, seal or otherwise secure the same, without undue delay. This action may be taken regardless of whether the inquiry necessary for summoning the opposing party has been fully concluded.

1244. If, during the course of the inquiry, it is established that there is a risk of misappropriation or dissipation of the property before the summary proceedings are concluded, and that any delay in securing an undertaking from the party in possession or the inadequacy of such security may subject the rightful owner to substantial risk, the District Judge shall have the authority to appoint one or more curators. The authority of such curators shall be governed by the terms specified in their respective appointments and shall not extend beyond the conclusion of the summary proceedings and the subsequent confirmation or transfer of possession. In cases involving immovable property, the Judge may delegate the curatorial powers to the Collector or to any officer subordinate to the Collector. Additionally, every appointment of a curator in respect of any property shall be duly publicized in an appropriate manner.

1245. The District Judge holds the authority to empower the curator to assume control of the property, either in a general capacity or until the party in possession furnishes adequate security, or until proper inventories of the property have been prepared, or for any other purpose deemed necessary to prevent misappropriation or waste. The Judge retains the discretion to permit the party in possession to maintain such possession, subject to the provision of security or otherwise. Any continuation of possession shall remain contingent upon the directives of the Judge, including but not limited to the preparation of inventories or the safeguarding of deeds and other relevant documents.

1246. Where a certificate has been issued under Part X of this Act or pursuant to the Succession Certificate Act, 1889, or where a grant of probate or letters of administration has been duly made, any curator appointed shall be precluded from exercising any authority that lawfully vests in the holder of such certificate, executor, or administrator.

1247. Any individual who has discharged debts or paid rents to a curator duly authorized by the Court to receive such payments shall be duly indemnified. The curator, in turn, shall be held accountable for the proper disbursement of such amounts to the rightful recipient, being the holder of the certificate, probate, or letters of administration, as the circumstances may require.

1248. The District Judge shall require the curator to furnish security ensuring the diligent and faithful execution of his duties and the proper rendering of accounts as prescribed herein. Additionally, the Judge may grant the curator authorization to receive reasonable remuneration from the estate, which shall not exceed 5% of the movable assets and the annual income derived from the immovable property, as deemed appropriate by the Court.

1249. Any excess funds collected by the curator shall be deposited in the Court and subsequently invested in public securities for the benefit of the rightful claimants, as determined upon the conclusion of the summary proceedings.

1250. The curator shall be required to furnish security without undue delay, and, where feasible, such security shall be taken in a general form to cover all future appointments of the curator. However, any delay in securing such bond shall not preclude the Judge from promptly conferring upon the curator the powers necessary to discharge his duties.

1251. Where the estate of the deceased comprises, in whole or in part, land subject to payment of revenue to the Government, the District Judge shall seek a report from the Collector on matters concerning the necessity of summoning the party in possession, appointing a curator, or selecting a suitable individual for such appointment. The Collector shall promptly provide the required report. However, in urgent circumstances, the Judge may, at his discretion, proceed without awaiting the report.

1252. The District Judge shall not be bound to adhere strictly to the recommendations contained in such a report. However, if the Judge chooses to act contrary to the report, he shall promptly submit a statement outlining his reasons to the High Court. Should the High Court find the stated reasons unsatisfactory, it may issue a directive requiring the Judge to proceed in accordance with the Collector's report.

1253. The curator shall remain under the authority of the District Judge in all matters concerning the initiation or defence of legal proceedings, and any such proceedings may be undertaken in the curator's name on behalf of the estate. However, explicit authorization must be granted in the curator's appointment order for the collection of debts or rents. Once such authority is conferred, the curator shall be empowered to issue a full discharge for any sums received under its purview.

1254. While the property remains under the custody of the curator, the District Judge may grant allowances to parties who appear to have a prima facie claim, as deemed appropriate upon a summary examination of their rights and circumstances. The Judge may also, at his discretion, require security for the repayment of such allowances, along with interest, should the final adjudication of the summary proceeding determine that the recipient was not lawfully entitled to them.

1255. The curator shall submit monthly abstract accounts and, upon the completion of every three-month period, if his administration extends for such duration, as well as upon relinquishing possession of the property, he shall furnish a comprehensive report detailing the administration of the estate to the satisfaction of the District Judge.

1256. The curator's accounts shall be accessible for inspection by all interested parties, and any such party shall have the right to designate a separate individual to maintain a duplicate record of all transactions, including receipts and disbursements made by the curator.

1257. If the curator's accounts are found to be overdue, inaccurate, or incomplete, or if he fails to present them as directed by the District Judge, he shall be liable to a fine not exceeding PKR 1,000 for each instance of such default.

1258. Where a District Judge appoints a curator for the entire estate of a deceased person, no other District Judge within the same Province shall appoint an additional curator. However, if a curator is appointed for a specific portion of the estate, the appointment of another curator for the remaining portions within the same Province shall not be precluded. Provided that no Judge shall appoint a curator or entertain a summary proceeding concerning property already subject to a summary proceeding initiated under Part VII of the Succession Act, 1925, before another Judge. If multiple curators are appointed by different Judges for distinct parts of the estate, the High Court may issue such directions as it deems appropriate for the appointment of a single curator for the entire estate.

1259. An application under Part VII of the Succession Act, 1925, seeking relief before the District Judge in respect of the estate of a deceased proprietor, whose property is claimed by right of succession, must be filed within a period of six months from the date of the proprietor's demise.

1260. Provided that nothing herein shall be construed to permit any violation of a public act of settlement or any lawful instructions left by a deceased proprietor regarding the disposition or possession of his property upon his demise, whether due to minority or any other circumstance. In every such instance, upon the satisfaction of the Judge having jurisdiction over the estate of the deceased as to the existence of such directions, the same shall be duly enforced.

1261. Nothing shall be deemed to authorize any disturbance of the possession of a Court of Wards of any property; and in case minor, or other disqualified person whose property is subject to the Court of Wards, is the party on whose behalf application is made under Part VII of the Succession Act, 1925, the District Judge, if he determines to summon the party in possession and to appoint a curator, shall invest the Court of Wards with the curatorship of the estate pending the proceeding without taking security as aforesaid: and if the minor or other disqualified person, upon the adjudication of the summary proceeding, appears to be entitled to the property, possession shall be delivered to the Court of Wards.

1262. No restriction shall be placed on the institution of a suit by a party whose application has been dismissed, whether prior to or subsequent to the summoning of the party in possession, or by a party who has been dispossessed under the provisions of Part VII of the Succession Act, 1925.

1263. The determination of a District Judge in a summary proceeding shall be conclusive only with respect to the question of actual possession and shall not extend beyond that scope; however, for this purpose, it shall be final and shall not be open to appeal or review.

1264. The Provincial Government designates public curators for one or more districts, and the District Judge with jurisdiction shall appoint such public curators in all instances where the selection of a curator is left to his discretion.

1265. Sections 211 to 216 of the Succession Act, 1925, govern the representative title to the property of a deceased person upon succession. The executor or administrator, as applicable, serves as the legal representative of the deceased for all purposes, and all assets of the deceased vest in such representative accordingly.

1266. In cases where the deceased was a Hindu, Muslim, Buddhist, Sikh, Jaina, Parsi, or any other exempted person, no provision herein shall be construed to vest in the executor or administrator any property of the deceased that would have otherwise devolved upon another person by the right of survivorship.

1267. No claim to any portion of the estate of a person who has died intestate shall be recognized or enforced by any Court of Law unless letters of administration have been duly obtained from a Court of competent jurisdiction. However, this requirement shall not be applicable in cases of intestacy concerning Hindus, Muslims, Buddhists, Sikhs, Jainas, Parsis, or Pakistan Christians.

1268. No claim as an executor or legatee shall be recognized or enforced by any Court of Law unless probate of the will, under which such right is asserted, has been duly granted by a Court of competent jurisdiction in Pakistan, or letters of administration have been issued with the will annexed or with an authenticated copy thereof.

1269. However, it shall not apply in the case of wills made by Muslims and Parsis, and shall only apply in the case of wills made by any Hindu Buddhist, Sikh or Jaina; such wills are of the classes specified in clauses (a) and (b) of section 57.

1270. No Court (a) passes a decree against a debtor of a deceased person for payment of his debt to a person claiming on succession to be entitled to the effects of the deceased in person or to any part thereof, or (b) proceed, upon an application of a person claiming to be so entitled, to execute against such a debtor a decree or order for the payment of his debt, except on the production, by the person so claiming, of: (i) a probate or letters of administration evidencing the grant to him of administration to the estate of the deceased; or (ii) a certificate granted under section 31 or section 32 of the Administrator Generals Act, 1913, and having the debt mentioned therein; or (iii) a succession certificate granted under Part X and having the debt specified therein; or (iv) a certificate granted under the Succession Certificate Act, 1989; or (v) a certificate granted under Sind Regulation No. VIII of 1827 and, if granted after the first day of May 1889, having the debt specified therein. The word 'debt' includes any debt except rent, revenue or profits payable in respect of land used for agricultural purposes.

1271. A grant of probate or letters of administration in respect of an estate shall be deemed to supersede any certificate previously granted under Part X or under the Succession Certificate Act, 1889 or Sind Regulation No. VIII of 1827, in respect of any debt or securities included in the estate. When at the time of the grant of the probate or letters any suit or other proceeding instituted by the holder of any such certificate regarding any such debt or security is pending, the person to whom the grant is made shall, on applying to the Court in which the suit or proceeding is pending, be entitled to take the place of the holder of the certificate in the suit or proceeding: Provided that, when any certificate is superseded, all payments made to the holder of such certificate in ignorance of such supersession shall be held good against claims under the probate or letters of administration.

1272. Once probate or letters of administration have been granted, no individual other than the grantee shall have the authority to initiate or continue any legal proceedings, or otherwise act in a representative capacity for the deceased, within the jurisdiction of the granting Province, unless and until such probate or letters of administration are revoked or set aside.

1273. Sections 218 to 236 of the Succession Act, 1925, govern the grant of probate and letters of administration. In cases where the deceased has died intestate and was a Hindu, Muslim, Buddhist, Sikh, Jaina, or an exempted person, the administration of the estate may be granted to any individual who, under the applicable rules of distribution, would be entitled to inherit the whole or a portion of the estate. If multiple such persons apply, the Court has the discretion to grant administration to one or more of them. In the absence of any such applicant, the Court may grant administration to a creditor of the deceased.

1274. If the deceased has died intestate and was not a person belonging to any of the classes referred to in section 218, those who are connected with him, either by marriage or by consanguinity, are entitled to obtain letters of administration of his estate and effects in the order and according to the rules hereinafter stated, namely: (a) If the deceased has, left a widow, administration shall be granted to the widow, unless the Court sees cause to exclude her, either on the ground of some personal disqualification, or because she has no interest in the estate of the deceased. Illustrations: (i) The widow is a lunatic or has committed adultery or has been barred by her marriage settlement of all interest in her husband estate. There is cause for excluding her from the administration. (ii) The widow has married again since the decease of her husband. This is not good cause for her exclusion. (b) If the Judge thinks proper, he may associate any person or persons with the widow in the administration who would be entitled solely to the administration if there were no widow. (c) If there is no widow, or if the Court sees cause to exclude the widow, it shall commit the administration to the person or persons who would be beneficially entitled to the estate according to the rules for the distribution of an intestates estate: Provided that, when the mother of the deceased is one of the class of persons so entitled, she shall be solely entitled to administration. (d) Those who stand in equal degree of kindred to the deceased are equally entitled to administration. (e) The husband surviving his wife has the same right of administration of her estate as the widow has in respect of the estate of her husband. (f) When there is no person connected with the deceased by marriage or consanguinity who is entitled to letters of administration and willing to act, they may be granted to a creditor. (g) Where the deceased has left property in Pakistan letters of administration shall be granted according to the foregoing rules, notwithstanding that he had his domicile in a country in which the law relating to testate and intestate succession differs from the law of Pakistan.

1275. Letters of administration confer upon the administrator all rights vested in the intestate, as if the grant had been made immediately upon the intestate's demise.

However, such letters do not validate any acts carried out by the administrator prior to their issuance if those acts result in the diminution or detriment of the intestate's estate.

1276. Probate is granted only to an executor appointed by the will. The appointment may be expressed or by necessary implication. Illustrations: (i) A, wills that C, be his executor if B will not. B is appointed executor by implication. (ii) A gives a legacy to B and several legacies to the other persons, among the rest to his daughter-in-law C, and adds 'but should the within-named C be not living I do constitute and appoint B my whole and sole executrix', C is appointed executrix by implication. (iii) A appoints several persons executors of his will and codicils and his nephew residuary legatee, and in another codicil are these words, 'I appoint my nephew my residuary legatee, to discharge all lawful demands against my will and codicils signed of different dates.' The nephew is appointed an executor by implication.

1277. Probate shall not be granted to any individual who is a minor or of unsound mind, nor to any group or association of individuals, except where such entity is a company that meets the conditions laid down by the rules established by the Provincial Government in this regard.

1278. When several executors are appointed, probate may be granted to them all simultaneously or at different times. Illustration: A is an executor of B's will by express appointment and C an executor of it by implication. Probate may be granted to A and C at the same time or to A first and then to C, or to C first and then to A.

1279. If a codicil is found after probate has been granted, a distinct probate for the codicil may be issued to the executor, provided it does not revoke the appointment of executors named in the will. However, if the codicil appoints different executors, the probate of the will shall be revoked, and a fresh probate shall be granted for both the will and the codicil collectively.

1280. When probate has been issued to multiple executors, and one of them passes away, the full authority to represent the testator devolves upon the remaining executor or executors. The grant of probate confirms the validity of the will from the date of the testator's death and legitimizes all intervening acts carried out by the executor in that capacity.

1281. When a will has been duly proved and lodged in a Court of competent jurisdiction outside the territorial limits of the Province, whether within or beyond Pakistan, and a duly authenticated copy of the will is presented, letters of administration may be issued with such authenticated copy annexed.

1282. If an individual designated as an executor has not formally renounced the executorship, no letters of administration shall be granted to any other person unless a citation has been issued, requiring the executor to either accept or renounce the role. However, if one or more among several appointed executors have obtained probate of the will, the Court may, upon the demise of the last surviving executor who had proved the will, grant letters of administration without the necessity of citing those who had not previously proved it.

1283. Renunciation may be effected either orally before the Judge or through a written declaration duly signed by the person renouncing. Once renounced, such person shall be permanently barred from seeking probate of the will under which they were appointed as executor.

1284. If an executor renounces or does not accept the executor-ship within the prescribed time, the will may be admitted to probate, and letters of administration with a copy of the will annexed may be issued to the individual who would have been entitled to administration in the event of intestacy.

1285. When (a) the deceased has made a will, but has not appointed an executor, or (b) the deceased has appointed an executor who is legally incapable or refuses to act, or who has died before the testator or before he has proved the will, or (c) the executor dies after having proved the will, but before he has administered all the estate of the deceased, an universal or a residuary legatee may be admitted to prove the will, and letters of administration with the will annexed may be granted to him of the whole estate, or of so much thereof as may be un-administered.

1286. If a residuary legatee with a beneficial interest outlives the testator but passes away before the complete administration of the estate, his legal representative shall have the same entitlement to administration with the will annexed as the original residuary legatee.

1287. In the absence of an executor, a residuary legatee, or the representative of a residuary legatee – or if such a person refuses, is incapable of acting, or cannot be located – those entitled to administer the estate in the event of intestacy, or any other legatee with a beneficial interest, or a creditor, may be permitted to prove the will, and letters of administration may be issued to such person or persons accordingly.

1288. Letters of administration with the will annexed shall only be granted to a legatee who is either a universal or residuary legatee, unless a citation has been issued and duly published, summoning the next-of-kin to either accept or decline the grant of letters of administration.

1289. Letters of administration shall not be issued to any individual who is a minor or of unsound mind, nor to any group or association of individuals, except in cases where the entity is a company that meets the requirements established by rules prescribed by the Provincial Government for this purpose.

§14. Gifts in Contemplation of Death

1290. Under section 191 of the Succession Act, 1925 a man may dispose, by gift made in contemplation of death, of any moveable property which he could dispose of by will. A gift said to be made in contemplation of death where a man, who is ill and expects to die shortly of his illness, delivers to another the possession of any moveable property to keep as a gift in case the donor shall die of that illness. Such a gift may be resumed by the giver and shall not take effect if he recovers from the illness during which it was made; nor if he survives the person to whom it was made. Illustrations: A, being ill, and in expectation of death, delivers to B, to be retained by him in case of A's death: a watch; a bond granted by C to A; a bank-note; a promissory note of the Federal Government endorsed in blank; a bill of exchange endorsed in blank; and certain mortgage-deeds. A dies of the illness during which he delivered these articles. B is entitled to: the watch; the debt secured by C's bond; the bank-note; the promissory note of the Federal Government; the bill of exchange; and the money secured by the mortgage-deeds.

1291. A, being ill, and in expectation of death, delivers to B the key of a trunk or the key of a warehouse in which goods of bulk belonging to A are deposited, with the intention of giving him the control over the contents of the trunk, or over the deposited goods, and desires him to keep them in case of A's death. A dies of the illness during which he delivered these articles. B is entitled to the trunk and its contents or to A's goods of bulk in the warehouse.

1292. A, being ill, and in expectation of death, puts aside certain articles in separate parcels and marks upon the parcels respectively the names of B and C. The parcels are not delivered during the life of A. A dies of the illness during which he set aside the parcels. B and C are not entitled to the contents of the parcel.

§15. Administrators or Executors

1293. Under sections 305 to 315 of the Succession Act, 1925, the authority of an executor or administrator is defined. The executor or administrator possesses the same legal capacity to initiate proceedings for all causes of action that survive the deceased and is vested with the same rights to recover debts as the deceased had during their lifetime.

1294. All demands whatsoever and all rights to prosecute or defend any action or special proceeding existing in favour of or against a person at the time of his decease, survive to and against his executors or administrator; except causes of action for defamation, assault, as deemed in the PPC, or other personal injuries not causing the death of the party; and except also cases where, after the death of the party, the relief sought could not be enjoyed or granting it would be nugatory. Illustrations: (i) A collision takes place on a railway in consequence of some neglect or default of an official, and a passenger is severely hurt, but not so as to cause death.

He afterwards dies without having brought any action. The cause of action does not survive. (ii) A sues for divorce. A dies. The cause of action does not survive to his representative.

1295. An executor or administrator has power to dispose of the property of the deceased, vested in him under section 211, either wholly or in part, in such manner as he may think fit. Illustrations: (i) The deceased has made a specific bequest of part of his property. The executor, not having assented to the bequest, sells the subject of it. The sale is valid. (ii) The executor in the exercise of his discretion mortgages a part of the immoveable estate of the deceased. The mortgage is valid. If the deceased was a Hindu, Muslim, Buddhist, Sikh or Jaina or an exempted person, shall be subject to the following restrictions and conditions, namely: (i) The power of an executor to dispose of immoveable property so vested in him is subject to any restriction which may be imposed in this behalf by the will appointing him, unless probate has been granted to him and the Court which granted the probate permits him by an order in writing, notwithstanding the restriction, to dispose of any immoveable property specified in the order in a manner permitted by the order. (ii) An administrator may not, without the previous permission of the Court by which the letters of administration were granted, (a) mortgage charge or transfer by sale, gift, exchange or otherwise any immoveable property for the time being vested in him under section 211, or (b) lease any such property for a term exceeding five years. (iii) A disposal of property by an executor or administrator in contravention of clause (i) or clause (ii), as the case may be, is voidable at the instance of any other person interested in the property.

1296. An executor or administrator may, in addition to, and not in derogation of, any other powers of expenditure lawfully exercisable by him, incur expenditure: (a) on such acts as may be necessary for the proper care or management of any property belonging to any estate administered by him; and (b) with the sanction of the High Court, on such religious, charitable and other objects, and on such improvements, as may be reasonable and proper in the case of such property.

1297. An executor or administrator shall not be permitted to claim or retain any commission or agency fees exceeding the rate prescribed for the Administrator General under the provisions of the Administrator General's Act, 1913, as applicable at the relevant time.

1298. If an executor or administrator acquires, whether directly or indirectly, any portion of the deceased's estate, such transaction shall be voidable at the discretion of any other party with an interest in the property.

1299. When there are several executors or administrators, the powers of all may, in the absence of any direction to the contrary, be exercised by any one of them who has proved the will or taken out administration. Illustrations: (i) One of several executors has power to release a debt due to the deceased. (ii) One has power to surrender a lease. (iii) One has power to sell the property of the deceased whether moveable or immoveable. (iv) One has power to assent to a legacy. (v) One has power to endorse a promissory note payable to the deceased. (vi) The will appoints A, B, C and D to be executors, and directs that two of them shall be a quorum. No act can be done by a single executor.

1300. In the event of the death of one or more executors or administrators, unless otherwise directed in the will or the grant of letters of administration, all authority and powers of the position shall devolve upon the remaining executor(s) or the sole survivor.

1301. An administrator of un-administered effects shall possess the same authority over such effects as the original executor or administrator. An administrator appointed during a minority shall have the full powers of a general administrator. In cases where probate or letters of administration are granted to a married woman, she shall exercise all the powers vested in an ordinary executor or administrator.

1302. An executor is responsible for ensuring that adequate funds are allocated for the deceased's funeral rites, conducted in a manner befitting the deceased's status, provided that the estate has sufficient assets to cover such expenses.

1303. An executor or administrator must, within six months from the grant of probate or letters of administration, or within any extended period allowed by the granting Court, submit to the Court a comprehensive inventory providing a complete and accurate valuation of all assets in possession, outstanding credits, and debts due to the estate. Similarly, within one year from the grant, or within any further time permitted by the Court, the executor or administrator shall present an account detailing the assets received and their subsequent application or disposal. The High Court may prescribe the format for such inventory or accounts. Failure to comply with a Court directive to furnish an inventory or account shall be considered an offence under section 176 of the PPC. Additionally, wilful submission of a false inventory or account shall constitute an offence under section 193 of the said Code.

1304. In every instance where probate or letters of administration have been granted with the intent to have effect throughout Pakistan, the executor or administrator shall ensure that the inventory of the deceased's estate includes all movable and immovable assets located within Pakistan. The inventory must distinctly specify the value of such assets in each Province. The probate or letters of administration shall be subject to a fee calculated based on the total value of the property covered under the grant, regardless of its location within Pakistan.

1305. The executor or administrator shall exercise due diligence in gathering the assets of the deceased and recovering any debts owed to the deceased at the time of his passing. Expenses incurred for the funeral, in an amount deemed reasonable and appropriate to the status and condition of the deceased, as well as deathbed charges including medical fees and costs for board and lodging for the month preceding death shall take precedence over all other debts in settlement.

1306. The costs associated with obtaining probate or letters of administration, including expenses incurred in any judicial proceedings necessary for the administration of the estate, shall be settled immediately after the payment of funeral expenses and deathbed charges.

1307. Wages owed for services provided to the deceased by any labourer, artisan, or domestic servant within the three months immediately preceding the death shall be paid next, followed by the settlement of other debts in accordance with their respective priorities, if any. Except as stated, no creditor shall be entitled to preference over another, and the executor or administrator shall discharge all known debts, including their own, in proportion and without preference, to the extent that the deceased's assets permit.

1308. If the domicile of the deceased was not in Pakistan, the application of his moveable property to the payment of his debts is to be regulated by the law of Pakistan. No creditor who has received payment of a part of his debt shall be entitled to share in the proceeds of the immoveable estate of the deceased unless he brings such payment into account for the benefit of the other creditors. This section shall not apply where the deceased was a Hindu, Muslim, Buddhist, Sikh or Jaina or an exempted person. Illustration: A dies, having his domicile in a country where instruments under seal have priority over instruments not under seal leaving moveable property to the value of PKR 5,000, and immoveable property to the value of PKR 10,000, debts on instruments under seal to the amount of PKR 10,000, and debts on instruments not under seal to the same amount. The creditors holding instruments under seal receive half of their debts out of the proceeds of the moveable estate. The proceeds of the immoveable estate are to be applied in payment of the debts on instruments not under seal until one-half such debts has been discharged. This will leave PKR 5,000 which are to be distributed ratably among all the creditors without distinction, in proportion to the amount which may remain due to them.

1309. All outstanding debts, regardless of their nature, must be satisfied before any legacy is distributed. If the deceased's estate is liable for any contingent obligations, the executor or administrator shall not be required to disburse any legacy unless an adequate indemnity is provided to cover such liabilities as and when they arise.

1310. If, after settling debts, necessary expenses, and specific legacies, the remaining assets are insufficient to satisfy all general legacies in full, such legacies shall be reduced proportionally. Unless otherwise directed by the will, the executor shall not prioritize one legatee over another, nor shall he withhold any funds in respect of a legacy to himself or any beneficiary for whom he acts as a trustee.

1311. When a specific legacy is bequeathed and the estate has adequate assets to cover debts and necessary expenses, the designated item shall be transferred to the legatee in its entirety, without any reduction.

1312. In the case of a demonstrative legacy, if the estate possesses sufficient assets to satisfy debts and necessary expenses, the legatee shall have a preferential right to receive payment from the specified fund until it is depleted. Should any portion of the legacy remain unpaid after the exhaustion of the designated fund, the legatee shall have a claim against the general assets for the outstanding balance, as if it were a general legacy.

1313. If the assets are not sufficient to answer the debts and the specific legacies, an abatement shall be made from the latter ratably in proportion to their respective amounts. Illustration: A has bequeathed to B a diamond ring valued at PKR 500, and to C & horse, valued at PKR 1,000. It is found necessary to sell all the effects of the testator; and his assets, after payment of debts, are only PKR 1,000. Of this sum PKR 333-5-4 are to be paid to B, and PKR 666-10-8 to C.

1314. For the purpose of abatement, a life legacy, a sum set aside by the will to generate an annuity, and the assessed value of an annuity where no specific sum has been allocated for its provision shall be regarded as general legacies.

1315. The Succession Act, 1925, sections 303 and 304 provide details about executors own wrong. A person who intermeddles with the estate of the deceased, or does any other act which belongs to the office of executor while there is no rightful executor or administrator in existence thereby makes himself an executor of his own wrong. Exceptions: (I) Intermeddling with the goods of the deceased for the purpose of preserving them or providing for his funeral or for the immediate necessities of his family or property, does not make an executor of his own wrong. Dealing in the ordinary course of business with goods of the deceased received from another does not make an executor of his own wrong. Illustrations: (i) A uses or gives away or sells some of the goods of the deceased, or takes them to satisfy his own debt or legacy or receives payment of the debts of the deceased. He is an executor of his own wrong. (ii) A, having been appointed agent by the deceased in his lifetime to collect his debts and sell his goods, continues to do so after he has become aware of his death. He is an executor of his own wrong in respect of acts done after he has become aware of the death of the deceased. (iii) A sues as executor of the deceased, not being such. He is an executor of his own wrong.

1316. A person who has acted in a manner that renders him an executor de son tort shall be liable to the rightful executor or administrator, or to any creditor or legatee of the deceased, to the extent of the assets that have come into his possession, after deducting any payments lawfully made to the rightful executor or administrator and those made in the due course of administration.

1317. Under sections 368 and 369 of the Succession Act, 1925, an executor or administrator who mismanages, misapplies, or causes loss or damage to the estate of the deceased shall be liable to compensate for the resulting harm. If the executor improperly pays an unfounded claim from the estate, he must make good the loss. Similarly, if the deceased held a valuable lease that required timely renewal through notice, and the executor fails to provide such notice, he shall be responsible for the resulting damage. Likewise, if the deceased had a lease with a rental obligation exceeding its value but terminable upon notice at a specific time, and the executor neglects to give such notice, he shall be accountable for the loss suffered by the estate. Illustrations:

(i) If the executor disburses funds from the estate to satisfy an unjustified claim, he shall be liable to restore the loss. (ii) If the deceased held a valuable lease that required timely renewal through notice, and the executor fails to give such notice, he shall be accountable for the resulting loss. (iii) If the deceased had a lease with a rental obligation exceeding its value, but which could have been terminated by giving notice at a specified time, and the executor fails to serve such notice, he shall be held liable for the loss incurred.

1318. When an executor or administrator occasions a loss to the estate by neglecting to get in any part of the property of the deceased, he is liable to make good the amount. Illustrations: (i) The executor absolutely releases a debt due to the deceased from a solvent person, or compounds with a debtor who is able to pay in full. The executor is liable to make good the amount. (ii) The executor neglects to sue for a debt till the debtor is able to plead that the claim is barred by limitation, and the debt is thereby lost to the estate. The executor is liable to make good the amount.

1319. Chapter IV, encompassing sections 264 to 302 of the Succession Act, 1925, governs the procedures for granting and revoking probates and letters of administration. The authority to grant and revoke probates and letters of administration within a district lies with the District Judge. However, except in cases covered under section 57, no court shall entertain applications for probate or letters of administration concerning a deceased person who was a Hindu, Muslim, Buddhist, Sikh, Jaina, or an exempted person unless the Provincial Government, through a notification in the Official Gazette, has conferred such authority.

1320. The High Court has the discretion to designate judicial officers within any district to act on behalf of the District Judge as Delegates for granting probate and letters of administration in uncontested matters, within the territorial limits it specifies. However, in the case of High Courts not constituted under a Royal Charter, such appointments shall require prior approval from the Provincial Government. The individuals appointed under this provision shall be referred to as 'District Delegates'.

1321. The District Judge shall possess the same powers and authority concerning the grant of probate and letters of administration, as well as all related matters, as are conferred upon him by law in respect of any civil suit or proceeding pending before his Court.

1322. The District Judge may require any individual to present and submit to the Court any document or writing that is or purports to be testamentary and is demonstrated to be in their possession or control. If it is not established that such a document is in their possession or control, but there is reasonable cause to believe they have knowledge of its existence, the Court may summon them for examination regarding the matter. Such an individual shall be obligated to truthfully respond to the Court's inquiries and, if directed, produce and submit the document. Failure to comply, including non-attendance, refusal to answer questions, or failure to produce the document, shall render them liable to penalties under the PPC, as would apply to a defaulting party in a legal suit. The allocation of costs for such proceedings shall be at the discretion of the Judge.

1323. The proceedings before the District Judge concerning the grant of probate and letters of administration shall, except where otherwise provided, be governed by the provisions of the Code of Civil Procedure, 1908, to the extent that the circumstances of the case allow.

1324. Until probate is granted for a deceased person's will or an administrator is appointed for their estate, the District Judge within whose jurisdiction any portion of the deceased's property is located shall have the authority and duty to take necessary measures for its protection. This may be done at the request of any individual claiming an interest in the property or in any other situation where the Judge deems the property to be at risk of loss or damage. For this purpose, the Judge may, if deemed appropriate, designate an officer to assume custody and safeguard the property. However, this provision shall not apply where the deceased was a Hindu, Muslim, Buddhist, Sikh, or Jaina, or an exempted person, nor shall it extend to the intestate property of a Pakistan Christian.

1325. A District Judge may grant probate of a will or letters of administration for the estate of a deceased individual under the seal of the Court, provided that the applicant submits a petition verified in the prescribed manner. The petition must establish that, at the time of death, the testator or intestate had a permanent residence or owned movable or immovable property within the jurisdiction of the Judge.

1326. If an application is submitted to the District Judge in a jurisdiction where the deceased did not have a permanent residence at the time of death, the Judge has the discretion to reject the application if he deems that it would be more appropriately or fairly adjudicated in another district. In cases where the application pertains to letters of administration, the Judge may either grant them without restriction or limit their scope to the assets located within his jurisdiction.

1327. A District Delegate may grant probate or letters of administration upon application, provided there is no dispute, if it is established through a verified petition that the testator or intestate had a permanent residence within the jurisdiction of the Delegate at the time of death.

1328. Probate or letters of administration shall have effect over all the property and estate, moveable or immoveable, of the deceased, throughout the Province in which the same is or are granted, and shall be conclusive as to the representative title against all debtors of the deceased, and all persons holding property which belongs to him, and shall afford full indemnity to all debtors, paying their debts and all persons delivering up such property to the person to whom such probate or letters of administration have been granted: Provided that probates and letters of administration granted (a) by a High Court, or (b) by a District Judge, where the deceased at the time of his death had a fixed place of abode situate within the jurisdiction of such Judge, and such Judge certifies that the value of the property and estate affected beyond the limits of the Province does not exceed PKR 10,000, shall, unless otherwise directed by the grant, have like effect brought-out Pakistan. The said proviso shall also apply in Pakistan after the separation of Pakistan from India to probates and letters of administration granted before the date of the separation, or on or after that date in proceedings pending at that date in any of the territories which on that date were comprised in India.

1329. Where probate or letters of administration has or have been granted by a High Court or District Judge with the effect referred to in the proviso to section 273, the High Court or District Judge shall send a certificate thereof to the following Courts, namely: (a) when the grant has been made by a High Court, to each of the other High Courts; (b) when the grant has been made by a District Judge, to the High Court to which such District Judge is subordinate and to each of the other High Courts. Every certificate referred above shall be made as nearly as circumstances admit in the form set forth in Schedule IV of the Succession Act, 1925, and such certificate shall be filed by the High Court receiving the same. Where any portion of the assets has been stated by the petitioner, as hereinafter provided in sections 276 and 278, to be situated within the jurisdiction of a District Judge in another Province, the Court required to send the certificate referred above to such District Judge, and such copy shall be filed by the District Judge receiving the same.

1330. An application for probate or letters of administration, if duly made and verified as prescribed, shall serve as sufficient authority for granting probate or administration. Such a grant shall not be challenged solely on the grounds that the testator or intestate had no fixed residence or assets within the district at the time of death, except through proceedings for revocation in cases where the grant was obtained by fraud upon the Court.

1331. Application for probate or for letters of administration, with the will annexed, shall be made by a petition distinctly written in English or in the language in ordinary use in proceedings before the Court in which the application is made, with the will or, in the cases mentioned in sections 237, 238, and 239, a copy, draft, or statement of the contents thereof, annexed, and stating (a) the time of the testators death, (b) that the writing annexed is his last will and testament, (c) that it was duly executed, (d) the amount of assets which are likely to come to the petitioners hands, and (e) when the application is for probate, that the petitioner is the executor named in the will. In addition to these particulars, the petition shall further state, (a) when the application is to the District Judge, that the deceased at the time of his death had a fixed place of abode, or had some property, situate within the jurisdiction of the Judge; and (b) when the application is to a District Delegate, that the deceased at the time of his death had a fixed place of abode within the jurisdiction of such Delegate. Where the application is to the District Judge and any portion of the assets likely to come to the petitioners hands is situate in another Province the petition shall further state the amount of such assets in each Province and the District Judges within whose jurisdiction such assets are situate.

1332. In cases wherein the will, copy or draft, is written in any language other than English or than that in ordinary use in proceedings before the Court, there shall be a translation thereof annexed to the petition by a translator of the Court, if the language be one for which a translator is appointed; or, if the will, copy or draft, is in any other language, then by any person competent to translate the same, in which case such translation shall be verified by that person in the following manner, namely: 'I (A.B.) do declare that I read and perfectly understand the language and character of the original, and that the above is a true and accurate translation thereof.'

1333. Application for letters of administration shall be made by petition distinctly written as aforesaid and stating: (a) the time and place of the deceased's death; (b) the family or other relatives of the deceased, and their respective residences; (c) the right in which the petitioner claims; (d) the amount of assets which are likely to come to the petitioners hands; (e) when the application is to the District Judge, that the deceased at the time of his death had a fixed place of abode, or had some property, situate within the jurisdiction of the Judge; and (f) when the application is to a District Delegate, that the deceased at the time of his death had a fixed place of abode within the jurisdiction of such Delegate. Where the application is to the District Judge and any portion of the assets likely to come to the petitioners hands is situate in another Province, the petition shall further state the amount of such assets in each Province and the District Judges within whose jurisdiction such assets are situate.

1334. Every person applying to any of the Courts mentioned in the proviso to section 273 for probate of a will or letters of administration of an estate intended to have effect throughout Pakistan, shall state in his petition, in addition to the matters respectively required by section 276 and section 278, that to the best of his belief no application has been made to any other Court for a probate of the same will or for letters of administration of the same estate, intended to have such effect as last aforesaid, or, where any such application has been made, the Court to which it was made, the person or persons by whom it was made and the proceedings (if any) had thereon. The Court to which any such application is made under the proviso to section 273 may, if it thinks fit, reject the same.

1335. The petition for probate or letters of administration shall in all cases be subscribed by the petitioner and his pleader, if any, and shall be verified by the petitioner in the following manner, namely: 'I (A.B.), the petitioner in the above petition, declare that what is stated therein is true to the best of my information and belief'.

1336. Where the application is for probate, the petition shall also be verified by at least one of the witnesses to the will (when procurable) in the manner or to the effect following, namely:

> I (C.D), one of the witnesses to the last will and testament of the testator mentioned in the above petition, declare that I was present and saw the said testator affix his signature (or mark) thereto (or that the said testator acknowledged the writing annexed to the above petition to be his last will and testament in my presence).

1337. If any petition or declaration that is required to be verified contains a statement that the person verifying knows or believes to be false, the person shall be considered to have committed an offence under section 193 of the PPC.

1338. In all cases the District Judge or District Delegate may, if he thinks proper: (a) examine the petitioner in person, upon oath; (b) require further evidence of the due execution of the will or the right of the petitioner to the letters of administration, as the case may be; (c) issue citations calling upon all persons claiming to have any interest in the estate of the deceased to come and see the proceedings before the grant of probate or letters of administration. The citation shall be fixed up in some conspicuous part of the court-house, and also in the office of the Collector of the district and otherwise published or made known in such manner as the Judge or District Delegate issuing the same may direct. Where any portion of the assets has been stated by the petitioner to be situate within the jurisdiction of a District Judge in another Province, the District Judge issuing the same shall cause a copy of the citation to be sent to such other District Judge, who shall publish the same in the same manner as if it were a citation issued by himself, and shall certify such publication to the District Judge who issued the citation.

1339. A caveat against the granting of probate or letters of administration may be filed with the District Judge or a District Delegate. Upon the filing of any caveat with a District Delegate, a copy shall be promptly forwarded to the District Judge. Similarly, when a caveat is filed with the District Judge, a copy shall be provided to the relevant District Delegate, if any, within whose jurisdiction the deceased is claimed to have had a fixed place of residence at the time of death, as well as to any other Judge or District Delegate to whom the District Judge deems it necessary to send the caveat. The caveat shall be filed in the form prescribed in Schedule V, as far as the circumstances permit.

1340. No action shall be taken on a petition for probate or letters of administration after a caveat has been filed with the Judge or District Delegate handling the application, or after notice of the caveat has been given to another Delegate, until reasonable notice has been provided to the person who entered the caveat, as deemed appropriate by the Court.

1341. A District Delegate shall refrain from granting probate or letters of administration in any case where there is a dispute regarding the grant, or where it appears to him that such a grant should not be made in his Court. Explanation: 'Dispute' refers to the presence of any individual, either personally, through an authorized agent, or a pleader duly appointed to represent them, opposing the proceedings.

1342. In any case where there is no dispute, but the District Delegate has doubts regarding the grant of probate or letters of administration, or when any issue arises in relation to the grant or application for such, the District Delegate may, if deemed appropriate, refer the matter to the District Judge. The District Judge may then provide instructions for the District Delegate to proceed with the application in accordance with the Judge's directions, or may prohibit any further action by the District Delegate, allowing the applicant to approach the Judge directly for the matter to be resolved.

1343. In any case where there is a dispute, or the District Delegate believes that probate or letters of administration should be denied in his Court, the petition, along with any supporting documents, shall be returned to the applicant for submission to the District Judge. However, if the District Delegate deems it necessary for the sake of justice, he is authorized to retain the petition and documents, and in such a case, the materials shall be forwarded to the District Judge for further consideration.

1344. When the District Judge or District Delegate determines that probate of a will should be issued, he shall grant it under the seal of his Court, using the form prescribed in Schedule VI.

1345. When the District Judge or District Delegate is satisfied that letters of administration to the estate of a deceased person, either with or without the annexed will, should be issued, he shall grant them under the seal of his Court, in the form specified in Schedule VII.

1346. Any individual to whom a grant of letters of administration, other than under section 241, is issued, must provide a bond to the District Judge, with one or more sureties, assuring the proper collection, management, and distribution of the deceased's estate. The form of the bond shall be determined by the District Judge through a general or specific order. In cases where the deceased was a Hindu, Muslim, Buddhist, Sikh, Jaina, or an exempted person: (a) the exception under section 241 regarding the bond requirement shall not apply, and (b) the District Judge may require a similar bond from anyone granted probate.

1347. The Court, upon receiving a petition and being satisfied that the bond's conditions have not been fulfilled, may assign the bond to a designated person, or their executors or administrators. The Court may impose conditions such as requiring security, directing that any funds received be deposited into the Court, or any other terms it deems appropriate. Once assigned, the person or their representatives will have the right to enforce the bond in their name, as if it had originally been made in their favour, and will be entitled to recover the full amount due for any breach of the bond, acting as trustees for all interested parties.

1348. No probate of a will shall be issued until at least seven clear days have passed since the testator's death, and no letters of administration shall be granted until fourteen clear days have elapsed from the date of the intestate's death.

1349. Each District Judge or District Delegate shall retain and preserve all original wills for which probate or letters of administration with the will annexed are granted, placing them in the records of the Court until a public registry for wills is established. The Provincial Government shall enact regulations regarding the preservation and inspection of the wills so stored.

1350. In any case, before the District Judge in which there is contention, the proceedings shall take, as nearly as may be, the form of a regular suit, according to the provisions of the Code of Civil Procedure, 1908 in which the petitioner for probate or letters of administration, as the case may be, shall be the plaintiff, and the person who has appeared to oppose the grant shall be the defendant.

1351. When a grant of probate or letters of administration is revoked or annulled under this Act, the person to whom the grant was made shall forthwith deliver up the probate or letters to the Court which made the grant. If such person wilfully and without reasonable cause omits so to deliver up the probate or letters, he shall be punishable with fine which may extend to PKR 1,000, or with imprisonment for a term which may extend to three months, or with both.

1352. When a grant of probate or letters of administration is revoked, any payments made in good faith to the executor or administrator under such grant prior to its revocation shall, despite the revocation, constitute a valid discharge for the person making the payment. Furthermore, the executor or administrator who acted under the revoked grant may retain and recover any payments made by them that the person subsequently granted probate or letters of administration could have lawfully made.

1353. Notwithstanding any provisions to the contrary, where the deceased was a Muslim, Buddhist, exempted person, or a Hindu, Sikh, or Jaina to whom section 57 does not apply, the Court shall have the discretion to refuse an application for letters of administration made under this Act, provided that the reasons for such refusal are recorded in writing.

1354. Every order made by a District Judge by virtue of the powers hereby conferred upon him shall be subject to appeal to the High Court in accordance with the provisions of the Code of Civil Procedure, 1908, applicable to appeals. The High Court shall have concurrent jurisdiction with the District Judge in the exercise of all the powers hereby conferred upon the District Judge. Except in cases to which section 57 applies, no High Court, in exercise of the concurrent jurisdiction hereby conferred over any local area shall, where the deceased is a Hindu, Muslim, Buddhist, Sikh or Jaina or an exempted person, receive applications for probate or letters of administration until the Provincial Government has, by a notification in the Official Gazette, authorized it to do so.

1355. The High Court, upon receiving an application, may suspend, remove, or discharge any private executor or administrator and appoint a successor to the office. The successor shall assume responsibility for the estate and be vested with all property belonging to the deceased's estate previously held by the removed executor or administrator.

1356. When probate or letters of administration for an estate have been granted under this Act, the High Court may, upon application, issue general or specific directions to the executor or administrator concerning the management or administration of the estate.

§16. Succession Certificates

1357. The Succession Act, 1925, sections 370~390 (Chapter-X) deals with the Succession Certificate. The District Judge within whose jurisdiction the deceased ordinarily resided at the time of his death, or, if at that time he had no fixed place of residence, the District Judge, within whose jurisdiction any part of the property of the deceased may be found, may grant a succession certificate.

1358. Application for such a certificate is made to the District Judge by a petition signed and verified by or on behalf of the applicant in the manner prescribed by the Code of Civil Procedure, 1908, for the signing and verification of a plaint by or on behalf of a plaintiff, and setting forth the following particulars, namely: (a) the time of the death of the deceased; (b) the ordinary residence of the deceased at the time of his death and, if such residence was not within the local limits of the jurisdiction of the Judge to whom the application is made, then the property of the deceased within those limits; (c) the family or other near relatives of the deceased and their respective residences; (d) the right in which the petitioner claims; (e) the absence of any impediment under section 370 or under any other provision of the Succession Act, 1925 or any other enactment, to the grant of the certificate or to the validity thereof if it were granted; and (f) the debts and securities in respect of which the certificate is applied for. If the petition contains any averment which the person verifying it knows or believes to be false, or does not believe to be true, that person shall be deemed to have committed an offence under section 198 of the PPC. Application for such a certificate may be made in respect of any debt or debts due to the deceased creditor or in respect of portions thereof.

1359. If the District Judge is satisfied that there is ground for entertaining the application, he shall fix a day for the hearing thereof and cause notice of the application and of the day fixed for the hearing (a) to be served on any person to whom, in the opinion of the Judge, special notice of the application should be given; and (b) to be posted on some conspicuous part of the court-house and published in such other manner, if any, as the Judge, subject to any rules made by the High Court in this behalf, thinks fit, and upon the day fixed, or as soon thereafter as may be practicable, shall proceed to decide in a summary manner the right to the certificate. When the Judge decides the right thereto to belong to the applicant, the Judge shall make an order for the grant of the certificate to him. If the Judge cannot decide the right to the certificate without determining questions of law or fact which seem to be too intricate and difficult for determination in a summary proceeding, he may nevertheless grant a certificate to the applicant if he appears to be the person having prima facie the best title thereto. When there are more applicants than one for a certificate, and it appears to the Judge that more than one of such applicants are interested in the estate of the deceased, the Judge may, in deciding to whom the certificate is to be granted, have regard to the extent of interest and the fitness in other respects of the applicants.

1360. When the District Judge grants a certificate, he specifies the debts and securities set forth in the application for the certificate, and may thereby empower the person to whom the certificate is granted (a) to receive interest or dividends on, or (b) to negotiate or transfer, or (c) both to receive interest or dividends on, and to negotiate or transfer, the securities or any of them.

1361. In any instance where the District Judge intends to proceed under section 373, and in any other case at his discretion, he may require the person to whom the certificate is to be granted to provide a bond with one or more sureties, or other adequate security. This bond shall ensure the proper accounting for debts and securities received and provide indemnity for individuals entitled to all or part of those debts and securities. Upon petition and sufficient cause shown, the Judge may assign the bond or other security to a suitable individual, who will then have the right to sue in their own name, as if the bond had originally been issued to them instead of the Judge. The appointed person may recover, as a trustee for all interested parties, the amount due under the bond or security, as the case may be.

1362. A District Judge may, upon the application of the certificate holder, authorize the extension of the certificate to include any debt or security not initially listed. Such an extension shall carry the same legal effect as if the debt or security had been specified in the original certificate. Following the extension, the Judge may grant powers regarding the receipt of interest or dividends, or the negotiation or transfer of any security included in the extension. Additionally, the Judge may require the provision of a bond, further bond, or other security as stipulated in section 375, in the same manner as required for the original issuance of the certificate.

1363. The Succession Certificate is granted, and extensions of certificates are made as per form set forth in Schedule-VIII of the Succession Act, 1925.

1364. If the District Judge has not granted the certificate holder any authority concerning a security listed in the certificate, or has only granted powers to receive interest or dividends, or to negotiate or transfer the security, the Judge may, upon receiving a petition and being satisfied with the reasons provided, amend the certificate. This amendment may include granting any of the powers outlined in section 374 or replacing one power with another, as the Judge deems appropriate.

1365. Every application for a succession certificate or its extension must be accompanied by a deposit equal to the fee required under the Court Fees Act, 1870, for the certificate or extension being sought. If the application is granted, the deposited sum shall be used, under the direction of the Judge, to purchase the stamp necessary to denote the fee payable. Any amount received that is not used for this purpose shall be refunded to the person who made the deposit.

1366. Succession certificates are valid throughout Pakistan. They also apply to certificates granted before the separation of Pakistan from India, as well as to those granted on or after that date in proceedings that were pending at the time of the separation, in any of the territories that were previously part of India.

1367. The certificate issued by the District Judge, concerning the debts and securities listed therein, shall be definitive and binding on those owing such debts or liable under such securities. It shall, despite any breach of section 370 or any other flaw, provide complete protection to all such individuals for any payments made or transactions conducted in good faith with the person to whom the certificate was granted, in relation to those debts or securities.

1368. If a Succession Certificate is issued to a resident of a Foreign State by the Pakistan diplomatic representative accredited to that State, or if such a certificate is extended in a similar manner by the representative, the certificate shall be deemed valid upon being stamped in accordance with the provisions of the Court Fees Act, 1870.

1369. A Succession Certificate can be revoked for any of the following causes, namely: (a) that the proceedings to obtain the certificate were defective in substance; (b) that the certificate was obtained fraudulently by the making of a false suggestion, or by the concealment from the Court of something material to the case; (c) that the certificate was obtained by means of an untrue allegation of a fact essential in point of law to justify the grant thereof, though such allegation was made in ignorance or inadvertently; (d) that the certificate has become useless and inoperative through circumstances; (e) that a decree or order made by a competent Court in a suit or other proceeding with respect to effects comprising debts or securities specified in the certificate renders it proper that the certificate should be revoked.

1370. An appeal may be made to the High Court from an order issued by a District Judge granting, refusing, or revoking a certificate. The High Court, at its discretion, may, through its order on the appeal, identify the rightful recipient of the certificate and instruct the District Judge, upon an appropriate application, to issue the certificate in accordance with its direction, overriding any previously granted certificate. Such an appeal must be filed within the time frame prescribed for appeals under the Code of Civil Procedure, 1908.

1371. Notwithstanding the other provisions of the Succession Act, 1925, any certificate issued under the Act for the effects of a deceased person shall be considered invalid if a prior certificate, probate, or letters of administration has already been granted concerning the deceased's estate, and such prior grant remains in effect.

1372. If a Succession Certificate is revoked under section 383, superseded by an appellate order under section 384, or rendered invalid due to the prior issuance of a certificate or for any other reason, any payments made or transactions conducted regarding debts and securities specified in the revoked or invalid certificate with the holder of such certificate, and made without knowledge of its revocation or invalidity, shall remain valid and protected against claims under any subsequent certificate.

§17. Case Laws

1373. Suit for declaration and injunction. Inheritance. The appellant, challenged the dismissal of his suit for declaration, permanent, and mandatory injunction against his daughter-in-law (respondent No. 5), concerning the inheritance of a property from his late son while still in service, and the appellant sought to claim his share in the property. He contested a 1999 letter from the Naval Headquarters that declared the property would be transferred solely to respondent No. 5, claiming that she was not his son's only legal heir. The appellant's argument was that the property should be inherited by all legal heirs according to Islamic law. Respondent No. 7, who purchased the property from respondent No. 5, argued that the property was allotted under the Navy Housing Scheme's terms, which provided that the house would go to the widow or next-of-kin if the member died during membership, and the appellant's claim to inheritance was invalid. However, the Court determined that the deceased did not own the property at the time of his death, and that the property was transferred to respondent No. 5 according to the Navy Housing Scheme's terms. The Court held that since the deceased was not the owner of any house in the Navy Housing Scheme at the time of his death, and the property was allotted to respondent No. 5 in accordance with the terms of the scheme, the suit property was not part of his estate. The appeal was dismissed, and the appellant was ordered to bear the costs of the contesting respondent. (sections 42 and 54. Specific Relief Act (I of 1877)) LHC (2024 MLD 75)

1374. Suit for declaration. Inheritance. Respondent filed a suit seeking a declaration regarding his inheritance share. He claimed that the petitioners had obtained inheritance mutation excluding his name from the list of legal heirs. The respondent alleged that the proceedings were conducted fraudulently, with the petitioners omitting his name from the inheritance record. However, there was no specific allegation in the plaint against any revenue officers (such as the Tehsildar, Girdawar, or Patwari) for their involvement in the alleged fraud or conspiracy related to the mutation. The petitioners contested the suit, filing a written statement, and after the trial, the suit was decreed in favour of the respondent. The petitioners appealed the decision, and during the appeal proceedings, they filed applications under Order I Rule 10, CPC, and for the settlement of additional issues. During the appeal, the petitioners filed the mentioned applications, arguing that certain revenue officers should be added as necessary parties due to allegations of fraud related to inheritance mutations. The petitioners contended that the court failed to exercise its jurisdiction by not including these officers as parties and not framing additional issues based on the pleadings. The respondent, however, did not appear in court, and the revision proceeded ex-parte. The court noted that the petitioners did not initially raise the issue of necessary revenue officers in the written statement or during the trial, and there were no specific allegations of fraud or connivance against the officers. Additionally, the application for impleading officers was made after a significant delay, which the court found unjustified. Regarding the framing of issues, the court found that the issues were properly settled earlier and that the petitioners did not raise any objections at the time. The additional issue regarding a compromise deed was not mentioned in the petitioners' written statement, and no explanation was provided for its omission. The court dismissed the Civil Revision, finding no illegality or irregularity in the Additional District Judge's order. (section 42. Specific Relief Act (I of 1877). O. XIV, R. 5. Civil Procedure Code (V of 1908)) LHC (2024 MLD 780)

1375. Suit for declaration and injunction. Inheritance. Dispute regarding the inheritance of deceased property, who passed away in 1937, leaving behind his widow and four daughters. Following his death, inheritance mutations were made, but three of the daughters were excluded from the inheritance in mutation. This exclusion was challenged by the heirs, particularly the husband of one daughter who sought to correct the record. The revenue officers, after remanding the case, did not properly incorporate the names of the excluded daughters in the inheritance records. The respondents filed a suit for declaration in Civil Court, arguing that the exclusion was against Islamic inheritance law, which mandates the equal distribution of property among heirs. The courts ruled in favour of the plaintiffs, decreeing that the inheritance record should be corrected to include all rightful heirs. The petitioners' objections regarding the timeliness of the suit were dismissed and the case was upheld on the grounds that the legal heirs automatically became owners of the estate upon Fateh Khan's death, regardless of the revenue record discrepancies. The civil revisions challenging the decisions were dismissed, and the concurrent findings of the lower courts were upheld. (section 42 and 54. Specific Relief Act (I of 1877); sections 42 and 45. Punjab Land Revenue Act (XVII of 1967)) LHC (2024 MLD 995).

1376. Inheritance. Dispute over the inheritance of the deceased, leaving behind two widows Before his death, two gift mutations were allegedly made by the deceased transferring his entire land to the petitioners, who were nephews of his one wife. The other wife filed a suit to claim her inheritance, which was decreed in her favour by the Appellate Court in January 2010. The petitioners attempted to argue that the wife had relinquished her inheritance rights through an undated Razi Nama, but it lacked consideration and was not executed with proper knowledge or consent. Despite these fraudulent actions, the High Court focused on peripheral issues, neglecting the core matter of inheritance. The case had been dragging on for twenty-five years, with the wife facing continuous obstacles in obtaining her rightful share. The inheritance rights, as prescribed in the Holy Qur'an, were being violated, with the petitioners using fraudulent tactics to deprive her of her share. The Court criticized the petitioners' actions and the delay in resolving the matter. The Supreme Court set aside the High Court's decision, restoring the 2010 decree in favour of the wife and directing the petitioners to pay her costs. The Court ordered the distribution of deceased estate according to Islamic law and instructed the revenue authorities to ensure compliance with the decree. SC (2025 SCMR 88).

Index

The numbers here refer to paragraph numbers.

Adoption, 68, 682, 701–712, 726–727
Adultery, 57, 298, 403, 460, 467, 633–639, 643, 650, 651, 655, 663, 667, 691, 694, 695, 699, 703, 1274
Age, 128–130, 155–157, 239–248, 251–253, 255–258, 714–716, 1137–1140, 1143–1145, 1221–1223
Appointment, 34, 46, 47, 52, 56, 104, 182, 191, 192, 194, 196, 204, 207, 294, 377, 714, 730, 731, 733, 735, 765, 1057, 1063, 1084, 1225, 1231, 1239, 1244, 1250, 1251, 1253, 1258, 1276, 1278, 1279, 1320
Arbitration Council, 72–84, 90, 249, 294, 415, 422, 466, 469, 470, 473, 502, 504–507, 509, 510, 512, 514, 515, 543, 552, 555, 562, 590, 592–594, 623
Bridal Gifts, 69, 228, 428–448
Children, 85–87, 131–133, 453–455, 482–493, 655–660, 687–701, 725–728, 737–745, 750–752, 768–771, 778–780, 808–810, 812–819, 1046–1048, 1089–1091, 1137–1139
Christian, 298–365, 631–665
Citizenship, 169–178, 698, 711
Constitution of Pakistan, 34–36, 40, 41, 44, 52, 53, 68, 95, 117–123, 155, 156, 271, 413, 415, 419, 421–424, 569, 576, 705, 727, 736, 737, 757, 927, 945, 954, 961, 976, 981, 993, 996, 1007, 1018, 1036
Constitution of the Islamic Republic of Pakistan, 33, 37, 68
Cruelty, 92, 220, 270, 298, 371, 445, 494, 526, 527, 529–534, 543, 565, 566, 579, 580, 584, 585, 587, 597, 630, 635, 638, 639, 643, 668
Custody, 657–661, 694–697, 713–789
Custody of child, 490, 765
Custody of minor, 487, 490, 492, 728, 747–750, 752, 760, 761, 763, 764, 769, 770, 782
Dissolution of marriage, 85, 87, 89, 92, 93, 127, 218, 220, 246, 249, 260, 370, 416, 420, 445, 451, 465, 481, 519, 524, 526, 528–531, 533, 535, 536, 543, 547, 551, 552, 560, 565–573, 575–586, 589, 595, 611, 613, 614, 630–632, 634, 636, 639, 650, 652, 655, 664, 666, 686, 742, 750
Divorce, 62–64, 68–70, 113–115, 385–387, 392–394, 396–407, 515–519, 543–671
Domicile, 171, 177–186, 385, 386, 792, 797, 1020, 1205, 1274, 1308
Dower, 85, 89, 93, 110, 249, 253, 281, 291, 292, 294, 406–431, 561–563
Dowry and Bridal Gifts (Restriction) Act, 69, 428–448
Duress, 270–275, 607
Family Courts, 85–94, 420–424, 443–445, 530–532, 749–752
Federal Government, 37, 46, 48, 68, 180, 442, 1128, 1161, 1168, 1176, 1177, 1181, 1290
Federal Shariat Court (FSC), 50, 57, 61, 95, 96, 280, 518, 557, 574, 627, 991
Fundamental Rights, 29, 35, 38, 50, 52, 54, 55, 70, 118, 266, 271, 463, 522, 687, 698, 742, 752, 757
Guardian, 102–104, 193–203, 254, 255, 262, 263, 268, 299, 315, 335, 353, 373, 377, 711–726, 728–741, 747–749, 751, 752, 754–757, 764–770, 772–776, 784–789
High Court, 50, 52, 55, 56, 84, 86, 88, 94, 135, 136, 155–157, 170, 171, 273, 274, 474–476, 530–532, 568–571, 741–743, 762–764, 769–771, 1016–1018

Index

Hindu, 11, 69, 71, 114, 116, 366–384, 791, 794, 799, 805, 1027, 1053, 1210, 1212, 1266, 1267, 1269, 1273, 1295, 1308, 1319, 1324, 1346, 1353, 1354
Iddat, 470, 474, 518, 530, 532, 568, 569, 574, 585, 596, 598–600, 615, 616, 618, 620, 625–630, 686, 1024, 1025
Illegitimate, 179, 374, 375, 454, 467, 619, 680, 683, 684, 686–688, 690, 692, 693, 696, 698, 900, 1070, 1091
Impotency, 445, 496, 498, 521–528
Insanity, 276–279, 497, 507, 535, 544, 642
Judicial divorce, 543, 560, 565
Juvenile, 69, 128–130, 134–160
Juvenile Court, 128, 129, 135–138, 140, 146–149, 151, 152, 154, 160
'*Khula*', 260, 420, 445, 455, 481, 519, 531, 565–589, 595, 611–614
Lahore High Court, 56
Legitimate, 123, 207, 221, 454, 467, 602, 607, 642, 680, 681, 683, 685, 686, 695, 697, 703, 710, 1028, 1070, 1091, 1141, 1242
Lunacy Act, 100, 102
Lunatics, 100, 190–212, 640, 661, 1274
Maintenance, 409, 412, 415, 421, 423, 463–493, 657–660, 692, 693
Marriage, 62–64, 68–71, 91–93, 106–116, 213–218, 551–553, 556, 557, 559, 560, 564–586, 594–596, 598, 599, 601, 602, 606–617, 619, 620, 626–684, 769–771, 791–794
Mental Health Ordinance, 100–105, 191, 759
Muslim Law, 106–112, 251, 270, 279, 280, 566, 707, 909, 938, 1009, 1011
Mutual consent, 219, 261, 266, 298, 467, 518, 543, 546–550, 750
Nikahnama, 107, 110, 244, 245, 261, 266, 281, 288–290, 293–296, 408, 411–413, 417–419, 421, 424, 427, 430, 511, 538, 543, 551, 559, 564, 592
Orphan, 250, 708–710, 727, 1135, 1142
Pakistan's Economy, 785–787
Parsi, 69, 71, 115, 116, 385–405, 666–671, 820, 1045–1051, 1266, 1267, 1269
Paternity, 626, 681–684, 689, 691, 699, 700, 703, 704
Polygamy, 249, 250, 299, 501–515
Puberty, 187, 244, 246, 247, 251–260, 262, 482, 487, 543, 565, 608, 673, 761, 782
Quran, 57, 64–67, 71, 95, 164, 167, 222, 233, 238, 242, 406, 407, 450, 452, 455, 458, 463, 464, 472, 482, 541, 566, 589, 602, 604, 610, 612, 687, 688, 693, 694, 701, 703, 704, 708–710, 900, 940, 991, 1052
Remarry, 373, 374, 376, 381, 516–520, 546, 574, 596, 599, 600, 602, 612, 615, 619, 620, 624–630, 1113
Resigns, 45
Second marriage, 82, 83, 249, 422, 492, 501–515, 539, 549, 584, 585, 629, 630, 633, 730, 761, 763, 764, 769, 771, 777, 779, 784
Special Courts and Tribunals, 61
Succession Act, 69, 98, 178, 179, 628, 647, 719, 733, 791–793, 797–799, 809, 813, 976, 1020, 1045, 1051–1055, 1060, 1068, 1092, 1096, 1098, 1102, 1114, 1115, 1123, 1127–1129, 1133, 1136, 1161, 1168, 1170, 1184, 1190, 1196, 1214, 1215, 1237, 1239, 1240, 1258, 1259, 1261, 1262, 1265, 1273, 1290, 1293, 1315, 1317, 1319, 1329, 1357, 1358, 1363, 1371
Supreme Court, 30, 50–56, 70, 258, 412, 415, 445, 468, 474, 730, 735, 765, 775, 786, 795, 901, 924, 925, 927, 928, 931, 935, 948, 964, 970, 974, 981, 982, 984, 987, 989, 1001, 1002, 1010, 1016, 1018, 1019, 1028, 1031, 1376
Surname, 161, 167–168, 308, 330, 702
Torture, 35, 479, 480, 530, 531, 588
Welfare of minor, 761, 769, 778, 780, 784
Woman, 175, 232–234, 270–273, 405, 406, 462, 463, 497, 499, 501, 520, 521, 528, 529, 566, 567, 602, 603, 615, 616, 624–630, 644, 645, 672–674, 699, 700, 1024, 1025
Zina, 56, 275, 280, 539, 549, 629, 672–678, 680, 681, 689, 691, 694, 695, 699, 700, 703